exploring psychology

FIFTH EDITION IN MODULES

Laura James, *The Chase*, acrylic, 1998.

Laura James is a self-taught painter living and working in Brooklyn, New York. *The Chase* is typical of her style—incorporating bright colors, intricate patterns, and sometimes surreal objects to display her unique vision. Ms. James is a member of the Jamaica Artist Alliance, the Bridgeman Art Library in London, and the National Conference of Black Artists. Her paintings are widely exhibited and have reached as far as Japan, Africa, Canada, and the Caribbean.

exploring psychology

FIFTH EDITION IN MODULES

DAVID G. MYERS

**HOPE COLLEGE,
HOLLAND, MICHIGAN**

WORTH PUBLISHERS

For Renee

Exploring Psychology Fifth Edition in Modules

ISBN: 0-7167-5549-1
          0-7167-5626-9 (spiral)
          0-7167-0121-9 (hardcover)
Third printing, 2004

Publisher: Catherine Woods
Development Editors: Christine Brune, Linda Strange
Executive Marketing Manager: Renee Altier
Associate Managing Editor: Tracey Kuehn
Production Manager: Sarah Segal
Art Director/Designer: Barbara Reingold
Photo Research Manager: Patricia Marx
Illustrations: John Collier, Alan Reingold, Shawn Kenney, Bonnie Hofkin and Demetrios Zangos
Composition: TSI Graphics
Printing and Binding: R.R. Donnelley and Sons
Cover art: Laura James, *The Chase,* acrylic, 1998

All royalties from the sale of this book are assigned to the David and Carol Myers Foundation, which exists to receive and distribute funds to other charitable organizations.

Worth Publishers
41 Madison Avenue
New York, New York 10010
www.worthpublishers.com

About the Author

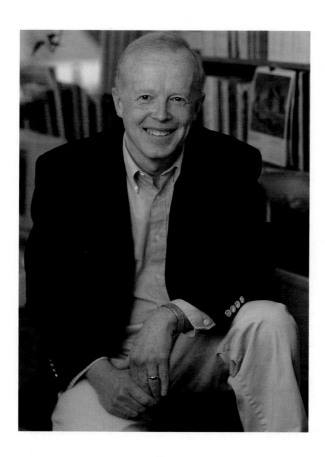

David G. Myers
is professor of psychology at Michigan's Hope College, where he has spent his career and been voted "outstanding professor" by students. His writings have appeared in more than four dozen journals and magazines, from *Science* to *Scientific American,* and in a dozen books.

Contents in Brief

Contents

Preface

Why Modular?

This new, 40-module version of my *Exploring Psychology,* fifth edition, is a longtime wish come true. It breaks out of the box by restructuring the text into a buffet of (a) short, digestible chapters (called modules), that (b) can be selected and assigned in any order.

Have we not all heard the familiar student complaint: "The chapters are too long!" Our typical 30- to 50-page chapters cannot be read in a single sitting before the eyes grow weary and the mind wanders. So why not parse the material into readable units? Ask your students whether they would prefer a 700-page book to be organized as fourteen 50-page chapters or as fifty 14-page chapters. You may be surprised at their overwhelming support for shorter chapters. Indeed, students digest material better when they process in smaller chunks—as "spaced" rather than massed practice.

I have equally often heard from instructors bemoaning the fact that they "just can't get to everything" in the book. Sometimes professors want to cover certain sections in a traditional, long chapter but not others. For example, in the typical States of Consciousness chapter, someone may want to cover Sleep and Hypnosis but not Drugs. In *Exploring Psychology Fifth Edition in Modules,* instructors could easily choose to cover Module 14, Waking and Sleeping Rhythms, and Module 15, Hypnosis, but not Module 16, Drugs.

How Is This Different from *Exploring Psychology,* Fifth Edition?

So, what are the primary differences between this book and *Exploring Psychology,* fifth edition? They are organization and independence of the modules.

Organization

Exploring Psychology Fifth Edition in Modules really IS *Exploring Psychology,* fifth edition—just in a different format. So, the modular book contains all the updated research and innovative new coverage from *Exploring Psychology,* fifth edition. A very few sections have moved around to accommodate the modular structure. For example, "Rates of Psychological Disorders" is a separate section at the end of the Psychological Disorders chapter in *Exploring Psychology,* fifth edition, but it is covered in the first of the Psychological Disorders and Their Treatment modules in the modular format. And "Improving Memory" is covered at the end of the Memory chapter in *Exploring Psychology,* fifth edition, but is covered at the end of the first memory module in *Exploring Psychology Fifth Edition in Modules.*

The Modules Are Independent

Each module in this book is now self-standing rather than dependent upon any other part of the book. Cross references to other modules have been replaced with brief explanations. In some cases, illustrations or key terms are repeated to avoid possible confusion. No assumptions are made about what students have read prior to each module. This independence gives instructors ultimate flexibility in deciding which modules to use, and in what order.

Table 1 Coverage of Evolution and Behavior Genetics

*In addition to the coverage found in new Module 5, **the evolutionary perspective** is covered on the following pages:*

Aging, pp. 131–132
Anxiety disorders, p. 505
Attraction, pp. 564, 566
Biological predispositions in learning, pp. 243–245
Charles Darwin, p. 2
Electromagnetic spectrum, sensitivity to, p. 149
Emotional expression, p. 145
Evolutionary perspective, defined, p. 5
Fear, pp. 402–403
Hearing, p. 159
Instincts, pp. 352–353

Intelligence, p. 343
Language, pp. 312, 314–315
Love, pp. 137–138
Need to belong, p. 384
Overconfidence, p. 308
Sensation, pp. 143, 162–163
Sensory adaptation, p. 147
Sleep, p. 204
Smell, p. 166
Stress and the immune system, pp. 430–431

*In addition to the coverage found in new Module 5, **behavior genetics** is covered on the following pages:*

Abuse, intergenerational transmission of, p. 259
Aggression, pp. 584–593
Biomedical therapies, pp. 552–557
Depth perception, pp. 172–173
Drives and incentives, p. 353
Drug use, pp. 230–231
Emotion and cognition, pp. 399–400
Happiness, pp. 415–420
Intelligence, pp. 336–347
Learning, pp. 243–245
Obesity and weight control, pp. 365–370
Perception, pp. 181–184

Personality traits, pp. 464–465
Psychological disorders:
    anxiety disorders, pp. 504–507
    bio-psycho-social perspective, p. 496
    depression, pp. 510–517
    personality disorders, pp. 518–521
    schizophrenia, pp. 527–528
Romantic love, pp. 137–138
Sexuality, pp. 374–376
Sexual orientation, pp. 379–383
Smell, p. 166
Stress, personality, and illness, pp. 424–433

What's New Since *Exploring Psychology,* Fourth Edition?

This new edition retains its predecessor's voice, and much of its content and organization. Yet change is reflected on every page. In addition to the several hundred new references in this edition and updates on every page, I have introduced the following major changes to this fifth edition:

NEW Module 5, The Nature and Nurture of Behavior

Introducing psychology in the new millennium calls for an understanding of the relative effects of nature and nurture on so many of our behaviors. This new module introduces students to the nature and nurture concepts that they will encounter throughout the book. I have taken a developmental approach, attempting to weave new thinking and research—from evolutionary psychology and behavior genetics on the "nature" side, and gender and cultural influences on the "nurture" side—into a coherent story of the origins of our human kinship and our human diversity. Later chapters apply these concepts when considering topics such as the evolutionary psychology of sleep, the genetics of altruism, gender and intelligence domains, and culture and physique. For a complete list of integrated coverage of these issues, see Tables 1, 2, and 3.

Increasingly Global Perspective on Psychology

For this and succeeding editions I also am working to offer a world-based psychology for our worldwide student readership. Thus, I continually search the world for research findings and text and photo examples, conscious that readers may be in Melbourne, Sheffield, Vancouver, or Nairobi. North American and European examples come easily, given that I reside in the United States, maintain contact with friends and colleagues in Canada, subscribe to several European periodicals, and live periodically in the United Kingdom. But this edition also offers 44 mentions of Australia and New Zealand. We are all citizens of a shrinking world, thanks to increased migration and the growing global economy. Thus, American students, too, benefit from information and examples that internationalize their world-consciousness. And if psychology seeks to explain *human* behavior (not just American or Canadian or Australian behavior), the broader the scope of studies presented, the more accurate is our picture of this world's people. My aim is to expose all students to the world beyond their own country. Thus, I continue to welcome input and suggestions from all readers.

Table 2 Coverage of the Psychology of Men and Women

Coverage of the psychology of women and men can be found on the following pages:

Arousal in REM sleep, pp. 200–201

Behavioral effects of gender, pp. 29–30

Biological sex/gender, pp. 89–90

Body image, pp. 358–362

Depression, p. 511

Dieting, pp. 367–368

Dream content, pp. 207–208

Eating disorders, pp. 360–361

Emotional expression, pp. 407–408

Empty nest, p. 138

Freud's views, p. 452

Gender and childrearing, pp. 91–92

Gender roles, pp. 90–91

Generic pronoun "he," p. 318

Happiness, p. 419

Heart disease, pp. 428–429

Help-receiving, p. 602

Hormones and
    aggression, p. 586
    sexual behavior, pp. 374–375
    sexual development, pp. 119–120

Immune system, pp. 430–431

Intelligence, pp. 343–345

Leadership, pp. 391–392

Life expectancy, p. 131

Maturation, pp. 119–120

Menarche, p. 120

Menopause, pp. 129–130

Midlife crisis, p. 136

Pornography, p. 375

Psychological disorders, rates of, pp. 500–501

Rape, pp. 246, 590–593

Sexual disorders, p. 377

Sexual fantasies, p. 196

Sexuality, pp. 375–376

Sexual orientation, pp. 379–383

Social connectedness, pp. 124–125

Stereotyping, p. 184

Suicide, p. 512

Weight discrimination, pp. 363–364

Women and work, p. 138

Table 3 Coverage of Culture and Multicultural Experience

Coverage of culture and multicultural experience permeates the chapters in the following discussions:

Aggression, p. 588

Alcoholism, pp. 500–501

Anger, pp. 413–415

Attractiveness, pp. 597–598

Behavioral effects of culture, pp. 29–30

Conformity, p. 570

Corporal punishment practices, pp. 253–254

Culture context effects, p. 184

Culture shock, pp. 479, 486

Deaf culture, pp. 65, 315, 317, 318

Depression, pp. 510–511

Development:
    adolescence, pp. 118–119
    attachment, pp. 114–115
    childrearing, p. 88

cognitive development, p. 105

developmental similarities, pp. 88–89

fetal alcohol syndrome, p. 101

moral development, pp. 121–122

motor development, pp. 104–105

social development, pp. 111–112

Drugs, psychological effects of, p. 223

Emotion:
    experiencing, pp. 413–415
    expressing, pp. 409–411

Human diversity/kinship, pp. 29–30

Hunger, pp. 358–362

Individualism/collectivism, pp. 479–481

Intelligence, pp. 335, 341–343

Language, pp. 317–319

Management styles, p. 392

Marriage, pp. 137–138

Obesity, pp. 362–364, 366

Participative management, p. 392

People with disabilities, pp. 415–416, 418–419

Perception, p. 184

Personal space, p. 87

Prejudice prototypes, pp. 302–303

Psychological disorders, pp. 497, 498
    dissociative personality disorder, pp. 520–521
    eating disorders, p. 361

schizophrenia, pp. 526–527

Psychotherapy, pp. 551–552

Self-esteem, p. 476

Self-serving bias, pp. 477–478

Sensory restriction, p. 181

Sexual orientation, pp. 379–380

Sexual standards, pp. 376–379

Smoking, pp. 224–225

Social clock, p. 136

Social-cultural perspective, p. 5

Suicide, pp. 512–513

Teen sexuality, pp. 376–379

Testing bias, pp. 346–347

Variations across cultures, pp. 86–87

Work-related values, p. 136

Enhanced Critical Thinking Coverage

I introduce students to critical thinking in a very natural way throughout the book, with even more in this edition to encourage active learning of critical thinking principles.

- *Module 2 takes a unique, critical thinking approach to introducing students to psychology's research methods,* emphasizing the fallacies of our everyday intuition and common sense and, thus, the need for psychological science. Critical thinking is introduced as a key term in this module (page 11).
- *"Thinking Critically About . . ." boxes* are found throughout the book, modeling for students a critical approach to some key issues in psychology. For example, see the new box "Thinking Critically About: Do Video Games Teach or Release Violence?" on page 592.
- *Detective-style stories* throughout the narrative get students thinking critically about psychology's key research questions.
- *"Apply this" style questions and activities* and *"Think about it" style discussions* keep students active in their study of each module.

Table 4 Critical Thinking Topics

Critical thinking coverage can be found on the following pages:

Thinking Critically About . . . boxes:

Hot and Cold Streaks in Basketball and the Stock Market, p. 24

Left Brain/Right Brain, p. 64

Hypnotic Age Regression: A True Story, p. 214

Risks—When Statistics Clash With Heuristics, p. 307

Lie Detection, p. 404

Alternative Medicine: New Ways to Health or Old Snake Oil?, p. 444

How to Be a "Successful" Astrologer or Palm Reader, pp. 470–471

Insanity and Responsibility, p. 499

Dissociation and Multiple Personalities, pp. 520–521

"Regressing" From Unusual to Usual, p. 543

Do Video Games Teach or Release Violence?, p. 592

Critical Examinations of Pop Psychology:

Perceiving order in random events, pp. 22–23

Can subliminal tapes improve your life?, pp. 27–28

Do we use only 10 percent of our brains?, p. 57

Critiquing the evolutionary explanation, pp. 73–74

How great is the power of parenting?, pp. 84–85

Sensory restriction, p. 181

Is there extrasensory perception?, pp. 186–189

Can hypnosis enhance recall? Coerce action? Be therapeutic? Alleviate pain?, pp. 211–216

Has the concept of "addiction" been stretched too far?, pp. 220–221

Near-death experiences, p. 227

Do animals exhibit language?, pp. 322–325

Is aerobic exercise therapeutic?, pp. 435–436

Spirituality and faith communities, pp. 441–446

Is repression a myth?, p. 459

How valid is the Rorschach test?, pp. 455–456

Is Freud credible?, pp. 460–461

Post-traumatic stress disorder, p. 506

Is psychotherapy effective?, pp. 543–546

Evaluating alternative therapies, pp. 547–549

Thinking Critically With Psychological Science:

The limits of intuition and common sense, pp. 8–9

"Critical thinking" introduced as a key term, pp. 11–12

The scientific attitude, pp. 10–11

The scientific method, pp. 16–17

Correlation and causation, p. 21

Illusory correlation, pp. 21–22

Evaluating therapies, pp. 26–27

Statistical reasoning, p. A-1

Making inferences, p. A-6

Scientific Detective Stories:

Language in the brain, pp. 58–60

Our divided brains, pp. 61–64

The twin and adoption studies, pp. 75–78

How a child's mind develops, pp. 105–111

Aging and intelligence, pp. 134–135

Parallel processing, pp. 153–154

How do we see in color?, pp. 155–157

Why do we sleep?, pp. 202–205

Why do we dream?, pp. 208–209

Is hypnosis an altered state of consciousness?, pp. 216–218

How do we store memories in our brains?, pp. 273–277

Memory construction, pp. 290–298

Do animals exhibit language?, pp. 322–325

Why do we feel hunger?, pp. 356–358

What determines sexual orientation?, pp. 380–383

The pursuit of happiness: Who is happy, and why?, pp. 415–420

Why—and in whom—does stress contribute to heart disease?, pp. 428–429

How and why is social support linked with health?, pp. 439–441

Self-esteem versus self-serving bias, pp. 475–479

What causes mood disorders?, pp. 510–517

Do prenatal viral infections increase risk of schizophrenia?, pp. 526–527

Is psychotherapy effective?, pp. 543–546

Why do people fail to help in emergencies?, pp. 601–602

- *Critical examinations of pop psychology* spark interest and provide important lessons in thinking critically about everyday topics.
- The Appendix on *Statistical Reasoning* encourages students to "focus on thinking smarter by applying simple statistical principles to everyday reasoning" (pp. A-1–A-8).
- Appendix B provides a *Critical Thinking Exercise* for each major topic in the book.

See Table 4 for a complete list of this text's coverage of critical thinking topics and Thinking Critically About boxes.

New, Comprehensive Online Teaching and Learning Resources

Wonderful new online resources authored by Thomas Ludwig (Hope College) and a team of contributors cover the key topics in *Exploring Psychology Fifth Edition in Modules*. With *PsychOnline* you pick and choose from a buffet of resources that can be used as a component of a more traditional lecture-based course, or as a complete online course.

Choose from 93 **interactive tutorials,** which review the key concepts in each module. Dozens of **Demonstrations, Simulations, Critical Thinking Activities,** and data-collecting **Research Projects** give students an opportunity to learn the core concepts hands-on (Figure 1). Students have many opportunities for review. *PsychOnline* includes hundreds of periodic **Concept Checks** within the tutorials, a **Practice Quiz** and key concept **Flashcards** at the end of each tutorial, and drag-and-drop-style **labeling** of anatomical and other art.

FIGURE 1
PsychOnline sample screens
The video in the screen at left (from the "Cognitive Development in Infancy and Childhood" tutorial) allows students to watch a baby displaying the beginnings of object permanence. At right (from a Demonstration activity in "Color Vision"), students can interact with wavelength, cone response, and experienced hue until they understand how and why they affect each other. Note in both screens that there is always just enough text to put the images and interactions into a meaningful context for students.

PsychOnline includes an **Instructor's Resource Library,** with numerous illustrations available in an easy-to-pick-up format for lecture presentations.

Additional resources within *PsychOnline* include:

- **Psychology in Everyday Life**—stories, jokes, and anecdotes related to teaching and learning specific, important topics in the introductory course
- **Psychology Around the Globe**—cross-cultural and international applications
- **Psychology on the Web**—carefully selected, informative sites keyed to important topics in this book
- **Psychology Forum**—with discussion topics designed to encourage student participation

Successful SQ3R Study Aids

1. *Myers in Modules' complete system of learning aids includes numbered "preview questions," which appear in this format throughout the book.*

Exploring Psychology Fifth Edition in Modules has retained its popular system of study aids, integrated into an SQ3R structure that augments the narrative without disrupting it. Each module opens with a module outline that enables students to quickly *survey* its major topics. Numbered preview *questions* at the start of each new major topic define the learning objectives that will guide students as they *read*. *Rehearse It* quizzes at the end of each major section will stimulate students to rehearse what they have learned (see sample on page xviii from Module 1). These test items offer a novel combination of crisp review of key ideas and practice with the multiple-choice test format. The module-ending *Review* answers each of the numbered preview questions and is followed by answers for each of the Rehearse It multiple-choice questions. All **key terms** are defined in the margins for ready reference while students are being introduced to the new term in the narrative (see sample at right). Periodic "Thinking Critically About," "Close-Up," and "Psychology Applied" boxes encourage development of critical thinking skills as well as application of the new concepts. "Critical Thinking Exercises" at the end of the book (Appendix B) allow practice of new skills as well as review of important module topics. The "Tips for Studying Psychology" section at the end of Module 1 explains the SQ3R-based system of study aids, suggesting how students can survey, question, read, rehearse, and review the material for maximum retention.

In the margins of this book, students will find interesting and informative review notes, and quotes from researchers and others that will encourage them to be active learners and apply what they are learning.

▶ **key terms** Look for a complete definition of each important term in the margin near its introduction in the narrative.

rehearse it!*

1. Psychology is the science of behavior and mental processes. The perspective in psychology that focuses on how behavior and thought differ from situation to situation and from culture to culture is the
   a. cognitive perspective.
   b. behavioral perspective.
   c. social-cultural perspective.
   d. neuroscience perspective.

2. In the history of psychology, one of the main debates has been over the nature-nurture issue. Nature is to nurture as
   a. personality is to intelligence.
   b. biology is to experience.
   c. intelligence is to biology.
   d. psychological traits are to behaviors.

3. The behavioral perspective in psychology emphasizes observable responses and how they are acquired and modified. A behavioral psychologist would be most likely to study
   a. the effect of school uniforms on classroom behaviors.
   b. the hidden meaning in children's themes and drawings.
   c. the age at which children can learn algebra.
   d. whether certain mathematical abilities appear to be inherited.

4. A psychologist who treats emotionally troubled adolescents at the local mental health agency is most likely to be a/an
   a. research psychologist.
   b. psychiatrist.

   c. industrial/organizational psychologist.
   d. clinical psychologist.

5. A psychologist who conducts basic research to expand psychology's knowledge base would be most likely to
   a. design a computer screen with limited glare and assess the effect on computer operators' eyes after a day's work.
   b. treat older people who are overcome by depression.
   c. observe 3- and 6-year-old children solving puzzles and analyze differences in their abilities.
   d. interview children with behavioral problems and suggest treatments.

Trademark Features

As a reporter, there is no beat I'd rather cover than psychology. Week by week, new information surprises us with discoveries about how the brain's chemical messengers control moods, about animal abilities, about unconscious ("automatic") thinking, about the roots and fruits of happiness, about the effects of stress on our capacity to fight disease. Indeed, this book, following the field, has changed dramatically since I set to work on the first edition 20 years ago. Today's psychological science is more attuned to the relative effects of nature and nurture, to gender and cultural diversity, and to the neuroscience revolution. We today can also harness new ways to present information, both in books and via electronic media. These changes are exhilarating! Keeping up with new discoveries and technologies fills each day and connects me with many colleagues and friends.

The thousands of instructors and millions of students across the globe who have studied this book have contributed immensely to its development. Much of this has occurred spontaneously, through correspondence and conversations. Dozens of formal reviews from teaching psychologists and researchers around the world have also aided each revision. I look forward to continuing feedback as we strive, over future editions, to create an ever better book.

Throughout its five editions, however, my vision for *Exploring Psychology* has not wavered: *to merge rigorous science with a broad human perspective in a book that engages both mind and heart.* My aim has been to create a state-of-the-art introduction to psychology, written with sensitivity to students' needs and interests. I aspire to help students understand and appreciate the wonder of important phenomena of their lives. I also want to convey the inquisitive, caring spirit in which psychologists do psychology. The study of psychology, I believe, enhances our abilities to restrain intuition with critical thinking, judgmentalism with compassion, and illusion with understanding.

Believing with Thoreau that "anything living is easily and naturally expressed in popular language," I seek to communicate psychology's scholarship with crisp narra-

---

*You can use these Rehearse It questions to gauge whether you are ready for the next section. The answers are always at the end of the chapter.

tive and vivid storytelling. Writing as a solo author, I hope to tell psychology's story in a way that is warmly personal as well as rigorously scientific. I love to reflect on connections between psychology and other realms, such as literature, philosophy, history, sports, religion, politics, and popular culture. And I love to provoke thought, to play with words, and to laugh.

Throughout this revision, as in this book's previous four editions, I have steadfastly followed eight principles:

1. **To exemplify the process of inquiry** I strive to show students not just the outcome of research, but how the research process works. Throughout, the book tries to excite the reader's curiosity. It invites readers to imagine themselves as participants in classic experiments. Several modules introduce research stories as mysteries that progressively unravel as one clue after another falls into place. (See, for example, the historical story of research on the brain's processing of language—pages 58–59.)

2. **To teach critical thinking** By presenting research as intellectual detective work, I exemplify an inquiring, analytical mind-set. Whether students are studying development, cognition, or statistics, they will become involved in, and see the rewards of, critical reasoning. Moreover, they will discover how an empirical approach can help them evaluate competing ideas and claims for highly publicized phenomena—ranging from subliminal persuasion, ESP, and alternative therapies to astrology, basketball streak-shooting, and repressed and recovered memories.

3. **To put facts in the service of concepts** My intention is not to fill students' intellectual file drawers with facts, but to reveal psychology's major concepts—to teach students how to think, and to offer psychological ideas worth thinking about. In each module I place emphasis on those concepts I hope students will carry with them long after they complete the course. Always, I try to follow Albert Einstein's dictum that "Everything should be made as simple as possible, but not simpler."

4. **To be as up to date as possible** Few things dampen students' interests as quickly as the sense that they are reading stale news. While retaining psychology's classic studies and concepts, I also present the discipline's most important recent developments. Nearly 492 references in this edition are dated 1998 to 2001.

5. **To integrate principles and applications** Throughout—by means of anecdotes, case histories, and the posing of hypothetical situations—I relate the findings of basic research to their applications and implications. Where psychology can illuminate pressing human issues—be they racism and sexism, health and happiness, or violence and war—I have not hesitated to shine its light.

6. **To enhance comprehension by providing continuity** Because the book has a single author, many significant issues—such as behavior genetics, cultural diversity, the bold thinking of intellectual pioneers, human rationality and irrationality, empathy for and understanding of troubled lives—weave throughout many modules, and students hear a consistent voice. "The uniformity of a work," observed Edward Gibbon, "denotes the hand of a single artist."

7. **To reinforce learning at every step** Everyday examples and rhetorical questions encourage students to process the material actively. Concepts are presented and then frequently applied to reinforce learning. The SQ3R system of pedagogical aids augments learning without interrupting the text narrative. A marginal glossary helps students master important terminology. Major sections begin with numbered preview questions and end with Rehearse It sections for self-testing on key concepts. End-of-module reviews repeat the preview questions and answer them.

8. ***To convey respect for human unity and diversity*** Time and again, readers will see evidence of our human kinship—our shared biological heritage, our common mechanisms of seeing and learning, hungering and feeling, loving and hating. They will also better understand the dimensions of our diversity—our *individual* diversity in development and aptitudes, temperament and personality, and disorder and health; and our *cultural* diversity in attitudes and expressive styles, childrearing and care for the elderly, and life priorities.

The Multimedia Supplements Package

Exploring Psychology Fifth Edition in Modules boasts a host of new electronic and print supplements titles.

NEW! PsychOnline offers comprehensive online resources for the introductory course. This impressive new project is detailed on p. xvii.

NEW! *Scientific American Presents: The Hidden Mind* In this special edition of *Scientific American* magazine, *The Hidden Mind* updates articles from some of the most notable neuroscientists studying the human brain, including Michael Gazzaniga, Antonio Damasio, Joseph LeDoux, Ursala Bellugi, and Doreen Kimura.

NEW! *Making Sense of Psychology on the Web* **with CD-ROM** by Connie K. Varnhagen (University of Alberta) is a brief booklet that helps students locate reliable information on the Web, evaluate sites, and organize research. The guide includes a CD-ROM containing Research HyperFolio, software that enables students to collect snippets of text, illustrations, video clips, and audio clips from the Web or other electronic sources and compile them into worksheets and an easily-accessible filing cabinet.

NEW! Worth Digital Media Archive CD-ROM This dual-platform Instructor's Presentation CD-ROM contains a rich collection of more than 40 digitized video clips of classic experiments and research. Footage includes Albert Bandura's Bobo doll experiment, Harold Takooshian's bystander studies, Piaget's conservation experiment, Harlow's monkey experiments, Milgram's obedience study, and Ulric Neisser's selective attention studies. The Digital Media Archive clips are compressed in MPEG format and are compatible with Microsoft PowerPoint software. The clips are also available in VHS format.

NEW! *Psychology: The Human Experience* Teaching Modules Available in VHS or DVD formats. This new Emmy-award-winning series includes more than three hours of footage from the new Introductory Psychology telecourse, Psychology: The Human Experience, produced by Coast Learning Systems in collaboration with Worth Publishers. These brief clips are ideal for lecture, and a faculty guide is available to help integrate each clip. Footage contains noted scholars, the latest research, and beautiful animations.

NEW! *PsychInquiry: Student Activities in Research and Critical Thinking* Developed by Thomas Ludwig (Hope College) and a team of contributors, this new CD-ROM contains dozens of highly interactive activities designed to help students learn about psychological research and to improve their critical thinking. These activities enable students to work hands-on with descriptive, correlational, and experiment research to help them hone the critical thinking mindset required for psychological research. *PsychInquiry* activities are complete with animations, video, fresh illustrations, and self-assessment instruments that draw students into the discipline. *PsychInquiry* also offers a handful of more extensive research activities for use as classroom projects or lab assignments.

A *Scientific American* Reader includes 12 articles I hand-selected from recent issues of *Scientific American*. I have written introductions for each article to tie them into key topics in this text.

Myers Psychology Web Companion (http://www.worthpublishers.com/ myers) provides a wide variety of activities and study aids organized by the modules in this book. Features include Module Overviews, Thinking Critically Exercises, Psychology in the News, Web links, simulations and demonstrations, online quizzes, and flashcards.

Online versions of Thomas Ludwig's (Hope College) award-winning programs, **PsychQuest** and **PsychSim,** are keyed to the appropriate Myers modules. Also available on CD-ROM.

Image and Lecture Gallery (http://www.worthpublishers.com) is Worth's convenient way to access electronic versions of lecture materials. Registered users can browse, search, and download illustrations from Worth titles and pre-built PowerPoint presentation files for specific chapters. Instructors can also create personal folders on a personalized home page for easy organization of the materials.

PowerPoint Slides are now available. They can be used as is, or customized to fit your needs. There are two pre-built versions for each module—one featuring module outlines only, the other featuring module art and illustrations.

Presentation Manager Pro 2.0 is an easy-to-operate CD-ROM that is compatible with most commercially available presentation software, such as PowerPoint. With Presentation Manager Pro, instructors can build classroom presentations using graphic material from the book and CD, and your own digital material (including video) imported from the Internet or other sources.

WebCT and **Blackboard** are available free to all adopters. With these course organizational software systems, instructors can create a course Web site and/or online course with content, threaded discussions, quizzing, an online grade book, a course calendar, and more! This book's graphic and media content is available in the WebCT and Blackboard formats.

Online Testing is now available with Diploma from the Brownstone Research Group. Instructors can now create and administer secure exams over a network and over the Internet with questions that incorporate multimedia and interactive exercises. The program includes impressive security features and grade book and result-analysis features.

Scientific American **Frontiers Video Collection, Second Edition** is a renowned series hosted by Alan Alda. These 10- to 12-minute modules provide an excellent way to show how psychological research is actually conducted, focusing on the work of Steve Sumi, Renee Baillargeon, Carl Rosengren, Laura Petitto, Steven Pinker, Barbara Rothbaum, Bob Stickgold, Irene Pepperberg, Marc Hauser, Linda Bartoshuk, and Michael Gazzaniga.

The Mind Video Teaching Modules, second edition, offer 35 brief, engaging video clips to enhance and illustrate lecture topics.

The Brain Video Teaching Modules, second edition, offer more engaging video clips to help you teach.

In addition to all these fabulous new resources, *Exploring Psychology Fifth Edition in Modules* is accompanied by smartly updated versions of the widely acclaimed print supplements package.

The updated and better-than-ever **Instructor's Resources** by Martin Bolt (Calvin College) has been hailed as the finest set of psychology teaching resources ever assembled, including ready-to-use demonstration handouts, detailed lecture/discussion ideas, student projects, classroom exercises, and video and film suggestions.

The **Student Study Guide** by Richard O. Straub (University of Michigan, Dearborn) follows the text's content and offers the following for every major section in the text: a new "Stepping Through the Section" feature, Self Tests, "Web Sightings" Internet activities, and "Cross-Check" crossword puzzles. The Guide also includes Cornelius Rea's (Douglas College, British Columbia) helpful "Focus on Vocabulary and Language" feature, designed to help clarify idioms and other phrases potentially unfamiliar to students for whom English is a second language.

The **Test Bank** by John Brink (Calvin College) is broken down into two banks, providing over 4000 multiple-choice factual/definitional and conceptual questions plus essay questions. Each question is page-referenced to the textbook, tied into the Instructor's Resources' list of learning objectives, and rated for level of difficulty. The second Test Bank includes optional questions on *PsychQuest* and *PsychSim* computer simulations and *The Brain* and *The Mind* videos.

The Critical Thinking Companion by Jane Halonen (James Madison University) and Cynthia Gray (Alverno College) is now available in a NEW second edition. This collection of engaging, challenging, and fun critical thinking exercises is tied to the main topics in *Exploring Psychology Fifth Edition in Modules.*

Our **Psychology Videodisc** will help you bring to life for your students all of the major topics in *Exploring Psychology Fifth Edition in Modules,* combining brief, exciting video clips and animated segments with a library of stills. This videodisc is accompanied by an extensive *Instructor's Guide,* by Martin Bolt and Richard O. Straub, and a presentation software package by Thomas Ludwig.

In Appreciation

If it is true that "whoever walks with the wise becomes wise" then I am wiser for all the wisdom and advice received from expert colleagues. Aided by several hundred consultants and reviewers over the last decade, this has become a better, more accurate book than one author alone (this author, at least) could write. My indebtedness continues to each of the teacher-scholars whose influence I acknowledged in the four previous editions.

My gratitude now extends to the colleagues who contributed criticism, corrections, and creative ideas related to the content of this new edition. For their expertise and encouragement, I thank the following reviewers:

Gary Anderson,
Camosun College
Marty Bourgeois,
University of Wyoming
Greg Cutler,
Bay de Noc Community College
David Entwistle,
Malone College
Elizabeth Garner,
University of North Florida
Jonathan Golding,
University of Kentucky
Carl Granrud,
University of Northern Colorado
Diedra Hayman,
Virginia Western Community College
Sherri Lynn Jackson,
Jacksonville University

Gary Levine,
Edinboro University of Pennsylvania
John Lindsay,
Georgia College and State University
Robert Mac Aleese,
Spring Hill College
Britt Mace,
Southern Utah University
Jean Raniseski,
Alvin Community College
Robert Rosenberg,
Community College of Philadelphia
Michael Scheible,
Gateway Area Technical College
Bryan Teixeira,
Camosun College
Richard Westley,
Massapequa High School

At Worth Publishers a host of people played key roles in creating this fifth edition. Christine Brune, Nancy Fleming, and Linda Strange offered just the right mix of encouragement, gentle admonition, attention to detail, and passion for excellence. An author could not ask for more. Christine and Nancy also guided the development of the new *PsychOnline* resources.

Publisher Catherine Woods helped construct and execute the plan for this new edition and was a trusted sounding board as we faced decisions along the way. Media and Supplements Editor Graig Donini coordinated production of the huge supplements package for this edition. Betty Probert efficiently edited and produced the print supplements. Editorial Assistant Miriam Beyer provided invaluable support in commissioning reviews, mailing information to professors, and numerous other daily tasks related to the book's development and production. Lee Mahler did a splendid job of laying out each page. Jennifer MacMillan, Tobi Zausner, and Patricia Marx located the myriad photographic illustrations.

Associate Managing Editor Tracey Kuehn displayed tenacity, commitment, and impressive organization in leading Worth's gifted artistic production team and coordinating editorial input throughout the production process. Senior Production Manager Sarah Segal masterfully kept the book to its tight schedule, and Babs Reingold created the distinctive design and art program. Production Manager Stacey Alexander did her usual excellent work of producing the many print supplements.

At Hope College, the supporting team members for this edition included Kathryn Brownson, who researched countless bits of information, proofed hundreds of pages, and with the assistance of Rachel Brownson and Jennifer Huber, prepared the References section. Typesetters Phyllis and Richard Vandervelde worked faithfully and joyfully to enter or revise every one of the more than 300,000 words, and finally to code them for electronic delivery.

Again, I gratefully acknowledge the influence and editing assistance of my writing coach, poet Jack Ridl, whose influence resides in the voice you will be hearing in the pages that follow. He more than anyone cultivated my delight in dancing with the language, and taught me to approach writing as a craft that shades into art.

After hearing countless dozens of people say that this book's supplements have taken their teaching to a new level, I reflect on how fortunate I am to be a part of a team on which everyone has produced on-time work marked by the highest professional standards. For their remarkable talents, their long-term dedication, and their friendship, I thank Martin Bolt, John Brink, Thomas Ludwig, and Richard Straub.

Finally, my gratitude extends to the many students and instructors who have written to offer suggestions, or just an encouraging word. It is for them, and those about to begin their study of psychology, that I have done my best to introduce the field I love.

When those who paint the Golden Gate Bridge finish, it is time to start over again. So with this book. The ink is barely dry before one begins envisioning the next edition. By the time you read this, I will be gathering information for the next edition. Your input will again influence how this book continues to evolve. So, please, do share your thoughts.

David Myers

Hope College
Holland, Michigan 49422-9000
USA
davidmyers.org

Introduction to the History and Science of Psychology

Hoping to satisfy their curiosity about people and to remedy their woes, millions of people turn to "psychology." They listen to talk shows featuring over-the-air counseling, read magazine columns on harnessing psychic powers, attend seminars on how to stop smoking through hypnosis, and browse self-help books on the meaning of dreams, the secrets of ecstatic love, and the roots of personal happiness.

Others, intrigued by claims of psychological truth, wonder: Do mothers and infants bond in the first hours after birth? Should we trust memories of child sexual abuse "recovered" in adulthood? Are first-born children more driven to achieve? Does handwriting give clues to personality? Does psychotherapy help?

For these questioners, as for most people whose exposure to psychology comes from popular books, magazines, and TV, psychologists analyze personality, offer counseling, and dispense child-rearing advice.

Do they? Yes, and much more. Consider some of psychology's questions that from time to time you may wonder about:

Have you ever found yourself reacting to something just as one of your parents would—perhaps in a way you vowed you never would—and then wondered how much of your personality you inherited? *To what extent is your parents' influence transmitted through their genes, to what extent through the home and neighborhood environments they gave you?*

Have you ever played peekaboo with a 6-month-old infant and wondered why the baby finds the game so delightful? The baby reacts as though, when you momentarily move behind a door, you actually disappear—only to reappear later out of thin air. *What do babies actually perceive and think?*

Have you ever awakened from a nightmare and, with a wave of relief, wondered why you had such a crazy dream? *How often, and why, do we dream?*

Have you ever wondered what leads to school and work success? Are some people just born smarter? *Does sheer intelligence explain why some people get richer, think more creatively, or relate more sensitively?*

Do you ever get depressed or anxious and wonder whether you'll ever feel "normal"? *What triggers our bad moods—and our good ones?*

Have you ever worried about how to act among people of a different culture, race, or gender? *In what ways are we alike as members of the human family? How do we differ?*

Such questions provide grist for psychology's mill (Module 1), because psychology is a science (Module 2) that seeks to answer all sorts of questions about us all: how we think, feel, and act.

1 The History and Scope of Psychology

Psychology's Roots

PREVIEW QUESTION 1 How did the science of psychology develop?[1]

To be human is to be curious about ourselves and the world around us. Psychology's ancestors therefore date to the world's early writings. Before 300 B.C., the Greek naturalist and philosopher Aristotle theorized about learning and memory, motivation and emotion, perception and personality. Today we chuckle at some of his guesses, like his suggestion that a meal makes us sleepy by causing gas and heat to collect around the source of our personality, the heart. But credit Aristotle with asking the right questions.

Philosophers' thinking about thinking continued until the birth of psychology as we know it, on a December day in 1879. In a small room on the third floor of a shabby building at Germany's University of Leipzig, two young men were helping a long-faced, austere, middle-aged professor, Wilhelm Wundt, create an experimental apparatus. Their machine measured the time lag between people's hearing a ball hit a platform and their pressing a telegraph key (Hunt, 1993). Later, the researchers compared this lag to the time required for slightly more complex tasks. Wundt was seeking to measure the "atoms of the mind"—the fastest and simplest mental processes. Thus began what many consider psychology's first experiment, launching the first psychological institute, staffed by Wundt and psychology's first graduate students.

The young science of psychology evolved from the more established fields of philosophy and biology. Wundt was both a philosopher and a physiologist. Charles Darwin, who proposed evolutionary psychology, was an English naturalist. Ivan Pavlov, who pioneered the study of learning, was a Russian physiologist. Sigmund Freud, renowned personality theorist, was an Austrian physician. Jean Piaget, the twentieth century's most influential observer of children, was a Swiss biologist. William James, author of an important 1890 psychology textbook, was an American philosopher. This list of pioneering psychologists—"Magellans of the mind," as Morton Hunt (1993) has called them—illustrates that psychology has its origins in many countries and disciplines (**FIGURE 1.1**).

A smile is a smile the world around
Psychology studies not only our cultural and gender diversity but also the similarities that define our shared human nature. Men and women in different cultures show differences in when and how often they smile, but a smile *means* the same thing anywhere in the world.

[1]A Preview Question will appear at the beginning of each major section of a module. Search actively for the answer to the question as you read through the section. Answers are available in the form of a numbered review at the end of the module.

FIGURE 1.1
A timeline of psychology's pioneers, 1879–1913

Hermann Ebbinghaus in Germany reports the first experiments on memory (1885).

Alfred Binet (shown) and **Théodore Simon** publish the first intelligence test for use with Parisian schoolchildren (1905).

Wilhelm Wundt establishes the first psychology laboratory at the University of Leipzig, Germany (1879).

Margaret Floy Washburn, the first woman to receive a Ph.D. in psychology, synthesizes research on animal behavior in *The Animal Mind* (1908).

Edward L. Thorndike in the United States conducts the first experiments on animal learning (1898).

American Psychological Association is founded (1892).

1875 1880 1885 1890 1895 1900 1905 1910 1915

G. Stanley Hall, a student of Wundt's, establishes what many consider the first American psychology laboratory at Johns Hopkins University (1883).

Sigmund Freud in Austria introduces his psychoanalytic theory in *The Interpretation of Dreams* (1900).

John B. Watson in the United States champions psychology as the science of behavior (1913).

William James publishes the widely used *Principles of Psychology* in the United States (1890).

Mary Whiton Calkins creates paired-associates technique for studying memory; becomes president of American Psychological Association (1905).

Ivan Pavlov in Russia begins to publish his classic studies of animal learning (1906).

So what is psychology? With activities ranging from psychotherapy to the study of nerve cell activity, psychology is not easily defined. Psychology began as the science of mental life. Wundt's basic research tool became introspection—self-examination of one's own emotional states and mental processes. Wundt focused on *inner* sensations, feelings, and images. Thus, until the 1920s, psychology was defined as "the science of mental life."

From the 1920s into the 1960s, American psychologists, initially led by flamboyant and provocative John B. Watson, dismissed introspection and redefined psychology as "the science of observable behavior." After all, said these *behaviorists,* science is rooted in observation. You cannot observe a sensation, a feeling, or a thought, but you *can* observe people's *behavior* as they respond to different situations.

In the 1960s, psychology began to recapture its initial interest in mental processes through studies of how our minds process and retain information. To encompass psychology's concern both with observable behavior and with inner thoughts and feelings, **psychology** has become *the science of behavior and mental processes.*

Let's unpack this definition. *Behavior* is anything an organism *does*—any action we can observe and record. Yelling, smiling, blinking, sweating, talking, and questionnaire-marking are all observable behaviors. *Mental processes* are the internal subjective experiences we infer from behavior—sensations, perceptions, dreams, thoughts, beliefs, and feelings.

For many psychologists, the key word in psychology's definition is *science.* Psychology, as I will emphasize throughout this book, is less a set of findings than a way of asking and answering questions. As a science, psychology attempts to sift opinions and evaluate ideas with careful observation and rigorous analysis. In its quest to describe and explain nature (human nature included), psychological science welcomes hunches and plausible-sounding theories. And it puts them to the test. If a theory works—if the data support its predictions—so much the better for that theory. If the predictions fail, the theory will be revised or rejected.

My aim in this text, then, is not merely to report results but also to show you how psychologists play the game. How do researchers sift contesting opinions and ideas? And how might all of us, whether scientists or simply curious people, think smarter when describing and explaining the events of our lives?

Of course, psychology also has content: Its scientific sifting of ideas has produced a smorgasbord of concepts and findings, from which we can only sample the fare. Once aware of psychology's well-researched ideas—about how body and mind connect, how a child's mind grows, how we construct our perceptions, how we remember (and misremember) our experiences, how people across the world differ (and are alike)—your mind may never again be quite the same.

Psychology's Perspectives

PREVIEW QUESTION 2 What theoretical perspectives do psychologists take?

During its short history, which we will explore in more detail as we progress through this book, psychology has wrestled with some issues that will reappear in many different contexts.

The biggest and most persistent issue concerns *the relative contributions of biology and experience.* Do our human traits develop through experience, or do we come equipped with them? Today's psychologists explore this **nature-nurture** debate by asking, for example:

- Are differences in intelligence, personality, and psychological disorders influenced more by heredity or by environment?
- Is children's grammar innate or formed by experience?

Throughout this book, important concepts are **boldfaced.** As you study, you can find these terms with their definitions in a nearby margin and also at the end of the book in the Glossary section.

■ **psychology** the science of behavior and mental processes.

■ **nature-nurture issue** the longstanding controversy over the relative contributions that genes and experience make to the development of psychological traits and behaviors.

- Are eating and sexual behavior more "pushed" by inner biology or "pulled" by external incentives?
- Is depression a brain disorder or a thought disorder?
- How are humans alike (because of their common biology) and different (because of their differing cultures)?
- Are gender differences biologically predisposed or socially constructed?
- To what extent are we humans alike because of our shared evolutionary history and different because of cultural shaping?

The debate continues. Yet over and over again we will see the nature-nurture tension dissolve: *Nurture works on what nature endows*. Our species is biologically endowed with an enormous capacity to learn and adapt. Moreover, every psychological event (every thought, every emotion) is simultaneously a biological event. Thus depression can be *both* a thought disorder and a brain disorder.

We can simultaneously view any psychological event from several perspectives (Table 1.1). Let's consider anger, for example.

Like peas in a pod
Because identical twins have the same genes, they are ideal participants in studies designed to shed light on hereditary and environmental influences on temperament, intelligence, and other traits. Studies of identical and fraternal twins provide a rich array of findings that underscore the importance of both nature and nurture.

TABLE 1.1

PSYCHOLOGY'S CURRENT PERSPECTIVES

Perspective	Focus	Sample Questions
Neuroscience	How the body and brain create emotions, memories, and sensory experiences	How are messages transmitted within the body? How is blood chemistry linked with moods and motives?
Evolutionary	How nature selects traits that promote the perpetuation of one's genes	How does evolution influence behavior tendencies?
Behavior-genetics	How much our genes, and our environment, influence our individual differences	To what extent are psychological traits such as intelligence, personality, sexual orientation, and depression attributable to our genes? To our environment?
Psychodynamic	How behavior springs from unconscious drives and conflicts	How can a person's personality traits and disorders be explained as the disguised effects of unconscious motivations and early childhood traumas?
Behavioral	How we learn observable responses	How do we learn to fear particular objects or situations? What is the most effective way to alter our behavior, say, to lose weight or stop smoking?
Cognitive	How we encode, process, store, and retrieve information	How do we use information in remembering? Reasoning? Solving problems?
Social-cultural	How behavior and thinking vary across situations and cultures	How are we—as Africans, Asians, Australians, or North Americans—alike as members of one human family? As products of different environmental contexts, how do we differ?

Views of anger
How would each of psychology's perspectives explain what's going on here?

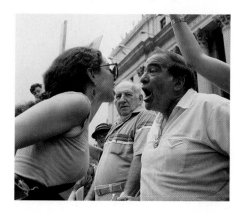

- Someone working from a *neuroscience perspective* might study the brain circuits that trigger the physical state of being "red in the face" and "hot under the collar."
- Someone working from an *evolutionary perspective* might analyze how anger facilitated the survival of our ancestors' genes.
- Someone working from a *behavior-genetics* perspective might study how heredity and experience influence our individual differences in temperament.
- Someone working from a *psychodynamic perspective* might view an outburst as an outlet for unconscious hostility.
- Someone working from a *behavioral perspective* might study the facial expressions and body gestures that accompany anger, or might attempt to determine which external stimuli result in angry responses or aggressive acts.
- Someone working from a *cognitive perspective* might study how our interpretation of a situation affects our anger and how our anger affects our thinking.
- Someone working from a *social-cultural perspective* might explore which situations produce the most anger, and how expressions of anger vary across cultural contexts.

Such perspectives needn't contradict one another. Rather, they are complementary outlooks on the same biological state. It's like explaining why grizzly bears hibernate. Is it because hibernation enhanced their ancestors' survival and reproduction? Because their inner physiology drives them to do so? Because cold environments hinder food gathering during winter? Such perspectives are complementary, because "everything is related to everything else" (Brewer, 1996).

So bear in mind psychology's limits. Don't expect it to answer the ultimate questions posed by Russian novelist Leo Tolstoy (1904): "Why should I live? Why should I do anything? Is there in life any purpose which the inevitable death that awaits me does not undo and destroy?" Instead, expect that psychology will help you understand why people think, feel, and act as they do. Then you should find the study of psychology both fascinating and useful.

Information sources, such as "Leo Tolstoy (1904)," are provided more fully in the References section at the book's end.

Psychology's Subfields

PREVIEW QUESTION 3 What are psychology's specialized subfields?

Picturing a chemist at work, you probably envision a white-coated scientist surrounded by glassware and high-tech equipment. Picture a psychologist at work and you would be right to envision

- a white-coated scientist probing a rat's brain.
- an intelligence researcher measuring how quickly an infant becomes bored with (looks away from) a familiar picture.
- an executive proposing a new "healthy life-styles" training program for employees.
- someone at a computer keyboard analyzing data on whether adopted teens' temperaments more closely resemble those of their adoptive parents or their biological parents.
- a therapist listening carefully to a client's depressed thoughts.
- a traveler en route to another culture to collect data on variations in human values and behaviors.
- a teacher or writer sharing the joy of psychology with others.

The cluster of subfields that we call psychology has less unity than most other sciences. But there is a payoff: Psychology is a meeting ground for different disciplines and is thus a perfect home for those with wide-ranging interests. In their diverse activities, from biological experimentation to cultural comparisons, psychologists share a common quest: describing and explaining behavior and the mental processes that underlie it.

"I'm a social scientist, Michael. That means I can't explain electricity or anything like that, but if you ever want to know about people I'm your man."

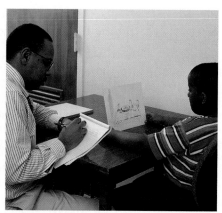

Psychology: A science and a profession
In their laboratories and consulting rooms, psychologists study and treat a wide range of human conditions. Here you see a face-to-face encounter typical of psychotherapy, a researcher introducing a participant to a laboratory experiment designed to test social judgment, and a psychologist testing a child.

Some psychologists conduct **basic research** that builds psychology's knowledge base. In the pages to follow we will meet a wide variety of such researchers:

- *Biological psychologists* exploring the links between brain and mind
- *Developmental psychologists* studying our changing abilities from womb to tomb
- *Cognitive psychologists* experimenting with how we perceive, think, and solve problems
- *Personality psychologists* investigating our inner traits
- *Social psychologists* exploring how we view and affect one another

Other psychologists conduct **applied research** that tackles practical problems. For example, *industrial/organizational psychologists* study and advise on behavior in the workplace. They use psychology's concepts and methods to help organizations and companies to select and train employees more effectively, to boost morale and productivity, to design products, and to implement systems.

Although most psychology textbooks focus on the methods and results of psychological science, psychology is also a helping profession devoted to such practical issues as how to have a happy marriage, how to overcome anxiety or depression, and how to raise thriving children. **Clinical psychologists** study, assess, and treat troubled people. After graduate school training, they administer and interpret tests, provide psychotherapy, manage mental health programs, and conduct research. By contrast, **psychiatrists,** who also often provide psychotherapy, are medical doctors licensed to prescribe drugs and otherwise treat physical causes of psychological disorders.

Today, psychology's researchers and students, like its historic pioneers, are citizens of many lands, from Australia to Western Europe to the developing nations. Worldwide, the number of psychologists—now well over 500,000—has doubled since 1980 (Rosenzweig, 1992). Sixty-four nations, from Argentina to Zimbabwe, participate in the International Union of Scientific Psychology (Rosenzweig, 1999).

■ **basic research** pure science that aims to increase the scientific knowledge base.

■ **applied research** scientific study that aims to solve practical problems.

■ **clinical psychology** a branch of psychology that studies, assesses, and treats people with psychological disorders.

■ **psychiatry** a branch of medicine dealing with psychological disorders; practiced by physicians who sometimes provide medical (for example, drug) treatments as well as psychological therapy.

I see you!
A biological psychologist might view this child's delighted response as evidence for brain maturation. A cognitive psychologist might see it as a demonstration of the baby's growing knowledge of his surroundings. For a cross-cultural psychologist, the role of grandparents in different societies might be the issue of interest.

rehearse it!

1. Psychology is the science of behavior and mental processes. The perspective in psychology that focuses on how behavior and thought differ from situation to situation and from culture to culture is the
   a. cognitive perspective.
   b. behavioral perspective.
   c. social-cultural perspective.
   d. neuroscience perspective.

2. In the history of psychology, one of the main debates has been over the nature-nurture issue. Nature is to nurture as
   a. personality is to intelligence.
   b. biology is to experience.
   c. intelligence is to biology.
   d. psychological traits are to behaviors.

3. The behavioral perspective in psychology emphasizes observable responses and how they are acquired and modified. A behavioral psychologist would be most likely to study
   a. the effect of school uniforms on classroom behaviors.
   b. the hidden meaning in children's themes and drawings.
   c. the age at which children can learn algebra.
   d. whether certain mathematical abilities appear to be inherited.

4. A psychologist who treats emotionally troubled adolescents at the local mental health agency is most likely to be a/an
   a. research psychologist.
   b. psychiatrist.

   c. industrial/organizational psychologist.
   d. clinical psychologist.

5. A psychologist who conducts basic research to expand psychology's knowledge base would be most likely to
   a. design a computer screen with limited glare and assess the effect on computer operators' eyes after a day's work.
   b. treat older people who are overcome by depression.
   c. observe 3- and 6-year-old children solving puzzles and analyze differences in their abilities.
   d. interview children with behavioral problems and suggest treatments.

You can use these Rehearse It questions to gauge whether you are ready for the next section. The answers are at the end of the module.

"What good fortune for those in power that people do not think."

Adolph Hitler, 1889–1945

Psychology's Scientific Strategies

Although in some ways we outsmart the smartest computers, our intuition often goes awry. To err is human. Enter psychological science. With its procedures for gathering and sifting evidence, science restrains error. As we familiarize ourselves with its strategies and incorporate its underlying principles into our daily thinking, we can think smarter. *Psychologists use the science of behavior and mental processes to better understand why people think, feel, and act as they do.*

What About Intuition and Common Sense?

PREVIEW QUESTION 4 What leads people to overestimate the value of common sense and underestimate the usefulness of psychological science?

In sifting reality from illusion, won't intuition and plain common sense suffice for everyday life? Some say psychology merely documents what people already know and dresses it in jargon: "So what else is new—you get paid for using fancy methods to prove what my grandmother knew?"

Others scorn a scientific approach because of their faith in human intuition. Advocates of "intuitive management" urge us to distrust statistical predictors and tune into our hunches when hiring, firing, and investing. Like *Star Wars'* Luke Skywalker, we should trust the force within.

Actually, as writer Madeline L'Engle noted (1973), "The naked intellect is an extraordinarily inaccurate instrument." Intuition can lead us astray. We sometimes err in presuming we could have foreseen what we know happened.

Did We Know It All Along? The Hindsight Bias

■ **hindsight bias** the tendency to believe, after learning an outcome, that one would have foreseen it. (Also known as the *I-knew-it-all-along phenomenon*.)

How easy it is to seem astute when drawing the bull's-eye after the arrow has struck. *After* each stock market downswing, for example, investment gurus say "the market was obviously overdue for a correction." Finding out that something has happened makes it seem inevitable. Psychologists call this 20/20 hindsight vision the **hindsight bias,** also known as the *I-knew-it-all-along phenomenon* (Slovic & Fischhoff, 1977; Wood, 1979).

This phenomenon is easy to demonstrate by giving half the members of a group some purported psychological finding, and the other half an opposite result. If you were in the first group, you might read, "Psychologists have found that separation weakens romantic attraction. As the saying goes, 'Out of sight, out of mind.'" Could you imagine why this might be true? Most people can, and nearly all will then regard this true finding as unsurprising.

But what if you had read the opposite: "Psychologists have found that separation strengthens romantic attraction. As the saying goes, 'Absence makes the heart grow fonder.'" People given this result can also easily explain it, and they overwhelmingly see it as unsurprising common sense. Obviously, when both a supposed finding and its opposite seem like common sense, there is a problem.

From our vantage point, it may in hindsight seem obvious that Eastern European countries would exchange communism for democracy. But it wasn't obvious to United Nations ambassador Jeanne Kirkpatrick in 1980 when she warned, "The history of this century provides no grounds for expecting that radical totalitarian regimes will transform themselves." The point is *not that common sense is usually wrong, but that it is often perceived after the fact. Common sense describes what *has happened* more easily than it predicts what *will happen.* As Dr. Watson said to Sherlock Holmes, "Anything seems commonplace, once explained."

Nevertheless, Grandmother is often right. As Yogi Berra once said, "You can observe a lot by watching." (We have Berra to thank for other gems, such as "Nobody ever comes here—it's too crowded," and "If the people don't want to come out to the ballpark, nobody's gonna stop 'em.") Because we're all behavior-watchers, it would be surprising if many of psychology's findings had *not* been foreseen. Many people believe that love breeds happiness, and they are right, according to researchers who have found that we humans have a deep "need to belong."

But sometimes Grandmother's intuition has it wrong. Informed by countless casual observations, our intuition may tell us that familiarity breeds contempt, that dreams predict the future, and that emotional reactions coincide with menstrual phase. The available evidence suggests that these common-sense ideas are wrong, wrong, and wrong. Throughout this book we will see how research has both inspired and overturned popular ideas—about aging, about sleep and dreams, about personality. And we will also see how it has surprised us with discoveries about how the brain's chemical messengers control our moods and memories, about animal abilities, and about the effects of stress on our capacity to fight disease.

The limits of intuition
Personnel interviewers tend to be overconfident of their gut feelings about job applicants. Their confidence stems partly from their recalling cases where their favorable impression proved right, and from their ignorance about rejected applicants who succeeded elsewhere.

"Life is lived forwards, but understood backwards."

Søren Kierkegaard, 1813–1855

"There are three things extremely hard, Steel, a Diamond, and to know one's self."

Benjamin Franklin, 1706–1790

© 1988 by Sidney Harris/American Scientist Magazine.

INSTITUTE for ADVANCED HINDSIGHT
RESEARCH INTO WHAT SHOULD HAVE BEEN

Overconfidence

Our everyday thinking is limited not only by our after-the-fact common sense but also by our human tendency toward overconfidence: We tend to think we know more than we do. Asked how sure we are of our answers to factual questions (is Boston north or south of Paris?), we tend to be more confident than correct.[1] Or consider these three anagrams, which Richard Goranson (1978) asked people to unscramble.

> WREAT → WATER
>
> ETRYN → ENTRY
>
> GRABE → BARGE

Reflect for a moment: About how many seconds do you think it would have taken you to unscramble each of these?

Once people know the target word, hindsight makes it seem obvious—so much so that they become overconfident. They think they would have seen the solution in only 10 seconds or so, when in reality the average subject spent 3 minutes, as you also might, given a similar anagram without the solution: OCHSA (see page 13 to check your answer).

Are we any better at predicting our social behavior? To find out, Robert Vallone and his associates (1990) had students predict at the beginning of the school year whether they would drop a course, vote in an upcoming election, call their parents more than twice a month, and so forth. On average, the students felt 84 percent confident in making these self-predictions. Later quizzes about their actual behavior showed their predictions were correct only 71 percent of the time. Even when they were 100 percent sure of themselves, their self-predictions erred 15 percent of the time.

The point to remember: Hindsight and overconfidence bias lead us to overestimate our intuition. But scientific inquiry, fed by skepticism and humility, helps us sift reality from illusion.

The Scientific Attitude

PREVIEW QUESTION 5 What attitudes characterize scientific inquiry?

Underlying all science is a hard-headed *curiosity,* a passion to explore and understand without misleading or being misled. Some questions (Is there life after death?) are beyond science. To answer them in any way requires a leap of faith. With many other ideas (Can some people demonstrate ESP?), the proof is in the

> "We don't like their sound. Groups of guitars are on their way out."
>
> **Decca Records, in turning down a recording contract with the Beatles in 1962**

> "Computers in the future may weigh no more than 1.5 tons."
>
> **Popular Mechanics, 1949**

> "The telephone may be appropriate for our American cousins, but not here, because we have an adequate supply of messenger boys."
>
> **British expert group evaluating the invention of the telephone**

> "They couldn't hit an elephant at this dist—."
>
> **General John Sedgwick's last words, uttered during a U.S. Civil War battle, 1864**

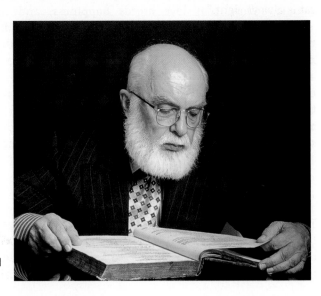

The amazing Randi
The magician James Randi exemplifies skepticism. He has tested and debunked a variety of psychic phenomena.

pudding. No matter how sensible or crazy-sounding an idea, the hard-headed question is, Does it work? When put to the test, can its predictions be confirmed?

This scientific approach has a long history. As ancient a figure as Moses used such an approach. How do you evaluate a self-proclaimed prophet? His answer: Put the prophet to the test. If the predicted event "does not take place or prove true," then so much the worse for the prophet (*Deuteronomy* 18:22). Magician James Randi uses Moses' approach when testing those claiming to see auras around people's bodies:

Aura-seer:	Yes, indeed.
Randi:	Do you see an aura around my head?
Aura-seer:	Yes, indeed.
Randi:	Can you still see the aura if I put this magazine in front of my face?
Aura-seer:	Of course.
Randi:	Then if I were to step behind a wall barely taller than I am, you could determine my location from the aura visible above my head, right?

Randi tells me that no aura-seer has yet agreed to take this simple test.

When subjected to such scrutiny, crazy-sounding ideas sometimes find support. More often, it relegates crazy-sounding ideas to the mountain of forgotten claims of perpetual motion machines, miracle cancer cures, and out-of-body travels into centuries past. To sift reality from fantasy, sense from nonsense, therefore requires a scientific attitude: being skeptical but not cynical, open but not gullible.

As scientists, psychologists approach the world of behavior with a curious *skepticism*. They persistently ask two questions: What do you mean? How do you know? Consider some familiar claims: that theater owners can make you hungry by flashing an imperceptibly brief message—EAT POPCORN; that lie detectors tell the truth; that astrologers can analyze your character and predict your future based on the position of the planets at your birth. As you will see in the pages that follow, we can test such claims. In the arena of competing ideas, skeptical testing can reveal which ones best match the facts. "To believe with certainty," says a Polish proverb, "we must begin by doubting."

Putting a scientific attitude into practice requires not only skepticism but also *humility* because we may have to reject our own ideas. In the last analysis, what matters is not my opinion or yours, but the truths nature reveals in response to our questioning. If people don't behave as our ideas predict, then so much the worse for our ideas. This is the humble attitude expressed in one of psychology's early mottos: "The rat is always right."

Historians of science tell us that these attitudes of curiosity, skepticism, and humility helped make modern science possible. Many of its founders were people whose religious convictions made them humble before nature and skeptical of any human authority (Hooykaas, 1972; Merton, 1938). Of course, scientists, like anyone else, can have big egos and may cling to their preconceptions. We all view nature through the spectacles of our preconceived ideas. Still, the ideal that unifies psychologists with all scientists is the skeptical yet humble scrutiny of competing ideas. As a community, scientists check and recheck one another's findings and conclusions.

Critical Thinking

This scientific attitude, with its principles for sifting reality from illusion, prepares us to think smarter. Smart thinking, called **critical thinking,** examines assumptions, discerns hidden values, evaluates evidence, and assesses conclusions. Whether reading a news report or listening to a conversation, critical thinkers ask questions. They

> "The scientist . . . must be free to ask any question, to doubt any assertion, to seek for any evidence, to correct any errors."
>
> **Physicist J. Robert Oppenheimer,** *Life,* October 10, 1949

> "A skeptic is one who is willing to question any truth claim, asking for clarity in definition, consistency in logic, and adequacy of evidence."
>
> **Philosopher Paul Kurtz,** *The Skeptical Inquirer,* 1994

> "My deeply held belief is that if a god anything like the traditional sort exists, our curiosity and intelligence are provided by such a god. We would be unappreciative of those gifts . . . if we suppressed our passion to explore the universe and ourselves."
>
> **Carl Sagan,** *Broca's Brain,* 1979

■ **critical thinking** thinking that does not blindly accept arguments and conclusions. Rather, it examines assumptions, discerns hidden values, evaluates evidence, and assesses conclusions.

Throughout this book, you will encounter Thinking Critically boxes. Each highlights careful thinking about some interesting or important issue.

wonder, How do they know that? What's this person's agenda? Is the conclusion based on anecdote and gut feelings, or on evidence? Does the evidence justify a cause-and-effect conclusion? What alternative explanations are possible? Carried to an extreme, healthy skepticism can degenerate into a negative cynicism that scorns any unproven idea. But a critical attitude can also produce humility—an awareness of our own vulnerability to error and an openness to surprises and new perspectives.

Has psychology's own critical inquiry indeed been open to surprising findings? The answer is plainly yes. Believe it or not . . .

- massive losses of brain tissue early in life may have minimal long-term effects.
- within days, newborns can recognize their mother's odor and voice.
- prolonged stress hinders the body's disease-fighting immune system, making people more vulnerable to physical illness.
- diverse groups—men and women, old and young, rich and working class, those with disabilities and without—report roughly comparable levels of personal happiness.
- electroconvulsive ("shock") therapy is often a very effective treatment for severe depression.

And has critical inquiry convincingly debunked popular presumptions? The answer is again yes. The available evidence indicates that . . .

- sleepwalkers are *not* acting out their dreams; sleeptalkers are *not* verbalizing their dreams.
- our past experiences are *not* all recorded verbatim in our brains; with brain stimulation or hypnosis, one *cannot* simply "play the tape" and relive long-buried or repressed memories.
- most people do *not* suffer from unrealistically low self-esteem.
- opposites do *not* generally attract.

"The real purpose of the scientific method is to make sure Nature hasn't misled you into thinking you know something you don't actually know."

Robert M. Pirsig, *Zen and the Art of Motorcycle Maintenance*, 1974

Tips for Studying Psychology

PREVIEW QUESTION 6 How can psychological principles help you as a student?

The investment you are making in studying psychology has the potential to enrich your life and enlarge your vision. Although many of life's significant questions are beyond psychology, some very important ones are illuminated by even a first course in psychology. Through painstaking research, psychologists have gained insights into brain and mind, depression and joy, dreams and memories. Even the unanswered questions can enrich us, by renewing our sense of mystery about "things too wonderful" for us yet to understand. What is more, your study of psychology can help teach you *how to ask important questions*—how to think critically as you evaluate competing ideas and pop psychology's claims.

Having your life enriched and your vision enlarged (and getting a decent grade, too) requires effective study. To master any subject you must *actively process* it. Your mind is not like your stomach, something to be filled passively; it is more like a muscle, which grows stronger with exercise. Countless experiments reveal that people learn and remember material best when they put it in their own words, rehearse it, and then review and rehearse it again.

The **SQ3R** study method incorporates these principles (Robinson, 1970). SQ3R is an acronym for its five steps: Survey, Question, Read, Rehearse, Review.

This book, unlike most psychology texts (including others that I have written), is organized by *short* chapters (modules) of readable length. To study a module, first *survey*, taking a bird's-eye view as you note its headings. Notice how the module is organized.

■ **SQ3R** a study method incorporating five steps: *Survey, Question, Read, Rehearse, Review.*

As you prepare to read each section, use its heading or the preview question to form a *question* that you should answer. For this section, you might have asked, "How can I most effectively and efficiently master the information in this book?"

Then *read* the section, actively searching for the answer. Relating what you are reading to your own life will improve understanding and retention. As you work through each module, reading the occasional Close-Up and Thinking Critically boxes will also help.

Having read a module, *rehearse* in your own words what you read. Test yourself by trying to answer your questions, rehearsing what you can recall, then glancing back over what you can't recall.

Finally, *review:* Read over any notes you have taken, again with an eye on the organization of the material, and quickly review the module.

Survey, question, read, rehearse, review. I have organized this book to facilitate your use of the SQ3R study system. Each module begins with an outline (a list of section headings) that aids your *survey*. Headings and preview *questions* suggest issues and concepts you should consider as you *read*. The material is organized into modules of readable length, and within each module are questions (Rehearse It!) that help you *rehearse* what you have learned. A *review* at the end of each module covers the module's essentials, and the list of key terms helps you check your mastery of important concepts. Survey, question, read. . . .

Five additional study tips may further boost your learning:

1. *Distribute your study time.* One of psychology's oldest findings is that "spaced practice" promotes better retention than "massed practice." You'll remember material better if you space your time over several study periods rather than cram it into one long study blitz. Better to give your study of this text one hour a day, with one day off a week, than six hours at a time. Doing this requires a disciplined approach to managing your time. (Richard Straub explains time management in *Discovering Psychology,* the study guide that accompanies this text.) For example, rather than trying to read several modules in a single sitting, read just one module and then turn to something else.

2. *Learn to think critically.* Whether reading or in class, note people's *assumptions and values.* What perspective or bias underlies an argument? *Evaluate evidence.* Is it anecdotal? Correlational? Experimental? *Assess conclusions.* Are there alternative explanations?

3. *In class, listen actively.* As psychologist William James urged a century ago, "No reception without reaction, no impression without . . . expression." Listen for the main ideas and subideas of a lecture. Write them down. Ask questions during and after class. In class, as in your private study, process the information actively and you will understand and retain it better.

4. *Overlearn.* Psychology tells us that overlearning improves retention. Most of us are prone to overestimating how much we know. You may understand a module as you read it, but by devoting extra study time to testing yourself and reviewing what you think you know, you will retain your new knowledge long into the future.

5. *Be a smart test-taker.* If a test contains both multiple-choice questions and an essay question, turn first to the essay. Read the question carefully, noting exactly what the instructor is asking. On the back of a page, pencil in a list of points you'd like to make and then organize them. Before writing, put aside the essay and work through the multiple-choice questions. (As you do so, your mind may continue to mull over the essay question. Sometimes the objective questions will bring pertinent thoughts to mind.) Then reread the essay question, rethink your answer, and start writing. When you've finished, proofread

Solution to anagram on page 10: CHAOS.

to eliminate spelling and grammatical errors that make you look less competent than you are. When reading multiple-choice questions, don't confuse yourself by trying to imagine how each of the alternatives might be right. Try instead to recall the answer *before* reading the alternatives given. Answer the question as if it were a fill-in-the-blank; first cover the answers and complete the sentence in your mind, and then find the alternative that best matches your own answer.

While exploring psychology, you will learn much more than effective study techniques. Psychology deepens our appreciation for how we humans perceive, think, feel, and act. By so doing it can indeed enrich our lives and enlarge our vision. Through this book I hope to help guide you toward that end. As educator Charles Eliot said a century ago: "Books are the quietest and most constant of friends, and the most patient of teachers."

rehearse it!

6. Psychology tells us what we already know from common sense, say some skeptics. Hindsight bias refers to our tendency to
   a. perceive events as obvious or inevitable after the fact.
   b. assume that two events happened because we wished them to happen.
   c. overestimate our abilities to predict the future.
   d. make judgments that fly in the face of common sense.

7. As scientists, psychologists view theories with skepticism, humility, and curiosity. This means that they
   a. approach research with a negative cynicism.
   b. assume that an article published in a reputable journal must be true.
   c. realize that some issues should not be studied.
   d. persistently ask questions and are willing to reject ideas that cannot be verified by research.

8. A newspaper article describes how a "cure for cancer has been found." A critical thinker probably will
   a. immediately dismiss the article as untrue because there is no evidence to back up the facts.
   b. accept the information as a wonderful breakthrough.
   c. question the article, evaluate the evidence, and assess the conclusions.
   d. question the article but quickly accept it as true due to the author's excellent reputation.

REVIEWING

The History and Scope of Psychology

1. How did the science of psychology develop?

Beginning with the first psychological laboratory, founded in 1879 by German philosopher and physiologist Wilhelm Wundt, psychology's modern roots can be found in many disciplines and countries. From its early definition as "the science of mental life," psychology became the behaviorists' "science of observable behavior." Psychology's historic perspectives and current activities are now combined in the present definition: "the science of behavior and mental processes."

2. What theoretical perspectives do psychologists take?

Psychologists view behavior and mental processes from various perspectives. These currently include the neuroscience, evolutionary, behavior-genetics, psychodynamic, behavioral, cognitive, and social-cultural perspectives.

3. What are psychology's specialized subfields?

Psychology's subfields encompass basic research (often done by biological, developmental, cognitive, personality, and social psychologists), applied research (sometimes conducted by organizational/industrial psychologists), and clinical applications.

4. What leads people to overestimate the value of common sense and underestimate the usefulness of psychological science?

If intuition and common sense were trustworthy, we would have less need for scientific inquiry and critical thinking. But without such thinking we readily succumb to *hindsight bias,* or the I-knew-it-all-along phenomenon. Learning the outcome of a study (or of an everyday happening) can make it seem like obvious common sense. But things seldom seem so obvious before the fact. We also are routinely *overconfident* of our judgments, thanks partly to our bias to seek information that confirms them. Such biases lead us to overestimate our unaided intuition. Although limited by the testable questions it can address, a scientific approach can help us sift reality from illusion.

5. What attitudes characterize scientific inquiry?

Scientific inquiry begins with an eagerness to *skeptically* scrutinize competing ideas and an open-minded humility before nature. Putting ideas, even crazy-sounding ideas, to the test helps us winnow sense from nonsense. The *curiosity* that drives us to test ideas and to expose their underlying assumptions carries into everyday life as critical thinking.

6. How can psychological principles help you as a student?

Experiments have shown that learning and memory are enhanced by active study. The SQ3R study method—survey, question, read, rehearse, and review—applies the principles derived from these experiments.

TERMS AND CONCEPTS TO REMEMBER

psychology, p. 4
nature-nurture issue, p. 4
basic research, p. 7

applied research, p. 7
clinical psychology, p. 7
psychiatry, p. 7

hindsight bias, p. 8
critical thinking, p. 11
SQ3R, p. 12

REHEARSE IT ANSWER KEY

1. c   2. b   3. a   4. d   5. c   6. a   7. d   8. c

Research Strategies: How Psychologists Ask and Answer Questions

The Scientific Method

PREVIEW QUESTION 1 How do psychologists use the scientific method to construct theories?

In everyday conversation, we tend to use "theory" to mean "mere hunch." In science, "theory" is linked with observation. A scientific **theory** *explains* through an integrated set of principles that *organizes* and *predicts* observable behaviors or events. By organizing isolated facts, a theory simplifies things. Psychologists now know so many facts about behavior that we could never hope to remember them all. By linking such observations and bridging them to deeper principles, a theory offers a useful summary. By connecting the observed dots, theories reveal a coherent picture.

A good theory of depression, for example, will first help us organize countless observations concerning depression into a much shorter list of principles. Say we observe over and over that people with depression describe themselves—their past, present, and future—in gloomy terms. We might therefore theorize that low self-esteem contributes to depression. So far so good: Our self-esteem principle neatly summarizes a long list of facts about people with depression.

Yet no matter how reasonable a theory may sound—and low self-esteem certainly seems a reasonable explanation of depression—we must put it to the test. A good theory doesn't just sound appealing. It must imply testable predictions, called **hypotheses.** By enabling us to test and reject or revise the theory, such predictions give direction to research. They specify in advance what results would support the theory and what results would disconfirm it. To test our self-esteem theory of depression, we might give people a test of self-esteem on which they respond to statements such as "I have good ideas." Then we could see whether, as we hypothesized, people who report poorer self-images are indeed more depressed (**FIGURE 2.1**).

FIGURE 2.1

The scientific method

A self-correcting process for asking questions and observing nature's answer.

(1) Theories
Example: Low self-esteem feeds depression.

generate or refine

lead to

(3) Research and Observations
Example: Administer tests of self-esteem and depression. See if a low score on one predicts a high score on the other.

(2) Hypotheses
Example: People with low self-esteem are more apt to feel depression.

lead to

In testing our theory, we should be aware that it can bias our observations. Having theorized that depression springs from low self-esteem, we may see what we expect to see. We may be tempted to perceive depressed people's comments as self-disparaging.

As one check on their biases, psychologists report their research precisely enough—with clear **operational definitions** of concepts—to allow others to **replicate** (repeat) their observations. If other researchers re-create the essence of a study with different participants and materials and get similar results, then our confidence in the reliability of the finding grows. The first study of hindsight bias aroused psychologists' curiosity. Now, after many successful replications with differing people and questions, we feel quite sure of the phenomenon's power.

In the end, our theory will be useful if it (1) effectively *organizes* a range of self-reports and observations and (2) implies clear *predictions* that anyone can use to check the theory or to derive practical applications. (If we boost people's self-esteem, will their depression lift?) Eventually, our research will probably lead to a revised theory that better organizes and predicts what we know about depression.

Our research strategies include descriptive, correlational, and experimental methods. We test hypotheses and refine our theories by making *observations* that *describe* behavior. We detect *correlations* that help *predict* behavior. And we do *experiments* that help *explain* behavior. To think critically about popularized psychology claims, we need to recognize these designs and to know how we can use them to sharpen our everyday thinking.

Description

PREVIEW QUESTION 2 How do psychologists observe and describe behavior?

The starting point of any science is description. In everyday life, all of us observe and describe people, often drawing conclusions about why they behave as they do. Professional psychologists do much the same, only more objectively and systematically.

The Case Study

Among the oldest research methods is the **case study,** in which psychologists study one or more individuals in great depth in the hope of revealing things true of us all. Some examples: Much of our early knowledge about the brain came from case studies of individuals who suffered a particular impairment after damage to a certain brain region. Sigmund Freud constructed his theory of personality from a handful of case studies. Developmental psychologist Jean Piaget taught us about children's thinking after carefully observing and questioning but a few children. Studies of only a few chimpanzees have revealed their capacity for understanding and language. Intensive case studies are sometimes very revealing.

Although case studies can also suggest hypotheses for further study, they sometimes mislead us: Any given individual may be atypical. Unrepresentative information can lead to mistaken judgments and false conclusions. Indeed, anytime a researcher mentions a finding ("Smokers die younger: 95 percent of men over 85 are nonsmokers") someone is sure to offer a contradictory case ("Well, I have

> - **theory** an explanation using an integrated set of principles that organizes and predicts observations.
> - **hypothesis** a testable prediction, often implied by a theory.
> - **operational definition** a statement of the procedures (operations) used to define research variables. For example, *intelligence* may be operationally defined as what an intelligence test measures.
> - **replication** repeating the essence of a research study, usually with different participants in different situations, to see whether the basic finding generalizes to other participants and circumstances.
> - **case study** an observation technique in which one person is studied in depth in the hope of revealing universal principles.

Good theories explain by

1. organizing and linking observed facts.
2. implying hypotheses that offer testable predictions and, sometimes, practical applications.

"'Well my dear,' said Miss Marple, 'human nature is very much the same everywhere, and of course, one has opportunities of observing it at closer quarters in a village.'"

Agatha Christie, *The Tuesday Club Murders*, 1933

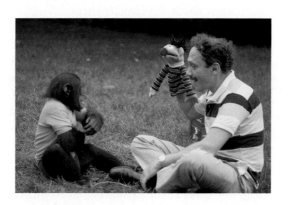

The case of the conversational chimpanzee

In intensive case studies of chimpanzees, psychologists have explored the intriguing question of whether language is uniquely human. Here Nim Chimpsky signs "hug" as his trainer, psychologist Herbert Terrace, shows him the puppet Ernie. But is Nim really capable of using language? Cognitive psychologists continue to debate this issue.

■ **survey** a technique for ascertaining the self-reported attitudes or behaviors of people, usually by questioning a representative, random sample of them.

an uncle who smoked two packs a day and lived to be 89"). Anecdotal cases—dramatic stories, personal experiences, even psychological case examples—have a way of overwhelming general truths. Numbers can be numbing (in one study of 1300 dream reports concerning a kidnapped child, only 5 percent correctly envisioned the child as dead). Anecdotes can be alarming ("But I know a man who dreamed his sister was in a car accident, and two days later she was badly injured").

The point to remember: Individual cases can suggest fruitful ideas. What's true of all of us can be glimpsed in any one of us. But to discern the general truths that cover individual cases, we must answer questions with other methods.

The Survey

The **survey** method, commonly used in both descriptive and correlational studies, looks at many cases in less depth. A survey asks people to report their behavior or opinions. Questions about everything from sexual practices to political opinions get put to the public. Harris and Gallup polls have revealed that 72 percent of Americans think there is too much TV violence, 84 percent favor equal job opportunities for homosexual people, 89 percent say they face high stress, 95 percent believe in God, and 96 percent would like to change something about their appearance.

Wording Effects

Asking questions is tricky. Even subtle changes in the order or wording of questions can have major effects. Should cigarette ads or pornography be allowed on television? People are much more likely to approve "not allowing" such things than "forbidding" or "censoring" them. In a recent national survey, only 27 percent of Americans approved of "government censorship" of media sex and violence, though 66 percent approved of "more restrictions on what is shown on television" (Lacayo, 1995). People are similarly much more approving of "aid to the needy" than of "welfare," of "affirmative action" than of "preferential treatment," and of "revenue enhancers" than of "taxes." Because wording questions is such a delicate matter, critical thinkers will reflect on how the phrasing of a question might have affected the opinions respondents expressed.

Sampling

You can describe human experience using common sense, dramatic anecdotes, personal experience, and arbitrary samples. But for an accurate picture of the experiences and attitudes of a whole population, there's only one game in town—the representative sample.

We can extend this point to everyday thinking, as we generalize from samples we observe. We meet a few students and attend a few classes during a visit to a college and infer from those instances how friendly the campus is and how good the teaching is. We observe the weather during a three-day visit to Copenhagen and then tell our friends about the climate there.

Overgeneralizing from such select samples is tempting, especially when they are vivid cases. Given (a) a statistical summary of a professor's student evaluations and (b) the vivid comments of two irate students, an administrator's impression of the professor may be influenced as much by the two unhappy students as by the many favorable evaluations in the statistical summary. Standing in the checkout line at the supermarket, George sees the woman in front of him pay with government-provided food stamps and then watches with dismay as she drives away in a fancy car. In both situations, the temptation to generalize from a few vivid but unrepresentative cases is nearly irresistible.

The point to remember: The best basis for generalizing is not from the exceptional cases one finds at the extremes, but from a representative sample of cases.

If you wished to survey the students at your college or university, how could you survey a sample that would represent the total student **population**—the whole group you wanted to study and describe? By making it a **random sample,** one in which every person in the entire group has an equal chance of participating.

To sample the students at your institution randomly, you would *not* send them all a questionnaire. (The conscientious people who return it would not be a random sample.) Rather, you would aim for a representative sample by, say, using a table of random numbers to pick participants from a student listing and then making sure you involve as many as possible. Large representative samples are better than small ones, but a small representative sample of 100 is better than an unrepresentative sample of 500.

The point to remember: Before believing survey findings, think critically: Consider the sample. You cannot compensate for an unrepresentative sample by simply adding more people.

The random-sampling principle also works in national surveys. Imagine that you had a giant barrel containing 60 million white beans mixed with 40 million red beans. A scoop that randomly sampled 1500 of them would contain about 60 percent white and 40 percent red beans, give or take 2 or 3 percent. Sampling voters in a national election survey is like sampling the beans; 1500 randomly sampled people, drawn from all areas of a country, provide a remarkably accurate snapshot of the opinions of a nation.

Because gathering a random sample can be a huge task, some don't make the effort. Shere Hite's book *Women and Love* reported survey findings based on only a 4.5 percent response rate from mailings to an unrepresentative sample of 100,000 women. The response was doubly unrepresentative because not only did she have a modest, self-selected return, but the women initially contacted were members of women's organizations. Nonetheless, "It's 4500 people. That's enough for me," reported Hite. And it was apparently enough for *Time* magazine, which made a cover story of her findings—that 70 percent of women married five or more years were having affairs, and that 95 percent of women felt emotionally harassed by the men they love (Wallis, 1987). Evidently it didn't matter that on less publicized surveys, *randomly* sampled American women expressed much higher levels of satisfaction: And only 1 in 7 reported having had an affair during their current marriage—a level of faithfulness replicated in British, French, and Danish surveys (Greeley, 1991, 1994). Without random sampling, large samples like Hite's—including call-in phone samples—merely give better estimates of a misleading number.

With very large samples, estimates become quite reliable. *E* is estimated to represent 12.7 percent of the letters in written English. *E*, in fact, is 12.3 percent of the 925,141 letters in Melville's *Moby Dick*, 12.4 percent of the 586,747 letters in Dickens' *A Tale of Two Cities*, and 12.1 percent of the 3,901,021 letters in 12 of Mark Twain's works (*Chance News*, 1997).

Drawing by D. Fradon; © 1969 The New Yorker Magazine, Inc.

"How would you like me to answer that question? As a member of my ethnic group, educational class, income group, or religious category?"

Naturalistic Observation

A third descriptive research method involves watching and recording the behavior of organisms in their natural environment and is known as **naturalistic observation.** Naturalistic observations range from watching chimpanzee societies in the jungle, to unobtrusive measures of parent-child interactions in different cultures, to recording students' self-seating patterns in the lunchrooms of multiracial schools.

Like the case study and survey methods, naturalistic observation does not *explain* behavior. It *describes* it. Nevertheless, description can be revealing. We once thought, for example, that only humans use tools. Then naturalistic observation revealed that chimpanzees sometimes insert a stick in a termite mound and withdraw it, eating the stick's load of termites. Such naturalistic observations, recalls chimpanzee observer

■ **population** all the cases in a group, from which samples may be drawn for a study.

■ **random sample** a sample that fairly represents a population because each member has an equal chance of inclusion.

■ **naturalistic observation** observing and recording behavior in naturally occurring situations without trying to manipulate and control the situation.

Naturalistic observation
Some psychologists study human and animal behavior in natural environments. As University of St. Andrews psychologist Richard Byrne observes an adult gorilla, recording its behavior on a hand-held computer, a curious infant approaches and investigates his camera lens cap.

Jane Goodall (1998), paved the way for later studies of animal thinking, language, and emotion. "Observations, made in the natural habitat, helped to show that the societies and behavior of animals are far more complex than previously supposed." We later learned that chimps and baboons also use deception to achieve their aims. Psychologists Andrew Whiten and Richard Byrne (1988) repeatedly saw one young baboon pretending to have been attacked by another as a tactic to get its mother to drive the other baboon away from its food.

Naturalistic observation also enabled Robert Levine and Ara Norenzayan (1999) to compare the pace of life in 31 countries. By operationally defining *pace of life* as walking speed, the speed with which postal clerks completed a simple request, and the accuracy of public clocks, they concluded that life is fastest-paced in Japan and Western Europe, and slower paced in economically less-developed countries. People in colder climates also live at a faster pace (and are more prone to die from heart disease). Naturalistic observation is often used to describe behavior. But this study, correlating pace of life with culture and climate, illustrates how it can also be used with correlational (and experimental) research.

Correlation

Describing behavior is a first step toward predicting it. When surveys and naturalistic observations reveal that one trait or behavior accompanies another, we say the two correlate. The **correlation coefficient** is a statistical measure of relationship. It reveals how closely two things vary together and thus how well either one *predicts* the other. Knowing how much aptitude test scores *correlate* with school success tells us how well the scores *predict* school success.

A *positive* correlation (between 0 and +1.00) indicates a *direct* relationship, meaning that two things increase together or decrease together. Some examples:

- According to some studies, the amount of violence viewed on television correlates about +.3 with aggressive social behavior; people's TV-viewing habits therefore modestly predict their aggressiveness (or vice versa).
- Genetically identical twins correlate about +.6 on tests of extraversion, which means that the outgoingness of either twin gives a reasonable clue to that of the other (Bouchard & others, 1990).
- University of Michigan surveys of 71,000 representatively sampled high school seniors revealed that the more hours students worked on a job, the less they slept and exercised and the more they used cigarettes, alcohol, and other drugs (ISR, 1994).

A *negative* correlation—equally predictive—indicates an *inverse* relationship: As one thing increases, the other decreases. Our earlier findings on self-esteem and depression illustrate a negative correlation: People who score *low* on self-esteem tend to score *high* on depression. Negative correlations could go as low as −1.00, which means that, like people on the opposite ends of a teeter-totter, one set of scores goes down precisely as the other goes up.

Though informative, psychology's correlations usually leave most of the variation among individuals unpredicted. As we will see, there is a correlation between parents' abusiveness and their children's later abusiveness when they become parents. But this does not mean that most abused children become abusive. The correlation simply indicates a statistical relationship: Although most abused children do not grow into abusers, nonabused children are even less likely to become abusive.

Likewise, early crime correlates with later crime. Boys arrested by age 14 are 18 times more likely to become chronic offenders than are boys who have not been arrested by that age, and chronic offenders are 14 times more likely to commit violent offenses. Yet two-thirds of boys arrested only once do *not* go on to commit violent crime (Forgatch, 1995). Correlations point us toward predictions, but usually imperfect ones.

■ **correlation coefficient** a statistical measure of the extent to which two factors vary together, and thus of how well either factor predicts the other.

Correlation and Causation

PREVIEW QUESTION 3 Why do correlations permit prediction but not explanation?

We have seen that correlations, however imperfect, do help us predict and restrain the illusions of our flawed intuition. Watching violence correlates with (and therefore predicts) aggression. But does that mean it *causes* aggression? Does low self-esteem *cause* depression? If, based on the correlational evidence, you assume that they do, you have much company. Among the most irresistible thinking errors made both by laypeople and by professional psychologists is assuming that correlation proves causation. And yet, no matter how strong the relationship, it does not! If watching TV violence correlates positively with aggressiveness, does this mean that watching TV violence influences aggressive behavior? Perhaps. But perhaps it means that aggressive people prefer violent programs. Or perhaps both are true.

And what about the negative correlation between self-esteem and depression? Perhaps low self-esteem does cause depression. But as **FIGURE 2.2** suggests, we'd get the same coincidence of low self-esteem and depression if depression caused people to be down on themselves or if something else—a third factor such as heredity or brain chemistry—caused both low self-esteem and depression. Among men, length of marriage correlates positively with hair loss—because both are associated with a third factor, age.

This point is so important—so basic to thinking smarter with psychology—that it merits one more example, from a survey of 12,118 adolescents: The more teens feel loved by their parents, the less likely they are to behave in unhealthy ways—having early sex, smoking, abusing alcohol and drugs, exhibiting violence (Resnick & others, 1997). "Adults have a powerful effect on their children's behavior right through the high school years," gushed an Associated Press story on the study. But the correlation comes with no built-in cause-and-effect arrow. Thus, the AP could as well have said, "Well-behaved teens feel their parents' love and approval; out-of-bounds teens more often think their parents are disapproving jerks."

The point to remember: Correlation indicates the *possibility* of a cause-and-effect relationship, *but it does not prove causation.* Knowing that two events are correlated need not tell us anything about causation. Remember this principle and you will be wiser as you see reports of scientific studies in the news and in this book.

Correlation need not mean causation
Length of marriage correlates with hair loss in men. Does this mean that marriage causes men to lose their hair (or that balding men make better husbands)? In this case, as in many others, a third factor obviously explains the correlation: Golden anniversaries and baldness both accompany aging.

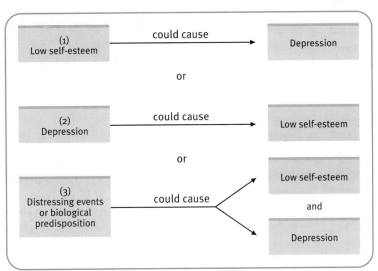

FIGURE 2.2

Three possible cause-and-effect relationships
People low in self-esteem are more likely to report depression than are those high in self-esteem. One possible explanation of this negative correlation is that a bad self-image causes depressed feelings. But, as the diagram indicates, other cause-and-effect relationships are possible.

Illusory Correlations

PREVIEW QUESTION 4 How accurately does the naked eye detect correlations?

Correlations make visible the relationships that we might otherwise miss. They also restrain our "seeing" relationships that actually don't exist. A perceived correlation that does not really exist is an **illusory correlation.** When we *believe* there is a relationship between two things, we are likely to *notice* and *recall* instances that confirm our belief (Trolier & Hamilton, 1986).

Illusory correlations help explain many a superstitious belief, such as the presumption that more babies are born when the moon is full or that infertile couples

■ **illusory correlation** the perception of a relationship where none exists.

FIGURE 2.3

Illusory correlation in everyday life
Many people believe infertile couples become more likely to conceive a child after adopting a baby. Their belief arises from their attention being drawn to such cases. The many couples who adopt without conceiving or conceive without adopting grab less attention. To determine whether there actually is a correlation between adoption and conception, we need data from all four cells in this figure. (From Gilovich, 1991)

	Conceive	Do not conceive
Adopt	confirming evidence	disconfirming evidence
Do not adopt	disconfirming evidence	confirming evidence

who adopt (**FIGURE 2.3**) become more likely to conceive (Gilovich, 1991). Such illusory thinking helps explain why for so many years people believed (and many still do) that sugar made children hyperactive, that getting cold and wet caused one to catch a cold, and that weather changes trigger arthritis pain. We are, it seems, prone to perceive patterns, whether they're there or not, and not so good at testing our hypotheses.

Because we are sensitive to dramatic or unusual events, we are especially likely to notice and remember the occurrence of two such events in sequence—say, a premonition of an unlikely phone call followed by the call. When the call does not follow the premonition, we are less likely to note and remember the nonevent.

The point to remember: When we notice random coincidences, we may forget that they are random and instead see them as correlated. Thus, we can easily deceive ourselves by seeing what is not there.

Perceiving Order in Random Events

Illusory correlations arise from our natural eagerness to make sense of our world—what poet Wallace Stevens called our "rage for order." Given even random data, we look for order, for meaningful patterns. And we usually find such, because *random sequences often don't look random.* Consider a random coin flip: If someone flipped a coin six times, which of the following sequences of heads (H) and tails (T) would be most likely: HHHTTT or HTTHTH or HHHHHH?

Daniel Kahneman and Amos Tversky (1972) found that most people believe HTTHTH would be the most likely random sequence. Actually, all are equally likely (or, we might say, equally unlikely) to occur. A bridge or poker hand of 10 through Ace, all of hearts, would seem extraordinary; actually, it would be no more or less likely than any other specific hand of cards (**FIGURE 2.4**).

Psychologists Thomas Holtgraves and James Skeel (1992) exposed people's perceptions of randomness in their bets placed in Indiana's Pick-3 Lottery. You can play, too: Make a pretend lottery pick of any three-digit number from 0 to 999.

Did your number have a repeated digit (as in 525)? Probably not. Only 14 percent of 2.24 million number strings chosen in July 1991 had a repeated digit. Although repeated digits actually occur in 28 percent of the available numbers, such numbers *look* less random (and people prefer to bet random-looking series). In actual random sequences, seeming patterns and streaks (such as repeating digits) occur more often than people expect. To demonstrate this phenomenon for myself (as you can do), I flipped a coin 51 times, with these results:

FIGURE 2.4

Two random sequences
Your chances of being dealt either of these hands is precisely the same: 1 in 2,598,960.

1. H	11. T	21. T	31. T	41. H	51. T
2. T	12. H	22. T	32. T	42. H	
3. T	13. H	23. H	33. T	43. H	
4. T	14. T	24. T	34. T	44. H	
5. H	15. T	25. T	35. T	45. T	
6. H	16. H	26. T	36. H	46. H	
7. H	17. T	27. H	37. T	47. H	
8. T	18. T	28. T	38. T	48. T	
9. T	19. H	29. H	39. H	49. T	
10. T	20. H	30. T	40. T	50. T	

Looking over the sequence, patterns jump out: Tosses 10 to 22 provided an almost perfect pattern of pairs of tails followed by pairs of heads. On tosses 30 to 38 I had a "cold hand," with only one head in nine tosses. But my fortunes immediately reversed with a "hot hand"—seven heads out of the next nine tosses.

What explains these patterns? Was I exercising some sort of paranormal control over my coin? Did I snap out of my tails funk and get in a heads groove? No such explanations are needed, for these are the sorts of streaks found in any random data. Comparing each toss to the next, 24 of the 50 comparisons yielded a changed result—just the sort of near 50-50 result we expect from coin tossing. Despite the seeming patterns in these data, the outcome of one toss gives no clue to the outcome of the next toss.

Failing to recognize random occurrences for what they are can predispose people to seek extraordinary explanations for ordinary events. Imagine that on one warm spring day 4000 college students gather for a coin-tossing contest. Their task is to flip heads. On the first toss, 2000 students do so and remain standing for a second round. As you would expect, about 1000 of these progress to a third round, 500 to a fourth, 250 to a fifth, 125 to a sixth, 62 to a seventh, 31 to an eighth, 15 to a ninth, and 8 amazing individuals, having flipped heads nine times in a row with ever-increasing displays of concentration and effort, remain standing for the tenth round.

By now, the crowd of losers is in awestruck silence as these expert coin tossers prepare to display their amazing ability yet again. The proceedings are temporarily halted. A panel of impartial scientists assembles to observe and document the incredible achievement of these gifted and talented individuals. Alas, on each succeeding toss half of those remaining flip a tail, until all have sat down. "Oh! Of course," their admirers say, "coin tossing is after all a highly sensitive skill. The tense, pressured atmosphere created by the scientists' scrutiny has disturbed their fragile gift."

However, some happenings seem so extraordinary that we struggle to conceive an ordinary, chance-related explanation (as applies to our coin-tosses). In such cases, statisticians often are less mystified. When Evelyn Marie Adams won the New Jersey lottery *twice*, newspapers reported the odds of her feat as 1 in 17 trillion. Bizarre? Actually, 1 in 17 trillion are the odds that a given person who buys a single ticket for two New Jersey lotteries will win both times. But statisticians Stephen Samuels and George McCabe (1989) report that, given the millions of people who buy U.S. state lottery tickets, it was "practically a sure thing" that someday, somewhere, someone would hit a state jackpot twice. Indeed, say fellow statisticians Persi Diaconis and Frederick Mosteller (1989), "with a large enough sample, any outrageous thing is likely to happen." (For two provocative instances of random sequences that don't look random, see Thinking Critically About Hot and Cold Streaks in Basketball and the Stock Market on page 24.)

We all experience events that make us feel astonished now and then. One day when my daughter bought two pairs of shoes, we later were astounded to discover that the two brand names were her first and last names. Checking out a photocopy

Bizarre-looking, perhaps. But actually no more unlikely than any other number sequence.

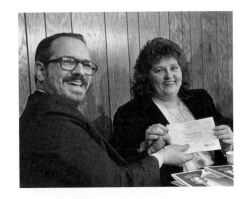

Given enough random events, something weird will happen
Evelyn Marie Adams was the beneficiary of one of those extraordinary, chance events when she won the New Jersey lottery a second time.

THINKING CRITICALLY ABOUT

HOT AND COLD STREAKS IN BASKETBALL AND THE STOCK MARKET

Misinterpreting random sequences is common in sports and investing. In both arenas, the statistical facts collide with common-sense intuition.

Basketball Players' "Hot Hands"

Every basketball player and every fan intuitively "knows" that players have hot and cold streaks. Players who have "hot hands" can't seem to miss. Those who have "cold" ones can't find the center of the hoop. When Thomas Gilovich, Robert Vallone, and Amos Tversky (1985) interviewed Philadelphia 76ers, the players estimated they were about 25 percent more likely to make a shot after they had just made one than after a miss. In one survey, 9 in 10 basketball fans agreed that a player "has a better chance of making a shot after having just *made* his last two or three shots than he does after having just *missed* his last two or three shots." Believing in shooting streaks, players will feed the ball to a teammate who has just made two or three shots in a row. Many coaches will bench the player who has just missed three in a row.

The only trouble is (believe it or not), it isn't true! When Gilovich and his collaborators studied detailed individual shooting records, they found that the 76ers—and the Boston Celtics, the New Jersey Nets, the New York Knicks, and Cornell University's men's and women's basketball players—were equally likely to score after a miss and after a basket. A typical 50 percent shooter averages 50 percent after just missing three shots, and 50 percent after just making three shots. It works with free throws, too. Celtics star Larry Bird made 88 percent of his free throws after making a free throw and 91 percent after missing. (Did this reduce Larry Bird to a mere puppet, manipulated by statistical laws? No, his skill was reflected in his 90 percent average.)

Why, then, do players and fans alike believe that players are more likely to score after scoring and to miss after missing? It's because streaks do occur, more than people expect in random sequences. In any series of 20 shots by a 50 percent shooter (or 20 flips of a coin), there is a 50-50 chance of four baskets (or heads) in a row, and it is quite possible that one person out of five will have a streak of 5 or 6. Players and fans notice these random streaks and so form the errant conclusion that "when you're hot, you're hot" (**FIGURE 2.5**).

Mutual Funds: Does Past Performance Predict Future Returns?

The same misinterpretation of random sequences occurs when investors believe that a mutual fund that has had a string of good years will likely outperform one that has had a string of bad years. Based on that assumption, investment magazines report mutual funds' perfor-mance. But, as economist Burton Malkiel (1989, 1995) documents, past performances of mutual funds do *not* predict their future performance. If on January 1 of each year since 1980 we had bought the previous year's top-performing funds, our hot funds would not have beaten the next year's market average. If we had put our money instead on the *Forbes* "Honor Roll" of funds each year for the two decades following 1975, we would have pulled in an annual return of 13.5 percent (compared with the market's overall 14.9 percent annual return). Of the top 81 Canadian funds during 1994, 40 performed above average and 41 below average during 1995 (Chalmers, 1995).

When funds have streaks of several good or bad years, we may nevertheless think that past success predicts future success. "Randomness is a difficult notion for people to accept," notes Malkiel. "When events come in clusters and streaks, people look for explanations and patterns. They refuse to believe that such patterns—which frequently occur in random data—could equally well be derived from tossing a coin. So it is in the stock market as well."

The point to remember: When watching basketball, choosing stocks, or flipping coins, remember that our intuition often misleads us. Random sequences frequently don't look random. Expect streaks.

FIGURE 2.5 Who is the chance shooter? Here are 21 consecutive shots, each scoring either a basket or a miss, by two players who each make 11. Within this sample of shots, which player's sequence looks more like what we would expect in a random sequence? (See page 27; adapted from Barry Ross, *Discover*, 1987.)

Player A

Player B

counter from our library, I confused the clerk when giving him my six-digit department charge number—which just happened at that moment to be identical to the counter's one-in-a-million number on which the last user had finished. Ron Vachon was astounded while sitting among thousands of fans at a September 1990 baseball game in Boston. Oakland A's outfielder Rickey Henderson hit two foul balls right to him, on successive pitches. That something like that should have happened to Vachon (who dropped them both) was incredibly unlikely. That it sometime would happen to someone was not. An event that happens to but one in 1 billion people every day occurs about six times a day, 2000 times a year.

On March 11, 1998, Utah's Ernie and Lynn Carey gained three new grandchildren when three of their daughters gave birth—on the same day (*Los Angeles Times*, 1998).

rehearse it!

1. In psychology a good theory implies hypotheses, or predictions that can be tested. When hypotheses are tested, the result is typically
   a. increased skepticism.
   b. rejection of the merely theoretical.
   c. confirmation or revision of the theory.
   d. personal bias on the part of the investigator.

2. Psychology's basic *research strategies* are description, correlation, and experimentation. Which of the following would you use in an attempt to predict college grades from high school grades?
   a. A case study
   b. Naturalistic observation
   c. Correlational research
   d. Experimental research

3. You wish to take an accurate poll in a certain country by questioning people who truly represent the country's adult population. Therefore, you need to make sure the people are
   a. at least 30 percent urban dwellers.
   b. registered voters.
   c. a very large sample of the population.
   d. a random sample of the population.

4. Suppose a psychologist finds that the *more* natural childbirth training classes a woman attends, the *less* pain medication she requires during childbirth. The relationship between the number of training sessions and the amount of pain medication required is a
   a. positive correlation (direct relationship).

   b. negative correlation (inverse relationship).
   c. cause-and-effect relationship.
   d. controlled experiment.

5. Knowing that two events are correlated does not tell us what is the cause and what is the effect. However, it does provide
   a. a basis for prediction.
   b. an explanation of events.
   c. proof that as one increases, the other also increases.
   d. an indication that an underlying third factor is at work.

6. Some people wrongly perceive that their dreams predict future events. This is an example of a/an
   a. negative correlation.
   b. positive correlation.
   c. illusory correlation.
   d. naturalistic correlation.

Experimentation

PREVIEW QUESTION 5 How do experiments clarify or reveal cause-and-effect relationships?

Happy are they "who have been able to perceive the causes of things," remarked the Roman poet Virgil. We endlessly wonder and debate *why* we act as we do. Why do people smoke? Have babies while they are still children? Do stupid things when drunk? Become troubled teens and gun down their classmates? Though psychology cannot answer these questions directly, it has helped us to understand what influences drug use, sexual behaviors, thinking when drinking, and aggression.

Many factors influence our everyday behavior. To isolate cause and effect—say, in looking for possible causes of depression—psychologists sometimes try to statistically control for other factors and study the sequence of events. For example, one group of Internet-use researchers found that people who feel lonely and depressed at the start of their study were not more likely to use the Internet. But two years later, those who had spent the most hours in cyberspace had become more lonely and depressed (Kraut & others, 1998).

The clearest and cleanest way to isolate cause and effect is, however, to **experiment.** Experiments enable a researcher to focus on the possible effects of one or more factors by (1) *manipulating the factors of interest* and (2) *holding constant ("con-*

■ **experiment** a research method in which an investigator manipulates one or more factors (independent variables) to observe the effect on some behavior or mental process (the dependent variable). By random assignment of participants, the experiment controls other relevant factors.

■ **placebo [pluh-SEE-bo; Latin for "I shall please"]** an inert substance or condition that may be administered instead of a presumed active agent, such as a drug, to see if it triggers the effects believed to characterize the active agent.

■ **double-blind procedure** an experimental procedure in which both the research participants and the research staff are ignorant (blind) about whether the research participants have received the treatment or a placebo. Commonly used in drug evaluation studies.

■ **placebo effect** any effect on behavior caused by a placebo.

■ **experimental condition** the condition of an experiment that exposes participants to the treatment, that is, to one version of the independent variable.

■ **control condition** the condition of an experiment that contrasts with the experimental condition and serves as a comparison for evaluating the effect of the treatment.

■ **random assignment** assigning participants to experimental and control conditions by chance, thus minimizing preexisting differences between those assigned to the different groups.

trolling") *other factors*. Imagine some researchers studying the effect of alcohol consumption on thinking ability. Before giving a thinking test, they would *manipulate* alcohol consumption (by giving some people a strong-tasting drink mixed with alcohol, others a drink that contained no alcohol but tasted the same). By randomly assigning people to the two conditions, which otherwise were similar, the researchers would hold all other factors constant. This would eliminate alternative explanations for why thinking might vary with drinking.

If behavior changes when we vary an experimental factor, such as alcohol, then we know that the factor is having an effect. *The important point to remember:* Unlike correlational studies, which uncover naturally occurring relationships, an experiment manipulates a factor to determine its effect.

Evaluating Therapies

Our tendencies to seek new remedies when we are ill or emotionally down can produce misleading testimonies. When our health or emotions return to normal, we attribute the return to something we have done. If three days into a cold we start taking vitamin C tablets and find our cold symptoms lessening, the pills may seem more potent than they are (an illusion of control). If, after nearly failing the first exam, we listen to a "peak learning" subliminal tape and then improve on the next exam, we may credit the tape rather than conclude that our performance has returned to our average. In the 1700s, blood-letting *seemed* effective. Sometimes people improved after the treatment; when they didn't, the practitioner inferred the disease was too far advanced to be reversed. So, whether or not a remedy is truly effective, enthusiastic users will probably endorse it. To find out whether it actually is effective, we must experiment.

And that is precisely how new drug treatments and new methods of psychological therapy are evaluated. In many of these studies, the participants are *blind* (uninformed) about what treatment, if any, they are receiving. One group receives the treatment. Others receive a pseudotreatment—an inert **placebo** (perhaps a pill with no drug in it). Often neither the participant nor the research assistant collecting the data knows whether the participant's group is receiving the treatment. This **double-blind procedure** enables researchers to check a treatment's actual effects apart from the research participants' (and their own) enthusiasm for it and from the healing power of belief. The **placebo effect** is well documented (Kirsch & Sapirstein, 1998). Just *thinking* one is getting a treatment can boost one's spirits, relax one's body, and lead to symptom relief.

The double-blind procedure creates an **experimental condition** in which people receive the treatment and a contrasting **control condition** without the treatment. **Random assignment** of people to the two conditions roughly equalizes the groups in age, attitudes, and every other characteristic. With random assignment, we can know that any later differences between people in the experimental and control conditions must be the result of the treatment.

A potent example: The drug Viagra was approved for use after 21 clinical trials, including an experiment in which researchers randomly assigned 329 men with impotence to either an experimental condition (Viagra) or a control condition (a placebo). Neither the men nor the person who gave them the pills knew which drug they were receiving. The result: At peak doses, 69 percent of Viagra-assisted attempts at intercourse were successful, compared with 22 percent for men receiving the placebo (Goldstein & others, 1998). Viagra worked.

This simple experiment manipulated just one drug factor. We call this experimental factor the **independent variable** because we can vary it independently of other factors, such as the men's age, weight, and personality (which random assignment controls). Experiments examine the effect of one or more independent variables on some measurable behavior, called the **dependent variable** because it can vary *depending* on what takes place during the experiment. Both variables are given precise operational definitions, which specify the procedures that manipulate the independent variable (the precise drug dosage and timing in this study) or measure the dependent variable (the questions that assessed the men's responses). Thus they answer the "What do you mean?" question with a level of precision that enables others to repeat the study.

Let's recap. An experiment has at least two different conditions: a comparison or control condition and an experimental condition. Random assignment equates the conditions before any treatment effects. In this way, an experiment tests the effect of at least one independent variable (what we manipulate) on at least one dependent variable (what we measure). Table 2.1 compares the features of psychology's research methods.

- **independent variable** the experimental factor that is manipulated; the variable whose effect is being studied.

- **dependent variable** the experimental factor—in psychology, the behavior or mental process—that is being measured; the variable that may change in response to manipulations of the independent variable.

Answer to Figure 2.5 (page 24): Player B, whose outcomes may look more random, actually has fewer streaks than would be expected by chance. For these players, chance shooting, like chance coin tossing, should produce a change in outcome about 50 percent of the time. But 70 percent of the time (14 times out of 20) Player B's outcome changes on successive shots. Player A is scoring more, as we would expect from a 50 percent shooter; 10 times out of 20, Player A's next outcome differs from the last.

TABLE 2.1

COMPARING RESEARCH METHODS

Research Method	Basic Purpose	How Conducted	What Is Manipulated
Descriptive	To observe and record behavior	Case studies, surveys, and naturalistic observations	Nothing
Correlational	To detect naturally occurring relationships; to assess how well one variable predicts another	Computing statistical association, sometimes among survey responses	Nothing
Experimental	To explore cause and effect	Manipulating one or more factors and using random assignment to eliminate preexisting differences among subjects	The independent variable(s)

Note the distinction between random *sampling* in surveys and random *assignment* in experiments. Random sampling helps us generalize to a larger population. Random assignment controls extraneous influences, which helps us infer cause and effect.

These concepts—experimental and control conditions, independent and dependent variables, random assignment—are important, yet easily confused. So let's put them to work with another intriguing set of experiments.

Can Subliminal Tapes Improve Your Life?

A new generation of entrepreneurs would have you believe so. We are bombarded by mail-order catalogs, cable television ads, and bookstores offering tapes whose imperceptibly faint messages supposedly "reprogram your unconscious mind for success and happiness." While struggling students listen to soothing music, subliminal messages (those below one's hearing threshold) are said to persuade the unconscious that "I am a good student. I love learning." Procrastinators can be similarly reprogrammed: "I set my priorities. I get things done ahead of time!"

Is there anything to these claims? Could positive subliminal messages help us, even a little? Research shows that subliminal *sensation* is for real: We, in fact, do process much information without conscious awareness. And under certain conditions, a stimulus too weak to recognize can affect us, *briefly*.

But does this subtle, fleeting effect extend to the powerful, enduring influence claimed by the subliminal tape merchants? Anthony Greenwald and his colleagues (1991) wanted to find out, so they randomly assigned university students to listen daily for five weeks to commercial subliminal tapes claiming to improve either self-esteem or memory. Then the researchers manipulated an experimental factor. On half the tapes they switched the labels. Some students *thought* they were receiving affirmations of self-esteem when they actually were hearing the memory enhancement tape. Others got the self-esteem tape but *thought* their memory was being recharged (**FIGURE 2.6**).

Were the tapes effective? Their scores on tests for both self-esteem and memory, taken before and after the five weeks, revealed zilch. No effects. None. And yet, those who *thought* they had heard a memory tape *believed* their memories had improved. A similar result occurred for those who thought they had heard a self-esteem tape. The tapes had no effects, yet the students *perceived* themselves receiving the benefits they *expected*. When reading this research, you can hear echoes of the testimonies that ooze from the mail-order tape catalogs. Many customers, having bought what is not supposed to be heard, and having indeed not heard it, actually write things like, "I really know that your tapes were invaluable in reprogramming my mind." Greenwald conducted 16 double-blind experiments evaluating subliminal self-help tapes over one 10-year period. His results were uniform: Not one had any therapeutic effect (Greenwald, 1992).

Experiments can also help us evaluate social programs. Do early childhood education programs boost impoverished children's chances for success? What are the effects of different antismoking campaigns? Does school sex education reduce teen pregnancies? To answer these questions, we can experiment: If an intervention is welcomed but resources are scarce, we could use a lottery to randomly assign some people (or regions) to experience the new program and others to a control condition. If later the two groups differ, there will be less to argue about (Passell, 1993).

FIGURE 2.6

Design of the subliminal tapes experiment

Students' self-esteem and memory abilities were assessed before and after listening to subliminal tapes purporting to increase either self-esteem or memory. Half the students, however, received deliberately mislabeled tapes. In this experiment, what was the independent variable? The dependent variable? (See page 30.)

rehearse it!

7. A researcher wants to determine whether noise level affects the blood pressure of elderly people. In one group she varies the level of noise in the environment and records blood pressures. In this experiment the level of noise is the
   a. control condition.
   b. dependent variable (the factor being measured).
   c. independent variable (the factor being manipulated).
   d. cause of any blood pressure variations.

8. To test the effect of a new drug on depression, we randomly assign people to control and experimental conditions. Those in the experimental condition take a pink pill containing the new medication; the control group takes a pink pill that contains no medication. Which statement is true?
   a. The medication is the dependent variable.
   b. Depression is the independent variable.
   c. Participants in the control group take a placebo.
   d. Neither the experimental nor the control group is told the purpose of the experiment.

9. To eliminate the biasing effect of a researcher's positive expectations on the outcome of a health clinic's research experiment,
   a. patients are randomly assigned to the control and experimental groups (random assignment).
   b. members of the experimental group are carefully matched for age, sex, income, and level of education with members of the control group (controlled selection).
   c. neither the patients nor the researcher will know whether a given person has been assigned to the experimental or control condition (double-blind procedure).
   d. people in the experimental group are chosen by selecting every tenth person in an alphabetical listing of all the clinic's patients (random selection).

10. Description is to explanation as case study is to
    a. correlation.
    b. naturalistic observation.
    c. experiment.
    d. survey.

Frequently Asked Questions About Psychology

We have seen how case studies, surveys, and naturalistic observations help us describe behavior. We have also noted that correlational studies, assessing the relationship between two factors, can indicate how, knowing one thing, we can predict another. We have examined the logic that underlies experiments, which use control conditions and random assignment of people to isolate the effects of an independent variable on a dependent variable. We have reflected on how a scientific approach, aided by statistics, can restrain biases.

You are now prepared to understand what lies ahead and to think critically about psychological matters. Yet, even knowing this much, you may still be approaching psychology with a mixture of curiosity and apprehension. So before we plunge in, let's engage some frequently asked questions.

PREVIEW QUESTION 6 Can laboratory experiments illuminate everyday life?

When you see or hear about psychological research, do you ever wonder whether people's behavior in the lab will predict their behavior in real life? For example, does detecting the blink of a faint red light in a dark room have anything useful to say about flying a plane at night? Does our tendency to remember best the first and last items in a list of unrelated words tell us anything about why we remember the names of certain people we meet at a party? After viewing a violent, sexually explicit film, does an aroused man's increased willingness to push buttons that he thinks will electrically shock a woman really say anything about whether violent pornography makes a man more likely to abuse a woman?

Before you answer, consider: The experimenter *intends* the laboratory environment to be a simplified reality—one in which important features of everyday life can be simulated and controlled. Just as an aeronautical wind tunnel enables an engineer to re-create atmospheric forces under controlled conditions, a laboratory experiment enables a psychologist to re-create psychological forces under controlled conditions.

The experiment's purpose, notes Douglas Mook (1983), is not to re-create the exact behaviors of everyday life but to test theoretical principles. *It is the resulting principles—not the specific findings—that help explain everyday behaviors.* When psychologists apply laboratory research on aggression to actual violence, they are applying theoretical *principles* of aggressive behavior, principles they have refined through many experiments. Similarly, it is the principles of the visual system, developed from experiments in artificial settings (such as looking at red lights in the dark), that we apply to more complex behaviors such as night flying. And many investigations show that principles derived in the laboratory *do* typically generalize to the everyday world (Anderson & others, 1999).

The point to remember: As psychologists, our concerns lie less with particular behaviors than with the general principles that help explain many behaviors.

PREVIEW QUESTION 7 Doesn't behavior depend on one's culture and gender?

If culture shapes behavior, what can psychological studies done in one culture, often with white North Americans, really tell us about people in general? As we will see time and again, **culture**—shared ideas and behaviors that one generation passes on to the next—matters. Our culture influences our standards of promptness and frankness, our attitudes toward premarital sex and varying body shapes, our tendencies to be casual or formal, and much, much more. Being aware of such differences, we can restrain our assumptions that others will—or necessarily

culture the enduring behaviors, ideas, attitudes, and traditions shared by a large group of people and transmitted from one generation to the next.

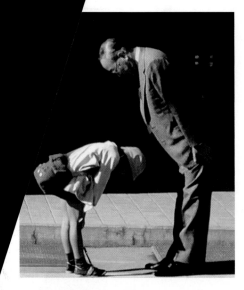

A cultured greeting
Because culture shapes people's understanding of social behavior, actions that seem ordinary to us may seem quite odd to visitors from far away. Yet underlying these differences are powerful similarities. Schoolchildren everywhere greet their teachers with respect, although not necessarily with the formality of this young Japanese schoolchild.

"All people are the same; only their habits differ."

Confucius, 551–479 B.C.

"Rats are very similar to humans except they are not stupid enough to purchase lottery tickets."

Dave Barry, 2000

Answer to Figure 2.6 (page 28): In the subliminal tapes experiment, the primary independent variable was the type of subliminal message, self-esteem versus memory. (This experiment actually had a second independent variable as well: people's beliefs about which tape they received.) The primary dependent variable was improvement on the self-esteem and memory measures.

should—think and act as we do. Given the growing mixing and clashing of cultures, our need for such awareness is urgent.

You will see throughout this book that gender matters, too. Researchers report gender differences in what we dream, in how we express and detect emotions, and in our risk of alcoholism, depression, and eating disorders. Not only is studying such differences interesting, it is also potentially beneficial. For example, many researchers believe that women carry on conversations more readily to build relationships; men usually talk to give information and advice (Tannen, 1990). Knowing this difference can help us prevent conflicts and misunderstandings in everyday relationships.

Likewise, it's important to remember that psychologically as well as biologically, women and men are overwhelmingly similar. Whether female or male, we learn to walk at about the same age; experience the same sensations of light and sound; feel the same pangs of hunger, desire, and fear; and exhibit similar overall intelligence and well-being. We also tend to exhibit and perceive the very behaviors our culture expects of males and females.

Our shared biological heritage does, however, unite us as a universal human family. The same underlying processes guide people everywhere. Variation in languages—spoken and gestured—may impede communication across cultures, yet all languages share deep principles of grammar, and people from opposite hemispheres can communicate with a smile or a frown. People in different cultures do vary in feelings of loneliness, but across cultures shyness and low self-esteem magnify loneliness (Jones & others, 1985). Japanese prefer their fish raw and North Americans prefer theirs cooked, but the same principles of hunger and taste influence both when they sit down to a meal. We are each in certain respects like all others, like some others, and like no other. Studying people of all races and cultures helps us discern our similarities and our differences.

The point to remember: Even when specific attitudes and behaviors vary across cultures, as they often do, the underlying processes are much the same. A children's song says it well: "We're all the same and different."

PREVIEW QUESTION 8 Why do psychologists study animals?

Many psychologists study animals because they find them fascinating. They want to understand how different species learn, think, and behave. Psychologists also study animals to learn about people, by doing experiments that are permissible only with animals. Because human physiology resembles that of many other animals, animal experiments have led to treatments for human diseases—insulin for diabetes, vaccines to prevent polio and rabies, transplants to replace defective organs. We humans are not like animals, we *are* animals.

Likewise, the same processes by which humans see, exhibit emotion, and become obese are present in rats and monkeys. To discover more about the basics of human learning, researchers even study sea slugs. To understand how a combustion engine works, you would do better to study the engine of a lawn mower than that of a Mercedes. Humans, like Mercedes, are complex. But it is precisely the simplicity of the sea slug's nervous system that makes it so revealing of the neural mechanisms of learning.

PREVIEW QUESTION 9 Is it ethical to experiment on animals?

If we share important similarities with other animals, then should we not respect them? "We cannot defend our scientific work with animals on the basis of the similarities between them and ourselves and then defend it morally on the basis of differences," notes Roger Ulrich (1991). The animal protection movement protests the use of animals in psychological, biological, and medical research—some 2 million Canadian, 3 million British, and 20 million American animals (Murkerjee, 1997; National Academy of Sciences, 1991). Researchers remind us that these 25 million animals are less than 1 percent of the 6 billion animals killed annually in these countries as a source of food (which means the average person eats 20 animals a year). While researchers each year conduct experiments on some 200,000 dogs and cats cared for under humane regulations, humane animal shelters are forced to kill 50 times that many.

Only 7 percent of psychology's studies have involved animals, 95 percent of which were rats, mice, rabbits, or birds. About 10 percent of these animal studies involved electric shock (Coile & Miller, 1984; Gallup & Suarez, 1985). In British psychology departments, where animal use dropped by two-thirds in the dozen years after 1977, electric shock had been used in only 4 percent of animal studies. All involved rats (Thomas & Blackman, 1991).

Animal protection organizations, such as Psychologists for the Ethical Treatment of Animals, advocate naturalistic observation of animals rather than laboratory manipulation. However, many researchers say this is not the morality of good versus evil but of compassion (for animals) versus compassion (for people). How many of us would have attacked Pasteur's experiments with rabies, which in causing some dogs to suffer led to a vaccine that spared millions of people, and dogs, from agonizing death? And would we really wish to have deprived ourselves of the animal research that led to effective methods of training children with mental disorders; of understanding aging; of relieving fears and depression; of controlling obesity, alcoholism, and stress-related pain and disease?

Out of this heated debate, two issues emerge. The basic one is whether it is right to place the well-being of humans above that of animals. In experiments on stress and cancer, is it right that mice get tumors in hopes that people might not? Is our use of other animals as natural as the behavior of carnivorous hawks, cats, and whales? (Animals themselves do not assign rights to other animals lower on the food chain.)

If we give human life first priority, the second issue is the priority given the well-being of animals. What safeguards should protect animals? Most researchers today feel ethically obligated to enhance the well-being of captive animals and protect them from needless suffering. Humane care also leads to more effective science, because pain and stress would distort the animals' behavior during experiments. Thus, researchers welcomed the national animal protection legislation updated by the United States in 1985 and by Britain in 1986, and they supported the accompanying regulations and laboratory inspections (Cherfas, 1990; Johnson, 1990).

Animals have themselves benefited from animal research. Studies have helped improve their care and management not only in laboratories and zoos but even in their natural habitats. By revealing our behavioral kinship with animals and the remarkable intelligence of some animals, experiments have also led to an increase in our empathy with them. At its best, a psychology concerned for humans and sensitive to animals serves the welfare of both.

PREVIEW QUESTION 10 Is it ethical to experiment on people?

If the image of animals or people receiving supposed electric shocks troubles you, you may find it a relief that most psychological research involves no such stress. Blinking lights, flashing words, and pleasant social interactions are the rule.

Occasionally, though, researchers do temporarily stress or deceive people, but only when they believe it is essential to a justifiable end, such as understanding and controlling violent behavior or studying mood swings. Such experiments wouldn't work if the participants knew all there was to know about the experiment beforehand. Either the procedures would be ineffective or the participants, wanting to be helpful, might try to confirm the researchers' predictions.

Ethical principles developed by the American Psychological Association (1992) and the British Psychological Society (1993) urge investigators to (1) obtain the in-

"I believe that to prevent, cripple, or needlessly complicate the research that can relieve animal and human suffering is profoundly inhuman, cruel, and immoral."

Psychologist Neal Miller (1983)

"The righteous know the needs of their animals."

Proverbs 12:10

"The greatness of a nation can be judged by the way its animals are treated."

Mahatma Gandhi, 1869–1948

Justifiable experimentation?
Is it right to use animals to advance our understanding of humans? For animal rights activists, no purpose justifies hurting, frightening, or (as here) manipulating an animal. For most psychologists and medical researchers, animal research is ethically justified so long as researchers observe strict standards and inflict no unnecessary pain.

FIGURE 2.7

What do you see?

People interpret ambiguous information to fit their preconceptions. Did you see a duck or a rabbit? Before showing some friends this image, ask them if they can see the duck lying on its back (or the bunny in the grass). (From Shepard, 1990.)

"It is doubtless impossible to approach any human problem with a mind free from bias."

Simone De Beauvoir, *The Second Sex*, 1953

formed consent of potential participants, (2) protect them from harm and discomfort, (3) treat information about individual participants confidentially, and (4) fully explain the research afterward. Moreover, most universities today screen research proposals through an ethics committee that safeguards the well-being of every participant.

PREVIEW QUESTION 11 Is psychology free of value judgments?

Psychology is definitely not value-free. Values affect what we study, how we study it, and how we interpret results. Consider: Researchers' values influence their choice of research topics—whether to study worker productivity or worker morale, sex discrimination or gender differences, conformity or independence. Values can even color "the facts." Our preconceptions can bias our observations and interpretations, leading us to see what we want or expect to see (**FIGURE 2.7**). Even the words we use to describe a phenomenon can reflect our values. Labeling the sex acts we do not practice as "perversions" or as "sexual variations" conveys a value judgment. The same holds true in everyday speech, when one person's "terrorists" are another's "freedom fighters," or one person's "faith" is another's "fanaticism." Our labeling someone as "firm" or "stubborn," "careful" or "picky," "discreet" or "secretive" reveals our feelings. Both in and out of psychology, labels describe and labels evaluate.

Popular applications of psychology also contain hidden values. If you defer to "professional" guidance about how to live—how to raise children, how to achieve self-fulfillment, what to do with sexual feelings, how to get ahead at work—you are accepting value-laden advice. A science of behavior and mental processes can certainly help us reach our goals, but it cannot decide them.

So, is psychology potentially dangerous? If some people see psychology as merely common sense, others have a different concern—that it is becoming dangerously powerful. Won't psychology be used to manipulate people?

Knowledge, like all powers, can be used for good or evil. Nuclear power has been used to light up cities—and to demolish them. Persuasive power has been used to educate people—and to deceive them. The power of mind-altering drugs has been used to restore sanity—and to destroy it.

Although psychology does indeed have the power to deceive, its purpose is to enlighten. Psychologists every day are exploring ways to enhance learning, creativity, and compassion. Psychology also speaks to many of our world's great problems—war, overpopulation, prejudice, family dysfunction, crime—all of which involve attitudes and behaviors. And psychology speaks to our deepest longings—for nourishment, for love, for happiness. True, psychology cannot address all of life's great questions, but it speaks to some mighty important ones.

rehearse it!

11. In a laboratory experiment, features of everyday life can be simulated, manipulated, and controlled. The laboratory environment is designed to help us
    a. exactly re-create the events of everyday life.
    b. re-create psychological forces under controlled conditions.
    c. create opportunities for naturalistic observation.
    d. minimize the use of animals and humans in psychological research.

12. Which of the following is true regarding gender differences and similarities?

a. Differences between the genders outweigh any similarities.
b. Despite some gender differences, the underlying processes of human behavior are the same.
c. Both similarities and differences between the genders depend more on biology than on environment.
d. Gender differences are so numerous, it is difficult to make meaningful comparisons.

13. The animal protection movement has protested the use of animals in all fields of scientific research. In defend-

ing their experimental research with animals, psychologists have noted that
a. animals' physiology and behavior can tell us much about our own.
b. they do not torture or needlessly exploit animals.
c. advancing the well-being of humans justifies animal experimentation.
d. All of the above

REVIEWING

Research Strategies: How Psychologists Ask and Answer Questions

1. How do psychologists use the scientific method to construct theories?

Research stimulates the construction of *theories,* which organize *observations* and imply predictive *hypotheses.* These hypotheses (predictions) are then tested to validate and refine the theory and to suggest practical applications. Precise operational definitions enable other researchers to replicate (repeat) observations.

2. How do psychologists observe and describe behavior?

Through individual case studies, surveys among random samples of a population, and naturalistic observations, psychologists observe and describe behavior and mental processes. In generalizing from observations, remember: Representative samples are a better guide than vivid examples.

3. Why do correlations permit prediction but not explanation?

The strength of the relationship between one factor and another is expressed in their *correlation coefficient.* Knowing how closely two things are positively or negatively correlated tells us how much one predicts the other. But correlation is only a measure of relationship; it does not reveal cause and effect.

4. How accurately does the naked eye detect correlations?

Correlations help us to see relationships that the naked eye might miss and to discount illusory correlations and random events that might otherwise look significant.

5. How do experiments clarify or reveal cause-and-effect relationships?

By constructing a controlled reality in an *experiment,* psychologists can manipulate one or more factors and discover how these independent variables affect a particular behavior, the dependent variable.

6. Can laboratory experiments illuminate everyday life?

By intentionally creating a controlled, artificial environment in the lab, researchers aim to test theoretical principles. These principles help us to understand, describe, explain, and predict everyday behaviors.

7. Doesn't behavior depend on one's culture and gender?

Although attitudes and behaviors vary across cultures, the principles that underlie them vary much less. Cross-cultural psychology explores both our cultural differences and the universal similarities that define our human kinship.

Gender is also a fact of life. Although gender differences tend to capture attention, it is important to remember the much greater similarities between men and women.

8. Why do psychologists study animals?

Some psychologists study animals out of an interest in animal behavior. Others do so because knowledge of the physiological and psychological processes of animals permits a better understanding of the similar processes operating in humans.

9. Is it ethical to experiment on animals?

Only about 7 percent of all psychological experiments involve animals, and under ethical and legal guidelines these animals rarely experience pain. Nevertheless, animal rights groups raise an important issue: Is an animal's temporary suffering justified if it leads to the relief of human suffering?

10. Is it ethical to experiment on people?

Occasionally researchers temporarily stress or deceive people in order to learn something important. Professional ethical standards provide guidelines for the treatment of human as well as animal participants.

11. Is psychology free of value judgments?

Psychology is not value-free. Psychologists' own values influence their choice of research topics, their theories and observations, their labels for behavior, and their professional advice.

Knowledge is power that can be used for good or evil. Applications of psychology's principles have so far been mostly for the good, and psychology addresses some of humanity's greatest problems and deepest longings.

TERMS AND CONCEPTS TO REMEMBER

theory, p. 16
hypothesis, p. 16
operational definition, p. 17
replication, p. 17
case study, p. 17
survey, p. 18

population, p. 19
random sample, p. 19
naturalistic observation, p. 19
correlation coefficient, p. 20
illusory correlation, p. 21
experiment, p. 25

placebo [pluh-SEE-bo], p. 26
double-blind procedure, p. 26
placebo effect, p. 26
experimental condition, p. 26
control condition, p. 26
random assignment, p. 26

independent variable, p. 27
dependent variable, p. 27
culture, p. 29

REHEARSE IT ANSWER KEY

1. c	3. d	5. a	7. c	9. c	11. b	13. d
2. c	4. b	6. c	8. c	10. c	12. b	

Biology and Behavior

N o principle is more central to today's psychology, or to this book, than this: *Everything psychological is simultaneously biological.* Your every idea, every mood, every urge is a biological happening. You think, feel, and act with your body. You relate to the world through your body. (Try laughing, crying, or loving without it.) Without your body—your genes, your brain, your body chemistry, your inner organs, your appearance—you are, indeed, nobody. Although we find it convenient to talk separately of biological and psychological influences on behavior, we need to remember: To think, feel, or act without a body is as plausible as running without legs.

As we enter the new century, science is riveted on the most amazing parts of our body—our brain, its component neural systems, and their genetic blueprints. The brain's ultimate challenge? To understand itself. How does our brain organize and communicate with itself? How does our heredity prewire the brain, and our experience modify it? How does the brain process the information we need to shoot a basketball? To delight in the nuances of a pianist's notes? To remember our first kiss?

Throughout this book you will find examples of how our biology underlies our behavior and mental processes. By studying the links between biological activity and psychological events, *biological psychologists* are gaining a better understanding of sleep and dreams, depression and schizophrenia, hunger and sex, stress and disease. (Some biological psychologists call themselves *behavioral neuroscientists, neuropsychologists, behavior geneticists, physiological psychologists,* or *biopsychologists.*) We therefore begin our study of psychology with a look at its biological roots.

We will start small and build—from neurons and their interconnections (Module 3), to the brain (Module 4), to the genetic and environmental influences that interact to affect our behavior (Module 5). At all levels, psychologists examine how we process information—how we take in information; how we organize, interpret, and store it; and how we use it. For scientists, it is a fortunate fact of nature that the information systems of humans and other animals operate similarly—so similarly, in fact, that you could not distinguish between small samples of brain tissue from a human and a monkey. This similarity allows researchers to study simple animals, such as squids and sea slugs, to discover how our neural systems operate, and to study mammals' brains to understand the organization of our own. Though human brains are more complex, they follow principles that govern all of the animal world.

3 Neural and Hormonal Systems

We are each a system composed of subsystems that are in turn composed of even smaller subsystems. Tiny cells organize to form such body organs as our stomach, heart, and brain. These organs in turn form larger systems for digestion, circulation, and information processing. And those systems are part of an even larger system—you, who in turn are a part of your family, community, and culture. We are *bio-psycho-social* systems, so to more deeply understand our behavior, we need to study how biological, psychological, and social systems work and interact.

Here, we look at the basics of the body's two communication systems: the nervous and hormone systems.

Neural Communication

Neurons

PREVIEW QUESTION 1 What are neurons, and how do they transmit information?

Our body's neural information system is complexity built from simplicity. Its building blocks are **neurons,** or nerve cells. There are many different types of neurons, but they are all variations on the same theme **(FIGURE 3.1).** Each consists of a cell body and its branching fibers. The fibers are of two types: The bushy **dendrites** receive information, and the **axons** pass it along to other neurons or to muscles or glands. Unlike the short dendrites, axons are sometimes very long, projecting several feet through the body. A neuron carrying orders to a leg muscle has a cell body and axon roughly on the scale of a basketball attached to a rope 4 miles long. A layer of fatty tissue, called the **myelin sheath,** insulates the axons of some neurons and helps speed their impulses. Evidence for the myelin sheath's importance appears in multiple sclerosis, a disease in which the myelin sheath degenerates. The result is a slowing of all communication to muscles and the eventual loss of muscle control.

FIGURE 3.1
A motor neuron

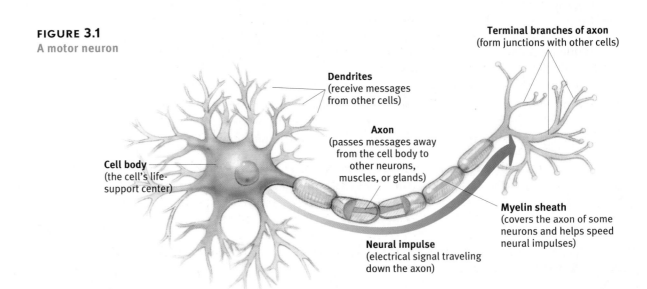

Dendrites
(receive messages from other cells)

Terminal branches of axon
(form junctions with other cells)

Axon
(passes messages away from the cell body to other neurons, muscles, or glands)

Cell body
(the cell's life-support center)

Myelin sheath
(covers the axon of some neurons and helps speed neural impulses)

Neural impulse
(electrical signal traveling down the axon)

Depending on the type of fiber, the neural impulse travels at speeds ranging from a sluggish 2 miles per hour to, in some myelinated fibers, a breakneck 200 or more miles per hour. But even this top speed is 3 million times slower than that of electricity through a wire. We measure brain activity in milliseconds (thousandths of a second) and computer activity in nanoseconds (billionths of a second). That helps to explain why, unlike the nearly instantaneous reactions of a high-speed computer, your reaction to a sudden event, such as a child darting in front of your car, may take a quarter-second or more.

A neuron fires an impulse when it receives signals from sense receptors stimulated by pressure, heat, or light, or when it is stimulated by chemical messages from adjacent neurons. The impulse, called the **action potential,** is a brief electrical charge that travels down the axon, rather like a line of dominoes falling, each one tripping the next. This is real electricity. A handful of neurons together produce enough power to light up a flashlight bulb.

The neuron is a miniature decision-making device that performs some complex calculations. From hundreds, even thousands, of other neurons, it receives signals on its dendrites and cell body. Some of these signals are *excitatory,* somewhat like pushing a neuron's accelerator. Other signals are *inhibitory,* more like pushing its brake. If excitatory signals minus inhibitory signals exceed a minimum intensity, called the **threshold,** the combined signals trigger an impulse. (Think of it this way: If the excitatory party animals outvote the inhibitory party poopers, the party's on.) The electrical impulse (the action potential) transmits down the axon, which branches into junctions with hundreds or thousands of other neurons and with the body's muscles and glands.

Increasing the stimulus above the threshold, however, will not increase the impulse's intensity. (The neuron's reaction is an *all-or-none response;* like guns, neurons either fire or they don't.) Nor does the strength of the stimulus affect the impulse's speed.

How then do we detect the intensity of a stimulus? How do we distinguish a gentle touch from a big hug? A strong stimulus cannot trigger a stronger or faster impulse in a neuron—squeezing a trigger harder won't make a bullet go faster. But a strong stimulus can trigger more neurons to fire, and to fire more often.

How Neurons Communicate

PREVIEW QUESTION 2 How do nerve cells communicate?

Neurons interweave so intricately that even with a microscope it is hard to see where one neuron ends and another begins. Scientists once believed that the branching axon of one cell fused with the dendrites of another in an uninterrupted fabric. Then a Spanish anatomist, Santiago Ramón y Cajal (1852–1934), described gaps between individual nerve cells and concluded that the individual neurons must function as independent agents within the nervous system. At the same time, the British physiologist Sir Charles Sherrington (1857–1952) noticed that neural impulses were taking an unexpectedly long time to travel a neural pathway. Sherrington inferred there must be a brief interruption in the transmission.

We now know that the axon terminal of one neuron is in fact separated from the receiving neuron by a gap less than a millionth of an inch wide. Sherrington called this junction the **synapse,** and the gap is called the *synaptic gap* or *cleft.* To Cajal, these near-unions of neurons—"protoplasmic kisses," he called them—were another of nature's marvels. How does the nerve impulse execute the protoplasmic kiss? How does it cross the tiny synaptic gap? The answer is one of the important scientific discoveries of our age.

- **neuron** a nerve cell; the basic building block of the nervous system.
- **dendrite** the bushy, branching extensions of a neuron that receive messages and conduct impulses toward the cell body.
- **axon** the extension of a neuron, ending in branching terminal fibers, through which messages are sent to other neurons or to muscles or glands.
- **myelin [MY-uh-lin] sheath** a layer of fatty tissue segmentally encasing the fibers of many neurons; enables vastly greater transmission speed of neural impulses as the impulse hops from one node to the next.
- **action potential** a neural impulse; a brief electrical charge that travels down an axon. The action potential is generated by the movement of positively charged atoms in and out of channels in the axon's membrane.
- **threshold** the level of stimulation required to trigger a neural impulse.
- **synapse [SIN-aps]** the junction between the axon tip of the sending neuron and the dendrite or cell body of the receiving neuron. The tiny gap at this junction is called the *synaptic gap* or *cleft.*

"All information processing in the brain involves neurons 'talking to' each other at synapses."

Neuroscientist Solomon H. Snyder (1984)

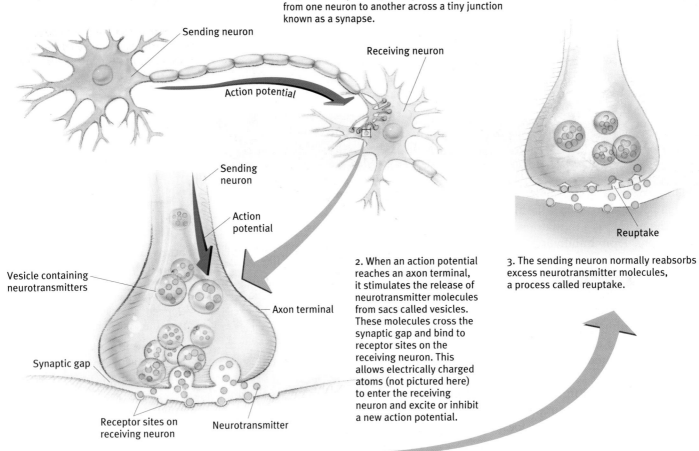

1. Electrical impulses (action potentials) travel from one neuron to another across a tiny junction known as a synapse.

Sending neuron

Receiving neuron

Action potential

Sending neuron

Action potential

Vesicle containing neurotransmitters

Axon terminal

Synaptic gap

Receptor sites on receiving neuron

Neurotransmitter

Reuptake

2. When an action potential reaches an axon terminal, it stimulates the release of neurotransmitter molecules from sacs called vesicles. These molecules cross the synaptic gap and bind to receptor sites on the receiving neuron. This allows electrically charged atoms (not pictured here) to enter the receiving neuron and excite or inhibit a new action potential.

3. The sending neuron normally reabsorbs excess neurotransmitter molecules, a process called reuptake.

FIGURE 3.2 How neurons communicate

■ **neurotransmitters** chemical messengers that traverse the synaptic gaps between neurons. When released by the sending neuron, neurotransmitters travel across the synapse and bind to receptor sites on the receiving neuron, thereby influencing whether that neuron will generate a neural impulse.

"When it comes to the brain, if you want to see the action, follow the neurotransmitters."

Neuroscientist Floyd Bloom (1993)

When the action potential reaches the knoblike terminals at an axon's end, it triggers the release of chemical messengers, called **neurotransmitters** (**FIGURE 3.2**). Within 1/10,000th of a second, the neurotransmitter molecules cross the synaptic gap and bind to receptor sites on the receiving neuron—as precisely as a key fits a lock. For an instant, the neurotransmitter unlocks tiny channels at the receiving site. This allows electrically charged atoms to enter the receiving neuron, thereby either exciting or inhibiting its readiness to fire. Excess neurotransmitters are reabsorbed by the sending neuron in a process called *reuptake*. Many drugs increase the availability of selected neurotransmitters by blocking their reuptake.

How Neurotransmitters Influence Us

PREVIEW QUESTION 3 How do neurotransmitters influence human behavior?

Researchers have discovered dozens of different neurotransmitters. That raises questions: Are certain neurotransmitters found only in specific places? What are their effects? Can we boost or diminish these effects through drugs or diet? Could such changes affect our moods, memories, or mental abilities?

Later in this book we examine the role of neurotransmitters in depression and euphoria, hunger and thinking, addictions and therapy. For now, let's glimpse how neurotransmitters influence our motions and our emotions. We now know that a particular neural pathway in the brain may use only one or two neurotransmitters

Dopamine pathways

Serotonin pathways

FIGURE 3.3
Neurotransmitter pathways
Each of the brain's differing chemical messengers has designated pathways where it operates, as shown here for dopamine and serotonin (Carter, 1998).

Sensory
↳ Afferent
↳ Motor
Efferent

(FIGURE 3.3), and that particular neurotransmitters may have particular effects on behavior and emotions. Some examples:

- *Dopamine* influences movement, learning, attention, and emotion. Excess activity at dopamine receptors has been linked with schizophrenia.
- *Serotonin* affects mood, hunger, sleep, and arousal. Prozac and similar antidepressant drugs raise serotonin levels.
- *Norepinephrine* helps control alertness and arousal.

The Endorphins

An exciting discovery about neurotransmitters occurred when Candace Pert and Solomon Snyder (1973) attached a radioactive tracer to morphine, showing them where in an animal's brain it was taken up. Their discovery: The morphine, an opiate drug that elevates mood and eases pain, was taken up by receptors in areas linked with mood and pain sensations.

It was hard to imagine why the brain would contain these "opiate receptors" unless it had its own naturally occurring opiates. Why would the brain have a chemical lock, unless it also had a corresponding key? Researchers soon confirmed that the brain does indeed contain several types of neurotransmitter molecules similar to morphine. Named **endorphins** (short for *endo*genous [produced within] m*orphin*e), these natural opiates are released in response to pain and vigorous exercise. They may therefore help explain all sorts of good feelings, such as the "runner's high," the painkilling effects of acupuncture, and the indifference to pain in some severely injured people, such as David Livingstone reported in his 1857 *Missionary Travels:*

> I heard a shout. Starting, and looking half round, I saw the lion just in the act of springing upon me. I was upon a little height, he caught my shoulder as he sprang, and we both came to the ground below together. Growling horribly close to my ear, he shook me as a terrier does a rat. The shock produced a stupor similar to that which seems to be felt by a mouse after the first shake of the cat. It caused a sort of dreaminess in which there was no sense of pain nor feeling of terror, though [I was] quite conscious of all that was happening. . . . This peculiar state is probably produced in all animals killed by the carnivora; and if so, is a merciful provision by our benevolent Creator for lessening the pain of death.

How Drugs and Other Chemicals Alter Neurotransmission

If indeed the endorphins lessen pain and boost mood, why not flood the brain with artificial opiates, thereby intensifying the brain's own "feel-good" chemistry? One problem is that when flooded with opiate drugs such as heroin and morphine, the brain may stop producing its own natural opiates. When the drug is withdrawn, the

Physician Lewis Thomas, on the endorphins:
"There it is, a biologically universal act of mercy. I cannot explain it, except to say that I would have put it in had I been around at the very beginning, sitting as a member of a planning committee."

The Youngest Science, 1983

■ **endorphins [en-DOR-fins]** "morphine within"—natural, opiatelike neurotransmitters linked to pain control and to pleasure.

■ **nervous system** the body's speedy, electrochemical communication system, consisting of all the nerve cells of the peripheral and central nervous systems.

■ **central nervous system (CNS)** the brain and spinal cord.

■ **peripheral nervous system (PNS)** the sensory and motor neurons that connect the central nervous system (CNS) to the rest of the body.

■ **nerves** neural "cables" containing many axons. These bundled axons, which are part of the peripheral nervous system, connect the central nervous system with muscles, glands, and sense organs.

■ **sensory neurons** neurons that carry incoming information from the sense receptors to the central nervous system.

brain may therefore be deprived of all forms of opiates. For a drug addict, the result is agony that persists until the brain resumes production of its natural opiates or receives more artificial opiates. Mood-altering drugs, from alcohol to nicotine to heroin, share this common effect: They trigger unpleasant, lingering aftereffects. For suppressing the body's own neurotransmitter production, nature charges a price.

Drugs affect communication at the synapse, often by exciting or inhibiting neuron firing. *Agonists* excite by mimicking a particular neurotransmitter or blocking its reuptake **(FIGURE 3.4)**. An agonist can be a drug molecule that is similar enough to the neurotransmitter to mimic its effects. Some opiate drugs, for example, produce a temporary "high" by amplifying normal sensations of arousal or pleasure. *Antagonists* inhibit by blocking neurotransmitters or by diminishing their release. An antagonist can be a drug molecule that is enough like the natural neurotransmitter to occupy its receptor site and block its effect but not similar enough to stimulate the receptor, rather like foreign coins that fit into, but won't operate, a soda or candy machine. Botulin poison causes paralysis by blocking receptors for acetylcholine (ACh), a neurotransmitter that produces muscle movement.

Neurotransmitter research is enabling the creation of new therapeutic drugs such as those used to alleviate depression. But designing a drug can be harder than it sounds. Scientists know, for example, that the tremors of Parkinson's disease result from the death of nerve cells that produce the neurotransmitter dopamine. Giving the patient dopamine as a drug doesn't help, though, because dopamine cannot cross the *blood-brain barrier,* by which the brain fences out unwanted chemicals circulating in the blood. But L-dopa, a raw material the brain can convert to dopamine, can sneak through the fence. Given L-dopa, many patients gain better muscular control.

FIGURE 3.4 Agonists and antagonists

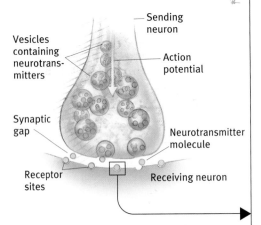

Neurotransmitters carry a message from a sending neuron across a synapse to receptor sites on a receiving neuron.

This neurotransmitter molecule has a molecular structure that precisely fits the receptor site on the receiving neuron, much as a key fits a lock.

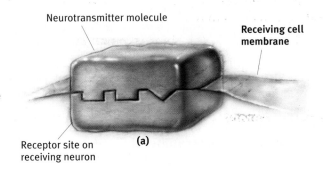

This agonist molecule excites. It is similar enough in structure to the neurotransmitter molecule that it mimics its effects on the receiving neuron. Morphine, for instance, mimics the action of endorphins by stimulating receptors in brain areas involved in mood and pain sensations.

This antagonist molecule inhibits. It has a structure similar enough to the neurotransmitter to occupy its receptor site and block its action, but not similar enough to stimulate the receptor. Botulin poisoning paralyzes its victims by blocking ACh receptors involved in muscle movement.

rehearse it!

1. The neuron fiber that carries messages to other neurons is the
   a. dendrite.
   b. axon.
   c. cell body.
   d. myelin.

2. The neuron's response to stimulation is an *all-or-none* response, meaning that the intensity of the stimulus de-termines
   a. whether or not an impulse is generated.
   b. how fast an impulse is transmitted.

   c. how intense an impulse will be.
   d. whether the stimulus is excitatory or inhibitory.

3. There is a minuscule space between the axon of a sending neuron and the dendrite or cell body of a receiving neuron. This small space is called the
   a. axon terminal.
   b. sac or vesicle.
   c. synaptic gap.
   d. threshold.

4. When the action potential reaches the axon terminal of a neuron, it triggers

   the release of chemical messengers called
   a. ions.
   b. synapses.
   c. neural impulses.
   d. neurotransmitters.

5. Endorphins are released in the brain in response to
   a. morphine or heroin.
   b. pain or vigorous exercise.
   c. antagonists.
   d. all of the above.

The Nervous System

PREVIEW QUESTION 4 What are the major divisions of the nervous system, and what are their basic functions?

Neurons communicating with other neurons form our body's primary information system, the **nervous system (FIGURE 3.5).** The brain and spinal cord form the **central nervous system (CNS).** The **peripheral nervous system (PNS)** links the central nervous system with the body's sense receptors, muscles, and glands. The sensory and motor axons carrying this PNS information are bundled into the electrical cables that we know as **nerves.** The optic nerve, for example, bundles nearly a million axon fibers into a single cable carrying the information that each eye sends to the brain.

Information travels in the nervous system through three types of neurons. The **sensory neurons** send information from the body's tissues and sensory organs

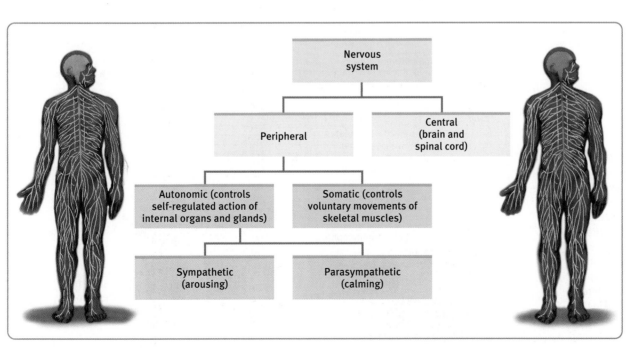

FIGURE 3.5
The functional divisions of the human nervous system

Nervous system

Peripheral

Central (brain and spinal cord)

Autonomic (controls self-regulated action of internal organs and glands)

Somatic (controls voluntary movements of skeletal muscles)

Sympathetic (arousing)

Parasympathetic (calming)

inward to the brain and spinal cord, which process the information. This processing involves a second class of neurons, the central nervous system's own **interneurons,** which enable its internal communication. The central nervous system then sends instructions out to the body's tissues via the **motor neurons.** Our complexity, though, resides mostly in our interneuron systems. Our nervous system has a few million sensory neurons, a few million motor neurons, but billions and billions of interneurons.

The Peripheral Nervous System

Our peripheral nervous system has two components—somatic and autonomic. The **somatic nervous system** controls the movements of our skeletal muscles. As you reach the bottom of this page, the somatic nervous system will report to your brain the current state of your skeletal muscles and carry instructions back, triggering your hand to turn the page.

Our **autonomic nervous system** controls the glands and the muscles of our internal organs. Like an automatic pilot, it may sometimes be consciously overridden. But usually it operates on its own to influence our internal functioning, including our heartbeat, digestion, and glandular activity. (*Autonomic* means "self-regulating.")

The autonomic nervous system is a dual system **(FIGURE 3.6)**. The **sympathetic nervous system** arouses us for defensive action. If something alarms or enrages you, the sympathetic system will accelerate your heartbeat, slow your digestion, raise your

Aggression triggered
Back arched and fur fluffed, this fierce cat is ready to attack. Which division of the autonomic nervous system is activated by such stimulation? (See page 44.)

FIGURE 3.6
The dual functions of the autonomic nervous system
The autonomic nervous system controls the more autonomous (or self-regulating) internal functions. Its sympathetic division arouses and expends energy. Its parasympathetic division calms and conserves energy, allowing routine maintenance activity. For example, sympathetic stimulation accelerates heartbeat, while parasympathetic stimulation slows it.

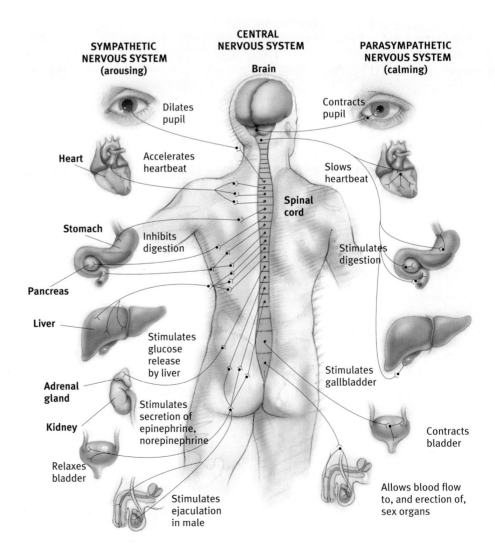

blood sugar, dilate your arteries, and cool you with perspiration, making you alert and ready for action. When the stress subsides, the **parasympathetic nervous system** produces opposite effects. It conserves energy as it calms you by decreasing your heartbeat, lowering your blood sugar, and so forth. In everyday situations, the sympathetic and parasympathetic nervous systems work together to keep us in a steady internal state.

The Central Nervous System

From the simplicity of neurons "talking" to other neurons arises the complexity of the central nervous system that enables our humanity—our thinking, feeling, and acting. Tens of billions of neurons, each communicating with thousands of other neurons, yield an ever-changing wiring diagram that dwarfs a powerful computer. One of the great remaining mysteries is how this neural machinery organizes itself into complex circuits capable of learning, feeling, and thinking.

Spinal Cord and Brain

The spinal cord is an information highway connecting the peripheral nervous system to the brain. Ascending neural tracts send up sensory information, and descending tracts send back motor-control information.

The neural pathways governing our **reflexes,** our automatic responses to stimuli, illustrate the spinal cord's work. One such pathway enables the pain reflex **(FIGURE 3.7).** When your fingers touch a flame, neural activity excited by the heat travels via sensory neurons to interneurons in your spinal cord. These interneurons respond by activating motor neurons to the muscles in your arm. That's why it feels as though your hand jerks away not by your choice, but on its own.

Because the simple pain reflex pathway runs through the spinal cord and out, your hand jerks from the candle's flame *before* your brain receives and responds to the information that causes you to feel pain. Information travels to and from the brain by way of the spinal cord. Were the top of your spinal cord severed, you would not feel such pain. Nor would you feel pleasure. Your brain would literally be out of touch with your body. You would lose all sensation and voluntary movement in body regions whose sensory and motor neurons connect with the spinal cord below its point of injury. Men paralyzed below the waist are usually capable of an erection (a simple

- **interneurons** central nervous system neurons that internally communicate and intervene between the sensory inputs and motor outputs.

- **motor neurons** the neurons that carry outgoing information from the central nervous system to the muscles and glands.

- **somatic nervous system** the division of the peripheral nervous system that controls the body's skeletal muscles. Also called the *skeletal nervous system.*

- **autonomic [aw-tuh-NAHM-ik] nervous system** the part of the peripheral nervous system that controls the glands and the muscles of the internal organs (such as the heart). Its sympathetic division arouses; its parasympathetic division calms.

- **sympathetic nervous system** the division of the autonomic nervous system that arouses the body, mobilizing its energy in stressful situations.

- **parasympathetic nervous system** the division of the autonomic nervous system that calms the body, conserving its energy.

- **reflex** a simple, automatic, inborn response to a sensory stimulus, such as the knee-jerk response.

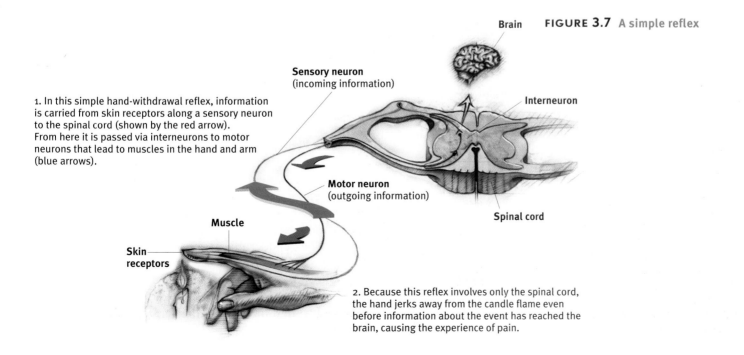

FIGURE 3.7 A simple reflex

Brain

Sensory neuron (incoming information)

Interneuron

1. In this simple hand-withdrawal reflex, information is carried from skin receptors along a sensory neuron to the spinal cord (shown by the red arrow). From here it is passed via interneurons to motor neurons that lead to muscles in the hand and arm (blue arrows).

Motor neuron (outgoing information)

Spinal cord

Muscle

Skin receptors

2. Because this reflex involves only the spinal cord, the hand jerks away from the candle flame even before information about the event has reached the brain, causing the experience of pain.

The cat on page 42 is aroused via its sympathetic nervous system.

reflex) if their genitals are stimulated. Females similarly paralyzed respond with vaginal lubrication. But, depending on where and how completely the spinal cord is severed, they may be genitally unresponsive to erotic images and have no genital feeling (Kennedy & Over, 1990; Sipski & Alexander, 1999). To produce bodily pain or pleasure, the sensory information must reach the brain.

rehearse it!

6. Information travels to and from the brain mostly by way of the spinal cord. The neurons of the spinal cord are called
   a. motor neurons.
   b. sensory neurons.
   c. sending neurons.
   d. interneurons.

7. The autonomic nervous system controls internal functions, such as heart

rate and glandular activity. The word *autonomic* means
   a. peripheral.
   b. voluntary.
   c. self-regulating.
   d. arousing.

8. Usually, the sympathetic nervous system arouses us for action and the parasympathetic nervous system calms us down. Together the two systems make up the

   a. autonomic nervous system.
   b. somatic nervous system.
   c. central nervous system.
   d. peripheral nervous system.

9. The neurons of the spinal cord are part of the
   a. somatic nervous system.
   b. central nervous system.
   c. autonomic nervous system.
   d. peripheral nervous system.

The Endocrine System

PREVIEW QUESTION 5 How does the endocrine system—the body's slower information system—transmit its messages?

FIGURE 3.8
The body's major endocrine glands

Hypothalamus
(brain region controlling the pituitary gland)

Thyroid gland
(affects metabolism, among other things)

Pituitary gland
(secretes many different hormones, some of which affect other glands)

Parathyroids
(help regulate the level of calcium in the blood)

Adrenal glands
(inner part, called the medulla, helps trigger the "fight or flight" response)

Pancreas
(regulates the level of sugar in the blood)

Ovary
(secretes female sex hormones)

Testis
(secretes male sex hormones)

Interconnected with the nervous system is the second of the body's communication systems, the **endocrine system (FIGURE 3.8).** The endocrine system's glands secrete another form of chemical messengers, **hormones.** Hormones originate in one tissue, travel through the bloodstream, and affect other tissues, including the brain. When they act on the brain, they influence our interest in sex, food, and aggression.

Some hormones are chemically identical to neurotransmitters. The endocrine system and the nervous system are therefore kindred systems: Both secrete molecules that activate receptors elsewhere. But unlike the speedy nervous system, zipping messages from eyes to brain to hand in a fraction of a second, endocrine messages trudge along. If the nervous system's communication delivers messages rather like e-mail, the endocrine system is the body's snail mail. Several seconds or more may elapse before the bloodstream carries a hormone from an endocrine gland to its target tissue. But these endocrine messages are often worth the wait because their effects usually last longer than the effects of a neural message.

The endocrine system's hormones influence many aspects of our lives—growth, reproduction, metabolism, mood—working to keep everything in balance while we respond to stress, exertion, and our own thoughts. In a moment of danger, for example, the autonomic nervous system orders the **adrenal glands** on top of the kidneys to release *epinephrine* and *norepinephrine* (also called *adrenaline* and *noradrenaline*). These hormones increase heart rate, blood pressure, and blood sugar, providing us with a surge of energy. When the emergency passes, the hormones—and the feelings of excitement—linger a while.

The most influential endocrine gland is the **pituitary gland,** a pea-sized structure located in the base of the brain, where it is controlled by an adjacent brain area called the *hypothalamus.* The pituitary releases hormones that influence growth, and its secretions also influence the release of hormones by other endocrine glands. The pituitary then is really a sort of master gland (whose own master is the hypothalamus). For example, under the brain's influence, the pituitary triggers your sex glands to release sex hormones. These may in turn influence your brain and behavior.

This feedback system (brain → pituitary → other glands → hormones → brain) reveals the intimate connection of the nervous and endocrine systems: the nervous system directing endocrine secretions, which then affect the nervous system. Conducting and coordinating this whole electrochemical orchestra is that maestro we call the brain.

- **endocrine [EN-duh-krin] system** the body's "slow" chemical communication system; a set of glands that secrete hormones into the bloodstream.

- **hormones** chemical messengers, mostly those manufactured by the endocrine glands, that are produced in one tissue and affect another.

- **adrenal [ah-DREEN-el] glands** a pair of endocrine glands just above the kidneys. The adrenals secrete the hormones epinephrine (adrenaline) and norepinephrine (noradrenaline), which help to arouse the body in times of stress.

- **pituitary gland** the endocrine system's most influential gland. Under the influence of the hypothalamus, the pituitary regulates growth and controls other endocrine glands.

rehearse it!

10. The endocrine system, the second and slower bodily communication system, produces chemical messengers that travel through the bloodstream and affect other tissues. These chemical substances are

   a. hormones.
   b. neurotransmitters.
   c. endorphins.
   d. glands.

11. The pituitary gland releases hormones that influence growth and the activity

of other glands. The pituitary gland is part of the
   a. endocrine system.
   b. peripheral nervous system.
   c. sympathetic nervous system.
   d. central nervous system.

REVIEWING

Neural and Hormonal Systems

1. What are neurons, and how do they transmit information?

The body's neural circuitry consists of billions of nerve cells, called neurons, which are the elementary components of the nervous system, the body's speedy electrochemical information system. A neuron receives signals from external stimuli and from other neurons through its branching dendrites and cell bodies, combines these signals in the cell body, and, if the signals exceed a certain threshold, transmits an electrical impulse (the action potential) down its axons. Some axons are covered by a myelin sheath, which helps speed the signal.

2. How do nerve cells communicate?

When electrical signals reach the end of the axon, they stimulate the release of chemical messengers called neurotransmitters. These molecules pass on their excitatory or inhibitory messages as they traverse the tiny gap (synapse) between neurons and combine with receptor sites on neighboring neurons.

3. How do neurotransmitters influence human behavior?

Dozens of different neurotransmitters have been discovered, and the functions of some are now well understood. Learning about endorphins, the feel-good neurotransmitters, has helped us understand how drugs affect our brain chemistry. Some drugs (agonists) mimic particular neurotransmitters; others (antagonists) block them.

4. What are the major divisions of the nervous system, and what are their basic functions?

The nervous system consists of the central nervous system (CNS) and the peripheral nervous system (PNS). The interneurons in the brain and spinal cord (the CNS) communicate with the sensory and motor neurons that form nerves in the PNS. The peripheral nervous system also has two main divisions, the somatic and the autonomic. The somatic nervous system directs voluntary movements and reflexes. The autonomic nervous system, through its sympathetic and parasympathetic divisions, controls our involuntary muscles and the glands of the internal organs.

TERMS AND CONCEPTS TO REMEMBER

neuron, p. 36
dendrite, p. 36
axon, p. 36
myelin [MY-uh-lin] sheath, p. 36
action potential, p. 37
threshold, p. 37
synapse [SIN-aps], p. 37
neurotransmitters, p. 38

endorphins [en-DOR-fins], p. 39
nervous system, p. 41
central nervous system (CNS), p. 41
peripheral nervous system (PNS), p. 41
nerves, p. 41
sensory neurons, p. 41

interneurons, p. 42
motor neurons, p. 42
somatic nervous system, p. 42
autonomic [aw-tuh-NAHM-ik] nervous system, p. 42
sympathetic nervous system, p. 42
parasympathetic nervous system, p. 43

reflex, p. 43
endocrine [EN-duh-krin] system, p. 44
hormones, p. 44
adrenal [ah-DREEN-el] glands, p. 45
pituitary gland, p. 45

REHEARSE IT ANSWER KEY

1. b
2. a
3. c
4. d
5. b
6. d
7. c
8. a
9. b
10. a
11. a

The Brain

In a jar on a display shelf in Cornell University's psychology department resides the well-preserved brain of Edward Bradford Titchener, a great early-twentieth-century psychologist and proponent of the study of consciousness. Imagine yourself gazing at that wrinkled mass of grayish tissue: Is Titchener in any sense still in there?[1]

You might answer that, without the living whir of electrochemical activity, there could be nothing of Titchener in his preserved brain. Consider then an experiment about which the inquisitive Titchener himself might have daydreamed. Imagine that just moments before his death, someone removed Titchener's brain from his body and kept it alive by pumping enriched blood through it as it floated in a tank of cerebral fluid. Would Titchener now still be in there? Further imagine, to carry our fantasy to its limit, that someone transplanted the still-living brain into the body of a person with severe brain damage. To whose home should the recovered patient return?

That we can imagine such questions illustrates how convinced we are that we live in our heads. And for good reason: The brain enables the mind: seeing, hearing, remembering, thinking, feeling, speaking, dreaming. Indeed, say neuroscientists, the *mind is what the brain does.* But precisely where and how are the mind's functions tied to the brain? (To see how scientists explore such questions, see the Close-Up on The Tools of Discovery on pages 48 and 49.)

> "I am a brain, Watson. The rest of me is a mere appendix."
>
> **Sherlock Holmes, in Arthur Conan Doyle's "The Adventure of the Mazarin Stone"**

Lower-Level Brain Structures

If you could open the skull and look inside, the first thing you might note is the brain's size. In dinosaurs, the brain represents 1/100,000th of the body's weight, in whales 1/10,000th, in elephants 1/600th, in humans 1/45th. It looks as though a principle is emerging. But keep on. In mice the brain is 1/40th the body's weight, and in marmosets 1/25th. So there are exceptions to the rule of thumb that the ratio of brain to body weight provides a clue to a species' intelligence.

More useful clues to an animal's capacities come from the brain's structures. In primitive vertebrate (backboned) animals, such as sharks, the brain primarily regulates basic survival functions: breathing, resting, and feeding. In lower mammals, such as rodents, a more complex brain enables emotion and greater memory. In advanced mammals, such as humans, the brain processes more information, enabling us to act with foresight.

Biological history has not greatly altered the basic mechanisms for survival. Rather, species have elaborated new brain systems on top of the old, much as the Earth's landscape covers the old with the new. Digging down, one discovers the fossil remnants of the past—brainstem components still performing much as they did for our distant ancestors. Starting with the brainstem and working up, let's now explore the brain.

Einstein's brain

For you and me, as well as for Albert Einstein (whose brain is shown here), this small wrinkled organ is far more complex than the most sophisticated computer. What you see here is only a portion of the brain's outer layer. Most of its surface lies hidden within its convoluted folds.

[1] Carl Sagan's *Broca's Brain* (1979) inspired this question.

CLOSE-UP:

THE TOOLS OF DISCOVERY

It is exciting to consider how fast and how far the neurosciences have progressed within a lifetime. For centuries, the human brain lay largely beyond the reach of science. The neuron was too small to study with the naked eye, its impulses too faint to record with ordinary electrodes. We were able to feel bumps on the skull, dissect and analyze lifeless brains, and observe the effects of specific brain diseases and injuries. But there were no tools high-powered yet gentle enough to explore the living brain. Now, that has changed. Whether in the interests of science or medicine, we can selectively **lesion** (destroy) tiny clusters of normal or defective brain cells, leaving their surroundings unharmed. We can probe the brain with tiny electrical pulses. We can snoop on the messages of individual neurons and on the mass action of billions of neurons. We can see color representations of the brain's energy-consuming activity. These new tools and techniques for peering into the brain while it works on mental tasks are doing for psychology what the telescope did for astronomy.

Clinical Observations

The oldest method of studying brain-mind connections is to observe the effects of brain diseases and injuries. Such observations were first recorded some 5000 years ago. But it was not until the last two centuries that physicians began systematically recording the results of damage to specific brain areas. Some noted that damage to one side of the brain often caused numbness or paralysis on the body's opposite side, suggesting that the right side of the body is wired to the brain's left side, and vice versa. Others noticed that damage to the back of the brain disrupted vision, and that damage to the left-front part of the brain produced speech difficulties. Gradually, the brain was being mapped.

Manipulating the Brain

Today's scientists, however, do not need to await brain injuries. They can electrically, chemically, or magnetically *stimulate* various parts of the brain and note the effects. They can also surgically lesion tissue in specific brain areas in animals. For example, a lesion in one area of the hypothalamus in a rat's brain reduces eating, causing the rat to starve unless force-fed. A lesion in another area produces *overeating*.

Recording the Brain's Electrical Activity

Right now, your mental activity is giving off telltale electrical, metabolic, and magnetic signals that would enable neuroscientists to eavesdrop on your brain with increasing precision. The tips of modern microelectrodes are so small they can detect the electrical pulse in a single neuron, making possible some astonishingly precise findings. For example, we can now detect exactly where the information goes after someone strokes a cat's whisker.

Electrical activity in the brain's billions of neurons sweeps in regular waves across its surface. The **electroencephalogram (EEG)** is an amplified tracing of such waves by an instrument called an *electroencephalograph*. Studying an EEG of the gross activity of the whole brain is like studying the activity of a car engine by listening to the hum of its motor. However, by presenting a stimulus repeatedly and having a computer filter out brain activity unrelated to the stimulus, one can identify the electrical wave evoked by the stimulus **(FIGURE 4.1)**.

Neuroimaging Techniques

Other new windows into the brain give us a Supermanlike ability to see inside the brain without lesioning it. For example, the **CT (computed tomogra-**

FIGURE 4.1
An electroencephalograph providing amplified tracings of waves of electrical activity in the brain
Here it is detecting brain response to sound, making possible an early evaluation of what may be a hearing impairment.

phy) scan examines the brain by taking x-ray photographs that can reveal brain damage. The **PET (positron emission tomography) scan (FIGURE 4.2)** depicts brain activity by showing each brain area's consumption of its chemical fuel, the sugar glucose (see Figure 4.14, page 59).

FIGURE 4.2
The PET scan
To obtain a PET scan, researchers inject volunteers with a low and harmless dose of a short-lived radioactive sugar. Detectors around the subject's head pick up the release of gamma rays from the sugar, which has concentrated in active brain areas. A computer then processes and translates these signals into a map of the brain at work.

"That's a lie, Morty! . . . Mom says you might have got the brains in the family, but I got the looks!"

Active neurons are glucose hogs. A person is given a temporarily radioactive form of glucose, and the PET scan locates and measures the radioactivity, thereby detecting where this "food for thought" goes. In this way, researchers can see which brain areas are most active as the person performs mathematical calculations, listens to music, or daydreams.

Another new way of looking into the living brain exploits the fact that the centers of atoms, including those in our brains, spin like tops. In **MRI (magnetic resonance imaging)** scans, the head is put in a strong magnetic field, which aligns the spinning atoms. Then a brief pulse of radio waves disorients the atoms momentarily. When the atoms return to their normal spin, they release detectable signals, which become computer-generated images of their concentrations. The result is a detailed picture of the brain's soft tissues. For example, MRI scans reveal enlarged fluid-filled brain areas in some patients who have schizophrenia, a disabling psychological disorder **(FIGURE 4.3)**.

By taking pictures less than a second apart, MRI scans can now show the brain lighting up (with increased oxygen-laden bloodflow) as a research participant performs different mental functions. As the person looks at a face, a *functional MRI* machine detects blood rushing to the back of the brain, which processes visual information (Figure 4.10, page 56). Ask the participant to solve a verbal analogy problem, and the part of the brain's left side near the front will light up. Such snapshots of the brain's activity provide new insights into how and where the brain divides its labor.

These new brain-imaging instruments are doing for psychological science what the microscope did for biology and the telescope for astronomy. To be learning about the neurosciences now is like studying world geography while Magellan was exploring the seas. Every year the explorers announce new discoveries, which also generate new interpretations of old discoveries. Here is a small sampling of new revelations:

- PET scans show that the brain areas that light up when people silently say the name of an animal differ from those that light up when they say the name of a tool (Martin & others, 1996).
- MRI scans reveal a larger-than-average neural area in the left

brain of musicians who display perfect pitch (Schlaug & others, 1995).
- MRI scans of bilingual people's brains reveal that second languages are represented in the same area as the first if learned early, and in differing areas if learned late (Kim & others, 1997).
- Functional MRI scans reveal that, during a rhyming task, men's brains have a distinctively active left brain area, whereas women's brains are active on both sides (Shawitz & others, 1995).

Data from different brain-imaging techniques are appearing faster than anyone can read and remember them. Researchers are assembling this information in computer databases. Clearly, this is the golden age of brain science.

FIGURE 4.3
MRI scan of a healthy individual (left) and a person with schizophrenia (right) Note the enlarged fluid-filled brain region in the image on the right.

- **lesion [LEE-zhuhn]** tissue destruction. A brain lesion is a naturally or experimentally caused destruction of brain tissue.

- **electroencephalogram (EEG)** an amplified recording of the waves of electrical activity that sweep across the brain's surface. These waves are measured by electrodes placed on the scalp.

- **CT (computed tomography) scan** a series of x-ray photographs taken from different angles and combined by computer into a composite representation of a slice through the body. Also called *CAT scan*.

- **PET (positron emission tomography) scan** a visual display of brain activity that detects where a radioactive form of glucose goes while the brain performs a given task.

- **MRI (magnetic resonance imaging)** a technique that uses magnetic fields and radio waves to produce computer-generated images that distinguish among different types of soft tissue; allows us to see structures within the brain.

- **brainstem** the oldest part and central core of the brain, beginning where the spinal cord swells as it enters the skull; the brainstem is responsible for automatic survival functions.

- **medulla [muh-DUL-uh]** the base of the brainstem; controls heartbeat and breathing.

- **reticular formation** a nerve network in the brainstem that plays an important role in controlling arousal.

- **neuron** a nerve cell; the basic building block of the nervous system.

- **thalamus [THAL-uh-muss]** the brain's sensory switchboard, located on top of the brainstem; it directs messages to the sensory receiving areas in the cortex and transmits replies to the cerebellum and medulla.

- **cerebellum [sehr-uh-BELL-um]** the "little brain" attached to the rear of the brainstem; it helps coordinate voluntary movement and balance.

The Brainstem and Its Associated Structures

PREVIEW QUESTION 1 What are the functions of the brainstem and its associated structures?

The Brainstem

The brain's basement—its oldest and innermost region—is the **brainstem.** It begins where the spinal cord enters the skull and swells slightly, forming the **medulla.** Here lie the controls for your heartbeat and breathing. If the top of a cat's brainstem is severed from the rest of the brain above it, the animal will still breathe and live—and even run, climb, and groom (Klemm, 1990). But cut off from the brain's higher region, it won't purposefully run or climb to get food.

The brainstem is also the crossover point, where most nerves to and from each side of the brain connect with the body's opposite side. This peculiar cross-wiring is but one of many surprises the brain has to offer.

Inside the brainstem, the **reticular** ("netlike") **formation,** a finger-shaped network of **neurons** (nerve cells), extends from the spinal cord right up to the thalamus **(FIGURE 4.4).** As the spinal cord's sensory input travels up to the thalamus, some of it branches off to the reticular formation, which filters incoming stimuli and relays important information to other areas of the brain. Among its other functions, the reticular formation helps control arousal.

In 1949, Giuseppe Moruzzi and Horace Magoun discovered that electrically stimulating the reticular formation of a sleeping cat almost instantly produced an awake, alert animal. Magoun also severed a cat's reticular formation from higher brain regions without damaging the nearby sensory pathways. The effect? The cat lapsed into a coma from which it never awakened.

The Thalamus

Atop the brainstem sits the brain's sensory switchboard, a joined pair of egg-shaped structures called the **thalamus** (Figure 4.4). It receives information from all the senses except smell and routes it to the higher brain regions that deal with seeing,

FIGURE 4.4

The brainstem and thalamus
The brainstem, including the medulla, is an extension of the spinal cord. The thalamus is attached to its top. The reticular formation passes through both structures.

Thalamus

Reticular formation

Medulla

hearing, tasting, and touching. Think of the thalamus as being to sensory input what London is to England's trains: a hub through which traffic passes en route to various destinations. The thalamus also receives some of the higher brain's replies, which it then directs to the cerebellum and medulla.

The Cerebellum

Extending from the rear of the brainstem is the **cerebellum,** meaning little brain, which is what its two wrinkled hemispheres rather look like **(FIGURE 4.5).** The cerebellum enables one type of nonverbal learning and memory, but its most obvious function is coordinating voluntary movement. When baseball great Sammy Sosa smacks a home run with a perfectly timed swing of the bat, give his cerebellum some credit. If you injured your cerebellum, you would likely have difficulty walking, keeping your balance, or shaking hands. Your movements would be jerky and exaggerated.

Note: These lower brain functions all occur without any conscious effort. This illustrates another of our recurring themes: *Our brain processes most information outside of our awareness.* We are aware of the *results* of our brain's labor (say, our current visual experience) but not of *how* we construct the visual image. Likewise, whether we are asleep or awake, our brainstem manages its life-sustaining functions, freeing our higher brain regions to dream or to think, talk, or savor a memory.

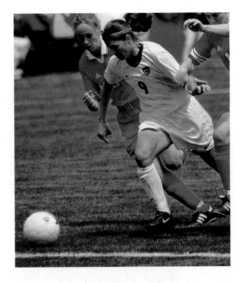

The brain's organ of agility
The cerebellum helps soccer football players such as Mia Hamm direct the ball precisely.

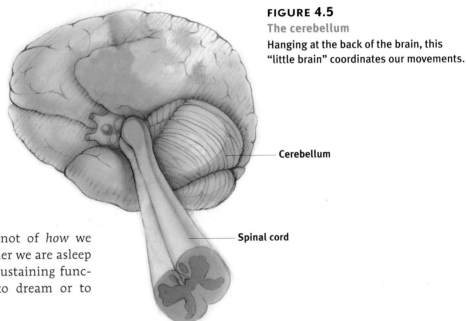

FIGURE 4.5
The cerebellum
Hanging at the back of the brain, this "little brain" coordinates our movements.

— Cerebellum

— Spinal cord

---

rehearse it!

1. The brainstem is the oldest and innermost region of the brain. The part of the brainstem that controls heartbeat and breathing is the
   a. cerebellum.
   b. medulla.
   c. cortex.
   d. thalamus.

2. The lower brain structure that governs arousal is the

   a. spinal cord.
   b. cerebellum.
   c. reticular formation.
   d. medulla.

3. The thalamus receives information from the sensory neurons and routes it to the higher brain regions that control the senses. The thalamus functions like a

   a. memory bank.
   b. pleasure center.
   c. breathing regulator.
   d. switchboard.

4. The part of the brain that coordinates voluntary movement is the
   a. cerebellum.
   b. medulla.
   c. thalamus.
   d. reticular formation.

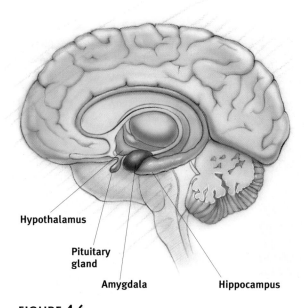

Hypothalamus

Pituitary gland

Amygdala   **Hippocampus**

FIGURE 4.6

The limbic system

Limbic structures form a doughnut-shaped neural system between the brain's older parts and its cerebral hemispheres. Although part of the hormonal (endocrine) system, not the brain, the pituitary gland is controlled by the limbic system's hypothalamus, just above it.

The hypothalamus

This small but important structure, colored red in this MRI brain scan photograph, helps keep the body's internal environment in a steady state by regulating thirst, hunger, and body temperature. Its activity also influences experiences of pleasureful reward.

The Limbic System

PREVIEW QUESTION 2 What are the functions of limbic system structures?

At the border ("limbus") of the brain's older parts and the cerebral hemispheres is a doughnut-shaped neural system, the **limbic system (FIGURE 4.6)**. One limbic system component, the *hippocampus,* is essential for memory processing. If animals or humans lose their hippocampus to surgery or injury, they become unable to lay down new memories of facts and episodes. The limbic system also has important links to emotions such as fear and anger, and to basic motives such as those for food and sex. The limbic system's influence on emotions and motives occurs partly through its control of the body's hormones.

The Amygdala

In the limbic system, two almond-shaped neural clusters, called the **amygdala,** influence aggression and fear. In 1939, psychologist Heinrich Klüver and neurosurgeon Paul Bucy surgically lesioned the part of a rhesus monkey's brain that included the amygdala. The result? The normally ill-tempered monkey turned into the most mellow of creatures. Poke it, pinch it, do virtually anything that normally would trigger a ferocious response, and still the animal remained placid. In later studies with other wild animals, including the lynx, wolverine, and wild rat, researchers noted the same effect. What then might happen if we electrically stimulated the amygdala in a normally placid domestic animal such as a cat? Do so in one spot and the cat prepares to attack, hissing with its back arched, its pupils dilated, its hair on end. Move the electrode only slightly within the amygdala, cage the cat with a small mouse, and now the cat cowers in terror.

These experiments affirm the amygdala's role in rage and fear, not to mention the perception of such emotions in others (Adolphs & others, 1994). Still, we must be careful not to think of the amygdala as *the* control center for aggression and fear. The brain is *not* neatly organized into structures that correspond to our categories of behavior. Actually, aggressive and fearful behavior both involve neural activity in all levels of the brain. Even within the limbic system, stimulating neural structures other than the amygdala can evoke such behavior. If you put a charge to your car's dead battery, you can activate your car's engine. That does not mean that the battery runs the car by itself. It is merely one link in an integrated system.

The Hypothalamus

Another of the limbic system's fascinating structures lies just below *(hypo)* the thalamus, and so is called the **hypothalamus.** Neuroscientists, by lesioning or stimulating different areas in the hypothalamus, have isolated within it neural networks that perform specific maintenance duties for the body. Some neural clusters influence hunger; still others regulate thirst, body temperature, and sexual behavior.

The hypothalamus both monitors blood chemistry and takes orders from other parts of the brain. For example, thinking about sex (in your brain's cerebral cortex) can stimulate your hypothalamus to secrete hormones. Through these hormones, the hypothalamus controls the adjacent "master gland," the pituitary (Figure 4.6), which in turn influences hormones release by other glands, which the hypothalamus monitors. (Note the interplay between the nervous and hormone systems: The brain influences the hormone system, which in turn influences the brain.) The powerful little hypothalamus also exerts control by triggering nervous system activity.

The story of a remarkable discovery about the hypothalamus illustrates how progress in scientific research often occurs—when curious, open-minded investigators make an unexpected observation. Two young McGill University neuropsychologists, James Olds and Peter Milner (1954), were trying to implant electrodes in the reticular formations of white rats when they made a magnificent mistake. In one rat, they incorrectly placed an electrode in what was later discovered to be a region of the hypothalamus (Olds, 1975). Curiously, the rat kept returning to the place on its tabletop enclosure where it had been stimulated by this misplaced electrode, as if seeking more stimulation. Upon discovering their mistake, they alertly recognized that they had stumbled upon a brain center that provides a pleasurable reward.

In a meticulous series of experiments, Olds (1958) went on to locate other "pleasure centers," as he called them. (What the rats actually experience only they know. And they aren't telling. Today's scientists do not want to attribute human feelings to rats, so they refer to reward centers, not "pleasure centers.") When Olds allowed rats to trigger their own stimulation in these areas by pressing a pedal, he noticed that they would sometimes do so at a feverish pace—up to 7000 times per hour—until they dropped from exhaustion. Moreover, they would do anything to get this stimulation, even cross an electrified floor that a starving rat would not cross even to reach food (FIGURE 4.7).

Similar reward centers in or near the hypothalamus were later discovered in many other species, including goldfish, dolphins, and monkeys. In fact, animal research has revealed both a general reward system that triggers the release of the neurotransmitter dopamine and specific centers associated with the pleasures of eating, drinking, and sex. Animals, it seems, come equipped with built-in systems that reward activities essential to survival.

These were dramatic findings. They led people to wonder whether humans, too, might have limbic centers for pleasure. Indeed we do. One neurosurgeon has used electrodes to calm violent patients. Stimulated patients reported mild pleasure; however, unlike rats, they were not driven to a frenzy by it (Deutsch, 1972; Hooper & Teresi, 1986). Some researchers believe that addictive disorders, such as alcoholism, drug abuse, and food binging, may stem from a *reward deficiency syndrome*—a genetically disposed deficiency in the natural brain systems for pleasure and well-being that leads people to crave whatever provides that missing pleasure or relieves negative feelings (Blum & others, 1996).

FIGURE 4.7
Rat with an implanted electrode
With an electrode implanted in a reward center of its hypothalamus, the rat readily crosses an electrified grid, accepting the painful shocks, to press a lever that sends electrical impulses to its "pleasure centers."

"If you were designing a robot vehicle to walk into the future and survive, . . . you'd wire it up so that behavior that ensured the survival of the self or the species—like sex and eating—would be naturally reinforcing."

Candace Pert (1986)

■ **limbic system** a doughnut-shaped system of neural structures at the border of the brainstem and cerebral hemispheres; associated with emotions such as fear and aggression and drives such as those for food and sex. Includes the hippocampus, amygdala, and hypothalamus.

■ **amygdala [ah-MIG-dah-la]** two almond-shaped neural clusters that are components of the limbic system and are linked to emotion.

■ **hypothalamus [hi-po-THAL-uh-muss]** a neural structure lying below (*hypo*) the thalamus; it directs several maintenance activities (eating, drinking, body temperature), helps govern the endocrine system via the pituitary gland, and is linked to emotion.

rehearse it!

5. The limbic system, a doughnut-shaped structure at the border of the brain's older parts and the cerebral hemispheres, is associated with basic motives, emotions, and memory functions. Two parts of the limbic system are the amygdala and the
   a. reticular formation.
   b. hippocampus.
   c. thalamus.
   d. medulla.

6. A ferocious response to electrical brain stimulation would lead you to suppose that the electrode had been touching the
   a. medulla.   c. hippocampus.
   b. pituitary.   d. amygdala.

7. The neural structure that most directly regulates eating, drinking, and body temperature is the
   a. cerebellum.

   b. hypothalamus.
   c. thalamus.
   d. amygdala.

8. The reward centers discovered by Olds and Milner were located in regions of the
   a. cerebral cortex.
   b. brainstem.
   c. hypothalamus.
   d. spinal cord.

The Cerebral Cortex

The **cerebral cortex** is an intricate covering of interconnected neural cells that, like bark on a tree, forms a thin surface layer on the cerebral hemispheres. It is our body's ultimate control and information-processing center.

With the elaboration of the cerebral cortex, tight genetic controls relax and the organism's adaptability increases. Frogs and other amphibians have a small cortex and operate extensively on preprogrammed genetic instructions; the larger cortex of mammals offers increased capacities for learning and thinking, enabling them to be more adaptable.

Structure of the Cortex

PREVIEW QUESTION 3 How is the cerebral cortex organized?

If you opened a human skull, exposing the brain, you would see a wrinkled organ, shaped somewhat like the meat of an oversized walnut. Without these wrinkles, a flattened cortex would require triple the area—roughly that of a very large pizza—to fit inside the skull. (To fit a thin pizza crust inside a skull, we would need to crumple it up.)

Eighty percent of the brain's weight lies in the ballooning left and right cerebral hemispheres, which are mostly filled with neural connections between the brain's surface and its other regions. The thin surface layer of the cerebral hemispheres is the cerebral cortex, a sheet of cells that is one-eighth of an inch thick and contains some 30 billion nerve cells and 300 trillion neural connections. Being human takes a lot of nerve. Supporting these billions of nerve cells are nine times as many **glial cells**—"glue cells" that guide neural connections, provide nutrients and an insulating covering (called the myelin sheath) for the nerve cells, and mop up ions and neurotransmitters (the chemicals that transmit messages between nerve cells). Some researchers believe that glial cells are more than neural nannies. By "chatting" with neurons they may also participate in information transmission and memory (Travis, 1994).

Each brain hemisphere is divided into four regions, or *lobes*. Starting at the front of your brain and going around over the top, there are the **frontal lobes** (behind your forehead), the **parietal lobes** (at the top and to the rear), the **occipital lobes** (at the back of your head), and the **temporal lobes** (just above your ears). These lobes are convenient geographic subdivisions separated by prominent folds **(FIGURE 4.8)**. Each lobe carries out many functions. Some functions require the interplay of several lobes.

Functions of the Cortex

PREVIEW QUESTION 4 What are the functions of the cerebral cortex?

More than a century ago, autopsies of people partially paralyzed or speechless revealed specific cortex areas that had been damaged. But this rather crude evidence did not convince researchers that specific parts of the cortex perform specific functions. After all, if control of speech and movement were diffused across the cortex, damage

The people who first dissected and labeled the brain used the language of scholars—Latin and Greek. Their words are actually attempts at graphic description: For example, *cortex* means "bark," *cerebellum* is "little brain," and *thalamus* is "inner chamber."

FIGURE 4.8
The basic subdivisions of the cortex

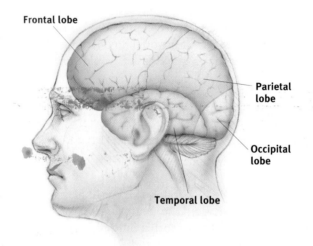

Frontal lobe
Parietal lobe
Occipital lobe
Temporal lobe

■ **cerebral [seh-REE-bruhl] cortex** the intricate fabric of interconnected neural cells that covers the cerebral hemispheres; the body's ultimate control and information-processing center.

■ **glial cells** cells in the nervous system that are not neurons but that support, nourish, and protect neurons.

■ **frontal lobes** the portion of the cerebral cortex lying just behind the forehead; involved in speaking and muscle movements and in making plans and judgments.

■ **parietal [puh-RYE-uh-tuhl] lobes** the portion of the cerebral cortex lying at the top of the head and toward the rear; includes the sensory cortex.

■ **occipital [ahk-SIP-uh-tuhl] lobes** the portion of the cerebral cortex lying at the back of the head; includes the visual areas, each of which receives visual information from the opposite visual field.

■ **temporal lobes** the portion of the cerebral cortex lying roughly above the ears; includes the auditory areas, each of which receives auditory information primarily from the opposite ear.

■ **motor cortex** an area at the rear of the frontal lobes that controls voluntary movements.

to almost any area might produce the same effect. A television would go dead with its power cord cut, but we would be deluding ourselves if we were to think we had "localized" the source of the picture in the cord.

This analogy reminds us how easy it is to err when trying to localize brain functions. We cannot draw lines around brain areas as in a meat market's beef chart; complex activities such as speaking, drawing, and shooting pool involve many brain areas. For example, our experience of listening to vocal music integrates brain activity in areas involved in speech and music processing. Mereille Besson and colleagues (1998) discovered this when recording electrical activity in the brains of French musicians listening to operatic solos sung a cappella (unaccompanied). The musicians' brains processed the lyrics and tunes in separate brain areas en route to their experiencing "the exquisite unity of vocal music."

Singing in the brain
Activities as seemingly simple as listening to a song or watching an orchestra play that song each involve multiple brain areas, including independent processing of the lyrics and the tune, as well as separate processing of the sight of the musicians.

Motor Functions

Scientists have, however, localized simpler brain functions. For example, in 1870, when German physicians Gustav Fritsch and Eduard Hitzig applied mild electrical stimulation to the cortexes of dogs, they made an important discovery: They could make different body parts move. The effects were selective: Stimulation caused movement only when applied to an arch-shaped region at the back of the frontal lobe, running roughly from ear to ear across the top of the brain. This arch we now call the **motor cortex (FIGURE 4.9).** Moreover, when the researchers stimulated specific parts of this region in the left or right hemisphere, specific body parts moved on the *opposite* side of the body.

FIGURE 4.9

Left-hemisphere tissue devoted to each body part in the motor cortex and the sensory cortex

As you can see, the amount of cortex devoted to a body part is not proportional to that part's size. Rather, the brain devotes more tissue to sensitive areas and to areas requiring precise control. Thus, the fingers have a greater representation in the cortex than does the upper arm. However, the neural wiring is complex. Individual muscles are linked with multiple neural clusters, which in turn may also link with other muscles.

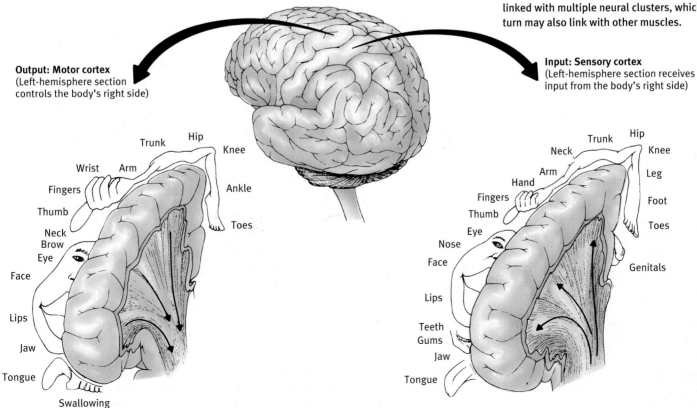

Output: Motor cortex
(Left-hemisphere section controls the body's right side)

Input: Sensory cortex
(Left-hemisphere section receives input from the body's right side)

■ **sensory cortex** the area at the front of the parietal lobes that registers and processes body sensations.

■ **association areas** areas of the cerebral cortex that are not involved in primary motor or sensory functions; rather, they are involved in higher mental functions such as learning, remembering, thinking, and speaking.

A half-century ago, neurosurgeons Otfrid Foerster in Germany and Wilder Penfield in Montreal mapped the motor cortex in hundreds of wide-awake patients. Before putting the knife to the brain, the surgeons needed to know the possible side effects of removing different parts of the cortex. They painlessly (the brain has no sensory receptors) stimulated different cortical areas and noted the body responses. Like Fritsch and Hitzig, they found that when they stimulated different areas of the motor cortex at the back of the frontal lobe, different body parts moved. They were now able to map the motor cortex according to the body parts it controlled (Figure 4.9). Interestingly, those areas of the body requiring precise control, such as the fingers and mouth, occupied the greatest amount of cortical space.

Neuroscientist José Delgado demonstrated the mechanics of motor behavior. In one monkey, he evoked a smiling response over 400,000 times. In a human patient, he stimulated a spot on the left motor cortex that triggered the right hand to make a fist. Asked to keep the fingers open during the next stimulation, the patient, whose fingers closed despite his best efforts, remarked, "I guess, Doctor, that your electricity is stronger than my will" (Delgado, 1969, p. 114). More recently, scientists have been able to predict a monkey's arm motion a tenth of a second before it moves—by repeatedly measuring motor cortex activity preceding specific arm movements (Gibbs, 1996).

As interesting as the early brain stimulation studies were, more recent research has revealed that the precise muscle-to-brain connections are not so simple as the early work suggested. In one recent study, researchers examined these connections using functional MRI scans to observe where the brain lights up when specific muscles are moved (Sanes & others, 1995). They found that a given finger or wrist movement, for example, would activate multiple and overlapping sites. Although it's true that certain areas of the cortex control certain areas of the body and that some areas require more brain tissue than others, the wiring pattern is complex—complex enough to enable the many different muscle combinations needed to produce specific gestures.

Sensory Functions

If the motor cortex sends messages out to the body, where are *incoming* messages received in the cortex? Penfield identified a cortical area that specializes in receiving information from the skin senses and from the movement of body parts. This area, parallel to the motor cortex and just behind it at the front of the parietal lobes, we now call the **sensory cortex** (Figure 4.9). Stimulate a point on the top of this band of tissue, and a person may report being touched on the shoulder; stimulate some point on the side, and the person may feel something on the face.

The more sensitive a body region, the greater the area of the sensory cortex devoted to it; your supersensitive lips project to a larger brain area than do your toes (Figure 4.9). (That's one reason we kiss with our lips rather than our toes.) Similarly, rats have a large area of the brain devoted to their whisker sensations, owls to their hearing sensations, and so forth. If a monkey or a human loses a finger, the region of the sensory cortex devoted to receiving input from that finger branches to receive sensory input from the adjacent fingers. They then become more sensitive (Fox, 1984). MRI scans show that well-practiced pianists likewise have a larger-than-usual auditory cortex area that encodes piano sounds (Pantev & others, 1998). The brain is sculpted not only by our genes but also by our experience.

Scientists explored further and identified areas where the cortex receives input from the other senses. At this moment you are receiving visual information in the occipital lobes at the very back of your brain **(FIGURE 4.10).** A bad enough bash there and you would go blind. Stimulated there, you might see flashes of light or dashes of color. In a sense, we *do* have eyes in the back of our head! From your occipital lobes, the visual information you are now processing goes to other areas that specialize in tasks such as identifying words, detecting emotions, and recognizing faces.

FIGURE 4.10

New technology shows the brain in action
This functional MRI scan shows the visual cortex—the occipital lobes—activated (color representation of increased bloodflow) as the subject looks at faces. When the person stops looking at faces, the region instantly calms down.

Any sound you are now hearing you processed with the auditory areas in your temporal lobes **(FIGURE 4.11).** Most of this auditory information travels a circuitous route from one ear to the auditory receiving area above your opposite ear. If you were stimulated there, you might hear a sound. The sound needn't be real. MRI scans of people with schizophrenia reveal that auditory areas of the temporal lobe are active during auditory hallucinations (Lennox & others, 1999). Even the phantom ringing sound experienced by people with hearing loss is—if heard in one ear—associated with activity in the temporal lobe on the brain's opposite side (Muhlnickel & others, 1998).

FIGURE 4.11
The visual cortex and auditory cortex
The occipital lobes at the rear of the brain receive input from the eyes. An auditory area of the temporal lobes receives information from the ears.

Visual cortex

Auditory cortex

Association Functions

So far, we have pointed out small areas of the cortex that either receive sensory information or direct muscular responses. In humans, that leaves a full three-fourths of the thin wrinkled layer, the cerebral cortex, uncommitted to sensory or muscular activity. What then goes on in this vast region of the brain? Neurons in these **association areas** (the light pink areas in **FIGURE 4.12)** integrate information. They associate various sensory inputs with stored memories—a very important part of thinking.

Electrically probing the association areas doesn't trigger any observable response. So, unlike the functions of the sensory and motor areas, those of the association areas are not so easily mapped. Their silence seems to be what someone had in mind when formulating one of pop psychology's most widespread falsehoods: that we ordinarily use only 10 percent of our brains. This fabrication—"one of the hardiest weeds in the garden of psychology," writes Donald McBurney (1996, p. 44)—implies that if we could activate our whole brain, we would be far smarter than those who drudge along on 10 percent brain power. But from observing surgically lesioned animals and brain-damaged humans, we know that the association areas are in fact not dormant. (The brain has no appendix—no apparently purposeless tissue.) Rather, the association areas interpret, integrate, and act on information processed by the sensory areas.

Our association areas in the frontal lobes enable us to judge, plan, and process new memories. People with damaged frontal lobes may have intact memories, score high on intelligence tests, and be able to bake a cake—yet be unable to plan ahead to *begin* baking the cake for the birthday party. After the sister of famed neurosurgeon Wilder Penfield suffered frontal lobe damage, she was unable to prepare the simplest of meals. She retained her knowledge of recipes, measurements,

The "10 percent myth"—which many people presume true because they have so often heard it—presumes that brain functions are neatly localized. But don't bother to hope that a bullet about to enter your brain would harmlessly damage only the unused 90 percent (Radford, 1999).

FIGURE 4.12
Areas of the cortex in four mammals
More intelligent animals have increased "uncommitted" or association areas of the cortex. These vast areas of the brain are responsible for integrating and acting on information received and processed by sensory areas. The frontal lobes are 4 percent of the brain surface in a cat, 17 percent in a chimp, and 29 percent in a human.

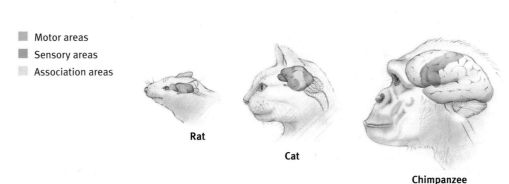

Motor areas
Sensory areas
Association areas

Rat

Cat

Chimpanzee

Human

Phineas Gage reconsidered
Using measurements of his skull (which was kept as a medical record) and modern neuroimaging techniques, researcher Hanna Damasio and her colleagues (1994) have reconstructed the probable path of the rod through Gage's brain.

■ **aphasia** impairment of language, usually caused by left hemisphere damage either to Broca's area (impairing speaking) or to Wernicke's area (impairing understanding).

■ **Broca's area** an area of the frontal lobe, usually in the left hemisphere, that directs the muscle movements involved in speech.

■ **Wernicke's area** a brain area involved in language comprehension and expression; usually in the left temporal lobe.

and techniques, but she could not decipher the order of steps in preparing the meal (Kimberg & others, 1998).

Frontal lobe damage also can alter personality, removing a person's inhibitions. Consider the classic case of railroad worker Phineas Gage. One afternoon in 1848, Gage, then 25 years old, was packing gunpowder into a rock with a tamping iron. A spark ignited the gunpowder, shooting the rod up through his left cheek and out the top of his skull, leaving his frontal lobes massively damaged. To everyone's amazement, Gage was immediately able to sit up and speak, and after the wound healed he returned to work. Although his mental abilities and memories were intact, his personality was not. The affable, soft-spoken Phineas Gage was now irritable, profane, and dishonest. He eventually lost his job and ended up earning his living as a fairground exhibit. This person, said his friends, was "no longer Gage." With his frontal lobes shish-kebabed, Gage's moral compass became disconnected from his behavior. The same loss of moral compass was recently discovered to be true of two people who as young children had experienced frontal lobe damage similar to Gage's. Both of these individuals recovered, but they also matured as morally deficient—stealing, lying, and abusing and neglecting their out-of-wedlock children without remorse (Dolan, 1999). Although raised in good homes, they seemingly didn't know right from wrong.

The association areas of the other lobes also perform mental functions. For example, the parietal lobes, parts of which were large and unusually shaped in Einstein's normal-weight brain, are involved in mathematical and spatial reasoning (Witelson & others, 1999). An area on the underside of the right temporal lobe enables us to recognize faces. If a stroke or head injury destroyed this area of your brain, you would still be able to describe facial features and to recognize someone's gender and approximate age, yet be strangely unable to identify the person as, say, Nelson Mandela or your next-door neighbor or even your spouse. But by and large, complex mental functions such as learning and memory don't reside in any one place. There is no one spot in a rat's small association cortex that, when damaged, will obliterate its ability to learn or remember a maze. Such functions are spread throughout much of the cortex.

Language

Complex human abilities, such as language, result from the intricate coordination of many brain areas. For example, consider this curious finding: Damage to any one of several cortical areas can cause **aphasia,** an impaired use of language. It is even more curious that some people with aphasia can speak fluently but cannot read (despite good vision), while others can comprehend what they read but cannot speak. Still others can write but not read, read but not write, read numbers but not letters, or sing but not speak. This all is very puzzling. After all, we think of speaking and reading, or writing and reading, or singing and speaking as merely different examples of the same general ability.

Researchers began to sort out how the brain processes language after a discovery by French physician Paul Broca in 1865. Broca discovered that after damage to a specific area of the left frontal lobe, later called **Broca's area,** a person would struggle to form words, yet often would be able to sing familiar songs with ease. A decade later, German investigator Karl Wernicke discovered that after damage to a specific area of the left temporal lobe **(Wernicke's area)** people could speak only meaningless words and were unable to comprehend others' words.

Norman Geschwind assembled these clues into an explanation of how we use language. When you read aloud, the words (1) register in the visual area, (2) are relayed to the angular gyrus that transforms the words into an auditory code that is (3) received and understood in the nearby Wernicke's area and (4) sent to Broca's area, which (5) controls the motor cortex, creating the pronounced word

FIGURE **4.13**
Specialization and integration in language

5. **Motor cortex**
(word is pronounced)

4. **Broca's area**
(controls speech muscles via the motor cortex)

2. **Angular gyrus**
(transforms visual representations into an auditory code)

1. **Visual cortex**
(receives written words as visual stimulation)

3. **Wernicke's area**
(interprets auditory code)

(FIGURES 4.13 and **4.14).** Depending on which link in this chain is damaged, a different form of aphasia occurs. Damage to the angular gyrus leaves the person able to speak and understand but unable to read. Damage to Wernicke's area disrupts understanding. Damage to Broca's area disrupts speaking. The general principle bears repeating: Complex abilities result from the intricate coordination of many brain areas.

Said another way, the brain operates by dividing its mental functions—speaking, perceiving, thinking, remembering—into subfunctions. Our conscious experience *seems* indivisible. Right now you are experiencing a whole visual scene as if your eyes were video cameras projecting the scene into your brain. Actually, researchers have discovered that your brain breaks vision into specialized subtasks, such as discerning color, depth, movement, and form. (After a localized stroke that destroys one of these neural work teams, people may lose just one aspect of vision, such as the ability to perceive movement.) These specialized neural networks, each having simultaneously done its own thing, then feed their information to "higher-level" networks that combine the atoms of experience and relay them to progressively higher-level association areas, enabling us to recognize a face as "Grandmother." The same is true of reading a word: The brain computes the word's form, sound, and meaning using different neural networks (Posner & Carr,

(a)
Hearing

(b)
Seeing

(c)
Speaking

FIGURE **4.14**
Brain activity when hearing, seeing, and speaking words
PET scans such as these detect the activity of different areas of the brain. The red blotches show where the brain is rapidly consuming the brain's normal fuel, glucose.

1992). Think about it: *What you experience as a continuous, indivisible stream of perception is actually but the visible tip of the information-processing iceberg, most of which lies beneath the surface of your conscious awareness.*

To sum up, the mind's subsystems are localized in particular brain regions, yet the brain acts as a unified whole. Moving your hand; recognizing faces; even perceiving color, motion, and depth all depend on specific neural networks. Yet complex functions such as language, learning, and loving involve the coordination of many brain areas. Both principles—specialization and integration—appear in research on the two brain hemispheres.

Brain Reorganization

PREVIEW QUESTION 5 Is the brain capable of reorganizing itself if damaged?

Nurture's sculpting of the ever-changing brain is evident in studies of the brain's **plasticity.** Most severed neurons will not regenerate (if your spinal cord were severed, you likely would be permanently paralyzed). But neural tissue can *reorganize in response to damage.*

In one experiment, neuroscientists severed the neural pathways for incoming information from a monkey's arm. The area of the sensory cortex that formerly received this input gradually shifted its function and began to respond when researchers touched the animal's face (Pons & others, 1991). Similarly, if a laser beam damages a spot in a cat's eye, the brain area that received input from that spot will soon begin responding to stimulation from nearby areas in the cat's eye. If a blind person uses one finger to read Braille, the brain area dedicated to that finger expands (Barinaga, 1992a). The sense of touch invades the part of the brain that normally helps people see. PET scans also reveal activation of the *visual* cortex when blind people read Braille (Sadato & others, 1996). Among deaf people who communicate with sign language, it is the temporal lobe area normally dedicated to auditory information that waits in vain for stimulation. Finally, it looks for other signals to process, such as those from the visual system.

Thus, the brain may not be as "hard-wired" as once thought. Unlike fixed computer circuits, brain hardware changes with time. In response to changing stimulation, the brain can either rewire itself with new synapses or (according to another theory) select new uses for its prewired circuits (Gazzaniga, 1992; Kolb & Whishaw, 1998). When one brain area is damaged, other areas may in time reorganize and take over some of its functions. If neurons are destroyed, nearby neurons may partly compensate for the damage by making new connections that replace the lost ones. These new connections are one way the brain struggles to recover from a minor stroke.

New evidence reveals that, contrary to long-held belief, adult humans can also generate new brain cells (Kempermann & Gage, 1999). Moreover, monkey brains have recently been discovered to form thousands of new neurons each day. These baby neurons originate deep in the brain and then migrate to the thinking frontal lobe and form connections with neighboring neurons (Gould & others, 1999). Such are the brain's ways of partially compensating for the gradual loss of neurons with age. Master "stem cells" that can develop into any type of brain cell have also been discovered in the fetal brain. These discoveries raise hopes that these recovery mecha-

Brain plasticity
Believe it or not, this 4-year-old is functioning with only half a brain. Her right hemisphere was surgically removed to eliminate seizures. Now neurons in her left hemisphere have made countless new connections to take over the tasks once performed by her right hemisphere.

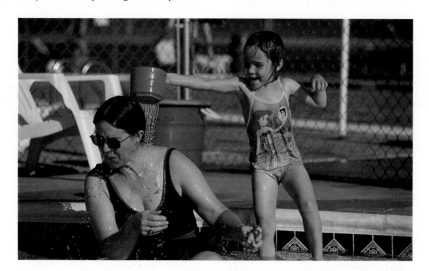

■ **plasticity** the brain's capacity for modification, as evident in brain reorganization following damage (especially in children) and in experiments on the effects of experience on brain development.

nisms might be enhanced to mend a disease-damaged brain. For example, if extracted, mass produced, and injected into a damaged brain, might stem cells turn themselves into replacements for damaged or dead brain cells?

Our brains are most plastic when we are young children (Kolb, 1989). Children are born with a surplus of neurons. If an injury destroys one part of a child's brain, the brain will compensate by putting other surplus areas to work. Thus, if the speech areas of an infant's left hemisphere are damaged, the right hemisphere will take over much of its language function.

As an extreme example of plasticity, consider a 5-year-old boy whose severe seizures, caused by a deteriorating left hemisphere, require removing the *entire* hemisphere. What hope for the future would such a child have? Is there any chance he might attend school and lead a normal life, or would he suffer permanent retardation?

Astonishingly, one such individual was at last report an executive. Half his skull is filled with nothing but cerebrospinal fluid—functionally it might as well be sawdust—yet he has scored well above average on intelligence tests, has completed college, and has attended graduate school (A. Smith, 1987; Smith & Sugar, 1975). Although paralyzed on the right side, this man (along with other such cases of "hemispherectomy") testifies to the brain's extraordinary powers of reorganization when damaged before it is fully developed. Indeed, one Johns Hopkins medical team, reflecting on the 58 child hemispherectomies they have performed, reports being "awed" by how well children retain their memory, personality, and humor after removal of either brain hemisphere (Vining & others, 1997).

rehearse it!

9. The motor cortex is the brain region that controls voluntary muscle movement. If a neurosurgeon stimulated your right motor cortex, you would most likely
   a. see light.
   b. hear a sound.
   c. feel a touch on the right arm.
   d. move your left leg.

10. The sensory cortex registers and processes body sensations, with the more sensitive body regions having the greatest representation. Which of the following has the greatest representation?
    a. Knee   c. Fingers
    b. Toes   d. Thumb

11. About three-fourths of the cerebral cortex is not committed to any specific sensory or muscular function. The "uncommitted" areas are called
    a. occipital lobes.
    b. fissures.
    c. association areas.
    d. Wernicke's area.

12. Judging and planning are enabled by the
    a. occipital lobes.
    b. parietal lobes.
    c. frontal lobes.
    d. temporal lobes.

13. The area in the brain that, if damaged, might impair your ability to form words is
    a. Wernicke's area.
    b. Broca's area.
    c. the left occipital lobe.
    d. the angular gyrus.

14. Plasticity refers to the brain's ability to reorganize itself after damage. Especially plastic are the brains of
    a. stroke patients.
    b. young adults.
    c. young children.
    d. deaf people.

Our Divided Brains

For more than a century, clinical evidence has shown that the brain's two sides serve differing functions. Accidents, strokes, and tumors in the left hemisphere generally impair reading, writing, speaking, arithmetic reasoning, and understanding. Similar lesions in the right hemisphere seldom have such dramatic effects.

It is small wonder that by 1960 the left hemisphere was well accepted as the "dominant" or "major" hemisphere, and its silent companion to the right as the "subordinate" or "minor" hemisphere. The verbal left hemisphere is rather like the moon's facing side—the one easiest to observe and study. But then researchers found that the "minor" right hemisphere was not so limited after all. The story of this discovery is a fascinating chapter in psychology's history.

■ **corpus callosum [KOR-pus kah-LOW-sum]** the large band of neural fibers connecting the two brain hemispheres and carrying messages between them.

■ **split brain** a condition in which the two hemispheres of the brain are isolated by cutting the connecting fibers (mainly those of the corpus callosum) between them.

In about one-fourth of left-handers, the right hemisphere controls speech.

Corpus callosum

FIGURE 4.15

The corpus callosum

This large band of neural fibers connects the two brain hemispheres. To photograph the half brain shown at top, the hemispheres were separated by cutting through the corpus callosum and lower brain regions. In the lower view, a surgeon has cut back brain tissue to expose the corpus callosum and bundles of fibers coming out from it.

Splitting the Brain

PREVIEW QUESTION 6 What is a split brain, and what does it reveal about brain functioning?

In 1961, two Los Angeles neurosurgeons, Philip Vogel and Joseph Bogen, speculated that major epileptic seizures were caused by an amplification of abnormal brain activity that reverberated between the two hemispheres. They therefore wondered whether they could reduce seizures in their patients with uncontrollable epilepsy by cutting communication between the hemispheres. To do this, Vogel and Bogen knew they would have to sever the **corpus callosum,** the wide band of axon fibers connecting the two hemispheres **(FIGURE 4.15).**

The surgeons had reason to believe such an operation would not be incapacitating. Psychologists Roger Sperry, Ronald Myers, and Michael Gazzaniga had divided the brains of cats and monkeys in this manner with no serious ill effects. So Vogel and Bogen operated. The result? The seizures were all but eliminated and the patients with these **split brains** were surprisingly normal, their personalities and intellect hardly affected. Waking from the surgery, one patient even managed to quip that he had a "splitting headache" (Gazzaniga, 1967).

Only a decade earlier, neuropsychologist Karl Lashley had jested that maybe the corpus callosum served only "to keep the hemispheres from sagging." The ingenious experiments of Sperry and Gazzaniga revealed that this broad band of more than 200 million nerve fibers, capable of transferring more than a billion bits of information per second between the hemispheres, has a more significant purpose. Their work provided a key to understanding the two hemispheres' complementary functions.

Sperry and Gazzaniga were not surprised that, after the split-brain operation, a patient could not identify an unseen object, such as a spoon, placed in his left hand. They knew that information travels from the left hand to the right hemisphere, and their animal split-brain experiments suggested that the right hemisphere would be unable to send this information to the left hemisphere (which in most humans controls speech). More extraordinary results came when Sperry and Gazzaniga conducted some perceptual tests.

Our eyes connect to our brains in such a way that, when we look straight ahead, the left half of our field of vision transmits through both eyes to our right hemisphere **(FIGURE 4.16).** Likewise, the right side of our field of vision transmits to our left hemisphere. In most of us with healthy, intact brains, information presented only to our right hemisphere is quickly sent to our left hemisphere, which names it. But what happens in a person whose corpus callosum has been severed? To find out, experimenters ask the person to look at a designated spot. Then they send information to either the left or right hemisphere (by flashing it to the spot's right or left). Finally, they quiz each hemisphere separately.

See if you can guess the results of an experiment using this procedure (Gazzaniga, 1967). While the patients stared at a dot, the word HEART was flashed across the visual field with HE in the left visual field and ART in the right. First, what did the patients *say* they saw? Second, asked to identify with their *left* hands what they had seen, did they *point* to HE or ART?

As **FIGURE 4.17** shows, the patients *said* they saw ART and so were startled when their left hands *pointed* to HE. Given an opportunity to express itself, each hemisphere reports only what it has seen.

Similarly, when a picture of a spoon was flashed to their right hemisphere, the patients could not say what they saw. But when asked to identify what they had seen by feeling with their left hands an assortment of objects hidden behind a screen, they readily selected the spoon. If the experimenter said, "Right!" the patient might reply,

"What? Right? How could I possibly pick out the right object when I don't know what I saw?" It is, of course, the left hemisphere doing the talking here, bewildered by what its nonverbal right hemisphere knows.

A few people who have had split-brain surgery have been for a time bothered by the unruly independence of their left hand, which might unbutton a shirt while the right hand buttoned it or put grocery store items back on the shelf after the right hand put them in the cart. It was as if each hemisphere was thinking "I've half a mind to wear my green (blue) shirt today." Indeed, said Sperry (1964), split-brain surgery leaves people "with two separate minds." (Reading these reports, I fantasize a split-brain person enjoying a solitary game of "rocks, paper, and scissors"—left versus right hand.)

When the "two minds" are at odds, the left hemisphere seems to act as the brain's press agent, doing mental gymnastics to rationalize reactions it does not understand. If a patient follows an order sent to the right hemisphere ("Walk"), the interpretive left hemisphere will offer a ready explanation ("I'm going into the house to get a Coke"). Thus, Michael Gazzaniga (1988) concludes that the left hemisphere is an "interpreter" that instantly constructs theories to explain our behavior.

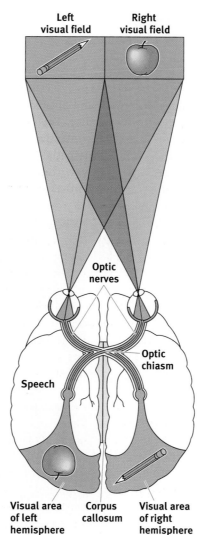

FIGURE 4.16

The information highway from eye to brain

Information from the left half of your field of vision goes to your right hemisphere, and information from the right half of your visual field goes to your left hemisphere, which in most people controls speech. (Note, however, that each eye receives sensory information from both the right and left visual fields.) The data received by either hemisphere are quickly transmitted to the other across the corpus callosum. In a person with a severed corpus callosum, this information sharing does not take place.

"Do not let your left hand know what your right hand is doing."

Matthew 6:3

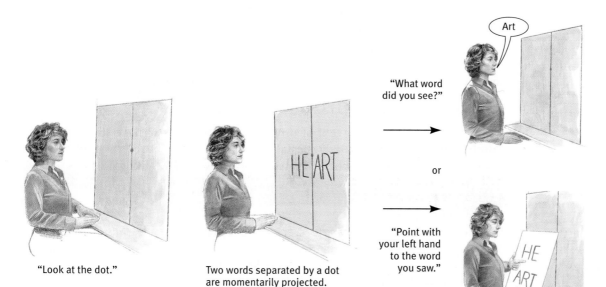

FIGURE 4.17

Testing the divided brain

When an experimenter flashes the word HEART across the visual field, the split-brain patient reports seeing the portion of the word transmitted to her left hemisphere. However, if asked to indicate with her left hand what she saw, she points to the portion of the word transmitted to her right hemisphere. (From Gazzaniga, 1983.)

LEFT BRAIN/RIGHT BRAIN

"Error flies from mouth to mouth, from pen to pen, and to destroy it takes ages."

—Voltaire, 1694–1778

You've heard or read it many times: Some people are "left-brained," others "right-brained." Leaping from the research on split and intact brains, educators, management advisers, and self-help writers urge us to harness the undeveloped half of our brain. Do you want to develop your creativity, music appreciation, or emotional empathy? Well, get your brain in balance. Awaken your dormant right hemisphere. Advocate "whole brain" education in your schools. Unleash intuitive, right-brained management from the chains of cold logic and statistics. Try *Drawing on the Right Side of the Brain* (the title of a million-copy bestseller translated into 10 languages).

What should we make of all this? By calling my friend Elsie "right-brained" have I explained why she's such a zany free spirit? And why her "left-brained" husband Bill is so coolly analytical? We've seen that research does show that each hemisphere serves special functions. The left is more logical, verbal, and able to deal with things in sequence. The right is more emotionally intuitive and expressive, skilled at spatial relations, and able to deal with things all at once. But neuroscientists raise a caution flag: Beware the fad of locating complex human abilities such as science or art in either hemisphere. "The left-right dichotomy in cognitive mode is an idea with which it is very easy to run wild," warned Sperry (1982). Actually, such complex activities as doing science or creating art require the integration of both hemispheres. Even when reading a story,

Left brain/right brain Is the artist a "right-brained" person? Such notions distort scientific findings regarding the cerebral hemispheres. While some areas of each hemisphere specialize in different tasks, the brain's two sides cooperate to enable the person in whatever he or she does.

Studying Hemispheric Differences in the Intact Brain

Question: If we flashed a red light to the right hemisphere of a split-brain patient and flashed a green light to the left hemisphere, would each observe its own color? Would the person be aware that the colors differ? What would the person verbally report seeing? (Answers on page 66.)

What about the 99.99+ percent of us with undivided brains? Have scientists found our hemispheres to be similarly specialized? Yes they have, in several different types of studies. For example, when a person performs a *perceptual* task, brain waves, bloodflow, and glucose consumption reveal increased activity in the *right* hemisphere; when a person speaks or calculates, activity increases in the *left* hemisphere.

On occasion, hemispheric specialization has been even more dramatically shown by briefly sedating an entire hemisphere. To check for the locus of language before surgery, a physician may inject a sedative into the neck artery that feeds blood to the hemisphere on its side of the body. Before the drug is injected, the patient is lying down, arms in the air, conversing easily. You can likely predict what happens we use both hemispheres—the left processing the words and finding meaning, the right appreciating humor, imagery, and emotional content (Hellige, 1993; Levy, 1985).

Why, then, do the popularizations of brain research so greatly exaggerate the findings? In *The Left-Hander Syndrome,* University of British Columbia psychologist Stanley Coren (1993) illustrates how journalism often oversimplifies and embellishes science. He recalls hearing a convention talk by Doreen Kimura, a psychologist at the University of Western Ontario in London, Ontario. Kimura reported that melodies fed to the left ear were more easily recognized than melodies fed to the right ear. Knowing that the left ear sends most of its information to the right hemisphere, she concluded that, among her right-handed student volunteers, the right brain was better at recognizing melodies.

A few days later, the *New York Times* reported that "Doreen Kimura, a psychologist from London, Ontario, has found that *musical ability* is controlled by the right side of the brain" (italics highlight the embellishment). Apparently drawing from the *Times* story, a syndicated newspaper story then reported that "London psychologist, Dr. Doreen Kimura, claims that musicians are right-brained!" (But Kimura studied university students, not musicians.) Later, a follow-up newspaper article further distorted the study: "An English psychologist has finally explained why there are so many great left-handed musicians."

Knowing that Kimura is not English, did not study musicians, and did not study left-handers, Coren recalled the words of an American editor: "Everything you read in the newspaper is absolutely true, except for the rare story of which you happen to have first-hand knowledge."

What can happen is this: As information flows from scientist to reader, it gets simplified as well as embellished, much as gossip does in passing from one person to the next. A TV network picks up an interesting finding, then reduces it to a 30-second report with an 11-second sound bite from the researcher. This alerts a major newspaper to a story angle, which in turn gets picked up by popular science magazines and, eventually, by supermarket magazines and tabloids.

At each step, notes Coren, "Ideas become more speculative and more distant from the actual research. . . . After a while, the neuropsychologist is no longer even visible in the communication chain." The rumors grow, accumulate, and evolve into scientific misinformation that becomes "'accepted truths,' which show up in conversation and writing in sentences that begin with, 'As everybody knows . . . ,' or 'Scientists have shown that. . . .'" In the end, sighs Coren, the public myth drowns out the voices of dissenting scientists.

The moral is not to discount everything you read, but to beware. Reporters want their stories to be newsworthy. When at their best, their ideal (and mine, in writing this book) is to extract the essence— to simplify without becoming simplistic. When at their worst, they distort a pretzel-shaped finding into a breadstick-shaped story: Some people are left-brained, others right-brained. . . .

when the drug flows into the artery going to the left hemisphere: Within seconds, the person's right arm falls limp and, if the left hemisphere controls language, the subject becomes speechless until the drug wears off. When the drug goes into the artery to the right hemisphere, the *left* arm falls limp, but the person can still speak.

Other tests also confirm hemispheric specialization. For example, most people recognize a picture faster and more accurately when it is flashed to the right hemisphere. But they recognize a word faster and more accurately when it is flashed to the left hemisphere. If a word is flashed to your right hemisphere, perception takes a fraction of a second longer—the length of time it takes to send the information through the corpus callosum to the more verbal left hemisphere.

Which hemisphere would you suppose enables sign language among deaf people? The right, because of its visual-spatial superiority? Or the left, because of its preparedness to process language? Studies reveal that, just as hearing people use the left hemisphere to process speech, deaf people use the left hemisphere to read signs

About 90 percent of the human population is right-handed. The remaining 10 percent (somewhat more among males, somewhat less among females) is left-handed. Tests reveal that about 95 percent of right-handers process speech primarily in the left hemisphere (Springer & Deutsch, 1985). Left-handers are more diverse. More than half process speech in the left hemisphere, as right-handers do. About one-quarter process language in the right hemisphere; the other quarter use both hemispheres more or less equally.

Answers to questions on page 64: Yes. No. Green.

(Corina & others, 1992). A stroke in the left hemisphere will disrupt a deaf person's signing much as it would disrupt a hearing person's speaking. Broca's area is similarly involved in both spoken and signed speech production (Corina, 1998). To the brain, language is language, whether spoken or signed.

Although the left hemisphere is adept at making quick, literal interpretations of language, the right hemisphere excels in making subtle inferences (Beeman & Chiarello, 1998; Beeman & others, 1994; Bowden & Beeman, 1998). If "primed" with the flashed word *foot*, the left hemisphere will be especially quick to then recognize the closely associated word *heel*. But if primed with *foot, cry,* and *glass,* the right hemisphere will more quickly recognize another word that is distantly related to all three (*cut*). And if given an insightlike problem—what word goes with *high, district,* and *house?*—the right hemisphere has better access to the solution. (The right hemisphere more quickly than the left recognizes that the solution is *school.*) As one patient explained after suffering right hemisphere stroke damage, "I understand words, but I'm missing the subtleties." Thus, the right hemisphere helps us modulate our speech to make meaning clear—as when we ask "What's that in the road ahead?" instead of "What's that in the road, a head?" (Heller, 1990).

From simply looking at the two hemispheres, which appear alike to the naked eye, who would suppose that they contribute so uniquely to the harmony of the whole? Yet a variety of observations—of people with split brains and people with normal brains—converge beautifully, leaving little doubt that we have unified brains with specialized parts.

We have glimpsed again the truth of our overriding principle: Everything psychological is simultaneously biological. This module has focused on how our thoughts, feelings, and actions arise from our specialized yet integrated brain. Throughout this book we will further explore the significance of the biological revolution in psychology.

Our knowledge of the brain and the mind has come a long way. Yet what is unknown still dwarfs what is known. We can describe the brain. We can learn the functions of its parts. We can study how the parts communicate. But how does the electrochemical whir in a hunk of tissue the size of a head of lettuce give rise to elation, a creative idea, or that memory of Grandmother?

The mind boggles both at what is known and what is not. Interviews with leading brain scientists reveal their own awe and wonder. Others ponder philosophical mysteries: How does the material brain give rise to consciousness? To what extent can a thing understand itself? The mind seeking to understand the brain—that is indeed among the ultimate scientific challenges.

> "If the human brain were so simple that we could understand it, we would be so simple that we couldn't."
>
> Emerson M. Pugh, quoted by George E. Pugh, *The Biological Origin of Human Values*, 1977

rehearse it!

15. The brain structure that enables the right and left hemispheres to communicate is
    a. the medulla.
    b. Broca's area.
    c. Wernicke's area.
    d. the corpus callosum.

16. An experimenter flashes the word HERON across the visual field of a split-brain patient. HER is transmitted to his right hemisphere and ON to his left hemisphere. When asked to indicate what he saw, the patient
    a. *says* he saw HER but *points* to ON.
    b. *says* he saw ON but *points* to HER.
    c. *says* he saw HERON but *points* to HER.
    d. *says* he saw HERON but *points* to ON.

17. The study of split-brain patients has allowed us to observe the special functions of each hemisphere of the brain. The left hemisphere excels in
    a. processing language.
    b. visual perceptions.
    c. recognition of emotion.
    d. recognition of faces.

18. Damage to the brain's right hemisphere is most likely to reduce a person's ability to
    a. recite the alphabet rapidly.
    b. recognize the emotional content of facial expressions.
    c. understand verbal instructions.
    d. solve arithmetic problems.

REVIEWING

The Brain

1. What are the functions of the brainstem and its associated structures?

Within the brainstem, the medulla controls heartbeat and breathing, and the reticular formation controls arousal and attention. The cerebellum, which is attached to the rear of the brainstem, coordinates muscle movement. On top of the brainstem is the thalamus, the brain's sensory switchboard. Methods of studying the brain include lesioning, electroencephalograms, and CT, PET, and MRI scans.

2. What are the functions of limbic system structures?

The limbic system has been linked primarily to memory, emotions, and drives. For example, one of its neural centers, the amygdala, is involved in aggressive and fearful responses. Another, the hypothalamus, has been linked to various bodily maintenance functions and to pleasurable rewards. The hypothalamus also controls the endocrine system.

3. How is the cerebral cortex organized?

The cerebral cortex is a thin, wrinkled sheet of neurons with trillions of interconnections. Glial cells support, nourish, and protect the neurons. The cortex covering each hemisphere can be viewed as having four geographical areas: the frontal, parietal, occipital, and temporal lobes, which are separated by prominent folds.

4. What are the functions of the cerebral cortex?

Small, well-defined regions within the cerebral lobes control muscle movement (the motor cortex) and receive information from the body senses (the sensory cortex). However, most of the cortex— its association areas—is uncommitted to such functions and is therefore free to process other information.

Some brain regions are known to serve specific functions. In general, however, human emotions, thoughts, and behaviors result from the intricate coordination of many brain areas. Language, for example, depends on a chain of events in several brain regions, particularly Broca's area and Wernicke's area. Damage to an area of the brain involved in language may cause one of several types of aphasia.

5. Is the brain capable of reorganizing itself if damaged?

If one hemisphere is damaged early in life (in the first five years), the other will pick up many of its functions, thus demonstrating the brain's plasticity. Unfortunately, the brain is less plastic later in life. However, nearby neurons can often at least partially compensate for damaged ones, as when a patient recovers from a minor stroke.

6. What is a split brain, and what does it reveal about brain functioning?

A split brain is one whose corpus callosum, the large band of nerve fibers connecting the two brain hemispheres, has been severed. Experiments on split-brain patients have refined our knowledge of each hemisphere's special functions. By testing the two hemispheres separately, researchers have confirmed that for most people the left hemisphere is the more verbal and that the right hemisphere excels in visual perception and the recognition of emotion. Studies of normal people with intact brains confirm that each hemisphere makes unique contributions to the integrated functioning of the brain.

TERMS AND CONCEPTS TO REMEMBER

lesion [LEE-zhuhn], p. 48
electroencephalogram (EEG), p. 48
CT (computed tomography) scan, p. 48
PET (positron emission tomography) scan, p. 48
MRI (magnetic resonance imaging), p. 49
brainstem, p. 50
medulla [muh-DUL-uh], p. 50

reticular formation, p. 50
neuron, p. 50
thalamus [THAL-uh-muss], p. 50
cerebellum [sehr-uh-BELL-um], p. 51
limbic system, p. 52
amygdala [ah-MIG-dah-la], p. 52
hypothalamus [hi-po-THAL-uh-muss], p. 52

cerebral [seh-REE-bruhl] cortex, p. 54
glial cells, p. 54
frontal lobes, p. 54
parietal [puh-RYE-uh-tuhl] lobes, p. 54
occipital [ahk-SIP-uh-tuhl] lobes, p. 54
temporal lobes, p. 54
motor cortex, p. 55

sensory cortex, p. 56
association areas, p. 57
aphasia, p. 58
Broca's area, p. 58
Wernicke's area, p. 58
plasticity, p. 60
corpus callosum [KOR-pus kah-LOW-sum], p. 62
split brain, p. 62

REHEARSE IT ANSWER KEY

1. b	3. d	5. b	7. b	9. d	11. c	13. b	15. d	17. a
2. c	4. a	6. d	8. c	10. d	12. c	14. c	16. b	18. b

5 The Nature and Nurture of Behavior

What makes you you? To answer, we must first understand how you come to be so much like everyone else. Whatever our differences, we are the leaves of one tree. Our human family shares not only a common biological heritage—cut us and we bleed—but also common behavioral tendencies. Our shared brain architecture predisposes us to sense the world, develop language, and feel hunger through identical mechanisms.

Our kinship appears in our social behaviors as well. Whether we live in the Arctic or the tropics, we prefer sweet tastes to sour, we divide the color spectrum into similar colors, and we feel drawn to behaviors that produce and protect offspring. Regardless of our culture or our gender, we regard female features that signify youth and health—and reproductive potential—as attractive. Whether our last name is Wong, Nkomo, Smith, or Gonzales, at about eight months we become wary of strangers, and as adults we prefer the company of those whose attitudes and attributes are similar to our own. Coming from different parts of the globe, we know how to read one another's smiles and frowns. As members of one species, we affiliate, conform, reciprocate favors, punish offenses, organize hierarchies of status, and mourn a child's death. A visitor from outer space could drop in anywhere and find humans dancing and feasting, singing and worshiping, playing sports and games, laughing and crying, living in families, and forming groups. Taken together, such universal behaviors reveal our human nature.

Telling the story of you also requires explaining your individuality. Why are you more or less intelligent? Happy? Aggressive? Why is one person gay or lesbian while another is straight? Why is one person unable to keep pounds off while another can't put them on? Also, what's the source of our *group* differences in whether we think plump is beautiful or unattractive, whether we hide or readily express anger, whether we tend to do our own thing or honor others' expectations?

Psychology's answer to these questions begins with a backward look at how our species developed the body-mind system—a system that enabled our distant ancestors to solve problems they faced while navigating their physical worlds, hunting, gathering food, encountering others, and reproducing. The story continues as we move forward to look at the genetic inheritance that designs each unique new body-mind system. Psychologists are exploring how—and how much—our individual heredity predisposes our differing personalities, preferences, and abilities. To what extent are we shaped by our heredity (our *nature*) and by our life history (including the *nurture* we have received since our conception)? Does our individual genetic makeup explain why one person is outgoing, another shy? Why one person is slow-witted and another quick? Or do we travel different developmental roads depending on our life experiences and our current environment?

The conclusions—that *nature* is crucially important, and that *nurture* is crucially important—are central to today's psychology. Genes—and the rest of our bodies—matter. Culture—and everything we experience from womb to tomb—matters. Consider, then, how nature and nurture together shape us.

The nurture of nature
Parents everywhere wonder: Will my baby grow up to be peaceful or aggressive? Homely or attractive? Successful or struggling at every step? What are children born with, and what is nurtured—and how?

Genes: Our Biological Blueprint

PREVIEW QUESTION 1 Our genes provide the blueprint for our biology; does this mean they determine our behaviors?

Behind the story of our body and our brain—surely the most awesome thing on our little planet—are the blueprints that design both our universal human attributes and our individual traits. Every cell nucleus in your body contains the genetic master code for the entire body. It's as if every room in the Tower of London had a bookcase containing the architect's plans for the entire building. These plans run to 46 books—23 donated by your mother (from her egg) and 23 by your father (from his sperm). These books, called **chromosomes,** are each composed of a coiled chain of the molecule **DNA (deoxyribonucleic acid).** Small segments of the giant DNA molecules, called **genes,** form the words of these chromosome books **(FIGURE 5.1).** All told, each of us has some 30,000 of these gene words. Each gene is a self-replicating unit capable of synthesizing proteins—the building blocks of our physical development.

Our genes are in turn defined by a four-letter alphabet of life, composed of biochemical letters called *nucleotides.* The smallest human chromosome (Y) has 50 million nucleotide "letters"; the largest has 250 million. Collectively, some 3 billion paired nucleotides define the genes that determine your individual biological development. To get a sense of the vast library of information contained in each of your cells, consider this: At 2000 nucleotide "letters" to a page, the 46 chromosome "books" containing your complete genetic code would need to run more than 30,000 pages each.

The sequence of the four nucleotide letters—A, T, C, and G—is virtually the same in all humans; genetically speaking, every human being is close to being your identical twin. The Human **Genome** Project has discovered the common sequence of nearly all the 3 billion letters within human DNA. It is this shared genetic profile that makes us humans, rather than dogs or tulips.

Geneticists and psychologists are also interested in the occasional variations found at particular gene sites in the DNA—variations that in their many combinations define each person's uniqueness. The differences are few. About 98.4 percent of our letter sequences match those of chimpanzees, and 99.9 percent match those of all other humans (Plomin & Crabbe, 2000). You and anyone else are near clones. But vive la différence! Our 1.6 percent difference from chimps has enabled space travel and the *Encyclopaedia Britannica.* And the 0.1 percent person-to-person variation from the common pattern gives clues to why one person has a disease that another does not, why one person is short and another tall, why one is happy and another depressed.

■ **chromosomes** threadlike structures made of DNA molecules that contain the genes.

■ **DNA (deoxyribonucleic acid)** a complex molecule containing the genetic information that makes up the chromosomes. (A DNA molecule has two strands—forming a "double helix"—held together by bonds between pairs of nucleotides.)

■ **genes** the biochemical units of heredity that make up the chromosomes; a segment of DNA capable of synthesizing a protein.

■ **genome** the complete instructions for making an organism, consisting of all the genetic material in its chromosomes. The human genome has 3 billion weakly bonded pairs of nucleotides organized as coiled chains of DNA.

"Thanks for almost everything, Dad."

Nucleus
(the inner area of a cell that houses chromosomes and genes)

Chromosome
(threadlike structure made largely of DNA molecules)

Gene
(segment of DNA containing the code for a particular protein; determines our individual biological development)

Cell
(the basic structural unit of a living thing)

DNA
(a spiraling, complex molecule containing genes)

FIGURE 5.1

The genes: Their location and composition

Contained in the nucleus of each of the trillions of cells in your body are chromosomes. Each chromosome contains a coiled chain of the molecule DNA. Genes are DNA segments that form templates for the production of proteins. By directing the manufacture of proteins, the genes determine our individual biological development.

Freed with DNA evidence
Donald Reynolds is all smiles in his attorney's office in 1997 after 11 years of false imprisonment on a rape charge. DNA evidence proved it was someone else who committed the crime.

Most human traits are influenced by many genes acting in concert. How tall you are, for example, reflects the height of your face, the size of your vertebrae, the length of your leg bones, and so forth—each of which may be influenced by different genes. Ditto for complex human traits such as intelligence, happiness, and aggressiveness. Still, researchers have discovered that variations in a single gene are part of the recipe for certain forms of Alzheimer's disease, for alcoholism, for schizophrenia, for reading disabilities, and the list grows.

Our genetic predispositions help explain both our shared human nature and our individual differences. Evolutionary psychology sheds light on what's universal, and behavior genetics illuminates our differences.

Evolutionary Psychology: Explaining Universal Behaviors

PREVIEW QUESTION 2 How do evolutionary psychologists use natural selection to explain behavior tendencies?

A fox is a wild and wary animal. If you capture a fox and try to befriend it, be careful. Stick your hand in the cage and, if the timid fox can't flee, it probably will make a snack of your fingers. Working at the Russian Academy of Science's Institute of Cytology and Genetics, Dmitry Belyaev was wondering how our human ancestors had domesticated dogs from their wolf forebears. Might he, within a comparatively short stretch of time, accomplish a similar feat by evolving the fearful fox into a friendly fox?

To find out, Belyaev set to work with 30 male and 100 female foxes. From their offspring he selected and mated the tamest 5 percent of males and 20 percent of females, measuring tameness by the foxes' responses to attempts to feed, handle, and stroke them. Over more than 30 generations, Belyaev and his successor, Lyudmila Trut, repeated that simple procedure. Today, 40 years and 45,000 foxes later, they have a new breed of foxes that, in Trut's (1999) words, are "docile, eager to please and unmistakably domesticated. . . . Before our eyes, 'the Beast' has turned into 'beauty,' as the aggressive behavior of our herd's wild [ancestors] entirely disappeared." So friendly and eager for human contact are they, so inclined to whimper to attract attention and to lick people like affectionate cats, that the cash-strapped institute has seized on a way to raise funds—by marketing its foxes to people as house pets.

As Belyaev and Trut demonstrated, when certain traits are *selected*—by conferring a reproductive advantage upon them—those traits, over time, come to prevail. Dog breeders, as Robert Plomin and his colleagues (1997) remind us, have given us sheepdogs that herd, retrievers that retrieve, trackers that track, and pointers that point. They also have given us placid clumber spaniels and aggressive pit bulls. Psychologists, too, have bred dogs, mice, and rats whose genes predispose them to be serene or reactive, quick learners or slow learners.

From beast to beauty
Forty years into the fox-breeding experiment, most of the offspring are devoted, affectionate, and capable of forming strong bonds with people.

Natural Selection

In natural environments, a mutant shark with keener than normal smell would find more prey, enabling it to live longer and leave more offspring. As nature continued over countless generations to give an edge to sharks best suited to their ecological niche, an exquisitely effective predator came into being.

Does **natural selection** also explain our shared human traits? Extended over many thousands of years and feeding off new gene combinations and **mutations**—random errors in gene replication—has natural selection favored advantageous variations? Do we tend to fear snakes and heights because our ancestors who feared them were more likely to survive and spread their genes?

Everyone agrees that the tight genetic leash that predisposes an ant's nest building, a dog's retrieving, or a cat's pouncing is looser on humans. Our genes provide more than a long leash; they endow us with a capacity to learn and therefore to adapt to life on the tundra or in the jungle. Yet in the big picture our lives are remarkably alike. Visit the international arrivals area at London's Heathrow Airport, a world hub where arriving passengers meet their excited loved ones. There you will see the same delighted joy in the faces of Kenyan grandmothers, Chinese children, and Canadian tourists. Although human differences grab our attention, our deep similarities also demand explanation.

These behavioral similarities arise from our biological similarity. Of our few genetic differences, only 6 percent are differences among races. Only 8 percent are differences among groups within a race. The rest—over 85 percent—are individual variations within local groups. The typical genetic difference between two Icelandic villagers or between two Kenyans is much greater than the *average* difference between the two groups. Thus, notes geneticist Richard Lewontin (1982), if after a worldwide catastrophe only Icelanders or Kenyans survived, the human species would suffer only "a trivial reduction" in its genetic diversity.

Why are we all so much alike? At the dawn of human history, our ancestors all faced certain questions: Who is my ally, who my foe? What food should I eat? With whom should I mate? Some individuals answered those questions more successfully than others. Those disposed to eat nourishing rather than poisonous food survived to contribute their genes to later generations. Similarly successful were those who mated with someone with whom they could produce and nurture offspring. Over generations, the genes of individuals not so disposed tended to be lost from the human gene pool. As further mutations occurred, genes providing an adaptive edge continued to be selected. This process, say **evolutionary psychologists,** led not only to muscles and bone structures but also behavioral tendencies and ways of thinking that prepared our Stone Age ancestors to survive, reproduce, and send their genes into the future. Nature selected the fittest adaptations.

As inheritors of this prehistoric genetic legacy, we love the taste of sweets and fats, which once were hard to come by but which prepared our ancestors to survive famines. Ironically, with famine rare in Western cultures, and sweets and fats beckoning us from store shelves, fast-food outlets, and vending machines, obesity has become a growing problem. We are, in some ways, biologically prepared for a world that no longer exists.

Evolution has been an organizing principle for biology for a long time. But only recently, in "the second Darwinian revolution," have psychologists attempted to harness evolutionary principles. Charles Darwin (1859) anticipated this application of evolutionary principles to psychology. In concluding *The Origin of Species*, he foresaw "open fields for far more important researches. Psychology will be based on a new foundation" (p. 346).

Psychologists, as we will see, are now using evolutionary principles to explore questions such as these:

- Why do infants become wary of strangers about the time they become mobile?
- Why do we so naturally divide people into categories—male and female, blacks and whites, geeks and studs?
- Why are most parents so passionately devoted to their children?
- Why do so many more people have phobias about spiders and snakes than about more dangerous guns and electricity?
- Why do we display greater empathy and helpfulness toward those who look, think, and act as we do?
- How and why do men and women differ? For example, why are men quicker than women to perceive friendliness as sexual interest, to initiate sexual relations, and to feel jealous rage over a mate's having sex with someone else?

To see how evolutionary psychologists think and reason, let's pause to explore this last question.

■ **natural selection** the principle that, among the range of inherited trait variations, those contributing to reproduction and survival will most likely be passed on to succeeding generations.

■ **mutation** a random error in gene replication that leads to a change in the sequence of *nucleotides*; the source of all genetic diversity.

■ **evolutionary psychology** the study of the evolution of behavior and the mind, using principles of natural selection. Natural selection is presumed to have favored genes that predisposed behavior tendencies and information-processing systems that solved adaptive problems faced by our ancestors, thus contributing to the survival and spread of their genes.

Those who are troubled by an apparent conflict between scientific and religious accounts of human origins may find it helpful to recall that different perspectives of life can be complementary. For example, the scientific account attempts to tell us *when* and *how;* religious creation stories usually aim to tell about an ultimate *who* and *why.* As Galileo explained to the Grand Duchess Christina, "The Bible teaches how to go to heaven, not how the heavens go."

■ **gender** in psychology, the characteristics, whether biologically or socially influenced, by which people define male and female.

Sexuality

"With few exceptions anywhere in the world," report cross-cultural psychologist Marshall Segall and his colleagues (1990, p. 244), "males are more likely than females to initiate sexual activity." Across 177 studies of some 130,000 people, men are much more accepting of casual sex, and they report masturbating much more often (Oliver & Hyde, 1993. This is among the largest of **gender** differences. There are others:

■ In a Canadian survey, 80 percent of 2350 customers of adults-only video stores were males (although half claimed to engage a partner in watching the movies [Jenish, 1993].) And if you have guessed that most hard-core pornography readers are male and most romance novel readers are female, you are right (Malamuth, 1996).

■ In a 1999 survey of 261,000 entering American college students, 53 percent of men but only 30 percent of women agreed that "if two people really like each other, it's all right for them to have sex even if they've known each other for a very short time" (Sax & others, 1999).

■ In a careful survey of 3432 U.S. 18- to 59-year-olds, 48 percent of the women but only 25 percent of the men cited affection as a reason for first intercourse. And how often do they think about sex? "Every day" or "several times a day," acknowledged 19 percent of the women and 54 percent of the men (Laumann & others, 1994).

■ Such gender differences characterize both heterosexual and homosexual people. Gay men report more interest in uncommitted sex, more responsiveness to visual sexual stimuli, and more concern with their partner's physical attractiveness than lesbians do (Bailey & others, 1994). (Aware of HIV risks, gay men were, however, having fewer partners in 1998 than in 1985 [Altman, 1999].)

■ Men also have a lower threshold for perceiving warm responses as a sexual come-on. In study after study, men more often than women attribute a woman's friendliness to sexual interest (Abbey, 1987; Johnson & others, 1991). Misattributing women's cordiality as a come-on helps explain men's greater sexual assertiveness (Kenrick & Trost, 1987). The unfortunate results can range from sexual harassment to date rape (Kanekar & Nazareth, 1988; Muehlenhard, 1988; Shotland, 1989).

"It's not that gay men are oversexed; they are simply men whose male desires bounce off other male desires rather than off female desires."

Steven Pinker, *How the Mind Works*, 1997

An Evolutionary Explanation

Evolutionary psychologists have a ready explanation for women's more relational and men's more recreational approaches to sex. It goes like this: Compared with eggs, sperm are cheap. Moreover, while a woman incubates and nurses one infant, a male can spread his genes by impregnating other females. (Aided by artificial insemination, one renowned Canadian bull sired more than 200,000 offspring before dying in 1998.) Our natural yearnings, argue evolutionary psychologists, are our genes' way of reproducing themselves. In our ancestral history, women most often sent their genes into the future by pairing wisely, men by pairing widely. "Humans are living fossils—collections of mechanisms produced by prior selection pressures," says evolutionary psychologist David Buss (1995).

And what do men and women find attractive in the other sex? Some aspects of attractiveness cross place and time. Men in 37 cultures, from Australia to Zambia, judge women as more attractive if they have a youthful appearance **(FIGURE 5.2)**. Evolutionary psychologists say that men drawn to healthy, fertile-appearing women—women whose smooth skin and youthful shape suggest many childbearing years to come—have stood a better chance of sending their genes into the future. From yesterday's Stone Age figurines to today's *Playboy* centerfolds and beauty pageant winners—and regardless of cultural variations in ideal weight—men feel most attracted to women whose waists are roughly a third narrower than their hips, a sign of youthful fertility (Singh, 1993).

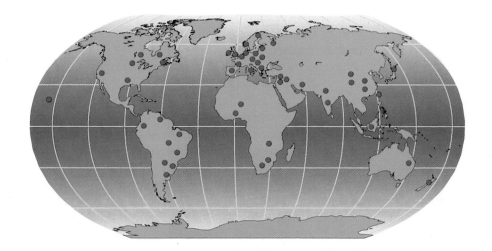

FIGURE 5.2
Worldwide mating preferences
David Buss and an international team of collaborators surveyed the mating preferences of 10,047 people in 37 countries depicted by the dots (from Buss, 1994b). Men everywhere preferred attractive physical features suggesting youth and health—and reproductive potential. Women everywhere preferred men with resources and social status. This gender difference, evolutionary psychologists believe, is the result of natural selection favoring those whose choices help perpetuate their genes.

Women also feel attracted to healthy-looking men, but especially to those who seem mature, dominant, and affluent (Singh, 1995). Such attributes, say the evolutionary psychologists, connote a capacity to support and protect (Buss, 1996; Geary, 1998). Presidential adviser Henry Kissinger had the same idea: "Power is the world's greatest aphrodisiac."

Evolutionary psychologists also note that each sex tends to advertise the qualities that maximize its odds of attracting desirable partners: women by spending time and money on appearance, men by trying to establish their status and dominance. In singles ads, for example, women tend to offer looks and seek status; men do the reverse (Rajecki & others, 1991). Why do even successful men lust after ever more money and power? Some evolutionary psychologists reason that such attributes are to men what antlers are to a stag or tail feathers to a male peacock. Men needn't consciously think, "I'm trying to outdo my male rivals in the competition for female attention." They're just hard-wired to want to outdo their rivals, because those who did so in the past put more of their genes into our human gene pool.

Women also prefer mates with the potential for long-term mating and investment in their joint offspring (Gangestad & Simpson, 2000). They prefer potential dads over likely cads. Thus, for men there are genetic tradeoffs between seeking to distribute one's genes widely and being willing to co-parent.

There is a principle at work here, say evolutionary psychologists: Nature selects behavioral tendencies that increase the likelihood of sending one's genes into the future. As mobile gene machines, we are predisposed to prefer whatever worked for our ancestors. They were predisposed to act in ways that would leave grandchildren—had they not been, we wouldn't be here. As carriers of their genetic legacy, so are we.

Critiquing the Evolutionary Explanation

Without disputing nature's selection of traits that enhance gene survival, critics see problems with evolutionary psychology. It often, they say, starts with an effect (such as the gender sexuality difference) and works backward to propose an explanation. If men were uniformly loyal to their mates, might we not reason that the children of committed, supportive fathers more often survived to perpetuate their genes? Might not men also be better off bonded to one woman—both to increase the otherwise slim odds of impregnation and to keep her from the advances of competing men? Might not a ritualized bond—a marriage—also spare women from chronic male harassment? (Such suggestions are, in fact, evolutionary explanations for why humans tend to pair off monogamously.) And what about those species, such as chimpanzees and bonobos, in which ardent females mate with numerous males? Is it so that the males, not knowing the true paternity of a female's offspring, will join in tolerating or protecting them? One can hardly lose at hindsight

"I contend that nature has given males the heaviest burden of all: the burden of always having to Make the First Move, and thereby risk getting Shot Down. I don't know WHY males get stuck with this burden, but it's true throughout the animal kingdom. . . . It's always the male bird who does the courting dance, making a total moron of himself, while the female bird just stands there, looking aloof, thinking about what she's going to tell her girlfriends. ('And then he hopped around on one foot! Like I'm supposed to be impressed by THAT!')."

Dave Barry, *Miami Herald*, 1999

"I had a nice time, Steve. Would you like to come in, settle down, and raise a family?"

explanation, which is, says paleontologist Stephen Jay Gould (1997), mere "speculation [and] guesswork in the cocktail party mode."

Moreover, says anthropologist Meredith Small (1999), evolutionary speculation about sex and gender "reinforces male-female stereotypes." Natalie Angier (1999) sees evolutionary psychology "glaring through an overwhelmingly masculinized lens. . . . Hard-core evolutionary psychology types go to extremes to argue in favor of the yawning chasm that separates the innate desires of women and men." But if women's sex drive is so much less wandering than men's, ask feminist researchers, then why must men go to such lengths to control women's sexuality? Why are women across the world beaten for promiscuity and adultery?

Critics also remind us that much of who we are is not hard-wired. Cultural expectations also bend the genders. For example, what's attractive varies somewhat with time and place. The voluptuous Marilyn Monroe ideal of the 1950s has been replaced by the turn-of-the-century leaner, athletic female image. Moreover, if socialized to value lifelong commitment, men may sexually bond with one partner; if socialized to accept casual sex, women may willingly have sex with many partners. Women's sexual variability is especially striking, notes Roy Baumeister (2000). Across time, across cultures, across situations, and across differing levels of education, religiosity, and peer influence, adult women's sexual drive and interests are more flexible and varying than adult men's—a phenomenon Baumeister calls the gender difference in "erotic plasticity." Women, more than men, for example, prefer to alternate periods of high sexual activity with periods of almost none.

Some gender differences in mate preferences indeed seem universal across cultures. But again, critics question whether such gender differences may to some extent be by-products of a culture's social and family structures. Show Alice Eagly and Wendy Wood (1999) a culture with gender inequality—where men are providers and women are homemakers—and they will show you a culture where men strongly desire youth and domestic skill in their potential mates, and women seek status and earning potential in their mates. Show Eagly and Wood a culture with gender equality, and they will show you a culture with smaller gender differences in mate preferences. They draw their conclusions from an analysis of the same 37 cultures studied earlier by David Buss.

Evolutionary psychologists respond to such criticisms by acknowledging our great human capacity for learning. (We come equipped to adapt and survive, whether living in igloos or tree houses.) They also point to the coherence of evolutionary principles and their ability to unify science. And they offer testable predictions (for example, that we will favor others to the extent they share our genes or can later reciprocate our favors). Some have even gleaned predictions for business. For example, given that early human communities apparently banded together in groups no larger than about 150, organizations today may function best if organized into family-size groups within work units no bigger than 150 (Nicholson, 1998).

rehearse it!

1. If nucleotides are the "letters," and genes are the "words," _____ is/are the "books" that hold all this information.
   a. DNA
   b. nuclei
   c. chromosomes
   d. cells

2. When the egg and sperm unite, each contributes
   a. one chromosome pair.
   b. 23 chromosomes.
   c. 23 chromosome pairs.
   d. an XY chromosome.

3. Evolutionary psychologists focus on
   a. how we differ from one another.
   b. the links between biology and behavior.
   c. natural selection of the fittest adaptations.
   d. random assignment of genes over several generations.

Behavior Genetics: Explaining Individual Differences

PREVIEW QUESTION 3 How do behavior geneticists explain individual differences?

While evolutionary psychologists apply Darwin's big idea in hopes of explaining our universal human tendencies, **behavior geneticists** explore our differences from one another. How much are our differences shaped by our differing genetic blueprints? By our upbringing? By our culture and current circumstances? And by how our **environment**—every external influence, from maternal nutrition while in the womb to social support while nearing the tomb—reacts to our genetic traits?

To disentangle the threads of heredity and environment, behavior geneticists often use two sets of tweezers: twin studies and adoption studies.

Twin Studies

To tease apart environment and heredity, it would be nice if we could control the home environment while varying heredity. Happily for our purposes, nature has given us ready-made subjects for this experiment: identical versus fraternal twins. **Identical twins,** who develop from a single fertilized egg that splits in two, are *genetically* identical **(FIGURE 5.3).** They are—millions and millions of them—nature's own human clones. (The possibility of laboratory human cloning raises new ethical issues but few new psychological issues.)

Fraternal twins, who develop from separate eggs, are genetically no more similar than ordinary brothers and sisters. A person whose identical twin has Alzheimer's disease has a 60 percent risk of sharing the disease; if the affected twin is fraternal, the risk is only 30 percent (Plomin & others, 1997). Such a difference suggests a genetic influence.

Behavior geneticists ask: Are identical twins, being genetic clones of one another, behaviorally more similar than fraternal twins? Studies of nearly 13,000 pairs of Swedish twins, of 7000 Finnish twin pairs, and of 3810 Australian twin pairs provide a consistent answer: On both extraversion (outgoingness) and neuroticism (emotional instability), identical twins are much more similar than fraternal twins. In explaining individual differences, genes matter.

Other dimensions of personality and ability also reflect genetic influences. When John Loehlin and Robert Nichols (1976) gave a battery of questionnaires to 850 U.S. twin pairs, identical twins were much more similar than fraternals in many ways—in abilities, personality traits, even interests. However, the identical twins, more than fraternal twins, also reported being treated alike. So, did their experience rather than their genes account for their similarity? No, said Loehlin and Nichols. Identical twins whose parents treated them alike were *not* psychologically more alike than identical twins who were treated less similarly.

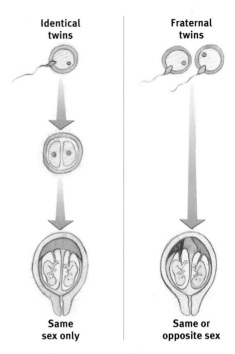

Identical twins   **Fraternal twins**

Same sex only   **Same or opposite sex**

FIGURE 5.3

Same egg, same genes; different eggs, different genes

Identical twins develop from a single fertilized egg, fraternal twins from two.

Twins Lorraine and Levinia Christmas, driving to deliver presents to each other near Flitcham, England, collided (Shepherd, 1997).

Benita Epstein

"The worst thing about being a clone is having no one to blame but myself."

■ **behavior genetics** the study of the relative power and limits of genetic and environmental influences on behavior.

■ **environment** every nongenetic influence, from prenatal nutrition to the people and things around us.

■ **identical twins** twins who develop from a single fertilized egg that splits in two, creating two genetically identical organisms.

■ **fraternal twins** twins who develop from separate eggs. They are genetically no closer than brothers and sisters, but they share a fetal environment.

Affable by nature?
Identical twins Gerald Levey and Mark Newman were separated at birth and raised in different homes. When reunited at age 31, they discovered that they both volunteered as firefighters. Research has shown remarkable similarities in the life choices of separated identical twins, lending support to the idea that genes influence personality.

"In some domains it looks as though our identical twins reared apart are . . . just as similar as identical twins reared together. Now that's an amazing finding and I can assure you none of us would have expected that degree of similarity."

Thomas Bouchard (1981)

Separated Twins

Imagine the following science fiction experiment: A mad scientist decides to separate identical twins at birth, then rear them in differing environments. Better yet, consider a true story:

On a chilly Ohio Saturday morning in February 1979, some time after divorcing his first wife, Linda, Jim Lewis awoke in his modest, middle-class home next to his second wife, Betty. Jim—a romantic, affectionate type—was determined that this marriage would work and made a habit of leaving love notes to Betty around the house. As Jim lay in bed he thought about others he had loved, including his son, James Alan, and his faithful dog, Toy.

Having outfitted a workshop in a corner of his basement, Jim looked forward to spending some of the day's free time on his woodworking hobby. He had derived many hours of satisfaction from building furniture, picture frames, and an assortment of other items, including a circular white bench around a tree in his front yard. Jim also liked to spend free time driving his Chevy, watching stock-car racing, and drinking Miller Lite beer.

Jim was basically healthy. Having undergone a vasectomy, he was done having children. His blood pressure was a little high, perhaps related to his chain-smoking habit. He chewed his fingernails to the nub. And he suffered occasional half-day migraine headaches— "like somebody's hitting you with a two-by-four in the back of the neck." He had become overweight a while back but had shed some of the pounds.

What was most extraordinary about Jim Lewis, however, was that at that same moment (I am not making this up) there existed another man—also named Jim—for whom all these things (right down to the dog's name) were also true.[1] This other Jim—Jim Springer—just happened, 38 years earlier, to have been his womb mate. Thirty-seven days after their birth, these two genetically identical twins were separated, adopted by blue-collar families, and reared with no contact or knowledge of the other's whereabouts until one February day when Jim Lewis' phone rang. The caller was his genetic clone (who, having been told he had a twin, set about to find him).

One month after that fateful encounter, the brothers became the first twin pair tested by University of Minnesota psychologist Thomas Bouchard and his colleagues, thus beginning a study of separated twins that extends to the present (Holden, 1980a,b; Wright, 1998). When given tests measuring their intelligence, personality, heart rate, and brain waves, the Jim twins—despite 38 years of separation—were virtually as alike as the same person tested twice. Their voice intonations and inflections were so similar that, hearing a playback of an earlier interview, Jim Springer guessed "That's me." Wrong—it was his brother.

Identical twins Oskar Stohr and Jack Yufe presented equally striking similarities. One was raised by his grandmother in Germany as a Catholic and a Nazi, while the other was raised by his father in the Caribbean as a Jew. Nevertheless, they share traits and habits galore. They like spicy foods and sweet liqueurs, have a habit of falling asleep in front of the television, flush the toilet before using it, store rubber bands on their wrists, and dip buttered toast in their coffee. Stohr is domineering toward women and yells at his wife, as did Yufe before he and his wife separated.

Aided by publicity in magazine and newspaper stories, Bouchard and his colleagues (1990; DiLalla & others, 1996; Segal, 1999) have located and studied more than 70 pairs of identical twins reared apart. They continue to find similarities not only of tastes and physical attributes but also of personality, abilities, attitudes, interests, and even fears.

[1]Actually, this description of the two Jims errs in one respect: Jim Lewis named his son James Alan. Jim Springer named his James Allan.

In Sweden, which has a national registry of 25,000 pairs of adult twins, Nancy Pedersen and her coworkers (1988) identified 99 separated identical twin pairs and more than 200 separated fraternal twin pairs. Compared with equivalent samples of identical twins reared together, the separated identical twins had more dissimilar personalities. Still, separated twins were more alike when genetically identical than when fraternal. Separation shortly after birth (rather than, say, at age 8) didn't amplify their personality differences. And what about twins of parents who misidentify their similar-appearing fraternal siblings as identical twins, or who misperceive their identical twins as fraternal twins? In both cases, their tested similarities have reflected what they really were, not what their parents thought them to be (Kendler, 1983). Parental perceptions hardly mattered.

The startling twin similarity stories do not impress Bouchard's critics. They contend that if any two strangers of the same sex and age were to spend hours comparing their behaviors and life histories, they would probably discover many coincidental similarities (although Bouchard's fraternal twins did not exhibit comparable similarities). Even the more impressive data from the personality assessments are clouded by the reunion of many of the separated twins some years before they were tested.

Moreover, separated twins shared an environment for at least their first nine months. They share an appearance, and the responses it evokes. And adoption agencies tend to place separated twins in similar homes. When environments are similar, the impact of environment looks smaller relative to heredity. Nevertheless, the twin studies illustrate why scientific thinking has shifted toward a greater appreciation of genetic influences. Genes-R-Us.

Coincidences are not unique to twins. Patricia Kern of Colorado was born March 13, 1941, and named Patricia Ann Campbell. Patricia DiBiasi of Oregon also was born March 13, 1941, and named Patricia Ann Campbell. Both had fathers named Robert, worked as bookkeepers, and had children ages 21 and 19. Both studied cosmetology, enjoyed oil painting as a hobby, and married military men, within 11 days of each other. They are not genetically related. (From an AP report, May 2, 1983)

Adoption Studies

Another real-life experiment, adoption, creates two groups of relatives: the adoptees' genetic relatives (biological parents and siblings) and environmental relatives (adoptive parents and siblings). For any given trait we can therefore ask whether adopted children are more like their adoptive parents, who contribute a home environment, or their biological parents, who contributed their genes. While sharing the same home environment, do adopted siblings come to share traits?

The stunning finding from studies of hundreds of adoptive families—toppling many of our cherished notions about parental influence—is that people who grow up together, whether biologically related or not, do not much resemble one another in personality (McGue & Bouchard, 1998; Plomin & others, 1998; Rowe, 1990). Adoptees' traits bear more similarities to their biological parents than to their caregiving adoptive parents.

If parental nurture mattered as much as most people suppose, then shouldn't people's personalities be more alike if they were reared in the same home? Shouldn't it matter whether the parents work or don't, fight or don't, drink or don't? Whether the house is a crowded apartment or a spacious estate? Whether the kitchen is stocked with green veggies or Twinkies, the family room with books or toy guns, the neighborhood school with computers or metal detectors? The finding is stunning enough to bear repeating: So far as personality development is concerned, environmental factors shared by a family's children have virtually no impact on their personalities. Two adopted children reared in the same home are no more likely to share personality traits with one another than with the child down the block.

What we have here is developmental psychology's biggest puzzle: Why are children in the same family so different? (Even nontwin biological brothers and sisters tend to be strikingly different.) Why do the shared genes and the shared family environment (the family's social class, the parents' personalities and marital status, day care versus home care, the neighborhood) have so little discernible effect on children's personalities? Is it because each sibling nevertheless has differing experiences—

Family ties

Studies of adoptive families have provided new clues to hereditary and environmental influences. How similar would you expect adopted children to be to their adoptive parents? To their biological parents?

■ **temperament** a person's characteristic emotional reactivity and intensity.

"The same fire that tempers steel melts butter."

The greater uniformity of adoptive homes—mostly healthy, nurturing homes—helps explain the lack of striking differences when comparing child outcomes of different adoptive homes (Stoolmiller, 1999).

Temperamental!

differing peer influences and life events (Dunn & Plomin, 1990; Hetherington & others, 1993)? Is it because siblings—despite sharing half their genes—have very different combinations of genes (Lykken & others, 1992)? Does parental influence therefore affect an easygoing child one way, an emotionally reactive child another? "Child-rearing is not something a parent does to a child," notes Judith Rich Harris (1998). "It is something the parent and the child do together. . . . I would have been pegged as a permissive parent with my first child, a bossy one with my second."

So, is adoptive parenting a fruitless venture? Adoption studies show that, although the personalities of adopted children do not much resemble those of their adoptive parents, adoption matters (Brodzinsky & Schechter, 1990). Although the genetic leash limits the family environment's influence on personality, parents do influence their children's attitudes, values, manners, faith, and politics. A pair of adopted children or identical twins *will* have more similar religious beliefs if reared in the same home (Kelley & De Graaf, 1997; Rohan & Zanna, 1996). Parenting matters!

Moreover, in adoptive homes, child neglect and abuse and even parental divorce are rare. (Adoptive parents are carefully screened; natural parents are not.) So it is not surprising that, despite a somewhat greater risk of psychological disorder, most adopted children thrive, especially when adopted as infants (Benson & others, 1994; Wierzbicki, 1993). They score higher than their biological parents on intelligence tests. Seven in eight report feeling strongly attached to one or both adoptive parents. They generally become happier and more stable people than they would have been in a stressed or neglectful environment. And as children of self-giving parents, they grow up to be more self-giving and altruistic than average (Sharma & others, 1998). In a Swedish study, infant adoptees grew up with fewer problems than were experienced by children whose biological mothers had initially registered them for adoption but then decided to raise the children themselves (Bohman & Sigvardsson, 1990). To benefit from adoption, children need not have personalities that resemble those of their adoptive parents.

Temperament Studies

As most parents will tell you after having their second child, babies differ even before gulping their first breath. Consider one quickly apparent aspect of personality. An infant's **temperament** includes inborn emotional excitability—whether reactive, intense, and fidgety, or easygoing, quiet, and placid. From the first weeks of life, "difficult" babies are more irritable, intense, and unpredictable. "Easy" babies are cheerful, relaxed, and predictable in feeding and sleeping (Chess & Thomas, 1987).

Temperament endures. Consider these findings:

- The most emotionally reactive newborns tend also to be the most reactive 9-month-olds (Wilson & Matheny, 1986; Worobey & Blajda, 1989).
- Four-month-olds who react to changing scenes with arched back, pumping legs, and crying are usually fearful and inhibited in their second year. Those who react with relaxed smiles are usually fearless and sociable in their second year (Kagan, 1990).
- Exceptionally inhibited and fearful 2-year-olds often are still relatively shy as 8-year-olds; about half will become introverted adolescents (Kagan & others, 1992, 1994).
- The most emotionally intense preschoolers tend to be relatively intense as young adults (Larsen & Diener, 1987). In one study that is following more than 900 New Zealanders through time, emotionally reactive and impulsive 3-year-olds developed into somewhat more impulsive, aggressive, and conflict-prone 21-year-olds (Newman & others, 1997).

Like human infants, infant monkeys vary in temperament. Some are timid and fearful, others more relaxed. Researcher Stephen Suomi (1987) placed infant monkeys that were genetically predisposed to be "uptight" or "easygoing" with foster mothers who were themselves uptight or easygoing. The result? Heredity overrode rearing. Compared with the easygoing monkeys, the uptight monkeys reacted more anxiously to stress, even when they were being raised by easygoing, nurturant foster mothers.

Heredity seems to predispose human temperament differences, too. Physiological tests reveal that anxious, high-strung human infants have high and variable heart rates and a reactive nervous system (Kagan & others, 1992). They become more physiologically aroused when facing new or strange situations. Compared with fraternal twins, twins who share identical genes are more likely to have similar temperaments (Emde & others, 1992; Gabbay, 1992; Robinson & others, 1992).

"Oh, he's cute, all right, but he's got the temperament of a car alarm."

Group Differences

If genetic influences help explain individual differences in traits such as aggressiveness, can the same be said of group differences between men and women, or between people of a different race? Not necessarily. Individual differences in height and weight are highly heritable. Yet nutritional rather than genetic influences explain why, as a group, today's adults are taller and heavier than those of a century ago. The two groups differ, but not because human genes have changed in a mere century's eyeblink of time. As with height and weight, so with personality and intelligence scores: Heritable individual differences need not imply heritable group differences. If some individuals are genetically disposed to be more aggressive than others, that needn't explain why some groups are more aggressive than others. Putting people in a new social context can change their aggressiveness.

Nature Enables Nurture

Among our similarities, the most important—the behavioral hallmark of our species—is our enormous capacity to adapt. Some human traits, such as having two eyes, develop the same in virtually every environment. But most psychologically interesting traits are expressed in particular environments. We all are driven to eat, but depending on our culturally learned tastes, we may have a yen for fish eyes, black bean salad, or chicken legs. Go barefoot for a summer and you will develop toughened, callused feet—a biological adaptation to friction. Meanwhile, your shoed neighbor will remain a tenderfoot. The difference between the two of you is, of course, an effect of environment. But it is also the product of a biological mechanism. Our shared biology enables our developed diversity (Buss, 1991).

An analogy may help: Genes and environment—nature and nurture—work together like two hands clapping, with the environment reacting to and shaping what nature predisposes. Thus, asking whether your intelligence or personality is more a product of your genes or environment is like asking whether the area of a field is more the result of its length or width. We could, however, ask whether the *differing* areas of various fields are more the result of differences in their length or width. For psychological traits, human differences are nearly always the result of both genetic and environmental variations. Thus (to give a preview of coming attractions), eating disorders are genetically influenced: Some individuals are more at risk than others. But culture also bends the twig, for eating disorders are a contemporary Western cultural phenomenon. Likewise, criminal and aggressive tendencies are known to be genetically influenced. But genetic changes did not explain the explosion in juvenile violence during the 1980s and early 1990s.

"To reveal and identify that which unites us rather than that which divides us [is] the principal challenge of the coming century and the coming millennium."

Václav Havel, *The Art of the Impossible*, 1997

■ **interaction** the effect of one factor (such as environment) depends on another factor (such as heredity).

■ **molecular genetics** the subfield of biology that studies the molecular structure and function of genes.

"Heredity deals the cards; environment plays the hand."

Psychologist Charles L. Brewer (1990)

"We predict that DNA will revolutionize psychological research and treatment early in the twenty-first century."

Robert Plomin and John Crabbe (2000)

Gene-Environment Interaction

To say that genes and experience are *both* important is true, but an oversimplification. More precisely, their effects intertwine. Imagine two babies, one genetically predisposed to be attractive, sociable, and easygoing, the other less so. Assume further that the first baby attracts more affectionate and stimulating care than the second and so develops into a warmer and more outgoing person. As the two children grow older, the more naturally outgoing one more often seeks activities and friends that encourage further social confidence.

What has caused their resulting personality differences? We can't say simply that individual personalities are *x* percent due to genes and *y* percent to experience, because neither heredity nor experience dances alone. Our genetically influenced traits *evoke* significant responses in others. Thus, an aggressive child may be yelled at by a teacher who talks warmly to the child's model classmates.

This helps explain why identical twins reared in different families recall their parents' warmth as remarkably similar—almost as similar as if they had had the same parents (Plomin & others, 1988, 1991, 1994). Fraternal twins recall their early family life more differently—even if reared in the same family! "Children experience us as different parents, depending on their own qualities," notes Sandra Scarr (1990). Moreover, as we grow older we also *select* environments well suited to our natures.

So, from conception onward, we are the product of a cascade of **interactions** between our genetic predispositions and our surrounding environments. Our genes affect how people react to and influence us. Biological appearances have social consequences. Asking whether genes or experiences are more important is therefore like asking whether an engine or a steering wheel is more important for driving a car. So, forget nature *versus* nurture; think nature *via* nurture.

Behavior geneticists have progressed from asking "Do genes influence behavior?" to asking "How much?" and "Which ones?" The new frontier of behavior-genetics research is the "bottom-up" **molecular genetics** quest to identify the *specific genes* that influence behavior. As psychologist Robert Plomin (1997) observes, "The DNA train [is] pulling out of the station," and psychologists are climbing aboard.

It seems clear that most human traits are influenced by a combination of genes. But genetic tests can now reveal who is at risk for at least a dozen diseases.

Genetic-environmental influence
People respond differently to a Woody Allen than to an Arnold Schwarzenegger.

Before long, researchers may also identify genes that influence depression, schizophrenia, aggressiveness, reading disability, alcoholism, body weight, and sexual orientation. Aided by new techniques for scanning relevant DNA snips, medical personnel may soon be able to give would-be parents a read-out on how their fetus's genes differ from the normal pattern and what this might mean. Such information will pose many difficult ethical dilemmas for parents and for society.

"I thought that sperm-bank donors remained anonymous."

rehearse it!

4. Fraternal twins result when
   a. a single egg is fertilized by a single sperm and then splits.
   b. a single egg is fertilized by two sperm and then splits.
   c. two eggs are fertilized by two sperm.
   d. two eggs are fertilized by a single sperm.

5. Adoption studies seek to reveal genetic influences on personality mainly by
   a. comparing adopted children with nonadopted children.
   b. evaluating whether adopted children more closely resemble their adoptive parents or their biological parents.
   c. studying the effect of prior neglect on adopted children.
   d. studying the effect of one's age at adoption.

6. Although development is lifelong, there is stability of personality over time. For example,
   a. most personality traits emerge in infancy and persist throughout life.
   b. temperament tends to remain stable throughout life.
   c. few people change significantly after adolescence.
   d. people tend to undergo greater personality changes as they age.

7. Molecular geneticists are now working with psychologists to ask
   a. do genes influence behavior?
   b. which genes influence which behaviors?
   c. how does culture bend the genetic influence?
   d. how many genes are there?

Environmental Influence

PREVIEW QUESTION 4 To what extent are our lives shaped by parental nurture, prenatal nutrition, early stimulation, and peer influences?

Genetic influences explain roughly 40 to 50 percent of our individual variations in many personality traits. When asked what accounts for the rest, many people presume it is parental nurture. But Peter Neubauer and Alexander Neubauer (1990, pp. 20–21) illustrate how, with hindsight, we may inappropriately credit or blame our parents:

> Identical twin men, now age thirty, were separated at birth and raised in different countries by their respective adoptive parents. Both kept their lives neat—neat to the point of pathology. Their clothes were preened, appointments met precisely on time, hands scrubbed regularly to a raw, red color. When the first was asked why he felt the need to be so clean, his answer was plain.

"My mother. When I was growing up she always kept the house perfectly ordered. She insisted on every little thing returned to its proper place, the clocks—we had dozens of clocks—each set to the same noonday chime. She insisted on this, you see. I learned from her. What else could I do?"

The man's identical twin, just as much a perfectionist with soap and water, explained his own behavior this way: "The reason is quite simple. I'm reacting to my mother, who was an absolute slob."

How Much Credit (or Blame) Do Parents Deserve?

Parents typically feel enormous pride in their children's successes, and guilt or shame over their failures. They beam when folks offer congratulations for the child who wins an award. They wonder where they went wrong with the child repeatedly called into the principal's office. Freudian psychiatry and psychology have been among the sources of such ideas, by blaming problems from asthma to schizophrenia on "bad mothering." And society reinforces such parent-blaming: Believing that parents shape their children as a potter molds clay, people readily praise parents for their children's virtues and blame them for their children's vices. Popular culture of the 1990s endlessly proclaimed the psychological harm parents inflict on their fragile children. "The major source of human misery" is the "neglected, wounded child" within each of us, claimed author-lecturer John Bradshaw (1990, p. 7). Having survived our "toxic" parents, today's "adult children" have swarmed to "recovery groups."

But do parents really produce future adults with a wounded child within by being (take your pick from the toxic lists) overbearing—or uninvolved? Pushy—or ineffectual? Overprotective—or distant? Are children really so easily wounded by well-meaning but occasionally exhausted parents who don't always successfully cross the psychological tightrope? If so, should we then blame our parents for our failings, and ourselves for our children's failings? Should we shame the parents of troubled children or pass city ordinances that punish them for their children's misdeeds?

If parental handling shapes children's personalities, then children who share the same parents should be somewhat similar, yes? But as we have seen, behavior geneticists have repeatedly found this to be untrue. Shared environmental influences—including the home influences that siblings share—typically account for less than 10 percent of their personality differences (though it accounts for more of their beliefs and values). In the words of behavior geneticists Robert Plomin and Denise Daniels (1987), "Two children in the same family [are on average] as different from one another as are pairs of children selected randomly from the population." To developmental psychologist Sandra Scarr (1993), this implies that "parents should be given less credit for kids who turn out great and blamed less for kids who don't." In procreation, a woman and a man shuffle their gene decks and deal a life-forming hand to their child-to-be, who is then subjected to countless influences beyond their control. And if our children are not formless blobs sculpted by parental nurture, then perhaps we parents can relax a bit more and love our children for who they are.

If parental influence on personality is more limited than popular psychology supposes, what aspects of the environment do matter? Here, for starters, are five: prenatal environment, early experience, peer influence, culture, and influences related to gender.

Even among chimpanzees, when one infant is hurt by another, the victim's mother will often attack the offender's mother (Goodall, 1968).

Who's to blame?
These deviant teenagers risk all by riding atop high-speed trains. Why? Although abuse and family collapse disturb many children, the surprising differences among children raised in the same home reveal the limits of parental influence. Genetic predispositions and social influences also shape children's lives.

"If you want to blame your parents for your own adult problems, you are entitled to blame the genes they gave you, but you are not entitled—by any facts I know—to blame the way they treated you. . . . We are not prisoners of our past."

Martin Seligman, *What You Can Change and What You Can't*, 1994

Prenatal Environment

"Nurture" begins in the womb, as embryos receive differing nutrition and varying levels of exposure to toxic agents. Even identical twins may receive not-so-identical prenatal nurture. Some identical twins share the same placenta, and thus a more similar prenatal environment (though one might get a richer blood supply and may weigh more at birth). Other twins have separate placentas **(FIGURE 5.4)**. In this arrangement, one placenta sometimes has a more advantageous placement that provides better nourishment and therefore a better placental barrier against viruses. Early indications are that, compared with same-placenta identical twins, those who develop with separate placentas are somewhat less similar in their psychological traits (Phelps & others, 1997).

Experience and Brain Development

Experience helps develop the brain's neural connections. Even if forgotten, early experience helps prepare our brains for thought and language, and also for later experiences. But how do early experiences leave their "marks" in the brain? Mark Rosenzweig and David Krech reared some young rats in solitary confinement and others in a communal playground **(FIGURE 5.5)**. When their brains were then analyzed, the rats who died with the most toys had won. Those living in the enriched environment, which simulated a natural environment, usually developed a heavier and thicker brain cortex (the *cerebral cortex* is the brain's control and information-processing center). Rosenzweig (1984; Renner & Rosenzweig, 1987) was so surprised by this discovery that he repeated the experiment several times before publishing his findings. The effects are great enough that, shown brief video clips of rats, you could tell from their activity and curiosity whether their rearing was impoverished or enriched (Renner & Renner, 1993). Bryan Kolb and Ian Whishaw (1998) report that rats housed for 60 days in enriched environments showed brain weight increases of 7 to 10 percent, and the number of neural connections mushroomed by about 20 percent— "an extraordinary change!" Such results have motivated improvements in the environments we provide for laboratory, farm, and zoo animals—and for children in institutions.

Several research teams have found that the stimulation of touch or massage benefits infant rats and premature babies (Field, 1998; Meaney & others, 1988). "Handled" infants of both species gain weight more rapidly and develop faster neurologically. William Greenough and his University of Illinois colleagues (1987) further discovered that repeated experiences modify a rat's neural tissue—at the very spot in

FIGURE 5.4

Two placental arrangements in identical twins

Identical twins may (a) have separate placentas and blood sources, as do all fraternal twins. Or they may (b) share the same placental blood. Researchers are now studying how this variation predicts later differences between identical twins. (From Davis & others, 1995.)

| Impoverished environment | Rat brain cell | Enriched environment | Rat brain cell |

FIGURE 5.5

Experience affects brain development

Mark Rosenzweig and David Krech reared rats either alone in an environment without playthings or with others in an environment enriched with playthings that were changed daily. In 14 of 16 repetitions of this basic experiment, the rats placed in the enriched environment developed significantly more cerebral cortex (relative to the rest of the brain's tissue) than did those in the impoverished environment. (From "Brain changes in response to experience" by M. R. Rosenzweig, E. L. Bennett, and M. C. Diamond. Copyright © 1972 Scientific American, Inc. All rights reserved.)

Stringing the circuits young
String musicians who started playing before age 12 have larger and more complex neuron circuits controlling the note-making left-hand fingers than do string musicians whose training started after age 13 (Elbert & others, 1995).

the brain that processes the experience. After brain maturation provides us with an abundance of neural connections, experience preserves our activated connections while allowing our unused connections to degenerate. The result by puberty is a massive loss of unemployed connections.

Here, then, at the juncture of nurture and nature, is where a child's enriched environment activates and preserves connections that, given impoverished experiences, might have died off from disuse. There is a biological reality to early childhood education. Consider:

- If given stimulating infant care, children from impoverished environments score better on intelligence tests given at age 12 (Ramey & Ramey, 1992).
- During early childhood—while the excess connections are still on call—youngsters can most easily master the grammar and accent of another language. Lacking any exposure to language before adolescence, the person will never master any language.
- Lacking visual experience during the early years, people whose vision is restored by cataract removal never achieve normal perceptions. The brain cells normally assigned to vision have died or been diverted to other uses.

So, for optimum brain development, normal stimulation during the early years is critical. Use it or lose it.

The brain's development does not, however, end with childhood. Throughout life our neural tissue is changing. Sights and smells, touches and tugs activate and strengthen some neural pathways while others weaken from disuse. Similar to pathways through a forest, less traveled paths gradually disappear, popular paths are broadened. Our genes dictate our overall brain architecture, but experience directs the details. If a monkey is trained to push a lever with a finger several thousand times a day, the brain tissue that controls the finger changes to reflect the experience. Human brains work similarly. The wiring of Eric Clapton's brain reflects the thousands of hours he has spent playing the guitar. Similarly, while learning to keyboard or rollerblade or perform a laboratory task, we perform with increasing skill as our brain incorporates the learning **(FIGURE 5.6)**. Experience nurtures nature.

FIGURE 5.6
A trained brain
A well-learned finger-tapping task activates more neurons in the region of the cortex controlling movement (orange area, right) than were active in the same brain before training (left).

Peer Influence

As children develop, experience sculpts their brains. But what types of experience are potent? Experiences with peers powerfully socialize children and youth, notes Judith Harris (1998). Consider:

- Preschoolers who disdain a certain food despite parents' urgings often will eat the food if put at a table with a group of children who like it.
- A child who hears English spoken with one accent at home and another in the neighborhood and at school will invariably adopt the accent of the peers, not the

parents. Moreover, immigrant children who are placed in peer groups of nonimmigrants quickly lose their parents' culture. "When in Rome, they become Romans," notes Harris. "Even if their parents happen to be British or Chinese or Mesquakie."

■ Direct parental influences on smoking are less important than many people suppose. More often, teens who start smoking typically have *friends* who model smoking, who suggest its pleasures, and who offer cigarettes (Rose & others, 1999).

Part of the similarity to peers may result from a "selection effect," as kids seek out peers with similar attitudes and interests. Those who smoke (or don't) may select as friends those who also smoke (or don't). Our sensitivity to peers makes biological sense, suggests Harris (1998). Parental nurture is essential to our early survival, and parental influence is especially discernible while children are in the home. But in the long run, we are destined to play with, work with, and mate with peers. Small wonder that nature predisposes us to be acutely sensitive to their styles and opinions (another example of how our evolved nature *enables* our cultural nurture). That being so, intervention programs for youth had best be aimed at a whole school or neighborhood and not just at isolated individuals. If the vapors of a toxic climate are seeping into a child's life, that climate—not just the child—needs reforming.

Peer power
As we develop we must play, work, mate, and partner with peers. No wonder children and youth are so sensitive and responsive to peer influences.

Predictably, other psychologists remind us that there is some power to parenting (Collins & others, 2000; Eisenberg & others, 1998a,b). Parenting's power to shape our differences is clearest at the extremes—the abused who become abusive, the neglected who become neglectful, the loved but firmly handled children who become self-confident and socially competent. The power of the family environment also shows up in the remarkable academic and vocational successes of children of the refugee Asian boat people—successes attributed to close-knit, supportive, even demanding families (Caplan & others, 1992).

Parental nurture is like nutrition. It may not matter much whether we get our protein from eating chicken or beans and rice, but we must have food. Likewise, it may not matter whether we grew up with parents who toilet trained us early or late, but it sure helps to have someone we belong to and who cares about us.

Howard Gardner (1998) concludes that parents and peers are complementary:

Parents are more important when it comes to education, discipline, responsibility, orderliness, charitableness, and ways of interacting with authority figures. Peers are more important for learning cooperation, for finding the road to popularity, for inventing styles of interaction among people of the same age. Youngsters may find their peers more interesting, but they will look to their parents when contemplating their own futures. Moreover, parents choose the neighborhoods and schools that supply the peers.

"You are the bows from which your children as living arrows are sent forth."

Kahlil Gibran, *The Prophet*, 1926

rehearse it!

8. Normal levels of stimulation are important during infancy and early childhood because during these years,
   a. a rich environment can override a child's genetic limits.
   b. experience activates and preserves neural connections that might otherwise die off from disuse.
   c. experience stimulates the growth of new brain cells.
   d. experience triggers the production of human growth hormones.

9. Children and youth are particularly responsive to influences of their
   a. peers.
   b. fathers.
   c. teachers and caretakers.
   d. mothers.

■ **culture** the enduring behaviors, ideas, attitudes, and traditions shared by a large group of people and transmitted from one generation to the next.

■ **norm** an understood rule for accepted and expected behavior. Norms prescribe "proper" behavior.

■ **personal space** the buffer zone we like to maintain around our bodies.

Culture

PREVIEW QUESTION 5 How do cultural norms affect our behavior?

Compared with the narrow path taken by flies, fish, and foxes, nature has built for us a longer, wider road along which environment drives us. The mark of our species—nature's great gift to us—is our ability to learn and adapt. We come equipped with a huge cerebral hard drive ready to receive many gigabytes of cultural software.

Culture is the behaviors, ideas, attitudes, and traditions shared by a large group of people and transmitted from one generation to the next (Brislin, 1988). If we all lived in homogeneous ethnic groups in separate regions of the world, as some people still do, cultural diversity would be less relevant. In Japan, 99 percent of the country's 126 million people are Japanese. Internal cultural differences are therefore minimal compared with those found in Los Angeles, where the public schools recently taught 82 different languages, or in Toronto or Vancouver, where minorities are one-third of the population and many are immigrants (as are 17 percent of all Canadians) (Iyer, 1993; Statistics Canada, 1999). I am ever mindful that the readers of this book are culturally diverse. You reach from Australia to Africa, from Singapore to Sweden.

Variation Across Cultures

We see our adaptability in cultural variations among our beliefs and our values, in how we raise our children and bury our dead, in what we wear (or whether we wear anything at all). Riding along with a unified culture is like riding a bike with the wind: As it carries us along, we hardly notice it is there. When we try riding *against* the wind we feel its force. Face to face with a different culture, we become aware of the cultural winds. Visiting Europe, most North Americans are struck by the smaller cars, the left-handed use of the fork, the uninhibited attire on the beaches. Stationed in Saudi Arabia, European and American soldiers alike realized how liberal their home cultures were. Arriving in North America, visitors from some cultures struggle to understand why many people wear their dirty *street* shoes in the house, or why people find it fun to eat a picnic lunch out in the woods amid flies and ants.

Each cultural group evolves its own **norms**—the rules for accepted and expected behavior. Muslims, for example, use only the right hand's fingers for eating. The Japanese have norms for taking off street shoes, and the British have a norm for orderly waiting in line. Sometimes social expectations seem oppressive: "Why should it matter how I dress?" Yet norms grease the social machinery. Prescribed, well-learned behaviors free us from self-preoccupation. When we know when to clap or bow, which fork to pick up first at the dinner party, and what sorts of gestures and compli-

Uniform requirements

People in individualist Western cultures sometimes see traditional Japanese culture as confining. But from the Japanese perspective the same tradition expresses a "serenity that comes to people who know exactly what to expect from each other" (Weisz & others, 1984).

ments are appropriate, we can relax and enjoy one another without fear of embarrassment or insult. Likewise, having a well-understood norm for greeting people in one's culture—by shaking hands or kissing each cheek—precludes awkward moments of indecision about whether to lead with one's hand or cheek.

When cultures collide, their differing norms often befuddle. For example, if someone invades our **personal space**—the portable buffer zone we like to maintain around our bodies—we feel uncomfortable. Scandinavians, North Americans, and the British prefer more personal space than do Latin Americans, Arabs, and the French (Sommer, 1969). At a social gathering, a Mexican seeking a comfortable conversation distance may end up walking around a room with a backpedaling American. (You can experience this at a party by playing space invader as you talk with someone.) To the American, the Mexican may seem intrusive; to the Mexican, the American may seem cold and standoffish.

Cultures also vary in their expressiveness. Those with roots in northern European culture often perceive people from Mediterranean cultures as warm and charming, but inefficient. The Mediterraneans, in turn, see northern Europeans as efficient, but cold and preoccupied with punctuality (Triandis, 1981).

Cultures vary in their pace of life, too. A British businessperson may feel frustrated by a Latin American client who arrives 30 minutes after the time set for lunch. People from time-conscious Japan—where bank clocks keep exact time, pedestrians walk briskly, and postal clerks fill requests speedily—may find themselves growing impatient when visiting Indonesia, where clocks keep less accurate time and the pace of life is more leisurely (Levine & Norenzayan, 1999). In adjusting to their host countries, the first wave of U.S. Peace Corps volunteers reported that two of their greatest culture shocks, after the language difference, were the differing pace of life and the people's differing sense of punctuality (Spradley & Phillips, 1972).

Variation Over Time

Consider, too, how rapidly cultures may change over time. English poet Geoffrey Chaucer (1342–1400) is separated from a modern Britisher by only 20 generations, but the two would converse with great difficulty. In the thinner slice of history since 1960, most Western cultures have changed with remarkable speed. Middle-class people fly to places they once only read about, e-mail those they once snail-mailed, and work in air-conditioned comfort where they once sweltered. They enjoy the convenience of on-line holiday shopping, make and take calls on pocket phones, and—enriched by doubled per-person real income—eat out two and a half times as often as did their parents back in the culture of 1960. With greater economic independence, today's women are more likely to marry for love and less likely to endure abusive relationships out of economic need. Various minorities enjoy expanded human rights.

But some changes seem not so wonderfully positive. Had you fallen asleep in the United States in 1960 and awakened near the end of the millennium, you would have opened your eyes to a culture with a doubled rate of divorce, a tripled rate of teen suicide, a quadrupled rate of reported juvenile violent crime, a quintupled prison population, and escalating depression (Myers, 2000). Americans also are spending more hours at work, fewer hours sleeping, and fewer hours with friends and family (Frank, 1999; Putnam, 2000). Similar cultural transformations have occurred in Canada, Britain, the European continent, Australia, and New Zealand.

Whether we love or loathe these changes, we cannot fail to be impressed by their breathtaking speed. And we cannot explain them by changes in the human gene pool, which evolves far too slowly to account for high-speed cultural transformations. Cultures vary. Cultures change. And cultures shape our lives.

Culture influences personal space
Behavior that is seen as appropriate in one culture may violate the norms of another group. In Arab countries people typically require less personal space than do members of some European and North American groups.

Cross-cultural communication can also suffer in translation, as in these signs for English-speaking tourists (Lederer, 1987; Triandis, 1994):

- **In a Greek tailor shop:** "Because of a big rush, we will execute customers in strict rotation."
- **An Italian laundry:** "Ladies, leave your clothes here and spend the afternoon having a good time."
- **A Danish airline:** "We take your bags and send them in all directions."
- **A Moscow hotel room:** "If this is your first visit to the USSR, you are welcome to it."
- **A detour sign in Japan:** "Stop: Drive Sideways."

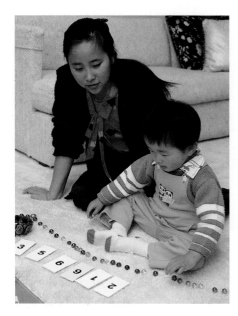

Parental involvement promotes development

Parents in every culture facilitate their children's discovery of their world, but cultures differ in what they deem important. Asian cultures place more emphasis on school and hard work than does North American culture. This may help explain why Japanese and Taiwanese children get higher scores on mathematics achievement tests.

Culture and Child-Rearing

Child-rearing practices are not immune to the variations in cultural values from one time and place to another. Do you prefer children who are independent or children who comply with what others think?

If you live in a Westernized culture, the odds are you prefer the former. Westernized countries derived from northern Europe are noted for their *individualism* (giving priority to personal goals and identity). Most parents in these societies want their children to think for themselves. "You are responsible for yourself," families and schools tell their children. "Follow your conscience. Be true to yourself. Discover your gifts. Think through your personal needs." But these cultural values represent change over time. A half-century ago, Western parents placed greater priority on obedience, respect, and sensitivity to others (Alwin, 1990; Remley, 1988). "Be true to your traditions," they taught their children. "Be loyal to your heritage and country. Show respect toward your parents and other superiors."

Unlike most Westerners, who now raise their children to be independent, many Asians and Africans favor *collectivism* (giving priority to group goals and identity). They tend to live in communal cultures, cultures that focus on cultivating emotional closeness. Rather than being given their own bedrooms and entrusted to day care, infants and toddlers typically sleep with their mothers and spend their days close to a family member (Morelli & others, 1992; Whiting & Edwards, 1988). Children of communal cultures grow up with a stronger sense of "family self"—a feeling that what shames the child shames the family, and what brings honor to the family, brings honor to the self. Compared with Westerners, people in Japanese and Chinese cultures, for example, exhibit greater shyness toward strangers and greater concern for social harmony and loyalty (Bond, 1988; Cheek & Melchior, 1990; Triandis, 1994). "My parents will be disappointed in me" is a concern of 7 percent of American and Italian teenagers and 14 percent of Australian teens, but of nearly 25 percent of teens in Taiwan and Japan (Atkinson, 1988).

Children across place and time have thrived under various child-rearing systems. Upper-class British parents traditionally handed off routine caregiving to nannies, then sent their children off to boarding school at about age 11 or 12. Their children generally grew up to be pillars of British society, just like their parents and their boarding-school peers. In the African Gusii society, babies nurse freely but spend most of the day on their mother's back—with lots of body contact but little face-to-face and language interaction. When the mother becomes pregnant, the toddler is weaned and handed over to someone else, often an older sibling. Westerners may wonder about the negative effects of this lack of verbal interaction, but then the African Gusii would in turn wonder about Western mothers pushing their babies around in strollers and leaving them in playpens and car seats (Small, 1997). Such diversity in child-rearing cautions us against presuming that our culture's way is the only way to rear children successfully.

Developmental Similarities Across Groups

Because we are so mindful of how others differ from us, we often fail to notice the similarities predisposed by our shared biology. Cross-cultural research can help us by leading us to appreciate both our cultural diversity *and* our human kinship. Compared with the person-to-person differences within groups, the differences between groups are small. Regardless of our culture, we humans share the same life cycle. We all speak to our infants in similar ways and respond similarly to their coos and cries (Bornstein & others, 1992a,b). All over the world, the children of parents who are warm and supportive feel better about themselves and are less hostile than are the children of parents who are punitive and rejecting (Rohner, 1986; Scott & others, 1991).

Within a culture, ethnic subgroups may behave differently yet be influenced similarly. Differences sometimes attributed to race may therefore actually result from other factors. David Rowe and his colleagues (1994, 1995) illustrate this with an analogy: Black men tend to have higher blood pressure than white men. Suppose that (1) in both groups salt consumption correlates with blood pressure, and (2) salt consumption is higher among black men than among white men. What then might we expect? A blood pressure "race difference" that may actually be a *diet* difference.

And that, say Rowe and his colleagues, parallels psychological findings: Behavior differences, like blood pressure differences, can result from differing inputs to the same process. Although American Hispanic, Asian, black, and white ethnic groups differ in school achievement and delinquency, the differences are "no more than skin deep." To the extent that family structure, peer influences, and parental education predicted behavior in one ethnic group, they did so for other groups as well.

So, in surface ways we may differ, but as members together of one species we seem subject to the same psychological forces. As members of different ethnic and cultural groups, our languages vary, yet they reflect universal principles of grammar. Our tastes vary, yet they reflect common principles of hunger. Our social behaviors vary, but they reflect pervasive principles of human influence.

"When someone has discovered why men on Bond Street wear black hats he will at the same moment have discovered why men in Timbuctoo wear red feathers."

G. K. Chesterton, 1874–1936

rehearse it!

10. In psychology, *personal space* refers to the portable buffer zone we like to maintain around our bodies. This space varies according to cultural norms. Which of the following prefer *less* personal space than the others?
    a. Americans
    b. British
    c. Arabs
    d. Scandinavians

11. Cultural values vary over time and place. Western cultures are to _____ as Asian and African cultures are to _____ .
    a. obedience; emotional closeness
    b. independence; social harmony
    c. loyalty; interdependence
    d. respect; morality

12. Human developmental processes tend to _____ from one group to another because we are members of _____ .
    a. be the same; the same ethnic group
    b. be the same; the same species
    c. differ; different species
    d. differ; different ethnic groups

Gender

PREVIEW QUESTION 6 How do nature and nurture interact to define us as male or female?

Earlier we considered one significant gender difference—in sexual interests and behaviors. Let's recap this module's theme—that nature and nurture together predispose our behavior—by considering other gender variations.

The Nature of Gender

In domains where men and women have faced similar challenges—regulating heat with sweat, developing tastes that nourish, growing calluses where the skin meets friction—the sexes are similar. Even when describing the ideal mate, both men and women put traits such as "kind," "honest," and "intelligent" at the top of their lists. But in some domains pertinent to mating, evolutionary psychologists contend, guys act like guys whether they are elephants or elephant seals, rural peasants or corporate presidents. Such differences between the sexes arise, genetically, from their differing sex chromosomes and, physiologically, from their differing concentrations of sex hormones.

Courtesy of Nick Downes.

■ **X chromosome** the sex chromosome found in both men and women. Females have two X chromosomes; males have one. An X chromosome from each parent produces a female.

■ **Y chromosome** the sex chromosome found only in males. When paired with an X sex chromosome from the mother, it produces a male child.

■ **testosterone** the most important of the male sex hormones. Both males and females have it, but the additional testosterone in males stimulates the growth of the male sex organs in the fetus and the development of the male sex characteristics during puberty.

■ **role** a set of expectations (norms) about a social position, defining how those in the position ought to behave.

■ **gender role** a set of expected behaviors for males and for females.

■ **gender identity** one's sense of being male or female.

■ **gender-typing** the acquisition of a traditional masculine or feminine role.

■ **social learning theory** the theory that we learn social behavior by observing and imitating and by being rewarded or punished.

■ **gender schema theory** the theory that children learn from their cultures a concept of what it means to be male and female and that they adjust their behavior accordingly.

"How is it gendered?"

Males and females are variations on a single form. Seven weeks after conception, you were anatomically indistinguishable from someone of the other sex. Then your genes activated your biological sex. Your sex was determined by your twenty-third pair of chromosomes, the sex chromosomes. The member of the pair that came from your mother was an **X chromosome.** From your father, you received the one chromosome out of 46 that is not unisex. This was either an X chromosome, making you a girl, or a **Y chromosome,** making you a boy. The Y chromosome contains a single gene that throws a master switch triggering the testes to develop and produce the principal male hormone, **testosterone,** which about the seventh week starts the development of external male sex organs. (Females have less testosterone.) Another key period for sexual differentiation falls during the fourth and fifth prenatal months, when different brain-wiring patterns for males and females develop under the influence of testosterone and the female's ovarian hormones (Fitch & Dennenberg, 1998).

The Nurture of Gender

Although biologically influenced, gender is also socially constructed. What biology initiates, culture accentuates.

Gender Roles

In psychology, as in the theater, a **role** refers to a cluster of prescribed actions—the behaviors we expect of those who occupy a particular social position. One set of norms defines our culture's **gender roles**—our expectations about the way men and women behave. Traditionally, men have initiated dates, driven the car, and picked up the check; women have decorated the house, bought and cared for the children's clothes, and selected the wedding gifts. In the United States, for example, married mothers do 90 percent of the laundry and 13 percent of the car maintenance (Acock & Demo, 1994). And, I do not have to tell you which parent, about 90 percent of the time in two-parent families, stays home with a sick child, arranges for the baby-sitter, or calls the doctor (Maccoby, 1995). Such formulas can smooth social relations, saving awkward decisions about who does what. But they often do so at a cost: If we deviate from such conventions, we may feel anxious.

Gender roles everywhere have tended to limit women's rights and power. "There are no human societies in which women dominate men," noted Felicia Pratto (1996). In 1997, women were 11.7 percent of the world's national legislators (Briscoe, 1997). Even in Israel's communal farms, the kibbutzim, where children have been reared together—dressed, bathed, and given toys without regard to gender—boys have grown up to do mostly "masculine" things and to dominate the leadership roles. Girls, although legally equal, play more with dolls and in adulthood seek more contact with children (Wilson, 1993).

Perhaps evolution predisposes men everywhere to be aggressive and dominant in order to serve their reproductive goals, and predisposes women to the interpersonal skills that serve their reproductive goals (Archer, 1996). But we know that gender roles are not rigidly fixed by evolution, because they vary across cultures. In nomadic societies of food-gathering people, there is minimal division of labor by sex. Boys and girls receive much the same upbringing. However, in agricultural societies, women remain close to home, working in the fields and staying with the children; men often roam more freely, herding cattle or sheep. Such societies typically socialize their children into distinct gender roles (Segall & others, 1990; Van Leeuwen, 1978).

Gender roles also vary among the industrialized countries. Women recently filled 48 percent of managerial positions in Switzerland, 28 percent in Austria,

17 percent in the United States, 3 percent in Ghana, and 2 percent in South Korea (Triandis, 1994). In North America, medicine and dentistry have been predominantly male occupations; in Russia, most medical doctors are women, as are most dentists in Denmark.

Gender roles vary over time as well as across cultures:

■ As we began the last century only one country—New Zealand—granted women the right to vote. As we ended it, only one democracy—Kuwait—did not (Briscoe, 1995).

■ With the flick of an apron, the number of U.S. college women hoping to be full-time homemakers plunged during the late 1960s and early 1970s **(FIGURE 5.7)**.

■ In developing countries, too, gender roles are changing. Between 1970 and 1992, girls' enrollment in schools rose from 38 to 68 percent, shrinking the gender gap (UNICEF, 1996).

Gender roles have changed, but not every male has changed with them.

FIGURE 5.7

Changing attitudes about gender roles
U.S. college students' endorsement of the traditional view of women's role has declined dramatically. Men's and women's attitudes have also converged. (From Dey & others, 1991; Sax & others, 1999.)

Gender and Child-Rearing

Society assigns each of us to a *gender*, the social category of male or female. The inevitable result is our strong **gender identity,** our sense of being male or female. To varying extents, we also become **gender-typed.** That is, some boys more than others exhibit traditionally masculine traits and interests, and some girls more than others become distinctly feminine.

Social learning theory assumes that children learn gender-linked behaviors by observing and imitating and by being rewarded or punished. "Nicole, you're such a good mommy to your dolls"; "Big boys don't cry, Alex." But modeling and rewarding is not done by parents alone, because the differences in the way parents rear boys and girls aren't enough to explain gender-typing (Lytton & Romney, 1991). In fact, even when their families discourage traditional gender-typing, children organize themselves into "boy worlds" and "girl worlds," each guided by rules for what boys and girls do.

Gender schema theory combines social learning theory with cognition: Out of your struggles to comprehend the world came concepts, or *schemas,* including a schema for your own gender (Bem, 1987, 1993). Gender became a lens (a

FIGURE 5.8

Two theories of gender-typing
Social learning theory proposes that gender-typing evolves through imitation and reinforcement. In gender schema theory, one's concept of maleness and femaleness influences one's perceptions and behavior.

schema) through which you view your experiences **(FIGURE 5.8)**. By age 3, language forces children to begin organizing their worlds on the basis of gender. English, for example, uses the pronouns *he* and *she*; other languages classify objects as masculine (*"le* train") or feminine (*"la* table"). Through language, dress, toys, and songs, social learning shapes gender schemas. Children then compare themselves with their concept of gender ("I am male—thus, masculine, strong, aggressive," or "I am female—therefore, feminine, sweet, and helpful") and adjust their behavior accordingly.

rehearse it!

13. The fertilized egg will develop into a boy if it receives
    a. an X chromosome from its mother.
    b. an X chromosome from its father.
    c. a Y chromosome from its mother.
    d. a Y chromosome from its father.

14. Gender roles vary across cultures and over time. "Gender role" refers to our

    a. sense of being male or female.
    b. expectations about the way men and women behave.
    c. biological sex.
    d. beliefs about how men and women should earn a living.

15. Psychologists differentiate between our biological sex and our gender. As a consequence of the gender assigned to

us by society, we develop a gender identity, which means that we

a. exhibit traditional masculine or feminine roles.
b. are socially categorized as male or female.
c. have a sense of being male or female.
d. have an ambiguous biological sex.

Postcript:
Reflections on Nature and Nurture

"There are trivial truths and great truths," reflected the physicist Niels Bohr on some of the paradoxes of modern science. "The opposite of a trivial truth is plainly false. The opposite of a great truth is also true." It appears true that our ancestral history helped form us as a species. Where there is variation, natural selection, and heredity, there will be, on some scale, evolution. The unique gene combination created when our mother's egg engulfed our father's sperm also helped form us, as individuals. Genes predispose both our shared humanity and our individual differences. This is a great truth about human nature. Genes form us.

But it also is true that our experiences help form us. In the womb, in our families, and in our other social relationships, we learn ways of thinking and acting. Even differences initiated by our nature may be amplified by our nurture. If men are inclined to roles that demand physical power, and women to more nurturing roles, each may then exhibit the actions expected of those who fill such roles and find themselves shaped accordingly. Presidents in time become more presidential, servants more servile. In such ways, our life experiences in local environments and surrounding cultures help form us. This, too, is a great truth about human nurture. Our genes and our experience together form who we are.

· · · · ·

If nature and nurture jointly form us, are we "nothing but" the product of nature and nurture?

We *are* the product of nature and nurture, but we are also an open system. Genes, for example, are all-pervasive but not all-powerful. Constrained by the dictates of their DNA, organisms construct themselves in particular places and times. Sometimes people defy their genetic bent to reproduce, by electing celibacy. Culture, too, is all-pervasive but not all-powerful. Sometimes people defy peer pressures, by asserting their freedom and doing the opposite. To excuse our failings by entirely blaming our nature and nurture is what philosopher-novelist Jean-Paul Sartre called "bad faith"—evading responsibility by blaming bad genes or bad influences for one's fate.

In reality, we are both the creatures and the creators of our worlds. We are—it is a great truth—the products of our genes and environments. Nevertheless—another great truth—the stream of causation that shapes the future runs through our present choices. Our decisions today design our environments tomorrow. The human environment is not like the weather—something that just happens. We are its architects. And that is what enables cultures to vary and to change so quickly.

· · · · ·

I know from my mail and from public opinion surveys that some readers feel troubled by the naturalism and evolutionism of contemporary science. They worry that a science of behavior (and evolutionary science in particular) will destroy our sense of the beauty, mystery, and spiritual significance of the human creature. For those concerned, I offer some reassuring thoughts.

When Isaac Newton explained the rainbow in terms of light of differing wavelengths, the poet Keats feared that Newton had destroyed the rainbow's mysterious beauty. Yet, notes Richard Dawkins (1998) in *Unweaving the Rainbow*, Newton's analysis led to Maxwell's theory of electromagnetism and onward to an even deeper mystery—Einstein's theory of special relativity. Moreover, nothing about Newton's optics need diminish our appreciation for the dramatic elegance of a rainbow arching across a rain-darkened sky.

When Galileo assembled evidence that the Earth revolved around the Sun, not vice versa, he did not offer irrefutable proof for his theory. Rather he offered a coher-

"Genes, by themselves, are like seeds dropped onto pavement: powerless to produce anything."

Primatologist Frans B. M. de Waal (1999)

"The causes of life's history [cannot] resolve the riddle of life's meaning."

Stephen Jay Gould, *Rocks of Ages: Science and Religion in the Fullness of Life*, 1999

"Let's hope that it's not true; but if it is true, let's hope that it doesn't become widely known."

Lady Ashley, commenting on Darwin's big idea

"Is it not stirring to understand how the world actually works—that white light is made of colors, that color measures light waves, that transparent air reflects light . . . ? It does no harm to the romance of the sunset to know a little about it."

Carl Sagan, *Skies of Other Worlds*, 1988

"The fairest thing we can experience is the mysterious. It is the fundamental emotion which stands at the cradle of true art and true science."

Albert Einstein, *The World as I See It*, 1949

"The larger the island of knowledge, the longer the shoreline of wonder."

Ralph W. Sockman

ent explanation for a variety of observations, such as the changing shadows cast by the Moon's mountains. His explanation eventually won the day because it described and explained things in a way that made sense, that hung together. Darwin's big idea likewise is a coherent view of natural history. It offers an organizing principle that unifies various observations.

Although some people of faith find the scientific idea of human origins troubling, many others find it congenial with their spirituality. In the fifth century, St. Augustine (quoted by Wilford, 1999) wrote, "The universe was brought into being in a less than fully formed state, but was gifted with the capacity to transform itself from unformed matter into a truly marvelous array of structures and life forms." Some 1600 years later, Pope John Paul II in 1996 welcomed science-religion dialogue, finding it noteworthy that evolutionary theory "has been progressively accepted by researchers, following a series of discoveries in various fields of knowledge." Evolution, he concluded, is "more than just a theory."

Meanwhile, many people of science are awestruck at the emerging understanding of the universe and the human creature. It boggles the mind—the entire universe popping out of a point some 14 billion years ago, and instantly inflating to cosmological size. Had the energy of this Big Bang been the tiniest bit less, the universe would have collapsed back on itself. Had it been the tiniest bit more, the result would have been a soup too thin to support life.

What caused this fine-tuned universe? Why is there something rather than nothing? What made it—like Baby Bear's porridge—"just right"? How did it come to be, in the words of Harvard-Smithsonian astrophysicist Owen Gingerich (1999), "so extraordinarily right, that it seemed the universe had been expressly designed to produce intelligent, sentient beings"? Is there a benevolent superintelligence behind it all? Or have there actually been an infinite number of universes born and we just happen to be the lucky inhabitants of one that, by chance, was exquisitely fine-tuned to give birth to us? On most of these questions, science is silent.

Rather than fearing or restraining science, we can welcome its enlarging our understanding and awakening our sense of awe. In *The Fragile Species*, Lewis Thomas (1992) described his utter amazement that the Earth in time gave rise to bacteria and eventually to Bach's Mass in B-Minor. In a short 4 billion years, life has come from nothing to structures as complex as a 6-billion-unit strand of DNA and the incomprehensible intricacy of the human brain. Nature, says cosmologist Paul Davies (1992, 1999), seems cunningly devised to produce extraordinary, self-replicating, information-processing systems—us. Although we appear to have been created from dust, over eons of time, the end result is a priceless creature, one rich with potentials beyond our imagining.

The Nature and Nurture of Behavior

1. Our genes provide the blueprint for our biology; does this mean they determine our behaviors?

Genes, segments of complex DNA molecules that form the chromosomes, are the biochemical units of heredity. They provide the blueprint for protein molecules, the building blocks of our physical and behavioral development. Our genetic predispositions help explain our behaviors, but they do not determine them.

2. How do evolutionary psychologists use natural selection to explain behavior tendencies?

Evolutionary psychologists study how natural selection has shaped our universal behavior tendencies. They reason that if organisms vary, if only some mature to produce surviving offspring, and if certain inherited behavior tendencies assist that survival, then nature must select those tendencies. Critics maintain that evolutionary psychologists make too many hindsight explanations.

3. How do behavior geneticists explain individual differences?

Behavior geneticists explore our individual differences using methods such as twin, adoption, and temperament studies. By such methods they identify the heritability of various traits and disorders. Studies of the inheritance of temperament, and of twins and adopted children, provide scientific support for the idea that nature and nurture influence one's developing personality. Genes and environment, biological and social factors, direct our life courses as their effects intertwine. Molecular geneticists are on a fast-moving frontier in their work to identify the specific genes that influence behaviors.

4. To what extent are our lives shaped by parental nurture, prenatal nutrition, early stimulation, and peer influences?

Genetic influences are pervasive, but so are prenatal environments, early experiences, peer influences, and cultures. Sculpted by experience, neural interconnections multiply rapidly after birth.

5. How do cultural norms affect our behavior?

Human variations across cultures and over time show how differing norms, or expectations, guide behavior. Cultures differ in their norms for personal space, expressiveness, and pace of life.

6. How do nature and nurture interact to define us as male or female?

Gender illustrates the interaction between nature and nurture. Although males and females share similarly adaptive bodily procedures, differing sex chromosomes and differing concentrations of sex hormones lead to significant physiological sex difference. Yet gender differences vary widely depending upon cultural socialization through social learning and gender schemas.

TERMS AND CONCEPTS TO REMEMBER

chromosomes, p. 69
DNA (deoxyribonucleic acid), p. 69
genes, p. 69
genome, p. 69
natural selection, p. 70
mutation, p. 70
evolutionary psychology, p. 71

gender, p. 72
behavior genetics, p. 75
environment, p. 75
identical twins, p. 75
fraternal twins, p. 75
temperament, p. 78
interaction, p. 80

molecular genetics, p.80
culture, p. 86
norm, p. 86
personal space, p. 87
X chromosome, p. 90
Y chromosome, p. 90
testosterone, p. 90

role, p. 90
gender role, p. 90
gender identity, p. 91
gender-typing, p. 91
social learning theory, p. 91
gender schema theory, p. 91

REHEARSE IT ANSWER KEY

1. c	3. c	5. b	7. b	9. a	11. b	13. d	15. c
2. b	4. c	6. b	8. b	10. c	12. b	14. b	

The Developing Person

In mid-1978, the newest astonishment in medicine . . . was the birth of an English baby nine months after conception in a dish. The older surprise, which should still be fazing us all, is that a solitary sperm and a single egg can fuse and become a human being. . . . This has been going on under our eyes for so long a time that we've gotten used to it; hence the outcries of amazement at this really minor technical modification of the general procedure—nothing much, really, beyond relocating the beginning of the process from the fallopian tube to a plastic container.

Lewis Thomas, *The Medusa and the Snail*, 1979

The developing person is no less a wonder after birth than in the womb. As we journey through life from womb to tomb, when and how do we change? We invariably notice how we differ. However, to *developmental psychologists*, who study physical, mental, and social changes throughout the human life cycle, discerning our commonalities is just as important. Virtually all of us began walking around age 1 and talking by age 2. As children, we each engaged in social play in preparation for life's work. As adults, we all smile and cry, love and loathe, and occasionally ponder the fact that someday we will die. Psychology's developmental perspective examines how people are continually developing, from infancy through old age. Much of its research centers on three major issues:

1. *Nature/nurture:* How much do genetic inheritance (our *nature*) and experience (the *nurture* we receive) influence our development?
2. *Continuity/stages:* Is development a gradual, continuous process like riding an escalator, or does it proceed through a sequence of separate stages, like climbing rungs on a ladder?
3. *Stability/change:* Do our early personality traits persist through life, or do we become different persons as we age?

We engaged the nature/nurture issue in Module 5. In Modules 6 through 9, we consider the other major developmental issues—continuity and stability—from prenatal development through adulthood.

"Nature is all that a man brings with him into the world; nurture is every influence that affects him after his birth."

Francis Galton, *English Men of Science*, 1874

6 Developmental Issues, Prenatal Development, and the Newborn

Introduction to Two Major Developmental Issues

PREVIEW QUESTION 1 What does research tell us about the issues of continuity versus stages and of stability versus change in lifelong development?

As researchers in **developmental psychology** study the physical, mental, and social changes occurring over the human life span, they consider two big questions: Do we develop through a gradual, continuous process or through a series of discrete stages? And as we develop, do our traits remain stable over time or do they change?

Continuity and Stages

Adults are vastly different from infants. But do they differ as a giant redwood differs from its seedling—a difference created by gradual, cumulative growth? Or do they differ as a butterfly differs from a caterpillar—a difference of distinct stages?

Generally speaking, researchers who emphasize experience and learning see development as a slow, continuous shaping process. Those who emphasize biological maturation tend to see development as a sequence of genetically predetermined stages or steps; although progress through the various stages may be quick or slow, everyone passes through the stages in the same order.

Are there clear-cut stages of psychological development, as there are physical stages such as crawling before walking? Several *stage theories* of development have been proposed and tested over the years. For example, developmental psychologist Jean Piaget (pronounced Pee-ah-ZHAY) proposed that all children pass through four discrete, age-linked stages of cognitive development, each stage with its own specific conceptual (thinking) abilities. But subsequent research has suggested that cognitive development, though occurring basically in the sequence Piaget proposed, is more continuous, with some conceptual abilities occurring at earlier ages than Piaget supposed. Similarly, research has tested other stage theories and found that life does not occur through a fixed, predictable series of steps.

Although research casts doubt on the idea that life proceeds through neatly defined, age-linked stages, the concept of stage remains useful. There are spurts of brain growth during childhood and puberty that correspond roughly to Piaget's stages (Thatcher & others, 1987). And stage theories contribute a developmental perspective on the whole life span, by suggesting how people of one age think and act differently when they arrive at a later age.

BEFORE   AFTER

As adults grow older, there is continuity of personality.

Stability and Change

This leads us to the next question: Over time, are people's personalities consistent, or do they change? If reunited with a long-lost grade school friend, would you instantly recognize that "it's the same old Andy"? Or does a person during one period of life seem like a different person at a later period?

Researchers who have followed lives through time have found evidence for both stability and change. There is continuity to personality and yet, happily for troubled

■ **developmental psychology** a branch of psychology that studies physical, cognitive, and social change throughout the life span.

children and adolescents, human development is life: The struggles of the present may be laying a foundation for a happier tomorrow. More specifically, researchers generally agree on the following points:

1. The first two years of life provide a poor basis for predicting a person's eventual traits (Kagan, 1978, 1998). Even children and adolescents often change: Many confused and troubled children have blossomed into mature, successful adults (Macfarlane, 1964; Thomas & Chess, 1986). As people grow older, however, continuity of personality does gradually increase (Costa & McCrae, 1989; Klohnen & Bera, 1998; Stein & others, 1986).

2. Some characteristics, such as temperament, are more stable than others, such as social attitudes (Moss & Susman, 1980). But attitudes, too, become more stable with age (Krosnick & Alwin, 1989).

3. In some ways, we all change with age. Most shy, fearful toddlers begin opening up by age 4, and during adulthood most of us mellow. In the years after college, most people become calmer and more self-disciplined (McCrae & Costa, 1994). Many a 20-year-old goof-off has matured into a 40-year-old business or cultural leader. Such changes can occur without changing a person's position *relative* to others of the same age. The hard-driving young adult may mellow by later life yet still be a relatively hard-driving senior citizen.

Finally, we should remember that life contains *both* stability and change. Stability enables us to depend on others, motivates our concern for the healthy development of children, and provides our identity. Change motivates our concerns about present influences, sustains our hope for a brighter future, and enables us to adapt and grow with experience.

"At 70, I would say the advantage is that you take life more calmly. You know that 'this, too, shall pass'!"

Eleanor Roosevelt, 1954

rehearse it!

1. Developmental researchers who emphasize learning and experience tend to believe in _____; those who emphasize biological maturation tend to believe in _____.
   a. nature; nurture
   b. continuity; stages
   c. stability; change
   d. randomness; predictability

2. Although development is lifelong, there is stability of personality over time. For example,
   a. most personality traits emerge in infancy and persist throughout life.
   b. temperament tends to remain stable throughout life.
   c. few people change significantly after adolescence.
   d. people tend to undergo greater personality changes as they age.

Prenatal Development

PREVIEW QUESTION 2 How does life develop before birth?

Conception

Nothing is more natural than a species reproducing itself. Yet nothing is more wondrous. Consider human reproduction. The process starts when a woman's ovary releases a mature egg, a cell roughly the size of the period at the end of this sentence, and when the 200 million or more sperm deposited during intercourse begin their race upstream toward it.

Like space voyagers approaching a huge planet, the sperm approach a cell 85,000 times their own size. The relatively few that make it to the egg release digestive enzymes that eat away the egg's protective coating, allowing a sperm to penetrate

(FIGURE 6.1). But the egg is hardly passive. As soon as one sperm begins to penetrate, the egg's surface blocks out the others. Meanwhile, fingerlike projections sprout around the successful sperm and pull it in. Before half a day elapses, the egg nucleus and the sperm nucleus fuse. The two have become one. Consider it your luckiest of moments. Among 200 million sperm, the one needed to make you, in combination with that one particular egg, won the race.

FIGURE 6.1

The union of egg and sperm

(a) A hoard of sperm cells surrounds an ovum. (b) As one sperm penetrates the egg's jellylike outer coating, a series of chemical events begins that will cause sperm and egg to fuse into a single cell. If all goes well, that cell will subdivide again and again to emerge 9 months later as a 100-trillion-cell human being.

(a)

(b)

Prenatal Development

Fewer than half of all fertilized eggs, called **zygotes,** survive beyond the first 2 weeks (Grobstein, 1979). But for you and me, good fortune prevailed. Beginning as one cell, each of us became two cells, then four—each cell just like the first. Then, within the first week, when this cell division had produced a zygote of some 100 cells, the cells began to *differentiate*—to specialize in structure and function. How identical cells do this—as if one decides "I'll become a brain, you become intestines!"—is a scientific puzzle that developmental biologists are just beginning to solve.

About 10 days after conception, the increasingly diverse cells attach to the mother's uterine wall, beginning approximately 37 weeks of the closest human relationship. The zygote's outer part attaches to the uterine wall, forming the placenta, through which nourishment passes. The inner cells become the **embryo (FIGURE 6.2).** Over the next 6 weeks, organs begin to form and function. The heart begins to beat and the liver begins to make red blood cells.

By 9 weeks after conception, the embryo looks unmistakably human. It is now a **fetus.** By the end of the sixth month, organs such as the stomach are sufficiently formed and functional to allow a prematurely born fetus a chance of survival.

At each prenatal stage, genetic *and* environmental factors affect our development. The placenta carries nutrients and oxygen from mother to fetus, while screening out many potentially harmful substances. But some substances slip by. The placental screen can admit **teratogens**—harmful agents such as particular viruses and drugs. If the mother is a heroin addict, her baby will be born a heroin addict. If she carries the AIDS virus, her baby may also. A pregnant woman never smokes alone; she and her fetus both experience reduced blood oxygen and a shot of nicotine. If she is a heavy smoker, her fetus may receive fewer nutrients and be born underweight. Heavy maternal smoking may also affect the fetal brain. That could help explain why a recent correlational study of 4169 Danish men found markedly increased

Prenatal development

zygote: conception to 2 weeks

embryo: 2 weeks through 8 weeks

fetus: 9 weeks to birth

(a)

(b)

(c)

(d)

FIGURE 6.2
Prenatal development
(a) The embryo grows and develops rapidly. At 40 days, the spine is visible and the arms and legs are beginning to grow. (b) Five days later, the inch-long embryo's proportions have begun to change. The rest of the body is now bigger than the head, and the arms and legs have grown noticeably. (c) By the end of the second month, when the fetal period begins, facial features, hands, and feet have formed. (d) As the fetus enters the fourth month, its 3 ounces could fit in the palm of your hand.

violent crime rates among men whose mothers smoked heavily during pregnancy—even after statistically controlling for other factors such as economic status and father criminality (Brennan & others, 1999).

There is no known safe amount of alcohol for a pregnant woman—even moderate drinking can affect the fetal brain (Braun, 1996). Alcohol enters the woman's bloodstream—and her fetus's—and depresses activity in both their central nervous systems. If she drinks heavily, her baby will be at risk for birth defects and mental retardation. For some infants, the effects are visible as **fetal alcohol syndrome (FAS)**, marked by a small, misproportioned head and lifelong brain abnormalities. Research with rats indicates that even a single drinking binge during the brain's growth-spurt period (in humans starting at six months gestation) can kill many millions of brain cells (Ikonomidou & others, 2000).

"You shall conceive and bear a son. So then drink no wine or strong drink."

Judges 13:7

The Competent Newborn

PREVIEW QUESTION 3 What are some of the newborn's abilities?

Having survived prenatal hazards, we as newborns come equipped with reflexes ideally suited for our survival. We withdraw a limb to escape pain. If a cloth over our face interferes with our breathing, we turn our head from side to side and swipe at it. New parents are often in awe of the coordinated sequence of reflexes by which their baby gets food. The **rooting reflex** illustrates this: When something touches their cheek, babies open their mouth and vigorously "root" for a nipple. Finding one, they automatically close on it and begin sucking—which itself requires a coordinated sequence of tonguing, swallowing, and breathing. Failing to find satisfaction, the hungry baby may cry—a behavior parents are predisposed to find highly unpleasant and very rewarding to relieve.

Moreover, psychologists have discovered that we are born preferring sights and sounds that facilitate social responsiveness. As newborns, we turn our heads in the direction of human voices. We gaze longer at a drawing of a facelike image **(FIGURE 6.3,** on page 102), than at a bull's-eye pattern; yet we gaze more at a bull's-eye pattern—which has contrasts much like that of the human eye—than at a solid disk (Fantz, 1961). We prefer to look at objects 8 to 12 inches away, which, wonder of wonders, just happens to be the approximate distance between a nursing infant's eyes and its mother's (Maurer & Maurer, 1988).

Our perceptual abilities develop continuously during the first months of life. Within days of birth, our brain's neural networks were stamped with the smell of

■ **zygote** the fertilized egg; it enters a 2-week period of rapid cell division and develops into an embryo.

■ **embryo** the developing human organism from about 2 weeks after fertilization through the second month.

■ **fetus** the developing human organism from 9 weeks after conception to birth.

■ **teratogens** agents, such as chemicals and viruses, that can reach the embryo or fetus during prenatal development and cause harm.

■ **fetal alcohol syndrome (FAS)** physical and cognitive abnormalities in children caused by a pregnant woman's heavy drinking. In severe cases, symptoms include noticeable facial misproportions.

■ **rooting reflex** a baby's tendency, when touched on the cheek, to open the mouth and search for the nipple.

FIGURE 6.3

Newborns' preference for faces

When shown these two stimuli with the same elements, Italian newborns spent nearly twice as many seconds looking at the facelike image (Morton & Johnson, 1991). Canadian newborns— average age 53 minutes in one study—displayed the same apparently inborn preference to look toward faces (Mondloch & others, 1999).

our mother's body. Thus, a week-old nursing baby, placed between a gauze pad from its mother's bra and one from another nursing mother, will usually turn toward the smell of its own mother's pad (MacFarlane, 1978). At 3 weeks, if given a pacifier that sometimes turns on recordings of its mother's voice and sometimes that of a female stranger's, an infant will suck more vigorously when it hears its now-familiar mother's voice (Mills & Melhuish, 1974). Newborns can also learn to turn their heads to the left or right to receive a sugar solution when their forehead is stroked (Lancioni, 1980). So not only can we as young infants see what we need to see, and smell and hear well, but we are already using our sensory equipment to learn.

rehearse it!

3. Developmental psychologists tend to focus on three major issues. Which of the following is *not* one of those issues?
   a. Nature/nurture
   b. Uniqueness/commonality
   c. Stability/change
   d. Continuity/stages

4. The 9 months of prenatal development prepare the individual for survival outside the womb. The body organs first begin to form and function during the period of the _____; within 6 months, during the period of the _____, the organs are sufficiently functional to allow a chance of survival.
   a. zygote; embryo
   b. zygote; fetus
   c. embryo; fetus
   d. placenta; fetus

5. Teratogens are chemicals that pass through the placenta's screen and may harm an embryo or fetus. Which of the following is *not* a teratogen?
   a. Oxygen
   b. Heroin
   c. Alcohol
   d. Nicotine

6. Stroke a newborn's cheek and he or she will root for a nipple. This illustrates
   a. a reflex.
   b. early learning.
   c. perceptual ability.
   d. a gender difference.

REVIEWING

Developmental Issues, Prenatal Development, and the Newborn

1. What does research tell us about the issues of continuity versus stages and of stability versus change in lifelong development?

Although the stage theories of development had to be modified in the light of later research, these theories usefully alert us to differences among people of different ages. The discovery that people's traits continue to change in later life has helped create a new emphasis on lifelong development. Nevertheless, there is also an underlying consistency to most people's temperament and personality traits.

2. How does life develop before birth?

By studying the human life span from conception to death, developmental psychologists examine how we develop physically, cognitively, and socially. The life cycle begins when one sperm cell, out of the some 200 million ejaculated, unites with an egg. The nuclei of the egg and sperm fuse to form a zygote. Attached to the uterine wall, the developing embryo begins to form body organs. By 9 weeks, the fetus is recognizably human. Along with nutrients, teratogens ingested by the mother can reach the developing child and place it at risk for birth defects and mental retardation.

3. What are some of the newborn's abilities?

Researchers have discovered that newborns are born with sensory equipment and reflexes—such as the rooting reflex—that facilitate their interacting with adults and securing nourishment. For example, they quickly learn to discriminate the smell and sound of their mothers.

TERMS AND CONCEPTS TO REMEMBER

developmental psychology, p. 98

zygote, p. 100
embryo, p. 100

fetus, p. 100
teratogens, p. 100

fetal alcohol syndrome (FAS), p. 101
rooting reflex, p. 101

REHEARSE IT ANSWER KEY

1. b   2. b   3. b   4. c   5. a   6. a

7 Infancy and Childhood

- **Physical Development**
- **Cognitive Development**
- **Social Development**

During infancy, a baby grows from newborn to toddler, and during childhood from toddler to teenager. We will see how we all travel this path and develop physically, cognitively, and socially. From infancy on, brain and mind, neural hardware and cognitive software, develop together. The regions of the brain linked with thinking, memory, and language are the last brain areas to develop. As they do, the child's mental abilities surge ahead (Chugani & Phelps, 1986; Thatcher & others, 1987).

Physical Development

PREVIEW QUESTION 1 How do the brain and motor skills develop during infancy and childhood?

Brain Development

While you resided in your mother's womb, your body was forming nerve cells (neurons) at the rate of nearly one-quarter million per *minute.* On the day you were born, you had most of the brain cells you would ever have. However, at birth your nervous system was immature: After birth, the neural networks that eventually enabled you to walk, talk, and remember had a wild growth spurt **(FIGURE 7.1).** Neural path-ways supporting language and agility continue developing into adolescence (Paus & others, 1999).

A flower unfolds in accord with its genetic blueprint. So do we, experiencing an orderly sequence of genetically designed biological growth processes called **maturation.** Maturation decrees many of our commonalities—from standing before walking, to using nouns before we use adjectives. Severe deprivation or abuse will retard development, and ample experiences with parents who talk and read to the child will help sculpt those important early neural connections. Yet the genetic growth tendencies are inborn. Maturation sets the basic course of development; experience adjusts it.

At birth 3 months 15 months

FIGURE 7.1

Drawings of neural connections in the human brain

In humans, the brain is immature at birth. As the child matures, the neural networks grow increasingly more complex.

Maturation and Infant Memory

The lack of neural connections helps explain why our earliest memories seldom pre-date our third birthdays (Howe & Courage, 1993; Nelson, 1993). We see this in the memories of a group of preschoolers who experienced an emergency fire evacuation caused by a burning popcorn maker. Seven years later they were able to recall the alarm and what caused it—*if* they were 4 to 5 years old at the time. Those who experienced the event as 3-year-olds could not remember the cause and usually misrecalled being already outside when the alarm sounded (Pillemer, 1995).

Motor Development

The developing brain also enables physical coordination. As an infant's muscles and nervous system mature, more complicated skills emerge. With minor exceptions, the sequence of physical (motor) development is universal. Babies roll over before they sit unsupported, and they creep on all fours before they walk. These behaviors reflect not imitation but a maturing nervous system; blind children, too, crawl and walk.

There are, however, individual differences in the timing of this sequence. In the United States, for example, 25 percent of all babies walk by age 11 months, and

- **maturation** biological growth processes that enable orderly changes in behavior, relatively uninfluenced by experience.

90 percent by age 15 months (Frankenburg & others, 1992). There are also cultural differences in timing. Ugandan babies, for example, usually walk by 10 months. Unlike babies from other cultures who spend much of the day lying in a crib, Ugandan babies experience more intimate and rhythmic physical contact (Bril, 1986).

Nature (genes) plays a major role, too. Identical twins typically begin sitting up and walking on nearly the same day (Wilson, 1979). Biological maturation—including the rapid development of the cerebellum, the structure at the back of the brain essential to motor coordination and balance—creates our readiness to learn walking at about age 1. Experience before that time has a limited effect. This is true for other physical skills, including bowel and bladder control. Before necessary muscular and neural maturation, no pleading, harassment, or punishment will produce successful toilet training.

Triumphant toddlers
Roll, crawl, walk, run—the sequence of these motor development milestones is the same the world around, though babies reach them at varying ages.

Cognitive Development

PREVIEW QUESTION 2 How did Piaget view the development of a child's mind, and what are current researchers' views?

"Who knows the thoughts of a child?" wondered poet Nora Perry. As much as anyone of his generation, developmental psychologist Jean Piaget (pronounced Pee-ah-ZHAY) knew. His interest began in 1920, when he was working in Paris to develop questions for children's intelligence tests. While administering tests to find out at what age children could answer certain questions correctly, Piaget became intrigued by children's *wrong* answers. Where others saw childish mistakes, Piaget saw intelligence at work. The errors made by children of a given age, he noted, were often strikingly similar.

A half-century spent with children convinced Piaget that a child's mind is not a miniature model of an adult's. As Copernicus revolutionized our understanding of the solar system, so Piaget revolutionized our understanding of children's minds, suggests William Damon (1995). Until Piaget, most people—forgetting their own preschool days—assumed children "simply knew less, not *differently,* than adults" (p. 100). Thanks partly to his work, we now understand that "children reason in wildly illogical ways about problems whose solutions are self-evident to adults" (Brainerd, 1996).

Piaget further believed that a child's mind develops through a series of stages, in an upward march from the newborn's simple reflexes to the adult's abstract reasoning power. An 8-year-old child therefore comprehends things that a 3-year-old cannot. An 8-year-old might grasp the analogy "getting an idea is like having a light turn on in your head." Trying to teach the same analogy to a 3-year-old would be fruitless. Our adult minds likewise engage in moral reasoning uncomprehended by 8-year-olds.

Piaget felt that the driving force behind this intellectual progression is our unceasing struggle to make sense of our experience. His core idea is that "children are

Jean Piaget
"If we examine the intellectual development of the individual or of the whole of humanity, we shall find that the human spirit goes through a certain number of stages, each different from the other" (1930).

Two-year-old Gabriella has learned the schema for "cow" from her picture books.

Gabriella sees a moose and calls it a "cow." She is trying to assimilate this new animal into an existing schema. Her mother tells her, "No, it's a moose."

Gabriella accommodates her schema for large, shaggy animals and continues to modify that schema to include "mommy moose," "baby moose," etc.

Pouring experience into mental molds
We use our existing schemas to assimilate new experiences. But sometimes we need to accommodate (adjust) our schemas to include new experiences.

An impossible object
Look carefully at the "devil's tuning fork" below. Now look away—no, better first study it some more—and then look away and draw it.... Not so easy, is it? Because this tuning fork is an impossible object, you have no schema for such an image.

active thinkers, constantly trying to construct more advanced understandings of the world" (Siegler & Ellis, 1996). To this end, the maturing brain builds concepts, which Piaget called **schemas.** Schemas (or schemes) are pliable mental molds into which we pour our experience, *accommodating* (adjusting) the mold to include new experiences when necessary. By adulthood we have built countless schemas ranging from knowing how to tie a knot to a concept of love.

Piaget's Theory and Current Thinking

Cognition refers to all the mental activities associated with thinking, knowing, remembering, and communicating. Piaget described cognitive development in four stages—sensorimotor, preoperational, concrete operational, and formal operational (Table 7.1). He believed that children experience spurts of change followed by greater stability as they move from one developmental plateau to the next. Each plateau has distinctive characteristics that permit specific kinds of thinking. To appreciate how a child's mind grows, let's look at Piaget's stages in the light of our current thinking about cognitive development.

TABLE 7.1

PIAGET'S STAGES OF COGNITIVE DEVELOPMENT

Typical Age Range	Description of Stage	Developmental Phenomena
Birth to nearly 2 years	*Sensorimotor* Experiencing the world through senses and actions (looking, hearing, touching, mouthing, and grasping)	• Object performance • Stranger anxiety
About 2 to 6 years	*Preoperational* Representing things with words and images but lacking logical reasoning	• Pretend play • Egocentrism • Language development
About 7 to 11 years	*Concrete operational* Thinking logically about concrete events; grasping concrete analogies and performing arithmetical operations	• Conservation • Mathematical transformation
About 12 through adulthood	*Formal operational* Abstract reasoning	• Abstract logic • Potential for mature moral reasoning

Sensorimotor Stage

During Piaget's **sensorimotor stage,** from birth to nearly age 2, babies take in the world through their sensory and motor interactions with objects—through looking, hearing, touching, mouthing, and grasping.

Very young babies seem to live in the present: What is out of sight is out of mind. In one of his tests, Piaget would show an infant an appealing toy and then flop his beret over it to see whether the infant searched for the toy. Before the age of 6 months, the infant did not. Young infants lack **object permanence**—the awareness that objects continue to exist when not perceived. By 8 months, infants begin exhibiting memory for things no longer seen. If you hide a toy, the infant will momentarily look for it. Within another month or two, the infant will look for it even after being restrained for several seconds.

But do children's cognitive abilities really grow through distinct stages? Does object permanence in fact blossom by 8 months, much as tulips blossom in spring? Today's researchers see development as more continuous. For example, they now view object permanence as unfolding gradually, as when young infants look for a toy where they saw it hidden a second before.

- **schema** a concept or framework that organizes and interprets information.

- **cognition** all the mental activities associated with thinking, knowing, and remembering.

- **sensorimotor stage** in Piaget's theory, the stage (from birth to about 2 years of age) during which infants know the world mostly in terms of their sensory impressions and motor activities.

- **object permanence** the awareness that things continue to exist even when not perceived.

  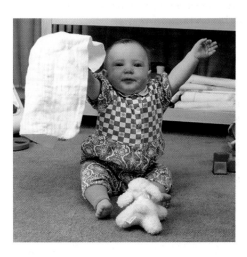

Object permanence
Infants younger than 6 months tend not to understand that things continue to exist when they are out of sight. But for this infant, out of sight is definitely not out of mind.

Consider some simple experiments on baby logic:

- Andrew Meltzoff and Richard Borton gave month-old babies one of two pacifiers to suck on without letting them see the objects **(FIGURE 7.2)**. When they were later shown both pacifiers, the infants *looked* mostly at the nipple they had *felt* in their mouth. Follow-up studies revealed the same amazing result with infants 12 hours old (Kaye & Bower, 1994).

- Like adults staring in disbelief at a magic trick, infants look longer at an unexpected scene of a car seeming to pass through a solid object, a ball stopping in midair, or an object violating object permanence by magically disappearing (Baillargeon, 1995, 1998; Wellman & Gelman, 1992). Babies seem to have a more intuitive grasp of simple laws of physics than Piaget realized.

- Babies also have a head for numbers. Karen Wynn (1992, 1998) showed 5-month-old infants one or two objects. Then she hid the objects behind a screen, sometimes removing or adding

FIGURE 7.2

Infants can think
After sucking on one of these two pacifiers, babies looked longer at the nipple they had felt in their mouth. (From Meltzoff & Borton, 1979.)

4. Possible outcome: Screen drops, revealing one object

FIGURE 7.3
Baby mathematics
Shown a numerically impossible outcome, infants stare longer. (From Wynn, 1992.)

1. Objects placed in case.   2. Screen comes up.   3. One object is removed.

4. Impossible outcome: Screen drops, revealing two objects.

one through a trap door **(FIGURE 7.3)**. When she lifted the screen, the infants sometimes did a double take, staring longer when shown a wrong number of objects. But were they just responding to a greater or smaller mass of objects, rather than a change in number? Later experiments showed that babies' number sense extends to such things as drumbeats and motions. If accustomed to a Daffy Duck puppet jumping three times on stage, they show surprise if it jumps only twice. Clearly, infants are smarter than Piaget appreciated.

> "It is a rare privilege to watch the birth, growth, and first feeble struggles of a living human mind."
>
> **Annie Sullivan, in Helen Keller's *The Story of My Life*, 1903**

Preoperational Stage

Piaget believed that during the preschool period and up to about age 6 or 7, children are in a **preoperational stage**—too young to perform mental operations. For a 5-year-old, the quantity of milk that is "too much" in a tall, narrow glass may become an acceptable amount if poured into a short, wide glass. This is because the child focuses only on the height dimension and is incapable of performing the *operation* of mentally pouring it back. A child lacks the concept of **conservation**—the principle that quantity remains the same despite changes in shape.

Piaget did not view the stage transitions as abrupt. Even so, symbolic thinking appears at an earlier age than he supposed. Judy DeLoache (1987) discovered this when she showed children a model of a room and hid a model toy in it (a miniature stuffed dog behind a miniature couch). The $2\frac{1}{2}$-year-olds easily remembered where to find the miniature toy, but they could not use the model to locate an actual stuffed

Piaget's test of conservation
This preoperational child does not yet understand the principle of conservation of substance. Closed beakers with identical volumes seem suddenly to hold different amounts after one is merely inverted.

dog behind a couch in a real room. Three-year-olds—only 6 months older—usually went right to the actual stuffed animal in the real room, showing that they *could* think of the model as a symbol for the room. Piaget probably would have been surprised.

Egocentrism Seen through the eyes of Piaget, preschool children are aware of themselves, of time, and of the permanence of objects. Yet they are **egocentric:** They cannot perceive things from another's point of view. They may think the Sun and Moon follow them around. Asked to "show Mommy your picture," 2-year-old Gabriella holds the picture up facing her own eyes. Three-year-old Rebecca hides under a table, assuming that if she can't see someone's eyes, they can't see her. Children's conversations also reveal their egocentrism, as one young boy demonstrated (Phillips, 1969, p. 61):

"Do you have a brother?"

"Yes."

"What's his name?"

"Jim."

"Does Jim have a brother?"

"No."

TV-watching preschoolers who block your view of the television assume that you see what they see. Preschoolers who ask you a question while you are on the phone assume that you hear no more than they hear. When relating to a young child, remember that such behaviors reflect a cognitive limitation: The egocentric preschoolers are not intentionally "selfish" or "inconsiderate." They simply have not developed the ability to take another's viewpoint. Parents who abuse their children generally have no understanding of these limits.

Theory of Mind Although still egocentric, preschoolers begin forming a **theory of mind.** Rather than thinking of people as breathing wind-up dolls, they come to realize that people have minds. When Little Red Riding Hood realizes her "grandmother" is really a wolf, she swiftly revises her ideas about the creature's intentions and races away.

As their ability to infer intentions and other mental states develops, children seek to understand what made a playmate angry, when a sibling will share, and what might make a parent buy a toy. The preschooler's growing ability to tease, empathize, and persuade stems from a growing ability to take another's perspective. Between 3 and 5, for example, children come to realize that others may hold false beliefs. Jennifer Jenkins and Janet Astington (1996) showed Toronto children a Band Aids (plasters) box and asked them what was inside. The children naturally expected Band Aids, and so were surprised to discover that the box actually contained pencils. Asked what a child who had never seen the box would think was inside, 3-year-olds typically answered "pencils." By age 4 to 5, the children's "theory of mind" had leapt forward, and they delighted in anticipating their friends' false belief that the box would hold Band Aids. Children with *autism,* a disorder characterized by deficient communication and social interaction, have difficulty understanding that another's state of mind differs from their own (Klein & Kihlstrom, 1998; Yirmiya & others, 1998).

Concrete Operational Stage

By the time children are about 6 or 7 years of age, said Piaget, they enter the **concrete operational stage.** Given concrete materials, they begin to grasp that change in shape does not mean change in quantity. They can mentally pour milk back and forth between glasses of different shapes. They enjoy jokes that allow them to use their new concepts, such as conservation:

> Mr. Jones went into a restaurant and ordered a whole pizza for his dinner. When the waiter asked if he wanted it cut into 6 or 8 pieces, Mr. Jones said, "Oh, you'd better make it 6, I could never eat 8 pieces!" (McGhee, 1976)

Question: If most 2½-year-olds do not understand how miniature dolls and toys can symbolize real objects, should anatomically correct dolls be used when questioning such children about alleged physical or sexual abuse? Judy DeLoache (1995) reports that "very young children do not find it natural or easy to use a doll as a representation of themselves."

■ **preoperational stage** in Piaget's theory, the stage (from about 2 to 6 or 7 years of age) during which a child learns to use language but does not yet comprehend the mental operations of concrete logic.

■ **conservation** the principle (which Piaget believed to be a part of concrete operational reasoning) that properties such as mass, volume, and number remain the same despite changes in the forms of objects.

■ **egocentrism** in Piaget's theory, the inability of the preoperational child to take another's point of view.

■ **theory of mind** people's ideas about their own and others' mental states—about their feelings, perceptions, and thoughts and the behavior these might predict.

■ **concrete operational stage** in Piaget's theory, the stage of cognitive development (from about 6 or 7 to 11 years of age) during which children gain the mental operations that enable them to think logically about concrete events.

■ **formal operational stage** in Piaget's theory, the stage of cognitive development (normally beginning about age 12) during which people begin to think logically about abstract concepts.

DENNIS THE MENACE

"Cut it up into a LOT of slices, Mom. I'm really hungry!"

During the concrete operational stage, said Piaget, children fully gain the mental ability to comprehend mathematical transformations and conservation. When my daughter Laura was 6, I was astonished at her inability to reverse arithmetic operations—until I considered Piaget's observation. Asked, "What is 8 plus 4?" she required 5 seconds to compute "12," and another 5 seconds to then compute 12 minus 4. By age 8, she could answer the second question instantly.

Formal Operational Stage

By age 12, our reasoning expands from the purely concrete (involving actual experience) to encompass abstract thinking (involving imagined realities and symbols). As children approach adolescence, said Piaget, many become capable of solving hypothetical propositions and deducing consequences: *If* this, *then* that. Systematic reasoning, what Piaget called **formal operational** thinking, is now within their grasp. Consider this simple problem:

> If John is in school, then Mary is in school. John is in school. What can you say about Mary?

Formal operational thinkers have no trouble answering correctly; nor do most 7-year-olds (Suppes, 1982). This illustrates, once again, why critics say the rudiments of Piaget's cognitive stages begin earlier than he realized.

Reflecting on Piaget's Theory

Piaget's stage theory is controversial. For some things, it gets high marks. Studies around the globe, from Australia to Algeria to North America, reveal that human cognition everywhere unfolds basically in the sequence he proposed (Segall & others, 1990). However, today's researchers see development as more continuous than did Piaget. By detecting the beginnings of each type of thinking at earlier ages, they have revealed conceptual abilities Piaget missed. Moreover, they see formal logic as a smaller part of cognition than he did.

"Assessing the impact of Piaget on developmental psychology is like assessing the impact of Shakespeare in English literature."

Developmental psychologist Harry Beilin (1992)

What remains of Piaget's ideas about the child's mind? Plenty—enough to merit his being singled out in 1999 by *Time* as one of that century's 20 most influential scientists and thinkers. Piaget identified significant cognitive milestones and stimulated worldwide interest in how the mind develops. His emphasis was less on the ages at which children typically reach specific milestones than on their sequence—a sequence that later research has shown is pretty much as he described (Lourenco & Machado, 1996). Piaget would not be surprised that today we are adapting his ideas to accommodate new findings—as part of our own cognitive development.

What are the implications of all this for parents and teachers? Piaget contended that children construct their understandings from their *interactions* with the world. This implies that children are not passive receptacles waiting to be filled with a teacher's knowledge. Teachers would do better to build on what children already know, engaging them in concrete demonstrations and stimulating them to think for themselves. Future parents and teachers, remember: Young children are incapable of adult logic. Realize that what is simple and obvious to you—that getting off a teeter-totter will cause their friend on the other end to crash—may be incomprehensible to a 3-year-old. And accept children's cognitive immaturity as adaptive—as nature's strategy for keeping children close to protective adults and providing time for learning and socialization (Bjorklund & Green, 1992).

■ **stranger anxiety** the fear of strangers that infants commonly display, beginning by about 8 months of age.

rehearse it!

1. The orderly sequence of biological growth is called maturation. Maturation explains why
   a. children differ greatly in temperament.
   b. most children have begun walking by about 12 months.
   c. enriching experiences may affect brain tissue.
   d. differences between the sexes are minimal.

2. Most of us remember nothing before our third birthday because
   a. we are not born with enough brain cells to form memories.
   b. we were not given the extra "handling" and environmental stimulation we needed.
   c. the connections between our brain cells had not yet become complex enough to form permanent memories.
   d. we do not enter the memory stage until our third year.

3. As the infant's muscles and nervous system mature, more complicated skills emerge. Which of the following is true of motor-skill development?
   a. It is determined solely by genetic factors.
   b. The sequence, but not the timing, is universal.
   c. Maturation has a limited effect if the environment is not right.
   d. Environment creates a readiness to learn.

4. According to Piaget, the preoperational stage extends from about age 2 to 6. During this period the young child's thinking is
   a. abstract.
   b. negative.
   c. conservative.
   d. egocentric.

5. The principle of conservation explains why a pint of milk remains a pint, whether poured into a tall thin glass or a round goblet. Children acquire the mental operations necessary to understand conservation during
   a. infancy.
   b. the sensorimotor stage.
   c. the preoperational stage.
   d. the concrete operational stage.

6. Piaget's stage theory continues to inform our understanding of cognitive development in childhood. However, many researchers believe that
   a. Piaget's "stages" begin earlier and development is more continuous than Piaget realized.
   b. children do not progress as rapidly as Piaget predicted.
   c. few children really progress to the concrete operational stage.
   d. there is no way of testing much of Piaget's theoretical work.

Social Development

PREVIEW QUESTION 3 How do the bonds of attachment form between parents and infants?

From birth, babies are social creatures. In all cultures, infants develop an intense bond with those who care for them. Beginning with a newborn's attraction to humans in general, infants soon come to prefer familiar faces and voices, then to coo and gurgle when given their mother's or father's attention. Soon after object permanence emerges and children become mobile enough to crawl into danger, a curious thing happens: They develop a fear of strangers, called **stranger anxiety.** Beginning at about 8 months, they tend to greet strangers by crying and reaching for their familiar caregivers. "No! Don't leave me!" their distress seems to say. At about this age, children have schemas for familiar faces; when they cannot assimilate the new face into these remembered schemas, they become distressed (Kagan, 1984). This illustrates an important principle: The brain, mind, and social-emotional behavior develop together.

Stranger anxiety
A newly emerging ability to evaluate people as unfamiliar and possibly threatening helps protect babies 8 months and older.

FIGURE 7.4

Harlow's mothers

Psychologist Harry Harlow reared monkeys with two artificial mothers—one a bare wire cylinder with a wooden head and an attached feeding bottle, the other a cylinder with no bottle but covered with foam rubber and wrapped with terry cloth. Harlow's discovery surprised many psychologists: The monkeys much preferred contact with the comfortable cloth mother, even while feeding from the nourishing mother.

Lee Kirkpatrick (1999) reports that for some people a perceived relationship with God functions as do other attachments—by providing a secure base for exploration and a safe haven when threatened.

At 12 months, many infants cling tightly to a parent when they are frightened or expect separation. Reunited after being separated, they shower the parent with smiles and hugs. No social behavior is more striking than this intense and mutual infant-parent bond. Called **attachment,** it is a powerful survival impulse that keeps infants close to their caregivers.

Origins of Attachment

A number of elements work to create the parent-infant bond. Infants become attached to those—typically their parents—who are comfortable, familiar, and responsive to their needs.

Body Contact

For many years, developmental psychologists reasoned that infants became attached to those who satisfied their need for nourishment. It only made sense. But an accidental finding revealed that this explanation is actually incomplete. During the 1950s, University of Wisconsin psychologist Harry Harlow bred monkeys for his learning studies. To equalize the infant monkeys' experiences and to prevent the spread of disease, he separated the monkeys from their mothers shortly after birth and raised them in sanitary individual cages, which included a cheesecloth baby blanket (Harlow & others, 1971). Surprisingly, the infants became intensely attached to their blankets: When the blankets were taken to be laundered, the monkeys became distressed.

Harlow soon recognized that this attachment to the blanket contradicted the idea that attachment derives from an association with nourishment. But how could he show this more convincingly? To pit the drawing power of a food source against the contact comfort of the blanket, Harlow created two artificial mothers. One was a bare wire cylinder with a wooden head, the other a cylinder wrapped with terry cloth. By attaching a bottle he could associate either with nourishment.

When reared with both a nourishing wire mother and a nonnourishing cloth mother, the monkeys overwhelmingly preferred the cloth mother **(FIGURE 7.4).** Like human infants clinging to their mothers, the monkeys would cling to their cloth mothers when anxious. They also used her as a secure base from which to venture into the environment, as if attached to the mother by an invisible elastic band that stretched so far and then pulled the infant back. Further studies revealed other qualities—rocking, warmth, and feeding—that made the cloth mother even more appealing.

Human infants, too, become attached to parents who are soft and warm and who rock, feed, and pat. And human attachment also consists of one person providing another with a *safe haven* when distressed and a *secure base* from which to explore the world. As we mature, our safe haven and secure base shift—from parents to peers and partners (Cassidy & Shaver, 1999). But at all ages we are social creatures. We gain strength when someone says to us, by words and actions, "I am here. I will be here. I am interested in what you do and what you think and feel. I will actively support you" (Crowell & Waters, 1994). We are "happiest and able to deploy [our] talents to best advantage," said attachment researcher John Bowlby (1979), when we know that one or more trusted friends will stand behind us, come what may.

Familiarity

Contact is one key to attachment. Another is familiarity. We know that nature opens windows of opportunity for wiring the brain for vision and language, then slams them shut. In many animals, attachments based on familiarity likewise form during a sensitive **critical period**—an optimal period shortly after birth when certain events must take place to facilitate proper development (Bornstein, 1989). The first moving object a gosling, duckling, or chick sees during the hours shortly after hatching is normally its mother. From then on, the young fowl follows her, and her alone.

This rigid attachment process, called **imprinting,** was explored by Konrad Lorenz (1937). He wondered: What would ducklings do if *he* was the first moving creature they observed? What they did was follow him around: Everywhere that Konrad went, the ducks were sure to go. Further tests revealed that although baby birds imprint best to their own species, they also will imprint to a variety of moving objects—an animal of another species, a box on wheels, a bouncing ball (Colombo, 1982; Johnson, 1992). And, once formed, this attachment is difficult to reverse.

Children do not imprint, but they do become attached to what they've known. Thus, they like to reread the same books, watch the same movies over again, reenact family traditions. They prefer to eat familiar foods, live in the same familiar neighborhood, attend school with the same old friends. Familiarity breeds content.

Responsive Parenting

In studies the world over, some babies seem more disposed to forming a secure attachment. Placed in a strange situation (usually a laboratory playroom), about 60 percent of infants display *secure attachment*. In their mother's presence they play comfortably, happily exploring their new environment. When she leaves, they are distressed; when she returns, they seek contact with her. Other infants show *insecure attachment*. They are less likely to explore their surroundings; they may even cling to their mother. When she leaves, they either cry loudly and remain upset or seem indifferent to their mother's going and returning (Ainsworth, 1973, 1989; Kagan, 1995; van IJzendoorn & Kroonenberg, 1988). What accounts for these differences?

One possible explanation is the mother's behavior. Female rats reared by relaxed, attentive adoptive mothers become more relaxed and attentive to their offspring than do those reared by stress-prone, inattentive adoptive mothers (Francis & others, 1999). Do human infants likewise pick up their mothers' tendencies?

Mary Ainsworth (1979) studied attachment differences by observing mother-infant pairs at home during their first six months. Later she observed the 1-year-old infants in a "strange situation" without their mothers—a strange little mini-drama that she and others came to believe gives insight into the child's emotional health and future relationships. Sensitive, responsive mothers—those who noticed what their babies were doing and responded appropriately—had infants who usually became securely attached. Insensitive, unresponsive mothers—mothers who attended to their babies when they felt like doing so but ignored them at other times—had infants who often became insecurely attached. Harlow's monkey studies, in which the artificial structures were certainly the ultimate unresponsive mothers, produced even more striking effects. When put in strange situations without their artificial mothers, the deprived infants were terrified **(FIGURE 7.5).**

Follow-up studies have confirmed that sensitive mothers—and fathers—tend to have securely attached infants (De Wolff & van IJzendoorn, 1997). But is attachment style the result of parenting or of genetically influenced temperament? By neglecting heredity, these studies are like "comparing foxhounds reared in kennels with poodles reared in apartments," chides Judith Harris (1998). So, to separate nature and nurture, Dutch researcher Dymphna van den Boom (1990) varied parenting while controlling temperament. (Pause and think: If you were the researcher, how might you have done this?)

Van den Boom's solution was to randomly assign one hundred 6- to 9-month-old temperamentally difficult infants to either an experimental condition, in which mothers received

- **attachment** an emotional tie with another person; shown in young children by their seeking closeness to the caregiver and showing distress on separation.

- **critical period** an optimal period shortly after birth when an organism's exposure to certain stimuli or experiences produces proper development.

- **imprinting** the process by which certain animals form attachments during a critical period very early in life.

FIGURE 7.5

Social deprivation and fear

Monkeys raised by artificial mothers were terror-stricken when placed in strange situations without their surrogate mothers. (Today's climate of greater respect for animal welfare prevents such primate studies.)

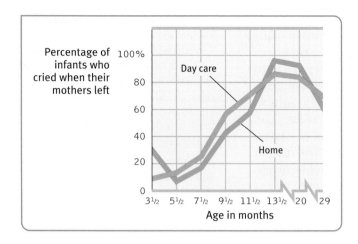

FIGURE 7.6

Infants' distress over separation from parents

In an experiment, groups of infants were left by their mothers in an unfamiliar room. In both groups, the percentage who cried when the mother left peaked at about 13 months. (From Kagan, 1976.) Whether the infant had experienced day care made little difference.

personal training in sensitive responding, or to an untreated control condition in which they did not. At age 1, 68 percent of the experimental-condition infants were rated securely attached; of the control-condition infants, only 28 percent were.

As these examples indicate, researchers have more often studied mother care than father care. Infants who lack a caring mother are said to suffer "maternal deprivation"; those lacking the care of a father are said merely to experience "father absence." "Fathering a child" has meant impregnating; "mothering" has meant nurturing. But evidence increasingly indicates that fathers are more than just mobile sperm banks. "Father absence"—resulting from nonmarital childbearing, separation, and divorce—puts children at increased risk for various psychological and social pathologies. This is true even after we control for income and educational differences between father-present and father-absent families (Myers, 2000).

Whether children are raised entirely at home or also in a day-care center, whether they live in North America, Guatemala, or the Kalahari Desert, anxiety over separation from parents peaks at around 13 months, then gradually declines **(FIGURE 7.6)**. Does this mean our need for and love of others also fades away? Hardly. Yet much of the life cycle story boils down to a poignant rhythm of attachment and separation—from the attachment of fetal life to the separation of birth, from infant attachment to adolescent separation, from the attachments of marriage and parenthood to the separation of death.

Effects of Attachment

PREVIEW QUESTION 4 What are the long-term effects of attachment bonds?

Does a trusting, secure attachment have lasting benefits? And what are the long-term effects when attachment bonds are absent or severed?

Secure Attachment Predicts Social Competence

At the University of Minnesota, Alan Sroufe and his colleagues (1983) identified infants who were securely attached at 12 to 18 months of age. Sroufe restudied these infants as 2- to 3-year-olds, and saw them functioning more confidently than other toddlers. Given challenging tasks, they were more enthusiastic and persistent. With other children they were more outgoing and responsive.

Developmental theorist Erik Erikson (1902–1994), in collaboration with his wife, Joan Erikson, said that securely attached children approach life with a sense of **basic trust**—a sense that the world is predictable and reliable. Erikson attributed basic trust not to one's continuing positive environment or inborn temperament, but to early parenting. He theorized that infants blessed with sensitive, loving caregivers form a lifelong attitude of trust rather than fear. Erikson would not have been surprised that as adults, our styles of romantic love exhibit either secure, trusting attachment; insecure, anxious attachment; or the avoidance of attachment (Feeney & Noller, 1990; Shaver & Hazan, 1993; Simpson & others, 1992). Although debate continues, many researchers now believe that our early attachment experiences lay the foundation for our adult relationships.

Deprivation of Attachment

If secure attachment nurtures social competence, what happens when circumstances prevent a child's forming attachments? In all of psychology, there's no sadder research literature. Babies reared in institutions without the stimulation and attention of a regular caregiver, or locked away at home under conditions of abuse or extreme neglect, are often withdrawn, frightened, even speechless. Those abandoned in Romanian or-

"Out of the conflict between trust and mistrust, the infant develops hope, which is the earliest form of what gradually becomes faith in adults."

Erik Erikson, 1983

phanages during the 1980s looked "frighteningly like Harlow's monkeys" (Carlson, 1995). If institutionalized more than 8 months, they often bore lasting scars (Chisholm, 1998; Malinosky-Rummell & Hansen, 1993; Rutter & others, 1998).

Harlow's monkeys similarly bore scars if reared in total isolation, without even an artificial mother. As adults, when placed with other monkeys their age, they either cowered in fright or lashed out in aggression. When they reached sexual maturity, most were incapable of mating. If artificially impregnated, females often were neglectful, abusive, even murderous toward their first-born. Similarly, some monkey mothers neglect or abuse their infants in the wild (Maestripieri & Carroll, 1998).

In humans, too, the unloved often become the unloving. Most abusive parents report having been neglected or battered as children (Kempe & Kempe, 1978). Many condemned murderers report the same. One study of 14 young men awaiting execution for juvenile crimes found that all but two had histories of brutal physical abuse (Lewis & others, 1988).

But does this mean that today's victim is predictably tomorrow's victimizer? The answer is no. Though most abusers were indeed abused, most abused children do *not* later become violent criminals or abusive parents. Even after years of banishment to a speechless attic environment, some children have matured—after adoption into loving homes—into normal adults with careers and families (Clarke & Clarke, 1998). But many children are not so dramatically resilient, especially those who experience no sharp break from their abusive past. Some 30 percent of those abused do abuse their children—a rate four times higher than the national rate of child abuse (Kaufman & Zigler, 1987; Widom, 1989a,b). Moreover, young children terrorized through sexual abuse, physical abuse, or wartime atrocities (being beaten, witnessing torture, and living in constant fear) may suffer other lasting wounds—often nightmares, depression, and a troubled adolescence involving substance abuse, binge eating, or aggression (Kendall-Tackett & others, 1993; Polusny & Follette, 1995; Trickett & McBride-Chang, 1995).

Such experiences can leave footprints on the brain. When normally placid golden hamsters are repeatedly threatened and attacked while young, the effects linger into their adult lives. They grow up to be cowards when caged with same-sized hamsters or bullies when caged with weaker ones (Ferris, 1996). Such animals show changes in such brain chemicals as serotonin, which calms aggressive impulses. A similarly sluggish serotonin response has been found in abused children who become aggressive teens and adults.

Child-Rearing Practices

Parenting styles vary. Some parents spank, some reason. Some are strict, some are lax. Some show little affection, some liberally hug and kiss. Do such differences affect children?

The most heavily researched aspect of parenting has been how, and to what extent, parents seek to control their children. Several investigators have identified three parenting styles:

1. *Authoritarian* parents impose rules and expect obedience: "Don't interrupt." "Do keep your room clean." "Don't stay out late or you'll be grounded." "Why? Because I said so."
2. *Permissive* parents submit to their children's desires, make few demands, and use little punishment.
3. *Authoritative* parents are both demanding and responsive. They exert control not only by setting rules and enforcing them but also by explaining the reasons and, especially with older children, encouraging open discussion and allowing exceptions when making the rules.

Too hard, too soft, and just right, these styles have been called. For studies by Stanley Coopersmith (1967), Diana Baumrind (1996), and John Buri and others

■ **basic trust** according to Erik Erikson, a sense that the world is predictable and trustworthy; said to be formed during infancy by appropriate experiences with responsive caregivers.

"What is learned in the cradle, lasts to the grave."

French proverb

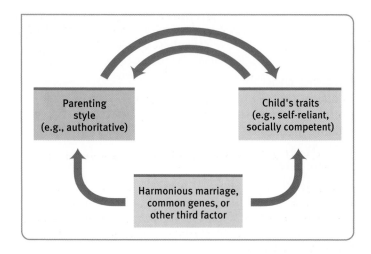

FIGURE 7.7

The correlation between authoritative parenting and social competence in children

Three possible explanations are (1) parenting may influence children's competence; (2) children's social competence may influence parenting; or (3) both may be influenced by an underlying third factor.

(1988) reveal that children with the highest self-esteem, self-reliance, and social competence usually have warm, concerned, *authoritative* parents. Although the participants in most studies have been middle-class white families, studies with families of other races and in more than 200 cultures worldwide confirm the social and academic benefits of loving and authoritative parenting (Baumrind, 1991; Rohner, 1994).

Of the three parenting styles, authoritative parenting provides children with the greatest sense of control. Authoritative parents openly discuss family rules by explaining them to younger children and reasoning about them with older children. When they feel that rules are more negotiated than imposed, older children feel more self-control (Baumrind, 1983; Lewis, 1981). And when parents enforce rules with consistent, predictable consequences, children feel they control the outcome.

But wait. Before jumping to conclusions about the results of different parenting styles, heed this caution: *Correlation is not causation.* The association between certain parenting styles (being firm but open) and certain childhood outcomes (social competence) is correlational. There are other possible explanations **(FIGURE 7.7)**. Perhaps children's traits influence parenting more than vice versa. Parental warmth and control vary somewhat from child to child even in the same family (Holden & Miller, 1999). So perhaps socially mature, agreeable, easygoing children *elicit* greater trust and warmth from their parents, and less competent and less cooperative children elicit less. This possibility is supported by twin studies (Kendler, 1996). Or there may be some underlying third factor. Perhaps, for example, competent parents and their competent children share genes that predispose social competence.

Parents struggling with conflicting advice and with the stresses of child-rearing should remember that *all advice reflects the advice-giver's values.* For those who prize unquestioning obedience from a child, an authoritarian style may have the desired effect. For those who value children's sociability and self-reliance, authoritative firm-but-open parenting is advisable.

The investment in raising a child buys many years not only of joy and love but of worry and irritation. Yet for most parents, a child is one's biological and social legacy—one's personal investment in the human future. To paraphrase psychiatrist Carl Jung, we reach backward into our parents and forward into our children, and through their children into a future we will never see, but about which we must therefore care.

rehearse it!

7. After about 8 months of age, infants develop schemas for familiar objects. Faced with a new baby-sitter, they will show distress, a behavior referred to as
   a. conservation.
   b. stranger anxiety.
   c. imprinting.
   d. maturation.

8. Body contact facilitates attachment between infant and parent. In a series of experiments, Harry Harlow found that monkeys raised with artifi-

cial mothers tended when afraid to cling to
   a. the wire mother.
   b. the cloth mother.
   c. whichever mother held the feeding bottle.
   d. none of the artificial mothers.

9. From the very first weeks of life, infants differ in their characteristic emotional reactions, with some infants being intense and anxious, while others are easygoing and relaxed. These differences are usually explained as differences in

   a. attachment.
   b. imprinting.
   c. temperament.
   d. parental responsiveness.

10. Children who in infancy formed secure attachments to their parents
    a. are likely to become good parents.
    b. prefer the company of adults to that of their peers.
    c. usually become socially competent youngsters.
    d. have less stranger anxiety.

Infancy and Childhood

1. How do the brain and motor skills develop during infancy and childhood?

Within the brain, nerve cells form before birth and, sculpted by experience, their interconnections continue to multiply after birth. The lack of neural connections in our earliest years helps explain why we lose conscious memories of our experiences from those years. Infants' more complex physical skills—sitting, standing, walking—develop in a predictable sequence whose actual timing is a function of individual maturation rate.

2. How did Piaget view the development of a child's mind, and what are current researchers' views?

Jean Piaget's observations of children convinced him—and almost everyone else—that the mind of a child is not that of a miniature adult. Piaget theorized that the mind develops by forming schemas that help us organize and interpret our experiences. In this way, children progress from the sensorimotor simplicity of the first two years to more complex stages of thinking.

Piaget believed that preschool children, in the preoperational stage, are egocentric and unable to perform simple logical operations. At about age 6 or 7 they enter the concrete operational stage and can perform concrete operations, such as those required to comprehend the principle of conservation. And by about age 12, children enter the formal operational stage, in which systematic reasoning is within their grasp.

Recent research supports the sequence Piaget proposed for the unfolding of human cognition, but it also shows that young children are more capable, and their development more continuous, than he believed. The cognitive abilities that emerge at each stage apparently begin developing in a rudimentary form in the previous stage.

3. How do the bonds of attachment form between parents and infants?

Infants become attached to their mothers and fathers not simply because mothers and fathers gratify biological needs but, more important, because they are comfortable, familiar, and responsive. In many animals, this attachment process, called imprinting, occurs during a critical period.

If denied responsive care, or if abused, both monkey and human infants may become pathetically withdrawn, anxious, and eventually abusive. Once an attachment forms, infants who are separated from their caregivers will, for a time, display stranger anxiety. Infants' differing attachment styles reflect both their individual temperament and the responsiveness of their parents and child-care providers.

4. What are the long-term effects of attachment bonds?

Attachment style in infancy predicts later social development. Human infants who display secure attachment to their mothers—and thus develop a sense of basic trust—generally become socially competent preschoolers. Parenting styles—permissive, authoritative, and authoritarian—reflect varying degrees of control. Children with the highest self-esteem, self-reliance, and social competence tend to have been reared by authoritative parents.

TERMS AND CONCEPTS TO REMEMBER

maturation, p. 104	object permanence, p. 107	theory of mind, p. 109	attachment, p. 112
schema, p. 106	preoperational stage, p. 108	concrete operational stage, p. 109	critical period, p. 112
cognition, p. 106	conservation, p. 108	formal operational stage, p. 110	imprinting, p. 113
sensorimotor stage, p. 107	egocentrism, p. 109	stranger anxiety, p. 111	basic trust, p. 114

REHEARSE IT ANSWER KEY

1. b	2. c	3. b	4. d	5. d	6. a	7. b	8. b	9. c	10. c

8 Adolescence

- **Physical Development**
- **Cognitive Development**
- **Social Development**

Tweens: Eleven going on fifteen
Sexual maturity and interests emerge at younger ages than a half-century ago, as reflected in preteens' toys, music, and clothes. "The 12- to 14-year-olds of yesterday are the 10 to 12's of today," says Bruce Friend (1998), Nickelodeon vice-president.

How will you look back on your life 10 years from now? Are you making choices that someday you will recollect with satisfaction? In one survey, adults' most common regret was not having taken their education more seriously (Kinnier & Metha, 1989).

- **developmental psychology** a branch of psychology that studies physical, cognitive, and social changes throughout the life span.

- **adolescence** the transition period from childhood to adulthood, extending from puberty to independence.

- **puberty** the period of sexual maturation, during which a person becomes capable of reproducing.

- **primary sex characteristics** the body structures (ovaries, testes, and external genitalia) that make sexual reproduction possible.

- **secondary sex characteristics** nonreproductive sexual characteristics, such as female breasts and hips, male voice quality, and body hair.

mong **developmental psychologists,** those who study physical, mental, and social changes occurring throughout the human life span, the view that childhood fixes our traits has given way to an awareness that as long as we live, we develop. At a five-year high school reunion, former soul mates may be surprised at the divergence of their paths; a decade later, they may have trouble keeping a conversation going.

As today's life-span perspective emerged, psychologists began to look at how maturation and experience shape us not only in infancy and childhood but also in adolescence and beyond. **Adolescence** is life between childhood and adulthood. It starts with the physical beginnings of sexual maturity and ends with the social achievement of independent adult status. In the Western world, this period now roughly corresponds to the teen years, but at earlier times—and in some developing countries today—adolescence was a brief interlude between the dependence of childhood and the responsibilities of adulthood (Baumeister & Tice, 1986). Shortly after sexual maturity, adult responsibilities and status were bestowed, often marked by an elaborate initiation. The new adult then worked, married, and had children.

Then, with improved nutrition, sexual maturity began to occur earlier in many countries. Both physically and socially, kids have been getting older younger. And influenced by compulsory schooling, adult independence began occurring later. As a result, the once brief interlude between biological maturity and social independence has widened **(FIGURE 8.1).** That gap—the years spent morphing from child to adult—is adolescence.

To G. Stanley Hall (1904), one of the first psychologists to describe adolescence, the tension between biological maturity and social dependence created a period of "storm and stress." Indeed, after age 30, many who grow up in independence-fostering Western cultures look back on their teenage years as a time they would not want to relive, a time when their peers' social approval was imperative, their sense of direction in life was in flux, and their feeling of alienation from their parents was deepest (Arnett, 1999; Macfarlane, 1964). Humorist Dave Barry (1996) is one such person:

> When my dad pulled up, wearing his poodle hat and driving his Nash Metropolitan—a comically tiny vehicle resembling those cars outside supermarkets that go up and down when you put in a quarter, except the Metropolitan looked sillier and had a smaller motor—I was mortified. I might as well have been getting picked up by a flying saucer piloted by some bizarre multi-tentacled stalk-eyed slobber-mouthed alien being that had somehow got hold of a Russian hat. I was horrified at what my peers might think of my dad; it never occurred to me that my peers didn't even notice my dad, because they were too busy being mortified by THEIR parents.

> Of course eventually my father stopped being a hideous embarrassment to me, and I, grasping the Torch of Dorkhood, became a hideous embarrassment to my son.

FIGURE 8.1

Adolescence is being stretched from both ends

In the 1890s the average interval between a woman's first menstrual period and marriage was about 7 years; today in industrialized countries it is nearly 12 years (Guttmacher, 2000).

Embarrassment is just one of the many adolescent moods. Despite the mood swings, adolescence can also be a time of vitality without the cares of adulthood, a time of rewarding friendships, of heightened idealism and a growing sense of life's exciting possibilities (Coleman, 1980). Nine of 10 high school seniors agree with the statement, "On the whole, I'm satisfied with myself" (*Public Opinion*, 1987).

Physical Development

PREVIEW QUESTION 1 What major physical changes occur during adolescence?

Adolescence begins with **puberty,** the time when one is maturing sexually. Puberty follows a surge of hormones, which may intensify moods and which trigger a two-year period of rapid physical development, usually beginning at about age 11 in girls and at about age 13 in boys. About the time of puberty, boys' growth propels them to greater height than their female counterparts **(FIGURE 8.2).** During this growth spurt, the **primary sex characteristics**—the reproductive organs and external genitalia—develop dramatically. So do **secondary sex characteristics,** the nonreproductive traits such as breasts and hips in girls, facial hair and deepened voice in boys, pubic and underarm hair in both sexes **(FIGURE 8.3,** on pg 120). A year or two before puberty, however, boys and girls often feel the first stirrings of attraction toward those of the other (or their own) sex (McClintock & Herdt, 1996).

In girls, puberty starts with breast development, which now often begins by age 10 (Brody, 1999). But puberty's landmarks are the first ejaculation in boys,

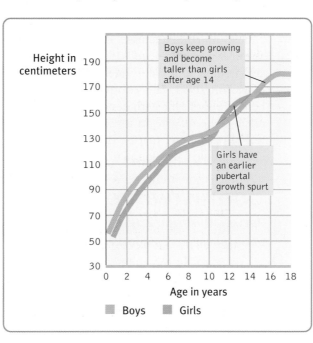

Height in centimeters

Boys keep growing and become taller than girls after age 14

Girls have an earlier pubertal growth spurt

Age in years

■ Boys   ■ Girls

FIGURE 8.2

Height differences

Throughout childhood, boys and girls are similar in height. At puberty, girls surge ahead briefly, but then boys overtake them at about age 14. (Data from Tanner, 1978.)

FIGURE 8.3

Body changes at puberty

At about age 10 or 11 in girls and age 13 in boys, a surge of hormones triggers a variety of physical changes. The pituitary gland, which controls the other hormone-secreting glands, is located in the base of the brain.

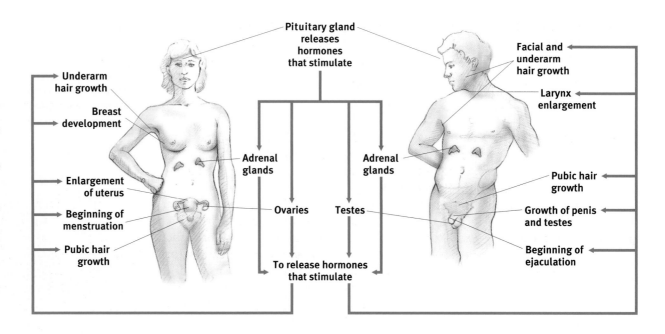

usually by about age 14, and the first menstrual period in girls, by about age 13. The first menstrual period, called **menarche** (meh-NAR-key), is usually a memorable event. Nearly all adult women recall it and remember experiencing a mixture of feelings—pride, excitement, embarrassment, and apprehension (Greif & Ulman, 1982; Woods & others, 1983). For the first few months many keep it a secret from friends. While most discuss it with their mothers, very few discuss it with their fathers (Brooks-Gunn, 1989). Girls who have been prepared for menarche usually experience it as a positive life transition. Afterward, regardless of their age, girls increasingly see and present themselves as different from boys and function more independently of their parents (Golub, 1983). Most men similarly recall their first ejaculation, which usually occurs as a nocturnal emission (Fuller & Downs, 1990).

Just as in the earlier life stages, the *sequence* of physical changes in puberty (for example, breast buds and visible pubic hair before menarche) is far more predictable than their *timing*. Some girls start their growth spurt at 9, some boys as late as age 16. Though such variations have little effect on height at maturity, they may have psychological consequences. Early maturation pays dividends for boys. Boys, being stronger and more athletic during their early teen years, tend to be more popular, self-assured, and independent. But for girls, early maturation can be stressful (Caspi & Moffitt, 1991; Ellis & others, 1999; Stattin & Magnusson, 1990). If a young girl's body is out of sync with her emotional maturity and with what her friends are experiencing, she may begin associating with older adolescents or may suffer teasing. It's not only when we mature that counts, but how people react to our genetically influenced physical development. Remember: *Heredity and environment interact.*

Cognitive Development

PREVIEW QUESTION 2 How did Piaget and Kohlberg describe cognitive and moral development during adolescence?

Adolescents' developing ability to reason gives them a new level of social awareness and moral judgment. As young teenagers become capable of thinking about their thinking, and of thinking about other people's thinking, they begin imagining what other people are thinking about *them*. (Adolescents might worry less about what oth-

■ **menarche [meh-NAR-key]** the first menstrual period.

ers think of them if they knew how similarly self-preoccupied their peers are.) As their cognitive abilities mature, many adolescents start to think about what is ideally possible, and they begin to criticize their society, their parents, and even their own shortcomings.

Developing Reasoning Power

During the early teen years, reasoning is often self-focused. Adolescents may think their private experiences are unique. They may assume their parents just can't understand what it feels like to be dating or to hate school: "But, Mother, *you* don't really know how it feels to be in love" (Elkind, 1978).

Gradually, though, most achieve the intellectual summit that developmental psychologist Jean Piaget (Pee-ah-ZHAY), in his theory of the stages of cognitive development, called *formal operations*. Preadolescents reason concretely, but adolescents become more capable of abstract logic: *If* this, *then* that. We can see this new abstract reasoning power as adolescents ponder and debate human nature, good and evil, truth and justice. Having perhaps envisioned God as an old man in the clouds when they were first capable of symbolic thinking in early childhood, they may now seek a deeper conception of God and existence (Elkind, 1970; Worthington, 1989). Adolescents' ability to reason hypothetically and deduce consequences also enables them to detect inconsistencies in others' reasoning and to spot hypocrisy. This can lead to heated debates with parents and silent vows never to lose sight of their own ideals (Peterson & others, 1986).

Developing Morality

A crucial task of childhood and adolescence is discerning right from wrong and developing character—the psychological muscles for controlling impulses. To be a moral person is to *think* morally and *act* accordingly. But as the German poet Goethe noted, "To put one's thoughts into action [is] the most difficult thing in the world."

Piaget (1932) believed that children's moral judgments build on their cognitive development. Agreeing with Piaget, Lawrence Kohlberg (1981, 1984) sought to describe the development of *moral reasoning,* the thinking that occurs as we consider right and wrong. Kohlberg posed moral dilemmas to children, adolescents, and adults, then analyzed their answers for evidence of stages of moral thinking. Consider his best-known dilemma:

> In Europe, a woman was near death from a very bad disease, a special kind of cancer. There was one drug that the doctors thought might save her. It was a form of radium that a druggist in the same town had recently discovered. The

"When the pilot told us to brace and grab our ankles, the first thing that went through my mind was that we must all look pretty stupid."

Jeremiah Rawlings, age 12, after a 1989 DC-10 crash in Sioux City, Iowa

© The New Yorker Collection 1992 Edward Koren from cartoonbank.com. All Rights Reserved.

"Ben is in his first year of high school, and he's questioning all the right things."

"It is a delightful harmony when doing and saying go together."

Michel de Montaigne (1533–1592)

Demonstrating their reasoning ability
Although on opposite sides of the abortion debate, these teens demonstrate their newfound ability to think logically about abstract topics. According to Piaget, they are in the final cognitive stage, formal operations.

drug was expensive to make, but the druggist was charging 10 times what the drug cost him to make. He paid $200 for the radium and charged $2000 for a small dose of the drug. The sick woman's husband, Heinz, went to everyone he knew to borrow the money, but he could get together only about $1000, which was half of what it cost. He told the druggist that his wife was dying and asked him to sell it cheaper or let him pay later. But the druggist said, "No, I discovered the drug and I'm going to make money from it." Heinz got desperate and broke into the man's store to steal the drug for his wife.

What do you think: Should Heinz have stolen the drug? Why was what he did right or wrong? Kohlberg would have been most interested in your reasoning, not your answer.

Kohlberg argued that as we develop intellectually we pass through as many as six stages of moral thinking, moving from the simplistic and concrete toward the more abstract and principled. He clustered these six stages into three basic levels: preconventional, conventional, and postconventional.

■ **Preconventional morality** Before age 9, most children have a preconventional morality of self-interest: They obey either to avoid punishment ("If you let your wife die, you will get in trouble") or to gain concrete rewards ("If you save your wife, you will be a hero").

■ **Conventional morality** By early adolescence, morality usually evolves to a more conventional level that cares for others and upholds laws and social rules simply because they are the laws and rules. Being able to take others' perspectives, adolescents may approve actions that will gain social approval or that will help maintain the social order ("If you steal the drug, everyone will think you are a criminal").

■ **Postconventional morality** Some of those who develop the abstract reasoning of formal operational thought may come to a third level. Postconventional morality affirms people's agreed-upon rights ("People have a right to live") or follows what one personally perceives as basic ethical principles ("If you steal the drug, you won't have lived up to your own ideals").

Kohlberg's claim was that these levels form a moral ladder, from the bottom rung of a young child's immature, preconventional morality, to the top rung of an adult's self-defined ethical principles, which only some attain. As with all stage theories, the sequence is unvarying. We begin on the bottom rung and ascend to varying heights.

Research confirms that children in various cultures progress from the level Kohlberg called preconventional into the stages of his conventional level (Edwards, 1981, 1982; Snarey, 1985, 1987). And as our *thinking* matures, our *behavior* also becomes less selfish and more caring (Krebs & Van Hesteren, 1994; Miller & others, 1996). However, the postconventional level is more controversial. It appears mostly in the European and North American educated middle class, which prizes *individualism*—giving priority to one's own goals rather than to group goals (Eckensberger, 1994; Miller & Bersoff, 1995). Critics therefore contend that the theory is biased against the moral reasoning of those in communal societies such as China and India—and also against Western women, whose morality may be based less on abstract, impersonal principles and more on caring relationships.

We can stimulate children's moral reasoning through discussions of moral issues and their implications. But sometimes talk is cheap. Morality is also *doing* the right thing. Thus, today's character education programs also teach children *empathy* for others' feelings. They teach them the self-discipline needed to restrain their impulses—to delay small gratifications now for the sake of bigger gratifications later. (Those who do learn to *delay gratification* become more socially responsible, academ-

"This might not be ethical. Is that a problem for anybody?"

"I am a bit suspicious of any theory that says that the highest moral stage is one in which people talk like college professors."

James Q. Wilson, *The Moral Sense*, 1993

ically successful, and productive [Funder & Block, 1989; Mischel & others, 1988, 1989].) And they engage students in responsible action through "service learning." When teens tutor, clean up their neighborhoods, and assist the elderly, their sense of competence and desire to serve increases and their school absenteeism and dropout rates diminish (Andersen, 1998).

Social Development

PREVIEW QUESTION 3 What tasks and challenges do adolescents face en route to mature adulthood, and are they the same for males and females?

Theorist Erik Erikson (1963) contended that each stage of life has its own "psychosocial" task, a crisis that needs resolution. Young children wrestle with issues of *trust,* then *autonomy* (independence), then *initiative* (Table 8.1). School-age children strive for *competence,* the sense that they are able and productive human beings. In adolescence, the task is to synthesize past, present, and future possibilities into a clearer sense of self. Adolescents wonder "Who am I as an individual? What do I want to do with my life? What values should I live by? What do I believe in?" Erikson called this quest to refine one's sense of self the adolescent's "search for identity."

TABLE 8.1

ERIKSON'S STAGES OF PSYCHOSOCIAL DEVELOPMENT

Identity Stage (approximate age)	Issues	Description of Task
Infancy (to 1 year)	Trust vs. mistrust	If needs are dependably met, infants develop a sense of basic trust.
Toddlerhood (1 to 2 years)	Autonomy vs. shame and doubt	Toddlers learn to exercise will and do things for themselves, or they doubt their abilities.
Preschooler (3 to 5 years)	Initiative vs. guilt	Preschoolers learn to initiate tasks and carry out plans, or they feel guilty about efforts to be independent.
Elementary school (6 years to puberty)	Competence vs. inferiority	Children learn the pleasure of applying themselves to tasks, or they feel inferior.
Adolescence (teen years into 20s)	Identity vs. role confusion	Teenagers work at refining a sense of self by testing roles and then integrating them to form a single identity, or they become confused about who they are.
Young adulthood (20s to early 40s)	Intimacy vs. isolation	Young adults struggle to form close relationships and to gain the capacity for intimate love, or they feel socially isolated.
Middle adulthood (40s to 60s)	Generativity vs. stagnation	The middle-aged discover a sense of contributing to the world, usually through family and work, or they may feel a lack of purpose.
Late adulthood (late 60s and up)	Integrity vs. despair	When reflecting on his or her life, the older adult may feel a sense of satisfaction or failure.

Forming an Identity

To refine their sense of identity, adolescents in Western cultures usually try out different "selves" in different situations—perhaps acting out one self at home, another with friends, and still another at school and work. If two of these situations overlap—as when a teenager brings home friends with whom he is Joe Cool—the discomfort can be considerable. The teen asks, "Which self should I be? Which is the real me?" Often, this role confusion is resolved by the gradual reshaping of a self-definition that unifies the various selves into a consistent and comfortable sense of who one is—an **identity.**

But not always. Erikson noticed that some adolescents forge their identity early, simply by taking on their parents' values and expectations. (Traditional, less individualistic cultures may inform adolescents who they are rather than leaving them to decide on their own.) Other adolescents may adopt a negative identity that defines itself in opposition to parents and society but in conformity with a particular peer group— the jocks, the preppies, the geeks, the goths. Still others never quite seem to find themselves or to develop strong commitments. For most, the identity question—Who am I?—continues past the teen years and reappears at turning points during adult life.

Who shall I be today?
By varying the way they look, adolescents try out different "selves." Although we eventually form a consistent and stable sense of identity, the "self" we present may change with the situation.

The late teen years, when many people begin attending college or working full time, provide new opportunities for trying out possible roles. As seniors, many college students have achieved a clearer identity than they had as first-year students (Waterman, 1988). Their identity typically incorporates an increasingly positive self-concept. In several nationwide studies, researchers have given young Americans tests of self-esteem. (Sample item: "I am able to do things as well as most other people.") Between ages 13 and 23, the self-concept usually becomes more positive, especially among boys and among those who belong to a satisfying peer group. A clearer, more self-affirming identity is forming, and with it comes a greater sense of control over one's future (Baumgardner, 1990; O'Malley & Bachman, 1983; Strange & Forsyth, 1993).

Developing Intimacy

Erikson contended that the adolescent identity stage is followed in young adulthood by a developing capacity for **intimacy,** the ability to form emotionally close relationships. Once you have a clear and comfortable sense of who you are, said Erikson, you are ready for close relationships.

Gender and Social Connectedness

To Carol Gilligan and her colleagues (1982, 1990), the "normal" struggle to create one's separate identity describes individualist males more than relationship-oriented females. Gilligan believes females differ from males both in being less concerned with viewing themselves as separate individuals and in being more concerned with "making connections."

■ **identity** one's sense of self; according to Erikson, the adolescent's task is to solidify a sense of self by testing and integrating various roles.

■ **intimacy** in Erikson's theory, the ability to form close, loving relationships; a primary developmental task in late adolescence and early adulthood.

These gender differences surface early, in children's play. Boys typically play in large groups with an activity focus and little intimate discussion. Girls usually play in smaller groups, often with one friend. Their play is less competitive than boys' and more imitative of social relationships. Both in play and other settings, females are more open and responsive to feedback than are males (Maccoby, 1990; Roberts, 1991). As teens, girls spend more time with friends and less time alone (Wong & Csikszentmihalyi, 1991).

The gender difference in connectedness carries into adulthood. Women, being more *interdependent,* use conversation to explore relationships; men use it to communicate solutions (Tannen, 1990). Studies of the job preferences of 640,000 people reveal some tendency for women more than men to value good hours, personal relationships, and opportunities to help others, and for men more than women to value earnings, promotions, challenge, and power (Konrad & others, 2000).

Women emphasize caring and provide most of the care to the very young and the very old. Women purchase 85 percent of greeting cards (*Time,* 1997). Although 69 percent of people say they have a close relationship with their father, 90 percent feel close to their mother (Hugick, 1989). Men, like empowered people generally, emphasize freedom and self-reliance. (That helps explain why at all ages men assign less importance to religion and pray less often than their female counterparts [Benson, 1992].)

Bonds and feelings of support are also stronger among women than among men (Rossi & Rossi, 1990). Women's ties—as mothers, daughters, sisters, aunts, and grandmothers—bind families together. As friends, women are more intimate than men; they talk more often and more openly (Berndt, 1992; Dindia & Allen, 1992).

In one survey of 4000 middle-aged twins, 78 percent of the women rated their "nurturance" above the men's average self-rating (Lykken, 1999), and both men and women report their friendships with women to be more intimate, enjoyable, and nurturing (Rubin, 1985; Sapadin, 1988). When wanting understanding and someone with whom to share worries and hurts, both men and women usually turn to women.

Gender differences in connectedness and other traits peak in late adolescence and early adulthood—the very years most commonly studied. As teenagers, girls become progressively less assertive and more flirtatious; boys become more domineering and unexpressive. But by age 50, these differences have diminished. Women become more assertive and self-confident and men more empathic and less domineering (Maccoby, 1998).

Some see biological wisdom in these changing gender roles. They speculate that, during courtship and early parenthood, social expectations lead both sexes to downplay traits that interfere with their roles. As long as men are expected to provide and protect, they forgo their more dependent and tender sides (Gutmann, 1977). As long as women are expected to nurture, they forgo their impulses to be assertive and independent. When they graduate from these early adult roles, men and women are freer to develop and express their previously inhibited tendencies.

> "What's the difference between a man and E.T.? E.T. phoned home."
>
> **Anonymous**

> "In the long years liker must they grow; The man be more of woman, she of man."
>
> **Alfred, Lord Tennyson, *The Princess*, 1847**

Separating From Parents

As adolescents seek to form their own identities, they begin to separate themselves from their parents (Paikoff & Brooks-Gunn, 1991). The preschooler who can't be close enough to mother, who loves to touch and cling to her, becomes the 14-year-old who wouldn't be caught dead holding hands with mom. The transition occurs gradually **(FIGURE 8.4,** on page 126). By adolescence, arguments occur more often, usually over mundane things—household chores, bedtime, homework (Tesser & others, 1989).

For a minority of parents and their adolescents, differences lead to estrangement. But for most, disagreement at the level of bickering is not destructive.

FIGURE 8.4

The changing parent-child relationship

Interviews from a large, national study of Canadian families reveal that the typically close, warm relationships between parents and preschoolers loosen as children age. (Data from Statistics Canada, 1999.)

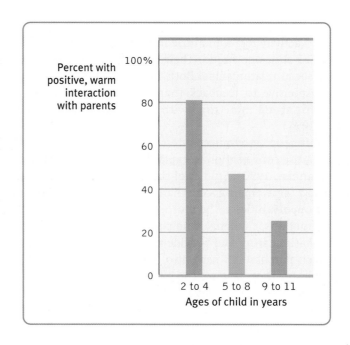

- A study of 6000 adolescents in 10 countries, from Australia to Bangladesh to Turkey, found that most liked their parents (Offer & others, 1988). "We usually get along but . . . ," adolescents often report (Galambos, 1992; Steinberg, 1987).
- In one survey of 25,000 middle-class teens worldwide, more than 80 percent rated family relationships as an "important" guiding principle for their lives, and more than half said it was *most* important—more significant than their "relationship with friends," "having fun," or "making the world a better place" (Stepp, 1996).
- A Gallup poll (1996) of American teens reported that 97 percent said they got along "fairly" or "very" well with their parents. Most, however, reported getting along better with Mom than with Dad. Positive relations with parents support positive peer relations. High school girls who have the most affectionate relationships with their mothers tend also to enjoy the most intimate friendships with girlfriends (Gold & Yanof, 1985). And teens who feel close to their parents tend to be healthy and happy and to do well in school (Resnick & others, 1997). (Of course, we can state this correlation the other way: Misbehaving teens are more likely to have tense parental relationships and to say their parents are jerks.) About half of the calls to teen hot lines concern peer relationships; the other half are about everything else—family problems, sex, school, self-esteem, and so forth (Boehm & others, 1999).

In Western cultures, adolescence is typically a time of diminishing parental influence and growing peer influence. Asked in a survey if they had "ever had a serious talk" with their child about illegal drugs, 85 percent of American *parents* answered yes. But the teens sometimes tuned out this earnest advice, for only 45 percent could recall such a talk (or saw it as less serious [Morin & Brossard, 1997]). Instead, what their friends are—what "everybody's doing"—they often become.

Heredity does much of the heavy lifting in forming individual differences in character and personality, and peer influences do much of the rest. Teens are herd animals. They talk, dress, and act more like their peers than their parents. But peers see their parents as having more influence in other areas—in shaping their religious faith and practices, and in thinking about college and career choices, for example (*Emerging Trends,* 1997).

As people mature in young adulthood, the emotional ties between parents and children continue to loosen. During their early twenties, many still lean heavily on

DOONESBURY

their parents. By their late twenties, most feel more comfortably independent of their parents and better able to empathize with them as fellow adults (Frank, 1988; White, 1983). As we enter the new millennium, this graduation from adolescence to adulthood is taking longer. From Europe to Australia, adolescents are taking more time to finish college, to leave the nest, to establish their careers. In the United States, for example, the average age at first marriage has increased nearly 4 years since 1960 (to 26 for men, 24 for women).

Parent–adolescent relations
For a relative few, adolescence means estrangement from parents.

rehearse it!

1. Adolescence is marked by the onset of
   a. an identity crisis.
   b. puberty.
   c. separation anxiety.
   d. parent-child conflict.

2. The adolescent growth spurt is marked by dramatic developments in the sex characteristics. Primary sex characteristics relate to _____; secondary sex characteristics refer to _____.
   a. ejaculation; menarche
   b. breasts and facial hair; ovaries and testes
   c. emotional maturity; hormone surges
   d. reproductive organs; nonreproductive traits

3. According to Piaget, the ability to think logically about abstractions indicates
   a. concrete operational thought.
   b. egocentrism.
   c. formal operational thought.
   d. conservation.

4. According to Kohlberg, preconventional morality focuses on _____; conventional morality is more concerned with _____.
   a. upholding laws and social rules; self-interest
   b. self-interest; basic ethical principles
   c. upholding laws and social rules; basic ethical principles
   d. self-interest; upholding laws and social rules

5. Erik Erikson contends that each stage of life has its own special psychosocial task or challenge. The primary task during adolescence is to
   a. attain formal operations.
   b. forge an identity.
   c. develop a sense of intimacy with another person.
   d. live independent of parents.

6. The differences among individuals of each sex are much greater than the differences between men and women. Nevertheless, women more than men exhibit a concern for
   a. independence and self-reliance.
   b. social connections.
   c. competitive achievement.
   d. social stereotyping.

Adolescence

1. What major physical changes occur during adolescence?

Adolescence begins at puberty with the onset of rapid growth and developing sexual maturity, and extends to adult independence. During this period, both primary and secondary sex characteristics develop dramatically. Girls, for example, experience menarche by about age 13. Boys seem to benefit from "early" maturation, girls from "late" maturation.

2. How did Piaget and Kohlberg describe cognitive and moral development during adolescence?

Piaget theorized that adolescents develop the capacity for formal operations, which enables them to reason abstractly. However, most developmentalists now believe that the rudiments of logic appear earlier than Piaget believed.

Following Piaget's lead, Lawrence Kohlberg contended that moral thinking likewise proceeds through a sequence of stages, from a preconventional morality of self-interest, to a conventional morality concerned with gaining others' approval or doing one's duty, to (in some people) a postconventional morality of agreed-upon rights or universal ethical principles. But morality also lies in actions. Moreover, say Kohlberg's critics, the postconventional level represents morality from the perspective of individualist, middle-class males.

3. What tasks and challenges do adolescents face en route to mature adulthood, and are they the same for males and females?

Erik Erikson theorized that a chief task of adolescence is to form one's identity, or sense of self. This often means "trying on" a number of different roles. For many people the struggle for identity continues in the adult years as new relationships emerge—as the capacity for intimacy develops—and new roles are assumed. Males and females differ in their social connectedness. Boys define themselves apart from their caregivers and playmates, girls through their social ties. Women typically become more caring, empathic, and sensitive to nonverbal cues, and men more independent and self-reliant.

TERMS AND CONCEPTS TO REMEMBER

developmental psychology, p. 118
adolescence, p. 118
puberty, p. 119

primary sex characteristics, p. 119
secondary sex characteristics, p. 119

menarche [meh-NAR-key], p. 120
identity, p. 124

intimacy, p. 124

REHEARSE IT ANSWER KEY

1. b   2. d   3. c   4. d   5. b   6. b

Adulthood

9

At one time, psychologists viewed adulthood, especially the center-of-life years between adolescence and old age, as one long plateau. No longer. Those who follow the unfolding of people's adult lives now believe our development continues. Physically, cognitively, and especially socially, people at age 50 differ from their 25-year-old selves.

It is more difficult to generalize about adulthood stages than about life's early years. If you know that James is a 1-year-old and Jamal is a 10-year-old, you could say a great deal about each child. Not so with adults who differ by a similar number of years. The boss may be 30 or 60; the marathon runner may be 20 or 50; your classmates may be teenagers or grandparents. Likewise, a 19-year-old can be a parent who supports a child or a child who gets an allowance. Yet our life courses are in some ways similar. Our bodies, our minds, and our relationships undergo some changes in common with those of our childhood friends, who in other ways now seem so very different.

"I am still learning."

Michelangelo, 1560, at age 85

Physical Changes

PREVIEW QUESTION 1 How do our bodies change in middle and late adulthood?

Our physical abilities—muscular strength, reaction time, sensory keenness, and cardiac output—all crest by the mid-twenties. Like the declining daylight after the summer solstice, declining physical prowess begins imperceptibly. Athletes are often the first to notice. World-class sprinters and swimmers peak in their teens or early twenties. Women, because they mature earlier than men, also peak earlier. But most of us—especially those of us whose daily lives do not require top physical performance—hardly perceive the early signs of decline.

Physical Changes in Middle Adulthood

Middle-aged athletes know all too well that physical decline gradually accelerates. As a 58-year-old who regularly plays basketball, I now find myself occasionally wondering whether my team really needs me down court. But even diminished vigor is sufficient for normal activities. Moreover, during early and middle adulthood, physical vigor has less to do with age than with a person's health and exercise habits. Many of today's physically fit 50-year-olds run 4 miles with ease, while sedentary 25-year-olds find themselves huffing and puffing up two flights of stairs. Even many 70-year-olds don't yet feel old.

For women, the foremost biological sign of aging is **menopause,** the ending of the menstrual cycle, usually beginning within a few years of age 50. Menopause and its physical symptoms accompany a reduction in the hormone estrogen. For 4 or 5 in 10 Canadian and U.S. women, but only 1 in 7 Japanese women, these include occasional hot flashes (Goode, 1999; Lock, 1998). Like the stereotype of adolescent storm and stress, the image of menopausal emotionality and depression clashes with reality: Menopause usually does *not* create psychological problems for women. One survey of 2500 middle-aged Massachusetts women, another that followed 541 middle-aged Pennsylvania women for 3 years, and yet another that followed 3049 middle-aged women over 10 years all found them no more or less depressed if experiencing menopause (Busch & others, 1994; Matthews, 1992; McKinlay & others, 1987a,b).

How old does a person have to be before you think of him or her as old? The average 18- to 29-year-old says 67. The average person 60 and over says 76 (Yankelovich, 1995).

menopause the time of natural cessation of menstruation; also refers to the biological changes a woman experiences as her ability to reproduce declines.

A woman's expectations and attitudes influence the emotional impact of menopause. Does she see it as a sign that she is losing her femininity and sexual attractiveness and growing old? Or does she view it as liberation from menstrual periods, fears of pregnancy, and children's demands?

Men experience no equivalent to menopause—no cessation of fertility, no sharp drop in sex hormones. They do experience a more gradual decline in sperm count, testosterone level, and speed of erection and ejaculation. Some may also experience psychological distress related to their perception of decreased virility and declining physical capacities. But most men age without such problems.

"Happy fortieth. I'll take the muscle tone in your upper arms, the girlish timbre of your voice, your amazing tolerance for caffeine, and your ability to digest french fries. The rest of you can stay."

After middle age, most men and women remain capable of satisfying sexual activity. When people over 60 were surveyed by the National Council on Aging, 39 percent expressed satisfaction with the amount of sex they were having and 39 percent said they wished for sex more frequently (Leary, 1998).

Physical Changes in Later Life

Is old age "more to be feared than death" (Juvenal, *Satires*)? Or is life "most delightful when it is on the downward slope" (Seneca, *Epistulae ad Lucilium*)? What is it like to grow old?

Sensory Abilities

As we have seen, physical decline begins in early adulthood, but we are not usually acutely aware of it until later life. Visual sharpness diminishes, and adaptation to changes in light level slows. Muscle strength, reaction time, and stamina also diminish noticeably, as do hearing, distance perception, and the sense of smell **(FIGURE 9.1)**. In later life, the stairs get steeper, the newsprint gets smaller, and people seem to mumble more.

With age, the eye's pupil shrinks and its lens becomes less transparent, reducing the amount of light reaching the retina. In fact, a 65-year-old retina receives only about one-third as much light as its 20-year-old counterpart (Kline & Schieber, 1985). Thus, to see as well as a 20-year-old when reading or driving, a 65-year-old-

Most stairway falls taken by older persons occur on the top step, precisely where the person typically descends from a window-lit hallway into the darker stairwell (Fozard & Popkin, 1978). Our knowledge of aging could be used to design environments that would reduce such accidents (National Research Council, 1990).

FIGURE 9.1

The aging senses
Sight, smell, and hearing all decline after age 70. (From Doty & others, 1984.)

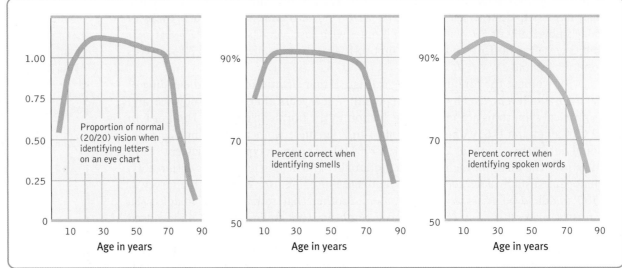

Proportion of normal (20/20) vision when identifying letters on an eye chart

Percent correct when identifying smells

Percent correct when identifying spoken words

Age in years

needs three times as much light—a reason for buying cars with untinted windshields. This also explains why older people sometimes ask younger people, "Don't you need better light for reading?"

Health

For those growing older, there is both good and bad news about health. The good news: Thanks partly to a lifetime's accumulation of antibodies, older people *less* often suffer short-term ailments, such as common flu and cold viruses. For example, those over 65 are half as likely as 20-year-olds and one-fifth as likely as preschoolers to suffer upper respiratory flu each year (National Center for Health Statistics, 1990). This is one reason why older workers have lower absenteeism rates (Rhodes, 1983). The bad news: The body's disease-fighting immune system weakens, making the elderly more susceptible to life-threatening ailments such as cancer and pneumonia.

Aging also levies a tax on the brain by slowing our neural processing. Up to the teen years, we process information with greater and greater speed (Fry & Hale, 1996; Kail, 1991). But compared with teens and young adults, older people take a bit more time to react, to solve perceptual puzzles, even to remember names (Bashore & others, 1997; Verhaeghen & Salthouse, 1997). And, as **FIGURE 9.2** indicates, car accident rates per mile sharply increase after age 75. By age 75, they reach the relatively high teenage level (National Research Council, 1990). Speed slows especially when the task becomes complex (Cerella, 1985; Poon, 1987). At video games, most 70-year-olds are no match for a 20-year-old.

During aging, brain regions important to memory begin to atrophy (Schacter, 1996). In young adulthood, a small, gradual net loss of brain cells begins, contributing to a 5 percent or so reduction of brain weight by age 80. Aging may proceed more slowly in women. Not only do women worldwide live four years longer than men, their brains shrink more slowly than men's (Coffey & others, 1998).

The birth of new cells and the proliferation of neural connections, especially in those who remain active, helps compensate for the cell loss (Coleman & Flood, 1986). Physical exercise enhances muscles, bones, and energy and helps prevent obesity and heart disease. It also, it now seems, stimulates brain cell development, thanks perhaps to increased oxygen and nutrient flow (Kempermann & others, 1998). And that may explain why sedentary older adults randomly assigned to a walking program exhibit enhanced memory and sharpened judgment (Kramer & others, 1999). We are more likely to rust from disuse than to wear out from overuse. "Use it or lose it" is sound advice.

"For some reason, possibly to save ink, the restaurants had started printing their menus in letters the height of bacteria."

Dave Barry, *Dave Barry Turns Fifty,* **1998**

Keeping the biological clock running smoothly
How quickly people age depends in part on their health habits. As this cheerful group makes clear, the more active people remain, the more vigor they retain.

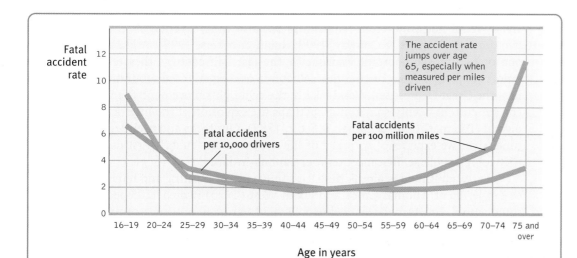

The accident rate jumps over age 65, especially when measured per miles driven

Fatal accidents per 10,000 drivers

Fatal accidents per 100 million miles

Age in years

FIGURE 9.2

Age and fatal accidents
Slowing reactions contribute to increased accident risks among those 75 and older (Stock, 1995). Would you favor driver exams based on performance, not age, to screen out those whose slow reactions or sensory impairments indicate accident risk?

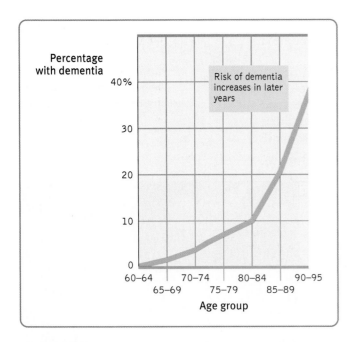

FIGURE 9.3

Incidence of dementia (mental disintegration) by age

Risk of mental loss due to Alzheimer's disease or a series of strokes doubles about every 5 years in later life. (From Jorm & others, 1987, based on 22 studies in industrial nations.)

If you are within five years of 20, what experiences from your last year will you likely never forget? If you are older, what do you remember most vividly from that era of your life?

■ **Alzheimer's disease** a progressive and irreversible brain disorder characterized by gradual deterioration of memory, reasoning, language, and, finally, physical functioning.

Dementia and Alzheimer's Disease

Some adults do, unfortunately, suffer a substantial loss of brain cells. Up to age 95, the incidence of mental disintegration doubles roughly every 5 years **(FIGURE 9.3).** A series of small strokes, a brain tumor, or alcoholism can progressively damage the brain, causing that mental erosion we call *dementia.* So, too, can the most feared of all brain ailments, **Alzheimer's disease,** which strikes 3 percent of the world's population by age 75. Alzheimer's symptoms are *not* the same as normal aging. (Occasionally forgetting where you laid the car keys is no cause for alarm; forgetting how to get home does suggest Alzheimer's.) Underlying the symptoms of Alzheimer's is a deterioration of neurons (nerve cells) that produce the substance acetylcholine, one of the chemicals that transmits messages between neurons. Deprived of this vital chemical messenger, memory and thinking suffer.

Alzheimer's destroys even the brightest of minds. First memory, then reasoning and language deteriorate. Robert Sayre (1979) recalls his father shouting at his afflicted mother to "think harder," while his mother, confused, embarrassed, on the verge of tears, randomly searched the house for lost objects. As Alzheimer's runs its course, after 5 to 20 years, the patient becomes emotionally flat, then disoriented, then incontinent, finally mentally vacant—a sort of living death, a mere body stripped of its humanity.

Cognitive Changes

PREVIEW QUESTION 2 In what ways do memory and intelligence change as we age?

Among the most controversial questions in the study of the human life span is whether adult cognitive abilities, such as memory, creativity, and intelligence, parallel the gradually accelerating decline of physical abilities. Employers, for example, may wonder whether they should encourage their senior workers to retire—or capitalize on their experience. Does the common perception that elderly people are generally less sharp (Kite & Johnson, 1988) lend truth to the proverb, "You can't teach an old dog new tricks"? Or does the evidence support another proverb: "You're never too old to learn"?

Aging and Memory

As we age, we remember some things well. Looking back in later life, people most vividly recall not only recent happenings but also their experiences in life's second two decades (Holmes & Conway, 1999; Rubin & others, 1998). Asked to recall the one or two most important events over the last half-century, they tend to name events from their teens or twenties. Whatever one experienced around this stage of life—the Great Depression, World War II, the civil rights movement, the Vietnam war (or, for current twenty-somethings, perhaps the explosion of the Internet)—becomes pivotal (Pillemer, 1998; Schuman & Scott, 1989). Our teens and twenties are also the time when we experience so many of life's memorable "firsts"—first date, first job, first going to college, first meeting your parents-in-law.

Early adulthood is a peak time for some types of learning and remembering. In one experiment, Thomas Crook and Robin West (1990) invited 1205 people to learn some names. Fourteen videotaped people said their names, using a common format: "Hi, I'm Larry." Then the same individuals reappeared and said, for example, "I'm from Philadelphia"—thus providing a visual and voice cue for remembering the person's name. As **FIGURE 9.4** shows, everyone remembered more names after a second and third replay of the introductions, but younger adults consistently surpassed older adults in their name recall. Similar results appear in other studies. Within hours after Prime Minister Margaret Thatcher announced her resignation, young and old British people recalled how they heard the news. When asked again 11 months later, 90 percent of the younger group but only 42 percent of the older group told the same story (Cohen & others, 1994).

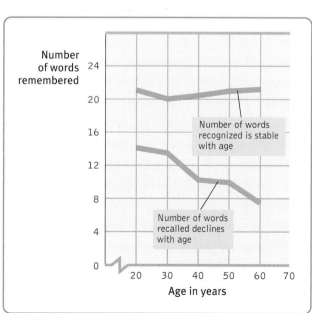

Percentage of names recalled

After three introductions

Older age groups have poorer performance

After two introductions

After one introduction

18–39 40–49 50–59 60–69 70–90

Age group

FIGURE 9.4

Tests of recall

Recalling new names introduced once, twice, or three times is easier for younger adults than for older ones. (Data from Crook & West, 1990.)

But consider another experiment. David Schonfield and Betty-Anne Robertson (1966) asked adults of various ages to learn a list of 24 words. Without giving any clues, the researchers asked some to recall as many words as they could from the list, and others simply to *recognize* words, using multiple-choice questions. As **FIGURE 9.5** shows, younger adults had better recall, but researchers found no similar memory decline with age on the recognition tests. Tests also reveal that recognition memory is better for older adults early rather than late in the day (May & others, 1993). So, how well older people remember depends: Are they being asked simply to *recognize* what they have tried to memorize (minimal decline) or to *recall* it without clues (greater decline)?

Forgetting seems also to depend on the type of information we are trying to remember. If you are asked to recall meaningless information—nonsense syllables or unimportant events—then the older you are, the more errors you are likely to make. However, if the information is meaningful and you are older, your rich web of existing knowledge will help you to catch it. Older people's capacity to learn and remember skills and *meaningful* material shows less decline (Graf, 1990; Labouvie-Vief & Schell, 1982; Perlmutter, 1983).

Those who study our capacity to learn and remember are aware of one other important complication: Right through our later years, we continue to diverge. If you think 20-year-olds differ widely in their abilities to learn and remember, consider this: 70-year-olds differ much more. Some 70-year-olds perform below nearly all 20-year-olds; other 70-year-olds match or outdo the average 20-year-old. Neuropsychologist Michela Gallagher (1990) has found that aging rats, too, vary much more than do young rats. Some old rats are as quick-witted as the smartest of young rats; others, for reasons related to brain deterioration, show their age.

Number of words remembered

Number of words recognized is stable with age

Number of words recalled declines with age

20 30 40 50 60 70

Age in years

FIGURE 9.5

Recall and recognition in adulthood

In this experiment, the ability to *recall* new information declined during early and middle adulthood, but the ability to *recognize* new information did not. (From Schonfield & Robertson, 1966.)

- **cross-sectional study** a study in which people of different ages are compared with one another.

- **longitudinal study** research in which the same people are restudied and retested over a long period.

Aging and Intelligence

What happens to our broader intellectual powers as we age? Do they gradually decline, as does our ability to recall new material? Or do they remain constant, as does our ability to recognize meaningful material? The evolving answer to this question makes an interesting research story, one that illustrates psychology's self-correcting process (Woodruff-Pak, 1989).

Phase I: Cross-Sectional Evidence for Intellectual Decline

In **cross-sectional studies,** researchers test and compare people of various ages. When giving intelligence tests to representative samples of people, researchers consistently find that older adults give fewer correct answers than do younger adults. David Wechsler (1972), creator of the most widely used adult intelligence test, therefore concluded that "the decline of mental ability with age is part of the general [aging] process of the organism as a whole."

Phase II: Longitudinal Evidence for Intellectual Stability

After colleges began giving intelligence tests to entering students about 1920, several psychologists saw their chance to study intelligence **longitudinally**—retesting the same people over a period of years. What they expected to find was a decrease in intelligence after about age 30 (Schaie & Geiwitz, 1982). What they actually found was a surprise: Until late in life, intelligence remained stable **(FIGURE 9.6).** On some tests, it even increased.

How then are we to account for the findings from the cross-sectional studies? In retrospect, researchers saw the problem. When a cross-sectional study compares 70-year-olds and 30-year-olds, it compares people not only of two different ages but of two different eras. It compares generally less-educated people (born, say, in the early 1900s) with better-educated people (born after 1950), people raised in large families with people raised in smaller families, people growing up in less affluent families with people raised in more affluent families.

FIGURE 9.6

Cross-sectional versus longitudinal testing of intelligence at various ages

In this test of one type of verbal intelligence (inductive reasoning), the cross-sectional method produced declining scores with age. The longitudinal method (in which the same people were retested over a period of years) produced a slight *rise* in scores well into adulthood. (Adapted from Schaie, 1994.)

"In youth we learn, in age we understand."

Marie Von Ebner-Eschenbach, *Aphorisms,* **1883**

Phase III: It All Depends

But the controversy continues. For one thing, longitudinal studies have their own pitfalls. Those who survive to the end of longitudinal studies may be bright, healthy people whose intelligence is least likely to decline. (Perhaps people who died younger and were removed from the study had declining intelligence.) Adjusting for the loss of subjects, as did a recent study following more than 2000 people over 75 in Cambridge, England, reveals a steeper intelligence decline. This is especially so as people age after 85 (Brayne & others, 1999).

Research is further complicated by the finding that intelligence is not a single trait but rather a number of distinct skills and abilities. Intelligence tests that assess speed of thinking may place older adults at a disadvantage because of their slower neural mechanisms for processing information. Meeting old friends on the street, names rise to the mind's surface more slowly—"like air bubbles in molasses" says David Lykken (1999). But slower need not mean less intelligent. Given other tests that assess general vocabulary, knowledge, and ability to integrate information, older adults generally hold their own.

German researcher Paul Baltes and his colleagues (1993, 1994, 1999) have developed "wisdom" tests that assess "expert knowledge about life in general and good judgment and advice about how to conduct oneself in the face of complex,

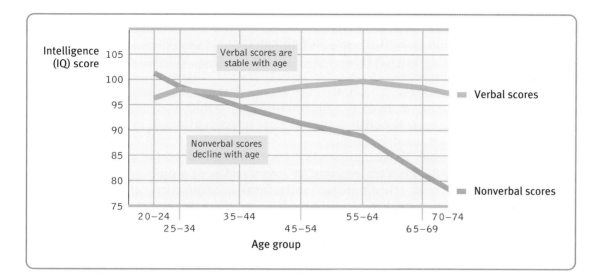

FIGURE 9.7
Intelligence and age
After adjustments for education, verbal intelligence scores hold steady with age, while nonverbal intelligence scores decline. (Intelligence scores from standardization sample of the Wechsler Adult Intelligence Scale, based on norms for 25- to 34-year-olds.) (Adapted from Kaufman & others, 1989.)

uncertain circumstances." Their results suggest that older adults more than hold their own on such tests. Thus, despite 30-year-olds' quick-thinking smarts, we usually select older people to be president of the company, the college, or the country. Age is sage. To paraphrase one 60-year-old, "Forty years ago I had a great memory, but I was a fool."

So, whether intelligence increases or decreases with age depends on the type of intellectual performance we measure. **Crystallized intelligence**—one's accumulated knowledge as reflected in vocabulary and analogies tests—*increases* up to old age. **Fluid intelligence**—one's ability to reason speedily and abstractly, as when solving novel logic problems—*decreases* slowly up to age 75 or so, then more rapidly, especially after age 85 (Cattell, 1963; Horn, 1982). We can see this pattern in the intelligence scores of a national sample of adults. After adjustments for education, verbal scores (reflecting crystallized intelligence) held relatively steady from ages 20 to 74. Nonverbal, puzzle-solving intelligence declined **(FIGURE 9.7).**

These cognitive differences help explain why mathematicians and scientists produce much of their most creative work during their late twenties or early thirties, whereas those in literature, history, and philosophy tend to produce their best work in their forties, fifties, and beyond, after accumulating more knowledge (Simonton, 1988, 1990). For example, poets (who depend on fluid intelligence) reach their peak output earlier than prose authors (who need a deeper knowledge reservoir)—a finding observed in every major literary tradition, for both living and dead languages. So, whether intellectual performance increases or decreases with age depends on how we assess it and on what we assess.

Age	Accomplishment
70	John Roch develops birth control pill
78	Grandma Moses begins painting (and continues until she is 100+)
81	Amos Alonzo Stagg is named coach of the year
89	Frank Lloyd Wright designs New York City's Guggenheim Museum

Social Changes

Many of the differences between younger and older adults are created not by the physical and cognitive changes that accompany aging but by life events associated with family relationships and work. A new job means new relationships, new expectations, and new demands. Marriage brings the joy of intimacy and the stress of merging your life with another's. The birth of a child introduces responsibilities and significantly alters your life focus. The death of a loved one creates an irreplaceable loss and a need to reaffirm your own life. Do these normal events of adult life shape a predictable sequence of life changes?

■ **crystallized intelligence** one's accumulated knowledge and verbal skills; tends to increase with age.

■ **fluid intelligence** one's ability to reason speedily and abstractly; tends to decrease during late adulthood.

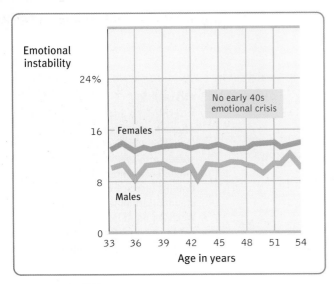

FIGURE 9.8

Early-forties midlife crises?

Among 10,000 people responding to a national health survey, there was no early-forties increase in emotional instability ("neuroticism") scores. (From McCrae & Costa, 1990.)

"Midway in the journey of our life I found myself in a dark wood, for the straight way was lost."

Dante, *The Divine Comedy*, 1314

Resetting the social clock

The social clock once prescribed that university graduation should occur around age 22. For this proud graduate, "standard time" is no longer the only setting.

"One can live magnificently in this world if one knows how to work and how to love."

Leo Tolstoy, 1856

Adulthood's Ages and Stages

PREVIEW QUESTION 3 Is the journey from adolescence to death marked by stages that serve as developmental milestones?

Some psychologists have argued that as people enter their forties, they undergo a "midlife transition" to middle adulthood, which for many is a crisis, a time of great struggle, of regret, or even of feeling struck down by life. The popular image of the midlife crisis is a man who forsakes his family for a younger girlfriend and a hot sports car. But the fact—reported by large samples of people—is that unhappiness, job dissatisfaction, marital dissatisfaction, divorce, anxiety, and suicide do not surge during the early forties (Hunter & Sundel, 1989; Mroczek & Kolarz, 1998). Divorce, for example, is most common among those in their twenties, suicide among those in their seventies and eighties. One study of emotional instability in nearly 10,000 men and women found "not the slightest evidence" that distress peaks anywhere in the midlife age range **(FIGURE 9.8).**

There is another reason skeptics question age-linked stages such as "midlife crisis." The **social clock**—the cultural prescription of "the right time" to leave home, get a job, marry, have children, and retire—varies from culture to culture and era to era. In Jordan, 40 percent of brides are in their teens; in Hong Kong, only 3 percent are (United Nations, 1992). In Western Europe, fewer than 10 percent of men over 65 remain in the work force, as do 16 percent in the United States, 36 percent in Japan, and 69 percent in Mexico (Davies & others, 1991). And the once rigid sequence for Western women—of student to worker to wife to at-home mom to older worker—has loosened. Contemporary women occupy these roles in any order or all at once. Given variations in the social clock and individual experience, the critics of stage theory are suspicious of any neat timetable of adult stages with ages.

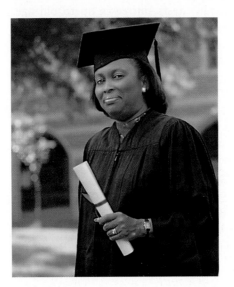

More important than one's chronological age are life events. Marriage, parenthood, vocational changes, divorce, nest emptying, relocation, and retirement mark transitions to new life stages whenever they occur—and increasingly they are occurring at unpredictable ages. The social clock still ticks, but people feel freer about being out of sync with it.

Adulthood's Commitments

PREVIEW QUESTION 4 What do psychologists view as adulthood's two primary commitments?

Two basic aspects of our lives do, however, dominate adulthood. Erik Erikson called them *intimacy* (forming close relationships) and *generativity* (being productive and supporting future generations). Researchers have chosen various terms—*affiliation* and *achievement, attachment* and *productivity, commitment* and *competence*. Sigmund Freud (1935) put it most simply: The healthy adult, he said, is one who can *love* and *work*. For most adults, love centers on family commitments toward partner, parents, and children. Work encompasses all our productive activities, whether for pay or not.

Love

Across time and place, human societies have nearly always included a relatively monogamous bond between men and women and a bond between parents and their children. We flirt, fall in love, and marry—one person at a time. "Pair-bonding is a trademark of the human animal," notes anthropologist Helen Fisher (1993). From an evolutionary perspective, the arrangement makes sense: Parents who cooperated to nurture their children to maturity were more likely to have their genes passed along to posterity than parents who didn't.

Research indicates that the bond of love is most satisfying and enduring when marked by a similarity of interests and values, a sharing of emotional and material support, and intimate self-disclosure. Women's marital satisfaction, even more than men's, is colored by their mate's social support (Acitelli & Antonucci, 1994). Happiness can occur in a relationship when one has a reassuring, respectful, caring, and mutually confiding partner.

Marriage bonds are more likely to last when couples marry after age 20 and are well educated. Compared with their counterparts of 40 years ago, people in Western countries *are* better educated and are marrying later. And yet, ironically, they are twice as likely to divorce than they would have been in 1960. This is in part because of rising expectations. We now not only hope for an enduring bond, but also for a mate who is a wage earner, caregiver, intimate friend, and warm and responsive lover. Women are also less dependent economically. To judge from the divorce rate—both Canada and the United States now have about one divorce for every two marriages—marriage has become a union that often defies management (Bureau of the Census, 1999). In Europe, divorce is only slightly less common.

Might test-driving life together in a "trial marriage" minimize divorce risk? It seems not. Ten studies in Europe, Canada, and the United States find a positive correlation between living together before marriage and risk of divorce after marriage. Compared with couples who do not cohabit with their spouses-to-be, those who do have markedly *higher* divorce rates (Myers, 2000). This correlation doesn't prove that cohabitation *causes* divorce, but it hardly seems to prevent it.

Nonetheless, the institution of marriage endures. More than 9 in 10 heterosexual adults marry. Of those who divorce, 75 percent remarry—and their second marriages are virtually as happy as the average first marriage (Vemer & others, 1989). Although the relatively few people who feel trapped in an unhappy marriage typically feel miserable, most married Europeans and most North Americans of both sexes feel happier than those who are unmarried, especially when compared with others who are separated and divorced (Inglehart, 1990). For example, surveys of more than 32,000 Americans since 1972 reveal that 23 percent of unmarried adults and 40 percent of married adults report being "very happy" (Myers, 2000). Lesbian women in couples, too, report greater well-being than those who are alone (Wayment & Peplau, 1995).

Marriages that last are not always devoid of conflict. Some couples fight but also shower one another with affection. Other couples never raise their voices yet also seldom praise one another or nuzzle. Both styles can last. After observing the interactions of 2000 couples, John Gottman (1994) reported a better indicator of likely marital success: at least a five-to-one ratio of positive to negative interactions. Stable marriages provide five times more instances of smiling, touching, complimenting, and laughing than of sarcasm, criticism, and insults. So, if you want to predict which newlyweds will stay together, do not pay attention to how passionately they are in love. The couples who make it are more often those who restrain putting down their partners. Put downs, unchecked, can take over a relationship (Notarius & Markman, 1993). To prevent a cancerous negativity, successful couples learn to fight fair (to state feelings without insulting) and to steer conflict away from chaos with comments like "I know it's not your fault" or "I'll just be quiet for a moment and listen."

Love
Intimacy, attachment, commitment—love by whatever name—is central to healthy and happy adulthood.

What do you think? Does marriage correlate with happiness because marital support and intimacy breed happiness, because happy people more often marry and stay married, or both?

■ **social clock** the culturally preferred timing of social events such as marriage, parenthood, and retirement.

Often, love bears children. For most people, the most enduring of life changes, having a child, is a happy event. However, when children begin to absorb time, money, and emotional energy, satisfaction with the marriage itself may decline. This is especially likely among employed women who, more than they expected, carry the traditional burden of doing the chores at home (Belsky & others, 1986; Hackel & Ruble, 1992). The effort to create an equitable relationship can pay double dividends, making for a more satisfying marriage, which also breeds better parent-child relations (Erel & Burman, 1995).

Although love bears children, children eventually leave home. This departure is a significant event, but seven national surveys reveal that the empty nest is for most people a happy place (Adelmann & others, 1989; Glenn, 1975). Compared with middle-aged women who still have children at home, those whose nest has emptied report greater happiness and greater enjoyment of their marriage. Many parents experience what sociologists Lynn White and John Edwards (1990) call a "postlaunch honeymoon," especially if they maintain close relationships with their children.

Work

For many adults, the answer to "Who are you?" depends a great deal on the answer to "What do you do?" Was Freud right? Does work, including a career, indeed contribute to self-fulfillment and life satisfaction? One approach to answering this question has been to compare the roughly equal numbers of North American women who are or are not employed. From their studies at the Wellesley College Center for Research on Women, Grace Baruch and Rosaline Barnett (1986) conclude that what matters is not which roles a woman occupies—whether it be as paid worker, wife, and/or mother—but the quality of her experience in those roles.

If you have left home, did your parents suffer the "empty nest syndrome"—a feeling of distress focusing on a loss of purpose and relationship? Did they mourn the lost joy of listening for you in the wee hours of Saturday morning? Or did they seem to discover a new freedom, relaxation, and (if still married) renewed satisfaction with their own relationship?

Job satisfaction and life satisfaction
Work can provide us with a sense of identity and competence and opportunities for accomplishment. Perhaps this is why challenging and interesting occupations enhance people's happiness.

For women and men, choosing a career path is difficult, especially in today's changing work environment. During the first two years of college or university, most students cannot predict their later careers. Most shift from their initially intended majors, many find their postcollege employment in fields not directly related to their majors, and most will change careers (Rothstein, 1980). In the end, happiness is about having work that fits your interests and provides you with a sense of competence and accomplishment. And for those who choose to marry, it is having a partner who is a close, supportive companion and who sees you as special, and/or having loving children whom you like and feel proud of.

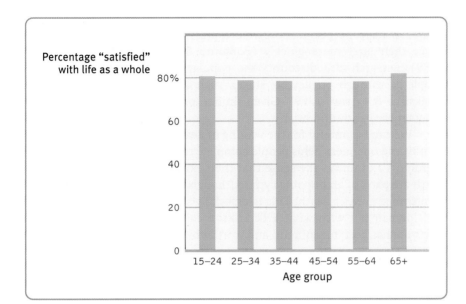

FIGURE 9.9

Age and life satisfaction
With the tasks of early adulthood behind them, many older adults have more time to pursue personal interests. No wonder their satisfaction with life remains high, especially if they are healthy and active. As this graph based on multinational surveys shows, age differences in life satisfaction are trivial. (Data from Inglehart, 1990.)

Well-Being Across the Life Span

To live is to grow older. That means we all can look back with satisfaction or regret, and forward with hope or dread. When people are asked what they would have done differently if they could relive their lives, their most common answer is "taken my education more seriously and worked harder at it." Other regrets—"I should have told my father I loved him," "I regret that I never went to Europe"—also focus less on mistakes made than on the things one *failed* to do (Gilovich & Medvec, 1995).

In later life, income shrinks, work is taken away, the body deteriorates, recall fades, energy wanes, family members and friends die or move away, and the great enemy, death, looms ever closer. Small wonder that many presume the over-65 years to be the worst of times (Freedman, 1978). But they are not, as Ronald Inglehart (1990) discovered when he amassed interviews conducted during the 1980s with representative samples of nearly 170,000 people in 16 nations. As **FIGURE 9.9** illustrates, older people report as much happiness and satisfaction with life as younger people do. Given that growing older is one sure consequence of living, an outcome most of us prefer to its alternative, we can all take comfort in this finding.

Death and Dying

Most of us will suffer and cope with the deaths of relatives and friends. Usually, the most difficult separation is from one's spouse—a loss suffered by five times more women than men. Grief is especially severe when the death of a loved one comes suddenly and before its expected time on the social clock. The accidental death of a child or the sudden illness that claims a 45-year-old spouse may trigger a year or more of mourning flooded with memories, eventually subsiding to a mild depression that sometimes continues for several years (Lehman & others, 1987). AIDS, which so often strikes down people in midlife and younger, has left countless grief-stricken partners experiencing such bereavement, as well as 11 million orphaned (and mostly African) children (Folkman & others, 1996; *New York Times*, 1999). In 1999, the disease killed 2.6 million people worldwide.

The normal range of reactions to a loved one's death is wider than most suppose. Some cultures encourage public weeping and wailing; others hide grief. Within

"Do not go gentle into that good night,
Old age should burn and rave at close of day;
Rage, rage against the dying of the light."

Dylan Thomas, "Do not go gentle into that good night," 1952, poem written to his father as he lay dying peacefully any culture some individuals grieve more intensely and openly; however, contrary to a popular misconception, those who express the strongest grief immediately do not purge their grief more quickly (Bonanno & Kaltman, 1999; Wortman & Silver, 1989). Research also discounts the popular idea that terminally ill and bereaved people go through predictable stages, such as denial, anger, and so forth (Nolen-Hoeksema & Larson, 1999). Given similar losses, some people grieve hard and long, others more lightly and briefly.

We can be grateful for the waning of death-denying attitudes. Facing death with dignity and openness helps people complete the life cycle with a sense of life's meaningfulness and unity—the sense that their existence has been good and that life and death are parts of an ongoing cycle. Although death may be unwelcome, life itself can be affirmed even at death. This is especially so for people who review their lives not with despair but with what Erik Erikson called a sense of *integrity*—a feeling that one's life has been meaningful and worthwhile.

"Consider, friend, as you pass by, as you are now, so once was I. As I am now, you too shall be. Prepare, therefore, to follow me."

Scottish tombstone epitaph

rehearse it!

1. By age 75, a person has experienced declining heart and muscular strength and losses in sight and hearing. However, this older adult is less likely than younger people to suffer from
   a. Alzheimer's disease.
   b. accidents and falls.
   c. short-term illnesses such as the flu.
   d. chronic illnesses such as diabetes.

2. Some types of learning and remembering peak in early adulthood. By age 65, a person would be most likely to experience a decline in the ability to
   a. recall and list all the items in the module's glossary.
   b. select the correct definition in a multiple-choice question.
   c. evaluate whether a statement is true or false.
   d. exercise sound judgment in answering an essay question.

3. In longitudinal studies the same people are retested at different ages. Longitudinal research suggests that intelligence
   a. steadily declines with age.
   b. peaks at age 25.
   c. generally increases in later life.
   d. remains stable until very late in life.

4. Freud defined the healthy adult as one who is able to love and work. Erikson agreed, observing that the adult struggles to attain intimacy and
   a. affiliation.
   b. identity.
   c. competence.
   d. generativity.

5. Most middle-aged adults define themselves in terms of their career. Which of the following has research shown to be true of women and work?

   a. Women who work for wages are happier than those who do not.
   b. Women whose roles are wife and mother are happier than those who also work for wages.
   c. The quality of a woman's experience in her role matters more than the role she occupies.
   d. A woman's age determines which role makes her happier.

6. Contrary to what many people assume,
   a. older people are much happier than adolescents.
   b. men in their forties express much greater dissatisfaction with life than do women of the same age.
   c. people of all ages report similar levels of happiness.
   d. those whose children have recently left home—the empty nesters—have the lowest level of happiness of all groups.

Adulthood

1. How do our bodies change in middle and late adulthood?

The barely perceptible physical declines of early adulthood begin to accelerate during middle adulthood. For women, a significant physical change of adult life is menopause, which generally seems to be a smooth rather than a rough transition. After 65, perceptual acuity, strength, and stamina decline, but short-term ailments such as colds and the flu are fewer. Neural processes slow, but the brain remains healthy, except for those who suffer brain disease, such as the progressive deterioration of Alzheimer's disease.

2. In what ways do memory and intelligence change as we age?

As the years pass, recall begins to decline, especially for meaningless information, but recognition memory remains strong. Research on how intelligence changes with age has progressed through several phases: cross-sectional studies suggesting a steady intellectual decline after early adulthood; longitudinal studies suggesting intellectual stability until very late in life; and today's view that fluid intelligence declines in later life but crystallized intelligence does not.

3. Is the journey from adolescence to death marked by stages that serve as developmental milestones?

Several theorists maintain that adults progress through an orderly sequence of age-related stages. Others contend that moving from one stage to the next entails recurring times of crisis, such as the early-forties time of transition to midlife. But it appears that people are not so predictable and that the social clock is no longer fixed.

4. What do psychologists view as adulthood's two primary commitments?

Adulthood's two major commitments are love (Erikson's *intimacy*—forming close relationships, especially with family) and work (productive activity, or what Erikson called *generativity*). Life events involving love and work influence adult development in unanticipated ways and vary with culture. Marriage seems more likely to last when people marry after age 20 and are well-educated, but Western couples who marry today are more than twice as likely to divorce as were those who married in 1960. Few people grow old gratefully, but most age gracefully, retaining a sense of well-being throughout life. Those who live to old age must, however, cope with the deaths of friends and family members and with the prospect of their own deaths. Erikson's view of the crisis of late adulthood pits integrity against despair.

TERMS AND CONCEPTS TO REMEMBER

menopause, p. 129	cross-sectional study, p. 134	crystallized intelligence, p. 135	social clock, p. 136
Alzheimer's disease, p. 132	longitudinal study, p. 134	fluid intelligence, p. 135	

REHEARSE IT ANSWER KEY

1. c   2. a   3. d   4. d   5. c   6. c

Sensation and Perception

Twenty-four hours a day, stimuli from the outside world bombard your body. Meanwhile, in a silent, cushioned, inner world, your brain floats in utter darkness. This raises a question, one that predates psychology by thousands of years and helped inspire its beginnings a century ago: *How does the world out there get in?*

To modernize the question: How do we construct our representations of the external world? How do we represent a campfire's flicker, crackle, and smoky scent as patterns of active neural connections? And how, from this living neurochemistry, do we create our conscious experience of the fire's motion and temperature, its aroma and beauty?

To represent the world in our head, we must detect physical energy from the environment and encode it as neural signals, a process traditionally called *sensation.* And we must select, organize, and interpret our sensations, a process traditionally called *perception.* In our everyday experiences, sensation and perception blend into one continuous process. In Modules 10 through 13 we slow down that process to study its parts.

We start with the sensory receptors (Modules 10 and 11) and work up to higher levels of processing. Psychologists refer to sensory analysis that starts at the entry level as *bottom-up processing.* Our minds also interpret what our senses detect (Modules 12 and 13). We construct perceptions drawing both on sensations coming bottom-up to the brain, and on our experience and expectations, which psychologists call *top-down processing.*

Failures of perception may occur anywhere between sensory detection and perceptual interpretation. For example, the eyes of a person born with cataracts may be unable to detect light, rendering the brain's higher-level visual processing equipment useless. People with brain damage reveal the importance of other links in the sensation-perception chain. After losing a temporal lobe area essential to recognizing faces, patient "E.H." suffers from a condition called *prosopagnosia.* She has complete sensation but incomplete perception. She can sense visual information—indeed may accurately report the features of a face—yet she is unable to recognize it. Shown an unfamiliar face, she does not react. Shown a familiar face, her autonomic nervous system responds with measurable perspiration. Still, she hasn't a clue who the person is. Shown her own face in a mirror, she is again stumped. Because of her brain damage, she cannot process top-down—she cannot relate her stored knowledge to the sensory input.

10 Introduction to Sensation and Perception: Vision

- **Sensing the World: Some Basic Principles**
- **Vision**

FIGURE 10.1

Top-down and bottom-up processing: "The Forest Has Eyes"

(Detail, "The Forest Has Eyes" by Bev Doolittle © The Greenwich Workshop, Inc., Trumbull, CT.)

- **sensation** the process by which our sensory receptors and nervous system receive and represent stimulus energies from our environment.

- **perception** the process of organizing and interpreting sensory information, enabling us to recognize meaningful objects and events.

- **bottom-up processing** analysis that begins with the sense receptors and works up to the brain's integration of sensory information.

- **top-down processing** information processing guided by higher-level mental processes, as when we construct perceptions drawing on our experience and expectations.

To construct the outside world in our heads, we must detect physical energy from the environment and encode it as neural signals (a process traditionally called **sensation**). And we must select, organize, and interpret our sensations (a process traditionally called **perception**). In our everyday experiences, we transform our sensations into perceptions. We create meaning.

Our sensory and perceptual processes work together to help us sort out the complex images in the painting in **FIGURE 10.1.** Through **bottom-up processing,** which begins with our sense receptors, we detect the lines, angles, and colors that form the horses, rider, and surroundings. And using **top-down processing,** drawing on our experiences and expectations, we consider the painting's title, notice the horses' and rider's apprehensive expressions, and then direct our attention to the aspects of the painting that give those observations meaning.

In this module we first look at some basic principles of sensation and perception, then consider vision—for humans, the major sense.

Sensing the World: Some Basic Principles

Sensory systems enable organisms to obtain needed information. Consider:

- A frog, which feeds on flying insects, has eyes with receptor cells that fire only in response to small, dark, moving objects. A frog could starve to death knee-deep in motionless flies. But let one zoom by and the frog's "bug detector" cells snap awake.
- A male silkworm moth has receptors so sensitive to the odor of the female sex-attractant that a single female silkworm moth need release only a billionth of an ounce per second to attract every male silkworm moth within a mile. That is why there continue to be silkworms.
- We are similarly designed to detect what are, for us, the important features of our environments. Our ears are most sensitive to sound frequencies that include human voice consonants and a baby's cry.

Nature's sensory gifts suit each recipient's needs.

Thresholds

PREVIEW QUESTION 1 What is an absolute threshold, and are we influenced by stimuli below it? How is our threshold for detecting differences affected by the magnitude of the stimuli?

We exist in a sea of energy. At this moment, you and I are being struck by x-rays and radio waves, ultraviolet and infrared light, and sound waves of very high and very low frequencies. But to all of these we are blind and deaf. The shades on our senses are open just a crack, allowing us only a restricted awareness of this vast sea. **Psychophysics** is the study of how this physical energy relates to our psychological experience. What stimuli can we detect? At what intensity? How sensitive are we to changing stimulation?

Absolute Thresholds

To some kinds of stimuli we are exquisitely sensitive. Standing atop a mountain on an utterly dark, clear night, we can, given normal senses, see a candle flame atop another mountain 30 miles away. In a silent room, we can hear a watch ticking 20 feet away. We can feel the wing of a bee falling on our cheek. We can even smell a single drop of perfume in a three-room apartment (Galanter, 1962).

Our awareness of these faint stimuli illustrates our **absolute threshold**—the minimum stimulation necessary to detect a particular stimulus (light, sound, odor, pressure, taste). Psychologists usually measure absolute threshold by recording the stimulation needed for us to pinpoint its appearance 50 percent of the time. To test your absolute threshold for sounds, a hearing specialist would expose each of your ears to varying sound levels. For each pitch, the hearing test defines where half the time you correctly detect the sound and half the time you do not. For each of the senses, that 50-50 point defines your absolute threshold.

Subliminal Stimulation

Can the stimuli that fall below our absolute threshold influence us? Some people claim they do. In 1956, controversy erupted over a false report that New Jersey movie audiences were unwittingly being influenced by imperceptible flashed messages to DRINK COCA-COLA and EAT POPCORN (Pratkanis, 1992). Many years later, the controversy erupted anew, this time over charges that rock music recordings contained "satanic messages," which could be heard if the recordings were played backward and which, when played forward, could unconsciously persuade the unwitting listener. Hoping to trespass on our unconscious, entrepreneurs have offered audiotapes to help us lose weight, stop smoking, or improve our memories. These tapes contain soothing ocean sounds that mask unheard messages such as, "I am thin," "Smoke tastes bad," or "I do well on tests. I have total recall of information." Claims like these make two assumptions: that unconsciously we can sense **subliminal** (literally, "below threshold") stimuli (**FIGURE 10.2**), and that, without our awareness, these stimuli have extraordinary suggestive powers. Can we? Do they?

Sensory limits
A mosquito's buzz can sound like a dive-bomber, thanks to our low threshold for sounds at its pitch. But a shrieking, dive-bombing bat will seem silent, its cries too high-pitched. Our ears are most sensitive to the pitch range of human speech.

- **psychophysics** the study of relationships between the physical characteristics of stimuli, such as their intensity, and our psychological experience of them.

- **absolute threshold** the minimum stimulation needed to detect a particular stimulus 50 percent of the time.

- **subliminal** below one's absolute threshold for conscious awareness.

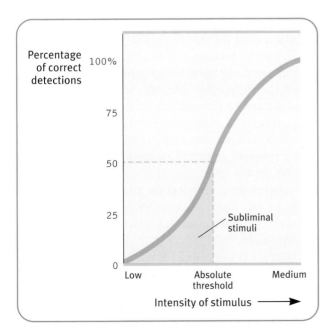

FIGURE 10.2
Absolute threshold
Do I smell it or not? When stimuli are detectable less than 50 percent of the time, they are "subliminal." Absolute threshold is the intensity at which we can detect a stimulus half the time.

The difference threshold

In this computer-generated copy of the Twenty-third Psalm, each line of the typeface changes imperceptibly. How many lines are required for you to experience a just noticeable difference?

The LORD is my shepherd;
      I shall not want.
He maketh me to lie down
         in green pastures:
      he leadeth me
         beside the still waters.
He restoreth my soul:
      he leadeth me
         in the paths of righteousness
            for his name's sake.
Yea, though I walk through the valley
            of the shadow of death,
      I will fear no evil:
   for thou art with me;
      thy rod and thy staff
         they comfort me.
Thou preparest a table before me
         in the presence of mine enemies:
   thou anointest my head with oil,
         my cup runneth over.
Surely goodness and mercy
            shall follow me
         all the days of my life:
   and I will dwell
      in the house of the LORD
         for ever.

■ **difference threshold** the minimum difference that a person can detect between two stimuli. We experience the difference threshold as a *just noticeable difference*. (Also called *just noticeable difference* or *jnd*.)

Can we be affected by stimuli so weak as to be unnoticed? Recent experiments hint that, under certain conditions, the answer may again be yes. One experiment subliminally flashed either emotionally positive scenes (such as kittens or a romantic couple) or negative scenes (such as a werewolf or a dead body) an instant before participants viewed slides of people (Krosnick & others, 1992). Although the participants consciously perceived only a flash of light, they gave more positive ratings to people whose photos had been associated with positive scenes. People somehow looked nicer if their photo immediately followed unperceived kittens rather than an unperceived werewolf. Chinese characters, too, seemed nicer if preceded by a flashed but unperceived smiling face rather than a scowling face (Murphy & Zajonc, 1993). Sometimes we *feel* what we do not know and cannot describe. And graduate students evaluate their research ideas more negatively shortly after viewing the unperceived scowling face of their adviser—as if a sense of the adviser's disapproval was lurking in the unconscious mind (Baldwin & others, 1991). An imperceptibly brief stimulus evidently triggers a weak response that evokes a feeling, though not a conscious awareness of the stimulus.

But does the fact of subliminal *sensation* verify entrepreneurial claims of subliminal *persuasion?* Can advertisers really manipulate us with "hidden persuasion"? The laboratory research reveals a *subtle, fleeting* effect on *thinking,* but the subliminal tape hucksters claim something different: a *powerful, enduring* effect on *behavior.* Experiments show that commercial subliminal tapes have no effect beyond that of a placebo—producing an effect because one believes they will do so (Moore, 1988; Pratkanis & others, 1994; Smith & Rogers, 1994).

For example, the Canadian Broadcasting Corporation used a popular Sunday night TV show to flash a subliminal message 352 times (*Advertising Age,* 1958). Asked to guess the message, not one of the almost 500 letter-writers did. Nearly half, however, reported feeling strangely hungry or thirsty during the show. But this was merely an effect of expectations. The actual message was TELEPHONE NOW. The effect of these 352 subliminal messages on Canadian telephone usage? Zilch.

Difference Thresholds

To function effectively, we need absolute thresholds low enough to allow us to detect important sights, sounds, textures, tastes, and smells. We also need to detect small differences among stimuli. A musician must detect minute discrepancies in an instrument's tuning. A wine taster must detect the slight flavor difference between two vintage wines. Parents must detect the sound of their own child's voice amid other children's voices.

The **difference threshold** (also called the *just noticeable difference,* or *jnd*) is the minimum difference a person can detect between any two stimuli. The difference threshold increases with the magnitude of the stimulus. Thus, if you add 10 grams to a 100-gram weight, you will detect the difference; add 10 grams to a 1-*kilogram* weight and you will not, because the difference threshold has increased. More than a century ago, Ernst Weber noted that regardless of their magnitude, two stimuli must differ by a constant proportion for their difference to be perceptible. This principle— that the difference threshold is not a constant amount but some constant *proportion* of the stimulus—is so simple and so widely applicable that we still refer to it as **Weber's law.** The exact proportion varies, depending on the stimulus. For the average person to perceive their differences, two lights must differ in intensity by 8 percent. Two objects must differ in weight by 2 percent. And two tones must differ in frequency by only 0.3 percent (Teghtsoonian, 1971).

Weber's law is a rough approximation. It works well for nonextreme sensory stimuli, and it parallels some of our life experiences. If the price of a 50-cent chocolate bar goes up by 5 cents, shoppers might notice the change; similarly, it might take a £4000 price hike in a £40,000 Mercedes to raise the eyebrows of its potential buyers. In both cases, the price went up by 10 percent. Weber's principle: Our thresholds for detecting differences are a roughly constant proportion of the size of the original stimulus.

Sensory Adaptation

PREVIEW QUESTION 2 **What function does sensory adaptation serve?**

Entering your neighbors' living room, you smell an unpleasant odor. You wonder how they can stand the stench, but within minutes you no longer notice it. Jumping into a swimming pool, you shiver and complain about how cold it is. A short while later a friend arrives and you exclaim, "C'mon in. Water's fine!" These examples illustrate **sensory adaptation**—our diminishing sensitivity to an unchanging stimulus. (To experience this phenomenon, move your watch up your wrist an inch: You will feel it— but only for a few moments.) After constant exposure to a stimulus, our nerve cells fire messages to our brain less frequently.

Why, then, if we stare at an object without flinching, does it not vanish from sight? Because, unnoticed by us, our eyes are always moving, quivering just enough to guarantee that retinal stimulation continually changes.

But what if we actually could stop our eyes from moving? Would sights seem to vanish, as odors do? To find out, psychologists have devised ingenious instruments for maintaining a constant image on the retina. Imagine that we fitted a volunteer, Mary, with one of these instruments—a miniature projector mounted on a contact lens (**FIGURE 10.3a**). When Mary's eye moves, the image from the projector moves as well. Thus, everywhere that Mary looks the scene is sure to go.

If we project the profile of a face through such an instrument, what will Mary see? At first, she will see the complete profile. But within a few seconds, as her sensory receptors begin to fatigue, things get weird. Bit by bit, the image vanishes, only later to reappear and then disappear—in recognizable fragments or as a whole (**FIGURE 10.3b**). Although sensory adaptation reduces our sensitivity, it offers an important benefit: It enables us to focus on *informative* changes in our environment without being distracted by the uninformative constant stimulation of garments, odors, and street noise. Our sensory receptors are alert to novelty; bore them with repetition and they free our attention for more important things. This reinforces a fundamental lesson: We perceive the world not exactly as it is, but as it is useful for us to perceive it.

Sensory thresholds and adaptation are not the only commonalities among the senses. All the senses receive sensory stimulation, transform it into neural information, and deliver that information to the brain. How do the senses work? How do we see? Hear? Smell? Taste? Feel pain? Let's start with vision, the sense people tend to prize the most.

- **Weber's law** the principle that, to be perceived as different, two stimuli must differ by a constant minimum percentage (rather than a constant amount).
- **sensory adaptation** diminished sensitivity as a consequence of constant stimulation.

"We need above all to know about changes; no one wants or needs to be reminded 16 hours a day that his shoes are on."

Neuroscientist David Hubel (1979)

For 9 in 10 people—but, curiously, for only 1 in 3 of those with schizophrenia— this eye flutter turns off when the eye is following a moving target (Holzman & Matthysse, 1990).

"My suspicion is that the universe is not only queerer than we suppose, but queerer than we can suppose."

J. B. S. Haldane, *Possible Worlds*, 1927

(a)

(b)

BEER PEER PEEP BEE BE

FIGURE 10.3

Now you see it, now you don't!
(a) A projector mounted on a contact lens makes the projected image move with the eye. (b) Initially the person sees the stabilized image, but soon she sees fragments fading and reappearing. (From "Stabilized images on the retina" by R. M. Pritchard. Copyright © 1961 Scientific American, Inc. All rights reserved.)

rehearse it!

1. To construct meaning out of our external environment, we select, organize, and interpret sensory information. This is the process of
   a. sensation.
   c. encoding.
   b. persuasion.
   d. perception.

2. Sensation is to _____ as perception is to _____.
   a. absolute threshold; difference threshold
   b. bottom-up processing; top-down processing
   c. interpretation; detection
   d. conscious awareness; persuasion

3. The absolute threshold is the minimum stimulation that a person can detect 50 percent of the time. Knowing your absolute threshold for sound tells you
   a. the smallest difference you can detect between two sounds.

   b. how likely you are to hear a particular faint sound.
   c. why you become used to background noise.
   d. whether you are being affected by subliminal stimulation.

4. People wonder whether subliminal stimuli, such as undetectably faint sights or sounds, influence us. Subliminal stimuli are
   a. too weak to be processed by the brain in any way.
   b. consciously perceived only 50 percent of the time.
   c. strong enough to affect our behavior.
   d. below the absolute threshold for conscious awareness.

5. To be perceived as different, two lights must differ in intensity by at least 8 percent. This illustrates a

   general principle called Weber's law, which states that for a difference to be perceived, two stimuli must differ by
   a. a fixed or constant amount.
   b. a constant minimum percentage.
   c. a constantly changing amount.
   d. more than 7 percent.

6. Sensory adaptation reduces our sensitivity to some stimuli in the environment, such as unpleasant smells. Sensory adaptation also has survival benefits. It helps us focus on
   a. the world as it really is.
   b. underlying phenomena and stimuli.
   c. constant features of the environment.
   d. important changes in the environment.

Vision

Part of our genius is our body's ability to convert one sort of energy to another. Our sensory systems convert stimulus energy into neural messages. Our eyes, for example, receive light energy and manage an amazing feat: They transduce (transform) the energy into neural messages that the brain then processes into what we consciously see. How does such a remarkable thing happen?

Differing eyes

When it comes to vision, humans and bees are on different wavelengths. Compare the way a flower is registered by a human's and a bee's eye. The bee detects reflected ultraviolet wavelengths, enabling it to see the pollen landing field. The differing ecological niches occupied by different species demand sensitivity to different stimuli.

The Stimulus Input: Light Energy

PREVIEW QUESTION 3 What are the characteristics of the wavelengths that we see as visible light?

Scientifically speaking, what strikes our eyes is not color but pulses of electromagnetic energy that our visual system experiences as color. What we see as visible light is but a thin slice of the whole spectrum of electromagnetic radiation. As **FIGURE 10.4** illustrates, this *electromagnetic spectrum* ranges from imperceptibly short pulses or waves of gamma rays, to the narrow band that we see as visible light, to the long waves of radio transmission. Two physical characteristics of light

FIGURE 10.4

The spectrum of electromagnetic energy

This spectrum ranges from gamma rays as short as the diameter of an atom to radio waves over a mile long. The narrow band of wavelengths visible to the human eye (shown enlarged) extends from the shorter waves of blue-violet light to the longer waves of red light. Other organisms are sensitive to differing portions of the spectrum. For instance, bees cannot see red but can see ultraviolet light (see photos on page 148).

White light

Prism

400　　500　　600　　700

Part of spectrum visible to humans

Gamma rays	X-rays	Ultra-violet rays		Infrared rays	Radar	Broadcast bands	AC circuits

10^{-5}　10^{-3}　10^{-1}　10^{1}　10^{3}　10^{5}　10^{7}　10^{9}　10^{11}　10^{13}　10^{15}　10^{17}

Wavelength in nanometers (billionths of a meter)

■ **wavelength** the distance from the peak of one light or sound wave to the peak of the next. Electromagnetic wavelengths vary from the short blips of cosmic rays to the long pulses of radio transmission.

■ **hue** the dimension of color that is determined by the wavelength of light; what we know as the color names *blue*, *green*, and so forth.

■ **intensity** the amount of energy in a light or sound wave, which we perceive as brightness or loudness, as determined by the wave's amplitude.

and sound help determine our sensory experience of them. Light's **wavelength**—the distance from one wave peak to the next (**FIGURE 10.5a**)—determines its **hue** (the color we experience, such as blue or green). **Intensity,** the amount of energy in light waves (determined by a wave's *amplitude,* or height), influences brightness (**FIGURE 10.5b**). To understand *how* we transform physical energy into a sensation of color, we first need to understand our mind's window, the eye.

FIGURE 10.5

The physical properties of waves

(a) Waves vary in wavelength, the distance between successive peaks. Frequency, the number of complete wavelengths that can pass a point in a given time, depends on the wavelength. The shorter the wavelength, the higher the frequency. (b) Waves also vary in amplitude, the height from peak to trough. Wave amplitude determines the intensity of colors and sounds.

Short wavelength = high frequency
(bluish colors, high-pitched sounds)

Long wavelength = low frequency
(reddish colors, low-pitched sounds)

(a)

Great amplitude
(bright colors, loud sounds)

Small amplitude
(dull colors, soft sounds)

(b)

FIGURE 10.6

The eye

Light rays reflected from the candle pass through the cornea, pupil, and lens. The curvature and thickness of the lens change to bring either nearby or distant objects into focus on the retina. Light rays travel in straight lines. So rays from the top of the candle strike the bottom of the retina and those from the left side of the candle strike the right side of the retina. The candle's retinal image is thus upside-down and reversed.

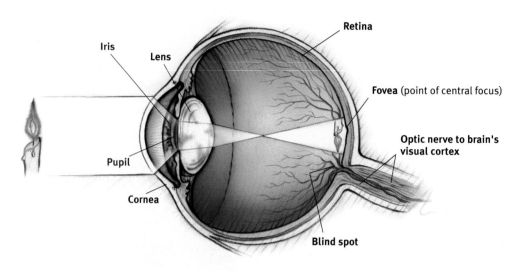

Iris
Lens
Retina
Fovea (point of central focus)
Optic nerve to brain's visual cortex
Pupil
Cornea
Blind spot

- **accommodation** the process by which the eye's lens changes shape to focus the image of near objects on the retina.

- **retina** the light-sensitive inner surface of the eye, containing the receptor rods and cones plus layers of neurons (nerve cells) that begin the processing of visual information.

- **rods** retinal receptors that detect black, white, and gray; necessary for peripheral and twilight vision, when cones don't respond.

- **cones** receptor cells that are concentrated near the center of the retina and that function in daylight or in well-lit conditions. The cones detect fine detail and give rise to color sensations.

- **optic nerve** the nerve that carries neural impulses from the eye to the brain.

The Eye

PREVIEW QUESTION 4 How does the eye transform light energy into neural messages?

Light enters the eye through the *cornea,* a transparent protector, then passes through the *pupil,* a small adjustable opening (**FIGURE 10.6**). The pupil's size, and therefore the amount of light entering the eye, is regulated by the *iris,* a colored muscle surrounding the pupil. The iris has a remarkable ability to adjust light intake by dilating and constricting in response to light intensity and even to inner emotions. When we're feeling amorous, our telltale dilated pupils subtly signal our interest. Behind the pupil is a *lens* that focuses the incoming rays into an image on the light-sensitive back surface. It does so by changing its curvature in a process called **accommodation.** The eyeball's light-sensitive surface on which the rays focus is a multilayered tissue, the **retina.**

For centuries, scientists have known that when the image of a candle passes through a small opening, its mirror image appears inverted on a dark wall behind (as in **FIGURE 10.6**). This fact was baffling. If the retina receives an upside-down image, how can we see the world right side up?

Eventually scientists discovered that the retina doesn't read the image as a whole. Rather, its millions of receptor cells convert light energy into neural impulses. These impulses are sent to the brain and constructed *there* into a perceived, upright-seeming image.

The Retina

If you followed a single particle of light energy into your eye, you would see that it first makes its way through the retina's outer layer of cells to its buried receptor cells,

Rod-shaped rods and cone-shaped cones

As this scanning electron microscope shows, rods and cones are well named. The rods are more sensitive to light than are the color-sensitive cones, which is why the world looks colorless at night. Some nocturnal animals, such as toads, mice, rats, and bats, have retinas made up almost entirely of rods, allowing them to function well in dim light. These creatures probably have very poor color vision.

the **rods** and **cones** (**FIGURE 10.7** and Table 10.1). Light energy striking the rods and cones produces chemical changes that generate neural signals. These signals activate the neighboring *bipolar cells,* which in turn activate the neighboring *ganglion cells.* The axons from the network of ganglion cells converge like the strands of a rope to form an **optic nerve** that carries information to your brain. Nearly a million messages can be sent by the optic nerve at once, through nearly 1 million ganglion fibers. (The auditory nerve, which enables hearing, carries much less infor-

FIGURE 10.7
The retina's reaction to light

2. Chemical reaction in turn activates bipolar cells.

1. Light entering eye triggers photochemical reaction in rods and cones at back of retina.

Light

Ganglion cell

Bipolar cell

Cross section of retina

Light

Cone

Neural impulse

Rod

To visual cortex

Optic nerve

3. Bipolar cells then activate the ganglion cells, the axons of which converge to form the optic nerve. This nerve transmits information to the visual cortex in the brain's occipital lobe.

TABLE 10.1

RECEPTORS IN THE HUMAN EYE

	Cones	Rods
Number	6 million	120 million
Location in retina	Center	Periphery
Sensitivity in dim light	Low	High
Color sensitive?	Yes	No
Detail sensitive?	Yes	No

mation through its mere 30,000 fibers.) Where the optic nerve leaves the eye there are no receptor cells—creating a **blind spot** (**FIGURE 10.8**).

Rods enable black-and-white vision; cones enable you to see color. If illumination diminishes, the cones become ineffectual. The rods, however, remain sensitive in dim light, because several rods will funnel their faint energy from dim light onto a single bipolar cell. That is why you do not see colors in dim light. Thus, cones and rods each provide a special sensitivity—cones to detail and rods to faint light.

When you enter a darkened theater or turn off the light at night, your pupils dilate to allow more light to reach the rods in the retina's periphery. It typically takes 20 minutes or more before our eyes fully adapt. You can demonstrate dark adaptation by closing or covering one eye for up to 20 minutes. Then make the light in the room not quite bright enough to read this book with your open eye. Now open the dark-adapted eye and read (easily). This period of dark adaptation is yet another instance of the remarkable adaptiveness of our sensory systems, for it parallels the average natural twilight transition between the sun's setting and darkness.

■ **blind spot** the point at which the optic nerve leaves the eye, creating a "blind" spot because no receptor cells are located there.

Knowing just this much about the eye, can you imagine why a cat sees so much better at night than you do? (See p. 153.)

FIGURE 10.8

The blind spot

Where the optic nerve leaves the eye (Figure 10.7), there are no receptor cells. This creates a blind spot in our vision. To demonstrate, close your left eye, look at the spot, and move the page to a distance from your face (about a foot) at which the car disappears. In everyday vision the blind spot doesn't impair your vision because your eyes are moving and because one eye catches what the other misses.

Visual Information Processing

PREVIEW QUESTION 5 How is visual information processed in the brain?

Turn your eyes to the left, close them, and then gently rub the right side of your right eyelid with your fingertip. Note the patch of light to the left, moving as your finger moves. Why do you see light? Why at the left? (See p. 155.)

Visual information percolates through progressively more abstract levels. At the entry level, the retina—which is actually a piece of the brain that migrates to the eye during early fetal development—processes information before routing it to the brain's cortex. The retina's neural layers are not just passing along electrical impulses; they also help to encode and analyze the sensory information. The third neural layer in a frog's eye, for example, contains the "bug detector" cells that fire only in response to flylike stimuli. In human eyes, the information from the retina's nearly 130 million receptor rods and cones is received and transmitted by the million or so ganglion cells, whose fibers make up the optic nerve. But most information processing occurs in the brain. Any given area of the retina relays its information to a corresponding location in the *visual cortex* at the back of the brain (**FIGURE 10.9**).

FIGURE 10.9

Pathway from the eyes to the visual cortex

Neurons in the optic nerves come together at the optic chiasm at the base of the brain and form the optic tracts, which run to nuclei in the thalamus (the brain's sensory switchboard), where they synapse on neurons that run to the visual cortex.

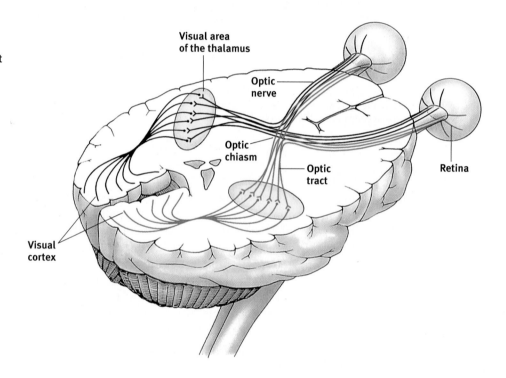

Feature Detection

When individual ganglion cells register information in their region of the visual field, they send signals to the visual cortex. Nobel Prize winners David Hubel and Torsten Wiesel (1979) demonstrated that when certain cortical neurons, called **feature detectors,** receive this information, they respond to specific features of a scene—to particular edges, lines, angles, and movements. From these elements the brain assembles the perceived image.

For example, Hubel and Wiesel report that a given brain cell might respond maximally to a bar flashed at a 2 o'clock tilt (**FIGURE 10.10**). If the bar is tilted further—say, to a 3 o'clock or 1 o'clock position—the cell quiets down. Thus, the feature detector cells record amazingly specific features taken in by the eye. Feature detector cells pass this information to other cells that respond only to more complex patterns. The basic idea is that perceptions arise from the interaction of many neuron systems, each performing a simple task.

■ **feature detectors** nerve cells in the brain that respond to specific features of the stimulus, such as shape, angle, or movement.

FIGURE 10.10
Electrodes record how individual cells in this monkey's visual cortex respond to different visual stimuli
Hubel and Wiesel won the Nobel Prize for their discovery that most cells in the visual cortex respond only to particular features—for example, to the edge of a surface or to a bar at a 30-degree angle in the upper right part of the field of vision. More complex features trigger higher-level detector cells, which integrate information from these simpler ones.

The visual cortex passes this information along to the temporal and parietal cortex, which includes higher-level brain cells that respond to specific visual scenes, such as a face or an arm movement in a particular direction. Psychologist David Perrett and his colleagues (1988, 1992, 1994) report that for biologically important objects and events, monkey brains (and surely ours as well) have a "vast visual encyclopedia" distributed as cells that respond to one stimulus but not to others. Perrett has identified nerve cells that specialize in responding to a specific gaze, head angle, posture, or body movement. Other supercell clusters integrate this information and fire only when the cues collectively indicate the direction of someone's attention and approach. This instant analysis, which aided our ancestors' survival, also helps a soccer goalkeeper anticipate the direction of an impending kick and a pedestrian anticipate another pedestrian's next movement.

Going left or right?
In the semifinal game of the 1996 European Cup, German goalkeeper Andreas Kopke anticipates the direction of Gareth Southgate's tiebreaker kick for England. Before Southgate's foot connects with the ball, Kopke's visual system has processed information from Southgate's eyes, posture, and movement, activating "going right" supercells. Kopke blocks the kick and Germany wins.

Parallel Processing

Consider some actual cases of peculiar visual disabilities produced by peculiar brain damage (from Hoffman, 1998).

- Looking at an American flag, Ms. W is able to see lines and stars. But "it's like you have one part here and one part there, and you put them together to see what they make."
- Mr. I, an artist until suffering a concussion at age 65, no longer perceives colors, only shades of gray. Tomatoes look black, flowers an assortment of grays. Even his once vivid imagination of colors is now gone.
- Ms. M, having suffered stroke damage near the rear of both sides of her brain, can no longer perceive movement. People moving about a room seem "suddenly here or there but I have not seen them moving." It's a challenge to pour tea into a cup because the fluid appears frozen and she cannot perceive the rising in the cup. (You could experience this same loss of motion if given disruptive magnetic stimulation to the corresponding neural area in your brain.)

These and other cases suggest that, unlike most computers, which do step-by-step serial processing, our brains engage in **parallel processing.** That means we can do several things at once. We construct our perceptions by integrating the work of different

Answer to question on p. 151:
There are at least two reasons: A cat's pupils can open much wider than yours, letting in more light; and a cat has a higher proportion of light-sensitive rods (Moser, 1987). But there is a trade-off: With fewer cones, a cat sees neither details nor color as well as you do.

■ **parallel processing** the processing of several aspects of a problem simultaneously; the brain's natural mode of information processing for many functions, including vision.

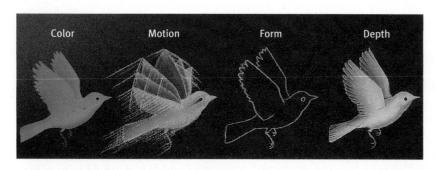

Parallel processing

Studies of brain-damaged patients suggest that the brain delegates the work of processing color, motion, form, and depth to different areas. After taking a scene apart, how does the brain integrate these subdimensions into the perceived image? The answer to this question is the Holy Grail of vision research.

FIGURE 10.11

A simplified summary of visual information processing

Abstraction:
Brain's higher-level cells respond to combined information from feature-detector cells

Feature detection:
Brain's detector cells respond to elementary features—bars, edges, or gradients of light

Recognition:
Brain matches the constructed image with stored images

Retinal processing:
Receptor rods and cones→bipolar cells → ganglion cells

Scene

"I am fearfully and wonderfully made."

King David, *Psalms* 139:14

visual teams, working in parallel. Destroy or disable the neural workstation for a visual subtask and something peculiar results.

The brain divides a visual scene into subdimensions such as color, depth, movement, and form and works on each aspect simultaneously (Livingstone & Hubel, 1988). This illustrates the remarkable powers of our human visual intelligence. Neural impulses travel a million times slower than a computer's internal messages, yet our brains humble any computer by recognizing a familiar face instantly. "You can buy a chess machine that beats a master," notes Donald Hoffman (1998, p. xiii), "but can't yet buy a vision machine that beats a toddler's vision."

The distribution of visual tasks to different neural work teams explains the peculiar cases. After her stroke damage, for example, Ms. M lost just one aspect of vision and was unable to perceive movement. When something moved, it disappeared until it stopped. Other brain-damaged patients can tell you all about the subdimensions of an object or person (a rose's color or a woman's height) but cannot name the object or the person. This reminds us once again of the startling truth: Our brains do many things at once, automatically and without our awareness.

Senses other than vision also process information with similar speed and intricacy. Opening the back door, you recognize the aroma wafting from the kitchen even before you step inside. Answering the phone, you recognize the friend calling from the moment she says "Hi." Within a fraction of a second after such events stimulate the senses, millions of neurons have simultaneously coordinated in extracting the essential features, comparing them with past experience and identifying the stimulus (Freeman, 1991).

This scientific understanding of sensory information processing is illustrated by neuropsychologist Roger Sperry's (1985) reflection: The "insights of science give added, not lessened, reasons for awe, respect, and reverence." Think about it: As you look at someone, the visual information is sent to your brain as millions of neural impulses, then constructed into its component features, and finally, in some as yet mysterious way, composed into a meaningful perceived image, which is then compared with previously stored images and recognized as, for example, your grandmother. The whole process (**FIGURE 10.11**) is more complex than taking a car apart, piece by piece, transporting it to a different location, then having specialized workers reconstruct it. That all of this happens instantly, effortlessly, and continuously is indeed awesome.

Color Vision

PREVIEW QUESTION 6 What theories contribute to our understanding of color vision, and how are we affected by color constancy?

We talk as though objects possess color. We say, "A tomato is red." Perhaps you have pondered the old question, "If a tree falls in the forest and no one hears it, does it make a sound?" We can ask the same of color: If no one sees the tomato, is it red?

The answer is no. First, the tomato is everything *but* red, because it *rejects* (reflects) the long wavelengths of red. Second, the tomato's color is our mental construction. As Isaac Newton (1704) noted, "The [light] rays are not coloured." Color, like all aspects of vision, resides not in the object but in the theater of our brains. Even while dreaming, we may perceive things in color.

In the study of vision, one of the most basic and intriguing mysteries is how we see the world in color. How, from the light energy striking the retina, does the brain manufacture our experience of color—and of such a multitude of colors? Our difference threshold for colors is so low that we can discriminate some 7 million different color variations (Geldard, 1972).

At least most of us can. For about 1 person in 50, vision is color-deficient—and that person is usually male, because the defect is genetically sex-linked. To understand why some people's vision is color-deficient, it will help to first understand how normal color vision works.

Modern detective work on the mystery of color vision began in the nineteenth century when Hermann von Helmholtz built on the insights of an English physicist, Thomas Young. Young and Helmholtz knew that any color can be created by combining the light waves of three primary colors—red, green, and blue. So, they inferred that the eye must have three types of receptors, one for each primary color of light.

Years later, researchers measured the response of various cones to different color stimuli and confirmed the **Young-Helmholtz trichromatic (three-color) theory,** which simply states that the retina has three types of color receptors, each especially sensitive to one of three colors. And surprise! Those colors are, indeed, red, green, or blue. When we stimulate combinations of these cones, we see other colors. For example, there are no receptors especially sensitive to yellow. Yet when both red- and green-sensitive cones are stimulated, we see yellow.

If you are trying to make sense of all this by thinking back to mixing paints, you had better think again. Mixing paints is *subtractive color mixing* because it *subtracts* wavelengths from the reflected light. The more colors you mix in, the fewer wavelengths can be reflected back. So, mixing blue and yellow paint leaves only green to be reflected back. Combining red, blue, and yellow means no light waves will be reflected and you will see brown or black. But mixing *lights,* as Young and Helmholtz did, is *additive color mixing,* because the process adds wavelengths and thus *increases* light—combining red, blue, and green lights makes white light (**FIGURE 10.12**).

■ **Young-Helmholtz trichromatic (three-color) theory** the theory that the retina contains three different color receptors—one most sensitive to red, one to green, one to blue—which when stimulated in combination can produce the perception of any color.

"Only mind has sight and hearing; all things else are deaf and blind."

Epicharmus, *Fragments*, 550 B.C.

Answer to question on p. 152: Your retinal cells are so responsive that even pressure triggers them. But your brain interprets their firing as light. Moreover, it interprets the light as coming from the left—the direction light normally comes from when it activates the right side of the retina.

FIGURE 10.12

Subtractive and additive color mixing Mixing paint colors subtracts wavelengths. Mixing all three primary colors leaves you with black. Mixing lights is additive, because wavelengths from each light in the mix reach the eye, and mixing all three primary light colors creates white.

Subtractive color mixing

Additive color mixing

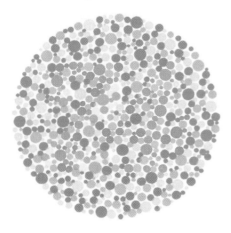

Most color-deficient people are not actually "colorblind." They simply lack functioning red- or green-sensitive cones. Their vision is dichromatic (two-color) instead of trichromatic, making it difficult to distinguish red and green, as in **FIGURE 10.13** (Boynton, 1979). Dogs, too, lack receptors for the wavelengths of red, giving them only limited, dichromatic color vision (Neitz & others, 1989).

Soon after Young and von Helmholtz proposed the trichromatic theory, physiologist Ewald Hering pointed out that other parts of the color vision mystery remained unsolved. For example, we see yellow when mixing red and green light. But how is it that those blind to red and green can often still see yellow? And why does yellow appear to be a pure color and not a mixture of red and green, the way purple is of red and blue?

Hering found a clue in the well-known occurrence of *afterimages*. When you stare at a green square for a while and then look at a white sheet of paper, you see red, green's *opponent color*. Stare at a yellow square and you will later see its opponent color, blue, on the white paper (as in the flag demonstration in **FIGURE 10.14**). Hering surmised that there were two additional color processes, one responsible for red versus green perception, and one for blue versus yellow.

A century later, researchers confirmed Hering's **opponent-process theory.** *After* leaving the receptor cells, visual information is analyzed in terms of the opponent colors red and green, blue and yellow, and also black and white. In the retina and in the thalamus (where impulses from the retina are relayed en route to the visual cortex) some neurons are turned "on" by red but turned "off" by green. Others are turned on by green but off by red (DeValois & DeValois, 1975). Opponent processes explain afterimages, such as in the flag demonstration, in which we tire our green response by staring at green. When we then stare at white (which contains all colors, including red), only the red part of the green/red pairing will fire normally.

The present solution to the mystery of color vision is therefore roughly this: Color processing occurs in two stages. The retina's red, green, and blue cones respond in varying degrees to different color stimuli, as the Young-Helmholtz trichromatic theory suggested. Their signals are then processed by the nervous system's opponent-process cells, en route to the visual cortex.

Color Constancy

Our experience of color depends on something more than the wavelength information received by our trichromatic cones and transmitted through the opponent-process cells.

That something more is the surrounding *context*. If you view only part of a tomato, its color will seem to change as the light changes. But if you see the whole tomato as one item in a bowl of fresh vegetables, its color will remain roughly constant as the lighting and wavelengths shift—a phenomenon known as **color con-**

- **opponent-process theory** the theory that opposing retinal processes (red-green, yellow-blue, white-black) enable color vision. For example, some cells are stimulated by green and inhibited by red; others are stimulated by red and inhibited by green.

- **color constancy** perceiving familiar objects as having consistent color, even if changing illumination alters the wavelengths reflected by the object.

stancy. Dorothea Jameson (1985) notes that a chip colored blue under indoor lighting matches the wavelengths reflected by a gold chip in the sunlight. Yet bring a bluebird indoors and it won't look like a goldfinch. Likewise, a green leaf hanging from a brown branch may, when the illumination changes, reflect the same light energy that formerly came from the brown branch. Yet to us the leaf stays greenish and the branch stays brownish. Put on yellow-tinted ski goggles and the snow, after a second, looks as white as before.

Though we take this color constancy for granted, the phenomenon is truly remarkable. It demonstrates that our experience of color comes not just from the object—the color is not in the isolated leaf—but from everything around it as well. You and I see color thanks to our brains' computations of the light reflected by any object *relative to its surrounding objects.*

In a context that does not vary, we maintain color constancy. But what if we change the context? Because the brain computes the color of an object relative to its context, the perceived color changes (as is dramatically apparent in **FIGURE 10.15**). This principle—that we perceive objects not in isolation but in their environmental context—is especially significant for artists, interior decorators, and clothing designers. Our perception of the color of a wall or of a swatch of paint on a canvas is determined not just by the paint in the can but by the surrounding colors.

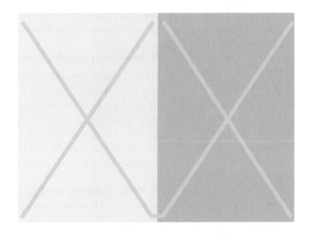

FIGURE 10.15

Color depends on context

In this painting by Joseph Albers (1975), the unchanging line seems to vary from gray to yellow as its surrounding context changes.

rehearse it!

7. Two physical characteristics of light help determine our sensory experience of it. The characteristic that determines the color we experience is
   a. intensity.
   b. wavelength.
   c. amplitude.
   d. hue.

8. The blind spot is located in the area of the retina in which
   a. there are rods but no cones.
   b. there are cones but no rods.
   c. the optic nerve leaves the eye.
   d. the bipolar cells meet the ganglion cells.

9. Rods and cones are the eye's receptor cells. Cones are especially sensitive to _____ light and are responsible for our _____ vision.
   a. bright; black-and-white
   b. dim; color
   c. bright; color
   d. dim; black-and-white

10. According to Hubel and Wiesel, the brain includes cells that respond maximally to certain bars, edges, and angles. These cells are called
   a. rods and cones.
   b. feature detector cells.
   c. bug detectors.
   d. ganglion cells.

11. Unlike most computers, the brain is capable of simultaneously processing separate aspects of an object or problem. We call this ability
   a. parallel processing.
   b. feature detection.
   c. recognition.
   d. accommodation.

12. Researchers today believe that the Young-Helmholtz and Hering theories together account for color vision. The Young-Helmholtz theory shows that the eye contains _____ and the Hering theory accounts for the brain's, having _____.
   a. opposing retinal processes; three pairs of color receptors
   b. opponent-process cells; three types of color receptors
   c. three pairs of color receptors; opposing retinal processes
   d. three types of color receptors; opponent-process cells

13. We perceive tomatoes and stringbeans as consistently red and green, respectively, even though shifting illumination may alter their reflective wavelengths. This demonstrates the phenomenon of
   a. afterimages.
   b. color constancy.
   c. trichromatic vision.
   d. color processing.

Introduction to Sensation and Perception: Vision

1. What is an absolute threshold, and are we influenced by stimuli below it? How is our threshold for detecting differences affected by the magnitude of the stimuli?

We—like other species—sense only a portion of the sea of energy that surrounds us, but to this portion, which enables us to survive and thrive, we are exquisitely sensitive. Our absolute threshold for any stimulus is the minimum stimulation detectable 50 percent of the time. Experiments reveal that we can process some information from subliminal (subthreshold) stimuli, but the restricted conditions under which this occurs would not enable unscrupulous opportunists to exploit us with subliminal messages.

To survive and thrive, an organism must have difference thresholds low enough to detect minute changes in important stimuli. In humans, a difference threshold (also called a just noticeable difference, or jnd) is a constant proportion of the magnitude of the stimulus—a principle known as Weber's law.

2. What function does sensory adaptation serve?

The phenomenon of sensory adaptation helps to focus our attention on changing stimulation by diminishing our sensitivity to constant or routine odors, sounds, and so forth.

3. What are the characteristics of the wavelengths that we see as visible light?

Each of our senses receives stimulation, transforms it into neural signals, and sends these neural messages to the brain. The energies we experience as visible light are a thin slice from the broad spectrum of electromagnetic radiation. The perceived hue (blue, green, and so on) of light depends on its wavelength. The brightness of light depends on its intensity.

4. How does the eye transform light energy into neural messages?

After entering the eye and being focused by a cameralike lens (through the process of accommodation), light waves strike the retina. The retina's light-sensitive rods and color-sensitive cones convert the light energy into neural impulses, which travel along the optic nerve to the brain. The point at which the optic nerve leaves the eye is the blind spot.

5. How is visual information processed in the brain?

Nerve cells in the retina process information before routing it to the brain. Within the cortex, individual feature detector cells respond to specific aspects of the visual stimulus, and their information is pooled by higher-level brain cells for interpretation. Subdimensions of vision (color, movement, depth, and form) are processed separately and simultaneously, illustrating our brain's capacity for parallel processing.

6. What theories contribute to our understanding of color vision, and how are we affected by color constancy?

Research on how we see color supports two nineteenth-century theories. First, as the Young-Helmholtz trichromatic (three-color) theory suggests, the retina contains three types of cones. Each is most sensitive to the wavelengths of one of the three primary colors (red, green, or blue). Second, as opponent-process theory maintains, the nervous system codes the color-related information from the cones into pairs of opponent colors, as demonstrated by the phenomenon of afterimages and as confirmed by measuring opponent processes within the retina and within visual neurons of the thalamus. The phenomenon of color constancy under varying illumination shows that our brains construct our experience of color.

TERMS AND CONCEPTS TO REMEMBER

sensation, p. 144	difference threshold, p. 146	retina, p. 150	Young-Helmholtz trichromatic
perception, p. 144	Weber's law, p. 146	rods, p. 150	(three-color) theory, p. 155
bottom-up processing, p. 144	sensory adaptation, p. 147	cones, p. 150	opponent-process theory, p. 156
top-down processing, p. 144	wavelength, p. 149	optic nerve, p. 150	color constancy, p. 156
psychophysics, p. 144	hue, p. 149	blind spot, p. 151	
absolute threshold, p. 145	intensity, p. 149	feature detectors, p. 152	
subliminal, p. 145	accommodation, p. 150	parallel processing, p. 153	

REHEARSE IT ANSWER KEY

1. d	3. b	5. b	7. b	9. c	11. a	13. b
2. b	4. d	6. d	8. c	10. b	12. d	

The Other Senses

■ Hearing

■ Touch and Pain

■ Taste

■ Smell

■ Body Position and Movement

For humans, vision is the major sense. More of our brain cortex is devoted to vision than to any other sense. Moreover, when there is a conflict between visual and other sensory information, vision tends to dominate or "capture" the other senses. This phenomenon of **visual capture** is an everyday experience. When viewing a movie for which the projector provides the sound, we nevertheless perceive the sound as coming from the screen, where we see the actors talking. While viewing a roller coaster ride on a giant wraparound movie screen, we may brace ourselves, even though our other senses tell us we're not moving. In both cases, vision has captured the other senses.

Yet without our senses of hearing, touch, taste, smell, and body motion and position, our capacities for experiencing the world would be vastly diminished.

Hearing

Like our other senses, our hearing, or **audition,** is highly adaptive. We hear a wide range of sounds, but we hear best those sounds having frequencies within a range that corresponds to the range of the human voice. And we also are remarkably sensitive to faint sounds, an obvious boon to our ancestors' survival when hunting or being hunted or detecting a child's whimper. (If our ears were much more sensitive, we would hear a constant hiss from the movement of air molecules.) We are also acutely sensitive to differences in sounds. We easily detect differences among thousands of human voices, helping us to recognize immediately the voice of almost anyone we know. How do we do it?

The Stimulus Input: Sound Waves

PREVIEW QUESTION 1 What are the characteristics of the air pressure waves that we hear as meaningful sounds?

Hit a piano key and the resulting stimulus energy is sound waves—jostling molecules of air, each bumping into the next, like a shove being transmitted through a concert hall's crowded exit tunnel. The resulting waves of compressed and expanded air are like the ripples on a pond circling out from where a stone has been tossed. As we swim in our ocean of moving air molecules, our ears detect these brief air pressure changes. They then transform them into nerve impulses, which our brain decodes as sounds. The strength, or amplitude, of sound waves determines their *loudness.* Sound waves also vary in **wavelength,** the distance from one wave peak

The sounds of music

A violin's short, fast waves create a high pitch; an accordion's longer, slower waves, a low pitch. Differences in the waves' height or amplitude also create differing degrees of loudness.

■ **visual capture** the tendency for vision to dominate the other senses, as when we perceive voices in films as coming from the screen we see rather than from the projector behind us.

■ **audition** the sense of hearing.

■ **wavelength** the distance from the peak of one light or sound wave to the peak of the next.

FIGURE 11.1

The physical properties of waves

(a) Waves vary in wavelength, the distance between successive peaks. Frequency, the number of complete wavelengths that can pass a point in a given time, depends on the wavelength. The shorter the wavelength, the higher the frequency. (b) Waves also vary in amplitude, the height from peak to trough. Wave amplitude determines intensity: the brightness of colors and the loudness of sounds.

(a) (b)

to the next, and therefore in **frequency** (**FIGURE 11.1**). Their frequency determines their **pitch:** The longer the waves (the lower their frequency), the lower the pitch; the shorter the waves (the higher their frequency), the higher the pitch. A piccolo produces much shorter sound waves than does a tuba.

Decibels are the measuring unit for sound energy. The *absolute threshold* for hearing, defined as the minimum stimulation needed to detect the stimulus (in this case the sound) 50 percent of the time, is arbitrarily defined as 0 decibels. Every 10 decibels correspond to a tenfold increase in sound. Thus, normal conversation (60 decibels) is 10,000 times louder than a 20-decibel whisper. And a tolerable 100-decibel passing subway train is 10 billion times louder than the faintest detectable sound. When prolonged, however, exposure to sounds above 85 decibels can produce hearing loss (**FIGURE 11.2**).

FIGURE 11.2

The intensity of some common sounds

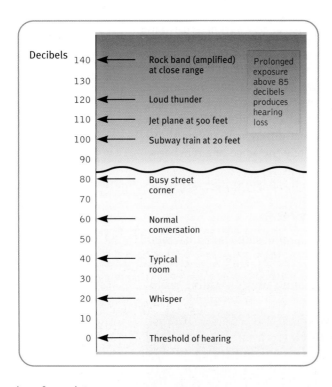

The Ear

PREVIEW QUESTION 2 How does the ear transform sound energy into neural messages?

To hear, we must somehow convert sound waves into neural activity. But how? The human ear accomplishes this feat through an intricate mechanical chain reaction. First, the visible outer ear channels the sound waves through the auditory canal to the *eardrum,* a tight membrane that vibrates with the waves (**FIGURE 11.3a**). The **middle ear** then transmits the eardrum's vibrations through a piston made of three tiny bones (the *hammer, anvil,* and *stirrup*) to a snail-shaped tube in the **inner ear** called the **cochlea** (KOHK-lee-uh). The incoming vibrations cause the cochlea's membrane (the *oval window*) to vibrate the fluid that fills the tube. This motion causes ripples in the *basilar membrane,* which is lined with *hair cells,* so named because of their tiny hairlike projections (**FIGURE 11.3b**). At the end of this sequence, the rippling of the basilar membrane bends these hair cells, not unlike the wind bending a wheat field. The movement of the hair cells triggers impulses in the adjacent nerve fibers, or axons, which in turn converge to form the auditory nerve. By means of this mechanical chain of events,

■ **frequency** the number of complete wavelengths that pass a point in a given time (for example, per second).

■ **pitch** a tone's highness or lowness; depends on frequency.

■ **middle ear** the chamber between the eardrum and cochlea containing three tiny bones (hammer, anvil, and stirrup) that concentrate the vibrations of the eardrum on the cochlea's oval window.

■ **inner ear** the innermost part of the ear, containing the cochlea, semicircular canals, and vestibular sacs.

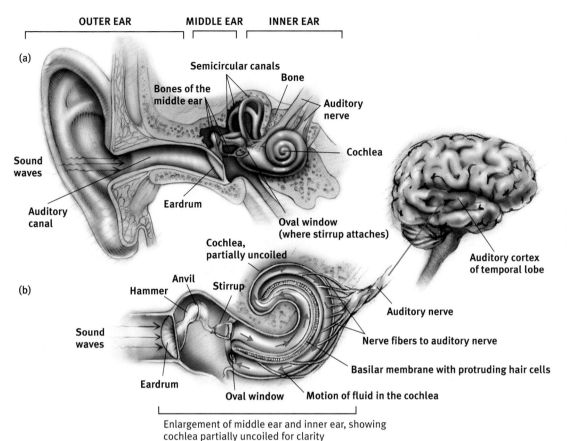

OUTER EAR   MIDDLE EAR   INNER EAR

(a)

Semicircular canals

Bones of the middle ear

Bone

Auditory nerve

Cochlea

Sound waves

Auditory canal

Eardrum

Oval window (where stirrup attaches)

Cochlea, partially uncoiled

Anvil

Hammer   Stirrup

(b)

Auditory cortex of temporal lobe

Sound waves

Auditory nerve

Nerve fibers to auditory nerve

Eardrum

Basilar membrane with protruding hair cells

Oval window   Motion of fluid in the cochlea

Enlargement of middle ear and inner ear, showing cochlea partially uncoiled for clarity

FIGURE 11.3

How we transform sound waves into nerve impulses that our brain interprets

(a) The outer ear funnels sound waves to the eardrum. The bones of the middle ear amplify and relay the eardrum's vibrations through the oval window into the fluid-filled cochlea. (b) The resulting pressure changes in the cochlear fluid cause the basilar membrane to ripple, bending the hair cells on the surface. Hair cell movements trigger impulses at the bases of the nerve cells, whose fibers converge to form the auditory nerve. (For clarity, the cochlea is shown partially uncoiled.)

sound waves cause the hair cells of the inner ear to send neural messages up to the temporal lobe's auditory cortex. From vibrating air to moving piston to fluid waves to electrical impulses to the brain: Voila! We hear.

My vote for the most magical part of the hearing process is the hair cells, damage to which accounts for most hearing loss. A 1997 Howard Hughes Medical Institute report on these "quivering bundles that let us hear" marvels at their "extreme sensitivity and extreme speed." A cochlea has only 16,000 of them, which sounds like a lot until we compare that with an eye's 100 million or so photoreceptors. But consider their responsiveness. Deflect the tiny bundles of cilia on the tip of a hair cell by the width of an atom—the equivalent of displacing the top of the Eiffel Tower by only half an inch—and the alert hair cell triggers a neural response. Moreover, at the highest perceived frequency they can turn neural current on and off 20,000 times per second!

As you might expect of something so sensitive, hair cells are delicate and fragile. Blast them with incessant jackhammer or headset sounds and a hair cell's cilia will begin to wither or fuse. As a general rule, if you cannot talk over a noise, it is potentially harmful, especially if prolonged (Roeser, 1998). Small wonder, then, that with industrialization, power tools, and loud recreations, the proportion of 45- to 64-year-old Americans who "cannot hear and understand normal speech" shot up by 87 percent in the two

Be kind to your inner ear's hair cells
When vibrating in response to sound, the 50 to 60 cilia shown here atop a hair cell produce an electrical signal.

■ **cochlea** [KOHK-lee-uh] a coiled, bony, fluid-filled tube in the inner ear through which sound waves trigger nerve impulses.

Pete Townshend of the Who acknowledged his hearing loss with a check for $10,000 to Hearing Education and Awareness for Rockers.

decades following 1971 (National Health Interview Survey, 1994). Although rock and roll may be here to stay, the sad truth for some rock musicians is that their hearing may not be.

People who spend their day behind a power mower or above a jackhammer should be wearing earplugs. And no matter what your occupation, if you experience ringing of the ears after exposure to loud machinery or music you have been bad to your unhappy hair cells. As pain alerts us to possible bodily harm, ringing of the ears alerts us to possible hearing damage. It is hearing's equivalent of bleeding. "Condoms or, safer yet, abstinence," say sex educators. "Earplugs or walk away," say hearing educators.

How Do We Locate Sounds?

Why don't we have one big ear—perhaps above our one nose? The better to hear you, as the wolf said to Red Riding Hood. Just as the placement of our two eyes allows us to sense visual depth, the placement of our two ears allows us to enjoy stereophonic ("three-dimensional") hearing. The slightly different messages sensed by the two microphones used in creating a stereophonic recording mimic the slightly different sound messages received by our two ears.

Two ears are better than one for at least two reasons. If a car to the right honks, your right ear receives a more *intense* sound slightly *sooner* than your left ear (**FIGURE 11.4**). Because sound travels 750 miles per hour and our ears are but 6 inches apart, the intensity difference and the time lag are extremely small. However, our sensitive auditory system can actually detect such minute differences (Brown & Deffenbacher, 1979; Middlebrooks & Green, 1991). A just noticeable difference in the direction from which two sounds come corresponds to a time difference of just 0.000027 seconds!

So how well do you suppose we do at locating sounds that are equidistant from our two ears, such as those that come from directly ahead, behind, overhead, or beneath us? Not very well. Why? Because such sounds strike the two ears simultaneously. Sit with closed eyes while a friend snaps fingers around your head. You will easily point to the sound when it comes from either side, but you will likely make some mistakes when it comes from directly ahead, behind, above, or below. That is why, when trying to pinpoint a sound, you cock your head, so that your two ears will receive slightly different messages.

FIGURE 11.4

How we locate sounds
Sound waves strike one ear sooner and more intensely than the other. From this information, our nimble brains compute the sound's location. As you might therefore expect, people who lose all hearing in one ear often have difficulty locating sounds.

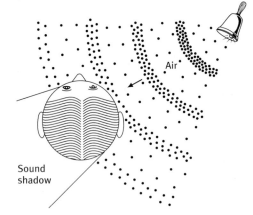

Touch and Pain

PREVIEW QUESTION 3 How do we sense touch and feel pain?

Touch

If you had to lose one sense, which would you prefer it to be? If you could have only one, which would you want?

Although not the first sense to come to mind, touch could be our priority sense. Right from the start, touch is essential to our development. Infant rats deprived of their mothers' grooming touch produce less growth hormone and have a lower metabolic rate—a good way to keep alive until the mother returns, but a reaction that stunts growth if she's delayed. Infant monkeys allowed to see, hear, and smell—but not touch—their mothers become desperately unhappy; those separated by a screen with holes that allow touching are much less miserable. Premature human babies gain weight faster and go home sooner if they are stimulated by hand massage. As lovers, we yearn to touch—to kiss, to stroke, to snuggle.

The precious sense of touch
As William James wrote in his *Principles of Psychology* (1890), "Touch is both the alpha and omega of affection."

Dave Barry may be right to say that the skin "keeps people from seeing the inside of your body, which is repulsive, and it prevents your organs from falling onto the ground." But skin does much more. Our "sense of touch" is actually a mix of at least four distinct skin senses—pressure, warmth, cold, and pain. Within the skin are different types of specialized nerve endings. Touching various spots on the skin with a soft hair, a warm or cool wire, and the point of a pin reveals that some spots are especially sensitive to pressure, others to warmth, others to cold, still others to pain.

Surprisingly, there is no simple relationship between what we feel at a given spot and the type of specialized nerve ending found there. Only pressure has identifiable receptors. The relationship between warmth, cold, and pain and the receptors that respond to them remains a mystery. Other skin sensations are variations of the basic four (pressure, warmth, cold, and pain):

- Stroking adjacent pressure spots creates a tickle.
- Repeated gentle stroking of a pain spot creates an itching sensation.
- Touching adjacent cold and pressure spots triggers a sense of wetness, which you can experience by touching dry, cold metal.

Touch sensations involve more than tactile stimulation, however. A self-produced tickle produces less somatosensory cortex activation than the same tickle from something or someone else (Blakemore & others, 1998). The brain is wise enough to be most sensitive to unexpected stimulation.

Pain

Be thankful for occasional pain. Pain is your body's way of telling you that something has gone wrong. Drawing your attention to a burn, a break, or a rupture, it tells you to change your behavior immediately. The rare people born without the ability to feel pain may experience severe injury without ever being alerted by pain's danger signals. Usually, they die by early adulthood. Without the discomfort that makes us occasionally shift position, their joints fail from excess strain, and without the warnings of pain, the effects of unchecked infections and injuries accumulate (Neese, 1991). More numerous are those who endure chronic pain. The suffering of people with persistent or recurring backaches, arthritis, headaches, and cancer-related pain prompts us to try to understand pain.

What Is Pain?

Pain is a property not only of the senses—of the region where we feel it—but of the brain as well. As the dreamer may see with eyes closed and the listener may hear a ringing during utter silence, so some 7 in 10 amputees may feel pain or movement in their nonexistent limbs (Melzack, 1992, 1993). Even those born without a limb sometimes perceive sensations from the absent limb. The brain, Melzack (1998) surmises, comes prepared to anticipate "that it will be getting information from a body that has limbs."

These *phantom limb sensations* indicate that with pain, as with sights and sounds, the brain can misinterpret the spontaneous central nervous system activity that occurs in the absence of normal sensory input. A similar phenomenon occurs with *tinnitus,* a ringing-in-the-ears sensation often experienced by people with hearing loss. Nerve damage in the taste system can produce taste phantoms, such as ice water seeming sickeningly sweet (Goode, 1999). Others have experienced phantom smells, such as nonexistent rotten food. The moral: To see, hear, taste, smell, and feel, we require not only a body but also a brain. No brain, no pain.

Unlike vision, however, the pain system is not located in a simple neural cord running from a sensing device to a definable area in the brain. Moreover, there is no one type of stimulus that triggers pains (as light triggers vision), and there are no special receptors (like the retina's light receptors) for pain. In fact, at low intensities, the stimuli

"When belly with bad pains doth swell, It matters naught what else goes well."

Sadi, *The Gulistan*, 1258

Putting pain out of mind
Vigorously rubbing sore feet helps reduce pain sensations, perhaps by stimulating the spinal cord's large fibers and closing the pain "gate" described in gate-control theory.

that produce pain also cause other sensations, including warmth or coolness, smoothness or roughness.

Although no theory of pain explains all the available findings, psychologist Ronald Melzack and biologist Patrick Wall's (1965, 1983) **gate-control theory** provides a useful model. Melzack and Wall believe that the spinal cord contains a neurological "gate" that either blocks pain signals or allows them to pass on to the brain. The spinal cord contains *small nerve fibers* that conduct most pain signals, and larger fibers that conduct most other sensory signals. When tissue is injured, the small fibers activate and open the neural gate, and you feel pain. Large-fiber activity closes the pain gate, turning pain off.

Thus, one way to treat chronic pain is to stimulate (electrically, by massage, or by acupuncture) "gate-closing" activity in the large neural fibers. Rubbing the area around your stubbed toe will create competing stimulation that will block some of the pain messages. If you place ice on a bruise, you not only will control the swelling but also will trigger cold messages that will close the gate on the pain signals. Some arthritic patients wear a small, portable electrical stimulation unit next to a painful area. When the unit stimulates nerves in the area, the patient feels a vibrating sensation rather than pain (T. Murphy, 1982).

Melzack and Wall believe the pain gate can also be closed by information from the brain. These brain-to-spinal-cord messages help explain some striking psychological influences on pain. When we are distracted from pain and soothed by the release of endorphins (our body's natural, opiatelike chemicals), our experience of pain may be greatly diminished. Sports injuries may go unnoticed, until the after-game shower. During a 1989 basketball game, Ohio State University player Jay Burson broke his neck—and kept playing. Clearly, there is more to pain than what stimulates the sense receptors.

> "Pain is increased by attending to it."
>
> Charles Darwin, *Expression of Emotions in Man and Animals,* 1872

There is also more to our *memories* of pain than the pain we experienced. In experiments, and after medical procedures, people overlook a pain's duration. Their memory snapshots instead record its peak moment and how much pain they felt at the end. Daniel Kahneman and his co-researchers (1993) discovered this when they asked people to immerse one hand in painfully cold water for 60 seconds, and then the other hand in the same painfully cold water for 60 seconds followed by a slightly less painful 30 seconds more. Curiously, when asked which trial they would prefer to repeat, most preferred the longer trial, with more net pain—but less pain at the end.

For medical personnel, the implication is clear: It's better to taper down a painful procedure than to switch it off abruptly. In one experiment, a physician did this for some patients undergoing colon exams—lengthening the discomfort by a minute, lessening its intensity

The pain in sprain is mainly in the brain
Kerri Strug had just sprained her left ankle so severely that she would be unable to do gymnastics for months afterward. Yet with this near-perfect vault, she helped carry her team to a 1996 Olympic gold medal. Because pain is a phenomenon of the conscious brain, athletes sometimes endure serious injuries while focusing their attention outside their bodies.

(Kahneman, 1999). Although this milder discomfort added to the net pain experience, patients given this "taper down" treatment later recalled the exam as less painful than those whose pain ended abruptly.

Pain Control

If pain is where body meets mind—if it is indeed a physical and a psychological phenomenon—then it should be treatable both physically and psychologically. Depending on the type of symptoms, pain control clinics select one or more therapies from a list that includes drugs, surgery, acupuncture, electrical stimulation, massage, exercise, hypnosis, relaxation training, and thought distraction. The Lamaze method of childbirth combines relaxation (through deep breathing and muscle relaxation), counterstimulation (through gentle massage), and distraction (through focusing attention on, say, a pleasant photograph).

Distracting people with pleasant images ("Think of a warm, comfortable environment") or drawing their attention away from the painful stimulation ("Count backward by 3s") is an especially effective way to increase pain tolerance (Fernandez & Turk, 1989; McCaul & Malott, 1984). The principle works in health care situations. A well-trained nurse may distract needle-shy patients by chatting with them and asking them to look away when inserting the needle. Because pain is in the brain, diverting the brain's attention may bring relief.

Taste

PREVIEW QUESTION 4 How do we experience taste?

Like touch, our sense of taste involves four basic sensations—sweet, sour, salty, and bitter (McBurney & Gent, 1979). Other tastes are mixtures of these. Investigators have, however, been frustrated in their search for specialized nerve fibers for each of these four basic taste sensations.

Taste is a chemical sense. Inside each little bump on the top and sides of your tongue are 200 or more taste buds, each containing a pore that catches food chemicals. These molecules are sensed by 50 taste receptor cells that project antennalike hairs into the pore. Some of these receptors respond mostly to sweet-tasting molecules, others to salty-, sour-, or bitter-tasting ones. It doesn't take much to trigger a response. If a stream of water is pumped across your tongue, the addition of a concentrated salty or sweet taste for but one-tenth of a second will get your attention (Kelling & Halpern, 1983). When a friend asks for "just a taste" of your soft drink, you can squeeze off the straw after a mere fraction of a second.

Taste receptors reproduce themselves every week or two, so if you burn your tongue with hot food it hardly matters. However, as you grow older, the number of taste buds decreases, as does taste sensitivity (Cowart, 1981). (No wonder adults enjoy strong-tasting foods that children resist.) Smoking and alcohol use accelerate the decline in taste buds and sensitivities.

Taste buds are certainly essential for taste, but there's more to taste than meets the tongue. Hold your nose, close your eyes, and have someone feed you various foods. A slice of apple may be indistinguishable from a chunk of raw potato; a piece of steak may taste like cardboard. To savor a taste, we normally breathe the aroma through our nose—which is why eating is not much fun when you have a bad cold, and why people who lose their sense of smell may think they have also lost their sense of taste. Smell not only adds to our perception of taste, it also changes it: A drink's strawberry odor enhances our perception of its sweetness. This is **sensory interaction** at work—the principle that one sense may influence another. Smell plus texture plus taste equals flavor. Similarly, we correctly perceive the location of the voice directly in front of us partly because we also see that the person is in front of us, not behind, above, or beneath us.

> "From there to here, from here to there, funny things are everywhere."
>
> **Dr. Seuss, *One Fish, Two Fish, Red Fish, Blue Fish*, 1960**

Although Lamaze training reduces labor pain, most Lamaze patients request a local anesthetic during labor. Some—having expected a "natural, painless birth"—feel needless guilt and failure (Melzack, 1984). Melzack therefore advocates—as does the Lamaze program itself—childbirth training that prepares a woman "to cope with an event which is often extremely painful and, at the same time, one of the most fulfilling peak experiences in her life."

■ **gate-control theory** theory that the spinal cord contains a neurological "gate" that blocks pain signals or allows them to pass on to the brain. The "gate" is opened by the activity of pain signals traveling up small nerve fibers and is closed by activity in larger fibers or by information coming from the brain.

■ **sensory interaction** the principle that one sense may influence another, as when the smell of food influences its taste.

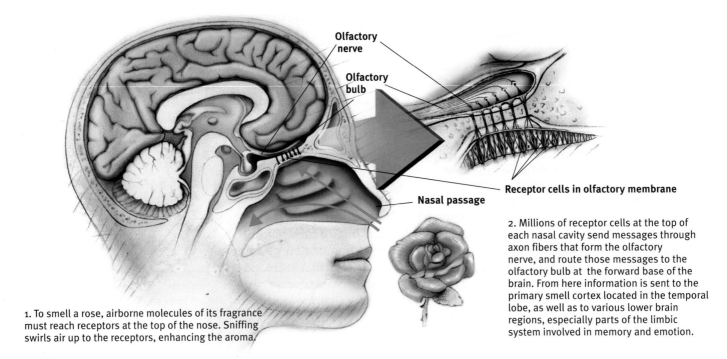

Olfactory nerve

Olfactory bulb

Receptor cells in olfactory membrane

Nasal passage

2. Millions of receptor cells at the top of each nasal cavity send messages through axon fibers that form the olfactory nerve, and route those messages to the olfactory bulb at the forward base of the brain. From here information is sent to the primary smell cortex located in the temporal lobe, as well as to various lower brain regions, especially parts of the limbic system involved in memory and emotion.

1. To smell a rose, airborne molecules of its fragrance must reach receptors at the top of the nose. Sniffing swirls air up to the receptors, enhancing the aroma.

FIGURE 11.5

The sense of smell

Smell

PREVIEW QUESTION 5 How does our sense of smell work?

Inhale, exhale. Inhale, exhale. Breaths come in pairs—except at two moments: birth and death. Each day, you inhale and exhale nearly 20,000 breaths of life-sustaining air, bathing your nostrils in a stream of scent-laden molecules. The resulting experiences of smell (*olfaction*) are strikingly intimate ones: You inhale something of whatever or whoever it is you smell.

Like taste, smell is a chemical sense. We smell something when molecules of a substance carried in the air reach a tiny cluster of 5 million receptor cells at the top of each nasal cavity (**FIGURE 11.5**). These olfactory receptor cells, waving like sea anemones on a reef, respond selectively—to the aroma of a cake baking, to a wisp of smoke, to a friend's fragrance. Instantly they alert the brain through their axon fibers. Even nursing infants and their mothers have a literal chemistry to their relationship. They quickly learn to recognize each other's scents (McCarthy, 1986). Aided by smell, a mother fur seal returning to a beach crowded with pups will find her own. Our own sense of smell is less impressive than the acuteness of our seeing and hearing. Looking out across a garden we see its forms and colors in exquisite detail and hear a variety of birds singing, yet we smell little of it without settling our nose into the blooms.

Precisely how olfactory receptors work remains a mystery. Unlike light, which can be separated into its spectral colors, an odor cannot be separated into more elemental odors. The olfaction system has no parallel to the retina, which detects myriad colors with sensory cells dedicated to red, green, or blue. Olfactory receptors recognize odors individually.

Odor molecules come in many shapes and sizes, so many in fact that it takes many different receptors to detect them. A large family of some 1000 genes—some 1 percent of all our genes—design the 1000 or so receptor proteins that recognize particular odor molecules (Axel, 1995). As a key slips into a lock, so odor molecules slip into these receptors. Yet we seem not to have a distinct receptor for each detectable odor. This suggests that some odors trigger a combination of receptors, whose activity the olfactory cortex interprets. As the alphabet's 26 letters can combine to form many words, so odor molecules bind to different receptor arrays, producing the 10,000 odors we can detect (Malnic & others, 1999).

Smell is primitive. A hotline runs between the brain area that gets information from the nose and the brain's ancient *limbic centers,* areas associated with memory and emotion. Eons before the elaborate analytical areas of our cerebral cortex had fully evolved, our mammalian ancestors sniffed for food—and for predators.

Odors also have the power to evoke memories and feelings. Laboratory studies confirm that, though it's difficult to recall odors by name, we have a remarkable capacity to recognize long-forgotten odors and their associated personal episodes (Engen, 1987; Schab, 1991). Students who do a word exercise while smelling the aroma of chocolate remember the words better the next day if the chocolate aroma is again present (Schab, 1990). And pleasant odors can evoke pleasant memories (Ehrlichman & Halpern, 1988). The smell of the sea, the scent of a perfume, or an aroma of a favorite relative's kitchen can bring to mind a happy time. Such is the power of an odor to switch on memories and to retrieve associated emotions. It's a phenomenon understood by the British travel agent chain, Lunn Poly. To evoke memories of lounging on sunny, warm beaches, the company recently began piping the aroma of coconut suntan oil into its shops (Fracassini, 2000).

The olfactory brain
Information from the taste buds (orange arrow) travels to an area of the temporal lobe not far from that where olfactory information is received. The brain's circuitry for smell (red arrow) also connects with areas involved in memory storage, which helps explain why a smell can trigger a memory explosion.

"The smell and taste of things bears unfaltering, in the tiny and almost impalpable drop of their essence, the vast structure of recollections."

French novelist Marcel Proust, *Remembrance of Things Past*, describing how the taste of a tea-soaked cake brought back long-forgotten memories of a bedroom in the old family house.

Body Position and Movement

PREVIEW QUESTION 6 How do our senses monitor our body's position and movement?

With only vision and the other familiar senses we have so far considered, we could not put food in our mouths, stand up, or reach out and touch someone. We would be helpless. To know just how to move your arms to grasp someone's hand, you first need to know the current position of your arms and hands and then be aware of their changing positions as you move them. For you to take just one step requires feedback from and instructions to some 200 muscles.

We come equipped with millions of position and motion sensors. They are all over our bodies—in the muscles, tendons, and joints—and they are continually providing information to our brains. If we twist our wrists one degree, the sensors immediately report it. This sense of our body parts' position and movement is **kinesthesis** (kin-ehs-THEE-sehs).

One can momentarily imagine being blind or deaf. Close your eyes, plug your ears, and experience the dark stillness. But what would it be like to live without touch or kinesthesis—without, therefore, being able to sense the positions of your limbs when awakening during the night? Ian Waterman of Hampshire, England, knows. In 1972, at age 19, Waterman contracted a rare viral infection that destroyed the nerves that enabled his sense of light touch and of body position and movement. People with this condition report feeling disembodied, as though their body is dead, not real, not theirs (Sacks, 1985). With prolonged practice Water-

■ **kinesthesis** [kin-ehs-THEE-sehs] the system for sensing the position and movement of individual body parts.

The intricate vestibular sense
Thank your inner ears for the information that enables your brain to monitor your body's position.

■ **vestibular sense** the sense of body movement and position, including the sense of balance.

man has learned to walk and eat—by visually focusing on his limbs and directing them accordingly. But if the lights go out, he crumples to the floor, unable to move until they come back on (Azar, 1998).

A companion **vestibular sense** monitors the head's (and thus the body's) position and movement. The biological gyroscopes for this sense of equilibrium are in the inner ear. In the semicircular canals, which look like a three-dimensional pretzel (**FIGURE 11.3a**, page 161), and the vestibular sacs, which connect the canals with the cochlea, are substances that move when the head rotates or tilts. This movement stimulates hairlike receptors which send the messages to the brain that enable us continually to sense our body position and to maintain our balance.

If you twirl around and then come to an abrupt halt, neither the fluid in your semicircular canals nor your kinesthetic receptors immediately return to their neutral state. The aftereffect fools your dizzy brain with the sensation that you're still spinning. This illustrates a principle that underlies research on perceptual illusions. Mechanisms that normally give us an accurate experience of the world can, under special conditions, fool us. Understanding how we get fooled provides clues to how our perceptual system works.

rehearse it!

1. The amplitude of a light wave determines our perception of brightness. The amplitude of a sound wave determines our perception of
   a. loudness.
   b. pitch.
   c. audition.
   d. frequency.

2. The frequency of sound waves determines their pitch. The _____ the waves are, the lower their frequency is and the _____ their pitch.
   a. shorter; higher
   b. longer; lower
   c. lower; longer
   d. higher; shorter

3. Sound waves pass through the auditory canal to a tight membrane. Vibrations of this membrane are transmitted by three tiny bones to a snail-shaped tube in the inner ear, where the waves are converted into neural activity. This tube is called the
   a. anvil.
   b. basilar membrane.
   c. cochlea.
   d. eardrum.

4. At least four skin senses—pressure, warmth, cold, and pain—make up our sense of touch. Of all the skin senses, the only one that has its own identifiable receptor cells is
   a. pressure.
   b. warmth.
   c. cold.
   d. pain.

5. There is no one type of stimulus that triggers pain and no one definable spot in the brain that interprets pain. Although no theory fully explains our experience of pain, the gate-control theory is useful. According to this theory,
   a. special pain receptors send signals directly to the brain.
   b. pain is a property of the senses, not of the brain.
   c. small nerve fibers in the spinal cord conduct most pain signals.
   d. the stimuli that produce pain are unrelated to other sensations.

6. The taste of the food we eat is greatly enhanced by its smell or aroma. One sense influencing another is referred to as
   a. sensory adaptation.
   b. chemical sensation.
   c. gate-control theory.
   d. sensory interaction.

7. Kinesthesis is the body's way of sensing its position and movement. The receptors for our companion vestibular sense are in the
   a. skin.
   b. brain.
   c. inner ear.
   d. skeletal muscles.

The Other Senses

1. What are the characteristics of the air pressure waves that we hear as meaningful sounds?

The pressure waves we experience as sound vary in frequency, which determines a tone's pitch (its highness or lowness). These waves also vary in amplitude, which determines their loudness. Sound energy is measured in decibels. Prolonged exposure to sounds above 85 decibels can produce hearing loss.

2. How does the ear transform sound energy into neural messages?

Through a mechanical chain of events, the sound waves traveling down the auditory canal cause minuscule vibrations in the eardrum. Transmitted via the bones of the middle ear to the fluid-filled cochlea in the inner ear, these vibrations create movement in tiny hair cells, triggering neural messages to the brain. We localize sound by detecting minute differences in the loudness and timing of the sounds received by each ear.

3. How do we sense touch and feel pain?

Our sense of touch is actually four senses—pressure, warmth, cold, and pain—that combine to produce other sensations, such as a tickle. The gate-control theory of pain proposes that a "gate" in the spinal cord opens when injury activates small nerve fibers, which pass pain signals on to the brain. The gate closes when large fibers conduct other sensory signals and block the passage of the pain signals. Because pain is both a physiological and a psychological phenomenon, it often can be controlled through a combination of physical and psychological treatments.

4. How do we experience taste?

Taste, a chemical sense, is a composite of four basic sensations—sweet, sour, salty, and bitter. Other tastes are mixtures of these four. Taste receptors are located in the taste buds. Our sense of smell affects our perception of taste, illustrating sensory interaction.

5. How does our sense of smell work?

Like taste, smell is a chemical sense. Airborne molecules activate receptor cells located at the top of each nasal cavity, which send messages to the brain. Odors have the power to switch on memories and their associated emotions.

6. How do our senses monitor our body's position and movement?

Our effective functioning requires a *kinesthetic sense,* which notifies the brain of the position and movement of body parts, and a *vestibular sense,* which monitors the position and movement of the whole body. Millions of position and motion sensors in the muscles, tendons, and joints are receptors for our kinesthetic sense. Receptors for the vestibular sense are located in the inner ear.

TERMS AND CONCEPTS TO REMEMBER

visual capture, p. 159
audition, p. 159
wavelength, p. 159
frequency, p. 160

pitch, p. 160
middle ear, p. 160
inner ear, p. 160
cochlea [KOHK-lee-uh], p. 160

gate-control theory, p. 164
sensory interaction, p. 165
kinesthesis [kin-ehs-THEE-sehs], p. 167

vestibular sense, p. 168

REHEARSE IT ANSWER KEY

1. a   2. b   3. c   4. a   5. c   6. d   7. c

Perceptual Organization

- ■ Form Perception
- ■ Depth Perception
- ■ Perceptual Constancy

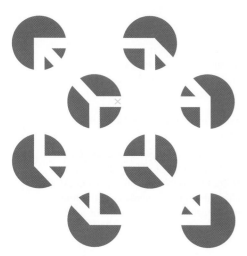

FIGURE 12.1

A Necker cube

What do you see: circles containing white lines, or a cube? If you stare at the cube, you may notice that it reverses location, moving the tiny X in the center from the front edge to the back. At times the cube may seem to float in front of the page, with circles behind it; other times the circles may become holes in the page through which the cube appears, as though it were floating behind the page. There is far more to perception than meets the senses.

FIGURE 12.2

Reversible figure and ground

PREVIEW QUESTION 1 What did the Gestalt psychologists contribute to our understanding of how the brain organizes sensations into perceptions?

We have examined the processes by which we sense sights and sounds, tastes and smells, touch and movement. Now our central question is, how do we see not just shapes and colors, but a rose in bloom, a familiar face, a sunset? How do we hear not just a mix of pitches and rhythms, but a child's cry of pain, the hum of distant traffic, a symphony? In short, how do we *organize* and *interpret* our sensations so that they become meaningful perceptions?

Early in the twentieth century, a group of German psychologists became intrigued with this question of how we organize sensations. Given a cluster of sensations, they believed, the human perceiver organizes them into a **gestalt,** a German word meaning a "form" or a "whole." The Gestalt psychologists provided compelling demonstrations of gestalt perception and described the principles underlying them. They also were fond of saying that in perception the whole may exceed the sum of its parts. Combine sodium, a corrosive metal, with chlorine, a poison gas, and something very different emerges—table salt. Likewise, a unique perceived form emerges from an object's components (Rock & Palmer, 1990), as it does in **FIGURE 12.1**. Note that the individual elements of the figure are really nothing but eight blue circles, each containing three converging white lines. But when we view them all together, we see a *whole* form, a "Necker cube."

As you read further about the Gestalt psychologists' organizational principles, keep in mind the fundamental truth they illustrate: Our brains do more than merely register information about the world. Perception is not just opening a shutter and letting a picture print itself on the brain. We constantly filter sensory information and infer perceptions in ways that make sense to us. Mind matters.

Form Perception

PREVIEW QUESTION 2 How do the principles of figure-ground and grouping contribute to our perception of form?

Imagine designing a video/computer system that, like your eye/brain system, could read handwritten addresses or recognize faces at a glance. (Postal services are, in fact, hoping to develop such a scanner.) What abilities would it need?

Figure and Ground

To start with, the system would need to recognize the addresses and faces as distinct from their backgrounds. Likewise, our first perceptual task is to perceive any object, called the *figure,* as distinct from its surroundings, called the *ground.* As you read, the words are the figure; the white paper, the ground. In **FIGURE 12.2**, the **figure-ground** relationship continually reverses—but always we organize the stimulus into a figure seen against a ground. (Is it a vase, or profiles of a younger Prince Philip and Queen Elizabeth?) Such reversible figure-and-ground illustrations demonstrate again that the same stimulus can trigger more than one perception. Curiously, though, if you do not *know* the figure is reversible, it is not so likely to reverse (Rock & others, 1994).

Grouping

Having discriminated figure from ground, we (and our video/computer system) then have to organize the figure into a meaningful form. Some basic features of a scene—such as color, movement, and light/dark contrast—we process instantly and automatically (Treisman, 1987). To bring order and form to these basic sensations, our minds follow certain rules for **grouping** stimuli together (**FIGURE 12.3**). The folowing rules, identified by the Gestalt psychologists, illustrate their idea that the perceived whole differs from the sum of its parts (Rock & Palmer, 1990).

■ **gestalt** an organized whole. Gestalt psychologists emphasized our tendency to integrate pieces of information into meaningful wholes.

■ **figure-ground** the organization of the visual field into objects (the *figures*) that stand out from their surroundings (the *ground*).

■ **grouping** the perceptual tendency to organize stimuli into coherent groups.

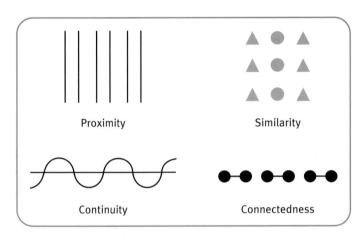

FIGURE 12.3

Organizing stimuli into groups
We could perceive the stimuli shown here in many ways, yet people everywhere see them similarly. The Gestalt psychologists believed this shows that the brain uses "rules" to order sensory information into wholes.

Proximity We group nearby figures together. We see not six separate lines, but three sets of two lines.

Similarity Figures similar to each other we group together. We see the triangles and circles as vertical columns of similar shapes, not as horizontal rows of dissimilar shapes.

Continuity We perceive smooth, continuous patterns rather than discontinuous ones. This pattern could be a series of alternating semicircles, but we perceive it as two continuous lines—one wavy, one straight.

Connectedness When they are uniform and linked, we perceive spots, lines, or areas as a single unit.

Closure We fill in gaps to create a complete, whole object. Thus we assume that the circles (near right) are complete but partially blocked by the (illusory) triangle. Add nothing more than little line segments that close off the circles (far right) and now your brain stops constructing a triangle.

FIGURE 12.4

Grouping principles
You probably perceive this doghouse as a gestalt—a whole (though impossible) structure. Actually, your brain imposes this sense of wholeness on the picture. As the photo on page 179 shows, gestalt grouping principles such as closure and continuity are at work here. (Reprinted from GAMES Magazine [810 Seventh Avenue, New York, NY 10019]. Copyright © 1983 PSC Games Limited Partnership.)

Usually, these grouping principles help us construct reality. Sometimes, however, they can lead us astray, as when we look at the doghouse in **FIGURE 12.4**.

Depth Perception

PREVIEW QUESTION 3 How do we see the world in three dimensions?

Two-dimensional images fall on our retinas, the light-sensitive inner surface of our eyes, yet we somehow organize three-dimensional perceptions. Seeing objects in three dimensions, called **depth perception,** enables us to estimate their distance from us. At a glance, we estimate the distance of an oncoming car or the height of a house. This ability is partly innate. Eleanor Gibson and Richard Walk (1960) discovered this using a miniature cliff with a drop-off covered by sturdy glass. Gibson's inspiration for these experiments occurred while she was picnicking on the rim of the Grand Canyon. She wondered: Would a toddler peering over the rim perceive the dangerous drop-off and draw back?

Back in their Cornell University laboratory, Gibson and Walk placed 6- to 14-month-old infants on the edge of a safe canyon—a **visual cliff** (**FIGURE 12.5**). The babies' mothers then coaxed them to crawl out onto the glass. Most refused to do so, indicating that they could perceive depth. Perhaps by crawling age the infants had *learned* to perceive depth. Yet newborn animals with virtually no visual experience—including young kittens, a day-old goat, and newly hatched chicks—respond similarly. Each species, by the time it is mobile, has the perceptual abilities it needs. What is more, during the first month of life, human infants turn to avoid objects coming directly at them but remain unbothered by anything approaching at an angle that would not hit them (Ball & Tronick, 1971).

Biological maturation predisposes our wariness of heights. Experience amplifies it. Infants' wariness increases with their experiences of crawling, no matter when they begin to crawl. When infants' movement is enhanced by a walker, they become even more wary of heights (Campos & others, 1992).

How do we do it? How do we transform two-dimensional retinal images into three-dimensional perceptions? Some depth cues—**binocular cues**—require both eyes. Others—**monocular cues**—are available to each eye separately.

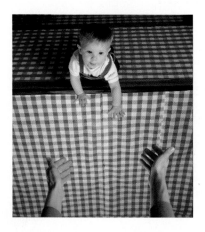

FIGURE 12.5

Visual cliff

Eleanor Gibson and Richard Walk devised this miniature cliff with a glass-covered drop-off to determine whether crawling infants and newborn animals can perceive depth. Even when coaxed, infants are reluctant to venture onto the glass over the cliff.

Binocular Cues

Because our eyes are about $2\frac{1}{2}$ inches apart, our retinas receive slightly different images of the world. When the brain compares these two images, the difference between them—their **retinal disparity**—provides an important cue to the relative distance of different objects. When you hold your finger directly in front of your nose, your retinas receive quite different views. (You can see this if you close one eye and then the other, or create a finger sausage as in **FIGURE 12.6.**) At a greater distance—say, when you hold your finger at arm's length—the disparity is smaller.

The creators of three-dimensional (3-D) movies simulate or exaggerate retinal disparity by photographing a scene with two cameras placed a few inches apart (a feature we might want to build into our seeing computer). When we view through spectacles or a device that allows the left eye to see only the image from the left

FIGURE 12.6

The floating finger sausage

Hold your two index fingers about 5 inches in front of your eyes, with their tips half an inch apart. Now look beyond them and note the weird result. Move your fingers out farther and the retinal disparity—and the finger sausage—will shrink.

camera and the right eye only the image from the right camera, the 3-D effect mimics normal retinal disparity. Computer-generated 3-D "stereogram" images do the same by making two slightly differing images available for the brain to fuse.

Can you find the three-dimensional Greek letter psi (ψ) in the stereogram in **FIGURE 12.7**? Cross your eyes slightly (or look at a pencil tip 3 inches or so above the page), and see if you can perceive the psi image (at which point you will no longer feel that your eyes are crossed). The image looks so real you may be able to measure its distance from the page with a ruler.

FIGURE 12.7
Two eyes + brain = depth
If you are having trouble seeing the 3-D image, try holding the picture close to your face, so that the center of it touches your nose, then slowly move it backward without changing the focus of your eyes. About a foot from your face, the 3-D image should emerge. The image appears because the picture contains two views of the psi, from slightly different angles. When the brain fuses these two into one, you see the image in three dimensions. (Some people are able to reverse the depth by relaxing and looking through the image, as if to a point behind it.)

But notice that you cannot trace the outline of the 3-D image on the page—because it isn't on the page. Notice also that if you close one eye, the image immediately disappears, illustrating that the image exists only in your brain. The perceived depth, from two slightly different images lying on top of one another, occurs as each eye focuses on one image and the brain integrates the two versions into a single 3-D image. This illustrates dramatically a fundamental lesson: Perception is not merely projecting the world onto our brains. Rather, sensations are disassembled into information bits that the brain then reassembles into its own functional model of the external world. *Our brains construct our perceptions.*

Another binocular cue to distance is **convergence,** a neuromuscular cue caused by the eyes' greater inward turn when they view a near object. The brain notes the angle of convergence, then computes whether you are focusing on this printed page or on something else across the room.

Monocular Cues

Try this: With both eyes open, hold two pens or pencils in front of you and touch their tips together. Now do so with one eye closed. The task should become noticeably more difficult, demonstrating the importance of binocular cues in judging the distance of nearby objects. Two eyes are better than one. How then do we judge whether a person is 10 or 100 meters away? In both cases, the retinal disparity while looking straight ahead is slight. At such distances we depend on monocular cues such as the following:

- **depth perception** the ability to see objects in three dimensions although the images that strike the retina are two-dimensional; allows us to judge distance.

- **visual cliff** a laboratory device for testing depth perception in infants and young animals.

- **binocular cues** depth cues, such as retinal disparity and convergence, that depend on the use of two eyes.

- **monocular cues** distance cues, such as linear perspective and overlap, available to either eye alone.

- **retinal disparity** a binocular cue for perceiving depth: The greater the disparity (difference) between the two images the retina receives of an object, the closer the object is to the viewer.

- **convergence** a binocular cue for perceiving depth; the extent to which the eyes converge inward when looking at an object.

Interposition

Relative size

Relative height

Relative motion   Direction of passenger's motion ➡

Interposition   If one object partially blocks our view of another, we perceive it as closer. The painting at left purposely confuses figure and ground by interposition.

Relative size   If we assume that two objects are similar in size, we perceive the one that casts the smaller retinal image as farther away.

Relative height   We perceive objects higher in our field of vision as farther away. (This reverses above the horizon, as when we perceive a higher bird as closer.) Relative height may contribute to the illusion that vertical dimensions are longer than identical horizontal dimensions. Is the vertical line here longer, shorter, or equal in length to the horizontal line? Measure and see.

Relative motion (motion parallax)   As we move, objects that are actually stable may appear to move. If while riding in a train you fix your gaze on some object—say, a house—the objects closer than the house (the fixation point) appear to move backward. The nearer an object is, the faster it seems to move. Objects beyond the fixation point appear to move with you at a decreasing speed as the object gets farther away. Your brain uses these speed and direction clues to compute the objects' relative distances.

Linear perspective   Parallel lines, such as railroad tracks, appear to converge with distance. The more

• **Fixation point**

the lines converge, the greater their perceived distance. Linear perspective can contribute to rail-crossing accidents, by leading people to overestimate a train's distance (Leibowitz, 1985). (A train's massive size also makes it appear to be moving more slowly than it is.)

Light and shadow Nearby objects reflect more light to our eyes. Thus, given two identical objects, the dimmer one seems farther away. This illusion can also contribute to accidents, as when a fog-shrouded vehicle, or one with only its parking lights on, seems farther away than it is. Shading, too, produces a sense of depth consistent with the assumed light source. Invert the illustration at the right and the hollow becomes a hill, because our brains follow a simple rule: *Assume that light comes from above.*

Artists use such monocular cues to convey depth on a flat canvas (**FIGURE 12.8**). So do people who must gauge depth with but one eye. In 1960, the University of Washington football team won the year's biggest game, thanks partly to the superb passing of Bob Schloredt. Schloredt, who was obviously skilled at judging his receiver's distance, used monocular cues for distance. He was blind in his left eye.

Linear perspective

Light and shadow
(From "Perceiving Shape from Shading" by Vilayanur S. Ramachandran. Copyright © 1988 by Scientific American, Inc. All rights reserved.)

FIGURE 12.8
Perspective techniques
By the time that "Bristol, Broad Quay" was painted (c. 1730, Anonymous), techniques for depicting three dimensions on a flat surface were well established. Note the effective use of distance cues such as interposition, linear perspective, and relative size and height.

■ **perceptual constancy** perceiving objects as unchanging (having consistent lightness, color, shape, and size) even as illumination and retinal images change.

Perceptual Constancy

PREVIEW QUESTION 4 How do perceptual constancies help us to organize our sensations into meaningful perceptions?

So far we have noted that our video/computer system must first perceive objects as we do—as having a distinct form, location, and perhaps motion. Its next task is even more challenging: to recognize the object without being deceived by changes in its size, shape, brightness, or color. **Perceptual constancy** enables us to perceive an object as unchanging even though the stimuli we receive from it change. You glance at someone ahead of you on the sidewalk and instantly recognize a classmate. In less time than it takes to draw a breath, information reaching your eyes has been sent to your brain, where work teams comprising millions of neurons have extracted the essential features, compared them with stored images, and identified the person. Replicating this human perceptual feat, which has intrigued perception researchers for decades, provides a monumental challenge for our seeing computer.

Shape and Size Constancies

Sometimes an object whose actual shape cannot change *seems* to change shape with the angle of our view (**FIGURE 12.9**). More often, thanks to *shape constancy,* we perceive the form of familiar objects as constant even while our retinal images of them change. When a door opens, it casts a changing shape on our retinas, yet we still manage to perceive the door as having a constant doorlike shape (**FIGURE 12.10**).

Thanks to *size constancy* we perceive objects as having a constant size, even while our distance from them varies. Size constancy leads us to perceive a car as large enough to carry people, even when we see its tiny image from two blocks away. This illustrates the close connection between an object's perceived *distance* and perceived *size.* Perceiving an object's distance gives us cues to its size. Likewise, knowing its general size—that the object is, say, a car—provides us with cues to its distance.

Size-Distance Relationship

It is a marvel how effortlessly size perception occurs. Given the perceived distance of an object and the size of its image on our retinas, we instantly and unconsciously infer the object's size. Although the monsters in **FIGURE 12.11a** cast the same retinal images, the linear perspective tells our brain that the monster in pursuit is farther away. We therefore perceive it as larger.

This interplay between perceived size and perceived distance helps explain several well-known illusions. For example, can you imagine why the moon looks up to 50 percent larger near the horizon than when high in the sky? For at least 22 centuries, scholars have wondered and have argued about reasons for the *moon illusion* (Hershenson, 1989). One reason is that cues to objects' distances at the horizon make the moon behind them seem farther away than a higher moon (Kaufman & Kaufman, 2000). Thus, the moon on the horizon seems larger, like the distant mon-

Box A   Box B

FIGURE 12.9

Perceiving shape

Do the tops of boxes A and B have different dimensions? They appear to. But—believe it or not—they are identical. (Measure and see.) With both boxes we adjust our perceptions relative to our viewing angle. (From Shepard, 1981.)

FIGURE 12.10

Shape constancy

A door casts an increasingly trapezoidal image on our retinas as it opens, yet we still perceive it as rectangular.

FIGURE 12.11

The interplay between perceived size and distance

(a) The monocular cues for distance make the pursuing monster look larger than the pursued. It isn't. (From Shepard, 1990.)
(b) This visual trick, called the Ponzo illusion, is based on the same principle as the fleeing monsters. The two red bars cast identical-sized images on our retinas. But experience tells us that a more distant object can create the same-sized image as a nearer one only if it is actually larger. As a result, we perceive the bar that seems farther away as larger.

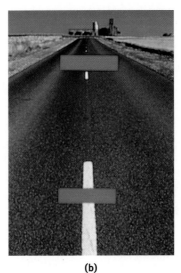

(a)   (b)

ster in Figure 12.11a and the distant bar in the *Ponzo illusion* in **FIGURE 12.11b.** Take away these distance cues—by looking at the horizon moon (or each monster or each bar) through a paper tube—and it immediately shrinks.

The size-distance relationship helps us understand this adaptation of a famous illusion (below right) created in 1889 by Franz Müller-Lyer. Does either line segment—AB or BC—appear longer? To most people the two segments appear to be the same length. Surprise! They are not. As your ruler can verify, line AB is a full one-third longer than line BC. Why did your eyes deceive you? One explanation for such illusions draws on our experience with the corners of rooms or buildings. This experience prompts us to interpret the vertical line on the ticket booth in **FIGURE 12.12a** as closer to us and therefore shorter, and the same-length vertical line by the door as farther away and therefore longer, although the two lines are equal. Thus, what appears as an illusion when isolated in a line drawing actually enables correct depth perception in our three-dimensional world.

A   B   C

(a)

FIGURE 12.12

The Müller-Lyer illusion

(a) Richard L. Gregory (1968) suggested that the corners in our rectangularly carpentered world teach us to interpret "outward" or "inward" pointing arrowheads at the ends of a line as a cue to the line's distance from us and so to its length. The red line defined by the corner at the ticket booth looks shorter than the red line defined by the corner to the left. But if you measure them, you will see that both are the same length. (b) There is more to the Müller-Lyer illusion than size constancy, however, for if we replace the arrowheads with circles and judge whether the black or blue line segment seems longer, we still get much the same effect. Here the two line segments are equal. Most people judge the black line as longer, apparently because they perceptually adjust the lengths of the lines toward the distance separating the figures. (From Day, 1984.)

(b)

FIGURE 12.13

The illusion of the shrinking and growing girls

This distorted room, designed by Adelbert Ames, appears to have a normal rectangular shape when viewed through a peephole with one eye. The girl in the near corner appears disproportionately large because we judge her size based on the false assumption that she is the same distance away as the girl in the far corner.

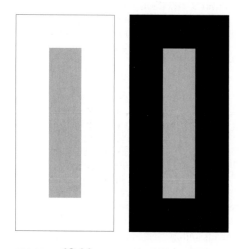

FIGURE 12.14

Brightness contrast

Although the interior rectangles are in fact identical, we perceive the right one as lighter because of the contrast with its dark surroundings. Like the effect of context on color perception, this phenomenon has great significance for artists and interior designers.

Size-distance relationships also explain why in **FIGURE 12.13** the two same-age girls seem so different in size. As the diagram reveals, the girls are actually about the same size, but the room is distorted. Viewed with one eye through a peephole, its trapezoidal walls produce the same images as those of a normal rectangular room viewed with both eyes. Presented with the camera's one-eyed view, the brain makes the reasonable assumption that the room is normal and that each of the girls is therefore the same distance from us. But given the different sizes of the images on the retina, our brain ends up calculating that the girls are very different in size.

Our occasional misperceptions reveal the workings of our normally effective perceptual processes. The perceived relationship between distance and size is generally valid, but under special circumstances it can lead us astray—as when helping to create the moon illusion, the Müller-Lyer illusion, and the Ames (distorted-room) illusion. Using distance cues to assess perceived size triggers illusions only if we aren't familiar with the object or if the distance cues are misleading. When we interpret the distance cues correctly—which we normally do—we also correctly perceive the object's size.

Lightness Constancy

White paper reflects 90 percent of the light falling on it; black paper, only 10 percent. In sunlight the black paper may reflect 100 times more light than does the white paper indoors, but it still looks black (McBurney & Collings, 1984). This illustrates *lightness constancy* (also called *brightness constancy*); we perceive an object as having a constant lightness even while its illumination varies. Perceived lightness depends on *relative luminance*—the amount of light an object reflects relative to its surroundings. If you view sunlit black paper through a narrow tube so nothing else is visible, it may look gray, because in bright sunshine it reflects a fair amount of light. View it without the tube and it is again black, because it reflects much less light than the objects around it. The phenomenon is similar to that of color constancy: As light changes, a red apple in a fruit bowl retains its redness, because our brain computes the light reflected by any object relative to its surrounding objects.

Perceived lightness stays roughly constant, given an unchanging context. But what happens when the surrounding context changes? As **FIGURE 12.14** shows, the visual system computes brightness and color relative to surrounding objects. Thus, perceived lightness changes with context.

Form perception, depth perception, and perceptual constancy illuminate how we organize our visual experiences. Perceptual organization applies to other senses, too. It explains why we perceive the clock's steady tick not as a tick-tick-tick but as grouped sounds, say, TICK-tick, TICK-tick. Listening to an unfamiliar language, we have trouble hearing where one word stops and the next one begins. Listening to our own language, we automatically hear distinct words. This, too, is a form of perceptual organization. But it is more, for we even organize a string of letters—THEDOGATEMEAT—into words that make an intelligible phrase, more likely "The dog ate meat" than "The do gate me at" (McBurney & Collings, 1984). This process involves not only organization but interpretation—discerning meaning in what we perceive.

The solution
Another view of the impossible doghouse in Figure 12.4 (page 171) reveals the secrets of this illusion. From the photo angle in Figure 12.4, the grouping principle of closure leads us to perceive the boards as continuous. (Reprinted from GAMES Magazine [810 Seventh Avenue, New York, NY 10019]. Copyright © 1983 PSC Games Limited Partnership.)

rehearse it!

1. Gestalt psychologists identified the principles by which we organize our perceptions. Our tendencies to fill in the gaps and to perceive a pattern as continuous are two different examples of the organizing principle called
   a. figure-ground.
   b. depth perception.
   c. shape constancy.
   d. grouping.

2. In their experiments, Gibson and Walk used a visual cliff to test depth perception in infants and young animals. Their results suggest that
   a. infants have not yet developed depth perception.
   b. crawling infants perceive depth.
   c. depth perception depends on experience.
   d. humans differ significantly from animals in being able to perceive depth in infancy.

3. The images that fall on our retinas are two-dimensional, or flat. Yet we perceive the world as having three-dimensional depth. Depth perception underlies our ability to
   a. discriminate figure from ground.
   b. perceive objects as having a constant shape or form.
   c. judge distances.
   d. fill in the gaps in a figure.

4. In estimating distances we use both binocular cues, which depend on both eyes, and monocular cues, which are available to either eye alone. Examples of monocular cues are interposition and
   a. closure.
   b. retinal disparity.
   c. linear perspective.
   d. convergence.

5. In the Müller-Lyer illusion, we misperceive the length of the lines between arrowheads. We do so partly because

a. distance cues do not help us assess size.
b. the visual distance cues (implied by the arrowheads) mislead us.
c. the perceived relationship between distance and size is generally illusory.
d. of our linear perspective.

6. Form perception and perceptual constancy are organizing principles that apply to hearing as well as vision. For example, in listening to a concerto, you follow the solo instrument and perceive the orchestra as accompaniment; this illustrates the organizing principle of
   a. figure-ground.
   b. shape constancy.
   c. grouping.
   d. depth or distance perception.

Perceptual Organization

1. What did the Gestalt psychologists contribute to our understanding of how the brain organizes sensations into perceptions?

The early Gestalt psychologists were impressed with the seemingly innate way in which we organize fragmentary sensory data into whole perceptions (gestalts). They studied how our minds structure the information that comes to us.

2. How do the principles of figure-ground and grouping contribute to our perception of form?

To recognize an object, we must first perceive it (see it as a figure) as distinct from its surroundings (the ground). We must also organize the figure into a meaningful form. Several gestalt principles of grouping—proximity, similarity, continuity, connectedness, and closure—describe this process.

3. How do we see the world in three dimensions?

Research on the visual cliff reveals that many species perceive the world in three dimensions at, or very soon after, birth. We transform two-dimensional retinal images into three-dimensional depth perceptions by use of binocular cues (such as retinal disparity and convergence) and monocular cues (such as interposition, relative size, relative height, relative motion, linear perspective, and light and shadow).

4. How do perceptual constancies help us to organize our sensations into meaningful perceptions?

Because of size, shape, and lightness constancy, objects appear to have unchanging characteristics regardless of their true distance from us or their actual shape or illumination. These perceptual constancies explain several well-known visual illusions, such as the moon and Müller-Lyer illusions.

TERMS AND CONCEPTS TO REMEMBER

gestalt, p. 170	depth perception, p. 172	monocular cues, p. 172	perceptual constancy, p. 176
figure-ground, p. 170	visual cliff, p. 172	retinal disparity, p. 172	
grouping, p. 171	binocular cues, p. 172	convergence, p. 173	

REHEARSE IT ANSWER KEY

1. d   2. b   3. c   4. c   5. b   6. a

Perceptual Interpretation

13

Philosophers have debated the origins of our perceptual abilities: Is it nature or nurture? German philosopher Immanuel Kant (1724–1804) maintained that knowledge comes from our *inborn* ways of organizing sensory experiences. Indeed, we come equipped to process sensory information. But British philosopher John Locke (1632–1704) argued that through our experiences we also *learn* to perceive the world. Indeed, we learn to link an object's distance with its size. So, just how important is experience? How radically does it shape our perceptual interpretations?

Sensory Deprivation and Restored Vision

PREVIEW QUESTION 1 What does research on sensory restriction and restored vision reveal about the effects of experience on perception?

Writing to John Locke (1690), William Molyneux wondered whether "a man *born* blind, and now adult, taught by his *touch* to distinguish between a cube and a sphere" could, if made to see, visually distinguish the two. Locke's answer was no, because the man would never have *learned* to see the difference.

Molyneux's hypothetical case has since been put to the test with dozens of adults who, though blind from birth, have gained sight (Gregory, 1978; von Senden, 1932). Most had been born with cataracts—clouded lenses that allowed them to see only diffused light, rather as you or I might see a diffuse fog through a Ping-Pong ball sliced in half. When their cataracts were surgically removed, the patients could distinguish objects from their surroundings (the so-called figure-ground relationship) and could sense colors—suggesting that these aspects of perception are innate. But much as Locke supposed, the formerly blind patients often could not recognize by sight objects that were familiar by touch.

Seeking to gain more control than is provided by clinical cases, researchers have conducted Molyneux's imaginary experiment with infant kittens and monkeys. In one experiment, they outfitted them with goggles through which the animals could see only diffuse, unpatterned light (Wiesel, 1982). After infancy, when their goggles were removed, these animals exhibited perceptual limitations much like those of humans born with cataracts. Their eyes had not degenerated; the light receptors in their retinas still relayed signals to their visual cortex. But lacking stimulation, the cortical cells had not developed normal connections. Thus, the animals remained functionally blind to shape.

In both humans and animals, a similar period of sensory restriction does no permanent harm if it occurs later in life. Cover the eye of an animal for several months during adulthood, and its vision will be unaffected after removing the eye patch. Remove cataracts that develop after early childhood, and a human, too, will enjoy normal vision. The effects of visual experiences during infancy in cats, monkeys, and humans suggest there is a *critical period* for normal sensory and perceptual development—an optimal time when experience must activate the brain's innate mechanisms if proper development is to take place. Experience indeed does guide the organization of the brain's neural connections.

Human infants born with an opaque lens (cataract) will typically have corrective surgery within a few months. The brain network responsible for the corrected eye

"Let us then suppose the mind to be, as we say, white paper void of all characters, without any ideas: How comes it to be furnished? . . . To this I answer, in one word, from EXPERIENCE."

John Locke, *An Essay Concerning Human Understanding*, 1690

then rapidly develops, enabling improved visual acuity with as little as one hour's visual experience (Mauer & others, 1999). Congenitally deaf kittens and human infants given cochlear implants to restore hearing exhibit a similar "awakening" of the pertinent brain area (Klinke & others, 1999; Siretenau, 1999). Nurture sculpts what nature has endowed.

Perceptual Adaptation

PREVIEW QUESTION 2 How adaptable is our ability to perceive the world around us?

Given a new pair of glasses, we may feel slightly disoriented, even dizzy. Within a day or two, we adjust. Our **perceptual adaptation** to changed visual input makes

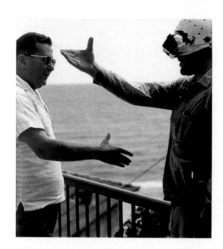

Perceptual adaptation
"Oops, missed," thinks Dr. Hubert Dolezal as he views the world through inverting goggles. Yet, believe it or not, kittens, monkeys, and humans can adapt to an inverted world.

the world seem normal again. But imagine a far more dramatic new pair of glasses—one that shifts the apparent location of objects 40 degrees to the left. When you first put them on and toss a ball to a friend, it sails off to the left. Walking forward to shake hands with the person, you veer to the left.

Could you adapt to this distorted world? Chicks cannot. When fitted with such lenses, they continue to peck where food grains *seem* to be (Hess, 1956; Rossi, 1968). But we humans adapt to distorting lenses quickly. Within a few minutes your throws would again be accurate, your stride on target. Remove the lenses and you would experience an aftereffect: At first your throws would err in the *opposite* direction, sailing off to the right; but again, within minutes you would readapt.

Indeed, given an even more radical pair of glasses—one that literally turns the world upside down—you could still adapt. Psychologist George Stratton (1896) experienced this when he invented, and for 8 days wore, optical headgear that flipped left to right *and* up to down, making him the first person to experience a right-side-up retinal image while standing upright (normally, our retinal images are inverted).

At first, Stratton felt disoriented. When he wanted to walk, he found himself searching for his feet, which were now "up." Eating was nearly impossible. He became nauseated and depressed. But Stratton persisted, and by the eighth day he could comfortably reach for something in the right direction and walk without bumping into things. When Stratton finally removed the headgear, he readapted quickly.

Later experiments replicated Stratton's experience (Dolezal, 1982; Kohler, 1962). After a period of adjustment, people wearing the optical gear have even been able to ride a motorcycle, ski the Alps, and fly an airplane. But how? Is it because through experience they perceptually reinvert their upside-down world to an upright position? Actually no. The street, ski slopes, and runway still seem above their heads. But by actively moving about in this topsy-turvy world, they adapt to the context and learn to coordinate their movements.

Perceptual Set

PREVIEW QUESTION 3 How do our assumptions, expectations, and contexts affect our perceptions?

As everyone knows, to see is to believe. As many people also know, but do not fully appreciate, to believe is to see. Our experiences, assumptions, and expectations may

- **perceptual adaptation** in vision, the ability to adjust to an artificially displaced or even inverted visual field.

- **perceptual set** a mental predisposition to perceive one thing and not another.

FIGURE 13.1

Perceptual set

What do you see in the center picture: a male saxophonist or a woman's face? Glancing first at one of the two unambiguous versions of the picture is likely to influence your interpretation. (From Shepard, 1990.)

give us a **perceptual set,** or mental predisposition, that greatly influences what we perceive. Is the image in the center picture of **FIGURE 13.1** a man playing the saxophone or a woman's face? What we see in such a drawing can be influenced by first looking at either of the two unambiguous versions (Boring, 1930).

Everyday examples of perceptual set abound. In 1972, a British newspaper published genuine, unretouched photographs of a "monster" in Scotland's Loch Ness—"the most amazing pictures ever taken," stated the paper. If this information creates in you the same perceptual set it did in most of the paper's readers, you, too, will see the monster in the photo reproduced in **FIGURE 13.2a**. But when Steuart Campbell (1986) approached the photos with a different perceptual set, he saw a curved tree trunk—very likely the same tree trunk others had seen in the water the day the photo was shot. Moreover, with this different perceptual set, you may now notice that the object is floating motionless, without any rippling water or wake around it—hardly what we would expect of a lively monster. Aided by apparent perceptual set, thousands of others have marveled at a face on the moon, Mother Teresa on a cinnamon bun, Jesus on a pancake, and the word *Allah* on a sliced potato.

Our perceptual set can influence what we hear as well as what we see. Consider the kindly airline pilot who, on a takeoff run, looked over at his depressed co-pilot and said, "Cheer up." The co-pilot heard the usual "Gear up" and promptly raised the wheels—before they had left the ground (Reason & Mycielska, 1982). People listening to rock music or a presidential speech played backward often perceive an evil message *if* specifically told what to listen for (Vokey & Read, 1985). One Web site (www.kissthisguy.com) has offered some 2000 examples of misperceptions such as "Little Miss Muffet sat on a tuffet eating her curtains away." Clearly, much of what we perceive comes not just from the world "out there" but also from what's behind our eyes and between our ears.

Even when listening to Disney movies, sex-sensitive viewers have perceived supposedly subliminal messages, such as the letters S-E-X in a cloud of dust stirred up by Simba in *The Lion King,* or "All good teenagers take off your clothes," murmured by a voice in *Aladdin.* The latter message was first perceived by a testosterone-laden male university student, who told his sister, who told her mother, who wrote to *Movie Guide,* whose report (later retracted) was picked up by the American Life League newsletter, whose allegation was reported by Virginia's *Newport News,* from where it was picked up by the Associated Press. "If somebody is [perceiving] something, that's their perception," responded Rick Rhoades, a spokesperson for Disney, which had been inundated with letters of protest. "There's nothing there" (Bannon, 1995). Some things must be believed to be seen.

What determines our perceptual set? Our preexisting concepts for male saxophonists and women's faces, for monsters and tree trunks, for airplane lights and UFOs, all influence how we interpret ambiguous sensations.

"The temptation to form premature theories upon insufficient data is the bane of our profession."

Sherlock Holmes, in Arthur Conan Doyle's *The Valley of Fear,* 1914

(a)

(b)

FIGURE 13.2

Believing is seeing

What do you perceive in these photos? (a) Is this Nessie, the Loch Ness monster, or a log? (b) Are these flying saucers or clouds? We often perceive what we expect to see.

FIGURE 13.3

Context effects: The magician's cabinet

Is the box in the far left frame lying on the floor or hanging from the ceiling? What about the one on the far right? In each case, the context defined by the inquisitive rabbits guides our perceptions. (From Shepard, 1990.)

Given a perceptual set—"this is a girl"—people see a more feminine baby.

Context Effects

A given stimulus may trigger radically different perceptions, partly because of our differing schemas, but also because of the immediate context. Some examples:

- Imagine hearing a noise interrupted by the words "eel is on the wagon." Likely, you would actually perceive the first word as *wheel.* Given "eel is on the orange," you would hear *peel.* This curious phenomenon, discovered by Richard Warren, suggests that the brain can work backward in time to allow a later stimulus to determine how we perceive an earlier one. The context creates an expectation that influences our perception as we match our sensory input against it (Grossberg, 1995).

- Is the "magician's cabinet" in **FIGURE 13.3** sitting on the floor or hanging from the ceiling? How we perceive it depends on the context defined by the rabbits.

- Did the speaker say "cults and sects" or "cults and sex"? Did the critic advocate "attacks" or "a tax" on our politicians? In both instances, we must discern the meaning from the surrounding words.

Even hearing sad rather than happy music can predispose people to perceive a sad meaning in spoken homophonic word meanings—*mourning* rather than *morning, die* rather than *dye, pain* rather than *pane* (Halberstadt & others, 1995).

In Seattle's county hospital where I was once an orderly, we occasionally faced the task of transporting a dead body through crowded hallways without alarming the patients or their visitors. Our solution was to create a context that matched people's schemas for sleeping and sedated patients: With the body's face uncovered and the sheet turned down in normal fashion, we could wheel an apparently "sleeping" body past the unsuspecting.

In everyday life, perceptual sets—for example, stereotypes about gender or culture—can color the context. Without the obvious cues of pink or blue, people will struggle over whether to call the new baby "he" or "she." But told an infant is "David," people (especially children) may perceive "him" as bigger and stronger than if the same infant is called "Diana" (Stern & Karraker, 1989). Some gender differences, it seems, exist merely in the eyes of their beholders.

The effects of perceptual sets and context show how experience helps us construct perception. "We hear and apprehend only what we already half know," said Thoreau. The river of perception is fed by two streams, sensation and cognition. To return to the question—is perception innate or learned?—we can answer: It's both. "Simple" perceptions are the brain's creative products. The Psychology Applied box illustrates how product designs influence human perception and behavior.

Culture and context effects

What is above the woman's head? In one study, nearly all the East Africans who were questioned said the woman was balancing a metal box or can on her head and that the family was sitting under a tree. Westerners, to whom corners and boxlike architecture are more common, were more likely to perceive the family as being indoors, with the woman sitting under a window. (Adapted from Gregory & Gombrich, 1973.)

THE HUMAN FACTOR IN OPERATING MACHINES

I love our VCR, though I still haven't figured out how to make it "express record." Our stove is wonderful, except for the moments I spend puzzling over which control works which burner. The push-bar doors on our campus buildings are sturdy, though occasionally frustrating when I push the wrong end. The extra buttons on my computer-linked phone are handy, though when transferring a call I still must look up which button to press.

Human factors psychologists help to design appliances, machines, and work settings that harness rather than confound our natural perceptions. Psychologist Donald Norman (1988) suggests how simple design changes could reduce some of our frustrations. For example, by exploiting "natural mapping," we could design stove controls that require no labels.

Understanding human factors can do more than enable us to design for reduced frustration; it can help avoid disaster. After beginning commercial flights in the late 1960s, the Boeing 727 was involved in several landing accidents caused by pilot error. Psychologist Conrad Kraft (1978) noted a common setting for these accidents: All took place at night, and all involved landing short of the runway after crossing a dark stretch of water or unilluminated ground. Kraft reasoned that, beyond the runway, city lights would project a larger retinal image if on a rising terrain. This would make the ground seem farther away than it was. By re-creating these conditions in flight simulations, Kraft discovered that pilots were deceived into thinking they were flying safely, higher than their actual altitudes (**FIGURE 13.4**). Aided by Kraft's finding, the airlines began corrective measures (such as requiring the co-pilot to monitor the altimeter and call out altitudes) and the accidents diminished.

Today's Boeing psychologists are at work on other human factors problems (Murray, 1998): How should airlines best train and manage mechanics to reduce the maintenance errors that underlie about 50 percent of flight delays and 15 percent of accidents? What illumination and typeface would make on-screen flight data easiest to read? How would warning messages be most effectively worded—as an action statement ("pull up") rather than a problem statement ("ground proximity")? In studying these and other human factors issues, psychologists strive to increase both safety and productivity.

(a) Traditional labeling

(b) Natural map

Better labels

(a) With traditionally positioned stove controls, a person must read the labels to figure out which knob works which burner. (b) By positioning the controls in a natural map, which the brain understands at a glance, we can eliminate the need to ponder written instructions just to boil water.

FIGURE 13.4

The human factor in misperception

Lacking distance cues when approaching a runway from over a dark surface, pilots simulating a night landing tended to fly too low. (From Kraft, 1978.)

rehearse it!

1. Locke believed that our perception of the world is learned through experience. Support for his view can be found in
   a. the writings of Immanuel Kant.
   b. research on the causes of cataracts.
   c. research on perceptual set and context.
   d. theories of color vision.

2. In some cases, surgeons have restored vision to patients who have been blind from birth. The newly sighted individuals were able to sense colors but had difficulty

   a. recognizing objects by touch.
   b. recognizing the shapes of objects.
   c. distinguishing figure from ground.
   d. distinguishing between bright and dim light.

3. Experiments in which volunteers wear glasses that displace or invert their visual fields show that, after a period of disorientation, they learn to function quite well. This ability is called
   a. context effect.
   b. perceptual set.
   c. sensory restriction.
   d. perceptual adaptation.

4. Our perceptual set influences what we perceive. This mental predisposition reflects our
   a. experiences, assumptions, and expectations.
   b. perceptual adaptation.
   c. objectivity, realism, and intelligence.
   d. perceptual constancy.

Is There Extrasensory Perception?

PREVIEW QUESTION 4 What claims are made for ESP, and can those claims withstand the demands of critical inquiry?

Can we perceive only what we sense? Or, without sensory input, are we capable of extrasensory perception? Half or a little more of British and American adults and Japanese university students say they believe in **extrasensory perception (ESP),** and another quarter aren't sure (Blackmore, 1997; Gallup & Newport, 1991; *George,* 1996; Nishizawa, 1996). The media overflow with reports of psychic wonders: crimes solved, dreams come true, futures foretold. Paranormal television (such as *Unsolved Mysteries* and *X-Files*) and movies (such as *The Sixth Sense* and *The Blair Witch Project*) are big business. The dial-a-psychic industry tops $1 billion a year, much of it from low-income people (Nisbet, 1998). Are there indeed people—any people—who can read minds, see through walls, or foretell the future?

In laboratory experiments, **parapsychologists**—those who study paranormal (literally, beyond the normal) occurrences—have at times been astonished at psychics who seem capable of discerning the contents of sealed envelopes, influencing the roll of a die, or drawing a picture of what someone else is viewing at an unknown remote location. But other research psychologists and scientists—including 96 percent of the scientists in the National Academy of Sciences—have been skeptical (McConnell, 1991). If ESP is real, we would need to overturn the scientific understanding that we are creatures whose minds are tied to our physical brains and whose perceptual experiences of the world are built of sensations. However, sometimes new evidence does overturn our scientific preconceptions. So let's critically evaluate claims for ESP.

Claims of ESP

Claims of paranormal phenomena include astrological predictions, psychic healing, reincarnation, communication with the dead, out-of-body experiences, and *psychokinesis* (moving objects via mind control). Of these, the most respectable, testable, and—for our discussion of perception—relevant claims are for three varieties of ESP:

- *Telepathy,* or mind-to-mind communication—one person sending thoughts to another or perceiving another's thoughts.
- *Clairvoyance,* or perceiving remote events, such as sensing that a friend's house is on fire.
- *Precognition,* or perceiving future events, such as a political leader's death or a sporting event's outcome.

■ **extrasensory perception (ESP)** the controversial claim that perception can occur apart from sensory input. Said to include *telepathy, clairvoyance,* and *precognition.*

■ **parapsychology** the study of paranormal phenomena, including ESP and psychokinesis.

Premonitions or Pretensions?

Can psychics see into the future? Although one might wish for a psychic stock forecaster, the tallied forecasts of "leading psychics" reveal meager accuracy. Between 1978 and 1985, the New Year's predictions of the *National Enquirer*'s favorite psychics yielded 2 accurate predictions out of 486 (Strentz, 1986). During the 1990s, tabloid psychics were all wrong in predicting surprising events (Madonna did not become a gospel singer, the Statue of Liberty did not lose both arms in a terrorist blast, Queen Elizabeth did not abdicate her throne to enter a convent). And they missed all the unexpected big-news events: How unfortunate that the psychic whom Princess Diana consulted shortly before her death did not foresee the danger that lay ahead.

Analyses of psychic visions offered to police departments reveal that these, too, are no more accurate than guesses made by others (Reiser, 1982). Psychics working with the police do, however, generate dozens or even hundreds of predictions. This increases the odds of an occasional correct guess, which psychics can then report to the media. Moreover, vague predictions can later be interpreted ("retrofitted") to match events that provide a perceptual set for interpreting them. Nostradamus, a sixteenth-century French psychic, explained in an unguarded moment that his ambiguous prophecies "could not possibly be understood till they were interpreted after the event and by it." Police departments are wise to all this. When Jane Ayers Sweat and Mark Durm (1993) asked the police departments of America's 50 largest cities whether they ever used psychics, 65 percent said they never had. Of those that had, not one had found it helpful.

Are the spontaneous "visions" of everyday people any more accurate? Consider our dreams. Do they foretell the future, as about half of university students believe (Messer & Griggs, 1989)? Or do they only seem to do so because we are more likely to recall or reconstruct dreams that seem to have come true? Over sixty years ago, two Harvard psychologists (Murray & Wheeler, 1937) tested the prophetic power of dreams. After aviator Charles Lindbergh's baby son was kidnapped and murdered but before the body was discovered, the researchers invited the public to report their dreams about the child. Of the 1300 dream reports submitted, how many accurately envisioned the child dead? Five percent. And how many also correctly anticipated the body's location—buried among trees? Only 4 of the 1300. Although this number was surely no better than chance, to those 4 dreamers the accuracy of their *apparent* precognitions must have seemed uncanny.

Which supposed psychic ability does the Psychic Pizza claim?

Throughout the day, each of us imagines many events. Occasionally an unlikely imagining is bound to occur and to astonish us when it does. If you tell everyone in a group of 100 to think "heads" before each tosses six coins, someone is likely to get heads every time (whether thinking heads or not) and to feel eerie afterward. Random sequences will at times contain weird conjunctions or streaks. Given the billions of events in the world each day, and given enough days, some stunning coincidences are sure to occur. With enough time, the improbable becomes inevitable.

One skeptic, magician James Randi, long offered $10,000 to anyone who could demonstrate "*any* paranormal ability" before a group of competent experts. With

"WOW"

"A person who talks a lot is sometimes right."

Spanish proverb

"Things that happen by chance are events in search of causes."

K. C. Cole, *The Universe and the Teacup*, **1998**

pledges from others, his offer—"to anyone who proves a genuine psychic power under proper observing conditions"—several years ago was upped to $1 million, on deposit with Goldman-Sachs (Randi, 1999). So far, no such person has emerged. Randi's offer has been publicized for three decades and dozens of people have been tested, sometimes under the scrutiny of an independent panel of judges. Still, nothing.

Putting ESP to Experimental Test

Finally, consider this, say the skeptics: If ESP existed, then surely someone out there could, when feeling the psychic spirit stirring, make millions in the stock market or occasionally pick winning lottery numbers or blackjack outcomes (becoming fabulously wealthy or generous). If someone—anyone—out there has accurate spontaneous premonitions, why did they not (for the sake of charity if not out of greed) predict the outcome of the $195 million multistate Powerball lottery in May 1998? Enough people certainly tried. Some 130 million tickets were purchased, each an effort at precognition. With 80 million-to-1 odds against specifying the correct string of numbers, that number of tickets would lead us to expect one or two winners by chance alone. And sure enough, Frank Capaci of Chicago was the one lucky winner—without any reported psychic help.

After thousands of experiments, *a reproducible ESP phenomenon has never been discovered, nor has anyone produced any individual who can convincingly demonstrate psychic ability.* A National Research Council investigation of ESP similarly concluded that "the best available evidence does not support the contention that these phenomena exist" (Druckman & Swets, 1988). And in 1995, a CIA-commissioned report evaluated 10 years of military testing of psychic spies (a program previously abandoned by the CIA after having produced nothing). Twenty million dollars had been invested. The result? The program produced nothing. Given so many disappointing laboratory results and vague or erroneous psychic visions, the psychic spy program was finally scrapped (Hyman, 1996; Waller, 1995).

In the past, there have existed all kinds of strange ideas—that bumps on the head reveal character traits, that bloodletting is a cure-all, that each sperm cell contains a miniature person. When faced with such claims—or with claims of mind reading or out-of-body travel or communication with the dead—how can we separate bizarre ideas from those that sound bizarre but are true? At the heart of science is a simple answer: Test them to see if they work. If they do, so much the better for the ideas. If they don't, so much the better for our skepticism.

This scientific attitude has led both believers and skeptics to agree that what parapsychology needs to give it credibility is a reproducible phenomenon and a theory to explain it. Seeking a phenomenon, how might we test ESP claims in a controlled experiment? An experiment differs from a staged demonstration. On stage, the "psychic," like a magician, controls what the audience sees and hears. The "effects" are typically mind-blowing. In the laboratory, the experimenter controls what the psychic sees and hears. Time and again, skeptics note, so-called psychics have exploited unquestioning audiences with amazing performances in which they *appeared* to communicate with the spirits of the dead, read minds, or levitate objects—only to have it revealed that their acts were a hoax, nothing more than the illusions of stage magicians.

Knowing how easily we can be deceived, and lacking reproducible results, most research psychologists remain skeptical. Indeed, they are dismayed by all the shows, books, and magazines on paranormal topics. But some have become newly intrigued by findings published by social psychologist Daryl Bem and parapsychologist Charles Honorton (1994) using the *ganzfeld procedure.* The procedure would place you in a reclining chair, play hissing white noise through headphones, and shine diffuse red

"At the heart of science is an essential tension between two seemingly contradictory attitudes—an openness to new ideas, no matter how bizarre or counterintuitive they may be, and the most ruthless skeptical scrutiny of all ideas, old and new."

Carl Sagan (1987)

"A psychic is an actor playing the role of a psychic."

Psychologist-Magician Daryl Bem (1984)

light through Ping-Pong ball halves strapped over your eyes. Ostensibly, this reduction of external distractions would put you in an ideal state to receive thoughts from someone else, which you may hear as small voices from within.

Building on earlier studies using this procedure, Bem and Honorton isolated a "sender" and "receiver" in separate, shielded chambers and had the sender concentrate for half an hour on one of four randomly selected visual images. The receivers were then asked which of four images best matched the images they experienced during the session. Over 11 studies, the receivers beat chance (25 percent accurately matched) by a bigger than usual margin (32 percent accurately matched).

Recall that psychology-based critical inquiry always asks two questions: What do you mean? And how do you know (what's your evidence)? Parapsychologists say the ganzfeld tests of ESP offer clear answers to both questions. Skeptic Ray Hyman (1994, 1996) granted that their methodology surpasses that of previous ESP experiments, but he questioned certain procedural details that may have introduced bias. Intrigued, other researchers set to work replicating these experiments. Would this be the first reliable ESP phenomenon? Or one more dashed hope?

Alas, Julie Milton and Richard Wiseman's (1999) statistical digest of 30 follow-up ganzfeld experiments found no effect. "We conclude that the ganzfeld technique does not at present offer a replicable method for producing ESP in the laboratory." But—hold the phone—one very recent study does find an effect (Milton, 1999).

Stay tuned, and remember: The scientific attitude blends curious skepticism with open-minded humility. It demands that extraordinary claims be supported by clear and reliable evidence. (If at 5′7″ and age 58 I claim to be able to dunk a basketball, the burden of proof would be on me to show that I can do it, not on you to prove that I couldn't.) Given such evidence, science is open to nature's occasional surprises.

As critical thinkers, we can be open to new ideas without being gullible, discerning without being cynical. We can be critical thinkers, yet—knowing that our understanding of nature is incomplete—we can agree with Shakespeare's Hamlet that "there are more things in heaven and earth, Horatio, than are dreamt of in your philosophy."

Some things that we assume to be true—the reality of another's love, the existence or nonexistence of God, the finality of death or the reality of life after death—are beyond science. After clearing the decks of tested and rejected pseudomysteries, we can therefore retain a humble sense of wonder regarding life's untestable mysteries.

Why, then, are so many people predisposed to believe that ESP, which *should* be testable by science, exists? In part, such beliefs may stem from understandable misperceptions, misinterpretations, and selective recall. But some people also have an unsatisfied hunger for wonderment, an itch to experience the magical. In Britain and the

The ganzfeld procedure
Hoping to detect faint telepathy signals, some parapsychologists use sensory deprivation to minimize distractions.

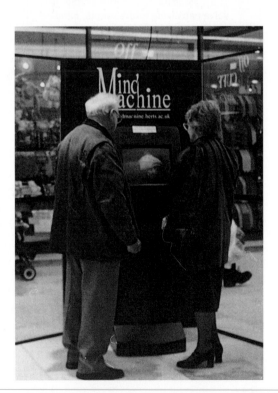

Testing psychic powers in the British population
Hertfordshire University psychologist Richard Wiseman created a "mind machine" to see if people could influence or predict a coin toss. Using a touch-sensitive screen, visitors to festivals around the country were given four attempts to call heads or tails. Using a random-number generator, a computer then decided the outcome. When the experiment concluded in January 2000, nearly 28,000 people had predicted 110,972 tosses—with 49.8 percent correct.

The Quigmans by Buddy Hickerson; © 1990, Los Angeles Times Syndicate. Reprinted with permission.

United States, the founders of parapsychology were mostly people who, having lost their religious faith, began searching for a scientific basis for believing in the meaning of life and life after death (Alcock, 1985; Beloff, 1985). In the upheaval since the collapse of autocratic rule in Russia, there has come an "avalanche of the mystical, occult and pseudoscientific" (Kapitza, 1991). In Russia as elsewhere, "extrasensorial" healers and seers fascinate the awestruck public. "Many people," declared a statement by 32 leading Russian scientists (1999), "believe in clairvoyance, astrology, and other superstitions to compensate for the psychological discomforts of our time."

To feel awe and to gain a deep reverence for life, we do not need to look any further than our own perceptual system and its capacity for organizing formless nerve impulses into colorful sights, vivid sounds, and evocative smells. Within our ordinary perceptual experiences lies much that is truly extraordinary—surely much more than has so far been dreamt of in our psychology. A century of research has revealed many of the secrets of sensation and perception, yet for future generations of researchers there remain profound and genuine mysteries to solve.

"I am fearfully and wonderfully made."

King David, Psalms 139:14

rehearse it!

5. More than half of Americans believe in the reality of ESP (extrasensory perception). The response of psychologists to these claims has been to
   a. deny the possibility of perception apart from sensation.
   b. doubt the existence of mysteries and extraordinary phenomena.
   c. test and critique ESP claims.
   d. devise a theory that explains why ESP exists.

6. The most testable varieties of ESP involve perceiving future events, mind-to-mind communication, and perceiving remote events. In order, these refer to
   a. clairvoyance, telepathy, and precognition.
   b. telepathy, clairvoyance, and precognition.
   c. precognition, telepathy, and clairvoyance.
   d. precognition, clairvoyance, and telepathy.

Perceptual Interpretation

1. What does research on sensory restriction and restored vision reveal about the effects of experience on perception?

For many species, infancy is a critical period during which experience must activate the brain's innate visual mechanisms. Although cataract removal may restore eyesight to adults who were blind from birth, these people remain unable to perceive the world normally. Generally, they can distinguish objects from their surroundings and can perceive colors, but they are unable to recognize shapes and forms. In controlled experiments, infant animals have been reared with severely restricted visual input. When their visual exposure is returned to normal, they, too, suffer enduring visual handicaps.

2. How adaptable is our ability to perceive the world around us?

Human vision is remarkably adaptable. For example, given glasses that shift the world slightly to the left or right, or even turn it upside down, people manage to adapt their movements and, with practice, to move about with ease.

3. How do our assumptions, expectations, and contexts affect our perceptions?

Clear evidence that perception is influenced by our learned assumptions and beliefs as well as by sensory input comes from the many demonstrations of perceptual set. Contexts plus the ideas we have stored in memory help us to interpret otherwise ambiguous stimuli. This helps explain why some of us "see" monsters, faces, and UFOs that others do not.

4. What claims are made for ESP, and can those claims withstand the demands of critical inquiry?

Parapsychologists have tried to document several forms of ESP—telepathy, clairvoyance, and precognition. But for several reasons, especially the lack of a reproducible ESP effect, most research psychologists remain skeptical. New studies using the ganzfeld procedure have recently raised hopes of a measurable telepathy phenomenon. Only one of more than 30 follow-up studies supports the phenomenon's reliability.

TERMS AND CONCEPTS TO REMEMBER

perceptual adaptation, p. 182

perceptual set, p. 183

extrasensory perception (ESP), p. 186

parapsychology, p. 186

REHEARSE IT ANSWER KEY

1. c   2. b   3. d   4. a   5. c   6. c

States of Consciousness

Now playing at an inner theater near you: the premiere showing of a sleeping person's vivid dream. This never-before-seen mental movie features captivating characters wrapped in a plot so original and unlikely, yet so intricate and so seemingly real, that the viewer later marvels at its creation.

Waking from a troubling dream, wrenched by its emotions, who among us has not wondered about this weird state of consciousness? How does our brain so creatively, colorfully, and completely construct this alternative, conscious world? In the shadowland between our dreaming and waking consciousness, we may even wonder for a moment which realm represents reality.

What is consciousness? What do we know about states of altered consciousness such as dreaming and daydreaming? These are the topics of Module 14. Then we look at what research tells us about other altered states of consciousness—hypnosis (Module 15) and drug-altered states (Module 16).

14 Waking and Sleeping Rhythms

- ■ Waking Consciousness
- ■ Sleep and Dreams

W hat is consciousness? In every science there are concepts so fundamental they are nearly impossible to define. Biologists agree on what is alive but not on precisely what life is. In physics, matter and energy elude simple definition. To psychologists, consciousness is similarly a fundamental yet slippery concept.

Waking Consciousness

PREVIEW QUESTION 1 What is consciousness and how does it function?

At its beginning, psychology was sometimes defined as "the description and explanation of states of consciousness" (Ladd, 1887). But the difficulty of scientifically studying consciousness led many psychologists during the first half of the twentieth century to turn to direct observations of behavior—an approach favored by an emerging school of psychology called *behaviorism*. By the 1960s, psychology no longer defined itself as the study of consciousness or "mental life" but rather as the science of behavior. Psychology had nearly lost consciousness. Consciousness was viewed as resembling a car's speedometer: "It doesn't make the car go, it just reflects what's happening" (Seligman, 1991, p. 24).

> "Psychology must discard all reference to consciousness."
>
> **Behaviorist John B. Watson (1913)**

By 1960, mental concepts began to reenter psychology. Advances in neuroscience made it possible to relate brain activity to various mental states—waking, sleeping, dreaming. Researchers began studying consciousness altered by hypnosis and drugs. Psychologists of all persuasions were affirming the importance of mental processes (cognition). Psychology was regaining consciousness.

For most psychologists today, **consciousness** is our awareness of ourselves and our environment. When we learn a complex concept or behavior—say, driving a car—consciousness focuses our concentration on the car and the traffic. This awareness varies with our attentional spotlight. With practice, driving becomes automatic and no longer requires our undivided attention—freeing our consciousness to focus on other things. Consciousness assembles information from various sources, enabling us to reflect on our past and plan for our future.

Consciousness
Our awareness of ourselves and our environment is but the visible surface of our brain's information processing.

Selective Attention

Perceptions come to us moment by moment, one perception vanishing as the next appears. Illusions—whether demonstrated in a psychology experiment or in a stage magician's act—rely on this important principle of perception: Our conscious attention is *selective*.

Selective attention means that at any moment we focus our awareness on only a limited aspect of all that we are capable of experiencing. Until reading this sentence, you have been unaware that your shoes are pressing against your feet or

- ■ **consciousness** our awareness of ourselves and our environments.
- ■ **selective attention** the focusing of conscious awareness on a particular stimulus, as in the cocktail party effect.

that your nose is in your line of vision. Now, suddenly, your attentional spotlight shifts. Your feet feel encased, your nose stubbornly intrudes on the page before you. While attending to these words, you've also been blocking from awareness information coming from your peripheral vision. But you can change that. While staring at the X below, notice what surrounds the book (the edges of the page, your desk top, and so forth).

X

Another example of selective attention, the *cocktail party effect,* is the ability to attend selectively to only one voice among many (as happens when you attend to one person at a party—until hearing your name spoken by someone else). Imagine hearing two conversations over a headset, one in each ear, and being asked to repeat the message in your left ear while it is spoken. When paying attention to what is being said in your left ear, you won't perceive what is said in your right. If you are asked later what language your right ear heard, you may draw a blank (though you could report the speaker's gender and loudness). At the level of conscious awareness, whatever has your attention pretty much has your undivided attention.

FIGURE 14.1

Testing selective attention

In this experiment, viewers who were attending to basketball tosses among the black-shirted players usually failed to notice the umbrella-toting woman sauntering across the screen. (From Neisser, 1979.)

It is true of the other senses, too. From the immense array of visual stimuli constantly before us, we select just a few to process. Ulric Neisser (1979) and Robert Becklen and Daniel Cervone (1983) demonstrated this dramatically. They showed people a one-minute videotape in which the images of three men in black shirts tossing a basketball were superimposed over the images of three men in white shirts doing the same thing. They asked the viewers to press a key every time the black-shirted players passed the ball. Midway through the tape, a young woman carrying an umbrella sauntered across the screen (**FIGURE 14.1**). Most had focused their attention so completely on the black-shirted players that they failed to notice the woman. When the researchers replayed the tape for them, they were astonished to see her.

Can stimuli that we do not notice affect us? Indeed yes. In one experiment, women students listened through headphones as a prose passage played in one ear. Their task was to repeat its words out loud and to check them against a written transcript (Wilson, 1979). Meanwhile, some simple, novel tunes played in the other ear. The tunes were not subliminal—the women could hear them easily. But with their attention selectively focused on the passage, the women were no more aware of the tunes than you normally are of your shoes. Thus, when they later heard these tunes interspersed among new ones, they could not recognize them (just as we cannot recall a conversation to which we paid no attention). Nevertheless, when asked to rate how much they liked each tune, they *preferred* the ones previously played. Their preferences revealed what their conscious memories could not.

Levels of Information Processing

Conscious awareness enables us to exert voluntary control and to communicate our mental states to others, yet consciousness is but the tip of the information-processing iceberg. Research reported throughout this book reveals that we process much information outside our awareness. We register and react to stimuli we do not consciously perceive. We perform well-learned tasks automatically, as when keyboarding without attending to where the letters are. When we meet someone, we instantly and unconsciously react to their gender, age, and appearance, and then become aware of our response. We change our attitudes and reconstruct our memories with no awareness of doing so.

Unlike the processing of subconscious information, which occurs simultaneously on many parallel tracks, conscious processing takes place in sequence (serially). Consciousness is relatively slow and has limited capacity, but is skilled at solving novel problems. It could be compared to a chief executive, whose many assistants automatically take care of routine business. Traveling a familiar route, your hands and feet do the driving while your mind engages in conversation. Running on automatic pilot allows consciousness—the mind's CEO—to monitor the whole system and deal with new challenges.

Novel tasks do, however, require our conscious attention. At the wheel for the first time in a country where people drive on the other side of the road, driving will command your attention. Or try this: If you are right-handed, you can move your right foot in a smooth counterclockwise circle, and you can write the number 3 repeatedly with your right hand—but probably not at the same time. (If you are musically inclined, try something equally difficult: Tap a steady three times with your left hand while tapping four times with your right hand.) Both tasks require conscious attention, which can be in only one place at a time. If time is nature's way of keeping everything from happening at once, then consciousness is nature's way of keeping us from thinking and doing everything at once.

Daydreams and Fantasies

PREVIEW QUESTION 2 What are the functions of daydreams and fantasies?

Consciousness occurs in varied states—among them, daydreams and fantasies. In James Thurber's classic story "The Secret Life of Walter Mitty," the bland existence of mild-mannered Walter Mitty is spiced with gratifying fantasies. As he drives past a hospital, Mitty imagines himself as Dr. Mitty, rushing to an operating room where two renowned specialists plead for his help. Again and again, the bumbling Walter Mitty relieves the tedium of his life by imagining himself as the triumphant Walter Mitty—now the world's greatest target shooter, now a heroic pilot.

Thurber's story became a classic because most of us can identify with Walter Mitty. From interview and questionnaire studies with hundreds of adults, clinical psychologist Jerome L. Singer (1975) reported that nearly everyone has daydreams or waking fantasies every day—on the job, in the classroom, walking down the street—in fact, almost anywhere at any time. Compared with older adults, young adults spend more time daydreaming and admit to more sexual fantasies (Cameron & Biber, 1973; Giambra, 1974). About 95 percent of both men and women say they have had sexual fantasies. But men (whether gay or straight) fantasize about sex more often, more physically, and less romantically—and these tendencies influence their preferences for books and videos (Leitenberg & Henning, 1995). Sexual fantasies do *not* indicate sexual problems or dissatisfaction. (If anything, sexually active and satisfied people have more sexual fantasies.)

Not all daydreaming is as overtly escapist or dramatic as Walter Mitty's. Mostly it involves the familiar details of our lives—perhaps imagining an alternative approach to something we have to do, or picturing ourselves explaining to an instructor why a paper will be late, or replaying in our minds personal encounters that we relish or wish had gone differently.

Some individuals—perhaps 4 percent of the population—fantasize so vividly they are said to have **fantasy-prone personalities.** One study of 26 women in this category found that as children they had enjoyed unusually intense make-believe play with their dolls, stuffed animals, or imaginary companions (Wilson & Barber, 1983). As adults, they reported spending more than half their time fantasizing. They would

Looking into the inner world
Daydreams and fantasies are a constructive part of everyone's repertoire of behaviors. For these Dutch commuters, daydreams may release tension, increase creativity, illuminate solutions to problems—and even lessen boredom.

■ **fantasy-prone personality** someone who imagines and recalls experiences with lifelike vividness and who spends considerable time fantasizing.

relive experiences or imagine scenes so vividly that occasionally they would later have trouble sorting out their remembered fantasies from their memories of actual events. When watching or imagining violent or frightening scenes, they sometimes even felt ill. Three-fourths had experienced orgasms solely by sexual fantasy. Many reported profound mystical or religious experiences.

Although few daydream this intensively, we all daydream. Are the hours we spend in fantasy a way of escaping rather than facing reality? Sometimes. But daydreaming can also be adaptive. Some daydreams help us prepare for future events by keeping us aware of our unfinished business and giving us the chance to mentally rehearse. Playful fantasies enhance the creativity of scientists, writers, and artists. For children, daydreaming in the form of imaginative play nourishes social and cognitive development—a fact that makes the diversion of watching television a concern to some developmental psychologists (Singer, 1986). "When I examined myself, and my methods of thought, I came to the conclusion that the gift of fantasy has meant more to me than my talent for absorbing positive knowledge" (Albert Einstein, 1879–1955).

Daydreams may also substitute for impulsive behavior. People who are prone to delinquency and violence or who seek the artificial highs of dangerous drugs have fewer vivid fantasies (Singer, 1976). Perhaps Walter Mitty's imaginative reveries not only rescued him from boredom but also allowed him to indulge his impulses within the safety of his inner world.

"This isn't a hasty decision. A lot of daydreaming went into it."

"The art of living requires us to steer a course between the two extremes of external and internal stimulation."

Psychologist Jerome L. Singer (1976)

rehearse it!

1. Consciousness involves selective attention to ongoing perceptions. An example of selective attention is the "cocktail party effect," which is the ability to
   a. drink without becoming intoxicated.
   b. follow many voices simultaneously.
   c. attend to but one voice among many other voices.
   d. be affected by unnoticed stimuli.

2. Most people daydream every day. These daydreams serve several functions: They provide an escape from reality, they help us prepare for the future, they enhance creativity, and they may substitute for
   a. a rich, complete life.
   b. impulsive behavior.
   c. night dreams.
   d. meditative time.

Sleep and Dreams

Sleep—the irresistible tempter to whom we must all succumb. Sleep—the mantle that covers human thought. Sleep—sweet, renewing, mysterious sleep. Sleep's age-old mysteries have intrigued us for centuries. Now, some of these mysteries are being solved. In laboratories throughout the world, thousands have slept attached to recording devices while others observe. By recording sleepers' brain waves and muscle movements, by observing and waking them from time to time, the sleep watchers glimpse things that a thousand years of common sense never told us. Perhaps you can anticipate some of their discoveries. Are the following statements true or false?

1. When people dream of performing some activity, their limbs often move in concert with the dream (page 202).
2. Sleepwalkers are acting out their dreams (page 206).
3. Sleep experts recommend treating insomnia with an occasional sleeping pill (page 205).
4. Some people dream every night; others seldom dream (page 202).

All these statements (adapted from Palladino & Carducci, 1983) are false. Let's see why.

"I love to sleep. Do you? Isn't it great? It really is the best of both worlds. You get to be alive and unconscious."

Comedian Rita Rudner, 1993

■ **circadian rhythm** [ser-KAY-dee-an] the biological clock; regular bodily rhythms (for example, of temperature and wakefulness) that occur on a 24-hour cycle.

■ **REM sleep** rapid eye movement sleep, a recurring sleep stage during which vivid dreams commonly occur. Also known as *paradoxical sleep* because the muscles are relaxed (except for minor twitches) but other body systems are active.

■ **alpha waves** the relatively slow brain waves of a relaxed, awake state.

■ **sleep** periodic, natural, reversible loss of consciousness—as distinct from unconsciousness resulting from a coma, general anesthesia, or hibernation (after Dement, 1999).

If our natural circadian rhythm were attuned to a 23-hour cycle, would we instead need to discipline ourselves to stay up later at night and sleep in longer in the morning? Do older adults, who typically prefer an earlier waking and bedtime than university students, have a shorter circadian rhythm?

Biological Rhythms and Sleep

PREVIEW QUESTION 3 How do our age-old biological rhythms influence our daily functioning and our sleep and dreams? What is the biological rhythm of our sleep?

Like the ocean, life has its rhythmic tides. Over varying periods of time, our bodies fluctuate, and with them, our minds. Let's look more closely at two of those biological rhythms—our 24-hour biological clock and our 90-minute sleep cycle.

Circadian Rhythm

The rhythm of the day parallels the rhythm of life—from our waking to a new day's birth to our nightly return to what Shakespeare called "death's counterfeit." Our bodies roughly synchronize with the 24-hour cycle of day and night through a biological clock called the **circadian rhythm** (from the Latin *circa,* "about," and *dies,* "day"). Our body temperature, for example, rises as morning approaches, peaks during the day, dips for a time in early afternoon (when many people take siestas), and then begins to drop again before we go to sleep. Awake at 4:00 A.M., with a depressed body, we may fret over concerns: Does a lovers' spat signal a split? Does a child's moodiness mean more trouble ahead? By midday, our body energized, we fret less. Pulling an all-nighter, we feel groggiest about 4:00 A.M., but we feel a second wind as our normal wake-up time arrives.

Recent evidence suggests that thinking is sharpest and memory most accurate when people are at their daily peak in circadian arousal. Some of us are morning-loving "larks," others evening-energized "owls." With age, we tend to shift from being owls to larks. Most university students are "evening persons," report Cynthia May and Lynn Hasher (1997). Their performance typically improves across the day. Most older adults are "morning persons," with their performance declining as the day wears on. In retirement homes, all is quiet by midevening; in university dorms, the day is far from over.

A transcontinental flight disrupts our circadian rhythm and we experience jet lag, mainly because we are awake when our circadian rhythm cries, "Sleep!" Studies in the laboratory and with shift workers reveal that bright light helps reset our biological clocks (Czeisler & others, 1986, 1989; Eastman & others, 1995). Thus, to speed the resetting of your biological clock after a long flight, spend the first day outdoors. Bright light in the morning facilitates awakening (and protects against depression). Bright light at night helps delay sleep (Oren & Terman, 1998).

We can also reset our biological clocks by adjusting our sleep schedules. If we stay up late and sleep in on weekends, we may end up with "Sunday night insomnia" and "Monday morning blues." Those who sleep till noon on Sunday and then go to bed just 11 hours later in preparation for the new workweek often find sleep elusive. They are like New Yorkers whose biology is on California time, or like someone who has just flown east from Perth to Sydney.

Curiously—given that our ancestors' body clocks were attuned to the rising and setting sun of the 24-hour day—young adults isolated without clocks or daylight typically adopt a 25-hour day. For this, we can thank (or blame) Thomas Edison, inventor of the light bulb. Being bathed in light, even in a cave, is like traveling one time zone west—it nudges our 24-hour biological clock back (Dement, 1999; Shanahan & others, 1999). This helps explain why rotating shift workers adapt better to progressively later shifts than to earlier ones, and why until our later years we must discipline ourselves to get to bed on time and force ourselves to get up. Most animals, too, when placed under unnatural constant illumination, exceed a 24-hour day. Artificial light delays sleep.

Sleep Stages

About every 90 or 100 minutes we pass through a cycle of five distinct sleep stages. This elementary fact was unknown until 8-year-old Armond Aserinsky went to bed

Left eye movements

Right eye movements

EMG (muscle tension)

EEG (brain waves)

FIGURE 14.2
Measuring sleep activity
Sleep researchers measure brain-wave activity, eye movements, and muscle tension by electrodes that pick up weak electrical signals from the brain, eye, and facial muscles. (From Dement, 1978.)

one night in 1952. His father, Eugene, a University of Chicago graduate student, needed to test an electroencephalograph he had been repairing during the day (Aserinsky, 1988; Seligman & Yellen, 1987). He placed electrodes near Armond's eyes to record the rolling eye movements believed to occur during sleep. Before long, the machine went wild, tracing deep zigzags on the graph paper. Aserinsky thought the machine was still broken. But as the night proceeded, the activity periodically recurred, indicating, Aserinsky finally realized, fast, jerky eye movements accompanied by energetic brain activity. When he awakened Armond during one such episode, the boy reported he was having a dream. Aserinsky had discovered what we now know as **REM sleep** (rapid *eye* *movement* sleep).

To find out if similar cycles occur during adult sleep, Nathaniel Kleitman (1960) and Aserinsky pioneered procedures that have now been used with thousands of volunteers. To appreciate both their methods and findings, imagine yourself as a participant. As the hour grows late, you begin to fight sleepiness and yawn in response to reduced brain metabolism. Yawning stretches your neck muscles and increases your heart rate, thus increasing the bloodflow to your brain and your alertness (Moorcroft, 1993). When you are ready for bed, the researcher glues electrodes to your scalp (to detect your brain waves), just outside the corners of your eyes (to detect eye movements), and on your chin (to detect muscle tension) (**FIGURE 14.2**). Other devices allow the researcher to record your heart rate, your respiration rate, and the degree of your genital arousal.

When you are in bed with your eyes closed, the researcher in the next room sees on the EEG the relatively slow **alpha waves** of your awake but relaxed state (**FIGURE 14.3**). As you adapt to all this equipment and grow tired, you slip into **sleep.** Sleep is a state that we do not know we are in until we

FIGURE 14.3
Brain waves and sleep stages
The regular alpha waves of an awake, relaxed stage are quite different from the slower, larger delta waves of deep Stage 4 sleep. Although the rapid REM sleep waves resemble the near-waking Stage 1 sleep waves, the body is more aroused during REM sleep than during Stage 1 sleep (from Dement, 1978).

Awake, relaxed

◀ Alpha waves ▶

Stage 1 sleep

Stage 2 sleep

Spindle (burst of activity)

Stage 3 sleep

Stage 4 sleep

◀ Delta waves ▶

REM sleep

Eye movement phase

FIGURE 14.4

The moment of sleep
We seem unaware of the moment we fall into sleep, but someone eavesdropping on our brain waves could tell (from Dement, 1999).

Can you recall the moment you fell asleep last night? Or, at best, your last moments of waking?

leave it. Our dive into sleep—marked by the slowed breathing and the irregular brain waves of Stage 1—happens in an unrecognized moment (**FIGURE 14.4**).

Sleep researcher William Dement (1999) observed the moment the perceptual door between the brain and outside world slammed shut in one of his 15,000 subjects. Dement asked this sleep-deprived young man, lying on his back with eyelids taped open, to press a button every time a strobe light flashed in his eyes (averaging about every 6 seconds). After a few minutes the subject missed one. Asked why, he said "because there was no flash." But there was a flash—which he missed because (his brain activity revealed) he had fallen asleep for two seconds. Unaware that he had done so, he had missed not only the flash 6 inches from his nose but also the abrupt moment of his entry into sleep.

During this brief Stage 1 sleep, you may experience fantastic images, resembling **hallucinations**—sensory experiences that occur without a sensory stimulus. You may have a sensation of falling (at which moment your body may suddenly jerk) or of floating weightlessly. Such "hypnogogic" sensations may later become incorporated into memories. People who claim to have been abducted by aliens—often shortly after getting in bed—commonly recall being floated off their beds.

Soon, you relax more deeply and begin about 20 minutes of Stage 2 sleep, characterized by the periodic appearance of *sleep spindles*—bursts of rapid, rhythmic brainwave activity. Although you can still be awakened without too much difficulty during this phase, you are now clearly asleep. Sleeptalking—usually garbled or nonsensical—can occur during this or any other sleep stage (Mahowald & Ettinger, 1990).

Then for the next few minutes you go through the transitional Stage 3 to the deep sleep of Stage 4. First in Stage 3, and increasingly in Stage 4, your brain emits large, slow **delta waves.** These stages together are called *slow-wave sleep.* They last for about 30 minutes, during which you are hard to awaken. Curiously, it is at the end of the deep sleep of Stage 4 that children may wet the bed or begin walking in their sleep. About 20 percent of 3- to 12-year-olds have at least one episode of sleepwalking, usually lasting 2 to 10 minutes; some 5 percent have repeated episodes (Giles & others, 1994).

Even when you are deeply asleep, your brain somehow processes the meaning of certain stimuli. You move around on your bed, but you manage not to fall out of it. If you sleep with your babies, you will not roll over and suffocate them (assuming you are not intoxicated). The occasional roar of passing vehicles may leave deep sleep undisturbed, but the cry from a baby's nursery quickly interrupts it. So does the sound of your name—a stimulus our selective attention is ever alert for. EEG recordings confirm that the brain's auditory cortex responds to sound stimuli even during sleep (Kutas, 1990). All this reminds us of one of this book's basic lessons: *We process most information outside of conscious awareness.*

REM Sleep

About an hour after you first fall asleep, a strange thing happens. Rather than continuing in deep slumber, you ascend from your initial sleep dive. Returning through Stage 3 and Stage 2 (where you spend about half your night), you enter the most intriguing sleep phase of all—REM sleep (**FIGURE 14.5**). For about 10 minutes, your brain waves become rapid and saw-toothed, more like those of the nearly awake Stage 1 sleep. But unlike Stage 1 sleep, REM sleep is a time when your heart rate rises, your breathing becomes rapid and irregular, and every half-minute or so your eyes dart around in a momentary burst of activity behind closed lids. Because anyone watching a sleeper's eyes can notice these REM bursts, it is amazing that science was ignorant of REM sleep until 1952.

■ **hallucinations** false sensory experiences, such as seeing something in the absence of an external visual stimulus.

■ **delta waves** the large, slow brain waves associated with deep sleep.

FIGURE 14.5

The stages in a typical night's sleep

Most people pass through the five-stage sleep cycle several times, with the periods of Stage 4 sleep and then Stage 3 sleep diminishing and REM sleep periods increasing in duration. The second graph plots this increasing REM sleep and decreasing deep sleep based on data from 30 young adults. (Cartwright, 1978; Webb, 1992)

During REM sleep, your genitals become aroused and you have an erection or increased vaginal lubrication and clitoral engorgement. For example, the common "morning erection" stems from the night's last REM period, often just before waking. Except during very scary dreams, genital arousal always occurs, regardless of whether the dream's content is sexual (Karacan & others, 1966). The phenomenon has been studied mostly in men, from whom measurements are more easily recorded. In young men, sleep-related erections outlast REM periods, lasting 30 to 45 minutes on average (Karacan & others, 1983; Schiavi & Schreiner-Engel, 1988). A typical 25-year-old man therefore has an erection during nearly half his night's sleep, a 65-year-old man for one-quarter. Many men troubled by "erectile disorder" (impotence) have morning erections, suggesting that the problem is not between their legs.

Although your brain's motor cortex, which controls voluntary movement, is active during REM sleep, your brainstem (the ancient part of the brain, responsible for automatic survival functions) blocks its messages, leaving your muscles relaxed—so relaxed that, except for an occasional finger, toe, or facial twitch, you are essentially paralyzed. Moreover, you cannot easily be awakened. Thus, REM sleep is sometimes called *paradoxical* sleep; internally the body is aroused while externally it appears calm.

Some sleep deeply, some not
The fluctuating sleep cycle enables safe sleep for soldiers on the battlefield. One benefit of communal sleeping is that someone will probably be awake or easily roused in the event of a threat during the night.

"Boy are my eyes tired! I had REM sleep all night long."

People rarely snore during dreams. When REM starts, snoring stops.

1993 Time/CNN poll: "How many hours do you sleep each night?"

Under six	12%
Six	26
Seven	30
Eight	28
Over eight	3

In 1989, Michael Doucette was named America's Safest Driving Teen. In 1990, while driving home from college, he fell asleep at the wheel and collided with an oncoming car, killing both himself and the other driver. Michael's driving instructor later acknowledged never having mentioned sleep deprivation and drowsy driving (Dement, 1999).

Even more intriguing than the paradoxical nature of REM sleep is what the rapid eye movements announce: the beginning of a dream. Even those who claim they never dream will, more than 80 percent of the time, recall a dream after being awakened during REM sleep. Unlike the fleeting images of Stage 1 sleep, REM sleep dreams are often emotional and usually storylike—but never acted out, thanks to REM's protective paralysis. (People occasionally recall dreams when awakened from stages other than REM sleep, but these dreams usually contain a single vague image, such as, "I was trying to borrow something from someone.")

The sleep cycle repeats itself about every 90 minutes. As the night wears on, deep Stage 4 sleep gets progressively briefer and then disappears. The REM sleep period gets longer. By morning, 20 to 25 percent of our average night's sleep—some 100 minutes—has been REM sleep. This means that those who say "I rarely dream" actually spend about 600 hours a year experiencing some 1500 dreams, or more than 100,000 dreams over a typical lifetime—dreams swallowed by the night.

Why Do We Sleep?

PREVIEW QUESTION 4 How does sleep loss affect us? What is sleep's function?

The idea that "everyone needs 8 hours of sleep" is not true. Newborns spend nearly two-thirds of their day asleep, most adults no more than one-third. Age-related differences in average time spent sleeping are rivaled by differences in the normal amount of sleep among individuals at any age. Some people thrive with fewer than 6 hours of sleep per night; others regularly sleep 9 hours or more. Sleep patterns may be genetically influenced. When Wilse Webb and Scott Campbell (1983) checked the pattern and duration of sleep among fraternal and identical twins, only the identical twins were strikingly similar.

Allowed to sleep unhindered, most humans will sleep 9 to 10 hours a night, reports Stanley Coren (1996). With that much sleep, we do not become groggy. We awake refreshed, sustain better moods, and perform more efficient and accurate work than do those who get less sleep. With a succession of 5-hour nights, however, we accumulate sleep debt that is not paid off by one 10-hour sleep—which explains why we can feel sleepy even after a long sleep. "The brain keeps an accurate count of sleep debt for at least two weeks," says William Dement (1999, p. 64). Deprived of sleep, we also begin to feel terrible, as our bodies yearn for sleep.

Obviously, then, we need sleep. Sleep commands roughly one-third of our lives—some 25 years, on average. But why? It seems an easy question to answer: Just keep people awake for several days and note how they deteriorate. If you were a volunteer in such an experiment, how do you think it would affect your body and mind?

Of course, you would become terribly drowsy at times—especially during the hours when your biological clock programs you to sleep. But could a lack of sleep physically damage you? Would it noticeably alter your biochemistry or body organs? Would you become emotionally disturbed? Intellectually disoriented?

Because of modern light bulbs, shift work, and social diversions, people in industrialized nations sleep less than they did a century ago. People who a century ago would have gone to bed at 9:00 P.M. are now up until 11:00 P.M. Thomas Edison (1948, pp. 52, 178) was pleased to accept credit for this. For him, lost sleep meant more time and opportunity.

> When I went through Switzerland in a motor-car, so that I could visit little towns and villages, I noted the effect of artificial light on the inhabitants. Where water power and electric light had been developed, everyone seemed normally intelligent. When these appliances did not exist, and the natives went to bed with the chickens, staying there till daylight, they were far less intelligent.

The Effects of Sleep Loss

Actually, a major effect of lessened sleep is not only sleepiness but a general malaise (Mikulincer & others, 1989). People today more than ever suffer from sleep patterns that thwart their having an energized feeling of well-being. Four in ten young adults say they are sleepy at work two or more days a week (National Sleep Foundation, 2000). Teenagers typically need 8 or 9 hours sleep, but they now average nearly 2 hours less sleep a night than their counterparts of 80 years ago (Holden, 1993; Maas, 1999). Many fill this need by using their first class for an early siesta and after-lunch study hall for a slumber party. Even when awake, they often function below their peak.

At Stanford University, William Dement (1997) reports, 80 percent of students are "dangerously sleep deprived." Such individuals "are at high risk for some sort of accident. . . . Sleep deprivation [entails] difficulty studying, diminished productivity, tendency to make mistakes, irritability, fatigue." A large sleep debt "makes you stupid," says Dement (1999, p. 231). But let's put this positively: To manage your life with enough sleep to awaken naturally and well rested is to be more alert, productive, healthy, and happy.

In experiments, the U.S. Navy and the National Institutes of Health have paid volunteers to spend 14 hours daily in bed for at least a week. For the first few days, the volunteers in both experiments averaged 12 hours sleep a day or more, apparently paying off a sleep debt that averaged 25 to 30 hours. That accomplished, they then settled back to 7.5 to 9 hours sleep a night and, with no sleep debt, felt energized and happier. "What this means to me," reflects Dement (1999, p. 72) "is that millions of us are living a less than optimal life and performing at a less than optimal level, impaired by an amount of sleep debt that we're not even aware we carry."

As a demonstration of the costs of widespread sleep deprivation among today's adolescents and adults, Stanley Coren capitalized on a naturally occurring experiment that manipulates sleep length—the "spring forward" to daylight time and "fall backward" to standard time. Searching millions of records, he found that in both Canada and the United States, accidents increase immediately after the shortened sleep associated with the spring time change. In Canada, for example, traffic accidents during 1991 and 1992 were 7 percent higher the Monday after the spring time change than on the Monday before, and they were 7 percent lower on the Monday following the extra sleep bestowed by the fall time change (**FIGURE 14.6**).

> "Tiger Woods said that one of the best things about his choice to leave Stanford for the professional golf circuit was that he could now get enough sleep."
>
> **Stanford sleep researcher William Dement**
> **(1997).**

FIGURE 14.6

Canadian traffic accidents, 1991 and 1992
The Monday after the spring time change, when people lose sleep, accidents increased as compared with the Monday before. After the fall time change, they dropped. (Adapted from Coren, 1996.)

"Drowsiness is red alert!"

William Dement, *The Promise of Sleep*, 1999

Sleepless and suffering
This fatigued, sleep-deprived person may also experience a depressed immune system, impaired concentration, and greater vulnerability to accidents.

Sleep deprivation can also be devastating for driving and piloting. Some 30 percent of Australian highway deaths occur when drivers fall asleep on long, monotonous roads (Maas, 1999). "Rest. That's what I need is rest," said Eastern Airlines Captain James Reeves to the control tower on a September 1974 morning— 30 minutes before crashing his airliner at low altitude, killing the crew and all 68 passengers (Moorcroft, 1993). Consider also the *Exxon Valdez* oil spill; Union Carbide's Bhopal, India, disaster; and the Three Mile Island and Chernobyl nuclear accidents—they all occurred after midnight, when operators in charge were likely to be drowsiest. Severely sleep-deprived, the *Exxon Valdez* mate at the helm was unresponsive to clear signals to turn his vessel back into the shipping lanes.

Other effects of sleep loss are subtle. One such effect is suppression of the disease-fighting immune system (Beardsley, 1996; Irwin & others, 1994). In rats, sleep deprivation increases the pathogens normally suppressed by the immune system. In humans, sleep deprivation suppresses immune cells that fight off viral infections and cancer, which helps explain why people who sleep 8 hours a night tend to outlive those chronically sleep-deprived (Dement, 1999). When infections do set in, we typically sleep more, boosting our immune cells. Chronic sleep debt also alters metabolic and hormonal functioning in ways that mimic aging and are conducive to obesity, hypertension, and memory impairment (Spiegel & others, 1999). Other effects include impaired creativity and concentration, slight hand tremors, irritability, slowed performance, and occasional misperceptions on monotonous tasks (Horne, 1989; Koslowsky & Babkoff, 1992).

TABLE 14.1

ARE YOU SLEEP DEPRIVED?

Cornell University psychologist James Maas reports that most college students suffer the consequences of sleeping less than they should. To see if you are in that group, answer the following true-false questions:

True	False	
☐	☐	1. I need an alarm clock in order to wake up at the appropriate time.
☐	☐	2. It's a struggle for me to get out of bed in the morning.
☐	☐	3. Weekday mornings I hit the snooze bar several times to get more sleep.
☐	☐	4. I feel tired, irritable, and stressed out during the week.
☐	☐	5. I have trouble concentrating and remembering.
☐	☐	6. I feel slow with critical thinking, problem solving, and being creative.
☐	☐	7. I often fall asleep watching TV.
☐	☐	8. I often fall asleep in boring meetings or lectures or in warm rooms.
☐	☐	9. I often fall asleep after heavy meals or after a low dose of alcohol.
☐	☐	10. I often fall asleep while relaxing after dinner.
☐	☐	11. I often fall asleep within five minutes of getting into bed.
☐	☐	12. I often feel drowsy while driving.
☐	☐	13. I often sleep extra hours on weekend mornings.
☐	☐	14. I often need a nap to get through the day.
☐	☐	15. I have dark circles around my eyes.

If you answered "true" to three or more items, you probably are not getting enough sleep. To determine your sleep needs, Maas recommends that you "go to bed 15 minutes earlier than usual every night for the next week—and continue this practice by adding 15 more minutes each week—until you wake without an alarm clock and feel alert all day."

(*Quiz reprinted with permission from James B. Maas,* Power sleep: The revolutionary program that prepares your mind and body for peak performance [*New York: Harper Collins, 1999*].)

Sleep Theories

Why, then, do we sleep? We have very few answers, but sleep may have evolved for at least two reasons: First, it suits our ecological niche. When darkness precluded our ancestors' hunting and food gathering and made travel treacherous, they were better off asleep in a cave, out of harm's way. Sleep *protects*. Animals with the most need to graze and the least ability to hide tend to sleep less. Elephants and horses sleep 3 to 4 hours a day, gorillas 12 hours, cats 15 hours, and bats 20 hours.

Second, sleep helps us recuperate. It helps *restore* body tissues, especially those of the brain. During the time we are awake our active brain produces the chemical adenosine, which inhibits certain neurons, making us sleepy. (Caffeine blocks adenosine's activity.) During sleep, adenosine concentration declines (Porkka-Heiskanen & others, 1997). As we sleep, our brain is nevertheless active, repairing and reorganizing itself and consolidating memories.

Sleep may also play a role in the *growth* process. During deep sleep, the pituitary gland releases a growth hormone. As adults grow older, they release less of this hormone, and they spend less time in deep sleep (Pekkanen, 1982). These physiological discoveries are only beginning to solve the ongoing riddle of sleep.

Sleep Disorders

PREVIEW QUESTION 5 What are the major sleep disorders?

No matter what their normal need for sleep is, some 10 to 15 percent of adults complain of **insomnia**—persistent problems in falling or staying asleep. True insomnia is not the occasional inability to sleep that we experience when anxious or excited. For any stressed organism, being vigilant is natural and adaptive. Moreover, from middle age on, sleep is seldom uninterrupted. Being occasionally awakened becomes the norm, not something to fret over or treat with medication.

Some people fret unnecessarily about their sleep (Coren, 1996). In laboratory studies, insomnia complainers do get less sleep than others, but they typically overestimate—by about double—how long it took them to fall asleep. They also underestimate by nearly half how long they actually slept. Even if we have been awake only an hour or two, we may *think* we have had very little sleep, because it's the waking part we remember. When researchers awaken people repeatedly during the night, some recall having slept soundly.

The most common quick fixes for true insomnia, sleeping pills and alcohol, can aggravate the problem. Both reduce REM sleep and can leave a person with next-day blahs. Relying on such, one comes to need bigger doses to get an effect. Then when the drug is discontinued, the insomnia can worsen. Scientists are searching for natural chemicals that are abundant during sleep, hoping they might be synthesized as a sleep aid without side effects. In the meantime, sleep experts offer other natural alternatives:

- Relax before bedtime, using dimmer light.
- Avoid caffeine (this includes chocolate) after late afternoon and avoid rich foods before bedtime. A glass of milk may help. (Milk provides raw materials for the manufacture of serotonin, a neurotransmitter that facilitates sleep.)
- Sleep on a regular schedule (rise at the same time even after a restless night) and avoid naps. A regular sleep schedule boosts daytime alertness, too, as shown in a recent experiment in which University of Arizona students slept 7.5 hours a night on either a varying or consistent schedule (Manber & others, 1996).
- Exercise regularly but not in the late evening (late afternoon is best).
- Reassure yourself that the temporary loss of sleep causes no great harm, certainly nothing worth losing sleep over. "Sleep is like love or happiness," notes Wilse Webb (1992, p. 170). "If you pursue it too ardently it will elude you."
- If nothing else works, aim for less sleep; go to bed later or get up earlier.

Rarer but also more severe than insomnia are the sleep disorders narcolepsy and sleep apnea. People who suffer **narcolepsy** (from *narco,* "numbness," and *lepsy,* "seizure") experience periodic, overwhelming sleepiness. This usually lasts less than 5 minutes, but sometimes occurs at the most inopportune times, perhaps just after taking a terrific swing at a softball or when laughing loudly, shouting angrily, or having sex (Dement, 1978, 1999). In severe cases, the person may collapse directly into a brief period of REM sleep, with its accompanying loss of muscular tension.

Those who suffer from narcolepsy—1 in 2000 people, estimates the Stanford University Center for Narcolepsy (1996)—must live with extra caution. As a traffic menace, "snoozing is second only to boozing," says the American Sleep Disorders Association, and those with narcolepsy are especially at risk (Aldrich, 1989). At the century's end, one team of researchers discovered a gene causing narcolepsy in dogs (Lin & others, 1999). Another team linked the disorder to the loss of a small group of

"Sleep faster, we need the pillows."

Yiddish proverb

"The lion and the lamb shall lie down together, but the lamb will not be very sleepy."

Woody Allen, in the movie *Love and Death*, 1975

"In 1757 Benjamin Franklin gave us the axiom, 'Early to bed, early to rise, makes a man healthy, wealthy, and wise.' It would be more accurate to say 'consistently to bed and consistently to rise . . .'"

James B. Maas (1999)

Imagine observing a person with narcolepsy in medieval times. Might such symptoms and their associated hallucinations have seemed like demon possession?

- **insomnia** recurring problems in falling or staying asleep.
- **narcolepsy** a sleep disorder characterized by uncontrollable sleep attacks. The sufferer may lapse directly into REM sleep, often at inopportune times.

■ **sleep apnea** a sleep disorder characterized by temporary cessations of breathing during sleep and consequent momentary reawakenings.

■ **night terrors** a sleep disorder characterized by high arousal and an appearance of being terrified; unlike nightmares, night terrors occur during Stage 4 sleep, within 2 or 3 hours of falling asleep, and are seldom remembered.

Night terrors and nightmares
Night terrors occur within 2 or 3 hours of falling asleep, during Stage 4 sleep. Nightmares occur toward morning, during REM sleep. (From Hartmann, 1984.)

brain cells that produce a needed neurotransmitter, one of the chemicals that relay messages between nerve cells (Peyron & others, 2000). Physicians also began prescribing a new drug, Modafinil, to relieve narcolepsy's sleepiness in humans.

The National Heart, Lung, and Blood Institute reports that 1 in 25 people (mostly overweight men) suffer from **sleep apnea**—a disorder that was unknown before modern sleep research. They intermittently stop breathing during sleep. (*Apnea* means "stopping respiration.") After an airless minute or so, decreased blood oxygen arouses the sleeper to awaken and snort in air for a few seconds. The process can repeat more than 400 times a night, depriving the person of slow-wave sleep. Apart from complaints of sleepiness and irritability during the day—and their mates' complaints about their loud "snoring"—apnea sufferers are often unaware of their disorder. Sleep apnea leaves people tired and sometimes irritable during the day and therefore, like those who suffer narcolepsy, at increased risk of traffic accidents (Teran-Santos & others, 1999). Anyone who snores at night, who feels tired during the day, and who possibly has high blood pressure as well, should be checked for apnea (Dement, 1999).

Other sleepers, mostly children, experience **night terrors.** The person might sit up or walk around, talk incoherently, experience a doubling of heart and breathing rates, and appear terrified (Hartmann, 1981). The night-terror sufferer seldom wakes up fully during the episode and recalls little or nothing the next morning—at most, a fleeting, frightening image. Night terrors are not nightmares (which, like other dreams, typically occur during early morning REM sleep). As with sleepwalking, night terrors usually occur during the first few hours of falling asleep, during Stage 4 sleep. Family members often try to awaken and reassure the person with night terrors.

Sleepwalking and sleeptalking run in families. Finnish twin studies reveal that occasional childhood sleepwalking occurs for about one-third of those with a sleepwalking fraternal twin and half of those with a sleepwalking identical twin. The same is true for sleeptalking (Hublin & others, 1997, 1998). Sleepwalking is usually harmless and unrecalled the next morning. Sleepwalkers typically return to bed on their own or are guided there by a family member. Young children, who have the deepest and lengthiest Stage 4 sleep, are most likely to experience both night terrors and sleepwalking. As we grow older and deep Stage 4 sleep diminishes, so do night terrors and sleepwalking. After age 40, sleepwalking is rare.

rehearse it!

3. Our body temperature tends to rise and fall in sync with a biological clock, which is referred to as
   a. the circadian rhythm.
   b. narcolepsy.
   c. REM sleep.
   d. hypnogogic sensations.

4. Stage 1 sleep is a twilight zone of light sleep. During Stage 1 sleep, a person is most likely to experience
   a. sleep spindles.
   b. hallucinations.
   c. night terrors or nightmares.
   d. rapid eye movements.

5. In the deepest stage of sleep—surprisingly, the stage when people sleepwalk—the brain emits large, slow delta waves. This deep stage of sleep is called

   a. Stage 2.
   b. Stage 4.
   c. REM sleep.
   d. paradoxical sleep.

6. An electroencephalograph shows that during sleep we pass through a cycle of five stages, each with characteristic brain waves. As the night progresses, the REM stage
   a. gradually disappears.
   b. becomes briefer and briefer.
   c. remains about the same.
   d. becomes progressively longer.

7. Various theories have been proposed to explain why we need sleep. They include all but which of the following?
   a. Sleep has survival value.
   b. Sleep helps us recuperate.

   c. Sleep rests the eyes.
   d. Sleep plays a role in the growth process.

8. Two relatively rare sleep disorders are narcolepsy and sleep apnea. With narcolepsy, the person _____; with sleep apnea, the person _____.
   a. has persistent problems falling asleep; experiences a doubling of heart and breathing rates
   b. experiences a doubling of heart and breathing rates; has persistent problems falling asleep
   c. intermittently stops breathing; suffers periodic, overwhelming sleepiness
   d. suffers periodic, overwhelming sleepiness; intermittently stops breathing

Dreams

PREVIEW QUESTION 6 What and why do we dream?

Discovering the link between REM sleep and dreaming opened a new era in dream research. Instead of relying on someone's hazy recall hours or days after having a dream, researchers could catch dreams as they happened. They could awaken people during a REM sleep period, or within 3 minutes afterward, and hear a vivid account.

What We Dream

REM dreams—"hallucinations of the sleeping mind"—are vivid, emotional, and bizarre. Several times a night, you are the creator and producer of a surrealistic mental movie, in which events frequently occur in a jumbled sequence, scenes change suddenly, people appear and disappear, and physical laws, such as gravity, may be violated. Yet **dreams** are so vivid we may confuse them with reality.

Occasionally, we may be sufficiently aware during a dream to wonder whether we are, in fact, dreaming. When experiencing such *lucid dreams,* some people are able to test their state of consciousness. If they can perform some absurd act, such as floating in the air, then they know they are dreaming.

We spend six years of our life in dreams, many of which are anything but sweet. For both women and men, 8 in 10 dreams are marked by negative emotions (Domhoff, 1999). People commonly dream of repeatedly failing in an attempt to do something; of being attacked, pursued, or rejected; or of experiencing misfortune (Hall & others, 1982). In the month after the 1989 San Francisco earthquake, 4 in 10 college students in the area (but only 1 in 20 students elsewhere) recalled one or more nightmares about an earthquake (Wood & others, 1992). And, when awakened during REM sleep, people report dreams with sexual imagery less often than you might think. In one study, only 1 in 10 dreams among young men and 1 in 30 among young women had sexual overtones (Domhoff, 1996.) More commonly, we dream of events in our daily lives, a meeting at work, taking an exam, relating to a family member or friend.

The story line of our dreams—what Sigmund Freud called their **manifest content**—often incorporates experiences and preoccupations from the day's events, especially in our first dreams of the night. People in hunter-gatherer societies often dream of animals; urban Japanese rarely do (Mestel, 1997). The sensory stimuli of our sleeping environment may also intrude. A particular odor or the telephone's ringing may be instantly and ingeniously woven into the dream story. In one experiment, William Dement and Edward Wolpert (1958) lightly sprayed cold water on dreamers' faces. Compared with sleepers who did not get the cold-water treatment, these sleepers were more likely to dream about water—about a waterfall, a leaky roof, or even about being sprayed by someone. Even while in REM sleep, focused on internal stimuli, we maintain some awareness of changes in our external environment.

So, could we learn a foreign language by listening to tapes while we sleep? If only it were so easy. While sleeping we can learn to associate a

> **dream** a sequence of images, emotions, and thoughts passing through a sleeping person's mind. Dreams are notable for their hallucinatory imagery, discontinuities, and incongruities, and for the dreamer's delusional acceptance of the content and later difficulties remembering it.

> **manifest content** according to Freud, the remembered story line of a dream (as distinct from its latent content).

Would you suppose that people dream if blind from birth? Studies of blind people in France, Hungary, Egypt, and the United States all found them dreaming of using their nonvisual senses—hearing, touching, smelling, tasting (Buquet, 1988; Taha, 1972; Vekassy, 1977).

"For what one has dwelt on by day, these things are seen in visions of the night."

Menander of Athens (342–292 b.c.), *Fragments*

Nocturnal mysteries

Marc Chagall's *I and the Village* captures the surrealism of many dreams. Psychologists study and debate why the brain creates such flights of fancy.

"I do not believe that I am now dreaming, but I cannot prove that I am not."

Philosopher Bertrand Russell (1872–1970)

sound with a mild electric shock (and to react to the sound accordingly). But we do not remember taped information played while we are soundly asleep (Eich, 1990; Wyatt & Bootzin, 1994). In fact, anything that happens during the 5 minutes just before we fall asleep is typically lost from memory (Roth & others, 1988). This explains why sleep apnea patients, who repeatedly awaken with a gasp and then immediately fall back to sleep, do not recall the episodes. It also explains why dreams that momentarily awaken us are mostly forgotten by morning. To remember a dream, get up and stay awake for a few minutes.

Why We Dream

In his landmark book *The Interpretation of Dreams,* published in 1900, Freud offered "the most valuable of all the discoveries it has been my good fortune to make." He argued that by fulfilling wishes, a dream provides a psychic safety valve that discharges otherwise unacceptable feelings. According to Freud, a dream's manifest content is a censored, symbolic version of its **latent content,** which consists of unconscious drives and wishes that would be threatening if expressed directly. Although most dreams have no overt sexual imagery, Freud nevertheless believed that most adult dreams can be "traced back by analysis to *erotic wishes.*" In Freud's view, a gun, for example, might be a disguised representation of a penis.

Freud considered dreams the key to understanding our inner conflicts. However, his critics say it is time to wake up from Freud's dream theory, which actually is one of his greatest failures. Dream interpretation, they say, is a nightmare. Some contend that even if dreams were symbolic, they could be interpreted any way one wished. Others maintain that dreams hide nothing. A dream about a gun is a dream about a gun. Legend has it that even Freud, who loved to smoke cigars, remarked that "sometimes, a cigar is just a cigar."

"When people interpret [a dream] as if it were meaningful and then sell those interpretations, it's quackery."

Sleep researcher J. Allan Hobson (1995)

Freud's wish-fulfillment theory of dreams has in large part given way to other theories. Researchers who see dreams as *information processing* believe that dreams may help sift, sort, and fix the day's experiences in our memory. We have known for some time that REM sleep increases following stressful experiences or intense learning periods (Palumbo, 1978) and that REM sleep facilitates memory (McGrath & Cohen, 1978). In experiments, people have heard unusual phrases or learned to find hidden visual images before bedtime. If awakened every time they began REM sleep, they remembered less the next morning than if awakened during other sleep stages (Empson & Clarke, 1970; Karni & Sagi, 1994). A night of solid sleep (and dreaming) does, it seems, have an important place in our lives. As we sleep, our bodies consolidate the day's important memories.

Another explanation proposes that dreams may also serve a *physiological function.* Perhaps dreams—or the associated brain activity of REM sleep—provide the sleeping brain with periodic stimulation. Research on rats raised in enriched or impoverished environments indicates that stimulating experiences develop and preserve the brain's neural pathways.

Rapid eye movements also stir the liquid behind the cornea; this delivers fresh oxygen to corneal cells, preventing their suffocation.

Other physiological theories propose that dreams erupt from neural activity that spreads upward from the brainstem (Antrobus, 1991; Hobson, 1988). According to one version—the *activation-synthesis* theory—this neural activity is random, and dreams are the brain's attempt to make sense of it. Much as a neurosurgeon can produce hallucinations by stimulating different parts of a patient's cortex, so can stimulation originating within the brain. Psychologists Martin Seligman and Amy Yellen (1987) note that the seconds-long bursts of rapid eye movements during REM sleep coincide with bursts of activity in the visual cortex. If awakened during one of these bursts of brain activity, people report vivid experiences, usually dramatic hallucinations.

Given these visual scenes, our cognitive machinery—influenced by its culture, age, gender, and current concerns—weaves a story line. As Freud might have expected, the brain's emotion-related limbic system also becomes active during REM sleep,

■ **latent content** according to Freud, the underlying meaning of a dream (as distinct from its manifest content). Freud believed that a dream's latent content functions as a safety valve.

while brain regions responsible for rational thought are idling. PET scans taken of sleeping people (if you can imagine sleeping while lying in a brain-scanning machine) reveal increased activity in several brain areas, especially the limbic system structure called the amygdala (Maquet & others, 1996). Add the limbic system's emotional tone to the brain's visual bursts and—voila!—we dream.

The activation-synthesis theory, then, is that dreams spring from the mind's relentless effort to make sense of unrelated visual bursts, which are given their emotional tone by the limbic system. Dreams are the brain's interpretation of its own activity.

There is one thing dream theorists agree on: We *need* REM sleep. Deprived of it by repeatedly being awakened, people return more and more quickly to the REM stage after falling back to sleep. When finally allowed to sleep undisturbed, they literally sleep like babies—with increased REM sleep, a phenomenon called **REM rebound.** Withdrawing REM-suppressing sleeping medications also increases REM sleep, but with accompanying nightmares.

Most other mammals also experience REM sleep and REM rebound. Animals' need for REM sleep suggests that its causes and functions are deeply biological. That REM sleep occurs in mammals (and not in animals such as fish, whose behavior is less influenced by learning) also fits the information-processing theory of dreams. All of this reminds us once again of a basic lesson: *Biological and psychological explanations of behavior are partners, not competitors.*

But if dreams lack the disguised meanings that Freud supposed, and instead serve physiological functions, are they therefore psychologically meaningless? Not necessarily. Every psychologically meaningful experience involves an active brain. Moreover, say advocates of dream reflection, dreams may be akin to abstract art—amenable to more than one meaningful interpretation, and illuminating to ponder.

■ **REM rebound** the tendency for REM sleep to increase following REM sleep deprivation (created by repeated awakenings during REM sleep).

A popular sleep myth: If you dream you are falling and hit the ground (or if you dream of dying), you die. (Unfortunately, those who could confirm these ideas are not around to do so. Some people, however, have had such dreams and are alive to report them.)

rehearse it!

9. According to Sigmund Freud, dreams are the key to the understanding of our inner conflicts. In interpreting dreams, Freud was most interested in their
   a. information-processing function.
   b. physiological function.
   c. manifest content, or story line.
   d. latent content, or symbolic meaning.

10. Some theories of dreaming propose that dreams serve a physiological purpose. One such theory suggests that dreams
    a. are the brain's attempt to make sense of random neural activity.
    b. enable neurons to make new connections.
    c. are manifestations of the sensory stimuli that intrude on our sleep.

    d. prevent the brain from being disturbed by periodic stimulations.

11. The tendency for REM sleep to increase following REM sleep deprivation is referred to as
    a. paradoxical sleep.
    b. deep sleep.
    c. REM rebound.
    d. slow-wave sleep.

REVIEWING

Waking and Sleeping Rhythms

1. What is consciousness and how does it function?

Psychology has returned to the study of consciousness—our awareness of ourselves and our environment. At any moment our selective attention makes us conscious of a very limited amount of all that we are capable of experiencing, as when we attend to one voice among many at a party (the cocktail party effect). Speedy, parallel processing handles subconscious information. Conscious processing of novel tasks is serial and much slower.

2. What are the functions of daydreams and fantasies?

Virtually everyone daydreams, especially fantasy-prone people and especially at times when attention can be freed from the tasks at hand. Daydreaming can be adaptive; it can help us prepare for future events and may substitute for impulsive behavior.

3. How do our age-old biological rhythms influence our daily functioning and our sleep and dreams? What is the biological rhythm of our sleep?

Our daily schedule of waking and sleeping is timed with a body clock known as the circadian rhythm. Each night's sleep also has a rhythm of its own. Beginning with the alpha waves of the awake but relaxed state, sleep cycles from transitional Stage 1 sleep, in which hallucinations may occur, to deep Stage 4 sleep, characterized by delta waves, and back up to the more internally active REM sleep stage. Periods of Stage 4 sleep progressively shorten and periods of dream-laden REM sleep lengthen through the night.

4. How does sleep loss affect us? What is sleep's function?

Depriving people of sleep has not conclusively revealed why, physiologically, we need sleep. Several theories have been pro-posed. One is that sleep has evolutionary value. Others are that sleep is linked with the release of pituitary growth hormone and that it may help to restore brain tissues and consolidate memories.

5. What are the major sleep disorders?

The disorders of sleep include insomnia (recurring wakefulness), narcolepsy (uncontrollable lapsing into REM sleep), sleep apnea (the temporary cessation of breathing while sleeping), and night terrors (high arousal and terrified appearance occurring during Stage 4 sleep).

6. What and why do we dream?

Although conscious thoughts can occur during any sleep stage, waking people during REM sleep yields predictable "dreamlike" reports; waking them during other sleep stages yields only an occasional fleeting image. Our dreams are mostly of ordinary events; they often relate to everyday experiences and more frequently involve anxiety or misfortune than triumphant achievements.

Freud believed that a dream's manifest content, or story line, is a censored version of its latent or hidden content, which gratifies our unconscious wishes. Newer explanations of why we dream suggest that dreams (1) help process information from the day and fix it in memory, (2) serve a physiological function, and/or (3) are the brain's efforts to string periodic hallucinations (from activity bursts in the visual cortex) into a story line. Despite their differences, most theorists agree that REM sleep and its associated dreams serve an important function, as shown by the REM rebound that occurs following REM deprivation.

TERMS AND CONCEPTS TO REMEMBER

consciousness, p. 194
selective attention, p. 194
fantasy-prone personality, p. 196
circadian [ser-KAY-dee-an] rhythm, p. 198

REM sleep, p. 199
alpha waves, p. 199
sleep, p. 199
hallucinations, p. 200
delta waves, p. 200

insomnia, p. 205
narcolepsy, p. 205
sleep apnea, p. 206
night terrors, p. 206
dream, p. 207

manifest content, p. 207
latent content, p. 208
REM rebound, p. 209

REHEARSE IT ANSWER KEY

1. c	3. a	5. b	7. c	9. d	11. c
2. b	4. b	6. d	8. d	10. a	

Hypnosis

Imagine you are about to be hypnotized. The hypnotist invites you to sit back, fix your gaze on a spot high on the wall, and relax. In a quiet, low voice the hypnotist suggests, "Your eyes are growing tired. . . . Your eyelids are becoming heavy . . . now heavier and heavier. . . . They are beginning to close. . . . You are becoming more deeply relaxed. . . . Your breathing is now deep and regular. . . . Your muscles are becoming more and more relaxed. Your whole body is beginning to feel like lead."

After a few minutes of this hypnotic induction, your eyes are probably closed and you may undergo **hypnosis**—a social interaction in which one person (the hypnotist) suggests to another (the subject) that certain perceptions, feelings, thoughts, or behaviors will spontaneously occur. When the hypnotist suggests, "Your eyelids are shutting so tight that you cannot open them even if you try," your eyelids may stay closed and it may seem beyond your control to open them. Told to forget the number 6, you may be puzzled when you count 11 fingers on your hands. Invited to smell a sensuous perfume that is actually ammonia, you may linger delightedly over its pungent odor. Asked to describe a nonexistent picture the hypnotist claims to be holding, you may talk about it in detail. Told that you cannot see a certain object, such as a chair, you may indeed report that it is not there, although you manage to avoid the chair when walking around.

And if instructed to forget all these happenings once out of the hypnotic state, you may later report **posthypnotic amnesia,** a temporary memory loss rather like being unable to recall a familiar name. Although people *say* they don't remember "forgotten" material, subtle tests have led skeptics to doubt their reported amnesia (Coe, 1989a). The material must be "in there," for it can affect later behavior and be recalled at a prearranged signal (Kihlstrom, 1985; Spanos & others, 1985).

Also working against the respectability of hypnosis were the grand claims made by its practitioners. Supposedly, mesmerized people could see with the backs of their heads, perceive others' internal organs, and communicate with the dead. Researchers now agree that hypnotized people can perform no such feats. Like unhypnotized people, those under hypnosis cannot leap tall buildings, run faster than a speeding bullet, or display superhuman strength. In experiments, their strength, stamina, learning, and perceptual abilities are like those of motivated unhypnotized people (Druckman & Bjork, 1994). Hypnotized people may surprise you by, say, extending their arms for 6 minutes straight—but unhypnotized people can also do this and other amazing feats (**FIGURE 15.1** on page 212).

Before considering whether the hypnotic state is actually an *altered* state of consciousness, let's first consider some areas of general agreement. Then, with the facts of hypnosis in mind, we can ponder two perplexing questions: What is hypnosis? And what does hypnosis tell us about human consciousness?

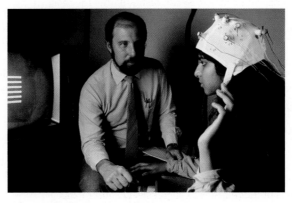

Subject to influence

As a deeply hypnotized woman sits before a TV screen, researcher David Spiegel asks her to imagine that a cardboard box is blocking the screen. When a stimulus appears on the screen, her brain waves do not display the normal response. Such findings, Spiegel argues, suggest that hypnosis can alter brain functioning.

- **hypnosis** a social interaction in which one person (the hypnotist) suggests to another (the subject) that certain perceptions, feelings, thoughts, or behaviors will spontaneously occur.

- **posthypnotic amnesia** supposed inability to recall what one experienced during hypnosis; induced by the hypnotist's suggestion.

Facts and Falsehoods About Hypnosis

PREVIEW QUESTION 1 What is hypnosis, and what powers does a hypnotist have over a hypnotized subject?

Can Hypnosis Work for Anyone?

Those who study hypnosis agree that its power resides not in the hypnotist but in the subject's openness to suggestion (Bowers, 1984). Hypnotists have no magical mind-control power; they merely engage people's ability to focus on certain images or behaviors. But what powers does hypnosis have?

Can Anyone Experience Hypnosis?

To some extent, nearly everyone is suggestible. When people standing upright with their eyes closed are told repeatedly that they are swaying back and forth, most will indeed sway a little. In fact, postural sway is one of the items on the Stanford Hypnotic Susceptibility Scale that assesses a person's hypnotizability. The people who respond to such suggestions without hypnosis are the people who respond with hypnosis—only a little more so (Kirsch & Lynn, 1998a). During hypnosis, a hypnotist gives a brief hypnotic induction and then presents a series of suggested experiences that range from easy (one's outstretched arms will move together) to difficult (with eyes open one will see a nonexistent person).

Those who are highly hypnotizable—say, the 20 percent who can carry out a suggestion not to smell or react to a bottle of ammonia held under the nose—are still likely to be the most hypnotizable 25 years later (Piccione & others, 1989). These hypnotically susceptible people frequently become deeply absorbed in imaginative activities (Lynn & Rhue, 1986; Silva & Kirsch, 1992). Typically, they have rich fantasy lives and easily become absorbed in the imaginary events of a novel or movie. Many researchers therefore refer to hypnotic "susceptibility" as hypnotic *ability,* a label with more positive connotations. Few of us would care to be "susceptible" to hypnosis, but most of us would be glad to have the "ability" to focus our attention totally on a task, to become imaginatively absorbed in it, to entertain fanciful possibilities. That is exactly what fantasy-prone people with hypnotic ability can do.

Can Hypnosis Enhance Recall of Forgotten Events?

Can hypnotic procedures enable people to relive earlier experiences? To recall kindergarten classmates? To retrieve forgotten or suppressed details of a crime? Should testimony obtained under hypnosis be admissible in court?

Most people believe that our experiences are all "in there," that everything that happens to us gets recorded in our brains and can be recalled if only we are able to break through our own defenses (Loftus, 1980). People tend to agree, for example, that "under hypnosis a person [can] recall childhood events with very high accuracy"—even events "as far back as birth" (Furnham, 1993; Johnson & Hauck, 1999). Testimonies to this come from *age regression* demonstrations, in which people supposedly relive experiences from their childhood. But 60 years of research dispute the claims of age regression: Hypnotized people are *not* more genuinely childlike than unhypnotized people who are asked to feign childlike behavior (Nash, 1987). As the Thinking Critically box on page 213 demonstrates, age-regressed people act as they *believe* children would, but they typically miss the mark by outperforming real children of the specified age (Silverman & Retzlaff, 1986). Age-regressed people may, for example, *feel* childlike and may print much as they know a 6-year-old would, but they

FIGURE 15.1

The "amazing" hypnotized "human plank"

Actually, unhypnotized people can also perform this feat.

"Excellent hypnotic subjects choose to become absorbed in suggestions in the same way that many people become absorbed in movies and novels."

Nicholas P. Spanos, *Multiple Identities and False Memories,* 1996 sometimes do so with perfect spelling and typically without any change in their adult brain waves, reflexes, and perceptions.

On rare occasions, the relaxed, focused state of hypnosis has enabled witnesses to produce leads in criminal investigations. One instance occurred in 1977, when 26 children and their bus driver, Ed Ray, were kidnapped and forced into an abandoned trailer truck buried 6 feet underground. After their rescue, Ray, under hypnosis, recalled all but one digit of the kidnapper's license plate. With this crucial information, police tracked down the abductors. This anecdote is atypical, and it is unclear whether hypnosis enabled Ray to retrieve the memory. Nevertheless, many researchers believe that hypnotic procedures may have some value—or at least do little harm—when used as an investigative tool.

The problem comes in putting on the witness stand someone whose memories are "hypnotically refreshed." Researchers have found that hypnotically refreshed memories combine fact with fiction. Thus, American, Australian, and British courts increasingly ban testimony from witnesses who have been hypnotized (Druckman & Bjork, 1994; Gibson, 1995; McConkey, 1995).

Hypnosis has unpredictable effects. Sometimes the relaxed reflection boosts recall. But often hypnosis contaminates memory with false recollections or even increases one's confidence in false memories (Lynn & others, 1997; McConkey, 1992). When pressed under hypnosis to recall details, perhaps to "zoom in on your visual memory screen," people use their imaginations to construct their memories. Without either person being aware of what is going on, the hypnotist's hints— "Did you hear loud noises?"—can become the subject's pseudomemory. Previously hypnotized witnesses may end up testifying confidently to events they never experienced (Laurence & Perry, 1988). And whether hypnotized or not, highly hypnotizable (fantasy-prone) people are especially vulnerable to false memory suggestions (Barnier & McConkey, 1992).

So, hypnosis cannot change the rules by which we form, store, and retrieve memories. It distresses memory researchers that many therapists do not appreciate the unreliability of hypnotically induced memories. When hypnosis researcher Michael Yapko (1994) surveyed 869 therapists attending various therapy conventions, 47 percent agreed that "psychotherapists can have greater faith in details of a traumatic event when obtained hypnotically than otherwise." And 54 percent agreed that "hypnosis can be used to recover memories of actual events as far back as birth." Such ignorance "of the facts" left Yapko aghast: "I am deeply concerned that psychotherapy patients will be led to believe destructive ideas that are untrue . . . all in the name of 'psychotherapy.'"

Striking examples of memories created under hypnosis come from the tens of thousands of people who since 1980 have reported being abducted by UFOs, abused in satanic cults, or adulated during a past life. Under hypnosis, one woman

> remembered a light and a voice calling her out of bed. She obeyed against her will and went to a muddy field as a saucer-shaped craft neared the ground. Through the windows she saw beings and a piercing sound prevented her from moving. A warm beam of light then pulled her inside the craft. She found herself inside a white hospital room. Two small beings with tiny mouths and compelling eyes, dressed as if in motorcycle jackets, told her without speaking to undress and lie down on a table. She resisted but eventually gave in . . . at last the doctor entered and gave her an injection. He then inserted a needle into her navel. . . . One being . . . undressed himself and rubbed her with a jelly. It warmed her [and he] then raped her. (Bullard, 1987)

Studies reveal that most reports of UFOs have come from people who are predisposed to believe in aliens, are fantasy prone, and have undergone hypnosis (Newman & Baumeister, 1996; Nickell, 1996).

"Hypnosis is not a psychological truth serum and to regard it as such has been a source of considerable mischief."

Researcher Kenneth Bowers (1987)

HYPNOTIC AGE REGRESSION: A TRUE STORY

Remembrances of Christmases Past?

What shall we make of a clever study by Robert True (1949)? He regressed hypnotized volunteers back to their Christmases and birthday parties at ages 10, 7, and 4. In each case, he asked them what day of the week it was. Without hypnosis, the odds that a person can name offhand the day of a long past date are but 1 in 7. Remarkably, the hypnotized subjects' answers were 82 percent correct.

But other investigators were unable to replicate True's results. When Martin Orne (1982) asked True why, he replied that *Science*, the journal that published his article, had shortened his key question to "What day is this?" Actually, he had asked his age-regressed subjects, "Is it Monday? Is it Tuesday?" and so forth until the subject stopped him with a yes. When Orne asked True if he knew the actual day of the week while posing the questions, True granted that he did but was puzzled why Orne would ask.

Can you see why? True's experiment appears to be a beautiful example of how hypnotists can subtly influence their subjects' memories. (It also illustrates how experimenters can subtly communicate their expectations and why they should be kept "blind" to the expected result.) "Given the eagerness of the hypnotized subject to fulfill the demands placed upon him," surmised Orne, it takes only the slightest change of inflection (in asking "Is it Wednesday?") for the subject to respond, "Yes."

The final blow to True's experiment came when Orne simply asked ten 4-year-olds what day of the week it was. To his surprise, none knew. If 4-year-olds typically do not know the day of the week, then True's adults were reporting information they probably didn't know when they were 4.

Remembrances of Lives Past?

If people's hypnotic regressions to childhood are partly imagined, then how believable are claims of hypnotic "regression to past lives"? Can the 25 percent of Americans who believe in reincarnation (Yankelovich, 1998) find support in such reports? Were the 36 percent of university students correct to agree, in a survey by Scott Brown and others (1996), that "certain people can be age regressed to recall past lives"?

Nicholas Spanos (1987–1988; Spanos & others, 1991) reported that, when hypnotized, fantasy-prone people who believe in reincarnation will offer vivid details of "past lives." But they nearly always report being their same race—unless the researcher has informed them that different races are common. They often report being someone famous rather than one of the countless "nobodies." Some contradict one another by claiming to have been the same person, such as Joan of Arc (Reveen, 1987–1988). Moreover, they typically do not know things that any person of that time would have known. One subject who "regressed" to a "previous life" as a Japanese fighter pilot in 1940 could not name the emperor of Japan and did not know that Japan was already at war. Hypnotic regressions to past lives offer no credible evidence of reincarnation.

Will the real Joan of Arc VIII please stand up?
Under hypnosis, people who claim to remember a past life too often report being someone famous.

MY NAME IS EUNICE. I HAVE LIVED MANY PAST LIVES, MOST OF THEM IN TRENTON, NEW JERSEY, ...

CHANNELLING ON THE CHEAP

Can Hypnosis Force People to Act Against Their Will?

Researchers Martin Orne and Frederick Evans (1965) demonstrated that hypnotized people *could* be induced to perform an apparently dangerous act. The participants followed a request to dip one hand briefly into fuming acid, then throw the "acid" in a research assistant's face. When interviewed a day later, they exhibited no memory of their acts and emphatically denied they would ever follow orders to commit such an act.

Had hypnosis given the hypnotist a special power to control these people against their will? To find out, Orne and Evans unleashed that enemy of so many illusory beliefs—the control group: Orne asked some other people to *pretend* they had been hypnotized. The laboratory experimenter, unaware that the control subjects had not been hypnotized, treated all the participants the same. The result? All the *unhypnotized* participants (perhaps believing that the laboratory context assured safety) performed the same acts as those who were hypnotized. Similarly, most hypnotized subjects can be induced to deface a sacred book, and a few will even steal an exam or sell illegal drugs. But most people asked to simulate hypnosis are equally likely to do the same (Levitt, 1986).

This illustrates a principle that is firmly established in social psychology's research findings: *An authoritative person in a legitimate context can induce people—hypnotized or not—to perform some unlikely acts.* Hypnosis researcher Spanos (1982) put it directly: "The overt behaviors of hypnotic subjects are well within normal limits."

Can Hypnosis Be Therapeutic?

Hypnotherapists do nothing magical. They simply try to help patients harness their own healing powers (Baker, 1987). Posthypnotic suggestions have helped alleviate headaches, asthma, warts, and stress-related skin disorders. One woman, who for more than 20 years suffered from open sores all over her body, was asked to imagine herself swimming in shimmering, sunlit liquids that would cleanse her skin and to experience her skin as smooth and unblemished. Within three months her sores had disappeared (Bowers, 1984).

When hypnosis is applied to such problems with self-control as nail biting and smoking, the most hypnotizable people show no greater benefit than those least hypnotizable. This suggests that the benefits are not a result of the hypnosis as such (Bowers & LeBaron, 1986). Should we also then question whether hypnosis is the therapeutic agent when we hear of improvements in problems unrelated to willpower, such as skin disorders? Do the benefits of hypnosis surpass those of simply encouraging people to relax and to form positive images?

The answer remains in doubt. For example, hypnosis speeds the disappearance of warts, but in controlled studies, so do the same positive suggestions given without hypnosis (Spanos, 1991, 1996). Hypnosis and positive suggestions, like placebos, change people's expectations. But unlike placebos, notes Irving Kirsch (1999), "hypnosis does not require deception in order to be effective."

Can Hypnosis Alleviate Pain?

Yes, hypnosis *can* relieve pain (Druckman & Bjork, 1994; Kihlstrom, 1985). When unhypnotized subjects put their arms in an ice bath, they feel intense pain within 25 seconds. When hypnotizable subjects do the same after being given suggestions to feel no pain, they indeed report feeling little pain. As some dentists know, even light hypnosis can reduce fear, and thus hypersensitivity to pain. Nearly 10 percent of us can become so deeply hypnotized that even major surgery can be performed without anesthesia. And half of us can gain some pain relief from hypnosis.

■ **dissociation** a split in consciousness, which allows some thoughts and behaviors to occur simultaneously with others.

The Lamaze method of childbirth
Like hypnosis, the Lamaze method uses breathing and concentration techniques that draw attention away from pain. Women for whom the method works tend to have high hypnotic ability (Venn, 1986).

How can this be? One theory of hypnotic pain relief finds the answer in **dissociation,** a split between different levels of consciousness. Hypnosis, it suggests, dissociates the sensation of the pain stimulus (of which the subject is still aware) from the emotional suffering that defines our experience of pain. The ice water therefore feels cold—very cold—but not painful.

Another theory proposes that hypnotic pain relief results from selective attention, as when an injured athlete, caught up in the competition, feels little or no pain until the game ends. Support for this view comes from several studies showing that hypnosis relieves pain no better than does merely relaxing and distracting people (Chaves, 1989). With their attention distracted during hypnosis, some women can experience childbirth with minimal pain; but so can some women without hypnosis, especially if given childbirth training (D'Eon, 1989).

Both views of pain assume that at some level a hypnotized person does experience the pain stimulus. Indeed, people who report feeling no pain nevertheless may respond with a pounding heart to electric shock or a surgeon's knife. Similar disparities between self-reports and behavior involve seeing and hearing. Following a suggestion that they are deaf, hypnotized people will deny being able to hear their own voices. But when they hear their voice over a headset with a half-second delay, they respond as unhypnotized people do: The delayed feedback disrupts their ability to speak fluently. If told they are colorblind, hypnotized people do not respond to colorblindness tests as do people with actual color-deficient vision. In each of these cases, the hypnotized subjects *report* perceiving no pain, sound, or color. Yet the stimuli have quite obviously registered within their sensory systems. Thus, hypnosis does *not* block sensory input. What people *say* they experience just doesn't fit with their behavior.

The unanswered question of how hypnosis relieves pain—by *dissociating* the pain sensation from conscious awareness, or merely by focusing *attention* on other things—brings us to the basic issue: Is hypnosis a unique psychological state?

Explaining the Hypnotized State

PREVIEW QUESTION 2 Is hypnosis an extension of normal consciousness or an altered state of consciousness?

We have seen that hypnosis involves heightened suggestibility. We have also seen that hypnotic procedures do not endow a person with special powers. But they can sometimes enhance a person's recall of real (and unreal) past events, aid in overcoming psychologically influenced ailments, and help alleviate pain. So, just what is hypnosis?

Hypnosis as a Social Phenomenon

Skeptics note that hypnosis is not a unique physiological state. Moreover, behaviors produced through hypnotic procedures can also be produced without them. This suggests that hypnotic phenomena may reflect the workings of normal consciousness (Lynn & others, 1990; Spanos & Coe, 1992).

We know that our interpretations of events exert a powerful influence on our ordinary perceptions. Especially in the case of pain, for which the effects of hypnosis seem most dramatic, our perceptions follow our attention. Moreover, imaginative people can manufacture vivid perceptions without hypnosis. Perhaps, then, "hypnotized" people are just acting the role of "good hypnotic subjects" and allowing the hypnotist to direct their fantasies.

It's not that people are consciously faking hypnosis. Rather, they're doing and reporting what's expected of them. Like actors who get caught up in their roles, they begin to feel and behave in ways appropriate to the hypnotic role. The more they like and trust the hypnotist and feel motivated to demonstrate hypnotic behavior, the more they do so (Gfeller & others, 1987). If told later to scratch their ear when they hear the word *psychology,* subjects will likely do so only if they think the experiment is still under way (and scratching is therefore expected). If an experimenter eliminates the motivation for their acting hypnotized—by stating that hypnosis reveals their "gullibility"—subjects become unresponsive.

Based on such findings, advocates of the *social influence theory* contend that hypnotic phenomena are *not* unique to hypnosis. They argue that hypnotic phenomena—like behavior associated with other supposed altered states, such as dissociative identity ("multiple personality") disorder and spirit or demon possession—are an extension of everyday social behavior (Spanos, 1994, 1996). In this view, hypnotic subjects are imaginative actors caught up in playing the role of hypnotic subject.

Hypnosis as Divided Consciousness

Most hypnosis researchers grant that normal social and cognitive processes play a part in hypnosis, but they nevertheless believe hypnosis is more than imaginative acting. For one thing, hypnotized subjects will *sometimes* carry out suggested behaviors on cue, even when they believe no one is watching (Perugini & others, 1998). Their doing so shows that more may be at work than merely trying to be a "good subject." Moreover, many practitioners remain convinced that certain phenomena *are* unique to hypnosis. What else explains hypnotic experiences such as pain reduction and compelling hallucinations (Bowers, 1990)? Skeptics reply that hypnotists' livelihoods depend on maintaining an aura of mysterious power (Coe, 1989b).

To veteran researcher Ernest Hilgard (1986, 1992), hypnosis involves not only social influence but also a special state of dissociated (divided) consciousness. Hilgard views hypnotic dissociation as a vivid form of everyday mind splits. Putting a child to bed, we might read *Goodnight Moon* for the fourteenth time while mentally organizing a busy schedule for the next day.

One version of dissociation theory emphasizes such separations of behavior from conscious control (Woody & Bowers, 1994). With practice, you could even read and comprehend a short story while copying dictated words, much as you can doodle while listening to a lecture or finish typing a sentence while starting a conversation, or as a skilled pianist can talk to an audience while playing a familiar piece (Hirst & others, 1978). In hypnosis as in life, *much of our behavior occurs on autopilot.* Thus, when hypnotized people write answers to questions about one

> "The total possible consciousness may be split into parts which co-exist but mutually ignore each other."
>
> William James, *Principles of Psychology,* 1890

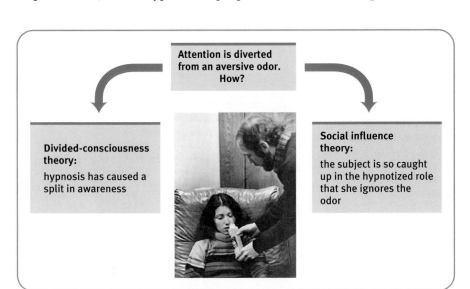

Attention is diverted from an aversive odor. How?

Divided-consciousness theory:
hypnosis has caused a split in awareness

Social influence theory:
the subject is so caught up in the hypnotized role that she ignores the odor

Explaining hypnosis
How can she do it? How can this hypnotized young woman show no reaction to the terrible smell of ammonia? Divided-consciousness theory and social influence theory offer possible explanations.

■ **hidden observer** Hilgard's term describing a hypnotized subject's awareness of experiences, such as pain, that go unreported during hypnosis.

topic while talking or reading about a different topic, they display an accentuated form of normal dissociation of cognition from behavior. So, when today's researchers refer to a "hypnotic state," note Irving Kirsch and Steven Jay Lynn (1995, 1998a,b), they merely refer to the subjective experience of hypnosis, not to a unique trance state.

This phenomenon spurred further inquiry. Hypnotized subjects, as we noted earlier, report far less pain than others when they place their arms in ice water. But when asked to press a key if "some part" of them does feel the pain, they invariably press the key. To Hilgard, this suggests that a dissociated consciousness, a **hidden observer,** is passively aware of what is happening.

The divided-consciousness theory of hypnosis provoked controversy, because what the "hidden observer" reports varies with what the experimenter seems to want. But this much seems clear: You and I process much information—while sensing, perceiving, learning, remembering, and thinking—without conscious awareness. Our information processing, which starts with selective attention, *is* divided into simultaneous conscious and subconscious realms. Without doubt, there is much more to thinking and acting than we are conscious of.

But still, there is also little doubt that social influences do play an important role in hypnosis. So, might the two views—social influence and divided consciousness—be bridged? Researchers John Kihlstrom and Kevin McConkey (1990) believe there is no contradiction between the two approaches, which are converging toward a "unified account of hypnosis." Hypnosis, they suggest, is an extension *both* of normal principles of social influence *and* of everyday dissociations between our conscious awareness and our automatic behaviors.

Demonstrating the "hidden observer"

A hypnotized subject being tested by Ernest Hilgard exhibits no pain when her arm is placed in an ice bath. But asked to press a key if some part of her feels the pain, she does so. To Hilgard, this suggests that hypnosis divides consciousness into one part that is unaware of pain and another part—a "hidden observer"—that is aware of it.

rehearse it!

1. Hypnosis is a social interaction in which a hypnotist suggests to a subject that certain perceptions, feelings, thoughts, or behaviors will spontaneously occur. Subjects who are hypnotizable and will carry out a hypnotic suggestion usually
   a. are fantasy-prone.
   b. have low self-esteem.
   c. are subject to hallucinations.
   d. are hidden observers.

2. Although experts differ in their understandings of hypnosis, most agree that hypnosis can be effectively used to
   a. elicit testimony about a "forgotten" event.
   b. re-create childhood experiences.
   c. relieve pain.
   d. alter personality.

3. Ernest Hilgard believes hypnosis is not merely an extension of normal social influence but involves dissociation, which means
   a. nonconformity to social pressure.
   b. a state of amnesia.
   c. a state of divided consciousness.
   d. conscious enactment of a hypnotic role.

Hypnosis

1. What is hypnosis, and what powers does a hypnotist have over a hypnotized subject?

Psychologists agree that hypnosis is a social interaction in which the hypnotist suggests to a subject that certain perceptions, feelings, thoughts, or behaviors will occur spontaneously. They also agree that people are suggestible in varying degrees, and that, although hypnotic procedures may help someone to recall past events, the hypnotist's beliefs frequently work their way into the subject's recollections. They further agree that hypnotized people can no more be made to act against their will than can nonhypnotized people. Hypnosis can be at least temporarily therapeutic (through posthypnotic suggestion), and hypnotizable people can enjoy significant pain relief (perhaps through dissociation). Psychologists do not believe, however, that posthypnotic amnesia really occurs.

2. Is hypnosis an extension of normal consciousness or an altered state of consciousness?

There is debate whether hypnosis is a by-product of normal social and cognitive processes or an altered state of consciousness, perhaps involving a dissociation between levels of consciousness (the hidden observer).

TERMS AND CONCEPTS TO REMEMBER

hypnosis, p. 211   posthypnotic amnesia, p. 211   dissociation, p. 216   hidden observer, p. 218

REHEARSE IT ANSWER KEY

1. a   2. c   3. c

16 Drugs and Consciousness

- Dependence and Addiction

- Psychoactive Drugs

- Influences on Drug Use

© 1992 by Sidney Harris.

"Just tell me where you kids got the idea to take so many drugs."

There is controversy about whether hypnosis alters consciousness, but there is little dispute that drugs do. **Psychoactive drugs** are chemicals that change perceptions and moods. Let's imagine a day in the life of a legal drug user. It begins with a wake-up latté. By midday, several cigarettes have calmed frazzled nerves. Leaving work early makes time for a happy-hour drink, providing a relaxing and sociable prelude to a dental appointment, where nitrous oxide makes an otherwise painful experience mildly pleasurable. A diet pill before dinner helps stem the appetite, and its stimulating effects can later be partially offset with two Tylenol PMs. Before drifting off into REM-depressed sleep, our hypothetical drug user is dismayed by a news report of "rising drug abuse."

Dependence and Addiction

PREVIEW QUESTION 1 What are dependence and addiction? Can substance abusers overcome their addictions?

Continued use of a psychoactive drug produces **tolerance:** The user requires larger and larger doses to experience the drug's effect. A person who rarely drinks alcohol might get tipsy on one can of beer, but an experienced drinker may not get tipsy until the second six-pack (**FIGURE 16.1**). Ironically, despite the connotations of "tolerance," alcoholics' brains, hearts, and livers suffer damage from the excessive alcohol they are "tolerating."

Users who stop taking psychoactive drugs may experience the undesirable side effects of **withdrawal.** As the body responds to the drug's absence, the user may feel physical pain and intense cravings, indicating a **physical dependence** on the drug. People can also develop **psychological dependence,** particularly for stress-relieving drugs. Although such drugs may not be physically addictive, they nevertheless become an important part of the user's life, often as a way of relieving negative emotions. With either physical addiction or psychological dependence, the user's primary focus becomes obtaining and using the drug.

Misconceptions About Addiction

An "addiction" has traditionally meant a craving for a substance, with physical symptoms such as aches, nausea, and distress following sudden withdrawal. In recent pop psychology, the supposedly irresistible seduction of addiction has been extended to cover many behaviors formerly considered bad habits or even sins. Has the concept been stretched too far? Are addictions as irresistible as com-

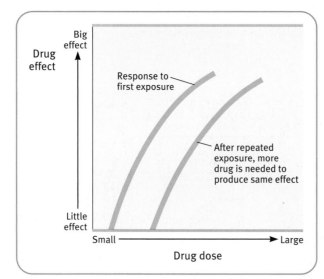

FIGURE 16.1

Drug tolerance

With repeated exposure to a psychoactive drug, the drug's effect lessens. Thus, it takes bigger doses to get the desired effect.

monly believed? Many drug researchers believe the following three myths about addiction are *false:*

1. ***Addictive drugs quickly corrupt; for example, morphine taken to control pain is powerfully addictive and often leads to heroin abuse.*** After taking a psychoactive drug, some people—perhaps 10 percent—do indeed have a hard time using it in moderation or stopping altogether. However, there are many more controlled, occasional users than addicts of drugs such as alcohol, marijuana, and cocaine (Gazzaniga, 1988; Siegel, 1990). Moreover, people typically don't become addicted when using drugs medically. Those given morphine to control pain rarely develop the cravings of the addict who uses morphine as a mood-altering drug (Melzack, 1990).

2. ***Addictions can't be overcome voluntarily; therapy is a must.*** Some addicts do benefit from treatment programs. Alcoholics Anonymous, for example, has supported many people in overcoming their alcohol dependence. But, say critics, the recovery rates of treated and untreated groups differ less than one might suppose. Therapy or group support may be helpful, but people often recover on their own.

   Moreover, viewing addiction as a disease, as diabetes is a disease, can undermine self-confidence and the will to change cravings that, without treatment, "one can't fight." And that, critics say, would be unfortunate, for many people do voluntarily stop using addictive drugs, without treatment. Some 70 percent of smokers who seek treatment for their addiction later return to smoking, whereas most of America's 41 million ex-smokers kicked the habit on their own.

3. ***We can extend the concept of addiction to cover not just drug dependencies, but a whole spectrum of repetitive, pleasure-seeking behaviors.*** We can, and we have, but should we? The addiction-as-disease-needing-treatment idea has been suggested for a host of driven behaviors, including overeating, shopping, exercise, sex, gambling, and work. Initially, we may use the term metaphorically ("I'm a science fiction addict"), but if we begin taking the metaphor as reality, addiction can become an all-purpose excuse. Those who embezzle to feed their "gambling addiction," who surf the Web half the night to satisfy their "Internet addiction," or who abuse or betray to indulge their "sex addiction" can then explain away their behavior as an illness.

   Sometimes, though, behaviors such as gambling do become compulsive and dysfunctional, much like abusive drug taking. Is there justification for stretching the addiction concept to cover social behaviors? Debates over the addiction-as-disease model continue.

psychoactive drug a chemical substance that alters perceptions and mood.

tolerance the diminishing effect with regular use of the same dose of a drug, requiring the user to take larger and larger doses before experiencing the drug's effect.

withdrawal the discomfort and distress that follow discontinuing the use of an addictive drug.

physical dependence a physiological need for a drug, marked by unpleasant withdrawal symptoms when the drug is discontinued.

psychological dependence a psychological need to use a drug, such as to relieve negative emotions.

"About 70 percent of Americans have tried illicit drugs, but . . . only a few percent have done so in the last month. . . . Past age 35, the casual use of illegal drugs virtually ceases." Having sampled the pleasures and their aftereffects, "most people eventually walk away."

Neuropsychologist Michael Gazzaniga (1997)

CALVIN AND HOBBES

■ **depressants** drugs (such as alcohol, barbiturates, and opiates) that reduce neural activity and slow body functions.

■ **stimulants** drugs (such as caffeine, nicotine, and the more powerful amphetamines and cocaine) that excite neural activity and speed up body functions.

■ **hallucinogens** psychedelic ("mind-manifesting") drugs, such as LSD, that distort perceptions and evoke sensory images in the absence of sensory input.

A University of Illinois campus survey showed that before sexual assaults, 80 percent of the male assailants and 70 percent of the female victims had been drinking (Camper, 1990). Another survey of 89,874 American collegians found alcohol or drugs involved in 79 percent of unwanted sexual intercourse experiences (Presley & others, 1997).

Facts: College and university students drink more alcohol than their nonstudent peers, and they spend more on alcohol than on books and other beverages combined. Fraternity and sorority members drink three times as much as other students (Atwell, 1986; Malloy & others, 1994). Although few university students believe they have an alcohol problem, many meet the criteria for alcohol abuse (Marlatt, 1991). As students mature with age, they drink less.

Psychoactive Drugs

There are at least three categories of psychoactive drugs:

■ **Depressants,** or "downers," calm neural activity and slow body functions.
■ **Stimulants,** or "uppers," temporarily excite neural activity and arouse body functions.
■ **Hallucinogens** distort perceptions and evoke sensory images in the absence of sensory input.

Drugs in all three categories do their work at the brain's synapses, the junctions between nerve cells, by stimulating, inhibiting, or mimicking the activity of neurotransmitters, the brain's chemical messengers.

Depressants

PREVIEW QUESTION 2 What are depressants, and what are their effects?

Let's look first at drugs such as alcohol, barbiturates (tranquilizers), and opiates, those that slow our body's functions.

Alcohol

True or false? In large amounts, alcohol is a depressant; in small amounts, it is a stimulant.

False. Small doses of "spirits" may, indeed, enliven a drinker, but they do so by slowing brain activity that controls judgment and inhibitions. When provoked, people under alcohol's influence respond more aggressively than usual. If asked to help, people under alcohol's influence respond more willingly than usual. In everyday life, alcohol is an equal-opportunity drug: It *increases* harmful tendencies—as when sexually coercive college men lower their dates' sexual inhibitions by getting them to drink (Abbey, 1991; Mosher & Anderson, 1986)—and it increases helpful tendencies—as when tipsy restaurant patrons leave extravagant tips (M. Lynn, 1988). Thus, alcohol makes us more aggressive or helpful or self-disclosing or sexually daring—when such tendencies are already present. *The urges you feel when sober are the ones you are more likely to act upon when intoxicated.*

Low doses of alcohol relax the drinker by slowing the sympathetic nervous system, the part of our nervous system that mobilizes our energy to react to stressful situations. With larger doses, alcohol can become a staggering problem: Reactions slow, speech slurs, and skilled performance deteriorates. Paired with sleep deprivation, alcohol becomes a potent sedative. (Although either sleep deprivation or booze can put a driver at risk, their combination is deadlier yet.) These physical effects, combined with lowered inhibitions, contribute to alcohol's worst consequences—the several hundred thousand lives claimed worldwide in alcohol-related accidents and violent crimes each year. Accidents occur despite most drinkers' belief (when sober) that driving while under the influence of alcohol is wrong and despite their insisting that they wouldn't do so. Yet as their blood-alcohol level rises, people's moral judgments become less mature, their qualms about drinking and driving lessen—and virtually all will drive home from a bar, even if given a breathalyzer test and told they are intoxicated (Denton & Krebs, 1990; MacDonald & others, 1995).

Alcohol not only affects judgment, it also affects memory. It impairs neither short-term recall for what just happened nor existing long-term memories. Rather, it disrupts the *processing* of recent experiences into long-term memories. Thus, the day after being intoxicated, heavy drinkers may not recall whom they met or what they said or did the night before. This memory blackout stems partly from an inability to transfer memories from the intoxicated to the sober state (Eich, 1980). Blackouts

Don't drink and drive
With billboards like this one that shows the appalling consequences of driving under the influence of alcohol, Mothers Against Drunk Driving (MADD) has vigorously promoted awareness of the dangers of alcohol abuse. The organization has also lobbied for stiffer penalties for drunk drivers.

after drinking may also result from the way alcohol suppresses REM (rapid eye movement) sleep. (Experiments have shown that people deprived of REM sleep have difficulty fixing their day's experiences into permanent memories.)

Alcohol has another intriguing effect on consciousness: It reduces self-awareness (Hull & others, 1986). Compared with people who feel good about themselves, those who want to suppress their awareness of failures or shortcomings are more likely to drink. Losing a business deal, a game, or a romance will sometimes elicit a drinking binge.

Alcohol also focuses one's attention on the immediate situation and away from any future consequences. This facilitates urges that a person might otherwise resist (Steele & Josephs, 1990). In surveys, over half of rapists acknowledge drinking before committing their offense (Seto & Barbaree, 1995). The effect reaches onto college campuses. Sexually active university students are less likely to use condoms when intoxicated in a sexually stimulating context (MacDonald & others, 1996, 1998, 2000). University women under alcohol's influence find an attractive but sexually promiscuous man a more appealing potential date than they do when sober. It seems, surmise Sheila Murphy and her colleagues (1998), "that when people have been drinking, the restraining forces of reason may weaken and yield under the pressure of their desires."

As with other psychoactive drugs, alcohol's behavioral effects stem not only from its alteration of brain chemistry but also from the user's expectations. Many studies have found that when people *believe* that alcohol affects social behavior in certain ways, and *believe*, rightly or wrongly, that they have been drinking alcohol, they will behave accordingly (Leigh, 1989).

Consider one such experiment by David Abrams and Terence Wilson (1983). They gave Rutgers University men who volunteered for a study on "alcohol and sexual stimulation" either an alcoholic or a nonalcoholic drink. (Both drinks had a strong taste that masked any alcohol.) In each group, half the participants thought they were drinking alcohol and half thought they were not. After being shown an erotic movie clip, the men who *thought* they had consumed alcohol were more likely to report having strong sexual fantasies and feeling guilt-free. Being able to *attribute* their sexual responses to alcohol released their inhibitions—whether they actually had drunk alcohol or not. If, as commonly believed, liquor is the quicker pick-her-upper, the effect lies partly in that powerful sex organ, the mind.

This research illustrates an important principle: A drug's psychological effects are powerfully influenced by the user's expectations. And that explains why drug ex-

"That is not one of the seven habits of highly effective people."

Fact: In a Harvard School of Public Health survey of 18,000 students at 140 colleges and universities, almost 9 in 10 students reported abuse by intoxicated peers, including sleep and study interruption, insults, sexual advances, and property damage (Wechsler & others, 1994).

Fact: Alcohol kills more people than all illegal drugs combined. So does tobacco (Siegel, 1990).

■ **barbiturates** drugs that depress the activity of the central nervous system, reducing anxiety but impairing memory and judgment.

■ **opiates** opium and its derivatives, such as morphine and heroin; they depress neural activity, temporarily lessening pain and anxiety.

■ **amphetamines** drugs that stimulate neural activity, causing speeded-up body functions and associated energy and mood changes.

periences vary with cultures (Ward, 1994). If one culture assumes that a particular drug produces euphoria (or aggression or sexual arousal) and another does not, each culture may find its expectations fulfilled.

Barbiturates

The **barbiturate** drugs, or *tranquilizers,* mimic the effects of alcohol. Because they depress sympathetic nervous system activity, barbiturates such as Nembutal and Seconal are sometimes prescribed to induce sleep or reduce anxiety. In larger doses, they can lead to impaired memory and judgment. In combination with alcohol—as when people take a sleeping pill after an evening of heavy drinking—the total depressive effect on body functions can be lethal. With sufficient doses, barbiturates by themselves can also cause death, which makes them the drugs often chosen by those attempting suicide.

Opiates

The **opiates**—opium and its derivatives, morphine and heroin—also depress neural functioning. The pupils constrict, the breathing slows, and the user becomes lethargic. For a few hours, blissful pleasure replaces pain and anxiety. But for short-term pleasure one pays a long-term price, which for the heroin user is the gnawing craving for another fix, the need for progressively larger doses, the week-long physical anguish of withdrawal—and for some, the ultimate price: death by overdose.

The pathway to addiction is treacherous. When repeatedly flooded with artificial opiates, the brain eventually stops producing its own opiates, the endorphins. If the drug is then withdrawn, the brain lacks the normal level of these painkilling neurotransmitters. The result is the agony of withdrawal.

Stimulants

PREVIEW QUESTION 3 What are stimulants, and what are their effects?

The most widely used stimulants are caffeine, nicotine, the powerful **amphetamines,** and the even more powerful cocaine. Stimulants speed up body functions, hence the nickname "speed" for amphetamines. Strong stimulants increase heart and breathing rates. Pupils dilate, appetite diminishes (because blood sugar rises), and energy and self-confidence rise. For these reasons, people use stimulants to stay awake, lose weight, or boost mood or athletic performance. As with other drugs, the benefits come with a price. When drug stimulation ends, the user experiences a compensating slowdown and may "crash" into fatigue, headaches, irritability, and depression. Like the depressants, stimulants—including coffee and caffeinated sodas—can be addictive (Silverman & others, 1992).

Nicotine

Imagine that cigarettes were harmless—except, once in every 50,000 packs, for an occasional innocent-looking one filled with dynamite. Not such a bad risk of having your head blown off, you might say. But with 250 million packs a day consumed worldwide, we could expect more than 5000 gruesome deaths daily—surely enough to have cigarettes banned everywhere.[1]

Ironically, the lost lives from these dynamite-loaded cigarettes would be far less than from today's actual cigarettes. Each year throughout the world, tobacco kills some 3 million of its best customers. That is equivalent to 20 loaded jumbo jets daily (Peto & others, 1992, 1994). And the worst is yet to come. Given present trends, according to a 1994 report by the World Health Organization and a 1999 update, the 3 million annual deaths will soon grow to 10 million, meaning that

Smokers repay society for the health, disability, and fire risk costs of their habit by dying earlier, which saves Social Security and retirement pension payments (Manning & others, 1989).

[1]This analogy, adapted here with world-based numbers, was suggested by mathematician Sam Saunders, as reported by K. C. Cole (1998).

half a billion people alive today will be killed by tobacco (Lopez, 1999). A teen-to-the-grave smoker has a 50 percent chance of dying from the habit, and the death is often agonizing and premature. Smoke a cigarette and nature will charge you 12 minutes—or 4 hours every pack—off your life expectancy (*Discover,* 1996). The elimination of smoking would do more to increase life expectancy than would any other preventive measure.

Nonsmokers not only live healthier, they live happier. Smoking correlates with higher rates of depression, chronic disabilities, and divorce (Doherty & Doherty, 1998; Vita & others, 1998). Nondepressed teens who smoke suffer a quadrupled risk of developing depression (Goodman & others, 2000). Healthy living seems to add both years to life and life to years.

Why do people not stop smoking? Three in four have tried (Niemi & others, 1989). However, once addicted to nicotine we find it very hard to quit. Tobacco products are as addictive as heroin and cocaine. Indeed, some who have kicked the heroin habit have been unable to also stop smoking. Surveys in Britain and the United States show that at least 1 in 3 of those who try cigarettes become hooked—a higher addiction rate than for heroin and cocaine (Heishman & others, 1997).

As with other addictions, the smoker becomes *dependent;* each year fewer than 1 of every 7 smokers who want to quit will do so. A smoker also develops *tolerance,* eventually needing larger and larger doses to get the same effect. Quitting causes *withdrawal* symptoms. Craving, insomnia, anxiety, and irritability all accompany nicotine withdrawal. And all it takes to relieve these aversive states is a cigarette (**FIGURE 16.2**). For those who endure, the acute craving and withdrawal symptoms of the first week or two gradually dissipate over the ensuing six months (Ward & others, 1997).

As with all addictive drugs, nicotine use is not only compulsive and mood-altering, it is also reinforcing. After an hour or a day without smoking, the habitual smoker finds a cigarette—a portable nicotine dispenser—powerfully reinforcing. Even if given low-nicotine cigarettes, the smoker will end up smoking more of them to maintain a roughly constant level of nicotine in the blood.

Smoking reinforces smoking by both terminating the aversive craving and offering a pleasurable lift. Nicotine triggers the release of the hormones epinephrine and norepinephrine, which in turn diminish appetite and boost alertness and mental efficiency. More importantly, nicotine also stimulates the central nervous system to release neurotransmitters that calm anxiety and reduce sensitivity to pain. For example, nicotine, like cocaine, increases the levels of the neurotransmitter dopamine—cocaine by blocking its reuptake, nicotine by stimulating its release (Nowak, 1994). Therefore, people who are anxious or depressed often find it especially hard to forgo smoking's rewards (Mansnerus, 1992). Over time, smokers who are abstaining feel increasing tension and stress, which a cigarette temporarily relieves (Parrott, 1999). These rewards keep people smoking even when they wish they could stop—indeed, even when they know they are committing slow-motion suicide. Although quitting seldom is easy, Centers for Disease Control reports that half of Americans who have ever smoked have quit. More than 90 percent did so on their own, often after repeated attempts.

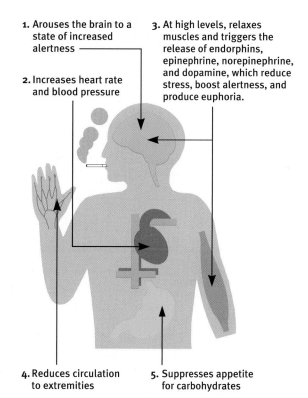

1. Arouses the brain to a state of increased alertness

2. Increases heart rate and blood pressure

3. At high levels, relaxes muscles and triggers the release of endorphins, epinephrine, norepinephrine, and dopamine, which reduce stress, boost alertness, and produce euphoria.

4. Reduces circulation to extremities

5. Suppresses appetite for carbohydrates

FIGURE 16.2

Where there's smoke . . . : The physiological effects of nicotine

Nicotine reaches the brain within 7 seconds, twice as fast as intravenous heroin. Within minutes, the amount in the blood soars.

The recipe for Coca-Cola originally included an extract of the coca plant, creating a cocaine tonic for tired elderly people. Between 1896 and 1905, Coke was indeed "the real thing."

Cocaine

In national surveys, 3 percent of U.S. adults and 3 percent of high school seniors reported having tried cocaine during the past year (Johnston & others, 1999; National Institute on Drug Abuse, 1999). Of the seniors, nearly half said they had smoked *crack,* a potent form of cocaine. During the 1990s the decade-long cocaine epidemic subsided, thanks partly to increased treatment and awareness and partly to the impoverishment, imprisonment, and deaths of many cocaine victims.

Cocaine addiction is a fast track from euphoria to crash. When animals and people chew coca leaves, only small amounts of cocaine enter the bloodstream, and they do so gradually, without seeming ill effects (Siegel, 1990). But when extracted cocaine is sniffed ("snorted"), and especially when injected or smoked ("freebased"), it enters the bloodstream quickly. The result: a "rush" of euphoria that lasts 15 to 30 minutes. Because the rush depletes the brain's supply of the neurotransmitters dopamine, serotonin, and norepinephrine, a crash of agitated depression occurs as the drug's effect wears off (**FIGURE 16.3**). Crack works even faster and produces a briefer but more intense high, a more intense crash, and a craving for more crack, which wanes after several hours but then returns several days later (Gawin, 1991).

To explore dopamine's role in cocaine addiction, researchers created a strain of mice in which they had "knocked out" the gene for a protein that mops up and recycles the excess dopamine released by a nerve cell (Giros & others, 1996). Like cocaine-hyped mice, these mice became hyperactive. They passed through a photocell beam five times as often as other mice. Moreover, cocaine did not affect the "knockout" mice. This suggests that cocaine raises dopamine concentrations by binding to the mop-up site, thus blocking its reuptake of dopamine. This effectively locks the brain's neural reward switches into the "on" position (Landry, 1997).

Regular cocaine users become addicted. Monkeys have become so strongly addicted that they will press a lever more than 12,000 times to gain each cocaine injection (Siegel, 1990). Human and animal cocaine users may experience emotional disturbance, suspiciousness, convulsions, cardiac arrest, or respiratory failure. In situations that trigger aggression, ingesting cocaine may increase aggressive reactions.

FIGURE 16.3
Cocaine euphoria and crash

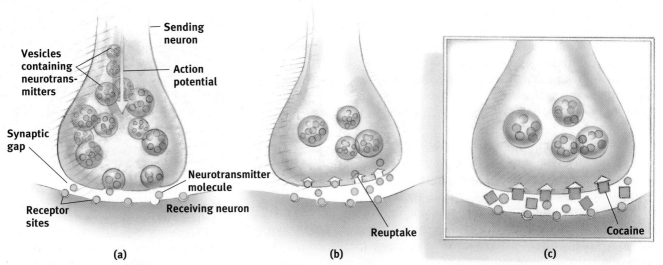

(a)
Neurotransmitters carry a message from a sending neuron across a synapse to receptor sites on a receiving neuron.

(b)
The sending neuron normally reabsorbs excess neurotransmitter molecules, a process called reuptake.

(c)
By binding to the sites that normally reabsorb neurotransmitter molecules, cocaine blocks reuptake of dopamine, norepinephrine, and serotonin (Ray & Ksir, 1990). The extra neurotransmitter molecules therefore remain in the synapse, intensifying their normal mood-altering effects and producing a euphoric rush. When the cocaine level drops, the absence of these neurotransmitters produces a crash.

Caged rats fight when given foot shocks, and they fight even more when given cocaine *and* foot shocks. Asked to determine how much electric shock one's opponent will receive in a laboratory competition, cocaine users who have ingested high-dose cocaine set higher levels than do those who have received a placebo (Licata & others, 1993).

As with all psychoactive drugs, cocaine's psychological effects depend not only on the dosage and form in which one takes the drug but also on one's expectations, one's personality, and the situation—a mix of factors. Given a placebo, cocaine users who *think* they are taking cocaine often have a cocainelike experience (Van Dyke & Byck, 1982).

Hallucinogens

PREVIEW QUESTION 4 What are hallucinogens, and what are their effects?

Hallucinogens are psychoactive drugs that distort perceptions and evoke vivid images in the absence of sensory input (which is why these drugs are also called *psychedelics,* meaning "mind-manifesting"). Some are natural substances, such as the mild hallucinogen marijuana. Others are synthetic, the two best known of which are PCP ("angel dust"), a potent painkiller that has highly unpredictable and sometimes devastating psychological effects, and LSD.

LSD

In 1943, chemist Albert Hofmann, the creator of **LSD** (*lysergic acid diethylamide*) took the first "acid trip." After accidentally ingesting some of the chemical, Hofmann reported that he "perceived an uninterrupted stream of fantastic pictures, extraordinary shapes with intense, kaleidoscopic play of colors" (Siegel, 1984). LSD and other powerful hallucinogens are chemically similar to (and therefore block the actions of) a subtype of the neurotransmitter serotonin (Jacobs, 1987).

The emotions of an LSD trip vary from euphoria to detachment to panic. As with all drug use, a person's current mood and expectations color the LSD experience. Despite emotional variations, the resulting perceptual distortions and hallucinations do have commonalities. The experience typically begins with simple geometric forms, such as a lattice, a cobweb, or a spiral. The next phase consists of more meaningful images; some may be superimposed on a tunnel or funnel, others may be replays of past emotional experiences. When the hallucinogenic experience peaks, people frequently feel separated from their bodies and experience dreamlike scenes as though they were real—so real that users may become panic-stricken or even harm themselves.

These hallucinatory sensations are strikingly similar to the **near-death experience** reported by about one-third of those who survive a brush with death, as when revived from cardiac arrest (Moody, 1976; Ring, 1980; Schnaper, 1980). Psychologist Ronald Siegel (1980) reports that one may experience visions of tunnels and bright lights or beings of light (**FIGURE 16.4**), a replay of old memories, and out-of-body sensations.

Given that oxygen deprivation and other insults to the brain are known to produce hallucinations, it is difficult to resist wondering whether near-death experiences are manufactured by the brain under stress. Patients who have experienced temporal lobe seizures have reported similarly profound mystical experiences, as have solitary sailors and polar explorers while enduring monotony, isolation, and cold (Suedfeld & Mocellin, 1987). Fantasy-prone persons are especially susceptible—or should we say *open*—to near-death and other out-of-body experiences, such as believing one has encountered or been abducted by aliens (Ring, 1992; Wilson & Barber, 1983).

- **LSD** a powerful hallucinogenic drug; also known as acid (*lysergic acid diethylamide*).

- **near-death experience** an altered state of consciousness reported after a close brush with death (such as through cardiac arrest); often similar to drug-induced hallucinations.

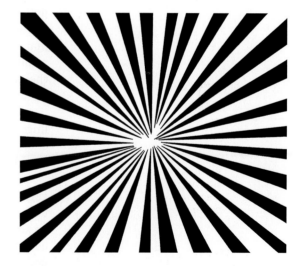

FIGURE 16.4

Near-death vision or hallucination?

Psychologist Ronald Siegel (1977) reports that people under the influence of hallucinogenic drugs often see "a bright light in the center of the field of vision.... The location of this point of light create[s] a tunnel-like perspective." Susan Blackmore (1991, 1993) offers an explanation of similar light during a near-death experience: As oxygen deprivation turns off the brain's inhibitory cells, neural activity increases in the visual cortex. The result is a growing patch of light, which looks much like what you would see moving through a tunnel. (From "Hallucinations" by R. K. Siegel. Copyright © 1977 Scientific American, Inc. All rights reserved.)

■ **THC** the major active ingredient in marijuana; triggers a variety of effects, including mild hallucinations.

Marijuana

Marijuana consists of the leaves and flowers of the hemp plant, which for 5000 years has been cultivated for its fiber. Marijuana's major active ingredient is **THC,** the everyday name of the complex organic molecule delta-9-tetrahydrocannabinol. Whether smoked or eaten, THC produces a mix of effects that makes the drug difficult to classify. (Smoking gets the drug into the brain in about 7 seconds, producing a greater effect than does eating the drug, which causes its peak concentration to be reached at a slower, unpredictable rate.) Like alcohol, marijuana relaxes, disinhibits, and may produce a euphoric high. But marijuana also acts as a mild hallucinogen by amplifying sensitivity to colors, sounds, tastes, and smells.

As with other drugs, the marijuana user's experience varies, depending on the situation. If the person feels anxious or depressed, taking the drug may intensify these feelings. In other situations, using marijuana can be not only pleasurable but therapeutic. For those who suffer the pain, nausea, and severe weight loss associated with AIDS, the discomfort of glaucoma, or the nausea that sometimes accompanies cancer chemotherapy, marijuana may spell relief (Watson & others, 2000). Such benefits have motivated legislation legalizing the drug for such patients. The medical uses are, however, compromised by the toxicity of marijuana smoke—which can cause cancer, lung damage, and pregnancy complications, reports the National Academy of Sciences (1999). If the drug becomes widely legalized for prescribed medical uses, capsules, patches, and inhalers may be developed to deliver the THC.

The National Academy of Sciences (1982, 1999) research reviews have identified other not-so-pleasant marijuana consequences. Like alcohol, marijuana impairs the motor coordination, perceptual skills, and reaction time necessary for safely operating an automobile or other machine. "THC causes animals to misjudge events," reports Ronald Siegel (1990, p. 163). "Pigeons wait too long to respond to buzzers or lights that tell them food is available for brief periods; and rats turn the wrong way in mazes." Marijuana also disrupts memory formation and interferes with immediate recall of information learned only a few minutes before. Such cognitive effects outlast the period of smoking (Pope & Yurgelun-Todd, 1996; Smith, 1995). Clearly, being stoned is not conducive to learning.

Unlike alcohol, which the body eliminates within hours, THC and its by-products linger in the body for a month or more. Thus, contrary to the usual tolerance phenomenon, regular users may achieve a high with smaller amounts of the drug than occasional users would take to get the same effect.

Uncertainty persists about marijuana's physical effects, but medical research suggests that long-term marijuana use may depress male sex hormone and sperm levels and damage the lungs more than does cigarette smoking (Wu & others, 1988). Large doses hasten the loss of brain cells (Landfield & others, 1988). Although marijuana is not as addictive as cocaine or nicotine, it changes brain chemistry, much as cocaine and heroin do, and it may make the brain more susceptible to cocaine and heroin addiction (Tanda & others, 1997). One study that followed 654 junior high students into their early twenties found that adolescents who heavily used marijuana developed more health and family problems than did nonusers (Newcomb & Bentler, 1988).

Despite their differences, the psychoactive drugs summarized in Table 16.1 share a common feature: They trigger negative aftereffects that offset their immediate positive effects. The aftereffects illustrate a more general principle: Emotions tend to produce opposing emotions, which linger after the original emotions disappear. With repetition, the opposing emotions grow stronger. This emotions-trigger-opposing-emotions principle parallels that of drug-induced pleasures; the pleasures wane as the drug exacts its compensatory price. That helps explain both tolerance and withdrawal. As the opposing, negative aftereffects get stronger, it takes larger and larger doses to produce the desired high (tolerance), causing the aftereffects to worsen in the drug's absence (withdrawal). This in turn creates a need to switch off the withdrawal symptoms by taking yet more of the drug.

"How strange would appear to be this thing that men call pleasure! And how curiously it is related to what is thought to be its opposite, pain! . . . Wherever the one is found, the other follows up behind."

Plato, *Phaedo*, Fourth Century B.C.

TABLE 16.1

A GUIDE TO SELECTED PSYCHOACTIVE DRUGS

Drug	Type	Pleasurable Effects	Adverse Effects
Alcohol	Depressant	Initial high followed by relaxation and disinhibition	Depression, memory loss, organ damage, impaired reactions
Heroin	Depressant	Rush of euphoria, relief from pain	Depressed physiology, agonizing withdrawal
Caffeine	Stimulant	Increased alertness and wakefulness	Anxiety, restlessness, and insomnia in high doses; uncomfortable withdrawal
Methamphet-amine ("speed," "crank," "ice")	Stimulant	Euphoria, alertness, energy	Irritability, insomnia, hypertension, seizures
Cocaine	Stimulant	Rush of euphoria, confidence, energy	Cardiovascular stress, suspiciousness, depressive crash
Nicotine	Stimulant	Arousal and relaxation, sense of well-being	Heart disease, cancer (from tars)
Marijuana	Mild hallucinogen	Enhanced sensation, relief of pain, distortion of time, relaxation	Lowered sex hormones, disrupted memory, lung damage from smoke

Influences on Drug Use

PREVIEW QUESTION 5 Why do some people become regular users of consciousness-altering drugs?

Drug use by North American youth increased during the 1970s. Then, with increased drug education and a more realistic and deglamorized media depiction of taking drugs, drug use declined sharply. But since the early 1990s the cultural antidrug voice has softened and drugs are once again being glamorized in some music and films. And drug use has rebounded, renewing public concern. Consider the trends:

- In the University of Michigan's annual survey of 15,000 high school seniors, the proportion who believed there is "great risk" in regular marijuana use rose from 35 percent in 1978 to 79 percent in 1991, then retreated to 57 percent in 1999 (Johnston & others, 1999).
- After peaking in 1978, marijuana use by this age group declined through 1992, but it has been rising since then (**FIGURE 16.5**).
- In the UCLA/American Council on Education annual survey of new college and university students, support for the legalization of marijuana dropped from 53 percent in 1977 to 17 percent in 1989; support rebounded to 34 percent in 1999 (Astin & others, 1997; Sax & others, 1999).

Similar changes in attitude and usage since the late 1970s appear in surveys of Canadian teens (Smart & others, 1991).

FIGURE 16.5

Trends in drug use

The percentage of high school seniors who report having used alcohol, marijuana, or cocaine during the past 30 days declined from the late 1970s to 1992. Since then drug use has been increasing and drug merchandise has become more openly available in stores and at concerts. (From Johnston & others, 1999.)

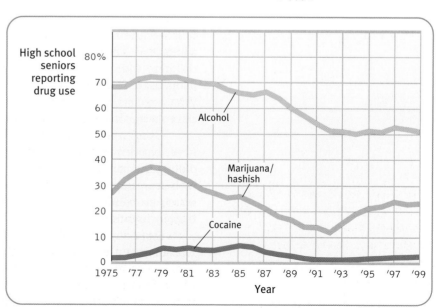

ANNUAL BEER AND WINE CONSUMPTION, LITERS PER PERSON		
	Beer	Wine
France	41	67
Germany	143	25
Italy	23	57
New Zealand	110	15
Australia	102	19
United Kingdom	106	12
United States	87	7
Sweden	59	12

Source: *Australian Social Trends*, 1995.

Warning signs of alcoholism

- Drinking binges
- Regretting things done or said when drunk
- Feeling low or guilty after drinking
- Failing to honor a resolve to drink less
- Drinking to alleviate depression or anxiety
- Avoiding family or friends when drinking

Other studies reveal a changing national attitude toward alcohol in the United States. More than at any time since Prohibition, health- and safety-conscious people see alcohol less as a beverage to be enjoyed than as a drug to be shunned. The number of new U.S. collegians who reported abstaining from drinking beer during the preceding year doubled, from 25 percent in 1981 to 49 percent in 1999. Four in 10 Americans declare themselves "a total abstainer" (Sourcebook, 1998).

The apparent lesson: Effectively inform people about the health hazards of using cocaine, marijuana, alcohol, or tobacco and—without therapy, support groups, or medicines—many will simply stop.

Biological Influences

Some people may be biologically vulnerable to alcohol. For example, evidence accumulates that heredity influences alcohol use problems:

- Adopted individuals are more susceptible to alcoholism if one or both of their biological parents have a history of alcoholism (Mirin & Weiss, 1989).
- Having an identical twin with alcoholism puts a male at especially increased risk for alcohol problems (McGue, 1999; Prescott & others, 1994).
- Boys who at age 6 are excitable, impulsive, and fearless (genetically influenced traits) are more likely as teens to smoke, drink, and use other drugs (Masse & Tremblay, 1997).
- Compared with other children, children whose parents abuse alcohol have a higher tolerance for multiple alcoholic drinks taken over an hour or two (Schuckit & Smith, 1996).
- Researchers have bred rats and mice that prefer alcoholic drinks to water (Azar, 1995; Goldman, 1996; Holden, 1991). One such strain has reduced levels of a brain chemical called NPY; mice engineered to overproduce NPY are very sensitive to alcohol's sedating effect and drink little (Thiele & others, 1998).
- Molecular geneticists have identified a gene on chromosome 11 that is more common among people with alcoholism, especially in severe cases (Noble, 1993).

Psychological and Cultural Influences

Psychological and social factors may also exert an important influence on alcohol and other drug use. In their studies of youth and young adults, Michael Newcomb and L. L. Harlow (1986) found that one psychological factor is the feeling that one's life is meaningless and directionless, a common feeling among school dropouts who subsist without job skills, without privilege, with little hope. When young unmarried adults leave home, alcohol and other drug use increases; when they marry and have children, it decreases (Bachman & others, 1997). Yet the ups and downs of marijuana usage seem not due to youth becoming more rebellious (which they have not). What predicts usage is instead the ups and downs in how risky the young people perceive marijuana use to be (Bachman & others, 1998, and **FIGURE 16.6**).

Other studies reveal that heavy users of alcohol, marijuana, and cocaine often have experienced significant stress or failure and are depressed. By temporarily dulling the pain of self-awareness, alcohol may offer a way to avoid having to cope with depression, anger, anxiety, or insomnia. The relief may be temporary, but as research on conditioning shows, behavior is often controlled more by its immediate than by its later consequences.

Especially for teenagers, drug use can also have social roots, evident in differing rates of drug use across cultural groups. In the United States, alcohol and other drug

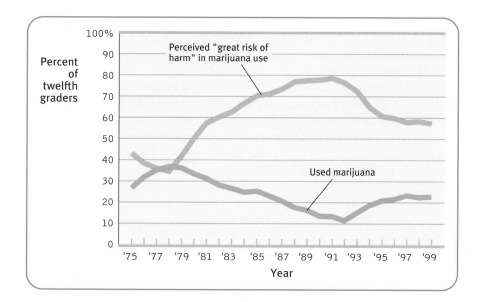

FIGURE 16.6

Perceived marijuana risk and actual use
As the percentage of twelfth graders perceiving a "great risk" in regular marijuana use increases, the percentage having used it in the previous 30 days decreases. (Data from Johnston & others, 1999.)

addiction rates are extremely low among the Amish, Mennonites, Mormons, and Orthodox Jews (Trimble, 1994). What do you suppose is the rate of drug usage among African-American students—low or high? One of psychology's best-kept secrets is that, contrary to popular stereotypes, African-American high school seniors "report the lowest rates of use for virtually all drugs" (Johnston & others, 1994, 1996). For example, nearly a third of white seniors, but only 13 percent of black seniors, report recently drinking heavily. Monthly smoking rates are 38 percent among white seniors, only 14 percent among black seniors. Although these data exclude high school dropouts, independent government studies of drug use in households nationwide and among 12,272 high schoolers in all 50 states confirm the finding: African-American teens have sharply lower rates of drinking, smoking, and cocaine use (Bass & Kane-Williams, 1993; Kann & others, 1993). (Curiously, however, cocaine-related arrests and emergency room visits occur more often among African-Americans [Bennett & DiIulio, 1996].)

Peer culture is a major social influence. By their words and examples, peers influence attitudes about drugs. They also throw the parties and provide the drugs. If an adolescent's friends use drugs, the odds are that he or she will, too. If the friends do not, the opportunity may not even arise.

Peer influence is not just a matter of what friends do and say but also of what adolescents *believe* their friends are doing and favoring. Young adolescents consume more alcohol when, as often happens, they overestimate their friends' use (Aas & Klepp, 1992; Graham & others, 1991). In one survey of sixth graders in 22 states, 14 percent believed their friends had smoked marijuana, though only 4 percent acknowledged doing so (Wren, 1999). At the university level, drinking dominates social occasions partly because students overestimate their fellow students' enthusiasm for alcohol (Prentice & Miller, 1993; Self, 1994). Thinking that few students share their concerns about the risks associated with alcohol, most students surrender to the perceived norm. Nearly half have engaged in binge drinking (Wechsler & others, 1994).

People are more likely to stop using drugs if their use was influenced by their peers (Kandel & Raveis, 1989). When friends stop or the social network changes, they typically stop. More than 9 in 10 soldiers who became drug-addicted while in Vietnam ceased their drug use after returning home (Robins & others, 1974). Teenagers who come from happy families and do well in school seldom use drugs,

In the real world, alcohol accounts for one-sixth or less of beverage use. In television's world, drinking alcohol occurs more often than the combined drinking of coffee, tea, soft drinks, and water (Gerbner, 1990).

Humorist Dave Barry (1995) recalling why he smoked his first cigarette the summer he turned 15: "Arguments against smoking: 'It's a repulsive addiction that slowly but surely turns you into a gasping, gray-skinned, tumor-ridden invalid, hacking up brownish gobs of toxic waste from your one remaining lung.' Arguments for smoking: 'Other teenagers are doing it.' Case closed! Let's light up!"

largely because they rarely associate with those who do (Oetting & Beauvais, 1987, 1990). As always with correlations, the traffic between friends' and one's own drug use may be two way: Our friends influence us, but we also select as friends those who share our likes and dislikes.

The findings suggest three possible channels of influence for drug prevention and treatment programs: (1) education about the long-term costs of a drug's temporary pleasures, (2) efforts to boost people's self-esteem and purpose in life, and (3) attempts to modify peer associations or to "inoculate" youth against peer pressures by training them in "refusal skills." Said more directly, people rarely abuse drugs if they understand the physical and psychological costs, feel good about themselves and the directions their lives are taking, and are in a peer group that disapproves of using drugs. These educational, psychological, and social factors help explain why 42 percent of American high school dropouts, but only 15 percent of college graduates, smoke (Ladd, 1998).

rehearse it!

1. Continued use of a psychoactive drug produces tolerance. This means that the user will
   a. feel physical pain and intense craving.
   b. be irreversibly addicted to the substance.
   c. need to take bigger doses to get the desired effect.
   d. be able to take smaller doses to get the desired effect.

2. Depressants are drugs that reduce neural activity and slow down body functions. The depressants include alcohol, barbiturates,
   a. and opiates.
   b. cocaine, and morphine.
   c. caffeine, nicotine, and marijuana.
   d. and amphetamines.

3. Alcohol is a depressant that, in significant doses, powerfully affects behavior. For example, drinking alcohol may make a person more helpful or more self-disclosing; conversely, it may make a person more aggressive or more sexually daring. These alcohol effects result from
   a. alcoholic blackouts or memory losses.
   b. deprivation of REM sleep.
   c. sensory arousal and hallucinations.
   d. the lowering of inhibitions.

4. Nicotine, caffeine, amphetamines, and cocaine stimulate neural activity, speed up body functions, and
   a. induce sensory hallucinations.
   b. interfere with memory.
   c. induce a temporary sense of well-being.
   d. lead to heroin use.

5. About one-third of those who have survived a brush with death have reported near-death experiences, which are strikingly similar to the hallucinations evoked by
   a. amphetamines.
   b. barbiturates.
   c. LSD.
   d. marijuana.

6. Smoking marijuana can relieve certain kinds of pain and nausea. It also
   a. impairs motor coordination, perception, reaction time, and memory.
   b. inhibits people's emotions.
   c. increases male sex hormone levels.
   d. stimulates brain cell development.

7. Drug use by young North Americans generally declined from the late 1970s until the early 1990s and then began to increase again. Social explanations for drug use today focus on the powerful effect of peer influence. An important *psychological* contributor to drug use is
   a. inflated self-esteem.
   b. the feeling that life is meaningless and directionless.
   c. academic and job pressures.
   d. overprotective parents.

Drugs and Consciousness

1. What are dependence and addiction? Can substance abusers overcome their addictions?

The use of psychoactive drugs often leads to tolerance and physical and/or psychological dependence. Users who are physically dependent will experience withdrawal when they try to stop taking the drug. The three types of psychoactive drugs are depressants, stimulants, and hallucinogens.

2. What are depressants, and what are their effects?

Alcohol, barbiturates, and the opiates are examples of depressants, which dampen neural activity and slow down body functions. Alcohol seems to enliven by disinhibiting both harmful and helpful tendencies and by impairing judgment. Alcohol also disrupts the processing of recent experiences into long-term memory and reduces self-awareness. User expectation strongly influences alcohol's behavioral effects. Barbiturates can be especially dangerous in combination with alcohol. The harmful aftereffects of opiates oppose and offset the temporary pleasure they induce.

3. What are stimulants, and what are their effects?

Caffeine, nicotine, the amphetamines, and cocaine are examples of stimulants, which stimulate neural activity and arouse body functions. The reinforcing effects of nicotine make smoking a difficult habit to kick, but increased knowledge of its devastating health effects has led to a decreasing percentage of Americans who smoke. All stimulants, but especially cocaine and crack, produce a crash of agitated depression as the drug wears off. This re-

inforces the use of increased amounts of the drug to get out of the depression, leading regular cocaine and crack users to become addicted. As with nearly all psychoactive drugs, stimulants act at the synapses by influencing the brain's neurotransmitters, and their effects depend on dosage and the user's personality and expectations.

4. What are hallucinogens, and what are their effects?

LSD and marijuana are examples of hallucinogens, which distort perception and evoke sensory images without sensory input. Both LSD and marijuana can distort the user's judgments of time and, depending on the setting in which they are taken, can alter sensation and perception. Similar hallucinations are reported in near-death experiences, perhaps as a result of oxygen deprivation in the brain. Although THC, the major active ingredient in marijuana, can be therapeutic for those enduring glaucoma or chemotherapy, it corrodes health, judgment, and memory.

5. Why do some people become regular users of consciousness-altering drugs?

Drug use among teenagers and young adults declined during the 1980s and early 1990s but has been increasing since. Nevertheless, psychological factors (such as stress, depression, and feelings of hopelessness) and social factors (such as peer pressure) combine to lead many people to experiment with—and become dependent on—drugs. Some people also appear to have a greater biological susceptibility to dependence on drugs such as alcohol.

TERMS AND CONCEPTS TO REMEMBER

psychoactive drugs, p. 220
tolerance, p. 220
withdrawal, p. 220
physical dependence, p. 220

psychological dependence, p. 220
depressants, p. 222
stimulants, p. 222

hallucinogens, p. 222
barbiturates, p. 224
opiates, p. 224
amphetamines, p. 224

LSD (*lysergic acid diethylamide*), p. 227
near-death experience, p. 227
THC, p. 228

REHEARSE IT ANSWER KEY

1. c   2. a   3. d   4. c   5. c   6. a   7. b

Learning and Memory

When a chinook salmon first emerges from its egg in the gravel bed of a stream, its genes provide many of the behavioral instructions it needs for life. It knows instinctively how and where to swim, what to eat, and how to protect itself from predators. Following this built-in plan, the young salmon soon begins its trek to the sea. After some four years in the ocean, the mature salmon returns to its birthplace. It navigates hundreds of miles to the mouth of its home river and then, guided by the scent of its home stream, begins an upstream odyssey to its ancestral spawning ground. Once there, the salmon seeks out the exact conditions of temperature, gravel, and water flow that will facilitate its breeding. It then mates and dies.

Unlike the salmon, we are not born with a genetic blueprint for life. Much of what we do we must learn from experience. Although we struggle to find the life direction a salmon is born with, our learning gives us more flexibility. We can learn how to build grass huts or snow shelters, and thereby adapt to almost any environment. Indeed, nature's most important gift to us may be our *adaptability*—our capacity to learn new behaviors that enable us to cope with changing circumstances.

In Module 17, we consider what we mean by *learning* and how humans learn by *classical conditioning* (learning to associate one stimulus with another), by *operant conditioning* (learning to associate our responses to their consequences), and by *observation* (learning from the experiences and examples of others).

The reservoir of our accumulated learning is our memory, our mind's storehouse. To a psychologist, *memory* is any indication that learning has persisted over time. It is our ability to store and retrieve information. In large part, we are what we remember.

Memory is the subject of Modules 18 and 19: what memory is, how we store and retrieve our memories, and how we can improve our memory (Module 18), and why we sometimes forget and how we construct our memories (Module 19).

17 Learning

Introduction to Learning

PREVIEW QUESTION 1 What is learning?

No topic is closer to the heart of psychology than **learning,** *a relatively permanent change in an organism's behavior due to experience.* Psychologists study the learning of moral ideas, of visual perceptions, of a drug's expected effect. And they study how learning shapes our thought and language, our motivations and emotions, our personalities and attitudes.

Learning in all such realms breeds hope. What is learnable, we can potentially teach—a fact that encourages parents, educators, coaches, and animal trainers. What has been learned we can potentially change by new learning—an assumption that underlies counseling, psychotherapy, and rehabilitation programs. No matter how unhappy, unsuccessful, or unloving we are, that need not be the end of our story.

By definition, experience is key to learning. More than 200 years ago, philosophers such as John Locke and David Hume echoed Aristotle's conclusion from 2000 years earlier: We learn by association. Our minds naturally connect events that occur in sequence: We *associate* them. If, after seeing and smelling freshly baked bread, you eat some and find it satisfying, then the next time you see and smell fresh bread, your experience will lead you to expect that eating it will be satisfying again. And if you associate a sound with a frightening consequence, then your fear may be aroused by the sound itself. As one 4-year-old exclaimed after watching a TV character get mugged, "If I had heard that music, I wouldn't have gone around the corner!" (Wells, 1981).

Simpler animals can learn simple associations. When disturbed by a squirt of water, the sea snail *Aplysia* will protectively withdraw its gill. If the squirts continue, as happens naturally in choppy water, the withdrawal response diminishes. (The snail's response "habituates.") But if the sea snail repeatedly receives an electric shock just after being squirted, its withdrawal response to the squirt alone becomes stronger. The animal associates the squirt with the impending shock. More complex animals can learn more complex associations, especially those that bring favorable consequences. Seals in an aquarium will repeat behaviors, such as slapping and barking, that prompt people to toss them a herring.

By linking two events that occur close together, both the sea snail and the seals exhibit **associative learning.** The sea snail associates the squirt with impending shock; the seals associate slapping and barking with receiving a herring (**FIGURE 17.1**). In both cases, the animals learned something important to their survival: to associate the past with the immediate future.

Nature without appropriate nurture
When captive-bred Mexican gray wolves were first freed, their life experience left them unprepared for self-protection and survival.

learning a relatively permanent change in an organism's behavior due to experience.

associative learning learning that certain events occur together. The events may be two stimuli (as in classical conditioning) or a response and its consequences (as in operant conditioning).

EVENT 1　　　　　　　　　　EVENT 2

Sea snail associates splash with a tail shock

Seal learns to expect a snack for its showy antics

FIGURE 17.1
Associative learning: Learning to associate two events

The significance of an animal's learning is illustrated by the challenges that captive-bred animals face when reintroduced to the wild. After being bred and raised in captivity, 11 Mexican gray wolves—extinct in the United States since 1977—were released in Arizona's Apache National Forest in 1998. Eight months later, the lone survivor of this initial effort was recaptured. The pen-reared wolves had learned how to hunt—and to move 100 feet away from people—but had not learned to run from a human with a gun. The gray wolves' experience is not unusual. Of 145 documented reintroductions of 115 species in the twentieth century, only 11 percent produced self-sustaining populations in the wild. Keiko—the killer whale of *Free Willy* fame—had all the right genes for being dropped right back into his Icelandic home waters, but not the life experience. Successful adaptation requires both nature (the biological predisposition) and nurture (a history of appropriate learning).

Conditioning is the process of learning associations. In *classical conditioning,* we learn to associate two stimuli and thus to anticipate events. We learn that a flash of lightning signals an impending crack of thunder, and so we start to brace ourselves when lightning flashes nearby (**FIGURE 17.2** on page 238).

In *operant conditioning,* we learn to associate a response and its consequence and thus to repeat acts followed by rewards and avoid acts followed by punishment. We learn that pushing a vending machine button, for example, relates to the delivery of a candy bar (**FIGURE 17.3** on page 238).

To simplify, we will consider these two types of associative learning separately. Often, though, they occur together in the same situation. A clever Japanese rancher re-

Which type of conditioning does the sea snail illustrate? What about the seal? (See page 241.)

FIGURE 17.2
Classical conditioning

FIGURE 17.3
Operant conditioning

portedly herds cattle by outfitting them with electronic pagers, which he calls from his portable phone. After a week of training, the cattle learned to associate two stimuli—the beep on their pager and the arrival of food (classical conditioning). But they also learned to associate their hustling to the food trough with the pleasure of eating (operant conditioning).

The concept of conditioning by association, however, leaves many questions: What principles influence the learning and the loss of associations? How can we apply these principles? And what really are the associations: Does the beep on a steer's pager evoke a cognitive representation of food, to which the steer responds by coming to the trough? Or does it make little sense to explain conditioned associations in terms of cognitive processes?

Conditioning is not the only form of learning. Through *observational learning,* we learn from others' experiences and examples. Complex animals, such as chimpanzees, sometimes learn behaviors merely by observing others perform them. If one animal watches another learn to solve a puzzle that gains a food reward, the observing animal may perform the trick more quickly.

In all these ways—by classical and operant conditioning and by observation—we humans learn and adapt to our environments. As this module will explain, we learn to expect and prepare for significant events such as food or pain (classical conditioning). We also learn to repeat acts that bring good results and to avoid acts that bring bad results (operant conditioning). By watching others, we learn new behaviors (observational learning). And, through language, we also learn things we have neither experienced nor observed. Of all the world's creatures, we humans are the most capable of changing through learning.

In searching for laws underlying learning, psychologist John B. Watson (1913) urged his colleagues to discard refer-

Most of us would be unable to name the order of the songs on our favorite CD. Yet hearing the end of one piece cues (by association) an anticipation of the next. Likewise, when singing your national anthem, you associate the end of each line with the beginning of the next. (Pick a line out of the middle and notice how much harder it is to recall the *previous* line.)

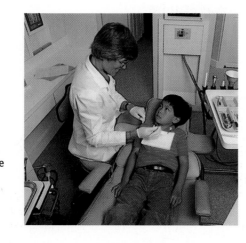

Conditioned fear
Because of pain experienced during previous visits to the dentist chair, this young patient has learned to expect discomfort.

ence to inner thoughts, feelings, and motives. The science of psychology should instead study how organisms respond to stimuli in their environments, said Watson. "Its theoretical goal is the prediction and control of behavior. Introspection forms no essential part of its methods." Simply said, psychology should be an objective science based on *observable behavior*. This view, which influenced North American psychology during the early twentieth century, Watson called **behaviorism.**

Classical Conditioning

Although the idea of learning associations had long generated philosophical discussion, it was only in the early twentieth century that psychology's most famous research verified it. For many people, the name Ivan Pavlov rings a bell. His experiments are classics, and the phenomenon he explored we justly call **classical conditioning** (or *Pavlovian conditioning*).

Pavlov's Experiments

PREVIEW QUESTION 2 How does classical conditioning demonstrate learning by association? How do the processes of acquisition, extinction, spontaneous recovery, generalization, and discrimination affect a conditioned response?

Pavlov was driven by a lifelong passion for research. After setting aside his initial plan to follow his father into the Russian Orthodox priesthood, Pavlov received a medical degree at age 33 and spent the next two decades studying the digestive system. This work earned him Russia's first Nobel Prize in 1904. But it was his novel experiments on learning, to which he devoted the last three decades of his life, that earned this feisty scientist his place in history.

Pavlov's new direction came when his creative mind seized on an incidental finding. After studying salivary secretion in dogs, he knew that when he put food in a dog's mouth the animal would invariably salivate. He also noticed that when he worked with the same dog repeatedly, the dog began salivating to stimuli associated with food—to the mere sight of the food, to the food dish, to the presence of the person who regularly brought the food, or even to the sound of that person's approaching footsteps. Because these "psychic secretions" interfered with his experiments on digestion, Pavlov considered them an annoyance—until he realized they pointed to a simple but important form of learning. From that time on, Pavlov studied learning, which he hoped might enable him to understand better the brain's workings.

At first, Pavlov and his assistants tried to imagine what the dog was thinking and feeling as it drooled in anticipation of the food. This only led them into fruitless debates. So to explore the phenomenon more objectively, they experimented. They paired various neutral stimuli with food in the mouth to see if the dog would begin salivating to the neutral stimuli alone. To eliminate the possible influence of extraneous stimuli, they isolated the dog in a small room, secured it in a harness, and attached a device that diverted its saliva to a measuring instrument (**FIGURE 17.4**). From an

- **behaviorism** the view that psychology (1) should be an objective science that (2) studies behavior without reference to mental processes. Most research psychologists today agree with (1) but not with (2).

- **classical conditioning** a type of learning in which an organism comes to associate stimuli. A neutral stimulus that signals an unconditioned stimulus (UCS) begins to produce a response that anticipates and prepares for the unconditioned stimulus. (Also called *Pavlovian conditioning*.)

Ivan Pavlov

"Experimental investigation . . . should lay a solid foundation for a future true science of psychology" (1927).

FIGURE 17.4
Pavlov's device for recording salivation
The dog's saliva was collected drop by drop in a tube.
(Adapted from Goodwin, 1991.)

BEFORE CONDITIONING

An unconditioned stimulus (UCS) produces an unconditioned response (UCR).

A neutral stimulus produces no salivation response.

DURING CONDITIONING

AFTER CONDITIONING

The unconditioned stimulus is repeatedly presented just after the neutral stimulus. The unconditioned stimulus continues to produce an unconditioned response.

The neutral stimulus alone now produces a conditioned response (CR), thereby becoming a conditioned stimulus (CS).

FIGURE 17.5

Pavlov's classic experiment

Pavlov presented a neutral stimulus (a tone) just before an unconditioned stimulus (food in mouth). The neutral stimulus then became a conditioned stimulus, producing a conditioned response.

■ **unconditioned response (UCR)** in classical conditioning, the unlearned, naturally occurring response to the unconditioned stimulus (UCS), such as salivation when food is in the mouth.

■ **unconditioned stimulus (UCS)** in classical conditioning, a stimulus that unconditionally—naturally and automatically— triggers a response.

■ **conditioned response (CR)** in classical conditioning, the learned response to a previously neutral conditioned stimulus (CS).

■ **conditioned stimulus (CS)** in classical conditioning, an originally irrelevant stimulus that, after association with an unconditioned stimulus (UCS), comes to trigger a conditioned response.

■ **acquisition** the initial stage in classical conditioning; the phase associating a neutral stimulus with an unconditioned stimulus so that the neutral stimulus comes to elicit a conditioned response. In operant conditioning, the strengthening of a reinforced response.

adjacent room they could present food—at first by sliding in a food bowl, later by blowing meat powder into the dog's mouth at a precise moment. If a neutral stimulus—something the dog could see or hear—now regularly signaled the arrival of food, would the dog associate the two stimuli? If so, would it begin salivating to the neutral stimulus in anticipation of the food?

The answers proved to be yes and yes. Just before placing food in the dog's mouth to produce salivation, Pavlov sounded a tone. After several pairings of tone and food, the dog began salivating to the tone alone, in anticipation of the meat powder. Using this procedure, Pavlov conditioned dogs to salivate to other stimuli—a buzzer, a light, a touch on the leg, even the sight of a circle. Because salivation in response to food in the mouth was unlearned, Pavlov called it an **unconditioned response (UCR).** Food in the mouth automatically, *unconditionally,* triggers a dog's salivary reflex (**FIGURE 17.5**). Thus, Pavlov called the food stimulus an **unconditioned stimulus (UCS).**

Salivation in response to the tone was *conditional* upon the dog's learning the association between the tone and the food. One translation of Pavlov therefore calls the salivation the "conditional reflex" (Todes, 1997). More commonly, this learned response is known as the **conditioned response (CR).** The previously irrelevant tone stimulus that now triggered the conditional salivation we call the **conditioned stimulus (CS).** It's easy to distinguish these two kinds of stimuli and responses. Just remember: conditioned = learned; *unconditioned = unlearned.*

If this demonstration of associative learning was so simple, what did Pavlov do for the next three decades? How did his research factory generate 532 papers on salivary conditioning (Windholz, 1997)? He and his associates explored the causes and effects of classical conditioning. Their experiments identified five major conditioning processes: acquisition, extinction, spontaneous recovery, generalization, and discrimination.

Acquisition

To understand the **acquisition,** or initial learning, of the stimulus-response relationship, Pavlov and his associates first had to confront the question of timing: How much time should elapse between presenting the neutral stimulus (the tone, the light, the touch, or whatever) and the unconditioned stimulus? They found that, in most cases, the answer was not much. With many species and procedures, half a second works well. What do you suppose would happen if the food (UCS) appeared *before* the tone (CS) rather than after? Would conditioning occur?

Not likely. Although there are exceptions, conditioning seldom occurs when the CS comes after the UCS. This finding fits the presumption that classical conditioning is biologically adaptive. It helps organisms *prepare* for good or bad events. Pavlov's tone (CS) signals an important biological event—the arrival of food (UCS). To a deer in the forest, the sound of a snapping twig (CS) may come to signal a predator (UCS). If the good or bad event had already occurred, the CS would not likely signal anything significant.

Michael Domjan (1992, 1994, 1997) showed how the CS signals an important biological event by conditioning the sexual arousal of male Japanese quail. Just before presenting an approachable female, the researchers turned on a red light. Over time, with the red light continuing to herald a female's impending arrival, it caused the male quail to become excited (and to copulate with her more quickly when she arrived). Moreover, the male quail developed a preference for their cage's red-light district. Exposure to sexually conditioned stimuli also caused them to release more semen and sperm (Domjan & others, 1998). All in all, the quail's capacity for classical conditioning gives it a reproductive edge. This illustrates the larger lesson that conditioning serves a function: It helps an animal survive and reproduce—by responding to cues that help it gain food, avoid dangers, defeat rivals, locate mates, and produce offspring (Hollis, 1997).

In humans, too, objects, smells, and sights associated with sexual pleasure become conditioned stimuli for sexual arousal. Psychologist Michael Tirrell (1990) recalls: "My first girlfriend loved onions, so I came to associate onion breath with kissing. Before long, onion breath sent tingles up and down my spine. Oh what a feeling!" (Questions: What is the unconditioned stimulus here? What is the conditioned response? See (**FIGURE 17.6**) In laboratory experiments, even a geometric figure can become sexually arousing if repeatedly associated with an erotic stimulus (Byrne, 1982). (Note that in this case the geometric figure is a CS, which gains its power to arouse by repeated pairing with a naturally erotic stimulus.)

Check yourself: If the aroma of cake baking sets your mouth to watering, what is the UCS? The CS? The CR? (See page 244.)

Remember:

UCS = UnConditioned Stimulus

UCR = UnConditioned Response

CS = Conditioned Stimulus

Answers to questions on page 237: The sea snail illustrates classical conditioning. The seal illustrates operant conditioning.

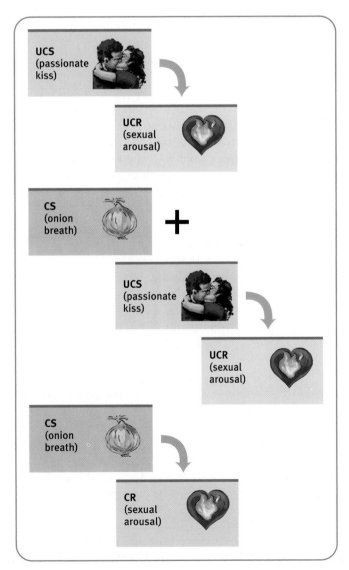

FIGURE 17.6

An unexpected CS

Onion breath does not usually produce sexual arousal. But when repeatedly paired with a passionate kiss it can become a CS and do just that.

■ **extinction** the diminishing of a conditioned response; occurs in classical conditioning when an unconditioned stimulus (UCS) does not follow a conditioned stimulus (CS); occurs in operant conditioning when a response is no longer reinforced.

■ **spontaneous recovery** the reappearance, after a rest period, of an extinguished conditioned response.

■ **generalization** the tendency, once a response has been conditioned, for stimuli similar to the conditioned stimulus to elicit similar responses.

Extinction and Spontaneous Recovery

After conditioning, what happens if the CS occurs repeatedly without the UCS? Will the CS continue to elicit the CR? Pavlov found that when he sounded the tone again and again without presenting food, the dogs salivated less and less. Their declining salivation illustrates **extinction,** the diminished responding that occurs when the CS (tone) no longer signals an impending UCS (food).

Pavlov found, however, that if he allowed several hours to elapse before sounding the tone again, the salivation to the tone would reappear spontaneously (**FIGURE 17.7**). This **spontaneous recovery**—the reappearance of a (weakened) CR after a rest pause—suggested to Pavlov that extinction was suppressing the CR rather than eliminating it.

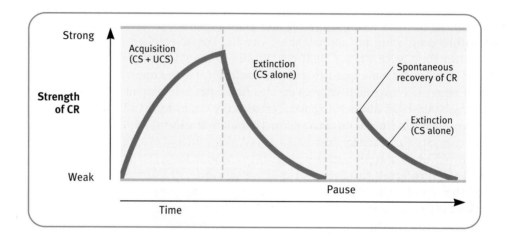

FIGURE 17.7

Idealized curve of acquisition, extinction, and spontaneous recovery
The rising curve shows that the CR rapidly grows stronger as the CS and UCS are repeatedly paired (acquisition), then weakens as the CS is presented alone (extinction). After a rest pause, the CR reappears (spontaneous recovery).

After breaking up with his fire-breathing heartthrob, Tirrell also experienced extinction and spontaneous recovery. He recalls that "the smell of onion breath (CS), no longer paired with the kissing (UCS), lost its ability to shiver my timbers. Occasionally, though, after not sensing the aroma for a long while, smelling onion breath awakens a small version of the emotional response I once felt."

Generalization

Pavlov and his students noticed that a dog conditioned to the sound of one tone also responded somewhat to the sound of a different tone never paired with food. Likewise, a dog conditioned to salivate when rubbed would also salivate some when scratched (Windholz, 1989) or when stimulated on a different body part (**FIGURE 17.8**). This tendency to respond to stimuli similar to the CS is called **generalization.**

Generalization can be adaptive, as when toddlers

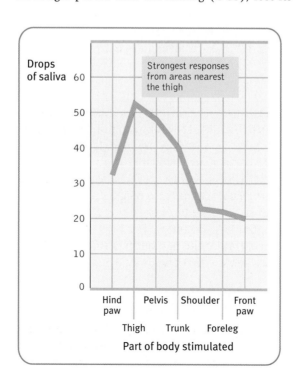

FIGURE 17.8

Generalization
Pavlov demonstrated generalization by attaching miniature vibrators to various parts of a dog's body. After conditioning salivation to stimulation of the thigh, he stimulated other areas. The closer a stimulated spot was to the thigh, the stronger the conditioned response. (From Pavlov, 1927.)

taught to fear moving cars in the street respond similarly to trucks and motorcycles. So automatic is the generalization that one Argentine writer who underwent torture still recoils with fear when he sees black shoes—his first glimpse of his torturers when they approached his cell. The phenomenon has been brought to the laboratory in studies comparing abused with nonabused children. Shown an angry face on a computer screen, abused children's brain-wave responses are dramatically stronger and longer lasting (Pollak & others, 1998).

Because of generalization, stimuli that are similar to naturally disgusting or appealing objects will, by association, evoke some disgust or liking. Normally desirable foods, such as fudge, are unappealing when presented in a disgusting form, as when shaped to resemble dog feces (Rozin & others, 1986). We perceive adults with childlike facial features (round face, large forehead, small chin, large eyes) as having childlike warmth, submissiveness, and naiveté (Berry & McArthur, 1986). In both cases, people's emotional reactions to one stimulus generalize to similar stimuli.

Discrimination

Pavlov's dogs also learned to respond to the sound of a particular tone and *not* to other tones. **Discrimination** is the learned ability to *distinguish* between a conditioned stimulus (which predicts the UCS) and other irrelevant stimuli. Like generalization, discrimination has survival value. Slightly different stimuli are at times followed by vastly different consequences. Being able to recognize these differences is adaptive. Confronted by a pit bull, your heart may race; confronted by a golden retriever, it likely will not. Facing an approaching group of skinheads, you may cross the street to avoid them; approaching some bald gentlemen, you don't.

Updating Pavlov's Understanding

PREVIEW QUESTION 3 How do cognitive processes and biological constraints affect classical conditioning?

Pavlov's dismissing "mentalistic" concepts such as consciousness has given way to a growing realization that he underestimated the importance of cognitive processes (thoughts, perceptions, expectations) and of biological constraints on an organism's learning capacity.

Cognitive Processes

The early behaviorists believed that the learned behaviors of various organisms could be reduced to mindless mechanisms. The idea that rats and dogs exhibit cognition therefore struck many psychologists as unnecessary. No longer. Robert Rescorla and Allan Wagner (1972) argued that when two significant events occur close together in time, an animal learns the *predictability* of the second event. If a shock always is preceded by a tone, and then sometimes also by a light that accompanies the tone, a rat will react with fear to the tone but not to the light. Although the light is always followed by the shock, the tone better predicts impending shock. The more predictable the association, the stronger the conditioned response. It's as if the animal learns an *expectancy,* an awareness of how likely it is that the UCS will occur.

This principle helps explain why classical conditioning treatments that ignore cognition often have limited success. For example, people receiving therapy for alcoholism sometimes are given alcohol spiked with a nauseating drug. Will they then associate alcohol with sickness? If classical conditioning were merely a matter of "stamping in" stimulus associations, we might hope so, and—to some extent—this

■ **discrimination** in classical conditioning, the learned ability to distinguish between a conditioned stimulus and other stimuli that do not signal an unconditioned stimulus.

Stimulus generalization:

"I don't care if she's a tape dispenser. I love her."

"All brains are, in essence, anticipation machines."

Daniel C. Dennett, *Consciousness Explained,*
1991

Answer to questions on page 241: The cake (and its taste) are the UCS. The associated aroma is the CS. Salivation to the aroma is the CR.

does occur. However, those receiving the drink are aware that they can blame their nausea on the drug, not on the alcohol. This cognition often weakens the association between alcohol and feeling sick. So, even in classical conditioning, it is not only the simple CS–UCS association but also the thought that counts.

Biological Predispositions

Ever since Darwin, scientists have assumed that all animals share a common evolutionary history and resulting commonalities in their makeup and functioning. Pavlov and Watson, for example, believed the basic laws of learning were essentially similar in all animals. So it should make little difference whether one studied pigeons or people. Moreover, it seemed that any natural response could be conditioned to any neutral stimulus. As learning researcher Gregory Kimble proclaimed in 1956, "Just about any activity of which the organism is capable can be conditioned and . . . these responses can be conditioned to any stimulus that the organism can perceive" (p. 195).

Twenty-five years later Kimble (1981) humbly acknowledged that "half a thousand" scientific reports had proven him wrong. More than the early behaviorists realized, an animal's capacity for conditioning is constrained by its biology. The biological predispositions of each species dispose it to learn the particular associations that enhance its survival. Environments are not the whole story.

Among those who challenged the prevailing behaviorist environmentalism was John Garcia. While researching the effects of radiation on laboratory animals, Garcia and Robert Koelling (1966) noticed that rats began to avoid drinking the water from the plastic bottles in radiation chambers. They wondered whether classical conditioning might be the culprit. Might the rats have linked the plastic-tasting water (a CS) to the sickness (UCR) triggered by the internal state (UCS)?

To test their hunch, Garcia and Koelling gave the rats a particular taste, sight, or sound (CS) and later also gave them radiation or drugs that led to nausea and vomiting (UCR). Two startling findings emerged: First, even if sickened as late as several hours after tasting a particular flavor, the rats thereafter avoided that flavor. This appeared to violate the notion that for conditioning to occur, the UCS must follow the CS immediately.

Second, the sickened rats developed aversions to the tastes but not to the sights or sounds. This contradicted the behaviorists' idea that any perceivable stimulus could serve as a CS. But it made adaptive sense, because for rats the easiest way to identify tainted food is to taste it. (If sickened after sampling a new food, they thereafter avoid the food—which makes it difficult to eradicate a population of "bait-shy" rats by poisoning.) Birds, which hunt by sight, appear biologically primed to develop aversions to the *sight* of tainted food (Nicolaus & others, 1983).

Humans, too, seem biologically prepared to learn some things rather than others. If you get violently ill four hours after eating contaminated mussels, you will probably develop an aversion to the taste of mussels but not to the sight of the associated restaurant, its plates, the people you were with, or the music you heard there. Similarly, we more easily learn an aversion to alcohol by associating its taste with nausea rather than with something unrelated to consumption, such as electric shock. We also more readily learn to fear snakes and spiders than to fear flowers (Cook & others, 1986). Again, it makes sense: Such animals harm us more frequently than do flowers.

All these cases support Darwin's principle that natural selection favors traits that aid survival. Nature prepares the members of each species to learn those things crucial to their survival. Someone who readily learns a taste aversion is unlikely to eat the same toxic food again and is more likely to survive and leave descendants. Indeed, all sorts of bad feelings, from nausea to anxiety to pain, serve good purposes. Like the low-oil light on a car dashboard, each alerts the body to a threat (Neese, 1991).

John Garcia

As the laboring son of California farmworkers, Garcia attended school only in the off-season during his early childhood years. After entering junior college in his late twenties, and earning his Ph.D. in his late forties, he received the American Psychological Association's Distinguished Scientific Contribution Award "for his highly original, pioneering research in conditioning and learning." He was also elected to the National Academy of Sciences.

Garcia and Koelling's provocative findings have been extended to other species. In one well-known study, coyotes and wolves that were tempted into eating sheep carcasses laced with a sickening poison developed an aversion to sheep meat (Gustavson & others, 1974, 1976). Two wolves that were later penned with a live sheep seemed actually to fear it.

Such research suggests possible humane ways for controlling predators and agricultural pests. This is but one instance in which psychological research that began with the discomfort of some laboratory animals enhanced the welfare of many more animals. In this case, the research saved the sheep from the coyotes. The coyotes in turn were saved from angry ranchers and farmers who, with their livestock no longer endangered, were less adamant about destroying the coyotes. Later experiments revealed that conditioned taste aversion could successfully prevent baboons from raiding African gardens, racoons from attacking chickens, and ravens and crows from feeding on crane eggs—all while preserving predators who occupy an important ecological niche (Garcia & Gustavson, 1997).

Has research on biological constraints compelled researchers to abandon the search for universal principles of learning that generalize across species? No. Biological predispositions affirm a deeper principle: *Learning enables animals to adapt to their environments.* Adaptation shows us why animals would be responsive to stimuli that announce significant events, such as food or pain. Animals are generally predisposed to associate a CS with a UCS that follows predictably and immediately—for causes often immediately precede effects.

Adaptation also helps explain exceptions, such as the taste-aversion finding. In this case, effect need not follow cause immediately—poisoned food usually causes sickness quite a while after the food has been eaten. Similarly, cancer patients who suffer nausea and vomiting beginning more than an hour following chemotherapy often develop classically conditioned nausea to stimuli associated with taking the drug (**FIGURE 17.9**). After four or five clinic visits, merely returning to the clinic's waiting room or seeing the nurses can provoke anxiety and anticipatory nausea (Burish & Carey, 1986; Davey, 1992; Hall, 1997). (Under normal circumstances, such revulsion to sickening stimuli is adaptive.)

Taste aversion

If you became violently ill after eating mussels, you probably would have a hard time eating them again. Their smell and taste would have become a CS for nausea. This learning occurs readily because our biology prepares us to learn taste aversions to toxic foods.

"Once bitten, twice shy."

G. F. Northall, *Folk-Phrases*, 1894

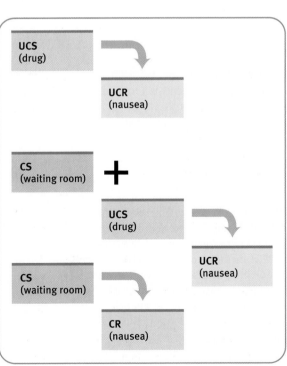

FIGURE 17.9

Nausea conditioning among cancer patients

Pavlov's Legacy

PREVIEW QUESTION 4 Why does Pavlov's work remain so important?

Judged by today's knowledge of cognitive processes and biological predispositions, Pavlov's ideas were incomplete. But if we see further than Pavlov did, it is because we stand on his shoulders. All the researchers we have met so far in this module agree that classical conditioning is a basic form of learning.

If Pavlov had taught us only that old dogs can learn new tricks, his experiments would long ago have been forgotten. Why should anyone care that a dog can be conditioned to drool at the sound of a tone? The importance lies first in this fact: Many other responses to many other stimuli can be classically conditioned in many other organisms—in fact, in every species tested, from earthworms to fish to dogs to monkeys to people (Schwartz, 1984). Thus, classical conditioning is one way that virtually all organisms learn to adapt to their environment.

Second, Pavlov showed us how a process such as learning can be studied objectively. Pavlov was proud that his methods involved virtually no subjective judgments or guesses about what went on in the dogs' minds. The salivary response is an overt behavior measurable as so many drops or cubic centimeters of saliva. Pavlov's success therefore suggested a scientific model for how the young discipline of psychology might proceed—by isolating the elementary building blocks of complex behaviors and studying them with objective laboratory procedures.

CLOSE-UP:

RAPE AS CLASSICAL CONDITIONING

"A burnt child dreads the fire," says a medieval proverb. Experiments with dogs reveal that, indeed, if a painful stimulus is sufficiently powerful, a single event is sometimes enough to traumatize the animal when it again faces the situation. The human counterparts to these experiments can be tragic, as illustrated by one woman's experience of being attacked and raped, and thereby conditioned to a life of fear. Her fear (CR) is most powerfully associated with particular locations and people (CS), but it generalizes to other places and people. Note, too, how her traumatic experience has robbed her of the normally relaxing associations with such stimuli as home and bed.

Four months ago I was raped. In the middle of the night I awoke to the sound of someone outside my bedroom. Thinking my housemate was coming home, I called out her name.

Someone began walking slowly toward me, and then I realized. I screamed and fought, but there were two of them. One held my legs, while the other put a hand over my mouth and a knife to my throat and said, "Shut up, bitch, or we'll kill you." Never have I been so terrified and helpless. They both raped me, one brutally. As they then searched my room for money and valuables, my housemate came home. They brought her into my room, raped her, and left us both tied up on my bed. We never slept another night in that apartment. We were too terrified. Still, when I go to bed at night—always with the bedroom light left on— the memory of them entering my room repeats itself endlessly. I was an independent person who had lived alone or with other women for four years; now I can't even think about spending a night alone. When I drive by our old apartment, or when I have to go into an empty house, my heart

pounds and I sweat. I am afraid of strangers, especially men, and the more they resemble my attackers the more I fear them. My housemate shares many of my fears, and is frightened when entering our new apartment. I'm afraid to stay in the same town, I'm afraid it will happen again, I'm afraid to go to bed. I dread falling asleep.

Eleven years later this woman could report—as do many trauma victims (Gluhoski & Wortman, 1996)— that her conditioned fears were gradually extinguishing:

The frequency and intensity of my fears have subsided. Still, I remain cautious about personal safety and occasionally have nightmares about my experience. But more important is my renewed ability to laugh, love, and trust—both old friends and new. Life is once again joyful. I have survived.

(From personal correspondence, with permission.)

Applications of Classical Conditioning

Psychologists have designed applications of Pavlov's principles of classical conditioning to improve human health and well-being in multiple contexts, including motivation, emotion, therapy for psychological disorders, and health problems. Here are a few examples:

- Former crack cocaine users often feel a craving when they again encounter cues (people, places) associated with previous highs. Thus, drug counselors advise addicts to steer clear of settings associated with the euphoria of previous drug use.

- Classical conditioning even works on the body's disease-fighting immune system. When a particular taste accompanies a drug that influences immune responses, the taste by itself may come to produce an immune response.

- Animals deprived of the neurotransmitter acetylcholine, essential for the transmission of certain nerve impulses, have difficulty being conditioned to blink in response to a tone that has previously signaled an impending air puff. Alzheimer's patients' brains are similarly short of acetylcholine, and they, too, have difficulty with this conditioning. Diana Woodruff-Pak and Michelle Papka (1999) report that older adults who condition easily rarely have Alzheimer's disease and are unlikely soon to develop it. These findings have motivated a new search for drugs that will enhance conditioning in animals—and perhaps help delay the onset of Alzheimer's (Azar, 1999).

Pavlov's work also provided a basis for John Watson's (1913) idea that human behavior, though biologically influenced, is mainly a bundle of conditioned responses. In one famous study, Watson and Rosalie Rayner (1920; Harris, 1979) showed how specific fears might be conditioned. Their subject was an 11-month-old infant named Albert. Like most infants, "Little Albert" feared loud noises but not white rats. Watson and Rayner presented him with a white rat and, as he reached to touch it, struck a hammer against a steel bar just behind his head. After seven repetitions of seeing the rat and then hearing the frightening noise, Albert burst into tears at the mere sight of the rat (an ethically troublesome study by today's standards). What is more, five days later Albert showed generalization of his conditioned response by reacting with fear to a rabbit, a dog, and a sealskin coat, but not to dissimilar objects such as toys (**FIGURE 17.10**).

Although Little Albert's fate is unknown, Watson's is not. After losing his professorship at Johns Hopkins University over an affair with Rayner (whom he later married), he became the J. Walter Thompson advertising agency's resident psychologist. There he used his knowledge of associative learning to conceive many successful campaigns, including one for Maxwell House that helped make the "coffee break" an American custom (Hunt, 1993).

Although some psychologists had difficulty repeating Watson and Rayner's findings with other children, the work with Little Albert has had legendary significance for many psychologists. Some have wondered if each of us might not be a walking repository of conditioned emotions (see Close-Up on page 246 on the

John B. Watson

Watson (1924) admitted to "going beyond my facts" when offering his famous boast: "Give me a dozen healthy infants, well-formed, and my own specified world to bring them up in and I'll guarantee to take any one at random and train him to become any type of specialist I might select—doctor, lawyer, artist, merchant-chief, and, yes, even beggar-man and thief, regardless of his talents, penchants, tendencies, abilities, vocations, and race of his ancestors."

FIGURE 17.10

Little Albert's conditioning

The pairing of a laboratory rat with a terribly loud noise gave Little Albert a conditioned fear (the CR) of both rats (the CS) and similar furry things (generalization).

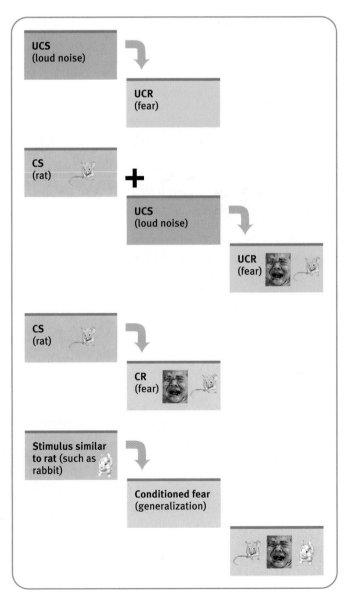

aftermath of rape). Might our worst emotions be controlled by the application of extinction procedures or by conditioning new responses to emotion-arousing stimuli? Psychologists who use behavioral techniques to treat emotional disorders believe they could be. One therapist told a patient, who for 30 years had feared going into an elevator alone, to force himself to enter 20 elevators a day. Within 10 days, his fear nearly vanished (Ellis & Becker, 1982).

rehearse it!

1. Learning is defined as "a relatively permanent change in behavior due to
   a. instinct."
   b. mental processes."
   c. experience with the environment."
   d. education or schooling."

2. Associative learning involves learning that certain events occur together. Two forms of associative learning are classical conditioning, in which the organism associates _____, and operant conditioning, in which the organism associates _____.
   a. two responses; a response and a consequence
   b. two stimuli; two responses
   c. two stimuli; a response and a consequence
   d. two responses; two stimuli

3. Working with dogs, Pavlov paired a tone or other neutral stimulus with food in the mouth. The dogs then came to salivate when presented with the neutral stimulus alone. Salivation in response to food in the mouth occurs naturally in dogs, without conditioning; food is therefore the uncondi-

tioned stimulus (UCS). Salivation in response to a tone must be learned; the tone is therefore a (an)
   a. conditioned stimulus.
   b. unconditioned stimulus.
   c. conditioned response.
   d. unconditioned response.

4. Dogs can learn to respond to one kind of stimulus and not to another—for example, to salivate at the sight of a circle (the CS) but not a square. Distinguishing between a CS and an irrelevant stimulus is
   a. generalization.
   b. discrimination.
   c. acquisition.
   d. spontaneous recovery.

5. Early behaviorists believed that for conditioning to occur, the unconditioned stimulus (UCS) must immediately follow the conditioned stimulus (CS). _____ demonstrated this was not always so.
   a. The Little Albert experiment
   b. Pavlov's experiments with dogs
   c. Watson's behaviorism theory
   d. Garcia and Koelling's taste-aversion studies

6. Research by Garcia and Koelling showed that rats developed aversions to certain tastes but not to sights or sounds, thus supporting
   a. Pavlov's demonstration of generalization.
   b. Darwin's principle that natural selection favors traits that aid survival.
   c. Watson's view that study should be limited to observable behavior.
   d. Kimble's original view that organisms can be conditioned to any stimulus.

7. Watson and Rayner classically conditioned a small child named Albert to fear a white rat. After Watson paired the rat with a frightening noise, Little Albert cried when the rat was presented (even without the noise). The child later showed fear in response to a rabbit, a dog, and a sealskin coat. Little Albert's fear of objects resembling the rat illustrates
   a. extinction.
   b. generalization of the conditioned response.
   c. spontaneous recovery.
   d. discrimination between two stimuli.

Operant Conditioning

PREVIEW QUESTION 5 What is operant conditioning, and how does it differ from classical conditioning?

Classical conditioning associates neutral stimuli with important stimuli that produce responses that are often automatic. It's one thing to teach an animal to salivate at the sound of a tone or a child to fear cars in the street; it's something else to teach an elephant to walk on its hind legs or a child to say *please*. Another type of associative learning explains—and trains—such behaviors. Through **operant conditioning** subjects associate behaviors with their consequences. Thus, they become more likely to repeat rewarded (reinforced) behaviors and less likely to repeat punished behaviors.

Both classical and operant conditioning involve acquisition, extinction, spontaneous recovery, generalization, and discrimination. Yet their difference is straightforward: Classical conditioning forms associations between stimuli (a CS and the UCS it signals). It also involves **respondent behavior**—behavior that occurs as an *automatic* response to some stimulus (such as salivating in response to meat powder and later

■ **operant conditioning** a type of learning in which behavior is strengthened if followed by reinforcement or diminished if followed by punishment.

■ **respondent behavior** behavior that occurs as an automatic response to some stimulus.

in response to a tone). Operant conditioning involves **operant behavior,** so-called because the act *operates* on the environment to produce rewarding or punishing stimuli. We can therefore distinguish classical from operant conditioning by asking: *Is the organism learning associations between events that it doesn't control (classical conditioning)? Or is it learning associations between its behavior and resulting events (operant conditioning)?*

Skinner's Experiments

PREVIEW QUESTION 6 How is behavior shaped?

B. F. Skinner (1904–1990) was a college English major and an aspiring writer who, seeking a new direction, entered graduate school in psychology. He went on to become modern behaviorism's most influential and controversial figure. Skinner's work elaborated a simple fact of life that psychologist Edward L. Thorndike (1874–1949) called the **law of effect:** *Rewarded behavior is likely to recur.* Using Thorndike's law of effect as a starting point, Skinner developed a "behavioral technology" that revealed principles of behavior control. These principles also enabled him to teach pigeons such unpigeonlike behaviors as walking in a figure 8, playing Ping-Pong, and keeping a missile on course by pecking at a target on a screen.

For his pioneering studies with rats (and later with pigeons), Skinner designed an **operant chamber,** popularly known as the *Skinner box.* The box is typically soundproof, with a bar or key that an animal presses or pecks to release a reward of food or water, and has an attached device that records the animal's responses.

Experiments by Skinner and other operant researchers did far more than teach us how to pull habits out of a rat. They explored the precise conditions that foster efficient and enduring learning.

Shaping

In his experiments, Skinner used **shaping,** a procedure in which reinforcers, such as food, gradually guide an animal's behavior toward a desired behavior. Imagine that you wanted to condition a rat to press a bar. After observing how the animal naturally behaves before training, you would build on its existing behaviors. You might give the rat a food reward each time it approaches the bar. Once the rat is approaching regularly, you would require it to move closer before rewarding it, then closer still; finally, you would require it to touch the bar before you gave it the food. With this method of *successive approximations,* you reward responses that are ever-closer to the final desired behavior, and you ignore all other responses. By making rewards contingent on desired behaviors, researchers and animal trainers gradually *shape* complex behaviors.

By shaping nonverbal organisms to discriminate between stimuli, a psychologist can also determine what they perceive. Can a dog distinguish colors? Can a baby discriminate sounds? If we can shape them to respond to one stimulus and not to an-

■ **operant behavior** behavior that operates on the environment, producing consequences.

■ **law of effect** Thorndike's principle that behaviors followed by favorable consequences become more likely.

■ **operant chamber** a chamber containing a bar or key that an animal can manipulate to obtain a food or water reinforcer, with attached devices to record the animal's rate of bar pressing or key pecking. Used in operant conditioning research (Also called Skinner box.)

■ **shaping** an operant conditioning procedure in which reinforcers guide behavior toward closer and closer approximations of a desired goal.

DENNIS THE MENACE

"I think Mom's using the can opener."

The law of effect at Stingray City
For 35 years, Cayman Islands fishing crews have gathered conch and cleaned them over this barrier reef. Stingrays in the surrounding bay gradually became accustomed to these yummy treats. Noticing the rays congregating, scuba divers then began feeding the increasingly friendly rays by hand. Today, tourists can do the same and can even pet the rays as they graze past them.

A discriminating creature
University of Windsor psychologist Dale Woodyard uses a food reward to train this manatee to discriminate between objects of different shapes, colors, and sizes. A manatee can remember such responses for as long as a year.

other, then obviously they can perceive the difference. Experiments show that some animals are remarkably capable of forming concepts; they demonstrate this by discriminating between classes of events or objects. If an experimenter reinforces a pigeon for pecking after seeing a human face, but not after seeing other images, the pigeon will learn to recognize a face (Herrnstein & Loveland, 1964). After being trained to discriminate among flowers, people, cars, and chairs, pigeons can usually identify in which of these categories a new pictured object belongs (Bhatt & others, 1988; Wasserman, 1993). With training, pigeons have even been taught to discriminate between Bach's music and Stravinsky's (Porter & Neuringer, 1984).

In the shaping procedure, the trainer builds on the organism's existing behaviors by expecting and immediately rewarding successively closer approximations of a desired behavior. In everyday life, too, we continually reward and shape the behavior of others, said Skinner, but we often do so unintentionally. Sometimes we unthinkingly reward behaviors we find annoying. Billy's whining, for example, annoys his mystified parents, but look how they typically deal with Billy.

Billy:	Could you tie my shoes?
Father:	(Continues reading paper.)
Billy:	Dad, I need my shoes tied.
Father:	Uh, yeah, just a minute.
Billy:	DAAAAD! TIE MY SHOES!
Father:	How many times have I told you not to whine? Now, which shoe do we do first?

Or consider the way some teachers use rewards. On a wall chart, the teacher pastes gold stars after the names of children scoring 100 percent on spelling tests. All children take the same tests. As everyone can then see, some children, the academic all-stars, easily get 100 percent. The others, no matter how hard they try or how much they improve, get no reward. The teacher would be better advised to apply the principles of operant conditioning—to reward all spellers for gradual improvements (successive approximations toward perfect spelling of words they find challenging).

Principles of Reinforcement

PREVIEW QUESTION 7 What are the basic types of reinforcers?

People often refer rather loosely to the power of "rewards." This idea gains a more precise meaning in Skinner's concept of **reinforcement,** any event that increases the frequency of a preceding response. A *positive* reinforcer may be a tangible reward. It may be praise or attention. Or it may be an activity—being able to use the car when the dishes are done, or to have a break after an hour of study.

Most people think of reinforcers as rewards. Actually, anything that serves to strengthen behavior is a reinforcer—even students being yelled at if yelling *increases* the offending behavior. There are two basic kinds of reinforcement (Table 17.1). One type (positive reinforcement) strengthens a response by *presenting* a stimulus after a response. Food is a positive reinforcer for animals; attention, approval, and money are positive reinforcers for most people. The other type (negative reinforcement) strengthens a response by reducing or *removing* an aversive stimulus. (Negative reinforcers, like negative numbers, subtract something.) Putting on a car seat belt may turn off the warning buzzer. Taking aspirin may relieve a headache. Dragging on a

TABLE 17.1

WAYS TO INCREASE BEHAVIOR

Operant Conditioning Term	Description	Example
Positive reinforcement	*Add* a positive stimulus	A hug, TV on
Negative reinforcement	*Remove* an aversive stimulus	Seat belt turns off buzzer

cigarette will reduce a nicotine addict's pangs. Pushing the snooze button silences the annoying alarm. All these involve negative reinforcement. When someone stops nagging or whining, that, too, is a reinforcer. (Note that contrary to popular usage, negative reinforcement is not aversive: It *removes* an aversive event.)

So imagine that whenever Billy throws a tantrum, his parents give in for the sake of peace and quiet. The child's tantrums will be reinforced when the parents give in. And the parents' behavior will be reinforced when Billy stops screaming. Or imagine a worried student who, after goofing off and getting a bad exam grade, studies harder for the next exam. The student's studying may be reinforced by reduced anxiety and by a better grade. Whether it works by giving something positive or by reducing something negative, *reinforcement is any consequence that strengthens behavior.*

PRIMARY AND CONDITIONED REINFORCERS **Primary reinforcers**—getting food or being relieved of electric shock—are innately satisfying. **Conditioned reinforcers,** also called *secondary reinforcers,* are learned. They get their power through association with primary reinforcers. If a rat in a Skinner box learns that a light reliably signals that food is coming, the rat will work to turn on the light. The light has become a secondary reinforcer associated with food. Our lives are filled with secondary reinforcers—money, good grades, a pleasant tone of voice, a word of praise—each of which has been linked with more basic rewards. Secondary reinforcers greatly enhance our ability to influence one another.

IMMEDIATE AND DELAYED REINFORCERS Let's return to the imaginary shaping experiment in which you were conditioning a rat to press a bar. Before performing this "wanted" behavior, the hungry rat will engage in a sequence of "unwanted" behaviors—scratching, sniffing, and moving around. Whichever of these behaviors immediately precedes the food reinforcer becomes more likely to recur. If you delay the reinforcement of bar pressing for longer than 30 seconds, allowing other behaviors to intervene and be reinforced, virtually no learning to press the bar will occur.

Unlike rats, humans do respond to reinforcers that are greatly delayed: the paycheck at the end of the week, the grade at the end of the semester, the trophy at the end of the season. Indeed, to function effectively we must learn to postpone immediate rewards for greater long-term rewards. Four-year-old children who in laboratory testing show an ability to delay gratification—who'd sooner have a big reward tomorrow than a small one right now—become more socially competent and more likely to be high achievers as adolescents (Mischel & others, 1989). A big step toward maturity—and toward gaining the most rewarding life—is learning to delay gratification, to control one's impulses in order to achieve more valued rewards (Logue, 1998a,b).

But to our detriment, small but immediate reinforcements are sometimes more alluring than big but delayed reinforcements. Smokers, alcoholics, and other drug users may know that their immediate pleasure—the kick that often comes within seconds—is more than offset by future ill effects. Still, immediate reinforcement prevails. Thus, hangovers do not prevent further drinking, and drugs such as nicotine and cocaine that provide the most immediate reinforcement are the most strongly addictive (Marlatt, 1991). Likewise, for many teens the immediate gratification of risky, unprotected sex in passionate moments prevails over the delayed gratifications of safe sex or saved sex (Loewenstein & Furstenberg, 1991). And the hour-long enjoyment of staying up to watch another TV show may seem to outweigh the prospect of tomorrow's day-long sluggishness.

Positive reinforcement
An A grade positively reinforces this boy's effort, as do his classmates' smiles and his teacher's praise.

HI AND LOIS

- **reinforcer** in operant conditioning, any event that *strengthens* the behavior it follows.

- **primary reinforcer** an innately reinforcing stimulus, such as one that satisfies a biological need.

- **conditioned reinforcer** a stimulus that gains its reinforcing power through its association with a primary reinforcer.(Also called secondary reinforcer.)

- **continuous reinforcement** reinforcing the desired response every time it occurs.
- **partial (intermittent) reinforcement** re-inforcing a response only part of the time; results in slower acquisition of a response but much greater resistance to extinction than does continuous reinforcement.
- **fixed-ratio schedule** in operant conditioning, a schedule of reinforcement that reinforces a response only after a specified number of responses.

"The charm of fishing is that it is the pursuit of what is elusive but attainable, a perpetual series of occasions for hope."

Scottish author John Buchan (1875–1940)

In operant conditioning, *acquisition* is the strengthening of a reinforced response. *Extinction* occurs when a response is no longer reinforced. *Generalization* and *discrimination* occur as organisms' responses to various stimuli that do or do not signal that a behavior will be reinforced.

Door-to-door salespeople are reinforced by which schedule? People checking the oven to see if the cookies are done are on which schedule? Airline frequent-flyer programs that offer a free flight after every 25,000 miles of travel use which reinforcement schedule? (See page 257.)

Reinforcement Schedules

PREVIEW QUESTION 8 How do different reinforcement schedules affect behavior?

So far, most of our examples assume **continuous reinforcement:** The desired response is reinforced every time it occurs. Under such conditions, learning occurs rapidly. But when the reinforcement stops—when we disconnect the food delivery chute—extinction also occurs rapidly. If the experimenter withholds food pellets, the rat soon stops pressing the bar. If a normally dependable candy machine fails to deliver a chocolate bar twice in a row, we stop putting money into it (although a week later we may exhibit spontaneous recovery by trying again).

Real life often does not provide continuous reinforcement. A salesperson does not make a sale with every pitch, nor does an angler get a bite with every cast. But they persist because their efforts have occasionally been rewarded. Researchers have explored several **partial (intermittent) reinforcement** schedules in which responses are sometimes reinforced, sometimes not (Nevin, 1988). Initial learning is typically slower with intermittent reinforcement, which makes continuous reinforcement preferable until a behavior is mastered. But intermittent reinforcement produces greater persistence—greater *resistance to extinction*—than is found with continuous reinforcement. Imagine a pigeon that has learned to peck a key to obtain food. When the experimenter gradually phases out the delivery of food until it occurs only rarely and unpredictably, pigeons may peck 150,000 times without a reward (Skinner, 1953). With intermittent reinforcement, hope springs eternal.

Corresponding human examples come readily to mind. Slot machines reward gamblers occasionally and unpredictably. This intermittent reinforcement affects them much as it affects pigeons: They keep trying, sometimes interminably. There is also a valuable lesson here for parents. *Occasionally* giving in to children's tantrums for the sake of peace and quiet puts the child on an intermittent reinforcement schedule. That is the very best procedure for making a behavior persist.

Skinner (1961) and his collaborators compared four schedules of partial reinforcement. Some are rigidly fixed, some unpredictably variable.

Fixed-ratio schedules reinforce behavior after a set number of responses. Like people paid on a piecework basis—say, for every 30 pieces—laboratory animals may be reinforced on a fixed ratio of, say, one reinforcer for every 30 responses. Once conditioned, the animal will pause only briefly after a reinforcer and will then return to a high rate of responding (**FIGURE 17.11**). Because resting while on a fixed-ratio schedule reduces rewards, employees often find such arrangements tiring. Unions have therefore pressured employers to replace piecework pay with hourly wage schedules.

Variable-ratio schedules provide reinforcers after an unpredictable number of responses. This is what gamblers and anglers experience—unpredictable reinforcement—and what makes gambling and fishing so hard to extinguish. Like the fixed-ratio schedule, the variable-ratio schedule produces high rates of responding, because reinforcers increase as the responding increases.

Fixed-interval schedules reinforce the first response after a fixed time period. Like people checking more frequently for the mail as the delivery time approaches, or checking to see if the cookies are done or the Jell-O is set, pigeons on a fixed-interval schedule peck a key more frequently as the anticipated time for reward draws near, producing a choppy stop-start pattern (Figure 17.11).

Variable-interval schedules reinforce the first response after *varying* time intervals. Like the unpredictable pop quiz that reinforces studying or the "Hello" that finally rewards persistence in redialing a busy phone number, variable-interval schedules tend to produce slow, steady responding. This makes sense, because there is no knowing when the waiting will be over. Should the pop quiz become predictable, students will begin the stop-start work pattern that characterizes fixed-interval schedules.

Animal behaviors differ, yet Skinner (1956) contended that these reinforcement principles of operant conditioning are universal. It matters little, he said, what response, what reinforcer, or what species you use. The effect of a given reinforcement schedule is pretty much the same: "Pigeon, rat, monkey, which is which? It doesn't matter. . . . Behavior shows astonishingly similar properties."

Punishment

PREVIEW QUESTION 9 How does punishment affect behavior?

The effect of **punishment** is opposite that of reinforcement. Reinforcement increases a behavior; punishment decreases it. Thus, a punisher is any consequence that *decreases* the frequency of a preceding behavior. Swift and sure punishers can powerfully restrain unwanted behavior. The dog that learns to come running at the sound of the electric can opener will learn to hide if its master starts running the can opener to attract and catch it for banishment to the basement. The rat that is shocked after touching the forbidden object and the child who loses a treat after running into the street will learn not to repeat the behavior.

Boys Town psychologist Robert Larzelere (1996, 1998, 1999) notes a problem with human punishment studies, which often find that spanked children are at increased risk for aggression, depression, and low self-esteem. Well, yes, says Larzelere, just as people who have received radiation treatments are more likely to die of cancer, and people who have undergone psychotherapy are more likely to suffer depression—because they had preexisting problems that triggered the treatments. If one adjusts for preexisting cancer or depression—or antisocial behavior—then radiation, psychotherapy, or an occasional single swat or two of misbehaving 2- to 6-year-olds looks more effective. That is especially so if the swat is combined with a generous dose of reasoning and positive parenting, and if it is used only as a backup to enhance the effectiveness of milder disciplinary tactics such as reasoning and time-out.

Nevertheless, say advocates of nonviolent parenting, physical punishment has drawbacks. Punished behavior is not forgotten; it is suppressed. This temporary suppression may (negatively) reinforce the parents' punishing behavior. The child swears, the parent swats, the parent hears no more swearing from the child, and the parent feels the punishment was successful in stopping the behavior. But was it? If the punishment is avoidable, the punished behavior may reappear in safe settings. The child may simply learn not to swear around the house but to swear elsewhere. The driver who is hit with a couple of speeding tickets may buy a radar detector and speed freely when no radar patrol is around.

Punishment may also increase aggressiveness by demonstrating that aggression is a way to cope with problems. This helps explain why so many aggressive delinquents and abusive parents come from abusive families (Straus & Gelles, 1980; Straus & others, 1997). Moreover, punishment can create fear; the person receiving the punishment may associate the fear not only with the undesirable behavior but also with the person who administers it or with the situation in which it occurs. Thus, a child may come to fear the punitive teacher and want to avoid school. For such

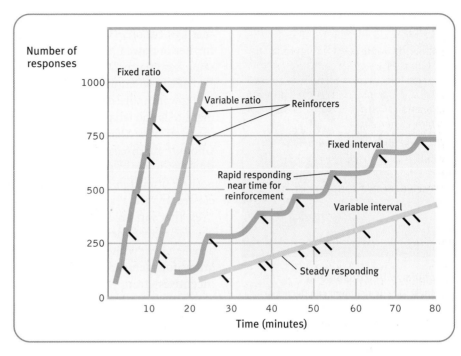

FIGURE 17.11

Intermittent reinforcement schedules Skinner's laboratory pigeons produced these response patterns to each of four reinforcement schedules. (Reinforcers are indicated by diagonal marks.) For people, as for pigeons, reinforcement linked to number of responses (a ratio schedule) produces a higher response rate than reinforcement linked to amount of time elapsed (interval schedule). But the predictability of the reward also matters. A predictable (fixed) schedule produces a higher response rate than an unpredictable (variable) schedule. (Adapted from "Teaching Machines" by B. F. Skinner. Copyright © 1961, Scientific American, Inc. All rights reserved.)

■ **variable-ratio schedule** in operant conditioning, a schedule of reinforcement that reinforces a response after an unpredictable number of responses.

■ **fixed-interval schedule** in operant conditioning, a schedule of reinforcement that reinforces a response only after a specified time has elapsed.

■ **variable-interval schedule** in operant conditioning, a schedule of reinforcement that reinforces a response at unpredictable time intervals.

■ **punishment** an event that decreases the behavior that it follows.

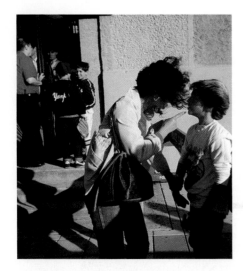

A problem with punishment
Swift and sure punishment can decrease unwanted behavior, but it can also evoke undesired responses, such as anger, fear, or resistance.

reasons, most European countries have banned hitting children in schools and child-care institutions (Leach, 1993, 1994). The Scandinavian countries and Austria have further outlawed physical punishment by parents, thereby extending to children the same legal protection given to spouses.

Even when punishment suppresses unwanted behavior, it often does not guide one toward more desirable behavior. Punishment tells you what *not* to do; reinforcement tells you what *to* do. Thus, punishment combined with reinforcement is usually more effective than punishment alone. This approach has been used with children who bite themselves or bang their heads. They may be mildly punished (say, with a squirt of water in the face) whenever they bite themselves, but also be rewarded with positive attention and food when they behave well. The approach also works in the classroom. The teacher whose feedback on a paper says "No, but try this . . . " and "Yes, that's it!" reduces unwanted behavior by reinforcing alternative behaviors.

Parents of delinquent youth often lack this awareness of how to reinforce desirable behavior without screaming or hitting (Patterson & others, 1982). Training programs for such parents help them reframe contingencies from dire threats to positive incentives—from "You clean up your room this minute or no dinner!" to "You're welcome at the dinner table after you get your room cleaned up." When you stop to think about it, many threats of punishment are just as forceful, and perhaps more effective, if rephrased positively. Thus, "If you don't get your homework done, there'll be no TV" would better be phrased as. . . .

To sum up, most psychologists favor an emphasis on reinforcement rather than on punishment. Notice people doing something right and affirm them for it.

Updating Skinner's Understanding

PREVIEW QUESTION 10 How do cognitive processes and biological constraints affect operant conditioning?

Skinner granted the existence of private processes and the biological underpinnings of behavior. Nevertheless, many psychologists criticized him for discounting the importance of these processes and predispositions.

Cognition and Operant Conditioning

A mere eight days before dying of leukemia, Skinner (1990) stood before the American Psychological Association convention for one final critique of "cognitive science," which he viewed as a throwback to early-twentieth-century introspectionism in psychology. Skinner died resisting the growing belief that cognitive processes—thoughts, perceptions, expectations—have a necessary place in the science of psychology and even in our understanding of conditioning. (He regarded thoughts and emotions as behaviors that follow the same laws as other behaviors.) Yet we have seen several hints that cognitive processes might be at work in operant learning. For example, animals on a fixed-interval reinforcement schedule respond more and more frequently as the time approaches when a response will produce a reinforcer. The animals behave as if they expect that repeating the response will soon produce the reward. (To a strict behaviorist, however, talk of "expectations" is unnecessary; it is enough to say that responses that are reinforced under certain conditions recur when those conditions recur.)

Evidence of cognitive processes has come from studying rats in mazes. Rats exploring a maze, with no obvious reward, are like people driving around a new town. The rats seem to develop a **cognitive map,** a mental representation of the maze. This occurs even if they are carried passively through the maze in a wire basket. When an experimenter then places a reward in the maze's goal box, the rats immediately perform as well as rats that have been reinforced with food for running the maze.

■ **cognitive map** a mental representation of the layout of one's environment. For example, after exploring a maze, rats act as if they have learned a cognitive map of it.

■ **latent learning** learning that occurs but is not apparent until there is an incentive to demonstrate it.

During their explorations, the rats seemingly experience **latent learning**—learning that becomes apparent only when there is some incentive to demonstrate it. The conclusion: Learning can occur without reinforcement. As the cognitive-mapping experiments suggest, there is more to learning than associating a response with a consequence. There is also cognition. Researchers have found striking evidence of animals' cognitive abilities in solving problems and in using aspects of language.

Biological Predispositions

As with classical conditioning, an animal's natural predispositions constrain its capacity for operant conditioning. When you reinforce a hamster's behavior with food, you can easily condition it to dig or to rear up, because these are among the animal's natural behaviors when searching for food. But it is difficult to use food as a reinforcer to shape hamster behaviors—such as face washing—that aren't normally associated with food or hunger (Shettleworth, 1973). Similarly, pigeons easily learn to flap their wings to avoid being shocked and to peck to obtain food, because it is natural for them to flee with their wings and eat with their beaks. However, they have a hard time learning to peck in order to avoid a shock or to flap their wings to obtain food (Foree & LoLordo, 1973). Biological constraints predispose organisms to learn associations that are naturally adaptive.

Skinner's former associates, Keller Breland and Marian Breland (1961), came to appreciate biological predispositions while using operant procedures to train animals for circuses, TV shows, and movies. The Brelands had originally assumed that operant principles would work on almost any response that any animal could make. But after training 6000 animals of 38 different species, from chickens to whales, they concluded that biological predispositions were more important than they had supposed. In one act, they trained pigs to pick up large wooden "dollars" and deposit them in a piggy bank. After learning this behavior, however, the animals began to drift back to their natural ways. They would drop the coin, push it with their snouts as pigs are prone to do, pick it up again, and then repeat the sequence—delaying their food reinforcer. As this "instinctive drift" illustrates, "misbehaviors" occurred when the animals reverted to their biologically predisposed patterns.

Skinner's Legacy:
Applications of Operant Conditioning

PREVIEW QUESTION 11 How might educators, business managers, and other individuals apply operant conditioning?

B. F. Skinner was one of the most controversial intellectual figures of the late twentieth century. He stirred a hornet's nest by repeatedly insisting that external influences (not internal thoughts and feelings) shape behavior and by urging the use of operant principles to influence people's behavior at school, work, and home. Recognizing that behavior is shaped by its consequences, we should administer rewards in ways that promote more desirable behavior.

Skinner's critics objected, saying that he dehumanized people by neglecting their personal freedom and by seeking to control their actions. Skinner's reply: People's behavior is already haphazardly controlled by external consequences, so why not administer those consequences for human betterment? In place of the punishments used in homes, schools, and prisons, would not reinforcers be more humanitarian? And if it is humbling to think that we are shaped by our histories, this very idea also gives us hope that we can shape our future.

Psychologists apply operant conditioning principles to problems ranging from high blood pressure to social withdrawal. Behavioral economists are applying operant principles to their study of consumer behavior and drug use and abuse. Reinforcement technologies are also at work in schools, businesses, and homes.

For more information on animal behavior, see books by (I am not making this up) Robin Fox and Lionel Tiger.

Natural athletes
Animals can most easily learn and retain behaviors that draw on their biological predispositions, such as cats' inborn tendency to leap high and land on their feet.

"Never try to teach a pig to sing. It wastes your time and annoys the pig."

Mark Twain (1835–1910)

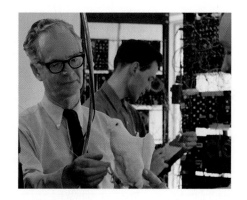

B. F. Skinner
"I am sometimes asked, 'Do you think of yourself as you think of the organisms you study?' The answer is yes. So far as I know, my behavior at any given moment has been nothing more than the product of my genetic endowment, my personal history, and the current setting" (1983).

Computer-assisted learning
Computers have helped realize Skinner's goal of individually paced instruction with immediate feedback.

At School

A generation ago, Skinner and others advocated teaching machines and textbooks that would shape learning in small steps and provide immediate reinforcement for correct responses. Such machines and texts, they said, would revolutionize education and free teachers to concentrate on their students' special needs.

To envision Skinner's idea, imagine two math teachers, each with a class of academically diverse students. Teacher A gives the whole class the same math lesson, knowing that some students will readily understand the concepts and that others will be frustrated. With so many different children, how can one teacher guide them individually? The whiz kids breeze through unchallenged; the slower learners experience failure. Faced with a similar class, Teacher B paces the material according to each student's rate of learning and provides prompt feedback with positive reinforcement to both slow and fast learners. Does the individualized instruction of Teacher B seem unrealistic?

Although the predicted revolution has not occurred, to the end of his life Skinner (1986, 1988, 1989) believed the ideal was achievable. "Good instruction demands two things," he said. "Students must be told immediately whether what they do is right or wrong and, when right, they must be directed to the step to be taken next." Computers were his final hope. For reading and math drills, the computer could be Teacher B—engaging the student actively, pacing material according to the student's rate of learning, quizzing the student to find gaps in understanding, providing immediate feedback, and keeping flawless records for the supervising teacher. With on-line testing systems improving and interactive student software and Web-based learning becoming available, we are closer than ever before to achieving Skinner's ideal.

At Work

Believing reinforcers influence productivity, business managers have capitalized on psychological research. Many companies now enable their employees to share profits and to participate in company ownership. When workers' productivity boosts rewards for everyone, their motivation, morale, and cooperative spirit often increase (Deutsch, 1991). Reinforcement for jobs well done is especially effective in boosting productivity when the desired performance is *well defined and achievable.* The message for managers? Reward is given for specific behaviors, not vaguely defined merit. Criticism, too, triggers the least resentment and the greatest performance boost when it is specific and considerate (Baron, 1988).

It is also wise to make the reinforcement *immediate.* When IBM legend Thomas Watson observed an achievement, he would write the employee a check on the spot (Peters & Waterman, 1982). But rewards need not be material, nor should they be so substantial that they become political and a source of discouragement to those who don't receive them. An effective manager may simply walk the floor and praise people for good work, or write notes of appreciation for a completed project. As Skinner said, "How much richer would the whole world be if the reinforcers in daily life were more effectively contingent on productive work?"

At Home

Parents can also take helpful advantage of operant conditioning. Parent-training researchers Michelle Wierson and Rex Forehand (1994) remind us that when parents say "get ready for bed" and then cave in to protests or defiance, they reinforce such behaviors. Eventually, exasperated, they may yell at their child or gesture menacingly, at which point the child's fearful compliance in turn reinforces the parents' angry behavior. Over time, a destructive parent-child relationship develops. To disrupt this cycle, the researchers have these recommendations for parents:

- Give children attention and other reinforcers when they are behaving *well.* Target a specific behavior, reward it, and watch it increase.
- Ignore whining. If whining has triggered attention in the past, it may temporarily increase when ignored. Over time, if not reinforced, it will diminish.
- When children misbehave or are defiant, do not yell at or hit them. Simply explain the misbehavior and give them *time-out*—remove them from any reinforcing surroundings for a specified time.

Finally, we can use operant conditioning on ourselves, by reinforcing our most desired behaviors and extinguishing those undesired. To take charge of your own behavior, psychologists suggest these step-by-step procedures:

1. *State your goal*—say, to stop smoking, eat less, or study or exercise more—in measurable terms, and make your intention public. You might, for example, aim to boost your study time by an hour a day and announce that goal to some supportive friends.
2. *Monitor* how often you engage in the behavior you wish to promote. You might log your current study time, noting under what conditions you do and don't study. (When I began writing textbooks, I logged my time and was astonished to discover how much time I was wasting.)
3. *Reinforce* the desired behavior. To increase your study time, allow yourself a snack (or some other reinforcing activity) only after specified periods of study. Agree with your friends that you will join them for weekend activities only if you have met your weekly studying goal.
4. *Reduce the incentives* gradually while giving yourself a mental pat on the back as your new behaviors become more habitual.

Contrasting Conditioning Techniques

The last four decades of research have changed psychologists' views of both classical and operant conditioning (summarized in Table 17.2). Learning, like so much else, depends on both nature and nurture. As we have seen, biological predispositions make learning some associations easier than learning others. Yet animals exhibit more sophisticated cognitive processes than once seemed likely. And rewarding people to do what they already enjoy may undermine their interest.

Answer to questions on page 252: Door-to-door salespeople are reinforced on a variable-ratio schedule (after varying numbers of rings). Cookie checkers are reinforced on a fixed-interval schedule. Frequent-flyer programs use a fixed-ratio schedule.

"O! This learning, what a thing it is."

William Shakespeare, *The Taming of the Shrew*, 1597

TABLE 17.2

COMPARISON OF CLASSICAL AND OPERANT CONDITIONING

	Classical Conditioning	Operant Conditioning
The response	Involuntary, automatic.	"Voluntary," operates on environment.
Acquisition	Associating events; CS announces UCS.	Associating response with a consequence (reinforcer or punisher).
Extinction	CR decreases when CS is repeatedly presented alone.	Responding decreases when reinforcement stops.
Cognitive processes	Organisms develop expectation that CS signals the arrival of UCS.	Organisms develop expectation that a response will be reinforced or punished; they also exhibit latent learning, without reinforcement.
Biological predispositions	Natural predispositions constrain which stimuli and responses can easily be associated.	Organisms best learn behaviors similar to their natural behaviors; unnatural behaviors instinctively drift back toward natural ones.

rehearse it!

8. Salivating in response to a tone paired with food is a (an) _____ ; pressing a bar to obtain food is a (an) _____ .
   a. primary reinforcer; secondary reinforcer
   b. secondary reinforcer; primary reinforcer
   c. operant behavior; respondent behavior
   d. respondent behavior; operant behavior

9. Thorndike's law of effect states that "rewarded behavior is likely to recur." This law became the basis for operant conditioning and the "behavioral technology" developed by
   a. Ivan Pavlov.
   b. John Garcia.
   c. B. F. Skinner.
   d. John B. Watson.

10. B. F. Skinner taught rats to press a bar to obtain a food pellet. To guide the rat's natural behavior toward the desired behavior, he used
   a. shaping.
   b. punishment.
   c. taste aversion.
   d. discrimination.

11. A reinforcer is any stimulus presented after a response that increases the frequency of that response. Imagine that your dog barks at every noise it hears. The barking disturbs you, so you put the dog outside when it starts to bark. The stopping of the barking is for you the termination of an aversive stimulus, or a
   a. positive reinforcer.
   b. negative reinforcer.
   c. punishment.
   d. primary reinforcer.

12. Continuous reinforcement—reinforcement of the desired response every time it occurs—makes for rapid learning and for rapid extinction when reinforcement stops. A partial reinforcement schedule that reinforces a response at unpredictable times is a
   a. fixed-interval schedule.
   b. variable-interval schedule.
   c. fixed-ratio schedule.
   d. variable-ratio schedule.

13. A medieval proverb notes that "a burnt child dreads the fire." In behavioral terms, the burning is an example of a

a. primary reinforcer.
b. negative reinforcer.
c. punisher.
d. positive reinforcer.

14. Most researchers today believe that cognitive processes can play an important role in learning. Evidence for the effect of cognition (thoughts, perceptions, and expectations) comes from studies in which rats
   a. spontaneously recover previously learned behavior.
   b. develop cognitive maps.
   c. exhibit respondent behavior.
   d. generalize responses.

15. Rats were carried passively through a maze and given no reward. In later trials involving food rewards, they immediately did as well as rats that had been reinforced for running the maze. The rats that had learned without reinforcement demonstrate
   a. modeling.
   b. biological predisposition.
   c. shaping.
   d. latent learning.

Learning by Observation

PREVIEW QUESTION 12 What is observational learning?

From drooling dogs, running rats, and pecking pigeons we have learned much about the basic processes of learning. But conditioning principles alone do not tell us the whole story. Among higher animals, especially humans, learning need not occur through direct experience. **Observational learning,** in which we observe and imitate others, also plays a big part. A child who sees his big sister burn her fingers on the stove has thereby learned not to touch it. The process of observing and imitating a specific behavior is often called **modeling.** We learn all kinds of social behaviors by observing and imitating models.

We can glimpse the roots of observational learning in other species. Shortly after a fight, stumptail macaque monkeys often reconcile with one another by approaching their opponent and making friendly contact. Rhesus macaque monkeys rarely make up quickly. If, however, rhesus monkeys grow up with forgiving older stumptails, then more often than not, their fights, too, are followed by reconciliation within three minutes (de Waal & Johanowicz, 1993). Monkey see, monkey do.

Imitation is all the more striking in humans. So many of our ideas, fashions, and habits pass by imitation that these transmitted cultural elements now have a name: *memes.* We humans are the supreme meme machines, notes Susan Blackmore (1999). Our catch phrases, hem lengths, ceremonies, foods, traditions, vices, and fads (think Pokémon) all spread by one person copying another.

The imitation of models shapes children's development. Shortly after birth, an infant may imitate an adult who sticks out his tongue. By 9 months, infants will im-

"Children need models more than they need critics."

Joseph Joubert, *Pensées*, 1842

■ **observational learning** learning by observing others.

■ **modeling** the process of observing and imitating a specific behavior.

itate novel play behaviors. And by age 14 months they will imitate acts modeled on television (Meltzoff, 1988; Meltzoff & Moore, 1989, 1997). To persuade children to smoke, simply expose them to parents, older youth, and attractive media models who smoke. To encourage children to read, read to them and surround them with books and people who read them. To increase the odds of your children practicing your religion, worship and attend other religious activities with them.

Bandura's Experiments

Picture this scene from a famous experiment devised by Albert Bandura, the pioneering researcher of observational learning (Bandura & others, 1961). A preschool child is at work on a drawing. An adult in another part of the room is working with some Tinkertoys. The adult then gets up and for nearly 10 minutes pounds, kicks, and throws a large inflated Bobo doll around the room, while yelling such remarks as, "Sock him in the nose. . . . Hit him down. . . . Kick him."

After observing this outburst, the child is taken to another room where there are many appealing toys. Soon the experimenter interrupts the child's play and explains that she has decided to save these good toys "for the other children." She now takes the frustrated child to an adjacent room containing a few toys, including a Bobo doll. Left alone, what does the child do?

Compared with children not exposed to the adult model, those who observed the model's aggressive outburst were much more likely to lash out at the doll. Apparently, observing the adult model beating up the doll lowered their inhibitions. But something more than lowered inhibitions was at work, for the children also imitated the very acts they had observed and used the very words they had heard.

Applications of Observational Learning

The bad news from such studies is that antisocial models—in one's family or neighborhood, or on TV—may have antisocial effects. In the first eight days after the 1999 Columbine High School massacre, every U.S. state except Vermont had to deal with copycat threats or incidents. Pennsylvania alone had 60 threats of school violence (Cooper, 1999).

Observational learning helps us understand how abusive parents might have aggressive children and why men who beat their wives often had wife-battering fathers. The lessons we learn as children are not easily unlearned as adults, and they are sometimes visited on future generations. Critics note that the intergenerational transmission of abuse could be genetic. But with monkeys, at least, we know it can be environmental. In study after study, young monkeys that received high levels of aggression when reared apart from their mothers grew up to be perpetrators of aggression (Chamove, 1980).

The good news is that **prosocial** (positive, helpful) models can have prosocial effects. People who exemplify nonviolent, helpful behavior can prompt similar behavior in others. Mahatma Gandhi and Martin Luther King, Jr., both drew on the power of modeling, making nonviolent action a powerful force for social change. Parents are powerful models. Research indicates that European Christians who risked their lives to rescue Jews from the Nazis usually had a close relationship with at least one parent who modeled a strong moral or humanitarian concern, as did the 1960s U.S. civil rights activists (London, 1970; Oliner & Oliner, 1988).

Models are most effective when their actions and words are consistent. Sometimes, however, models say one thing and do another. Many parents seem to operate according to the principle "Do as I *say*, not as I *do*." Experiments suggest that children learn to do both (Rice & Grusec, 1975; Rushton, 1975). When exposed to a hypocrite, they tend to imitate the hypocrisy by doing what the model did and saying what the model said.

■ **prosocial behavior** positive, constructive, helpful behavior. The opposite of antisocial behavior.

Albert Bandura

"Learning would be exceedingly laborious, not to mention hazardous, if people had to rely solely on the effects of their own actions to inform them what to do" (1977).

Learning from observation

This 14-month-old boy in Andrew Meltzoff's laboratory is imitating behavior he has seen on TV. In the top photo the infant leans forward and carefully watches the adult pull apart a toy. In the middle photo he has been given the toy. In the bottom photo he pulls the toy apart, imitating what he has seen the adult do.

A model grandma

This boy is learning to cook by observing his grandmother. As the sixteenth-century proverb states, "Example is better than precept."

What determines whether we will imitate a model? Bandura believes part of the answer is reinforcements and punishments—those received by the model as well as by the imitator. We look and we learn. By looking, we learn to anticipate a behavior's consequences in situations like those we are observing. By watching TV programs, children may "learn" that physical intimidation is an effective way to control others, that free and easy sex brings pleasure without later misery or disease, or that men are supposed to be tough and women gentle. We are especially likely to imitate those we perceive as similar to ourselves, as successful, or as admirable.

Our knowledge of learning principles comes from the work of thousands of investigators. This module has focused on the ideas of a few pioneers—Pavlov, Watson, Skinner, and Bandura. They illustrate the impact that can result from single-minded devotion to a few well-defined problems and ideas. These researchers defined the issues and impressed on us the importance of learning. As their legacy demonstrates, intellectual history is often made by people who risk going to extremes in pushing ideas to their limits.

rehearse it!

16. Children learn many social behaviors by imitating parents and other models. This type of learning is called
    a. observational learning.
    b. reinforced learning.
    c. operant conditioning.
    d. classical conditioning.

17. Parents are powerful models of behavior. They are most effective in getting their children to imitate them if
    a. their words and actions are consistent.
    b. they have outgoing personalities.
    c. the father works and the mother stays home to care for the children.
    d. they carefully explain why a behavior is acceptable in adults but not in children.

18. Bandura believes that modeling is not automatic. Whether a child will imitate a model depends in part on the
    a. child's closeness to the model.
    b. child's ability to distinguish right from wrong.
    c. rewards and punishments received by the model and by the imitator.
    d. child's age in relation to that of the model.

REVIEWING

Learning

1. What is learning?

All animals, especially humans, adapt to their environments aided by learning. Through associative learning, we come to link certain events. The process of learning associations between events is called *conditioning*. Through *classical conditioning,* we learn to anticipate important events, such as impending food or pain. Through *operant conditioning,* we learn to repeat acts that bring desired results and to avoid acts that bring punishment. Through *observational learning,* we learn from the experience and example of others.

2. How does classical conditioning demonstrate learning by association? How do the processes of acquisition, extinction, spontaneous recovery, generalization, and discrimination affect a conditioned response?

Although associative learning had been discussed for centuries, it remained for Ivan Pavlov to capture the phenomenon of classical conditioning. Pavlov repeatedly presented a neutral stimulus (such as a tone) just before an unconditioned stimulus (UCS, such

as food) triggered an unconditioned response (UCR, such as salivation). After several repetitions, the tone alone (now the conditioned stimulus—CS) began triggering a conditioned response (CR, such as salivation). Further experiments on acquisition revealed that classical conditioning was usually greatest when the CS was presented just before the UCS, thus preparing the organism for what was coming.

The first stage in response learning involves the association of a CS with the UCS (acquisition). Responses are subsequently weakened if they are not reinforced (extinction), but they may reappear after a rest pause (spontaneous recovery). Responses may be triggered by stimuli similar to the CS (generalization) but not by dissimilar stimuli (discrimination).

3. How do cognitive processes and biological constraints affect classical conditioning?

The behaviorists' optimism that learning principles would generalize from one response to another and from one species to another has been tempered. Conditioning principles, we now know, are cognitively and biologically constrained. In classical conditioning, animals learn when to "expect" an unconditioned stimulus. Moreover, biological predispositions make learning some associations easier than learning others. For example, rats are biologically predisposed to learn associations between, say, a peculiar taste and a sickness-producing drink, which they will then avoid. But they don't learn to avoid a sickening drink announced by a noise.

4. Why does Pavlov's work remain so important?

Pavlov's conditioning principles generalize to many species and are applicable to humans, especially to the learning of emotions such as fear. His objective methods illustrated how psychology could proceed as a science.

Pavlov's work laid a foundation for John B. Watson's emerging belief that, to be an objective science, psychology should study only overt behavior, without considering unobservable mental activity. Watson called this position *behaviorism*.

5. What is operant conditioning, and how does it differ from classical conditioning?

Through classical (Pavlovian) conditioning, an organism associates different stimuli that it does not control and responds automatically (respondent behavior). Through operant conditioning, the organism associates its operant behaviors with their consequences.

6. How is behavior shaped?

Expanding on Edward Thorndike's law of effect, B. F. Skinner and other researchers found that the behavior of rats or pigeons placed in a Skinner box can be shaped by rewarding closer and closer approximations of the desired behavior.

7. What are the basic types of reinforcers?

Reinforcers can be positive (when presented after a response) or negative (when an aversive stimulus is withdrawn); primary (unlearned) or secondary (learned through association with primary reinforcers); and immediate or delayed. Regardless of type, all reinforcers strengthen the behaviors that they follow.

8. How do different reinforcement schedules affect behavior?

Partial reinforcement schedules (fixed-interval, fixed-ratio, variable-interval, and variable-ratio) produce slower acquisition of the target behavior than does continuous reinforcement. They also produce greater resistance to extinction.

9. How does punishment affect behavior?

Like reinforcement, punishment is most swiftly effective when strong, immediate, and consistent. Although punishment decreases the frequency of the behavior it follows, it is not simply the logical opposite of reinforcement, for punishment can result in several undesirable side effects, such as increased aggression and fear of the punisher.

10. How do cognitive processes and biological constraints affect operant conditioning?

Many psychologists have criticized behaviorists such as Skinner for underestimating the importance of cognitive and biological processes in operant conditioning. Research on cognitive mapping and latent learning points to the importance of cognitive processes in learning. Research has also made it clear that biological predispositions constrain what an animal can be taught.

11. How might educators, business managers, and other individuals apply operant conditioning?

Operant principles are applied successfully in schools, in the workplace, and at home. Computer-assisted instruction both shapes and reinforces learning; immediate reinforcement boosts worker productivity; individuals can strengthen their own desired behavior and extinguish unwanted behavior.

12. What is observational learning?

Observational learning results from watching others' behavior and imitating it. In experiments, children tend to imitate what a model both does and says, whether the behavior is prosocial (positive and helpful) or antisocial. Such experiments have stimulated research on the effects of social modeling in the home, on television, and within peer groups.

TERMS AND CONCEPTS TO REMEMBER

learning, p. 236
associative learning, p. 236
behaviorism, p. 239
classical conditioning, p. 239
unconditioned response (UCR), p. 240
unconditioned stimulus (UCS), p. 240
conditioned response (CR), p. 240
conditioned stimulus (CS), p. 240

acquisition, p. 240
extinction, p. 242
spontaneous recovery, p. 242
generalization, p. 242
discrimination, p. 243
operant conditioning, p. 248
respondent behavior, p. 248
operant behavior, p. 249
law of effect, p. 249
operant chamber, p. 249

shaping, p. 249
reinforcer, p. 250
primary reinforcer, p. 251
conditional reinforcer, p. 251
continuous reinforcement, p. 252
partial (intermittent) reinforcement, p. 252
fixed-ratio schedule, p. 252
variable-ratio schedule, p. 252

fixed-interval schedule, p. 252
variable-interval schedule, p. 252
punishment, p. 253
cognitive map, p. 254
latent learning, p. 255
observational learning, p. 258
modeling, p. 258
prosocial behavior, p. 259

REHEARSE IT ANSWER KEY

1. c	3. a	5. d	7. b	9. c	11. b	13. c	15. d	17. a
2. c	4. b	6. b	8. d	10. a	12. b	14. b	16. a	18. c

18 Information Processing

Be thankful for memory. We take it for granted, except when it malfunctions. But it's our memory, notes Rebecca Rupp (1998, p. xvii), that "allows us to recognize friends, neighbors, and acquaintances and call them by their names; to knit, type, drive, and play the piano; to speak English, Spanish, or Mandarin Chinese." It's our memory that accounts for time and defines our life. It's our memory that enables us to sing our national anthem, find our way home, and locate the food and water we need for survival. It's our shared memories that bind us together as Muslims, Christians, or Jews; as Irish or Aussies; as Serbs or Albanians. And it is our memories that occasionally pit us against those whose offenses we cannot forget.

In large part, you are what you remember. Without memory, there would be no savoring joyful moments past, no guilt or anger over painful recollections. You would instead live in an enduring present. Each moment would be fresh. But each person would be a stranger, every language foreign, every task—dressing, cooking, biking—a novel challenge. You would even be a stranger to yourself, lacking that continuous sense of self that extends from your distant past to your momentary present.

The Phenomenon of Memory

Your memory is your mind's storehouse, the reservoir of your accumulated learning. To the Roman statesman Cicero, memory was "the treasury and guardian of all things." To a psychologist, **memory** is any indication that learning has persisted over time. It is our ability to store and retrieve information.

Studying memory's extremes has helped researchers understand this phenomenon. Talking with John, a former graduate student, you would be impressed by his wit, his intelligence (he might explain his master's thesis), and his skill at tasks such as typing. It might be some time before you noticed that John suffers a tragic defect, caused by a brain injury suffered in a motorcycle accident. He cannot form new memories. Although John remembers his life before the accident, he otherwise lives in an eternal present. Each morning when his rehabilitation therapist greets him, she must reintroduce herself. She must listen patiently as over and over he retells anecdotes from his preaccident life. Each time the need arises, he inquires, "Where is the bathroom?" and is told anew.

"Waiter, I'd like to order, unless I've eaten, in which case bring me the check."

Memory lost and found

Larry Treadgold, an engineer, invented a paging system that serves as a kind of artificial memory for his son Adrian. Brain-injured in an auto accident, the young man can retain information for as long as he pays attention. But as soon as he is distracted, the information fades. The paging system allows a central computer to take over memory functions, reminding him, for example, to "take your 8:00 A.M. medications; call 123–4567 to confirm." If Adrian fails to confirm, the computer continues to page him and eventually contacts an emergency number.

At the other extreme are some people who would be medal winners in a memory Olympics, such as Russian journalist Shereshevskii, or S, as psychologist Alexander Luria (1968) called him. S's memory not only allowed him merely to listen while other reporters were scribbling notes, it also earned him a place in virtually every modern book on memory. You and I can repeat back a string of about 7 digits—almost surely no more than 9. S could repeat up to 70 digits or words, provided they were read about 3 seconds apart in an otherwise silent room. Moreover, he could recall them backward as easily as forward. His accuracy was unerring, even when he was asked to recall a list as much as 15 years later, after having memorized hundreds of other lists. "Yes, yes," he might recall. "This was a series you gave me once when we were in your apartment. . . . You were sitting at the table and I in the rocking chair. . . . You were wearing a gray suit and you looked at me like this. . . ."

Do these memory feats make your own memory seem feeble? If so, just think: Your capacity for remembering countless voices, sounds, and songs; tastes, smells, and textures; faces, places, and happenings is pretty staggering in itself. Imagine viewing more than 2500 slides of faces and places, for only 10 seconds each. Later you see 280 of these slides one at a time, paired with a previously unseen slide. If you are like the participants in this experiment by Ralph Haber (1970), you would recognize 90 percent of those you had seen before.

Your memory ability is perhaps most apparent in your recall of unique and highly emotional moments in your past. One of my vivid memories is of my only hit in an entire season of Little League baseball. Perhaps yours is of a car accident, your first romantic kiss, your first day as an immigrant in a new country, or your surroundings when you heard some tragic news. Most Americans over 50 feel sure of exactly what they were doing when they heard the news of President Kennedy's assassination (Brown & Kulik, 1982). Seven months after Princess Diana's death, most Britishers could still recall what they had also reported the day after her death—their whereabouts on hearing the news (Wynn & Gilhooly, 1999). This clarity for our memories of surprising, significant events leads some psychologists to call them **flashbulb memories,** because it's as if the brain commands, "Capture this!"

How do we accomplish such memory feats? How can we remember things we have not thought about for years, yet forget the name of someone we met a minute ago? How can two people's memories of the same event be so different? How are memories stored in our brains? Why can even our flashbulb memories sometimes prove dead wrong? Why will you be likely later in this module to misrecall this sentence: *"The angry rioter threw the rock at the window"?* How can we improve our memories? These will be our questions as we review a century of research on memory. To think about memory, we first need a model of how it works.

Information Processing

PREVIEW QUESTION 1 How do psychologists describe the human memory system?

Building a memory is in some ways like my information processing in creating this book. For each edition I first glimpse countless items of information, including some 100,000 journal article titles. Most of it I ignore, but some things merit temporary storage in my briefcase for more detailed processing later. Most of these items I eventually discard. The rest—about 3000 articles and news items—gets organized and filed for long-term storage. Later, I retrieve this information and draw from it as I spin the story of today's psychology. In forming memories, you, too, must select, process, store, and retrieve information. You follow this process not only in the "cramming" you do to study in your college courses, but also in your processing of countless daily events.

Our memory is also in some ways like a computer's information-processing system. To remember any event requires that we *get information into our brain* **(encoding),** *retain* that information **(storage),** and later *get it back out* **(retrieval).** Consider how a computer *encodes, stores,* and *retrieves* information. First, it translates input (keystrokes) into an electronic language, much as the brain encodes

MR. TOTAL RECALL

© The New Yorker Collection 1987 W. Miller from cartoonbank.com. All Rights Reserved.

Which is more important—your experiences or your memories of them?

Hours after the space shuttle *Challenger* explosion in 1986, people recalled where they had heard the news. Yet they were sometimes wildly inaccurate when again recalling their whereabouts 1 to 3 years later (McCloskey & others, 1988; Neisser, 1997). One woman recalled hearing it from someone running through her dorm screaming, "The space shuttle blew up." Actually, she had learned about it from friends over lunch.

■ **memory** the persistence of learning over time through the storage and retrieval of information.

■ **flashbulb memory** a clear memory of an emotionally significant moment or event.

■ **encoding** the processing of information into the memory system—for example, by extracting meaning.

■ **storage** the retention of encoded information over time.

■ **retrieval** the process of getting information out of memory storage.

- **sensory memory** the immediate, initial recording of sensory information in the memory system.

- **short-term memory** activated memory that holds a few items briefly, such as the seven digits of a phone number while dialing, before the information is stored or forgotten. *Working memory* is a similar concept that focuses more on the processing of briefly stored information.

- **long-term memory** the relatively permanent and limitless storehouse of the memory system.

- **working memory** a concept of memory similar to *short-term memory* but focusing more on the processing of briefly stored information.

sensory information into a neural language. The computer permanently stores vast amounts of information on a disk, from which it can later be retrieved.

Like all analogies, the computer model has its limits, however. Our memories are less literal and more fragile than a computer's. Moreover, most computers process information sequentially but fast. The brain is slower but does many things at once—in parallel.

Here we will use Richard Atkinson and Richard Shiffrin's classic and influential *three-stage processing* model of memory (1968), which suggests that we give birth to memories through three stages. We first record to-be-remembered information as a fleeting **sensory memory,** from which it is processed into a **short-term memory** bin, where we encode it for **long-term memory** and later retrieval (**FIGURE 18.1**).

This three-step process is limited and fallible. Bombarded with information, we cannot possibly focus on everything at once. Instead we shine the flashlight beam of our attention on certain incoming stimuli—often novel or important stimuli. These incoming stimuli, along with images we retrieve from our long-term memory, get displayed on our mental screen as conscious short-term memories. These rapidly decay unless used or rehearsed.

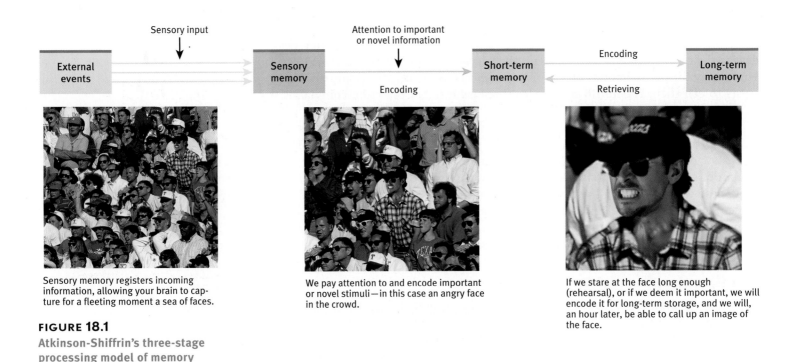

Sensory memory registers incoming information, allowing your brain to capture for a fleeting moment a sea of faces.

We pay attention to and encode important or novel stimuli—in this case an angry face in the crowd.

If we stare at the face long enough (rehearsal), or if we deem it important, we will encode it for long-term storage, and we will, an hour later, be able to call up an image of the face.

FIGURE 18.1
Atkinson-Shiffrin's three-stage processing model of memory

The newer concept of **working memory** clarifies the short-term memory concept by focusing more on our behind-the-scenes information processing. We do not just display information on-screen, we actively associate new and old information and solve problems. Working memory is roughly like a computer's random-access memory (RAM), which integrates information coming in from our keyboard with that retrieved from long-term storage on the hard drive. Part of this working memory is visible on our short-term screen.

Like short-term memory, working memory is quite limited. Alan Baddeley (1992) notes that working memory has a visual and a verbal component. These separate mental subsystems allow us to process images and words simultaneously en route to storage. Because each subsystem is limited, we cannot effectively engage in two conversations at once, though we can talk while playing chess.

repeat up to 70 digits or words, provided they were read about 3 seconds apart in an otherwise silent room. Moreover, he could recall them backward as easily as forward. His accuracy was unerring, even when he was asked to recall a list as much as 15 years later, after having memorized hundreds of other lists. "Yes, yes," he might recall. "This was a series you gave me once when we were in your apartment. . . . You were sitting at the table and I in the rocking chair. . . . You were wearing a gray suit and you looked at me like this. . . ."

Do these memory feats make your own memory seem feeble? If so, just think: Your capacity for remembering countless voices, sounds, and songs; tastes, smells, and textures; faces, places, and happenings is pretty staggering in itself. Imagine viewing more than 2500 slides of faces and places, for only 10 seconds each. Later you see 280 of these slides one at a time, paired with a previously unseen slide. If you are like the participants in this experiment by Ralph Haber (1970), you would recognize 90 percent of those you had seen before.

Your memory ability is perhaps most apparent in your recall of unique and highly emotional moments in your past. One of my vivid memories is of my only hit in an entire season of Little League baseball. Perhaps yours is of a car accident, your first romantic kiss, your first day as an immigrant in a new country, or your surroundings when you heard some tragic news. Most Americans over 50 feel sure of exactly what they were doing when they heard the news of President Kennedy's assassination (Brown & Kulik, 1982). Seven months after Princess Diana's death, most Britishers could still recall what they had also reported the day after her death—their whereabouts on hearing the news (Wynn & Gilhooly, 1999). This clarity for our memories of surprising, significant events leads some psychologists to call them **flashbulb memories,** because it's as if the brain commands, "Capture this!"

How do we accomplish such memory feats? How can we remember things we have not thought about for years, yet forget the name of someone we met a minute ago? How can two people's memories of the same event be so different? How are memories stored in our brains? Why can even our flashbulb memories sometimes prove dead wrong? Why will you be likely later in this module to misrecall this sentence: *"The angry rioter threw the rock at the window"?* How can we improve our memories? These will be our questions as we review a century of research on memory. To think about memory, we first need a model of how it works.

Information Processing

PREVIEW QUESTION 1 How do psychologists describe the human memory system?

Building a memory is in some ways like my information processing in creating this book. For each edition I first glimpse countless items of information, including some 100,000 journal article titles. Most of it I ignore, but some things merit temporary storage in my briefcase for more detailed processing later. Most of these items I eventually discard. The rest—about 3000 articles and news items—gets organized and filed for long-term storage. Later, I retrieve this information and draw from it as I spin the story of today's psychology. In forming memories, you, too, must select, process, store, and retrieve information. You follow this process not only in the "cramming" you do to study in your college courses, but also in your processing of countless daily events.

Our memory is also in some ways like a computer's information-processing system. To remember any event requires that we *get information into our brain* **(encoding),** *retain* that information **(storage),** and later *get it back out* **(retrieval).** Consider how a computer *encodes, stores,* and *retrieves* information. First, it translates input (keystrokes) into an electronic language, much as the brain encodes

Which is more important—your experiences or your memories of them?

Hours after the space shuttle *Challenger* explosion in 1986, people recalled where they had heard the news. Yet they were sometimes wildly inaccurate when again recalling their whereabouts 1 to 3 years later (McCloskey & others, 1988; Neisser, 1997). One woman recalled hearing it from someone running through her dorm screaming, "The space shuttle blew up." Actually, she had learned about it from friends over lunch.

■ **memory** the persistence of learning over time through the storage and retrieval of information.

■ **flashbulb memory** a clear memory of an emotionally significant moment or event.

■ **encoding** the processing of information into the memory system—for example, by extracting meaning.

■ **storage** the retention of encoded information over time.

■ **retrieval** the process of getting information out of memory storage.

- **sensory memory** the immediate, initial recording of sensory information in the memory system.

- **short-term memory** activated memory that holds a few items briefly, such as the seven digits of a phone number while dialing, before the information is stored or forgotten. *Working memory* is a similar concept that focuses more on the processing of briefly stored information.

- **long-term memory** the relatively permanent and limitless storehouse of the memory system.

- **working memory** a concept of memory similar to *short-term memory* but focusing more on the processing of briefly stored information.

sensory information into a neural language. The computer permanently stores vast amounts of information on a disk, from which it can later be retrieved.

Like all analogies, the computer model has its limits, however. Our memories are less literal and more fragile than a computer's. Moreover, most computers process information sequentially but fast. The brain is slower but does many things at once—in parallel.

Here we will use Richard Atkinson and Richard Shiffrin's classic and influential *three-stage processing* model of memory (1968), which suggests that we give birth to memories through three stages. We first record to-be-remembered information as a fleeting **sensory memory**, from which it is processed into a **short-term memory** bin, where we encode it for **long-term memory** and later retrieval (**FIGURE 18.1**).

This three-step process is limited and fallible. Bombarded with information, we cannot possibly focus on everything at once. Instead we shine the flashlight beam of our attention on certain incoming stimuli—often novel or important stimuli. These incoming stimuli, along with images we retrieve from our long-term memory, get displayed on our mental screen as conscious short-term memories. These rapidly decay unless used or rehearsed.

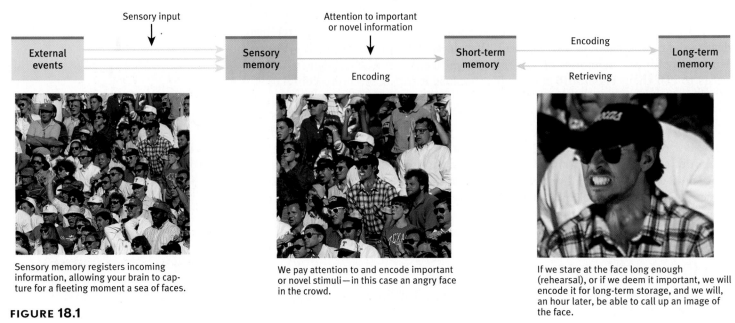

Sensory memory registers incoming information, allowing your brain to capture for a fleeting moment a sea of faces.

FIGURE 18.1
Atkinson-Shiffrin's three-stage processing model of memory

We pay attention to and encode important or novel stimuli—in this case an angry face in the crowd.

If we stare at the face long enough (rehearsal), or if we deem it important, we will encode it for long-term storage, and we will, an hour later, be able to call up an image of the face.

The newer concept of **working memory** clarifies the short-term memory concept by focusing more on our behind-the-scenes information processing. We do not just display information on-screen, we actively associate new and old information and solve problems. Working memory is roughly like a computer's random-access memory (RAM), which integrates information coming in from our keyboard with that retrieved from long-term storage on the hard drive. Part of this working memory is visible on our short-term screen.

Like short-term memory, working memory is quite limited. Alan Baddeley (1992) notes that working memory has a visual and a verbal component. These separate mental subsystems allow us to process images and words simultaneously en route to storage. Because each subsystem is limited, we cannot effectively engage in two conversations at once, though we can talk while playing chess.

Encoding: Getting Information In

PREVIEW QUESTION 2 How do the sights, sounds, and other sensations we experience get selectively encoded and transferred into the memory system?

Some encoding occurs automatically, freeing your attention to simultaneously process information that requires effort. Thus, your memory for the route you walked to your last class is handled by **automatic processing.** Your learning of this module's concepts requires **effortful processing** (**FIGURE 18.2**).

Automatic Processing

With little or no effort, you encode an enormous amount of information about *space, time,* and *frequency:* During an exam, you may recall the place on the textbook page where forgotten material appears. To guess where you left your coat, you can re-create a sequence of the day's events. You may realize that "this is the third time I've run into you this afternoon." Memories like these form almost automatically. In fact, not only does *automatic processing* occur effortlessly, it is difficult to shut off. When you hear or read a word in your native language, whether an insult or a compliment, it is virtually impossible not to register its meaning automatically.

Some types of automatic processing we learn. For example, learning to read reversed sentences at first requires effort:

.citamotua emoceb nac gnissecorp luftroffE

After practice, some *effortful processing* becomes more automatic, much as reading from right to left becomes easy for students of Hebrew (Kolers, 1975).

Effortful Processing

PREVIEW QUESTION 3 How much does rehearsal aid in forming memories?

We encode and retain vast amounts of information automatically, without any intentional effort. Other types of information, however, we remember only with effort and attention. When learning novel information such as names, we can boost our memory through **rehearsal,** or conscious repetition. This was shown long ago by the pioneering researcher of verbal memory, German philosopher Hermann Ebbinghaus (1850–1909). Ebbinghaus became impatient with philosophical speculations about memory and decided to study it scientifically. To do so, he chose to study his own learning and forgetting of novel verbal materials.

Ebbinghaus needed to find verbal material that was not familiar. His solution was to form a list of all possible nonsense syllables created by sandwiching a vowel between two consonants. Then, for a particular experiment, he would randomly select a sample of the syllables. To get a feel for how Ebbinghaus tested himself, rapidly read aloud, eight times over, the following list (from Baddeley, 1982). Then try to recall the items:

JIH, BAZ, FUB, YOX, SUJ, XIR, DAX, LEQ, VUM, PID, KEL, WAV, TUV, ZOF, GEK, HIW.

FIGURE 18.2
Automatic versus effortful processing
Some information, such as this module's concepts, requires effort to encode and remember. Other information, like where you ate dinner yesterday, you process automatically.

■ **automatic processing** unconscious encoding of incidental information, such as space, time, and frequency, and of well-learned information, such as word meanings.

■ **effortful processing** encoding that requires attention and conscious effort.

■ **rehearsal** the conscious repetition of information, either to maintain it in consciousness or to encode it for storage.

FIGURE 18.3

Ebbinghaus' retention curve
Ebbinghaus found that the more times he practiced a list of nonsense syllables on day 1, the fewer repetitions he required to relearn it on day 2. Said simply, the more time we spend learning novel information, the more we retain. (From Baddeley, 1982.)

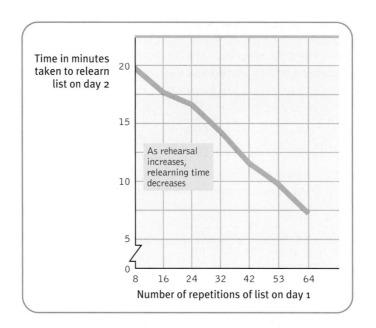

The day after learning such a list, Ebbinghaus could recall few of the syllables. But were they entirely forgotten? As **FIGURE 18.3** portrays, the more frequently he repeated the list aloud on day 1, the fewer repetitions he required to relearn the list on day 2. Here, then, was a simple beginning principle: *The amount remembered depends on the time spent learning.* Even after we learn material, additional rehearsal *(over-learning)* increases retention.

The point to remember is that for novel verbal information, practice—effortful processing—does indeed make perfect. And that helps us understand some other interesting phenomena:

- The *next-in-line effect:* When people go around a circle reading words or saying their names, their poorest memories are for what was said by the person just before them (Bond & others, 1991; Brenner, 1973). When we are next in line, we focus on our own performance and often fail to process the last person's words.
- Information presented in the seconds just before sleep seldom is remembered (Wyatt & Bootzin, 1994). When our consciousness fades before we've processed the information, all is lost. Information presented in the *hour* before sleep, as we will see, is well remembered.
- Taped information played during sleep is registered by the ears but is not remembered (Wood & others, 1992). Without opportunity for rehearsal, "sleep learning" doesn't occur.

We also retain information better when our rehearsal is distributed over time (as when learning classmates' names), a phenomenon called the **spacing effect** (Dempster, 1988).

In a 9-year experiment, Bahrick (1993) and three of his family members practiced foreign language word translations for a given number of times, at intervals ranging from 14 to 56 days. Their consistent finding: The longer the space between practice sessions, the better their retention, up to 5 years later. Reflecting on the spacing effect, Bahrick saw a practical implication: Restudying material for comprehensive final exams, capstone review courses, and senior examinations will enhance lifelong retention. Spreading out learning—say, over a semester or a year, rather than over shorter terms—should also help. *Spaced study beats cramming.*

A phenomenon you have surely experienced further illustrates the benefits of rehearsal. Experimenters have shown people a list of items (words, names, dates) and then immediately asked them to recall the items in any order. As people struggle to recall

"The mind is slow in unlearning what it has been long in learning."

Roman philosopher Seneca (4 B.C.–A.D. 65)

the list, they often demonstrate the **serial position effect:** They remember the last and first items better than they do those in the middle (**FIGURE 18.4**). Perhaps because the last items are still in short-term memory, people briefly recall them especially quickly and well. But after a delay—after they shift their attention from the last items—their recall is best for the first items. As an everyday parallel, imagine being introduced to several people. As you meet each person, you repeat (rehearse) all their names starting from the beginning. By the time you meet the last person, you will have spent more time rehearsing the earlier names than the later ones; thus, the next day you will probably more easily recall the earlier names. Also, learning the first few names may interfere with your learning the later ones.

Rehearsal will not encode all information equally well. Sometimes merely repeating information, such as the new phone number we are about to dial, is not enough to store it for later recall (Craik & Watkins, 1973; Greene, 1987). How, then, do we encode information for processing into long-term memory? Processing our sensory input is like sorting through the day's mail. Some items we instantly discard. Others we process more thoughtfully: We open, read, and retain them. Our memory system processes information not just by repetitive rehearsal but also by encoding its significant features.

Encoding Strategies

PREVIEW QUESTION 4 What strategies and devices help us remember information that requires effortful processing?

We process information in three key ways—by encoding its meaning, by visualizing it, and by mentally organizing it. To some extent we do these things automatically. But in each case there are effortful strategies for enhancing memory.

Encoding Meaning

Do you recall (from page 263) the sentence about the rioter? Can you now repeat that sentence: "The angry rioter threw . . ."? Your memory of the sentence may be affected by the way you stored it. When processing verbal information for storage, we usually encode its meaning (*semantic encoding*). For example, we associate it with what we already know or imagine. Whether we hear "eye-screem" as "ice cream" or "I scream" depends on how the context and our experience guide us to interpret the sounds.

Perhaps, then, like the subjects in an experiment by William Brewer (1977), you recalled the rioter sentence as the meaning you encoded when you read it (for example, "The angry rioter threw the rock *through* the window") and not as it was written ("The angry rioter threw the rock *at* the window"). As such recall indicates, we tend not to remember things exactly as they were. Rather, *we remember what we encoded.* Studying for an exam, you may remember your lecture notes rather than the lecture itself. Likewise, as we hear or read about a situation, our minds construct a model of it. Gordon Bower and Daniel Morrow (1990) liken our minds to theater directors who, given a raw script, imagine a finished stage production. Asked later to recall what we heard or read, we recall not the literal text but the mental model we constructed from it.

Here is another sentence I will ask you about later: *"The fish attacked the swimmer."*

To experience the importance of meaning for verbal memory, put yourself in the place of the students whom John Bransford and Marcia Johnson (1972) asked to remember the following recorded passage:

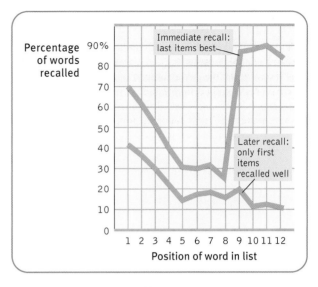

FIGURE 18.4

The serial position effect

After being presented with a list of words or names, people immediately recall the last items well (perhaps because they are still "on-screen"), and quite often the first few items nearly as well. But later they recall the first items best. (From Craik & Watkins, 1973.)

How many *Fs* are in the following sentence? FINISHED FILES ARE THE RESULTS OF YEARS OF SCIENTIFIC STUDY COMBINED WITH THE EXPERIENCE OF YEARS. (See page 269.)

■ **spacing effect** the tendency for distributed study or practice to yield better long-term retention than is achieved through massed study or practice.

■ **serial position effect** our tendency to recall the last and first items in a list better than those in the middle.

■ **imagery** mental pictures; a powerful aid to effortful processing, especially when combined with semantic encoding.

■ **mnemonics [nih-MON-iks]** memory aids, especially those techniques that use vivid imagery and organizational devices.

The procedure is actually quite simple. First you arrange things into different groups. Of course, one pile may be sufficient depending on how much there is to do. . . . After the procedure is completed one arranges the materials into different groups again. Then they can be put into their appropriate places. Eventually they will be used once more and the whole cycle will then have to be repeated. However, that is part of life.

When the students heard the paragraph you have just read, without a meaningful context, they remembered little of it. When told that the paragraph was about washing clothes (something additionally meaningful to them), they remembered much more of it—as you probably could now after rereading it.

Such research suggests the benefits of rephrasing what we read and hear into meaningful terms. From his experiments on himself, Ebbinghaus estimated that, compared with learning nonsense material, learning meaningful material required only one-tenth the effort. As memory researcher Wayne Wickelgren (1977, p. 346) noted, "The time you spend thinking about material you are reading and relating it to previously stored material is about the most useful thing you can do in learning any new subject matter."

Encoding Imagery

We struggle to memorize formulas, definitions, and dates, yet we can easily picture where we were yesterday, who was with us, where we sat, and what we wore. Our earliest memories—probably of something that happened at age 3 or 4—almost surely involve visual **imagery,** or mental pictures.

In a variety of experiments, researchers have documented the benefits of mental images. For example, we remember words that lend themselves to picture images better than we remember abstract, low-imagery words. (When I quiz you later, which three of these words—*typewriter, void, cigarette, inherent, fire, process*—will you most likely recall?) Similarly, you probably still recall the sentence about the rock-throwing rioter, not only because of the meaning you encoded but also because the sentence lent itself to a visual image. As the example suggests, and as certain memory experts believe, memory for concrete nouns is aided by encoding them *both* semantically and visually (Marschark & others, 1987; Paivio, 1986). Two codes are better than one.

> "A thing when heard, remember, strikes less keen on the spectator's mind than when 'tis seen."
>
> Horace, *Ars Poetica*, 8 B.C.

Thanks to the durability of our most vivid images, we recall our experiences with mental snapshots of their best or worst moments. Thus, the best moment of a pleasure or joy, and the worst moment of a pain or frustration, often colors our memories more than does its duration (Fredrickson & Kahneman, 1993). Recalling the high points while forgetting the mundane moments may explain a phenomenon that Terrence Mitchell, Leigh Thompson, Erika Peterson, and Randy Cronk (1997) call *rosy retrospection:* People tend to recall events such as a camping holiday more positively than they evaluated them at the time. They remember their visit to Disney World less for the muggy heat and long lines than for the surroundings, food, and rides.

Imagery is at the heart of many memory aids. **Mnemonic** (nih-MON-ik) devices (so named after the Greek word for memory) were developed by ancient Greek scholars and orators as aids to

Rosy retrospection

SALLY FORTH ®

The imagery principle
Plastic surgery researcher Darrick Antell observes that "You can talk until you're blue in the face about all the health hazards" of tanning and smoking. But show people photos of identical twins, only one of whom has aged under the influence of tanning and smoking, and they will learn and remember. Sixty-year-old Gay Black, left, was an avid tanner and onetime smoker, unlike her younger-looking identical twin, Gwen Sirota, right.

remembering lengthy passages and speeches. Using the "method of loci," they imagined themselves moving through a familiar series of locations, associating each place with a visual representation of the to-be-remembered topic. Then, when speaking, the orator would mentally revisit each location and retrieve the associated image.

A variation on this method uses vivid stories to organize words to be memorized. Gordon Bower and Michael Clark (1969), using lists of unrelated nouns, asked one group to study the lists and another group to invent stories using the nouns. (A sample made-up story: "A LUMBERJACK DARTed out of a forest, SKATEd around a HEDGE past a COLONY of DUCKs. He tripped on some FURNITURE, tearing his STOCKING while hastening toward the PILLOW where his MISTRESS lay.") After working through 12 lists of 10 words each, the group that studied each list struggled to recall 13 percent of the words; the group that invented vivid stories recalled an astounding 93 percent.

Other mnemonic devices involve both acoustic and visual codes. For example, the "peg-word" system requires that you first memorize a jingle: *"One is a bun; two is a shoe; three is a tree; four is a door; five is a hive; six is sticks; seven is heaven; eight is a gate; nine is swine; ten is a hen."* Without much effort, you will soon be able to count by peg-words instead of numbers: bun, shoe, tree . . . and then to visually associate the peg-words with to-be-remembered items. Now you are ready to challenge anyone to give you a grocery list to remember. Carrots? Imagine them stuck into a bun. Milk? Fill the shoe with it. Paper towels? Drape them over the tree branch. Think "bun, shoe, tree" and you see their associated images: carrots, milk, paper towels. With few errors (Bugelski & others, 1968), you will be able to recall the items in any order and to name any given item. Such mnemonic systems are often the secret used by feats-of-memory experts who repeat long lists of names and objects.

Organizing Information for Encoding

Meaning and imagery enhance our memory partly by helping us organize information. When Bransford and Johnson's laundry paragraph (page 268) became meaningful, its sentences formed a sequence. Mnemonic devices help organize material for our later retrieval.

CHUNKING To experience the importance of organization, glance for a few seconds at row 1 of **FIGURE 18.5,** then look away and try to reproduce what you saw. Impossible, yes? But you can easily reproduce the second row, which is no less complex. Similarly, I bet you found row 4 much easier to remember than row 3, although both contain the same letters. And you could remember the sixth cluster more easily than the fifth, although both contain the same words.

Answer to question on page 267: Partly because your initial processing of the letters was primarily acoustic rather than visual, you probably missed some of the six *F*s, especially those that sound like a *V* rather than an *F*.

FIGURE 18.5

Effects of chunking on memory
When we organize information into meaningful units, such as letters, words, and phrases, we recall it more easily. (From Hintzman, 1978.)

1. ꓯꓵꓛꓱꓵꓲꓠꓲ
2. K L C I S N E

3. KLCISNE NVESE YNA NI CSTTIH TNDO
4. NICKELS SEVEN ANY IN STITCH DONT

5. NICKELS SEVEN ANY IN STITCH DONT SAVES AGO A SCORE TIME AND NINE WOODEN FOUR YEARS TAKE

6. DONT TAKE ANY WOODEN NICKELS FOUR SCORE AND SEVEN YEARS AGO A STITCH IN TIME SAVES NINE

As this demonstrates, we organize easily remembered information into meaningful units, or chunks. **Chunking** information into meaningful units occurs so naturally that we take it for granted. If you are a native English speaker, you can reproduce perfectly the 150 or so line segments that make up the words in the three phrases of item 6 in Figure 18.5. It would astonish someone unfamiliar with the language.

I am similarly awed at the ability of someone literate in Chinese to glance at **FIGURE 18.6** and then to reproduce all the strokes; or of a chess master who, after a 5-second look at the board during a game, can recall the exact positions of most of the pieces (Chase & Simon, 1973); or of a varsity basketball player who, given a 4-second glance at a basketball play, can recall the positions of the players (Allard & Burnett, 1985). We all remember information best when we can organize it into personally meaningful arrangements.

Chunking also aids our recall of unfamiliar material. One mnemonic technique organizes it into a more familiar form by creating words (called *acronyms*) or sentences from the first letters of words to be remembered. Should you ever need to recall the names of North America's five Great Lakes, just remember HOMES (*Huron, Ontario, Michigan, Erie, Superior*). Want to remember the colors of the rainbow in order of wavelength? Think of ROY G. BIV (*red, orange, yellow, green, blue, indigo, violet*).

HIERARCHIES When people develop expertise in an area, they process information not only in chunks but also in hierarchies composed of a few broad concepts divided and subdivided into narrower concepts and facts. By organizing knowledge in hierarchies, we, too, can retrieve information efficiently. For example, this module aims not only to teach you the elementary facts of memory but also to help you organize these facts around broad principles, such as encoding; subprinciples, such as automatic and effortful processing; and still more specific concepts, such as meaning, imagery, and organization (**FIGURE 18.7**).

FIGURE 18.7
Organization benefits memory
When we organize words or concepts into hierarchical groups, as illustrated here with concepts in this module, we remember them better than when we see them presented randomly.

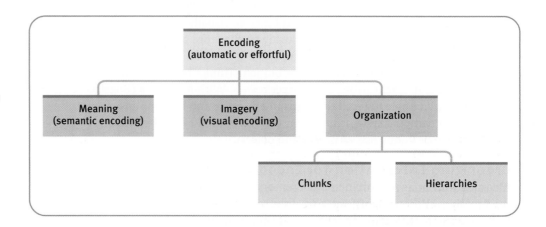

■ **chunking** organizing items into familiar, manageable units; often occurs automatically.

■ **iconic memory** a momentary sensory memory of visual stimuli; a photographic or picture-image memory lasting no more than a few tenths of a second.

Gordon Bower and his colleagues (1969) demonstrated the benefits of hierarchical organization. They presented words either randomly or grouped into categories. When the words were organized into groups, recall was two to three times better. Such results show the benefits of organizing what you study—of giving special attention to outlines, headings, previews, and review paragraphs and questions. If you can master concepts within a module's overall organization, your recall should be effective at test time. Taking lecture and text notes in outline format—a type of hierarchical organization—may also prove helpful.

rehearse it!

1. Human memory involves information processing. We take information in, retain it, and later get it back out. In psychological terms, these steps are
   a. retrieval, encoding, and storage.
   b. encoding, storage, and retrieval.
   c. storage, encoding, and retrieval.
   d. retrieval, storage, and encoding.

2. Short-term memory is an intermediate stage of memory where information is held before it is stored or forgotten. The newer concept of *working memory*
   a. clarifies the idea of short-term memory by focusing on behind-the-scenes information processing.
   b. splits short-term memory into two substages—sensory memory and working memory.
   c. splits short-term memory into two areas—working (retrievable) memory and inaccessible memory.
   d. clarifies the idea of short-term memory by introducing the element of rehearsal.

3. Rehearsal is the conscious repetition of information a person wants to remember, either in the short or long term. Rehearsal is part of
   a. automatic processing.
   b. effortful processing.
   c. forgetting.
   d. retrieval.

4. Psychologists have found that when people are shown a list of words and are immediately tested, they tend to recall the first and last items on the list more readily than those in the middle (called the *serial position effect*). When people are *retested* after a delay, they are most likely to recall
   a. the first items on the list.
   b. the first and last items on the list.
   c. a few items at random.
   d. the last items on the list.

5. Many people use visual imagery to help them remember material that would otherwise be difficult to master. Memory aids that use visual imagery, peg-words, or other organizational devices are called
   a. acronyms.
   b. nonsense material.
   c. mental pictures.
   d. mnemonics.

6. Chunking is a way of organizing information into familiar and manageable units. A related technique involves organizing material into broad categories, which are then divided into subcategories. This technique, used in organizational charts, is called
   a. serial position.
   b. peg-words.
   c. hierarchial organization.
   d. mental pictures.

Storage: Retaining Information

If you later recall something you experienced, you must, somehow, have stored and retrieved it. Anything stored in long-term memory lies dormant, waiting to be reawakened by a cue. What is our temporary and our long-term memory storage capacity? Let's start with the first memory store noted in the three-stage processing model (Figure 18.1 on page 264)—our fleeting sensory memory.

Sensory Memory

PREVIEW QUESTION 5 How does sensory memory work?

Consider what one intriguing memory experiment revealed about our sensory memory—the initial recording of sensory information in the memory system. As part of his doctoral research, George Sperling (1960) showed people three rows of three letters each for only 1/20th of a second (**FIGURE 18.8**). It was harder than reading by flashes of lightning. After the nine letters disappeared from the screen, the subjects could recall only about half of them.

Was it because they had insufficient time to glimpse them? No, Sperling cleverly demonstrated that even at faster than lightning-flash speed, people actually *can* see and recall all the letters, but only momentarily. Rather than ask them to recall all nine letters at once, Sperling would sound a high, medium, or low tone immediately *after* flashing the nine letters. This cue directed the subject to report only the letters of the top, middle, or bottom row, respectively. Now the subjects rarely missed a letter, showing that all nine letters were momentarily available for recall.

Sperling's experiment revealed that we have a fleeting photographic memory called **iconic memory.** For an instant, our eyes register an exact representation of

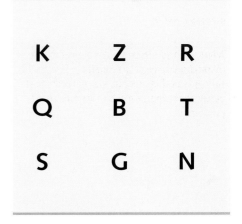

FIGURE 18.8

Momentary photographic memory
When George Sperling flashed a group of letters similar to this for 1/20th of a second, people could recall only about half of the letters. But when signaled to recall a particular row *immediately* after the letters had disappeared, they could do so with near-perfect accuracy.

FIGURE 18.9

Short-term memory decay
Unless rehearsed, verbal information may be quickly forgotten. (From Peterson & Peterson, 1959.)

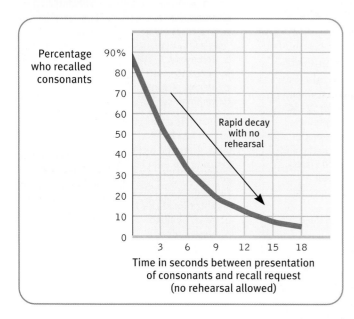

How many of the six quiz words on page 268 can you now recall? Of these, how many are high-imagery words? How many are low-imagery?

■ **echoic memory** a momentary sensory memory of auditory stimuli; if attention is elsewhere, sounds and words can still be recalled within 3 or 4 seconds.

a scene and we can recall any part of it in amazing detail—but only for a few tenths of a second. If Sperling delayed the tone signal by more than half a second, the iconic memory was gone and the subjects once again recalled only about half the letters. As cars or sidewalk pedestrians pass by, our visual screen clears quickly, as it must, so that new images can be superimposed over old ones.

We also have an impeccable, though fleeting, memory for auditory sensory images, called **echoic memory** (Cowan, 1988; Lu & others, 1992). However, if partially interpreted, the auditory echo disappears more slowly. The last few words spoken seem to linger for 3 or 4 seconds. Sometimes, just as you ask, "What did you say?" you can hear in your mind the echo of what was said.

Short-Term Memory

PREVIEW QUESTION 6 What are the limits of short-term memory?

Among the vast amounts of information registered by our sensory memory, we illuminate some with our attentional flashlight. We also retrieve information from long-term storage for "on-screen" display. But unless we meaningfully encode or rehearse that information, it quickly disappears. During your finger's trip from the phone book to the phone, your memory of a friend's number may evaporate.

To find out how quickly a short-term memory will disappear, Lloyd Peterson and Margaret Peterson (1959) asked people to remember three-consonant groups, such as *CHJ*. To prevent subjects' rehearsal of the letters, the researchers asked them, for example, to start at 100 and count aloud backwards by threes. After 3 seconds people recalled the letters only about half the time; after 12 seconds they seldom recalled them at all (**FIGURE 18.9**). Without active processing, short-term memories have a limited life.

Short-term memory is limited not only in duration but also in capacity, typically storing but seven or so chunks of information (give or take two). This recall capacity has been enshrined in psychology as the *Magical Number Seven, plus or minus two* (Miller, 1956).

Our short-term recall is slightly better for random digits (such as those of a phone number) than for random letters, which sometimes have similar sounds. It is slightly better for information we hear than for images we see. Both children and adults have short-term recall for roughly as many words as they can speak in 2 seconds (Cowan, 1994; Hulme & Tordoff, 1989). The basic principle: *At any given moment, we can consciously process only a very limited amount of information.*

Long-Term Memory

PREVIEW QUESTION 7 How large and durable is our long-term memory?

In Arthur Conan Doyle's *A Study in Scarlet,* Sherlock Holmes offers a popular theory of memory capacity:

I consider that a man's brain originally is like a little empty attic, and you have to stock it with such furniture as you choose. . . . It is a mistake to think that that little room has elastic walls and can distend to any extent. Depend upon it, there comes a time when for every addition of knowledge you forget something that you knew before.

Contrary to Sherlock Holmes' belief, our capacity for storing long-term memories is essentially limitless. By one careful estimate, the average adult has about a billion bits of information in memory and a storage capacity that is probably a thousand to a million times greater (Landauer, 1986). So, our brains are *not* like attics, which once filled can store more items only if we discard old ones.

The point is vividly illustrated by those who have performed phenomenal memory feats. Consider Rajan Mahadevan, a University of Tennessee psychologist. Give him a block of 10 digits from the first 30,000 or so digits of pi and, after a few moments of mental searching for the string, he'll pick up the series from there, firing numbers like a machine gun (Delaney & others, 1999; Thompson & others, 1993). He also can repeat 50 random digits—backwards. It is not a genetic gift, he says; anyone could learn to do it. But given the genetic influence on so many human traits, and knowing that Rajan's father memorized Shakespeare's complete works, one wonders.

Storing Memories in the Brain

PREVIEW QUESTION 8 How and where does the brain physically store memories?

I marveled at my aging mother-in-law, a retired pianist and organist. At age 88 her blind eyes could no longer read music. But let her sit at a keyboard and she would flawlessly play any of hundreds of hymns, including ones she had not thought of for 20 years. Where did her brain store those thousands of sequenced notes? For a time, some memory researchers believed that brain stimulation during surgery provided evidence that our whole past, and not just well-practiced music, is "in there," in complete detail, just waiting to be relived. Even today, 6 in 10 university students agree that "everything we learn is permanently stored," although sometimes inaccessible (Brown & others, 1996). Perhaps some of them have heard of the brain surgery experiments performed by Wilder Penfield and other neurosurgeons. To predict possible side effects of such surgery, Penfield (1969) helped map the brain's motor cortex by electrically stimulating wide-awake patients. Occasionally, Penfield's patients would report hearing things, such as "a mother calling her little boy." Penfield assumed that he was activating long-lost experiences etched permanently on the brain.

Scrutinizing these famous reports, memory researchers Elizabeth Loftus and Geoffrey Loftus (1980) discovered that these flashbacks were extremely rare, occurring in only a handful of Penfield's 1100 stimulated patients. Moreover, the content of these few recollections suggested that the experiences were not being relived but were being invented. As if they had been dreaming, people would recall being in locations they had never visited. Although the brain's storage capacity may be essentially unlimited, Penfield's evidence did *not* suggest that we store most information with the exactness of a tape recorder. Rather, say memory researchers, forgetting occurs as new experiences interfere with our retrieval and as the physical memory trace gradually decays.

But what exactly is the "memory trace"? Since 1980, new clues to the physical basis of long-term memory have surfaced rapidly. While cognitive psychologists study our memory "software," neuroscientists are gaining new insights into our memory "hardware"—how and where we physically store information in our brains.

For several decades, neuroscientists have searched the brain for physical evidence of memory. The search has at times been exasperating. One psychologist, Karl Lashley (1950), trained rats to solve a maze, then cut out pieces of the rats' cerebral cortexes and retested their memory of the maze. He hoped eventually to locate where memory of the maze was stored. Alas, no matter what part of the cortex he removed, the rats retained at least a partial memory of how to solve the maze. Lashley's conclusion: Memories do not reside in single, specific spots.

Clark's Nutcracker
Among animals, one contender for champion memorist would be a mere birdbrain—the Clark's Nutcracker—which during winter and early spring can locate up to 6000 caches of buried pine seeds (Shettleworth, 1993).

"Our memories are flexible and superimposable, a panoramic blackboard with an endless supply of chalk and erasers."

Elizabeth Loftus and Katherine Ketcham, *The Myth of Repressed Memory*, 1994

■ **long-term potentiation (LTP)** an increase in a synapse's firing potential after brief, rapid stimulation. Believed to be a neural basis for learning and memory.

■ **amnesia** the loss of memory.

Are memories instead rooted in the brain's ongoing electrical activity? If so, then temporarily shutting down that activity should eliminate them, much as a power failure eliminates the settings on a digital clock radio. To test this, Ralph Gerard (1953) trained hamsters to turn right or left to get food. Then he lowered their body temperature until the brain's electrical activity ceased. When the hamsters were revived and their brains were active again, would they remember which way to turn? Yes. Their long-term memories survived the electrical blackout. In commenting on the elusiveness of the memory trace, one memory researcher, with tongue only partly in cheek, said "I must admit that memories are more of a spiritual than a physical reality. When you try to touch them, they turn to mist and disappear" (Loftus & Ketcham, 1994, p. 4). To know how our brain stores and effortlessly retrieves a flood of details "defies comprehension," says one awestruck neuroscientist (Doty, 1998).

Recently, the search for the physical basis of memory—information incarnated in matter—has focused on the firing potential of the synapses.

Synaptic Changes

Neuroscientists are expanding the search for the location of memories by exploring changes within and between single neurons. Memories begin as impulses whizzing through brain circuits, somehow leaving permanent neural traces. Where does the neural change occur? The available clues point to the synapses—the sites where nerve cells communicate with one another through their neurotransmitter messengers. We know that experience modifies the brain's neural networks: Given increased activity in a particular pathway, neural interconnections form or strengthen.

Eric Kandel and James Schwartz (1982) observed actual changes in the sending neurons. By observing sea snails' neural connections before and after conditioning, the researchers were able to pinpoint changes. When learning occurs, the snail releases more of the neurotransmitter serotonin at certain synapses. These synapses then become more efficient at transmitting signals.

Increased synaptic efficiency makes for more efficient neural circuits. In experiments, rapidly stimulating certain memory-circuit connections has increased their sensitivity for hours or even weeks to come. The sending neuron now needs less prompting to release its neurotransmitter, and receptor sites on the receiving neuron may increase (**FIGURE 18.10**). This prolonged strengthening of potential neural firing, called **long-term potentiation (LTP),** provides a neural basis for learning and remembering associations. We know now that drugs that block LTP interfere with learning (Lynch & Staubli, 1991). Mutant mice engineered to lack an enzyme needed for LTP can't learn their way out of a maze (Silva & others, 1992). And rats given a drug that enhances LTP will learn a maze with half the usual number of mistakes (Service, 1994). These findings raise hopes that researchers may someday discover a drug to enhance human memory, especially for those whose memory is fading.

After long-term potentiation has occurred, passing an electric current through the brain won't disrupt old memories. But the current will wipe out very recent experiences. Such is the experience both of laboratory animals and of depressed people given electroconvulsive therapy. A blow to the head can do the same. When football players who have been dazed or momentarily knocked unconscious are interviewed a few minutes later, they typically cannot recall the name of the play during which the incident occurred (Yarnell & Lynch, 1970). Likewise, a boxer knocked out in round 2 may have no memory of the round. (They are like sleepers who can't remember what they heard just before losing consciousness.) The information in short-term memory before the blow did not have time to consolidate into long-term memory.

Drugs that block neurotransmitters will also disrupt information storage (Squire, 1987). For example, alcohol impairs memory formation by disrupting serotonin's messenger activity (Weingartner & others, 1983). The morning after a night of heavy drinking, a person may have trouble remembering the previous evening.

FIGURE 18.10

Doubled receptor sites

Electron microscope images show just one receptor site (white) reaching toward a sending neuron before long-term potentiation (top) and two afterward (bottom). (From Toni & others, 1999.)

Stress Hormones and Memory

The stress hormones that humans and animals produce when excited or stressed make more glucose energy available to fuel brain activity. This hormone surge signals the brain that something important has happened. The arousal sears the events onto the brain. Conversely, people given a drug that blocks stress hormones will later have more trouble remembering the details of an upsetting story (Cahill & others, 1994). No emotion means weaker memories.

Emotion-triggered hormonal changes help explain why we long remember exciting or shocking events, such as our first kiss, a political assassination, or an earthquake. People who have suffered traumatic experiences often relive the experience with vivid flashbacks. And people who experienced the 1989 San Francisco earthquake had perfect recall a year and a half later of where they were and what they were doing (as they had recorded within a day or two of the quake). Others' memories for the circumstances under which they *heard* about the quake were prone to errors (Neisser & others, 1991; Palmer & others, 1991). (A second important reason for the durability of dramatic experiences is our reliving and rehearsing them—as did most people who experienced the earthquake and told their stories to countless others.)

The point to remember, according to James McGaugh (1994), is that "stronger emotional experiences make for stronger, more reliable memories." After traumatic experiences—a wartime ambush, a house fire, a rape—vivid recollections of the horrific event intrude again and again. It is as if they were burned in.

Stress hormones and memory
When we are greatly aroused, as with these people trying to escape a life-threatening storm, our stress hormones help make memories indelible.

Storing Implicit and Explicit Memories

A memory-to-be enters the cortex through the senses, then winds its way into the brain's depths. Precisely where it goes depends on the type of information, as dramatically illustrated in the special **amnesic** patients similar to John, whom we met at the beginning of this module.

Neurologist Oliver Sacks (1985, pp. 26–27) describes another such patient, Jimmie, who had brain damage. Jimmie had no memories—thus, no sense of elapsed time—beyond his injury in 1945. Asked in 1975 to name the U.S. President (Gerald Ford), he replied, "FDR's dead. Truman's at the helm."

When Jimmie gave his age as 19, Sacks set a mirror before him: "Look in the mirror and tell me what you see. Is that a 19-year-old looking out from the mirror?"

Jimmie turned ashen, gripped the chair, cursed, then became frantic: "What's going on? What's happened to me? Is this a nightmare? Am I crazy? Is this a joke?" When his attention was diverted to some children playing baseball, his panic ended, the dreadful mirror forgotten.

Sacks showed Jimmie a photo from *National Geographic*. "What is this?" he asked.

"It's the Moon," Jimmie replied.

"No, it's not," Sacks answered. "It's a picture of the Earth taken from the Moon."

"Doc, you're kidding? Someone would've had to get a camera up there!"

"Naturally."

"Hell! You're joking—how the hell would you do that?" Jimmie's wonder was that of a bright young man from 56 years ago reacting with amazement to his travel back to the future.

Careful testing of people with amnesia reveals something even stranger: Although incapable of recalling new facts or anything they have recently done, Jimmie and other similarly amnesic people can learn. Shown hard-to-find figures in pictures (where's Waldo?), they can quickly spot them again later. They can learn to read mirror-image writing or do a jigsaw puzzle, and they have even been taught complicated job skills (Schacter, 1992, 1996; Squire, 1987). However, *they do all these things with absolutely no awareness of having learned them.*

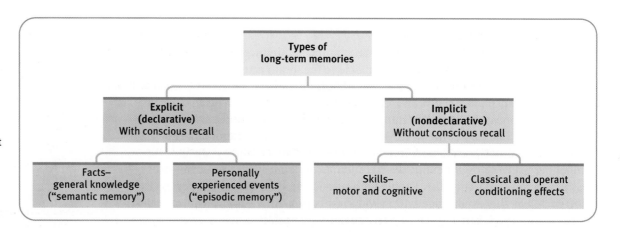

FIGURE 18.11

Memory subsystems
We process and store our explicit and implicit memories separately. Thus, one may lose explicit memory (becoming amnesic), yet display implicit memory for material one cannot consciously recall.

The two-track memory system reinforces an important principle of the way the brain handles information via parallel processing: Mental feats such as vision, thinking, and memory may seem to be single abilities, but they are not. Rather, we split information into different components for separate and simultaneous processing.

"[Brain-scanning] technologies are revolutionizing the study of the brain and mind in the same way that the telescope revolutionized the study of the heavens."

Endel Tulving (1996)

FIGURE 18.12

The hippocampus
Explicit memories for facts and episodes are processed in the hippocampus and fed to other brain regions for storage.

Consider what happens when such patients have learned to solve a Tower of Hanoi puzzle, which requires moving rings from one pole to another until they are stacked in order of size. Amnesia victims will deny having seen the puzzle before, insist it is silly for them to try, and then, like practiced experts, proceed to solve it.

These curious findings challenge the idea that memory is a single, unified system. Instead, we seem to have two memory systems operating in tandem (**FIGURE 18.11**). Whatever has destroyed conscious recall in these individuals with amnesia has not destroyed their unconscious capacity for learning. They can learn *how* to do something—called **implicit memory** (*procedural memory*). But they cannot know and declare *that* they know—called **explicit memory** (*declarative memory*). Having read a story once, they will read it faster a second time, showing implicit memory. But there will be no explicit memory, for they cannot recall having seen the story before. Having played golf on a new course, they will forget it completely, yet the more they play the course, the more their game will improve. If repeatedly shown the word *perfume,* they will not recall having seen it. But if asked the first word that comes to mind in response to the letters *per,* they surprise themselves by saying *perfume,* readily displaying their learning. They retain their past but do not explicitly recall it.

One way to discover how memory works is to study its malfunctions. For example, these remarkable patients provoke us to wonder: Do our explicit and implicit memory systems involve separate brain regions?

THE HIPPOCAMPUS Scans of the brain in action, and autopsies of people who had amnesia, reveal that new explicit memories of names, images, and events are laid down via a brain structure called the **hippocampus** (**FIGURE 18.12**). When brain scans capture the brain giving birth to a memory, they reveal activity in the hippocampus as well as in certain areas of the frontal lobes (Wagner & others, 1998). The hippocampus again lights up on a PET scan when people recall words (using explicit memory) (Squire, 1992).

Damage to the hippocampus disrupts some types of memory. Chickadees and other birds can store food in hundreds of places and return to these unmarked caches months later, but not if their hippocampus has been removed (Sherry & Vaccarino, 1989). Among experienced London taxi drivers, the back of the hippocampus, the part associated with spatial memory, is enlarged (Maguire & others, 2000). Like the cortex, the hippocampus is lateralized. (You've got two of them, one just above each ear and about an inch and a half straight in.) Damage to the left or right hippocampus seems to produce different results. Patients with left hippocampus damage have trouble remembering verbal information, but they have no trouble recalling visual designs and locations. For those with right hippocampus damage, the problem is reversed (Schacter, 1996).

Monkeys who lose their hippocampus to surgery also lose most of their recall for things learned during the preceding month, though their older memories remain intact (Squire & Zola-Morgan, 1991). The hippocampus seems to act as a convergence zone where the brain registers and temporarily stores the elements of a remembered episode—

the smells, feels, sounds, and place. It is also a play-back system that reactivates neurons that fired when we experienced the event, as if helping the brain strengthen connections among them (Skaggs & McNaughton, 1996).

Our brain's librarian assigns different information to different regions. Brain scans reveal that, once stored, our mental encores of past experience activate various parts of the frontal and temporal lobes (Fink & others, 1996; Gabrieli & others, 1996; Markowitsch, 1995). Calling up a telephone number and holding it in working memory activates a region of the left frontal cortex; recalling a party scene would more likely activate a region of the right hemisphere.

THE CEREBELLUM Although your hippocampus is a temporary processing site for your explicit memories, you could lose it and still lay down memories for skills and conditioned associations. Hoping to locate such implicit memories, psychologist Richard Thompson and his fellow explorers David Krupa and Judith Thompson studied how a rabbit's brain learns to associate a tone with an impending air puff in the eye (and thus to blink in anticipation of the puff). First, they traced the pathway connecting the brain's reception of the tone with the blink response. They discovered that it runs to the brainstem through a part of the **cerebellum** (at the back of the head) and that if they cut this pathway, the learned response would be lost. It was like cutting the cords to your stereo speakers, which would confirm the cord's part in the electronic path but might still leave you wondering where the music is stored. Their next step was to administer a drug during the rabbits' eyeblink training, temporarily deadening different parts of the neural pathway. This pinpointed the implicit memory—in the cerebellum. The rejuvenated rabbits failed to display the learned response only when the cerebellum was deactivated during training (Green & Woodruff-Pak, 2000). Human patients with a damaged cerebellum are likewise incapable of eyeblink conditioning (Daum & Schugens, 1996).

This dual explicit-implicit memory system helps explain infantile amnesia: The reactions and skills we learned during infancy reach far into our future, yet as adults we recall nothing (explicitly) of our first three years. Our conscious minds are blank, not only because we index so much of our explicit memory by words that nonspeaking children have not learned, but also because the hippocampus is one of the last brain structures to mature.

■ **implicit memory** retention without conscious recollection (of skills and dispositions). (Also called *procedural memory*.)

■ **explicit memory** memory of facts and experiences that one can consciously know and "declare." (Also called *declarative memory*.)

■ **hippocampus** a neural center located in the limbic system that helps process explicit memories for storage.

■ **cerebellum [sehr-uh-BELL-um]** the "little brain" attached to the rear of the brainstem; it helps coordinate voluntary movement and balance.

rehearse it!

7. Sensory information is initially recorded in our sensory memory. This memory may be visual (_____ memory) or auditory (_____ memory).
   a. implicit; explicit
   b. iconic; echoic
   c. declarative; nondeclarative
   d. long-term; short-term

8. Our capacity for storing long-term memories is essentially limitless. However, our short-term memory for new information is limited. When confronted with a list of novel items, most people can immediately recall
   a. only the first items on the list.
   b. a series of about 20 items.
   c. a series of about 7 items.
   d. only meaningful items.

9. Researchers have found that long-term potentiation (LTP) provides a neural basis for learning and memory. LTP refers to
   a. emotion-triggered hormonal changes.
   b. the role of the hippocampus in processing explicit memories.
   c. an increase in a synapse's firing potential after brief, rapid stimulation.
   d. aging people's potential for learning.

10. A patient who has amnesia and has suffered damage to the hippocampus typically has difficulties in learning new facts and recalling recent events. However, the person may well be able to recall the more distant past and certain well-learned skills, such as how to ride a bicycle or hem a dress. Memories of skills are
   a. explicit memories.
   b. implicit memories.
   c. iconic memories.
   d. echoic memories.

11. The physical basis of memory—how and where memories are physically stored in the brain—is not yet well understood. However, research suggests that the hippocampus plays an important role. The hippocampus may function as
   a. a way station between short-term and long-term explicit memories.
   b. a computer's hard disk.
   c. the cortex.
   d. a processing center for implicit memories.

Remembering things past
Even if Madonna and Paul Newman had not become famous, their high school classmates would most likely still recognize their yearbook photos.

"Memory is not like a container that gradually fills up; it is more like a tree growing hooks onto which memories are hung."

Psychologist Peter Russell, *The Brain Book*, 1979

Multiple-choice questions test our

a. recall.

b. recognition.

c. relearning.

Fill-in-the-blank questions test our

_____.

(See page 280.)

Retrieval: Getting Information Out

PREVIEW QUESTION 9 What cues or associations help us access our stored memories?

To most people, memory is **recall,** the ability to retrieve information not in conscious awareness. To a psychologist, memory is any sign that something learned has been retained. So *recognizing* or more quickly *relearning* information also indicates memory.

Long after you cannot recall most of the people in your high school graduating class, you may still be able to recognize their yearbook pictures from a photographic lineup and pick their names from a list of names. Harry Bahrick and his colleagues (1975) reported that people who graduated 25 years earlier could not *recall* many of their old classmates, but they could *recognize* 90 percent of their pictures and names.

Our speed at relearning can reveal memory. If you once learned something and then forgot it, you probably will relearn it more quickly than you originally learned it. When you study for a final exam or resurrect a language used in early childhood, the relearning is easier. Tests of **recognition** and of time spent **relearning** reveal that we remember more than we can recall.

Our recognition memory is impressively quick and vast. "Is your friend wearing a new or old outfit?" "Old." "Is this seconds-long movie clip from a film you've ever seen?" "Yes." "Have you ever before seen this person—this minor variation on the same old human features (two eyes, one nose, and so on)?" "No." Before the mouth can form our answer to any of millions of such questions, the mind knows, and knows that it knows.

Retrieval Cues

To retrieve a fact from a library, you need a way to access it. In recognition tests, *retrieval cues* (such as photographs) provide reminders of information (classmates' names) we could not otherwise recall. Retrieval cues also guide us to where to look. If you want to know what the pyramid on the back of an American dollar signifies, you might look in *Collier's Encyclopedia* under "dollar," "currency," or "money." But your efforts would be futile. To get the information you want, you would have to look under "Great Seal of the United States" (Hayes, 1981). Like information stored in encyclopedias, memories can't be accessed unless we have the right cues for retrieving them. Do you recall the gist of the second sentence I asked you to remember (on page 267)? If not, does the word *shark* help? Experiments show that *shark* more readily retrieves the image you stored than does the sentence's actual word, *fish* (Anderson & others, 1976).

You can think of a memory as held in storage by a web of associations. To retrieve a specific memory, you first need to identify one of the strands that leads to it, a process called **priming.** Philosopher-psychologist William James referred to priming as the "wakening of associations." Often our associations are activated, or primed, without our awareness. As **FIGURE 18.13** indicates, seeing or hearing the word *rabbit* primes associations with *hare* even though we may not recall having seen or heard *rabbit*.

FIGURE 18.13

Priming—awakening associations

After seeing or hearing *rabbit*, we are later more likely to spell the spoken word *hair/hare* as *h-a-r-e*. The spreading of associations unconsciously activates related associations. This phenomenon is called priming. (Adapted from Bower, 1986.)

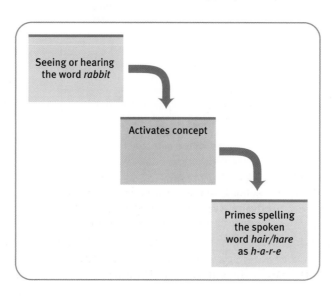

Seeing or hearing the word *rabbit*

Activates concept

Primes spelling the spoken word *hair/hare* as *h-a-r-e*

Priming has been called "memoryless memory"—memory without remembering, invisible memory. If, walking down a hallway, you see a poster of a missing child, you will then be "primed" to interpret an ambiguous adult-child interaction as a possible kidnapping (James, 1986). Although you don't consciously remember the poster, it predisposes your interpretation. (Researchers have shown that even subliminal stimuli can briefly prime responses to later stimuli.)

Retrieval cues often prime our memories of earlier experiences. But the best retrieval cues come from the associations formed at the time we encode a memory. Those cues can be words (such as the mnemonic device ROY G. BIV), or experiences (such as tastes, smells, and sights) that evoke our recall of associated episodes. To call up visual cues when trying to recall something, we may mentally place ourselves in the original context. For British theologian John Hull (1990, p. 174) this became difficult after losing his sight. On one occasion when his wife asked him what he had done that day he had difficulty recalling. "I knew I had been somewhere, and had done particular things with certain people, but where? I could not put the conversations I had had into a context. There was no background, no features against which to identify the place. Normally, the memories of people you have spoken to during the day are stored in frames which include the background."

Context Effects

It does help to put yourself back in the context where you experienced something. Duncan Godden and Alan Baddeley (1975) discovered this when they had scuba divers listen to a list of words in two different settings, either 10 feet underwater or sitting on the beach. As **FIGURE 18.14** illustrates, the divers recalled more words when they were retested in the same place.

> Ask a friend two rapid-fire questions: (a) How do you pronounce the word spelled by the letters *s-h-o-p*? (b) What do you do when you come to a green light? If your friend answers "stop" to the second question, you have demonstrated priming.

FIGURE 18.14
The effects of context on memory
Words heard underwater are best recalled underwater; words heard on land are best recalled on land. (Adapted from Godden & Baddeley, 1975.)

Percentage of words recalled

Chart showing percentage of words recalled:
- Water/land: ~22%
- Land/water: ~21%
- Water/water: ~31%
- Land/land: ~40%

Greater recall when learning and testing contexts are the same

Different contexts for hearing and recall | Same contexts for hearing and recall

You have probably experienced similar context effects. You return to where you once lived or to the school you once attended and are flooded with retrieval cues and memories. Even taking an exam in the same room where you are taught may help a little. In several experiments, Carolyn Rovee-Collier (1993) found that a familiar context activates memories even in 3-month-olds. After infants learned that kicking a crib mobile would make it move (via a connecting ribbon from the ankle), the infants kicked more when tested again in the same crib with the same bumper.

■ **recall** a measure of memory in which the person must retrieve information learned earlier, as on a fill-in-the-blank test.

■ **recognition** a measure of memory in which the person need only identify items previously learned, as on a multiple-choice test.

■ **relearning** a memory measure that assesses the amount of time saved when learning material for a second time.

■ **priming** the activation, often unconsciously, of particular associations in memory.

Distributed by Levin Represents.

CALLAHAN

"I wonder if you'd mind giving me directions. I've never been sober in this part of town before."

Sometimes, being in a context similar to one we've been in before may trigger the experience of **déjà vu** (French for "already seen")—that eerie sense that "I've been in this exact situation before." The 60 percent of people who report having had this experience (McAneny, 1996) often wonder, "How could I recognize a situation that I'm experiencing for the first time?" Those who suppose something paranormal is occurring may think of reincarnation ("I must have experienced this in a previous life") or precognition ("I viewed this scene in my mind before experiencing it"). If we pose the question differently ("Why do I feel as if I recognize this situation?"), we can see how our memory system might produce déjà vu (Alcock, 1981). If we have previously been in a similar situation, the current situation may be loaded with cues that unconsciously retrieve the earlier experience. Thus, if in such a context you see a stranger who looks and walks like one of your friends, the similarity may give rise to an eerie feeling of recognition. Because the feeling conflicts with your knowing that the person is a stranger, you may think, "I've seen that person in this situation before."

Moods and Memories

Associated words, events, and contexts are not the only retrieval cues. Events in the past may have aroused a specific emotion that later can prime us to recall its associated events. Cognitive psychologist Gordon Bower (1983) explained it this

Mood and memory
Elated, we remember other happy times. Mood serves as a retrieval cue, activating other memories tinged with the same emotion. These memories help sustain the current mood.

way: "A specific emotional state is like a specific room in a library into which the subject places memory records, and he can most easily retrieve those records by returning to that same room or emotional state." What we learn in one state—be it joyful or sad, drunk or sober—is sometimes more easily recalled when we are again in the same state, a subtle phenomenon called *state-dependent memory.* What is learned when depressed, high, or drunk is not recalled well in *any* state (depression and certain drugs interfere with encoding, and alcohol disrupts storage). But it is recalled slightly better when again drunk, high, or depressed. Someone who hides money when drunk may forget the location until drunk again.

More striking is the way our memories are *biased* by our moods (Eich, 1995; Ellis & Ashbrook, 1989; Matt & others, 1992). We seem to associate good or bad events with their accompanying emotions, which become retrieval cues. Thus, our memories are somewhat **mood-congruent.** Being depressed sours memories by priming negative associations, which we then use to explain our current mood. Conversely, if people are put in a buoyant mood—whether under hypnosis or just by the day's events (a World Cup soccer victory for the German subjects of one study)—they recall the world through rose-colored glasses (Forgas & others, 1984; Schwarz & others, 1987). They judge themselves competent and effective, other people benevolent, and life in general wonderful.

Knowing this connection, we should not be surprised that in some studies *currently* depressed people recall their parents as rejecting, punitive, and guilt-promoting, whereas *formerly* depressed people describe their parents much as do those who have never suffered depression (Lewinsohn & Rosenbaum, 1987; Lewis, 1992). No wonder Robert Bornstein and others (1991) report that adolescents' ratings of parental warmth give little clue to how the same adolescents will rate their parents six weeks later. When teenagers are down, their world, including their parents, seems inhuman; as their mood brightens, their parents morph from devils into angels. You and I may nod our heads knowingly. Yet, in a good or bad mood, we persist in attributing to reality our own changing judgments and memories.

Answers to questions on page 278:
Multiple-choice questions test recognition.
Fill-in-the-blank questions test recall.

■ **déjà vu** that eerie sense that "I've experienced this before." Cues from the current situation may subconsciously trigger retrieval of an earlier experience.

■ **mood-congruent memory** the tendency to recall experiences that are consistent with one's current good or bad mood.

Moods also influence how we *interpret* other people's behavior. In a bad mood we read someone's look as a glare; in a good mood we encode the same look as interest. How we perceive the world depends on our mood. Passions exaggerate.

Your mood's effect on retrieval helps explain why moods persist. When happy, you recall happy events, which helps prolong the good mood. When depressed, you recall sad events, which in turn darkens your interpretations of current events. Unfortunately for those suffering from depression, this process maintains depression's vicious cycle.

Improving Memory

PREVIEW QUESTION 10 How might we apply memory principles to everyday situations, such as remembering a person's name or the material we are studying?

Now and then we are dismayed at our forgetfulness—at our embarrassing inability to recall someone's name, at forgetting to bring up a point in conversation, at forgetting to bring along something important, at finding ourselves standing in a room unable to recall why we are there (Herrmann, 1982). Is there anything we can do to minimize such misdeeds of our memory system? Much as biology benefits medicine and botany benefits agriculture, so can the psychology of memory benefit education. Sprinkled throughout this module and summarized here for easy reference are concrete suggestions for improving memory.

Study repeatedly to boost long-term recall. Overlearn. To learn a name, say it to yourself after being introduced; wait a few seconds and say it again; wait longer and say it again. Provide yourself with many separate study sessions by taking advantage of life's little intervals—riding on the bus, walking across campus, waiting for class to start.

Spend more time rehearsing or actively thinking about the material. Speed-reading (skimming) complex material—with minimal rehearsal—yields little retention. Rehearsal and critical reflection help more. It pays to study actively!

Make the material personally meaningful. To build a network of retrieval cues, take thorough text and class notes in your own words. Mindlessly repeating information is relatively ineffective. It is better to form images, understand and organize information, relate the material to what you already know or have experienced, and put it in your own words. Without such cues, you may find yourself stuck when a question uses phrasing different from the rote forms you memorized. To increase retrieval cues, form as many associations as possible.

To remember a list of unfamiliar items, use mnemonic devices. Associate items with peg-words. Make up a story that incorporates vivid images of the items. Chunk information into acronyms.

Refresh your memory by activating retrieval cues. Mentally re-create the situation and the mood in which the original learning occurred. Return to the same location. Jog your memory by allowing one thought to cue the next.

Minimize interference. Study before sleeping. Do not study in close proximity topics that are likely to interfere with each other, such as Spanish and French.

Test your own knowledge, both to rehearse it and to help determine what you do not yet know. If you must *recall* information later, do not be lulled into overconfidence by your ability to *recognize* it. Test your recall. In using this or any other text, outline each module or chapter section on a blank page. For terms and concepts listed at the end of a module or chapter, attempt to define each term *before* turning back to its definition. Take practice tests; the study guides that accompany many texts, including this one, can help.

"When a feeling was there, they felt as if it would never go; when it was gone, they felt as if it had never been; when it returned, they felt as if it had never gone."

George MacDonald, *What's Mine's Mine*, 1886

Thinking and memory
Most of what we know is not the result of efforts to memorize. We learn because we're curious and because we spend time thinking about our experiences. Actively thinking as we read, by rehearsing and relating ideas, yields the best retention.

"Knit each new thing on to some acquisition already there."

William James, *Principles of Psychology*, 1890

rehearse it!

12. To measure long-term memory, psychologists test a person's ability to recall information. They also test ability to recognize what has been learned, and they measure relearning time. A psychologist who asks you to write down as many objects as you can remember having seen a few minutes earlier is testing your
    a. recall.
    b. recognition.
    c. recall and recognition.
    d. relearning.

13. To gain access to a memory, a person activates an association that leads to that memory. The association may be activated by a specific odor, visual image, or mnemonic; all of these are examples of
    a. relearning.
    b. déjà vu.
    c. declarative memories.
    d. retrieval cues.

14. To retrieve a memory, it sometimes helps to return to the setting where the event occurred. In some cases, retrieval may be enhanced by a context similar to one you have already experienced. The resulting feeling that "you've been there before" is known as
    a. déjà vu.
    b. mood-congruent memory.
    c. relearning.
    d. the misinformation effect.

15. When happy, we tend to recall happy times. When depressed, we more often recall depressing events. This tendency to recall experiences that are consistent with our current emotions is called
    a. mnemonics.
    b. chunking.
    c. repression.
    d. mood-congruent memory.

REVIEWING

Information Processing

1. How do psychologists describe the human memory system?

Memory is the persistence of learning over time. We are particularly likely to remember vivid events that form flashbulb memories. The computer is one convenient model for thinking about human memory. Both systems must *encode, store,* and *retrieve* information. Both feature *long-term memory,* from which we can activate information into a *working memory;* in computers, part of this working memory is displayed on screen. On-screen memory is similar to our *short-term memory;* unless used or rehearsed, it quickly disappears. We experience *sensory memory* when sensory information is immediately recorded in our memory system.

2. How do the sights, sounds, and other sensations we experience get selectively encoded and transferred into the memory system?

Some types of information, notably concerning space, time, and frequency, we encode mostly automatically (automatic processing). Other types of information, including much of our processing of meaning, imagery, and organization, require effortful processing.

3. How much does rehearsal aid in forming memories?

Without rehearsal, much information (such as a new phone number) is lost within three seconds. The more we rehearse information, the better we retain it—especially if our rehearsal is spaced out over time (spacing effect) rather than massed. When learning a list of words or names, our later recall is often best for those learned first, which we may have rehearsed more (the serial position effect).

4. What strategies and devices help us remember information that requires effortful processing?

Effortful encoding of meaning, imagery, and organization enhances long-term retention. Mnemonic devices exploit the memorability of visual images and of information that is organized into chunks (chunking). Organizing information into hierarchies also aids memory.

5. How does sensory memory work?

Information first enters the memory system through the senses. We have a precise but fleeting iconic (photographic) memory for visual stimuli and a slightly longer-lasting echoic memory for auditory stimuli.

6. What are the limits of short-term memory?

Our short-term memory span for information just presented is very limited—a seconds-long retention of about seven items, depending on the information and how it is presented.

7. How large and durable is our long-term memory?

Our capacity for storing information permanently in long-term memory is essentially unlimited. Nevertheless, most of what we learn is soon forgotten; the brain does not store information with the durability and exactness of a tape recorder.

8. How and where does the brain physically store memories?

The search for the physical basis of memory has recently focused on brain circuits, synapses (through long-term potentiation), neurotransmitters, and hormones. As demonstrated in studies of people with amnesia, one brain structure, the hippocampus, processes explicit memories; implicit memories involve different brain mechanisms. This suggests a dual memory system.

9. What cues or associations help us access our stored memories?

To be remembered, information that is "in there" must be retrieved, as measured by recall, recognition, or relearning. This occurs with the aid of associations (cues) formed through priming; for example, sometimes a familiar context causes us to believe we have experienced an event at an earlier time (déjà vu). Our memory is often mood-congruent. Mood can serve as a retrieval cue, leading us to recall happy times when happy, sad times when sad.

Moods can also interfere with our recall, as when preoccupation with our feelings—sad or happy—makes us less attentive to new information.

10. How might we apply memory principles to everyday situations, such as remembering a person's name or the material we are studying?

The psychology of memory suggests concrete strategies for improving memory. These include repeated, spaced study; active rehearsal; encoding of well-organized, vivid, meaningful associations; mnemonic techniques; the return to contexts and moods that are rich with associations; minimizing interference; and self-testing and rehearsal.

TERMS AND CONCEPTS TO REMEMBER

memory, p. 262
flashbulb memory, p. 263
encoding, p. 263
storage, p. 263
retrieval, p. 263
sensory memory, p. 264
short-term memory, p. 264
long-term memory, p. 264
working memory, p. 264

automatic processing, p. 265
effortful processing, p. 265
rehearsal, p. 265
spacing effect, p. 266
serial position effect, p. 267
imagery, p. 268
mnemonics [nih-MON-iks], p. 268
chunking, p. 270
iconic memory, p. 271

echoic memory, p. 272
long-term potentiation (LTP), p. 274
amnesia, p. 275
implicit memory, p. 276
explicit memory, p. 276
hippocampus, p. 276
cerebellum [sehr-uh-BELL-um], p. 277

recall, p. 278
recognition, p. 278
relearning, p. 278
priming, p. 278
déjà vu, p. 280
mood-congruent memory, p. 280

REHEARSE IT ANSWER KEY

| 1. b | 3. b | 5. d | 7. b | 9. c | 11. a | 13. d | 15. d |
| 2. a | 4. a | 6. c | 8. c | 10. b | 12. a | 14. a | |

19 Forgetting and Memory Construction

- Forgetting
- Memory Construction

Forgetting

PREVIEW QUESTION 1 Why do we forget? At what points in the memory system can our memory fail us?

Amid all the applause for memory—all the efforts to understand it, all the books on how to improve it—have any voices been heard in praise of forgetting? William James (1890, p. 680) was such a voice: "If we remembered everything, we should on most occasions be as ill off as if we remembered nothing." To discard the clutter of useless or out-of-date information—where we parked the car yesterday, a friend's old phone number, restaurant orders already cooked and served—is surely a blessing (Bjork, 1978). A good memory is helpful, but so is the ability to forget.

More often, however, our memory dismays and frustrates us. Memories are quirky. My own memory can easily call up episodes like that wonderful first kiss with the woman I love or trivial facts like Sammy Sosa's current home run total. Then it abandons me when I'm trying to recall that new colleague's name or where I left my sunglasses.

To remember any event requires that we get information into our brain (*encoding*), retain that information (*storage*), and later get it back out (*retrieval*). Richard Atkinson and Richard Shiffrin (1968), in their classic and influential *three-stage processing* model of memory, suggest that we give birth to memories through three stages. We first record to-be-remembered information as a fleeting *sensory memory*, from which it is processed into *short-term memory*, which holds the information briefly before we encode it for *long-term memory* and later retrieval.

Memory failures can occur in any of the stages of the memory system. They may be failures of encoding (the information never gets in), of storage (fading of the memory record), or of retrieval (from a lack of retrieval cues or from the interfering effects of other learning). Our memories may also become distorted or too persistent. Memory researcher Daniel Schacter (1999) enumerates seven ways our memories fail us—the seven sins of memory, he calls them:

Three sins of forgetting:

- *Absent-mindedness*—inattention to details produces encoding failure (our mind is elsewhere as we lay down the car keys).
- *Transience*—storage decay over time (unused information fades).
- *Blocking*—inaccessibility of stored information (it may be on the tip of our tongue, but we experience retrieval failure—we cannot get it out).

Three sins of distortion:

- *Misattribution*—confusing the source of information (putting words in someone else's mouth or remembering a movie scene as an actual happening).
- *Suggestibility*—the lingering effects of misinformation (a leading question— "Did Mr. Jones touch your private parts?"—later becomes a young child's false memory).
- *Bias*—belief-colored recollections (what were your initial feelings toward your fiancé?).

One sin of intrusion:

- *Persistence*—unwanted memories (being haunted by images of a sexual assault).

Let's first consider the sins of forgetting, then those of distortion and persistence.

Encoding Failure

What causes us to forget? One answer is that we failed to encode the information (**FIGURE 19.1**). Thus, it never entered long-term memory. The same brain areas that jump into action when young adults are encoding new information are less responsive among older adults. This slower encoding helps explain age-related memory decline (Grady & others, 1995). (Although older people tend to recall less than younger adults do, they usually remember as well as younger people when given reminders or a recognition test.)

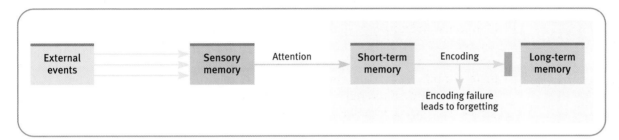

FIGURE 19.1

Forgetting as encoding failure We cannot remember what we have not encoded.

But no matter how young we are, we simply cannot attend to more than a few of the myriad sights and sounds continually bombarding us. In fact, much of what we sense we never even notice. Consider something you have looked at countless times: What letters accompany the number 5 on your telephone? Or where is the number 0 on your calculator? For most of us these are surprisingly difficult questions.

If you live in North America, Britain, or Australia, you have probably also looked at thousands of pennies in your lifetime. You can surely recall the features (color and size) you use to distinguish coins. But can you recall what the side with the head looks like? If not, let's make the memory test easier: If you are familiar with U.S. coins, can you recognize the real thing in **FIGURE 19.2**? Raymond Nickerson and Marilyn Adams (1979) discovered that most people cannot. Likewise, few British people can draw from memory the one-pence coin they have seen thousands of times (Richardson, 1993). The details of a penny are not very meaningful—nor are they essential for distinguishing pennies from other coins—and few of us have made the effort to encode them. We encode some information automatically; other types of information require *effortful* processing. Without attention and conscious effort, many memories never form.

Storage Decay

Even after encoding something well, we sometimes later forget it. To study the durability of our stored memories, Hermann Ebbinghaus (1885) learned lists of nonsense syllables and measured how much he retained when relearning each list, from

(a) (b) (c) (d) (e)
(f) (g) (h) (i) (j)
(k) (l) (m) (n) (o)

FIGURE 19.2

Test your memory Which one of these pennies is the real thing? (If you live outside the United States, try drawing your own country's penny.) (From Nickerson & Adams, 1979.) (See page 287.)

FIGURE 19.3

Ebbinghaus' forgetting curve

After learning lists of nonsense syllables, Ebbinghaus studied how much he retained up to 30 days later. He found that memory for novel information fades quickly, then levels out. (Adapted from Ebbinghaus, 1885.)

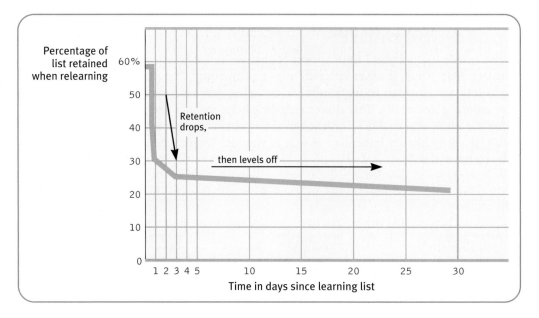

20 minutes to 30 days later. His famous "forgetting curve" (**FIGURE 19.3**) indicates that much of what we learn we may indeed quickly forget. Later experiments made the forgetting curve into one of psychology's laws: The course of forgetting is initially rapid, then levels off with time (Wixted & Ebbesen, 1991).

Harry Bahrick (1984) extended Ebbinghaus's finding. He examined the forgetting curve for Spanish vocabulary learned in school. By using the cross-sectional method (comparing people from different age groups), Bahrick compared the knowledge of Spanish among people who had just taken Spanish with the knowledge of those who had studied it up to 50 years before. Compared with those just completing a high school or college Spanish course, those who had been out of school for 3 years had forgotten much of what they had learned (**FIGURE 19.4**). However, after roughly 3 years, their forgetting leveled off; what people remembered then, they still remembered 25 and more years later, even if they had not used their Spanish at all.

FIGURE 19.4

The forgetting curve for Spanish learned in school

Compared with people just completing a Spanish course, those 3 years out of the course remembered much less. Compared with the 3-year group, however, those who studied Spanish even longer ago did not forget much more. (Adapted from Bahrick, 1984b.)

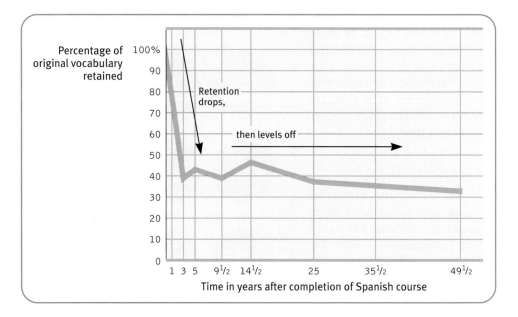

One explanation for these forgetting curves is a gradual fading of the physical memory trace. As we learn more about the physical storage of memory, we may come to understand better how memory storage can decay. But memories also fade because of the accumulation of other learning that disrupts our retrieval.

Retrieval Failure

We have seen that when we fail to encode information and when our stored memories decay, we forget. Forgotten events are like books you can't find in your campus library—some because they were never acquired, others because they were discarded.

But there is a third possibility: Even if the book is stored and available, it may be inaccessible. Perhaps you don't have the information needed to look it up and retrieve it. Information sometimes gets into our brain and, though we know it is there, we cannot get it out (**FIGURE 19.5**). A name may lie poised on the tip of the tongue, waiting to be retrieved. When people who cannot recall information get retrieval cues ("It begins with an *M*"), they often remember what they could not recall. Retrieval problems also lie behind the occasional memory failures of older adults. Forgetting is often not memories discarded but memories hard to find.

Answer to question on page 285: The first penny (a) is the real penny.

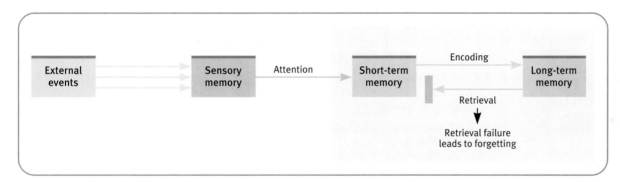

FIGURE 19.5
Retrieval failure
We store in long-term memory what's important to us, or what we've rehearsed. But sometimes even stored information cannot be accessed, which leads to forgetting.

Interference

Learning some items may interfere with retrieving others, especially when the items are similar. If someone gives you a phone number, you may be able to recall it later. But if two more people give you their numbers, each successive number will be more difficult to recall. Such **proactive** *(forward-acting)* **interference** occurs when something you learned earlier disrupts your recall of something you experience later. As you collect more and more information, your mental attic never fills, but it certainly gets cluttered.

For example, if you buy a new combination lock or get a new phone number, the old one may interfere. Benton Underwood (1957) found that those who learn different lists of words on successive days have more and more difficulty remembering each new list the next day. This proactive interference explains why Ebbinghaus, after memorizing countless lists of nonsense syllables during his career, could remember only about one-fourth of a new list of syllables on the day after he learned it—far fewer than you as a novice could remember after learning a single list.

Retroactive *(backward-acting)* **interference** occurs when new information makes it harder to recall something you learned earlier (**FIGURE 19.6**). For example,

■ **proactive interference** the disruptive effect of prior learning on the recall of new information.

■ **retroactive interference** the disruptive effect of new learning on the recall of old information.

FIGURE 19.6
Proactive and retroactive interference

French, learned beforehand, interferes proactively

Study French — papier livre plume école

Study Spanish — papel libro pluma escuela

proactive interference

Spanish 101
Mid-term
exam

Spanish, learned afterward, interferes retroactively

Study French — papier livre plume école

Study Spanish — papel libro pluma escuela

retroactive interference

French 101
Mid-term
exam

learning new students' names typically interferes with a teacher's recall of the names of previous students.

You can minimize retroactive interference by reducing the number of interfering events—say, by going to sleep shortly after learning new information. This is what John Jenkins and Karl Dallenbach (1924) found in a classic experiment. Day after day, two people each learned some nonsense syllables, then tried to recall them after up to eight hours of being awake or asleep at night. As **FIGURE 19.7** shows, forgetting occurred more rapidly after being awake and involved with other activities. The investigators surmised that "forgetting is not so much a matter of the decay of old impressions and associations as it is a matter of interference, inhibition, or obliteration of the old by the new" (1924, p. 612). Later experiments have confirmed that the hour before a night's sleep (but not the minute before sleep) is a good time to commit information to memory (Fowler & others, 1973).

Interference is an important cause of forgetting, but we should not overstate the point. Sometimes old information can facilitate our learning of new information. Knowing Latin may help us to learn French—a phenomenon called *positive transfer.* It is when old and new information compete with each other that interference occurs.

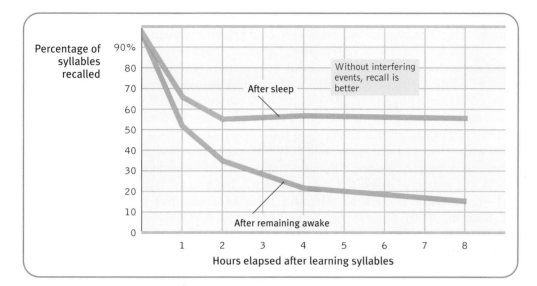

FIGURE 19.7
Retroactive interference
More forgetting occurred when a person stayed awake and experienced other new material. (From Jenkins & Dallenbach, 1924.)

Motivated Forgetting

The huge cookie jar in our kitchen was jammed with freshly baked chocolate chip cookies. Still more were cooling across racks on the counter. Twenty-four hours later, not a crumb was left. Who had taken them? During that time, my wife, three children, and I were the only people in the house. So while memories were still fresh, I conducted a little memory test. Andy acknowledged wolfing down as many as 20. Peter admitted eating 15. Laura guessed she had stuffed her then-6-year-old body with 15 cookies. My wife, Carol, recalled eating 6, and I remembered consuming 15 and taking 18 more to the office. We sheepishly accepted responsibility for 89 cookies. Still, we had not come close; there had been 160.

In experiments that parallel the cookie-memory phenomenon, Michael Ross and his colleagues (1981) found that people unknowingly revise their own histories. After Ross persuaded a group of people that brushing their teeth frequently is desirable, they (more than other people) recalled having frequently brushed their teeth in the last two weeks. Having taken a highly touted study skills course, students later inflated their estimates of self-improvement. By *de*flating their evaluations of their previous study habits, they convinced themselves that they had really benefited (Conway & Ross, 1984). To remember our past is often to revise it. By recalling events as we wish, we protect and enhance our self-images.

Why do our memories fail us? Why did my family and I not encode, store, and retrieve the actual number of cookies each of us ate? As **FIGURE 19.8** reminds us, we automatically encode sensory information in amazing detail. So was it a storage problem? Might our memories of cookies, like Ebbinghaus' memory of nonsense syllables,

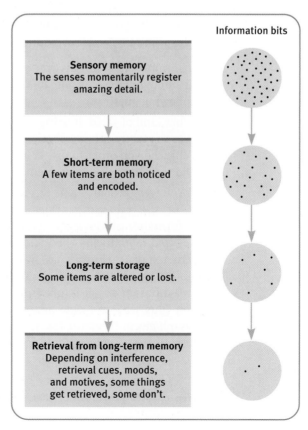

FIGURE 19.8
When do we forget?
Forgetting can occur at any memory stage. As we process information, we filter, alter, or lose much of it.

have vanished almost as fast as the cookies themselves? Or might the information still be intact but irretrievable because it would be embarrassing to remember?[1]

With his concept of **repression,** Sigmund Freud proposed that our memory systems do indeed self-censor painful information. To protect our self-concepts and to minimize anxiety, we supposedly repress painful memories. But the submerged memory lingers, said Freud, and with patience and effort may be retrieved by some later cue or during therapy. One reported case involved a woman with an intense, unexplained fear of running water. One day an aunt solved the mystery. She whispered, "I have never told." The words relit a blown-out candle in the mind; they cued the woman's memory of an incident when, as a disobedient young child, she wandered away from a family picnic and became trapped under a waterfall—until being rescued by her aunt, who promised not to tell her parents (Kihlstrom, 1990). Such stories have fed the now-common belief, shared by 9 in 10 university students, that "memories for painful experiences are sometimes pushed into unconsciousness" (Brown & others, 1996). Repression was central to Freud's psychology and became part of psychology's lore. Most everyone believes it. Therapists assume it often. Yet increasing numbers of memory researchers think repression rarely, if ever, occurs.

Memory Construction

PREVIEW QUESTION 2 How accurate are our memories?

Picture yourself having this experience:

> You go to a fancy restaurant for dinner. You are seated at a table with a white tablecloth. You study the menu. You tell the server you want prime rib, medium rare, a baked potato with sour cream, and a salad with blue cheese dressing. You also order some red wine from the wine list. A few minutes later the server returns with your salad. Later the rest of the meal arrives. You enjoy it all, except the prime rib is a bit overdone.

Were I immediately to quiz you on this paragraph (adapted from Hyde, 1983), you could surely retrieve considerable detail. For example, without looking back, answer the following questions:

1. What kind of salad dressing did you order?
2. Was the tablecloth red checked?
3. What did you order to drink?
4. Did the server give you a menu?

You were probably able to recall exactly what you ordered, and maybe even the color of the tablecloth. Does retrieval therefore consist merely of "reading" the information stored in our brain's library? We do have an enormous capacity for storing and reproducing the incidental details of our daily experience. But we often construct our memories as we encode them, and we may also alter our memories as we withdraw them from the memory bank. Like a scientist who infers a dinosaur's appearance from its remains, we infer our past from stored information plus what we now assume. Did the server give you a menu? Not in the paragraph given. Nevertheless, many answer yes. By filtering information and filling in missing pieces, your schema for restaurants directed your memory construction.

repression in psychoanalytic theory, the basic defense mechanism that banishes anxiety-arousing thoughts, feelings, and memories from consciousness.

misinformation effect incorporating misleading information into one's memory of an event.

[1]One of my cookie-scarfing sons, on reading this in his father's textbook years later, confessed that he had fibbed "a little."

Misinformation and Imagination Effects

In more than 200 experiments, involving more than 20,000 people, Elizabeth Loftus has shown how eyewitnesses similarly reconstruct their memories when questioned. In one experiment with John Palmer, Loftus showed a film of a traffic accident and then quizzed the viewers about what they saw (Loftus & Palmer, 1974). Those asked, "How fast were the cars going when they *smashed* into each other?" gave higher speed estimates than those asked, "How fast were the cars going when they *hit* each other?" A week later, the researchers asked the viewers if they recalled seeing any broken glass. Compared with those who had been asked the question with *hit,* those asked the question with *smashed* were more than twice as likely to say yes, they had seen broken glass (**FIGURE 19.9**). In fact, the film showed no broken glass.

In many follow-up experiments around the world, people have witnessed an event, received or not received misleading information about it, and then taken a memory test. The repeated result is a **misinformation effect:** After exposure to subtle misinformation, many people misremember. They have misrecalled a yield (give way) sign as a stop sign, hammers as screwdrivers, Coke cans as peanut cans, *Vogue* magazine as *Mademoiselle,* "Dr. Henderson" as "Dr. Davidson," breakfast cereal as eggs, and a clean-shaven man as a man with a mustache (Loftus & others, 1992). As a memory fades with time following an event, the injection of misinformation becomes easier (Loftus, 1992).

So unwitting is the misinformation effect that people later find it nearly impossible to discriminate between their memories of real and suggested events (Schooler & others, 1986). This difficulty was strikingly true among those who three years later misrecalled where they were when they heard of the space shuttle *Challenger's* explosion (Neisser & Harsch, 1992). When shown their own accounts, handwritten the day after the explosion, many were surprised. Some felt so sure of their false memories that they insisted their original version must have been flawed.

As we recount an experience, we fill in memory gaps with plausible guesses and assumptions. After more retellings, we often recall the guessed details, which have now been absorbed into our memories, as if we had actually observed them (Roediger & others, 1993). Others' vivid retelling of an event may also implant false memories.

Even repeatedly *imagining* nonexistent actions and events can create false memories. In one laboratory experiment, students who repeatedly imagined simple acts such as breaking a toothpick or picking up a stapler later experienced "imagination inflation"; they were more likely to think they had actually done such things during the experiment's first phase (Goff & Roediger, 1998). In another experi-

Depiction of actual accident

Leading question:
"About how fast were the cars going when they *smashed* into each other?"

Memory construction

FIGURE 19.9

Memory construction

When people who saw the film of a car accident were asked a leading question, they recalled a more serious accident than they had witnessed. (From Loftus, 1979.)

"Memory is insubstantial. Things keep replacing it. Your batch of snapshots will both fix and ruin your memory. . . . You can't remember anything from your trip except the wretched collection of snapshots."

Annie Dillard, "To Fashion a Text," 1988

ment, by Maryanne Garry and others (1996), university students noted whether they had experienced certain childhood events, such as breaking a window with their hand. Two weeks later, half were asked to imagine themselves experiencing four of these events—for example, running, tripping, falling, and cutting their hand as it crashed through a window. After vividly imagining the fictional event, one-fourth of them became more likely to believe that such events may actually have happened during their childhood.

Ira Hyman and his co-workers (1995, 1996) invited Western Washington University students to recall actual childhood events (reported to the researchers by their parents), along with a suggested false event, such as spilling a punch bowl at a wedding. By a third interview (after being encouraged to think about the events between interviews), one-fourth of the students had constructed false memories. For example, they were asked to recall something that happened "when you were six years old and you were attending a wedding." One student recalled, "It was an outdoor wedding and I think we were running around and knocked something over like the punch bowl or something and made a big mess and of course got yelled at for it." The take-home point: *Given time, the mind's search for a fact may create a fiction.*

To see how far the mind will go in creating a fiction, Richard Wiseman and his University of Hertfordshire colleagues (1999) staged eight seances, each attended by 25 curious people. During the supposed seance, the medium—actually a professional actor and magician—asked everyone to concentrate on the moving table. Although it never moved, he suggested that it had: "That's good. Lift the table up. That's good. Keep concentrating. Keep the table in the air." When questioned two weeks later, 34 percent of the participants recalled having actually seen the table levitate.

"It isn't so astonishing, the number of things I can remember, as the number of things I can remember that aren't so."

Mark Twain (1835–1910)

DOONESBURY

Memory construction helps explain why "hypnotically refreshed" memories of crimes so easily incorporate errors, some of which originate with the hypnotist's leading questions. ("Did you hear loud noises?") It explains why dating partners who fall in love *over*estimate their first impressions of one another ("It was love at first sight"), while those who break up *under*estimate their earlier liking ("We never really clicked") (McFarland & Ross, 1987). And it explains why people who are asked how they felt 10 years ago about marijuana or gender issues recall attitudes closer to their current views than to the views they actually reported a decade earlier (Markus,1986).

"Memory isn't like reading a book; it's more like writing a book from fragmentary notes."

Psychologist John F. Kihlstrom (1994)

Source Amnesia

When we encode memories, we distribute different aspects of them to different parts of the brain. Among the frailest parts of a memory is its source. Thus, we may recognize someone but have no idea where we have seen the person. Or we imagine or dream an event and later aren't sure if it really happened. In both cases, we retain the image, but not the context in which we acquired it.

An example: Australian psychologist Donald Thompson found his own work on memory distortion ironically haunting him when authorities brought him in for questioning about a rape. Although he was a near-perfect match to the victim's memory of the rapist, he had an airtight alibi. Just before the rape occurred Thompson was being interviewed on live television. He could not possibly have made it to the crime scene. Then it came to light that the victim had been watching the interview—ironically about face recognition—and had experienced **source amnesia,** confusing her memories of Thompson with those of the rapist (Schacter, 1996).

Debra Poole and Stephen Lindsay (1995) experimented with source amnesia (also called *source misattribution*). They had preschoolers interact with "Mr. Science," who engaged them in demonstrations such as blowing up a balloon with baking soda and vinegar. Three months later, their parents on three successive days read them a story about themselves and Mr. Science. The stories described some things they had experienced and some they had not. When asked by a new interviewer what Mr. Science had done with them, 4 in 10 children spontaneously recalled Mr. Science doing things that were only in the story.

Authors and songwriters sometimes suffer source amnesia. They think an idea came from their own creative imagination, when in fact they are unintentionally plagiarizing something they earlier read or heard.

Children's Eyewitness Recall

Because memory is reconstruction as well as reproduction, we can't be sure whether a memory is real by how real it feels. Much as perceptual illusions may seem like real perceptions, unreal memories feel like real memories. If memories can be sincere, yet sincerely wrong, might children's recollections of sexual abuse be prone to err? Who is most often victimized—abused children whose recollections are disbelieved or falsely accused adults whose reputations are ruined?

At issue is the credibility of children's reports. As we have seen, interviewers who ask leading questions can plant false memories of a story they expect to hear. We also know that children sometimes are credible eyewitnesses in criminal cases, but that they tend to be suggestible. In 90 percent of studies making age comparisons, preschoolers were more suggestible than were older children or adults (Bruck & Ceci, 1999). In these studies, many young children have falsely reported that a nurse had licked their knee, a man had put "something yucky" in their mouth, their doctor had put a stick in their genitals, and someone had touched their private parts. When suggestive interview techniques are combined, most preschoolers can be induced to report false events such as seeing a thief steal food in their day-care center (Bruck & others, 1998). Nevertheless, if questioned about

■ **source amnesia** attributing to the wrong source an event that we have experienced, heard about, read about, or imagined. (Also called *source misattribution*.) Source amnesia, along with the misinformation effect, is at the heart of many false memories.

their experiences in words they understand, children often accurately recall what happened and who did it (Goodman & others, 1990; Howe, 1997; Pipe, 1996). Children are especially credible when involved adults have not talked with them prior to the interview and when their disclosure is made in a first interview with a neutral person who asks nonleading questions.

So, depending on the questioning, children may or may not produce accurate eyewitness reports. To the children, both feel real. No wonder trained professionals, after viewing videotaped interviews, cannot discriminate between children's false and accurate reports (Bruck & Ceci, 1997).

Stephen Ceci (1993) thinks "it would be truly awful to ever lose sight of the enormity of child abuse." Yet Ceci and Maggie Bruck's (1993a, 1995) studies of children's memories have sensitized them to children's suggestibility. In one study, they asked 3-year-olds to show on anatomically correct dolls where a pediatrician had touched them. Fifty-five percent of the children who had not received genital examinations pointed to either genital or anal areas.

In another study, Ceci and Bruck had a child choose a card from a deck of possible happenings and an adult then read from the card. For example, "Think real hard, and tell me if this ever happened to you. Can you remember going to the hospital with a mousetrap on your finger?" After 10 weekly interviews, with the same adult repeatedly asking children to think about several real and fictitious events, a new adult asked the same question. The stunning result: 58 percent of preschoolers produced false (often vivid) stories regarding one or more events they had never experienced. Here is one from a boy who initially had denied the mousetrap incident (Ceci & others, 1994):

> My brother Colin was trying to get Blowtorch [an action figure] from me, and I wouldn't let him take it from me, so he pushed me into the wood pile where the mousetrap was. And then my finger got caught in it. And then we went to the hospital, and my mommy, daddy, and Colin drove me there, to the hospital in our van, because it was far away. And the doctor put a bandage on this finger.

> "[The] research leads me to worry about the possibility of false allegations. It is not a tribute to one's scientific integrity to walk down the middle of the road if the data are more to one side."
>
> **Stephen Ceci (1993)**

Given such detailed stories, professional psychologists who specialize in interviewing children were often fooled. They could not reliably separate real from false memories. Nor could the children themselves. The above child, reminded that his parents had told him several times that the mousetrap incident never happened—that he had imagined it—protested, "But it really did happen. I remember it!"

Repressed or Constructed Memories of Abuse?

During the 1990s, psychology's most intense controversy—the "memory wars"—concerned reports of repressed and recovered memories of childhood sexual abuse. Are clinicians who have guided people in "recovering" such memories triggering false memories that break apart families, or are they uncovering the truth? Without disputing the all-too-common reality and horror of such abuse, critics use principles of memory construction to question the reality of repressed and recovered memories.

Traumatic events *are* sometimes forgotten, perhaps aided by the toxic effects of sustained stress (Nadel & Jacobs, 1998). In 1974, four-year-old Rachel (not her real name) and two others were molested by her uncle. Rachel told her mother, who informed the mother of one of the others, who then stabbed and killed the uncle. Seventeen years later, psychologist Linda Meyer Williams (1995) tracked down Rachel and 128 other women who were recorded as having experienced childhood sexual abuse (sexual intercourse or fondling). When asked whether she had ever been sexually abused as a child or whether any family members had ever gotten into trouble for their sexual behavior, Rachel calmly said no, then added: "Oh wait a minute. . . . My uncle sexually assaulted someone. . . . I never met my uncle (my mother's brother), he died before I was born. You see, he molested a little boy. When the little boy's mother found out, she took a butcher knife and stabbed my uncle in the heart, killing him." Rachel was one of 49 victims—38 percent of those interviewed—who did not spontaneously recall the specific reported incident of their own abuse. (Most did recall experiencing other sexual traumas.)

Cognitive psychologist Jennifer Freyd (1996, 1998, 1999) theorizes that memories may remain vivid for life-threatening traumas such as a hurricane or car accident, yet be dulled or blocked for traumas that involve repeated betrayal. Consider Eva Hart, who 84 years after surviving the sinking of the *Titanic* still remembers the event with chilling clarity: "I saw it, heard it, and nobody could possibly forget it" (Rupp, 1998, p. 70). But then there are Rachel and the others, who have not remembered. By repressing their knowledge of a caregiver's sexual abuse, perhaps dependent children maintain their relationship with the caregiver and ensure their own survival.

Some who have forgotten claim later to have also *recovered* memories of abuse. In one recent five-year period in Washington State, 682 people who claimed repressed memories of sexual abuse and other crimes sought money for their therapy bills from the state's victim compensation fund (Hallinan, 1997).

Ellen Bass and Laura Davis (1988), authors of the popular incest-recovery manual *The Courage to Heal*, encouraged recovering and reporting such memories. They offered a long list of incest-survivor characteristics, including feelings of shame, powerlessness, unworthiness, vulnerability, perfectionism, and deficient goals and motivation. If you have some of these feelings, some therapists have said, don't be surprised if you have no memory of sexual abuse, because "denial" and "repression" are common. "If you are unable to remember any specific instances . . . but still have a feeling that something abusive happened to you, it probably did," said Bass and Davis (pp. 21–22). "If you think you were abused and your life shows the symptoms, then you were."

Accepting this, some therapists have reasoned with patients that "people who've been abused often have your symptoms, so you probably were abused. Let's see if, aided by hypnosis or drugs, or helped to dig back and visualize your trauma, you can recover it." In one American survey, the average therapist estimated that 11 percent of the population—some 34 million people—have repressed memories of childhood sexual abuse (Kamena, 1998). In another survey, of British and American doctoral-level therapists, 7 in 10 said they had used techniques such as hypnosis or drugs to help clients recover suspected repressed memories of childhood sexual abuse (Poole & others, 1995).

As we might expect from the research on source amnesia and the misinformation effect, many patients exposed to such techniques do form an image of a threatening person. With further visualization, the image grows more vivid, leaving the patient stunned, angry, and ready to confront or sue the equally stunned and devastated parent or other relative, who, as the therapist has predicted, vigorously denies the accusation. One woman in her thirty-second therapy session recalled that her father had abused her at age 15 months. After such aided recall, actress Roseanne Barr (1991) claimed to recall sexual abuse beginning in infancy.

Understandably, persuading adult women that their fathers or mothers were incestuous has torn apart many families. Thousands of such families have sought advice from the False Memory Syndrome Foundation. The foundation takes its name from the term that John Kihlstrom (1996) defines as a disruptive condition in which a person's identity and relationships center around a false but strongly believed memory of traumatic experience. The person resists disconfirming information and may become so focused on the memory as to avoid coping with the real problems.

> "Spend time imagining that you were sexually abused, without worrying about accuracy, proving anything, or having your ideas make sense. As you give rein to your imagination, let your intuitions guide your thoughts."
>
> **Wendy Maltz, *The Sexual Healing Journey*, 1991**

Without questioning the professionalism of most therapists, skeptics compare the uncorroborated accusations suggested by some therapists to a 1990s reenactment of the Salem witch trials. Clinicians who use "memory work" techniques such as "guided imagery," hypnosis, and dream analysis to recover such memories "are nothing more than merchants of mental chaos, and, in fact, constitute a blight on the entire field of psychotherapy," charged some scientific critics (Loftus & others, 1995). Moreover, women who report recovering memories of childhood sexual abuse are more prone to false memories in laboratory tests (Clancy & others, 2000). Irate clinicians countered that those who dispute recovered memories of abuse add to abused women's trauma and play into the hands of child molesters.

The trouble with inferring child abuse from adult symptoms is that the symptom list is "general enough to include everybody at least sometimes," notes Carol Tavris (1993). People feel unworthy, ashamed, and perfectionistic for so many reasons that the symptoms hardly prove any one cause. And, as Stephen Lindsay (1995) notes, all the ingredients for cooking false memories are potentially present in the therapy setting: a credible authority, repeated suggestions, imagination-enhancing techniques, and affirmation for one's budding suspicions.

In an effort to find a sensible common ground that might resolve this ideological battle, study panels have been convened and public statements made by the American Medical, American Psychological, and American Psychiatric Associations; the Australian Psychological Society; the British Psychological Society; and the Canadian Psychiatric Association. Those committed to protecting abused children and those committed to protecting wrongly accused adults agree on the following:

- **Injustice happens.** Some innocent people have been falsely convicted. And some guilty people have evaded responsibility by casting doubt on their truth-telling accusers.
- **Incest happens.** And it happens more often than we once supposed. There is no characteristic "survivor syndrome" (Kendall-Tackett & others, 1993). However, sexual abuse can leave its victims predisposed to problems ranging from sexual dysfunction to depression.
- **Forgetting happens.** Like Rachel, notes Elizabeth Loftus (1995), many of the women interviewed by Linda Meyer Williams either were very young when abused or may not have understood the meaning of their experience—circumstances under which forgetting is "utterly common." Forgetting isolated past events, both negative and positive, is an ordinary part of everyday life. With all sorts of memories, we tend over time to lose the peripheral details and retain the gist of the experience (Howe, 1998).
- **Recovered memories are commonplace.** Cued by a remark or an experience, we recover memories of long-forgotten events, both pleasant and unpleasant. What is debated is whether the unconscious mind sometimes forcibly represses painful experiences and, if so, whether these can be retrieved by certain therapist-aided techniques.
- **Memories "recovered" under hypnosis or the influence of drugs are especially unreliable.** "Age-regressed" hypnotized subjects, for example, incorporate suggestions into their memories, even memories of "past lives."
- **Memories of things happening before age 3 are also unreliable.** People do not reliably recall happenings of any sort from their first 3 years—a phenomenon called *infantile amnesia.*
- **Memories, whether real or false, can be emotionally upsetting.** If a false memory of abuse becomes a real part of one's history, the client as well as the family may suffer. Like real traumas, such experiences can then cause lasting suffering.

"When memories are 'recovered' after long periods of amnesia, particularly when extraordinary means were used to secure the recovery of memory, there is a high probability that the memories are false."

Royal College of Psychiatrists Working Group on Reported Recovered Memories of Child Sexual Abuse (Brandon & others, 1998).

At the end of 1999, the False Memory Syndrome Foundation was tracking 800 lawsuits, 70 percent against accused parents (Freyd, 1999). Nine in ten accusers are women, most between ages 25 and 45. Eleven suits by former patients against therapists had gone to trial, with nine ending in a verdict against the therapist. Fifty-six more such suits were settled out of court.

Without knowing a person's initial experience (as we do in memory experiments) it is difficult to assess the validity of a person's memory. As Mark Pendergrast (1996) notes, "It is ironic that no one can ethically conduct an experiment to replicate what is happening throughout the UK and the US in private therapy settings."

To more closely approximate therapist-aided recall, Elizabeth Loftus and her colleagues (1996) have experimentally implanted false memories of childhood traumas. In one study, she had a trusted family member recall for a teenager three real childhood experiences and a false one—a vivid account of the child's being lost for an extended time in a shopping mall at age 5 until being rescued by an elderly person. Two days later, one subject, Chris, said, "That day I was so scared that I would never see my family again." Two days after that he began to visualize the flannel shirt, bald head, and glasses of the old man who supposedly had found him. Told the story was made up, Chris was incredulous: "I thought I remembered being lost . . . and looking around for the guys. I do remember that, and then crying, and Mom coming up and saying, 'Where were you? Don't you . . . ever do that again.'"

TODAY'S SPECIAL GUEST

BRUNDAGE MORNALD, OF BATTLE CREEK, MONTANA

UNDER HYPNOSIS, MR. MORNALD RECOVERED LONG-BURIED MEMORIES OF A PERFECTLY NORMAL, HAPPY CHILDHOOD.

Such is the memory construction process by which people can recall being abducted by UFOs, victimized by a satanic cult, molested in a crib, or living a past life. Thousands of seemingly healthy people, notes Loftus, "speak in terror-stricken voices about their experience aboard flying saucers. They *remember,* clearly and vividly, being abducted by aliens. Or consider the fact that thousands of reasonable, normally functioning human beings relate in calm voices and with deeply felt conviction their past-life experiences. They *remember* having lived before" (Loftus & Ketcham, 1994, p. 66).

Loftus knows firsthand the phenomenon she studies. At a family reunion, an uncle told her that at age 14, she found her mother's drowned body. Shocked, she denied it. But the uncle was adamant, and over the next three days she began to wonder if *she* had a repressed memory. "Maybe that's why I'm so obsessed with this topic." As the now-upset Loftus pondered her uncle's suggestion, she "recovered" an image of her mother lying in the pool, face down, and of herself finding the body. "I started putting everything into place. Maybe that's why I'm such a workaholic. Maybe that's why I'm so emotional when I think about her even though she died in 1959."

Then her brother called and said there was a mistake. Her uncle had later remembered what other relatives now confirmed. Aunt Pearl, not Loftus, had found the body (Loftus & Ketcham, 1994; Monaghan, 1992).

Elizabeth Loftus

"People in general and jurors in particular have a lot of misconceptions about the way memory works" (quoted by Monaghan, 1992).

But then again, Loftus also knows firsthand the reality of sexual abuse. A male baby-sitter molested her when she was 6 years old. She has not forgotten. And that makes her wary of those whom she sees as trivializing real abuse by suggesting and seeking out uncorroborated traumatic experiences, then accepting them uncritically as fact. The enemies of the truly victimized are not only those who prey and those who deny, she says, but those whose writings and allegations "are bound to lead to an increased likelihood that society in general will disbelieve the genuine cases of childhood sexual abuse that truly deserve our sustained attention" (Loftus, 1993).

So, does repression ever occur? Psychologists continue to have heated debates on this topic, which is the cornerstone of Freud's theory and a recurring theme in so much popular psychology. But this much now appears certain: The most common response to a traumatic experience (witnessing the murder of a parent, experiencing the horrors of a Nazi death camp, being terrorized by a hijacker or a rapist) is not banishment of the experience into an active but inaccessible unconscious. Rather, such experiences are typically etched on the mind as vivid, persistent, haunting memories. "The things we remember best," noted Baltasar Gracian in 1647, "are those better forgotten."

rehearse it!

1. In some cases, forgetting may be due to encoding failure. That is, meaningless information may not be transferred from
   a. the environment into sensory memory.
   b. sensory memory into long-term memory.
   c. long-term memory into short-term memory.
   d. short-term memory into long-term memory.

2. Forgetting may result from storage decay. Ebbinghaus found that after about three days after a session of learning nonsense syllables, people have forgotten much of what they learned. Ebbinghaus' "forgetting curve" shows that as time goes on, retention of the nonsense syllables tends to
   a. increase slightly.
   b. decrease noticeably.
   c. decrease greatly.
   d. level out.

3. Experiments show that the hour before sleep is a good time to memorize information. For example, studying a vocabulary list before going to sleep minimizes the disrupting effects of all the other new words and terms that might, in the course of a school day, claim our attention. Going to sleep after learning new material minimizes
   a. the misinformation effect.
   b. amnesia.
   c. retroactive interference.
   d. proactive interference.

4. People unknowingly revise or rearrange their memories of events. According to Sigmund Freud, painful or unacceptable memories are self-censored, or blocked from consciousness, through a mechanism called
   a. repression.
   b. proactive interference.
   c. anxiety.
   d. physical decay of the memory trace.

5. Because we often alter information as we encode it and because we tend to fill in memory gaps with our assumptions about events, our memories are generally not exact reproductions of events. One reason for this memory reconstruction is
   a. proactive interference.
   b. the misinformation effect.
   c. retroactive interference.
   d. the eyewitness recall effect.

6. Aspects of our memories are distributed to different parts of the brain. Thus, while we may recognize a face in the crowd, we may not be able to recall where we know the person from. This is called
   a. the misinformation effect.
   b. amnesia.
   c. source amnesia.
   d. repression.

REVIEWING

Forgetting and Memory Construction

1. Why do we forget? At what points in the memory system can our memory fail us?

Memory failures can occur in any of the stages of the memory system. When we fail to encode information, it never enters long-term memory and therefore is not available for retrieval. We can attend to only a few of the sights and sounds that bombard our senses. Also, without effortful processing, much of what we sense we never notice or process.

Some of what we encode is altered or lost in memory storage. Forgetting curves may reflect gradual fading of the physical memory trace, which is a topic of ongoing research.

Retrieval failure may be caused by proactive or retroactive interference, by insufficient cues, or even by motivated forgetting (repression).

2. How accurate are our memories?

Memories are not stored as exact copies, and they certainly are not retrieved as such. Rather, we construct our memories, using both stored and new information. Thus, when eyewitnesses are subtly exposed to misinformation after an event, they often believe they saw the misleading details as part of the event. This seems especially true of young children. Source amnesia occurs when we misattribute an event or statement.

TERMS AND CONCEPTS TO REMEMBER

proactive interference, p. 287
retroactive interference, p. 287

repression, p. 290

misinformation effect, p. 291

source amnesia, p. 293

REHEARSE IT ANSWER KEY

1. d   2. d   3. c   4. a   5. b   6. c

Thinking, Language, and Intelligence

Throughout history, we humans have deplored our foolishness and celebrated our wisdom. The poet T. S. Eliot was struck by "the hollow men . . . Headpiece filled with straw." But Shakespeare's Hamlet extolled the human species as "noble in reason! . . . infinite in faculties! . . . in apprehension how like a god!" Psychologists, too, sometimes marvel at our capabilities, sometimes at our propensity to err.

We study the human brain—a mere 3 pounds of tissue containing circuitry more complex than the planet's telephone networks. We marvel at the competence of newborn infants. We study the human sensory system, which disassembles visual stimuli into millions of nerve impulses, distributes them for parallel processing, and then reassembles them into clear and colorful perceived images. We are aware of the seemingly limitless capacity of human memory and the ease with which we process information, consciously and unconsciously. Little wonder, then, that our species, by accumulating and refining ideas over time, has the collective genius to invent the camera, the car, and the computer; to unlock the atom and crack the genetic code; to travel into space and probe the oceans' depths.

At the same time, we have found that our species is kin to the other animals, influenced by the same principles that produce learning in rats and pigeons. We know that we assimilate reality into our preconceptions, succumb to perceptual illusions, and easily deceive ourselves about pseudopsychic claims, hypnotic regression, and false memories. It is also little wonder, then, that we sometimes imagine we can read minds and travel outside our bodies; that we form distorted images of other ethnic, age, and gender groups; that we are bound by the same biological principles as other creatures.

In Modules 20 through 22 we encounter further instances of these two images of the human condition—the rational and the irrational. We will see how we form concepts, solve problems, and make judgments (Module 20). We will look at our flair for language and ask whether our species alone has this capability (Module 21). And we will consider the roots of our intelligence (Module 22).

As you read through these modules, take some time to reflect on how deserving we are of our name *Homo sapiens*—wise human. How would we do on our report card? On decision making and judgment, our error-prone species might rate a C+. On problem solving, where humans are inventive yet vulnerable to fixation, we would probably receive better marks, perhaps a B. On cognitive efficiency, our fallible but quick heuristics earn us an A. And when it comes to learning and using language, the awestruck experts would surely award the human species an A+.

20 Thinking

- Concepts
- Solving Problems
- Making Decisions and Forming Judgments

We have a seemingly limitless capacity to receive, perceive, store, and retrieve information. How does our cognitive system use this information? Thinking, or **cognition,** refers to all the mental activities associated with processing, understanding, and communicating. *Cognitive psychologists* study these mental activities, including the logical and sometimes illogical ways in which we create concepts, solve problems, make decisions, and form judgments. We begin our study with concepts, the building blocks of thinking.

Concepts

PREVIEW QUESTION 1 What are the functions of concepts?

To think about the countless events, objects, and people in our world, we simplify things. We form **concepts**—mental groupings of similar objects, events, and people. The concept *chair* sums up a variety of items—a baby's high chair, a reclining chair, the chairs around a dining room table, a dentist's chair.

Imagine life without concepts. We would need a different name for every object and idea. We could not ask a child to "throw the ball" because there would be no concept of *ball*. Instead of saying, "They were angry," we would have to describe facial expressions, vocal intensities, gestures, and words. Such concepts as *ball* and *angry* provide us with much information without much cognitive effort.

Animals, too, are capable of feats of concept formation. Pigeons—mere bird brains—can sort objects according to their similarity. Shown pictures of cars, cats, chairs, and flowers, they readily learn to identify the categories. Shown a picture of a never-before-seen chair, the pigeon will reliably peck a key that represents "chairs" (Wasserman, 1995).

To simplify things further, humans organize concepts into hierarchies. Cab drivers organize their cities into geographical sectors, which subdivide into neighborhoods and again into blocks. The earliest naturalists simplified and ordered the overwhelming complexity of some 5 million living species by clustering them into two basic categories—the plant and animal kingdoms. Then they divided these basic categories into smaller and smaller subcategories—vertebrates, bony fish, and Atlantic salmon, for instance.

We form some concepts by definition. Told the rule that a triangle has three sides, we thereafter classify all three-sided geometric forms as triangles. More often, however, we form our concepts by developing **prototypes**—a mental image or best example that incorporates all the features we associate with a category (Rosch, 1978). The more closely something matches our prototype of a concept, the more readily we recognize it as an example of the concept. A robin and a goose both satisfy our definition of *bird:* an animal that has wings and feathers and hatches from an egg. Yet people agree more quickly that "A robin is a bird" than that "A goose is a bird." For most of us, the robin is the birdier bird; it more closely resembles our bird prototype. Likewise, "maternal love" and "self-love" both qualify as love. But people more instantly agree that "maternal love is a type of love," because it better matches their love prototype (Fehr & Russell, 1991).

If something fails to match our prototype, we may have trouble classifying it. Thus, we might be slow to recognize nonflying penguins and kiwis as birds. Simi-

"Attention, everyone! I'd like to introduce the newest member of our family."

- **cognition** the mental activities associated with thinking, knowing, and remembering.

- **concept** a mental grouping of similar objects, events, ideas, or people.

- **prototype** a mental image or best example of a category. Matching new items to the prototype provides a quick and easy method for including items in a category (as when comparing feathered creatures to a prototypical bird, such as a robin).

- **algorithm** a methodical, logical rule or procedure that guarantees solving a particular problem. Contrasts with the usually speedier—but also more error-prone—use of *heuristics*.

- **heuristic** a rule-of-thumb strategy that often allows us to make judgments and solve problems efficiently; usually speedier but also more error-prone than *algorithms*.

- **insight** a sudden and often novel realization of the solution to a problem; it contrasts with strategy-based solutions.

RISKS—WHEN STATISTICS CLASH WITH HEURISTICS

THINKING CRITICALLY ABOUT

"Most people reason dramatically, not quantitatively," said Oliver Wendell Holmes. With horrific television and magazine images of air crashes in mind, many people, petrified of air travel, prefer the safety of their own cars. One Gallup study (*Gallup Report,* 1989) found that, of those who do fly, 44 percent reported feeling fearful and 63 percent had "lost confidence" in airline safety. After the four crashed planes of September 11, many more fearful people understandably turned from flying to driving.

Ironically, the statistical reality is that air travel is safer than ever. Mile for mile, U.S. travelers during the last half of the 1990s were 37 times more likely to die in a car crash than on a commercial flight (National Safety Council, 2001). In the 27 months following March 22, 1992, major U.S. airlines carried more than 1 billion passengers on 16 *million* flights without a single death (Tolchin, 1994). For most air travelers, the most dangerous part of the journey is the drive to the airport. When a friend tells me of revising her will before flying, I cannot resist saying, "Much better to have done so before you drove to Kansas." For even if she were to board a random jet every day, she

would (if her experience matched the average) have to live 21,000 years before crashing to her death (Barnett, 1996).

The images of September 11, forever etched on our minds, left most people more anxious about flying than driving. The fact, however, is that driving is far more dangerous—so much so that if terrorists at the end of 2001 had taken down 50 more planes with 60 passengers each, Americans would still have ended the year safer in planes than on the road.

Still, when overall statistics vie with vivid images of helpless crash victims, many find the memorable instances more persuasive. It is like judging the likelihood of shark attacks after watching the *Jaws* movies: Regardless of statistics, memorable images have a way of heightening swimmers' feelings of risk. People may *know* their fears are irrational, but no matter. Nightmarish images from horror movies may linger for months or years, causing anxiety over a creaking house. The available images of a plane death—which is 6900 times more likely to make the *New York Times* front page than a cancer death (Barnett, 1990)—protrude into consciousness. Even smokers (whose habit shortens their lives by about five years) may senselessly

fret before flying (which shortens the average person's life by one day).

The 1988 terrorist bomb that exploded Pan Am Flight 103 and the 1996 fiery explosion of TWA Flight 800 caused many would-be international vacationers to stay home and risk the more dangerous highways. The same fearful public continues to smoke billions of cigarettes a year, guzzle alcohol, and devour foods that put people at risk for the greatest of killers—heart disease. All because *perceptions* of risk are virtually unrelated to actual risk (Slovic, 1987)—a phenomenon due partly to our greater fear of things we cannot control and partly to our overestimating the likelihood of dreaded, publicized, and cognitively available events. Thus, the public dreads a catastrophic nuclear accident (which after the 1986 Chernobyl disaster we can readily visualize). Yet it accepts the less dramatic risks of coal-generated power quietly fueling acid rain and global warming.

The point to remember: Whether making travel plans or choosing foods, defining safety standards or evaluating environmental hazards, smart thinkers will define risks based not on mentally available media images but on statistical reality.

The availability heuristic affects our social judgments, as Ruth Hamill and her co-workers demonstrated (1980). They presented people with a single, vivid case of welfare abuse, in which a long-term welfare recipient had several unruly children. Statistically, this case was exceptional: Most people who received welfare did so for four years or less (Duncan & others, 1988). Yet when the statistical reality was pitted against the single vivid case, the memorable case had greater influence on people's opinions about welfare recipients.

A memorable picture sometimes overwhelms a thousand statistics. When a little girl, Jessica McClure, fell into a Texas well, the attention of hundreds of millions of people worldwide was riveted on her three-day rescue. During those three days, more than 100,000 invisible children—"mere statistics" on some world health ledger—died of preventable starvation, diarrhea, and disease (Gore, 1992).

"The human understanding is most excited by that which strikes and enters the mind at once and suddenly, and by which the imagination is immediately filled and inflated. It then begins almost imperceptibly to conceive and suppose that everything is similar to the few objects which have taken possession of the mind."

Francis Bacon, *Novum Organum,* 1620

- **overconfidence** the tendency to be more confident than correct—to overestimate the accuracy of one's beliefs and judgments.

- **framing** the way an issue is posed; how an issue is framed can significantly affect decisions and judgments.

- **belief perseverance** clinging to one's initial conceptions after the basis on which they were formed has been discredited. (*Confirmation bias*—searching for belief-support information—contributes to belief perseverance.)

FIGURE 20.4
Solution to the candle-mounting problem
Solving this problem requires recognizing that a box need not always serve as a container. (From Duncker, 1945.)

"When you know a thing, to hold that you know it; and when you do not know a thing, to allow that you do not know it; this is knowledge."

Confucius (551–479 B.C.), *Analects*

Overconfidence

Our use of intuitive heuristics when forming judgments, our eagerness to confirm the beliefs we already hold, and our knack for explaining away failures combine to create **overconfidence,** a tendency to overestimate the accuracy of our knowledge and judgments. Across various tasks, people overestimate what their performance was, is, or will be (Metcalfe, 1998).

People are also more confident than correct when answering such questions as, "Is absinthe a liqueur or a precious stone?" (It's a licorice-flavored liqueur.) On questions where only 60 percent of people answer correctly, respondents typically feel 75 percent confident. Even when people feel 100 percent certain of their answers to such questions, they err about 15 percent of the time (Fischhoff & others, 1977).

Overconfidence plagues decisions outside the laboratory, too. It was an overconfident Hitler who invaded Russia, an overconfident Lyndon Johnson who waged war with North Vietnam, an overconfident Slobodan Milosovich who marched into Kosovo. Stockbrokers and investment managers market their services with confidence that they can outperform the market average in picking stocks, despite overwhelming evidence to the contrary (Malkiel, 1985, 1995). A purchase of stock X, recommended by a broker who judges this to be the time to buy, is usually balanced by a sale made by someone who judges this to be the time to sell. Despite their confidence, buyer and seller can't both be right.

Roger Buehler and his colleagues (1994) were struck by how routinely planners exhibit overconfidence in estimating how quickly and inexpensively they can do a project. In 1957, they predicted the Sydney Opera House would be completed in 1963 for $7 million. A reduced version actually opened in 1973 at a cost of $102 million. (Even as I wrote this we were moving into a new kitchen that our architect estimated would take one month, that our contractor estimated would take three months, and that actually took five months.) Students, too, are routinely overconfident about how quickly they can do assignments and write papers, Buehler reports; they typically expect to finish projects ahead of schedule. But in fact, the projects generally get finished after about twice the number of days they predicted. Although people know they have often underestimated completion times, they remain overly confident of their next prediction.

Overconfidence does have adaptive value. Failing to appreciate one's potential for error when making military, economic, or political judgments can have devastating consequences, but so can a lack of self-confidence. People who err on the side of overconfidence live more happily and find it easier to make tough decisions (Baumeister, 1989; Taylor, 1989). Moreover, when given prompt and clear feedback on the accuracy of their judgments—as weather forecasters are after each day's predictions—people soon learn to assess their accuracy more realistically (Fischhoff, 1982). The wisdom to know when we know a thing and when we do not is born of experience.

Framing Decisions

A further test of rationality is whether the same issue, presented in two different but logically equivalent ways, will elicit the same answer. For example, one surgeon tells someone that 10 percent of people die while undergoing a particular surgery. Another tells someone that 90 percent survive. The information is the same. The effect is not. The risk seems greater to those who hear that 10 percent will die (Marteau, 1989; Rothman & Salovey, 1997).

The way we present an issue is called **framing,** and its effects are sometimes striking. Consumers respond more positively to ground beef described as "75 percent lean" rather than "25 percent fat" (Levin & Gaeth, 1988). People express more surprise when a "1 in 20" event happens than when an equivalent "10 in 200" event happens (Denes-Raj & others, 1995). And 9 in 10 college students rate a condom as effective if it has a supposed "95 percent success rate" in stopping the AIDS virus; only 4 in 10 think it successful when given a "5 percent failure rate" (Linville & others, 1992).

Consider how the framing effect influences economic and business decisions:

- Merchants mark up their "regular prices" to appear to offer huge savings on "sale prices." A $100 coat marked down from $150 by Store X can seem like a better deal than the same coat priced regularly at $100 by Store Y (Urbany & others, 1988).
- Many find taking a 7 percent pay cut in a period of zero inflation much more objectionable than receiving a 5 percent pay raise when inflation is 12 percent (Kahneman & others, 1986).
- FedEx doesn't charge extra to pick up at your door; instead, they offer a "drop-off discount." Likewise, my dentist doesn't charge more if we pay later, though she does offer a 5 percent discount for immediate cash payment. FedEx and my dentist both understand that a fee framed as a forfeited discount irritates customers less than one framed as a surcharge, although they add up to the same thing.

That our judgments can flip-flop so dramatically is startling. It suggests that our judgments and decisions may not be well reasoned, and that those who understand the power of framing can use it to influence important decisions—for example, by framing survey questions to support or reject a particular viewpoint. Subtle wording differences have potentially powerful effects.

"This CD player costs less than players selling for twice as much."

The Belief Perseverance Phenomenon

PREVIEW QUESTION 4 How do our preexisting beliefs influence our decision making?

An additional source of irrationality is **belief perseverance,** our tendency to cling to our beliefs in the face of contrary evidence. Belief perseverance often fuels social conflict. Charles Lord and his colleagues (1979) revealed how this happens when they studied people with opposing views of capital punishment. Those on both sides studied two supposedly new research findings, one supporting and the other refuting the claim that the death penalty deters crime. Each side was more impressed by the study that supported its beliefs, and each readily disputed the other study. Thus, showing the pro- and anti–capital-punishment groups the *same* mixed evidence actually *increased* their disagreement.

If you want to rein in the belief perseverance phenomenon, a simple remedy exists: *Consider the opposite.* When Lord and his colleagues (1984) repeated the capital-punishment study, they asked some of their participants to be "as *objective* and *unbiased* as possible." The plea did nothing to reduce the biased evaluation of evidence. They asked another group to consider "whether you would have made the same high or low evaluations had exactly the same study produced results on the *other* side of the issue." Having imagined and pondered *opposite* findings, these people were much less biased in their evaluations of the evidence.

"Once you have a belief, it influences how you perceive all other relevant information. Once you see a country as hostile, you are likely to interpret ambiguous actions on their part as signifying their hostility."

Political scientist Robert Jervis (1985)

"I'm happy to say that my final judgment of a case is almost always consistent with my prejudgment of the case."

Belief perseverance
Do risk takers or cautious people make better fire fighters? Once we've formed opinions on a question like this and developed reasons for our views, we tend to cling to our beliefs—even if the basis for our opinion is undermined.

If people interpret ambiguous evidence as supporting their preexisting belief, would their belief be demolished by information that clearly discredits its basis? Not necessarily. Craig Anderson and Lee Ross discovered that it can be surprisingly difficult to change a false belief once a person has ideas that support it. In one study with Mark Lepper (1980), they asked people to consider whether risk-taking or cautious people make better fire fighters. Then they told half the people about a risk taker who was an excellent fire fighter and about a cautious person who was a poor fire fighter. From these cases, the participants surmised that risk takers tend to be better fire fighters. "Risk takers are braver," was the typical explanation. The researchers gave the other participants two cases suggesting the opposite conclusion, that cautious people are better fire fighters. These participants typically reasoned, "Cautious people think before they act. They're less likely to make foolish mistakes."

The researchers then discredited the basis for the beliefs by truthfully informing both groups that the cases were simply made up for the experiment. Did discrediting the evidence undermine the participants' newly formed beliefs? Not by much, because they held on to their explanations for why these new beliefs made sense. Although the evidence was gone, their theory survived.

The more we come to appreciate why our beliefs might be true, the more tightly we cling to them. Once people have explained to themselves why they believe that a child is "gifted" or "learning disabled," or that candidate X or Y will be more likely to preserve peace or start a war, or that women or men are naturally superior, they tend to ignore the evidence that undermines that belief. Prejudice persists.

> "To begin with, it was only tentatively that I put forward the views I have developed . . . but in the course of time they have gained such a hold upon me that I can no longer think in any other way."
>
> Sigmund Freud, *Civilization and Its Discontents*, 1930

We have seen how our irrational thinking can plague our efforts to solve problems, make wise decisions, form valid judgments, and reason logically. From this we might conclude that our heads are indeed filled with straw. All in all, these and many other findings suggest "bleak implications for human rationality" (Nisbett & Borgida, 1975). Still, we should not forget that our cognition can be effective and wonderfully efficient: It enables our survival and our inventive genius.

Moreover, even the most sophisticated computers are ironically dwarfed by the most ordinary of human mental abilities—recognizing a face; distinguishing a cat from a dog; knowing whether the word *line* refers to a rope or a fragment of poetry or a social come-on.

A computer's capabilities exceed our own at tasks that use its unique strengths—vast memory and precise logic and retrieval. But computers have not duplicated the wide-ranging intelligence of a human mind, which can *all at once* converse naturally, recognize a caricatured face, use common sense, experience emotion, and consciously reflect on its own existence.

> "Even though I am not religious, the amazement and wonder I have about the human mind is closer to religious awe than dispassionate analysis."
>
> Bill Gates, 1997

1. We use the concept *bird* to think and talk about a variety of creatures, all of which have wings and feathers. A concept is
   a. a mental grouping of similar things.
   b. an example of insight.
   c. a fixation on certain characteristics.
   d. another word for "prototype."

2. Sometimes we solve problems through trial and error, trying hundreds or even thousands of solutions before finding one that works. At other times we are more methodical or systematic. The most systematic procedure for solving a problem is
   a. heuristics.   c. insight.
   b. an algorithm.   d. intuition.

3. A major obstacle to problem solving is the confirmation bias, the tendency to search for information that confirms our preconceptions while ignoring information that might prove us wrong. Another obstacle to problem solving is fixation, which is

   a. an error we make when we base our judgments on certain vivid memories.
   b. the art of framing the same question in two different ways.
   c. the inability to view a problem from a new perspective.
   d. a rule of thumb for judging the likelihood of an event in terms of our mental image of it.

4. You move into a new neighborhood and notice that your next-door neighbor is very neatly dressed, wears glasses, and is reading a Greek play. Given a choice between her being a librarian and a store clerk, you incorrectly guess that she is a librarian. Your incorrect judgment is probably due to
   a. the availability heuristic.
   b. confirmation bias.
   c. overconfidence.
   d. the representativeness heuristic.

5. After a New York City bombing by foreign-born terrorists in 1993, many observers incorrectly assumed that the 1995 bombing of a federal building in Oklahoma City was probably the work of foreign-born terrorists. This assumption illustrates
   a. belief perseverance.
   b. the availability heuristic.
   c. functional fixedness.
   d. confirmation bias.

6. The way an issue is posed can affect our decisions and judgments. For example, one study found that people perceived student cheating to be worse if told that 65 percent of students had cheated than if told that 35 percent of students had not cheated. In this case people's reactions were influenced by
   a. belief perseverance.
   b. fixation.
   c. confirmation bias.
   d. framing.

REVIEWING

Thinking

1. What are the functions of concepts?

Concepts are one of the building blocks of thinking. They serve to simplify and order the world by organizing it into a hierarchy of categories. Concepts often form around prototypes, or best examples of a category.

2. What strategies do we use to solve problems, and what obstacles hinder our problem solving?

When faced with new situations for which no well-learned response suffices, we may use any of several strategies, such as trial and error, algorithms, and rule-of-thumb heuristics. Insight, a sudden and often novel realization, can also offer solutions to problems. We do, however, face certain obstacles to successful problem solving. The confirmation bias predisposes us to verify rather than challenge our hypotheses. And fixations such as functional fixedness may prevent our taking a needed fresh perspective on a problem.

3. How do heuristics, overconfidence, and framing influence our decisions and judgments?

Our use of heuristics, such as the representativeness and availability heuristics, provides highly efficient but occasionally misleading guides for making quick decisions and forming intuitive judgments. Our tendencies to seek confirmation of our hypotheses and to use quick and easy heuristics can blind us to our vulnerability to error, a phenomenon known as overconfidence. Framing—the way a question is presented—can significantly affect our thinking.

4. How do our preexisting beliefs influence our decision making?

As the belief perseverance phenomenon indicates, we sometimes cling to our ideas after their basis has been discredited, because the explanation for their apparent validity lingers in our minds. In general, people tend to accept as more logical those conclusions that agree with their beliefs.

TERMS AND CONCEPTS TO REMEMBER

cognition, p. 302
concept, p. 302
prototype, p. 302
algorithm, p. 303

heuristic, p. 303
insight, p. 303
confirmation bias, p. 304
fixation, p. 304

functional fixedness, p. 305
representativeness heuristic, p. 305
availability heuristic, p. 306

overconfidence, p. 308
framing, p. 308
belief perseverance, p. 309

REHEARSE IT ANSWER KEY

1. a   2. b   3. c   4. d   5. b   6. d

21 Language and Thought

The most tangible indication of our thinking power is **language**—our spoken, written, or gestured words and the ways we combine them as we think and communicate. Humans have long and proudly proclaimed that language sets us above all other animals. "When we study human language," asserted linguist Noam Chomsky (1972), "we are approaching what some might call the 'human essence,' the qualities of mind that are, so far as we know, unique" to humans. To cognitive scientist Steven Pinker (1990), language is "the jewel in the crown of cognition." When the human vocal tract evolved the capacity to utter vowels, our capacity for language exploded, catapulting our species forward (Diamond, 1989). Whether spoken, written, or signed, language enables us to communicate complex ideas from person to person and to transmit civilization's accumulated knowledge across generations.

Language Development

PREVIEW QUESTION 1 When do children acquire language, and how do they master this complex task?

Make a quick guess: How many words did you learn in one average day during the years between your first birthday and your high school graduation?

The average secondary school graduate knows some 80,000 words (Miller & Gildea, 1987). That averages (after age 1) to nearly 5000 words learned each year, or 13 each day! How you did it—how the 5000 words a year you learned could so far outnumber the roughly 200 words a year that your schoolteachers consciously taught you—is one of the great human wonders. Before children can add 2 + 2, they are creating their own original and grammatically appropriate sentences. Most parents would have trouble stating the rules of syntax. Yet their preschoolers comprehend and speak with a facility that puts to shame a college student struggling to learn a foreign language or a scientist struggling to simulate natural language on a computer. As we converse, words effortlessly spill out of our mouths with perfect syntax (pretty amazing, given how many ways there are to mess up). There are, it sometimes seems, servants down in our heads' basement busily hammering together sentences that get piped up and shoved out of our mouth. How does our astonishing facility for language unfold, and how can we explain it?

Acquiring Language

Children's language development moves from simplicity to complexity. Infants start without language (*in fantis* means "not speaking"). Yet by 4 months of age, babies can read lips and discriminate speech sounds. They prefer to look at a face that matches a sound, so we know they can recognize that *ah* comes from wide open lips and *ee* from a mouth with corners pulled back (Kuhl & Meltzoff, 1982). At about this age, babies enter a **babbling stage** in which they spontaneously utter a variety of sounds such as *ah-goo, da-da,* and *na-na*—easily formed sounds likely to be found in most languages.

Babbling is not an imitation of adult speech, for it includes sounds from various languages, even sounds that do not occur in the household's language. From this early babbling, a listener could not identify an infant as being, say, French, Korean, or

Although you probably know about 80,000 words, you use only 150 words for about half of what you say.

■ **language** our spoken, written, or gestured words and the ways we combine them to communicate meaning.

■ **babbling stage** beginning by 4 months, the stage of speech development in which the infant spontaneously utters various sounds at first unrelated to the household language.

Ethiopian. Deaf infants babble (repeat syllablelike gestures), too (Petitto & Marentette, 1991). It seems, then, that before nurture molds our speech, nature enables a wide range of possible sounds.

Eventually our babbling comes to resemble the characteristic sounds and intonations of our household language. By the time infants are about 10 months old, their babbling has changed so that a trained ear can identify the language of the household (de Boysson-Bardies & others, 1989). Sounds outside the infant's native tongue begin to disappear. And infants gradually lose their ability to discriminate sounds they never hear. Clever experiments by Janet Werker (1989) reveal that at 6 months infants can perceive subtle sound differences in other languages, but by 12 months they cannot (**FIGURE 21.1**). Without exposure to other languages, we became functionally deaf to speech sounds outside our native language. Thus, by adulthood those who speak only English cannot discriminate certain Japanese sounds. Nor can Japanese adults with no training in English distinguish between the English *r* and *l*. Thus (believe it or not), *la-la-ra-ra* may sound like the same repeated syllable to a Japanese adult. This makes life challenging for the Japanese tourist who is told the train station is "just after the next light." The next what? After the street veering right or farther down, after the traffic light?

■ **one-word stage** the stage in speech development, from about age 1 to 2, during which a child speaks mostly in single words.

■ **two-word stage** beginning about age 2, the stage in speech development during which a child speaks mostly two-word statements.

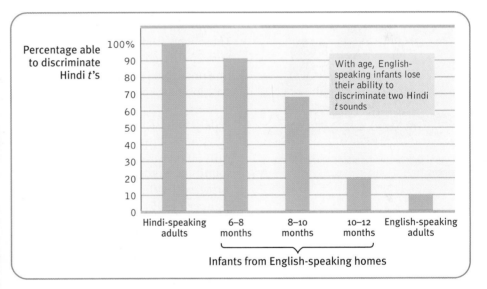

FIGURE 21.1

Testing for speech sound perception
We are all born with the ability to recognize speech sounds from all the world's languages. In Janet Werker's lab, an infant is reinforced with applause and by activating toy animals when he looks to the right after hearing a changed sound (as in *ba, ba, ba, ba, da, da*). Adult Hindi speakers and young infants from English-speaking homes can easily discriminate two Hindi *t* sounds not spoken in English. By about age 1, however, English-speaking listeners rarely perceive the sound difference. (Adapted from Werker, 1989.)

Around the first birthday (the exact age varies from child to child), most children enter the **one-word stage.** Having already learned that sounds carry meanings, they begin to use sounds to communicate meaning. Their first words usually contain only one syllable—*ma* or *da,* for instance—and may be barely recognizable. But family members quickly learn to understand the infant's language, and gradually it conforms more and more to the family's language. At this one-word stage, an inflected word may equal a sentence. "Doggy!" may mean "Look at the dog out there!"

Children typically use more and more single words during the second year. At about 18 months, their word learning begins to explode, from a word per week to a word per day. Before their second birthday, they usually enter the **two-word stage,** when they start uttering two-word sentences (Table 21.1). Language at this stage is characterized by **telegraphic speech:** Like telegrams (TERMS ACCEPTED. SEND MONEY), this early form of speech contains mostly nouns and verbs (*Want juice*). Also like telegrams, it follows rules of syntax; the words are in a sensible order. The English-speaking child typically says adjectives before nouns—*big doggy* rather than *doggy big*.

There seems to be no "three-word stage." Once children move out of the two-word stage, they quickly begin uttering longer phrases (Fromkin & Rodman, 1983). Although the sentences may still resemble a telegraphed message, they continue to follow the rules of syntax *(Mommy get ball)*. By early elementary school, the child understands complex sentences and begins to enjoy the humor conveyed by double meanings: "You never starve in the desert because of all the sand-which-is there."

TABLE 21.1

SUMMARY OF LANGUAGE DEVELOPMENT

Month (approximate)	Stage
4	Babbles many speech sounds.
10	Babbling reveals household language.
12	One-word stage.
24	Two-word, telegraphic speech.
24+	Language develops rapidly into complete sentences.

© 1994 by Sidney Harris.

"Got idea. Talk better. Combine words. Make sentences."

■ **telegraphic speech** early speech stage in which the child speaks like a telegram—"go car"—using mostly nouns and verbs and omitting "auxiliary" words.

Explaining Language Development

Those who study language acquisition inevitably wonder how we do it. Attempts to answer this question have sparked a spirited intellectual controversy. The nature-nurture debate surfaces again and, here as elsewhere, appreciation for innate predisposition has grown.

Skinner: Operant Learning

Behaviorist B. F. Skinner (1957) believed that we can explain language development with familiar learning principles, such as *association* (of the sights of things with the sounds of words); *imitation* (of the words and syntax modeled by others); and *reinforcement* (with success, smiles, and hugs when the child says something right). Thus, Skinner (1985) argued, babies learn to talk in many of the same ways that animals learn to peck keys and press bars: "Verbal behavior evidently came into existence when, through a critical step in the evolution of the human species, the vocal musculature became susceptible to operant conditioning."

Chomsky: Inborn Universal Grammar

The learning perspective in language goes well beyond Skinner's ideas, which linguist Noam Chomsky (1959, 1987) thinks were naive. Surely, Chomsky has said, a Martian scientist observing children in a single-language community would conclude that language is almost entirely inborn. But it isn't. Children do learn the language used in their environment. However, the rate at which they acquire words and grammar without being taught is too extraordinary to be explained solely by learning principles. Children generate all sorts of sentences they have never heard and, therefore, could not be imitating. (No parent teaches the sentence, "I hate you, Daddy.") There are 3,628,800 ways to arrange this sentence's 10 words. Only a handful of them make any sense. Yet any 4-year-old could pick them out from among the 3,628,700+ nonsensical orderings.

Moreover, many of the errors young children make result from overgeneralizing logical grammatical rules, such as adding *-ed* to make the past tense (from de Cuevas, 1990):

Child: My teacher holded the baby rabbits and we petted them.

Mother: Did you say your teacher held the baby rabbits?

Child: Yes.

Mother: Did you say she held them tightly?

Child: No, she holded them loosely.

Chomsky (1987) likens the behaviorist view of how language develops to filling a bottle with water. He instead views language development as "helping a flower to grow in its own way." It is, he believes, akin to sexual maturation: Given adequate nurture, it just "happens to the child." All human languages have the same grammatical building blocks, such as nouns and verbs, subjects and objects, negations and questions. Even sign language, whether produced by deaf Chinese or American children, has structural similarities (Goldin-Meadow & Mylander, 1998).

Our 5000 human languages are therefore dialects of the "universal grammar" for which our brains are prewired. Thanks to our inborn universal grammar, we readily learn the specific grammar of whatever language we hear. It happens so naturally—as naturally as birds learning to fly—that training hardly helps. Expose children to language and they will soak it up. If not exposed to a language, a group of children will make up their own. Without exposure to language, deaf children, too, will spontaneously create one with gestures, complete with sophisticated grammar (Horgan, 1995; Pinker, 1995).

Other worlds may have languages that, for us humans, are unlearnable, but our world does not. Chomsky maintains that our language acquisition capacity is like a box—a "language acquisition device"—in which grammar switches are thrown as children experience their language. Thus, English-speaking children learn to put the object of a sentence last ("She ate an apple"). Japanese-speaking children put the object before the verb ("She an apple ate"). We are born with the hardware and an operating system; experience writes the software (**FIGURE 21.2**).

Creating a language
Brought together as if on a desert island (actually a school), Nicaragua's young deaf children created their own Nicaraguan Sign Language, complete with words and intricate grammar. Our biological predisposition to language does not create language in a vacuum. But activated by a social context, nature and nurture worked creatively together (Osborne, 1999).

FIGURE 21.2
Nature and nurture
Genes design the mechanisms for a language, and experience activates them as it modifies the brain. Grow up in Paris and you will speak French (environment matters), but not if you are a cat (genes matter).

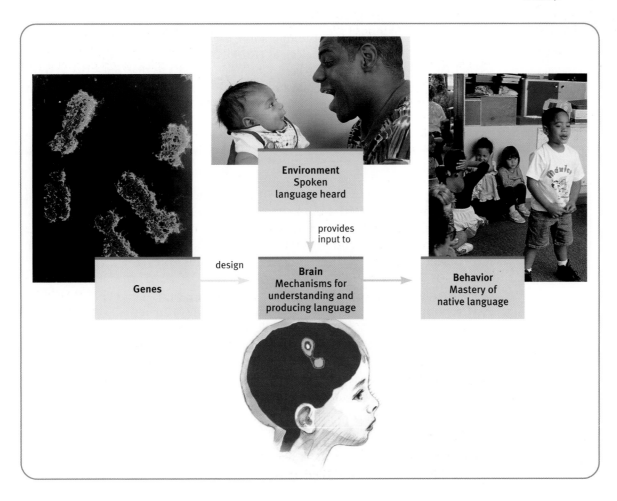

Genes → design → Brain: Mechanisms for understanding and producing language → Behavior: Mastery of native language

Environment: Spoken language heard → provides input to → Brain

LIttle statistician

Human infants come with a remarkable capacity to statistically analyze language and discern words and grammatical rules. This is a tribute to both nature and nurture—to our biological machinery for learning language.

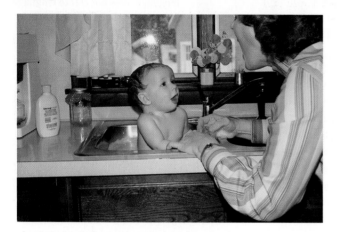

Brain scans reveal a difference in how the brain records a second language learned early versus later in life. Adults who learned a second language early in life use the same patch of frontal lobe tissue when recounting an event in one language, then another. Those who learned their second tongue after childhood display activity in an adjacent brain area while using their second language (Kim & others, 1997).

Cognitive Scientists: Statistical Learning

Human infants display a remarkable ability to learn statistical aspects of human speech. When you or I listen to an unfamiliar language, the syllables all run together. Someone unfamiliar with English might, for example, hear the "United Nations" as the "Uneye Tednay Shuns." Before our first birthday, our brains were discerning word breaks by statistically analyzing which syllables most often go together. Jenny Saffran and her colleagues (1996) showed this by exposing 8-month-old infants to a computer voice speaking an unbroken, monotone string of nonsense syllables (*bidakupadotigolabubidaku . . .*). After just two minutes of exposure, the infants were able to recognize (as indicated by their attention) three-syllable sequences that appeared repeatedly.

Follow-up research offers further testimony to infants' surprising knack for soaking up language. Seven-month-old infants can learn simple sentence structures. After repeatedly hearing syllable sequences that follow one rule, such as *ga-ti-ga* and *li-na-li* (an ABA pattern), they listen longer to syllables in a different sequence, such as *wo-fe-fe* (an ABB pattern) rather than *wo-fe-wo*. Their detecting the difference between the two patterns suggests that babies come with a built-in readiness to learn grammatical rules (Marcus & others, 1999).

Childhood is the critical period for mastering grammar. Those who learn a second language as adults usually speak it with the accent of their first language. Do they master the foreign grammar better than the accent? To find out, Jacqueline Johnson and Elissa Newport (1991) gave Korean and Chinese immigrants to the United States a grammar test, requiring them to identify each of 276 sentences ("Yesterday the hunter shoots a deer") as grammatically correct or incorrect. Some of the test-takers had immigrated in early childhood, others as adults. Regardless of their age at immigration, each had been in the United States for approximately 10 years. Nevertheless, as **FIGURE 21.3** reveals, those who learned their second language early learned it best. Chomsky would say that once the grammar switches are thrown during a child's developing years, mastering another grammar becomes more difficult.

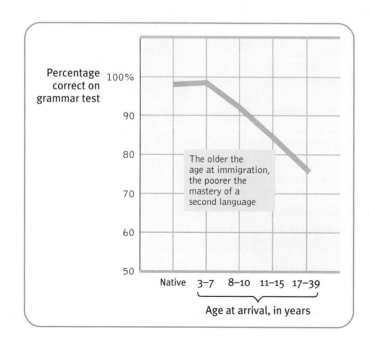

Percentage correct on grammar test

The older the age at immigration, the poorer the mastery of a second language

Native 3–7 8–10 11–15 17–39

Age at arrival, in years

FIGURE 21.3

New language learning gets harder with age

Young children have a readiness to learn language. Ten years after coming to the United States, Asian immigrants took a grammar test. Those who arrived before age 8 understood grammar as well as native speakers. Those who arrived later did not. (From Johnson & Newport, 1991.)

The impact of early experience is also evident in comparisons of deaf and hearing children. Hearing children of hearing-speaking parents and deaf children of deaf-signing parents have much in common. Both groups babble as infants—hearing children by repeating sounds, deaf children by repeating elementary sign gestures (Petitto & Marentette, 1991). Both groups develop vocabularies at comparable rates (Meier, 1991). For both groups, later-than-usual exposure to language (at age 2 or 3) unleashes their brain's idle language capacity, producing a rush of language. But consider the 90+ percent of deaf children born to hearing-nonsigning parents. These children typically do not experience language during their early years. Compared with deaf children exposed to sign language from birth, those who learn to sign as teens or adults are like immigrants who learn English after childhood. They can master the basic words and learn to order them, but they never become as fluent as native signers in producing and comprehending subtle grammatical differences (Newport, 1990).

To summarize, children's genes design complex brain wiring that prepares them to learn language as they interact with their caregivers. Skinner's emphasis on learning helps explain why infants acquire the language they hear and how they add new words. (So does infants' ability to learn statistical probabilities in speech.) Chomsky's emphasis on our built-in readiness to learn grammar rules helps explain why preschoolers acquire language so readily and use grammar so well. Once again, we see biology and experience working together.

Thinking and Language

PREVIEW QUESTION 2 What is the relationship between thinking and language?

Thinking and language intricately intertwine. Asking which comes first is one of psychology's chicken-and-egg questions. Do our ideas come first and we wait for words to name them? Or are our thoughts conceived in words and therefore unthinkable without them?

Language Influences Thinking

Linguist Benjamin Lee Whorf contended that language determines the way we think. According to Whorf's (1956) **linguistic relativity** hypothesis, different languages impose different conceptions of reality: "Language itself shapes a man's basic ideas." The Hopi, Whorf noted, have no past tense for their verbs. Therefore, he contended, a Hopi could not so readily *think* about the past.

Whorf's relativity hypothesis would probably not occur to people who speak only one language and view that language as simply a vehicle for thought. But to those who speak two dissimilar languages, such as English and Japanese, it seems obvious that a person thinks differently in different languages (Brown, 1986). Unlike English, which has a rich vocabulary for self-focused emotions such as anger, Japanese has many words for interpersonal emotions such as sympathy (Markus & Kitayama, 1991). Many bilinguals report that they even have a different sense of self, depending on which language they are using (Matsumoto, 1994). After emigrating from Asia to North America, bilinguals may even reveal different personalities when taking the same personality test in their two languages (Dinges & Hull, 1992). Learn a language and you learn about a culture. When a language becomes extinct—the likely fate of most of the world's 5000 remaining languages—the world loses the culture and thinking that hang on that language. "To destroy a people, destroy their language," observed poet Joy Hajo.

But to say that language *determines* the way we think, as Whorf did, is much too strong. People who speak the same language often think very differently. A conserva-

"Childhood is the time for language, no doubt about it. Young children, the younger the better, are good at it; it is child's play. It is a onetime gift to the species."

Lewis Thomas, *The Fragile Species*, 1992

No means no! No matter how you say it Deaf children of deaf-signing parents and hearing children of hearing parents have much in common. They develop language skills at about the same rate, and they are equally effective at opposing parental wishes and demanding their way.

"All words are pegs to hang ideas on."

Henry Ward Beecher, *Proverbs From Plymouth Pulpit*, 1887

■ **linguistic relativity** Whorf's hypothesis that language determines the way we think.

tive and a liberal may know the same words, use the same grammar, yet have conflicting attitudes. Moreover, a Papua New Guinean without our words for shapes and colors nevertheless perceives them much as we do (Rosch, 1974).

Our words do, however, have some *influence* on what we think (Hardin & Banaji, 1993). Whether living in Britain or New Guinea, people use their language when classifying and remembering colors (Davidoff & others, 1999). Imagine that while viewing three colors you called (using your color words) two of them yellow and one of them blue. Later you would likely see and recall the yellows as being more similar. People in the Berinmo tribe, which has different words for two shades of yellow, would better recall the distinctions between the two yellows.

Given the subtle influence of words on thinking, we do well to choose our words carefully. Referring to women as *girls*—as in "the girls at the office"—perpetuates a view of women's having lower status, does it not? Or consider the generic use of the pronoun *he*. Does it make any difference whether I write "A child learns language as *he* interacts with *his* caregivers" or "Children learn language as *they* interact with *their* caregivers"? Some argue it makes no difference because every reader knows "the masculine gender shall be deemed and taken to include females" (as the British Parliament declared in 1850).

But is the generic *he* always taken to include females? Twenty studies consistently found that it is not (Henley, 1989). For example, Janet Hyde (1984) asked children to finish stories for which she gave them a first line, such as "When a kid goes to school, _____ often feels excited on the first day." When Hyde used *he* in the blank, the children's stories were nearly always about males. *He or she* in the blank resulted in female characters about one-third of the time. Studies with adolescents and adults in North America and New Zealand have found similar effects of the generic *he* (Hamilton, 1988; Martyna, 1978; Ng, 1990). Sentences about "the artist and his work" tend to conjure up images of a man. Similarly, ambiguous actions taken by a "chairman of the board" seem to reveal an assertive and independent personality. The same actions taken by a "chairperson of the board" seem to reveal a warmer, more caring personality (McConnell & Fazio, 1996).

Consider, too, that people use generic pronouns selectively, as in "the doctor . . . he" and "the secretary . . . she" (MacKay, 1983). If *he* and *his* were truly gender-free, we shouldn't skip a beat when hearing that "a nurse must answer his calls" or that "man, like other mammals, nurses his young." That we are startled indicates that *his* carries a gender connotation that clashes with our idea of *nurse*.

Language's power to influence thought makes vocabulary building a crucial part of education. To expand language is to expand the ability to think. In young children, thinking develops hand in hand with language (Gopnik & Meltzoff, 1986). And what is true for preschoolers is true for everyone: *It pays to increase your word power.* That's why most textbooks, including this one, introduce new words—to teach new ideas and new ways of thinking.

A safe sign

We have outfielder William Hoy to thank for baseball sign language. The first deaf player to join the major leagues, in 1892, he invented hand signals for "Strike!" "Safe!" (shown here) and "Yerr Out!" (Pollard, 1992). Such gestures worked so well that referees in all sports now use invented signs, and fans are fluent in sports sign language.

Increased word power helps explain what McGill University researcher Wallace Lambert (1992; Lambert & others, 1993) calls the "bilingual advantage." Bilingual children in Canada, Switzerland, Israel, South Africa, and Singapore outperform monolinguals on intelligence tests. Knowing this, Lambert helped devise a Canadian program that enables English-speaking children to be immersed in French. (From 1981 to 1999, the number of non-Quebec Canadian children immersed in French rose from 65,000 to 280,000 [Commissioner, 1999].) For most of their first three years in school, the English-speaking children are taught entirely in French, and thereafter gradually shift by the end of their schooling to classes mostly in English. Not surprisingly, the children attain a natural French fluency unrivaled by other methods of language teaching. Moreover, compared with similarly capable children in control conditions, they do so without detriment to their English fluency, and with increased aptitude scores, math scores, and appreciation for French-Canadian culture.

So, for English-speaking Canadians, immersion followed by bilingual education pays dividends. Does bilingual education for children in a linguistic minority also pay dividends? Advocates of "English-only" education doubt it. They argue that bilingual programs are expensive, ineffective, and detrimental to non–English-speaking children's assimilation into their English-based cultures (Porter, 1998). But some studies find that such children benefit from bilingual education if in "two-way" schools where they, together with English-speaking children, experience half their classes in English and half in their native language. Compared with non–English-speaking children dropped into English-only schools, those in the two-way schools tend to develop higher self-esteem. They drop out less frequently. And they eventually attain higher levels of academic achievement and English proficiency (August & Hakuta, 1998; Padilla & Benavides, 1992; Thomas & Collier, 1998).

Increasing word power through sign language has also had great benefits for deaf people, who for thousands of years were viewed as incompetent to inherit property, marry, be educated, or have challenging work (Sacks, 1990). Since the spread of signed instruction, deaf people have shown that, when exposed to signing as preschoolers and then schooled in their language, they become fully literate. Deaf children with native sign fluency—learned, for example, as children of signing deaf parents—outperform other signing deaf children on measures of intelligence and academic achievement (Isham & Kamin, 1993). Whether we are deaf or hearing, language transforms experience. Language connects us to the past and the future. Language fuels our imagination. Language links us to one another.

Thinking Without Language

When you are alone, do you talk to yourself? Is "thinking" simply conversing with yourself? Without a doubt, words convey ideas. But aren't there times when ideas precede words? To turn on the cold water in your bathroom, in which direction do you turn the handle? To answer this question, you probably thought not in words but with a mental picture. Indeed, we often think in images. Artists think in images. So do composers, poets, mathematicians, athletes, and scientists. Albert Einstein reported that he achieved some of his greatest insights through visual images and later put them into words.

Pianist Liu Chi Kung showed the value of thinking in images. One year after placing second in the 1958 Tchaikovsky piano competition, Liu was imprisoned during China's cultural revolution. Soon after his release, after seven years without touching a piano, he was back on tour, the critics judging his musicianship better than ever. How did he continue to develop without practice? "I did practice," said Liu,

Mental practice
Before each turn at bat during his 70–home-run season, Mark McGwire would imagine the pitcher throwing the baseball, imagine how the ball would move, and "imagine smashing the ball with his Paul Bunyan swing" (Olney, 1998).

A thoughtful art
Playing the piano engages thinking without language. In the absence of a piano, mental practice can sustain one's skill.

"every day. I rehearsed every piece I had ever played, note by note, in my mind" (Garfield, 1986).

Athletes in many fields now supplement physical with mental practice. For Olympic athletes, "mental practice has become a standard part of training," reports Richard Suinn (1997). Golf great Jack Nicklaus has said that he would "watch a movie" in his head before each shot. In a laboratory test, Georgia Nigro (1984) demonstrated the wisdom of mental practice. She had people actually throw darts 24 times at a target, then had half the people throw 24 darts mentally, and, finally, had everyone throw another 24 darts. Only those who had mentally practiced showed any improvement.

Young members of the U.S. Figure Skating Association have exhibited similar improvement in their performance ratings for jumps and spins following mental practice while listening to their skating music (Garza & Feltz, 1998). And several experiments on mental practice and basketball foul shooting have found comparable benefits. In one such experiment (Savoy & Beitel, 1996), conducted with the University of Tennessee women's team over 35 games, the team's free-throw shooting increased from approximately 52 percent in games following standard physical practice to some 65 percent after mental practice. During the mental practice, players repeatedly imagined making foul shots under various conditions, including being "trash-talked" by their opposition. The experiment's dramatic conclusion occurred when Tennessee won the national championship game in overtime, thanks in part to their foul shooting.

Mental rehearsal can also help you achieve an academic goal. In one study, Shelley Taylor and her UCLA colleagues (1998) engaged introductory psychology students who were a week away from facing a midterm exam. Some were told to visualize themselves scanning the posted grade list, seeing their A, beaming with joy, and feeling proud. Repeating this "outcome simulation" 5 minutes each day until the exam had little effect, adding only 2 points to their exam scores, compared with scores of student counterparts not engaging in any mental simulation. But the researchers had another group visualize themselves effectively studying—reading their textbook chapters, going over notes, eliminating distractions, declining an offer to go out. Repeating this "process simulation" for 5 minutes each day had a beneficial effect. Compared with the control students, this second group of students began studying sooner, spent more time at it, and beat the control group average by 8 points. From such experiments, the researchers conclude that it is better to spend your fantasy time planning how to get somewhere than to dwell on the imagined destination.

Psychologists have found further evidence of thinking without language. Much of our information processing occurs outside of consciousness, beyond language. Inside the ever-active brain, many streams of activity flow in parallel, function automatically, are remembered implicitly, and only occasionally surface as conscious words. "Thinking lite," this unconscious processing has been called—"one-fourth the effort of regular thinking." So, yes, there certainly is cognition without language.

What, then, should we say about the relationship between thinking and language? As we have seen, language does influence our thinking. But if thinking did not also affect language, there would never be any new words. And new words and new combinations of old words express new ideas. The basketball term *slam dunk* was coined after the act itself had become fairly common. So, let us say that *thinking affects our language, which then affects our thought.*

Psychological research on thinking and language mirrors the mixed reviews given our species in literature and religion. The human

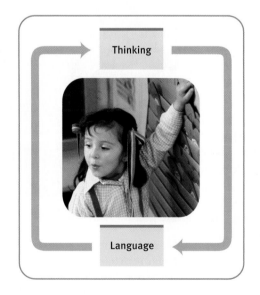

The interplay of thought and language
The traffic runs both ways between thinking and language. Thinking affects our language, which affects our thought.

Thinking

Language

mind is simultaneously capable of striking intellectual failures and of vast intellectual power. Some misjudgments have disastrous consequences, so we do well to appreciate our capacity for error. Yet our heuristics often serve us well, and they certainly are efficient. Moreover, our ingenuity at problem solving and our extraordinary power of language surely, among the animals, rank humankind as almost "infinite in faculties."

rehearse it!

1. Children progress from babbling to sentences of two and then four, five, six, or more words. The one-word stage of speech development is usually reached at about
   a. 4 months.
   b. 6 months.
   c. 1 year.
   d. 2 years.

2. B. F. Skinner believed that we learn language the same way we learn other behaviors—through association, imitation, and reinforcement. Skinner's behaviorist view is most helpful in explaining
   a. the onset of babbling.
   b. the speech behavior of deaf infants.
   c. the seemingly effortless mastery of grammatical rules by very young children.
   d. why children learn their household's language.

3. According to Noam Chomsky, we are biologically prepared to acquire language and are born with a readiness to learn the grammatical rules of the language we hear. He believes all we need to acquire language is
   a. instruction in grammar.
   b. exposure to language in early childhood.
   c. reinforcement for babbling and other early verbal behaviors.
   d. imitation and drill.

4. Benjamin Lee Whorf proposed that our language determines the way we perceive and think about the world. Although we now know that language influences, rather than determines, our thinking, Whorf's linguistic relativity hypothesis does help explain why
   a. a person who learns a second language thinks differently in that language.
   b. children have a built-in readiness to learn grammatical rules.
   c. apes are able to communicate through sign language.
   d. artists, athletes, and others are able to think in visual images.

Animal Thinking and Language

PREVIEW QUESTION 3 Do animals—in some sense that we can identify with—think? Do they even exhibit language?

If in our use of language we humans are, as the psalmist long ago rhapsodized, "little lower than God," where do other animals fit in the scheme of things? Are they "little lower than human"? In part, the answer lies in the extent to which animals share our capacity for thinking and language.

Do Animals Think?

Animals, especially the great apes, display remarkable capacities for thinking (Hauser, 2000). Some experimenters have monkeyed with numbers. In one, monkeys were shown four screens containing one to four objects each (perhaps two bananas, one triangle, four apples, and three hearts). Across variations in sizes and shapes, the monkeys quickly learned to touch pictures in ascending numerical order and then to receive a food reward. When then shown a display containing five to nine objects, they could order these, too (Brannon & Terrace, 1998). One female chimpanzee named Ai could even order five random numbers between 0 and 9 after they were hidden (Kawai & Matsuzawa, 2000). After the first number was touched, the four others were covered by white squares on a screen. More than 90 percent of the time, Ai could remember and order the numbers by touching squares in the right sequence. Monkey see, monkey count.

We aren't the only creatures that display insight. German psychologist Wolfgang Köhler (1925) observed apparent insight while studying chimpanzees placed on an is-

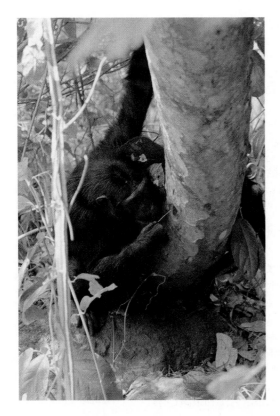

Chimpanzee inventiveness
A wild chimp shows ingenuity by using a stick to fish for ants living in the tree.

Smart bird brain
Alex, an African gray parrot trained and tested by University of Arizona professor Irene Pepperberg (1994, 2000), displays numerical competence when shown novel assortments of objects. Asked, for example, "How many red blocks?" or "How many green balls?" Alex, with a brain the size of a walnut, answers correctly more than 80 percent of the time.

land off the coast of Africa. In one experiment with a caged chimp named Sultan, Köhler placed a piece of fruit and a long stick well beyond reach, and a short stick inside the cage. Spying the short stick, the chimp grabbed it and tried to reach the fruit. But the stick, by design, was too short. After several unsuccessful attempts, Sultan dropped the stick and paused to survey the situation. Then suddenly, as if thinking "Aha!" he jumped up, seized the short stick again, and used it to pull in the longer stick—which he then used to reach the fruit. Sultan's actions displayed animal cognition, claimed Köhler, and showed that there is more to learning than conditioning.

Thanks to problem solving shaped by reinforcement, forest-dwelling chimpanzees have become natural tool users (Boesch-Achermann & Boesch, 1993). They can select appropriate branches or stones to use as hammers in cracking nuts. They can also break off a reed or a stick, strip the twigs and leaves, carry it to a termite mound, fish for termites by twisting it just so, and then carefully remove it without scraping off many termites. One anthropologist, trying to mimic the chimpanzee's deft termite fishing, failed miserably.

Researchers have found at least 39 local customs related to chimp tool use, grooming, and courtship (Gibbons, 1992; Whiten & others, 1999). One group of chimps may slurp ants directly from the stick, while another plucks them off individually. One group may break nuts with a stone hammer, another with a wooden hammer. Such group differences, along with differing dialects and hunting styles, occur within subspecies and thus seem not to be genetic. Rather, they are the chimpanzee equivalent of cultural diversity. Like humans, chimps—often younger chimps—invent customs and pass them on to their peers.

If primates can count, exhibit insight, use tools, and transmit cultural innovations, do they have what developmental psychologists call a "theory of mind"? Can they infer mental states in themselves and their peers? Chimps and orangutans have been observed using mirrors to inspect themselves and touching a colored spot that a researcher has dabbed on their face (Gallup, 1998). Chimps and baboons have also been observed using deception, as when a young baboon feigns having been attacked as a seeming tactic for getting its mother to drive a competing baboon away from its food (Whiten & Byrne, 1988). Do such observations indicate that primates are capable of self-recognition and of comprehending others' perceptions? Many researchers think yes, but some behaviorists are unconvinced (Heyes, 1998). For example, unlike young children, chimpanzees do not know to beg for food from someone who can see them—someone who has a blindfold over the mouth rather than the eyes (Povinelli, 1999).

Do Animals Exhibit Language?

Without doubt, animals communicate. Vervet monkeys have different alarm cries for different predators: a barking call for a leopard, a cough for an eagle, and a chuttering for a snake. Hearing the leopard alarm, other vervets climb the nearest tree. Hearing the eagle alarm, they rush into the bushes. Hearing the snake chutter, they stand up and scan the ground (Byrne, 1991). Whales also communicate, with clicks and wails.

The question is, however, do animals' communications make up a language?

The Case of the Apes

The greatest challenge to humanity's claim to be the only language-using species has come from reports of apes that "talk" with people. Genetically speaking, our closest relatives are the chimpanzees, and the chimpanzees' closest relatives are not other apes, but us (Sagan & Druyan, 1992). Knowing that chimpanzees could not vocalize more than a few words, University of Nevada researchers Allen Gardner and Beatrice Gardner (1969) tried to teach sign language words to a chimp named Washoe, as though she were a deaf human child. After four years, Washoe could use 132 signs. At age 32, Washoe had a vocabulary of 181 signs (Sanz & others, 1998). The Gardners' announcement of the success of their efforts aroused enormous scientific and public interest. One *New York Times* reporter, having learned sign language from his deaf parents, visited Washoe and exclaimed, "Suddenly I realized I was conversing with a member of another species in my native tongue."

Human language appears to have evolved from gestured communications (Corballis, 1999). So it is no wonder that our ape relatives have produced many gestured words but few spoken words. It is no wonder that gestures survive as part of hearing people's speech (even when talking on the phone!). It is no wonder that signing so readily developed among deaf people as an alternative to speech. It is no wonder that congenitally blind people produce gestures similar to those of sighted people, even if they believe the listener is also blind (Iverson & Goldin-Meadow, 1998). And it is no wonder that prohibiting gestures disrupts speech that has spatial content (for example, when describing an apartment layout). For both humans and apes, communication entails gestures.

Further evidence of gestured "ape language" surfaced during the 1970s. Usually apes signed just single words, but sometimes they strung signs together to form intelligible sentences. Washoe signed, "You me go out, please." Apes even appeared to combine words creatively. Washoe designated a swan as a "water bird." Koko, a gorilla trained by Francine Patterson (1978), reportedly described a long-nosed Pinocchio doll as an "elephant baby." Lana is a chimpanzee that "talks" by punching buttons wired to a computer that then translates her punches into English. One day, she wanted her trainer's orange, but she had no word for *orange*. She did however

But is this language?
The ability of chimpanzees to express themselves in American Sign Language (ASL) raises questions about the very nature of language. Here, the trainer is asking, "What is this?" The sign in response is "Baby." Does the response constitute language?

Seeing a doll floating in her water, Washoe signed, "Baby in my drink."

Gesture researcher Robert Krauss (1998) recalls his grandfather telling of two men walking on a bitter winter day. One chattered away while the second nodded, saying nothing. "Schmuel, why aren't you saying anything?" the first friend finally wondered. "Because," replied Schmuel, "I forgot my gloves."

Gestured communication
For hearing people, today's gestures may be less central to communication than for those who first used hand signals. Yet gestures remain naturally associated with spontaneous speech, especially speech that has spatial content.

know her colors and the word for *apple,* so she improvised: "?Tim give apple which-is orange" (Rumbaugh, 1977).

As reports of ape language accumulated, it seemed that they might indeed be "little lower than human." Granted, their vocabularies and sentences are simple, rather like those of a 2-year-old child, yet the apes do seem to share what we humans have considered our unique ability.

But Can Apes Really Talk?

By the late 1970s, fascination with "talking apes" turned toward cynicism: Were the chimps language champs or were the researchers chumps? The ape language researchers were making monkeys out of themselves, said the skeptics, who raised the following arguments:

- Apes gain their limited vocabularies only with great difficulty. They are hardly like speaking or signing children, who effortlessly soak up dozens of new words a week. Saying that apes can learn language because they can sign words is like saying humans can fly because they can jump.
- Chimps can make signs or push buttons in sequence to get a reward, just as Moscow circus bears can learn to ride unicycles. But pigeons, too, can peck a sequence of keys to get grain (Straub & others, 1979). No one says the pigeon is "talking."
- Apes can certainly use symbols meaningfully. But "Give orange me give eat orange me eat orange . . ." is a far cry from the exquisite syntax of a 3-year-old (Pinker, 1995). To the child, "you tickle" and "tickle you" communicate different ideas. A chimp might sign the phrases interchangeably.
- After training a chimp whom he named Nim Chimsky, Herbert Terrace (1979) concluded that much of chimpanzees' signing is nothing more than apes aping their trainers' signs.
- Presented with ambiguous information, people tend to see what they want or expect to see, a concept known as *perceptual set.* Interpreting chimpanzee signs as language may be little more than wishful thinking on the part of their trainers, claimed Terrace. (When Washoe signed *water bird,* she perhaps was separately naming *water* and *bird.*)

"Chimps do not develop language," concludes Steven Pinker (1995). "But that is no shame on them; humans would surely do no better if trained to hoot and shriek like chimps, to perform the waggle-dance of the bee, or any of the other wonderful feats in nature's talent show."

In science as in politics, controversy can stimulate progress. The provocative claim that "apes share our capacity for language" and the skeptical rejoinder that "apes no use language" (as Washoe might have put it) have moved psychologists toward a greater appreciation of both apes' remarkable capabilities and our own. Everyone agrees: Humans alone possess language, if by the term we mean verbal or signed expression of complex grammar. If we mean, more simply, the ability to communicate through a meaningful sequence of symbols, then apes are indeed capable of language.

Although chimpanzees do not have our facility for language, their abilities to think and communicate continue to impress their trainers. After her second infant died, a depressed Washoe repeatedly asked "Baby?" and became withdrawn when told "Baby dead, baby gone, baby finished." Two weeks later, caretaker-researcher Roger Fouts (1992, 1997) had better news for Washoe: "I have baby for you." Washoe reacted to the signed news with instant excitement, her hair on end, swaggering and

Another "talking" chimpanzee
Lana has learned to speak by punching word symbols on a computer keyboard. When she presses a key, the symbol lights up.

© 1979 by Sidney Harris/American Scientist magazine.

"Although humans make sounds with their mouths and occasionally look at each other, there is no solid evidence that they actually communicate with each other."

panting while signing over and again, "Baby, my baby." When Fouts then introduced the foster infant, Loulis, it took several hours for them to warm to each other, whereupon Washoe broke the ice by signing, "Come baby" and cuddling Loulis. In the months that followed, Loulis picked up 68 signs simply by observing Washoe and three other language-trained chimps.

Moreover, Washoe, Loulis, and the others now sign spontaneously. They ask one another to *chase, tickle, hug, come,* or *groom.* People who sign can actually eavesdrop on these chimp-to-chimp conversations with near-perfect agreement about what the chimps are saying, 90 percent of which pertains to social interaction, reassurance, or play (Fouts & Bodamer, 1987). The chimps are even modestly bilingual; they can translate spoken English words into signs (Shaw, 1989–1990).

More stunning is the discovery by Sue Savage-Rumbaugh and her colleagues (1993) that pygmy chimpanzees can learn to comprehend the semantic nuances of spoken English. Kanzi, one such chimp with the grammatical abilities of a 2½-year-old, happened onto language while observing his adoptive mother being language trained. Kanzi behaves intelligently whether asked, "Can you show me the light?" or "Can you bring me the [flash]light?" or "Can you turn the light on?" Kanzi also knows the spoken words *snake, bite,* and *dog.* Given stuffed animals and asked—for the first time—to "make the dog bite the snake," he put the snake to the dog's mouth. For chimps as for humans, early life is the critical time for learning language. If raised without early exposure to speech or word symbols, the chimps are unable as adults to gain language competence (Rumbaugh & Savage-Rumbaugh, 1994).

Yes, trained apes' language capabilities are modest by human standards. Yet their cognitive powers remain impressive. If Kanzi "had a vocal tract, he would be talking," exclaims Duane Rumbaugh (1994). Realizing this, we see once again how animal research can increase our respect for the creatures studied. Believing that animals could not think, Descartes and other philosophers argued that they were living robots without any moral rights. Animals, it has been said at one time or another, cannot plan, conceptualize, count, use tools, show compassion, or use language (Thorpe, 1974). Today, we know better. We have seen primates exhibit insight, show family loyalty, communicate with one another, display altruism, transmit cultural patterns across generations, and comprehend the syntax of human speech. Accepting and working out the moral implications of all this is an unfinished task for our own thinking species.

> "[Our] egocentric view that [we are] unique from all other forms of animal life is being jarred to the core."
>
> **Duane Rumbaugh and Sue Savage-Rumbaugh**
> **(1978)**

"He says he wants a lawyer."

---

rehearse it!

5. Insight is defined as a sudden and often novel realization of a problem's solution. Of the examples discussed in this section, the problem-solving behavior that most closely resembled insight was
   a. Alex the parrot's answer to questions about colors and numbers.
   b. Sultan the chimpanzee's use of a short stick to pull in a long stick.
   c. the young baboon's pretending to have been attacked in order to get its mother to drive away another baboon competing for food.
   d. Washoe the chimpanzee's use of sign language to request food.

6. There is much controversy over whether apes can be taught to use language in the way that humans do.

However, most researchers of ape sign language agree that apes can
   a. communicate through symbols.
   b. reproduce most human speech sounds.
   c. create new sentences and meanings.
   d. surpass a human 3-year-old in language skills.

Language and Thought

1. When do children acquire language, and how do they master this complex task?

Among the marvels of nature is a child's ability to acquire language. The ease with which children progress from the babbling stage through the one-word stage to the telegraphic speech of the two-word stage and beyond has sparked a lively debate concerning how they do it. Behaviorist B. F. Skinner proposed that we learn language by the familiar principles of association, imitation, and reinforcement. Challenging this claim, linguist Noam Chomsky argues that children are biologically prepared to learn words and use grammar. For mastery of grammar, the learning that occurs during life's first few years is, however, critical.

2. What is the relationship between thinking and language?

Language facilitates and expresses our thoughts. There is no disputing that words convey ideas and that different languages can embody different ways of thinking. Although the linguistic relativity hypothesis suggests that language *determines* thought, it is more accurate to say that language *influences* thought. Studies of the effects of using the generic pronoun *he,* for example, reveal the influence of words.

However, some ideas, such as the ability to perceive and remember different colors, do not depend on language. We sometimes think in images rather than in words, and we invent new words to describe new ideas. So we might say that our thinking affects our language, which then affects our thought.

3. Do animals—in some sense that we can identify with—think? Do they even exhibit language?

Another vigorously debated issue is whether language is a uniquely human ability. Several teams of psychologists provoked enormous interest by teaching various apes, including a number of chimpanzees, to communicate with humans by using sign language or by pushing buttons wired to a computer. The animals have developed considerable vocabularies and are able to string words together to express meaning and requests. Skeptics point out significant differences between apes and humans in their facility with language, especially in their respective abilities to order words grammatically. Nevertheless, these studies have revealed that apes possess considerable cognitive ability.

TERMS AND CONCEPTS TO REMEMBER

language, p. 312	one-word stage, p. 313	telegraphic speech, p. 314	linguistic relativity, p. 317
babbling stage, p. 312	two-word stage, p. 313		

REHEARSE IT ANSWER KEY

1. c   2. d   3. b   4. a   5. b   6. a

Intelligence

No controversy in psychology has been more heated than the question of whether there exists in each person a general intellectual capacity that can be measured and quantified as a number. And the debate goes beyond science as school boards and the courts debate the usefulness and fairness of intelligence and aptitude tests. Should such tests be used to rank individuals and to determine whether to admit them to a particular college or to hire them in a particular job? Do groups differ in native intelligence?

Let's therefore consider: What is intelligence? How is it assessed? And to what extent does it result from nature (heredity) rather than nurture (environment)? Is intelligence testing society's best means of identifying those who would benefit from special opportunities? Or is intelligence testing a potent discriminatory weapon camouflaged as science?

The Origins of Intelligence Testing

PREVIEW QUESTION 1 When and why were intelligence tests created?

Intelligence is a concept intended to explain why some people perform better than others on cognitive tasks. Robert Sternberg (1997) speaks for many experts in viewing **intelligence** as the mental abilities needed to select, adapt to, and shape environments. Intelligent behavior reflects a capacity to learn from experience, to solve problems, and to reason clearly. To understand the concept of intelligence, it helps first to know the history of intelligence testing.

Alfred Binet: Predicting School Achievement

The modern intelligence-testing movement began at the turn of the twentieth century when the French government passed a law requiring that all children attend school. Teachers soon faced an overwhelming range of individual differences. Some children, including many newcomers to Paris, seemed incapable of benefiting from the regular school curriculum and in need of special classes. But how could the schools objectively identify children with special needs?

The government was reluctant to trust teachers' subjective judgments of children's learning potential. Academic slowness might merely reflect inadequate prior education. Also, teachers might prejudge children on the basis of their social backgrounds. To minimize bias, France's minister of public education in 1904 commissioned Alfred Binet (1857–1911) and others to study the problem.

Binet and his collaborator, Théodore Simon, began by assuming that all children follow the same course of intellectual development but that some develop more rapidly. On tests, therefore, a "dull" child should perform as does a typical younger child, and a "bright" child as does a typical older child.

Binet and Simon set out to measure what came to be called a child's **mental age,** the chronological age typical of a given level of performance. The average 9-year-old has a mental age of 9. But many 9-year-olds have mental ages below or above 9. Children below average, such as 9-year-olds who perform at the level of a typical 7-year-old, would struggle with schoolwork considered normal for their age.

Alfred Binet
"The scale, properly speaking, does not permit the measure of intelligence, because intellectual qualities . . . cannot be measured as linear surfaces are measured" (Binet & Simon, 1905).

- **intelligence** the mental abilities needed to select, adapt to, and shape environments. It involves the abilities to profit from experience, solve problems, reason, and successfully meet challenges and achieve goals.

- **mental age** a measure of intelligence test performance devised by Binet; the chronological age typical of a given level of performance. Thus, a child who does as well as the average 8-year-old is said to have a mental age of 8.

"The IQ test was invented to predict academic performance, nothing else. If we wanted something that would predict life success, we'd have to invent another test completely."

Social psychologist Robert Zajonc (1984b)

To measure mental age, Binet and Simon developed varied reasoning and problem-solving questions that might predict school achievement. By testing "bright" and "backward" Parisian schoolchildren on these questions, Binet and Simon succeeded: They found items that did predict how well the children handled schoolwork. Binet hoped his test would be used to improve children's education, but he also feared it would be used to label children and limit their opportunities (Gould, 1981).

Lewis Terman: The Innate IQ

Binet might have been dismayed to discover that the test he designed as a practical guide for identifying slow learners in need of special help would soon be used as a numerical measure of inherited intelligence. After Binet's death in 1911, Stanford University professor Lewis Terman (1877–1956) attempted to use Binet's test but found that the Paris-developed age norms worked poorly with California schoolchildren. So Terman revised the test. He adapted some of Binet's original items, added others, established new age norms, and extended the upper end of the test's range from teenagers to "superior adults." Terman gave his revision the name it retains today—the **Stanford-Binet.**

For such tests, German psychologist William Stern derived the famous **intelligence quotient,** or **IQ.** The IQ was simply a person's mental age divided by chronological age and multiplied by 100 to get rid of the decimal point:

$$IQ = \frac{\text{mental age}}{\text{chronological age}} \times 100$$

"You did very well on your IQ test. You're a man of 49 with the intelligence of a man of 53."

Thus, an average child, whose mental and chronological ages are the same, has an IQ of 100. But an 8-year-old who answers questions as would a typical 10-year-old has an IQ of 125.

Most current intelligence tests, including the Stanford-Binet, no longer compute an IQ. The original IQ formula works fairly well for children but not for adults. Consider: Should a 40-year-old who does as well on the test as an average 20-year-old be assigned an IQ of only 50? Obviously, something is out of whack. Today's intelligence tests therefore produce a mental ability score based on the test-taker's performance relative to the average performance of others the same age. As on the original Stanford-Binet, current tests define this score so that 100 is average, with about two-thirds of all people scoring between 85 and 115. Although there is no longer any intelligence *quotient,* the term "IQ" still lingers in everyday vocabulary as a shorthand expression for "intelligence test score."

What Is Intelligence?

PREVIEW QUESTION 2 Is intelligence a single general ability or several distinct abilities?

Reading all the conflicting ideas about intelligence can leave you feeling as Alice in Wonderland felt after reading "Jabberwocky": "Somehow it seems to fill my head with ideas—only I don't exactly know what they are." So let's see if we can refine the concept.

One General Ability or Several Specific Abilities?

We all know some people talented in science, others in the humanities, and still others in athletics, art, music, or dance. Perhaps you have known a talented artist who is

■ **Stanford-Binet** the widely used American revision (by Terman at Stanford University) of Binet's original intelligence test.

■ **intelligence quotient (IQ)** defined originally as the ratio of mental age *(ma)* to chronological age *(ca)* multiplied by 100 (thus, IQ = *ma/ca* × 100). On contemporary intelligence tests, the average performance for a given age is assigned a score of 100.

■ **factor analysis** a statistical procedure that identifies clusters of related items (called *factors*) on a test; used to identify different dimensions of performance that underlie one's total score.

dumbfounded by the simplest mathematical problems, or a brilliant math student who has little aptitude for literary discussion. We may therefore wonder whether people's mental abilities are too diverse to justify labeling them with the single word *intelligence* or quantifying them with a number from some single scale.

To find out whether there might be a general ability factor that runs throughout our specific mental abilities, psychologists study how various abilities relate to one another. A statistical method called **factor analysis** enables researchers to identify clusters of test items that measure a common ability. For example, people who do well on vocabulary items often do well on paragraph comprehension, a cluster that helps define a verbal intelligence factor. Other clusters include a spatial ability factor and a reasoning ability factor.

Charles Spearman (1863–1945), who helped develop factor analysis, believed there is also a **general intelligence,** or **g,** factor that underlies the specific factors. Spearman granted that people often have special abilities that stand out. But he also noted that those who score high on one factor, such as verbal intelligence, typically score higher than average on other factors, such as spatial or reasoning ability. So there is at least a tendency for different abilities to come in the same package. Spearman believed that this commonality, the *g* factor, underlies all of our intelligent behavior, from navigating the sea to excelling in school.

Howard Gardner (1983, 1993a,b, 1995) is a modern representative of the view that intelligence nevertheless comes in different packages. These different abilities, he observes, enabled our ancestors to cope with different environmental challenges (finding their way home, reading others' emotions, solving problems). Gardner finds support for his view in the fact that brain damage may diminish one type of ability but not others. He also notes that people with **savant syndrome** often score low on intelligence tests but have an island of brilliance—some incredible ability, as in computation, drawing, or musical memory (**FIGURE 22.1**). These people may have virtually no language ability, yet may be able to compute numbers as quickly and accurately as an electronic calculator, or identify almost instantly the day of the week that corresponds to any given date in history (Miller, 1999).

Using such evidence, Gardner argues that we do not have *an* intelligence, but instead have *multiple* intelligences, each relatively independent of the others. In addition to the verbal and mathematical aptitudes assessed by the standard tests, he identifies

- **general intelligence (*g*)** a general intelligence factor that Spearman and others believed underlies specific mental abilities and is therefore measured by every task on an intelligence test.

- **savant syndrome** a condition in which a person otherwise limited in mental ability has an exceptional specific skill, such as in computation or drawing.

"*g* is one of the most reliable and valid measures in the behavioural domain . . . and it predicts important social outcomes such as educational and occupational levels far better than any other trait."

Robert Plomin (1999)

FIGURE 22.1

Savant syndrome

Although hardly able to speak coherently, Britain's Stephen Wiltshire can draw intricate scenes after just one good look. This drawing is of St. Mark's Cathedral in Venice, Italy. By age 13, Stephen was famous for his ability to "draw, with greatest ease, any street he had seen; but he could not, unaided, cross one by himself" (Sacks, 1995).

Gardner (1998) also speculates about a ninth possible intelligence—"existential intelligence"—the ability "to ponder large questions about life, death, existence."

distinct aptitudes for musical accomplishment, for spatially analyzing the visual world, for mastering movement skills (as in dance), and for insightfully understanding ourselves, others, and our natural environment. In simple words, you can think of these eight intelligences as word smarts, number smarts, music smarts, space smarts, body smarts, self smarts, people smarts, and nature smarts. If you are not a candidate for the high-IQ group, MENSA, you might still have a genius for leadership.

As exemplars of these alternative intellects Gardner offers poet T. S. Eliot, scientist Albert Einstein, composer Igor Stravinsky, artist Pablo Picasso, dancer Martha Graham, psychiatrist Sigmund Freud, leader Mahatma Gandhi, and naturalist Charles Darwin. According to Gardner (1998), the computer programmer, the poet, the street-smart adolescent who becomes a crafty executive, and the point guard on the basketball team exhibit different kinds of intelligence. He notes that

> If a person is strong (or weak) in telling stories, solving mathematical proofs, navigating around unfamiliar terrain, learning an unfamiliar song, mastering a new game that entails dexterity, understanding others, or understanding himself, one simply does not know whether comparable strengths (or weaknesses) will be found in other areas.

A general intelligence score is therefore like the overall rating of a city—which doesn't give you much specific information about its schools, streets, or nightlife.

Wouldn't it be wonderful if the world were so just, responds intelligence researcher Sandra Scarr (1989), that being weak in any area would often be compensated by genius in some other area? Alas, the world is not just, for there remains some tendency for different skills to correlate. For example, people with mental disadvantages often have lesser physical abilities as well; thus, we hold Special Olympics to give them a chance to enjoy fair competition.

While Robert Sternberg (1985, 1997) agrees with Gardner's idea of multiple intelligences, he distinguishes more simply among three aspects of intelligence:

- **Analytical (academic problem-solving) intelligence**—assessed by intelligence tests, which present well-defined problems having a single right answer.
- **Creative intelligence**—demonstrated in reacting adaptively to novel situations and generating novel ideas.
- **Practical intelligence**—often required for everyday tasks, which are frequently ill-defined, with multiple solutions.

Traditional intelligence tests assess academic intelligence. They predict school grades reasonably well but do less well in predicting vocational success. Managerial success, for example, depends less on the academic abilities assessed by an intelligence test score (assuming the score is average or above) than on keen practical intelligence—a shrewd ability to manage oneself, one's tasks, and other people. Sternberg and Richard Wagner's (1993, 1995) test of practical managerial intelligence measures whether the test-taker knows how to write effective memos, how to motivate people, when to delegate tasks and responsibilities, how to read people, and how to promote his or her own career. Business executives who score high on this test tend to earn higher salaries and receive better performance ratings than do those who score low. In a similar finding, Stephen Ceci and Jeffrey Liker (1986) report that racetrack fans' expertise in handicapping horses—a practical but complex cognitive task—is unrelated to their intelligence test scores.

Although Sternberg (1998, 1999) and Gardner (1998) differ on specific points, they agree that multiple abilities can contribute to life success. They also agree that the differing varieties of giftedness add spice to life and challenges for education. Under Gardner's or Sternberg's influence, many teachers have been trained to appreciate the varieties of ability and to apply multiple intelligence theory in their classrooms. Evaluations of these programs are under way.

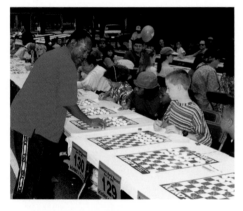

Spatial intelligence genius
In 1998, World Checkers Champion Ron "Suki" King of Barbados set a new record by simultaneously playing 385 players in 3 hours and 44 minutes. Thus, while his opponents often had hours to plot their game moves, King could devote only about 35 seconds to each game. Yet he still managed to win all 385 games!

"You have to be careful, if you're good at something, to make sure you don't think you're good at other things that you aren't necessarily so good at. . . . Because I've been very successful at [software development] people come in and expect that I have wisdom about topics that I don't."

Bill Gates (1998)

Creativity and Intelligence

PREVIEW QUESTION 3 What is creativity, and what fosters this ability?

Creativity is the ability to produce ideas that are both novel and valuable. The forms for creativity vary by culture. Samoan culture encourages creativity in dance, Balinese culture in music, the African Ashanti culture in wood carvings (Lubart, 1990). In each, creativity means expressing familiar themes in novel and valuable ways.

Results from tests of intelligence and creativity suggest that a certain level of aptitude is necessary but not sufficient for creativity. In general, people with high scores on intelligence tests also do well on creativity tests. ("How many uses can you think of for a brick?") But beyond a certain level—an intelligence test score of about 120—the correlation between intelligence and creativity shrivels. Exceptionally creative architects, mathematicians, scientists, and engineers usually score no higher on intelligence tests than do their less creative peers (MacKinnon & Hall, 1972). So clearly there is more to creativity than that which intelligence tests reveal. Studies of creative people suggest five other components of creativity (Sternberg, 1988; Sternberg & Lubart, 1991, 1992):

- *Expertise* provides a well-developed base of knowledge. "Chance favors only the prepared mind," observed Louis Pasteur. The more ideas, images, and phrases we have to work with, through our accumulated learning, the more chances we have to combine these mental building blocks in novel ways.

- *Imaginative thinking skills* provide the ability to see things in new ways, to recognize patterns, to make connections. To be creative you must first master the basic elements of a problem, then redefine or explore the problem in a new way. Copernicus first developed expertise regarding the solar system and its planets and then defined the system as revolving around the Sun, not the Earth.

- A *venturesome personality* tolerates ambiguity and risk, perseveres in overcoming obstacles, and seeks new experiences rather than following the pack. Inventors, for example, have a willingness to persist after failures. Thomas Edison tried countless substances for his light bulb filament.

- *Intrinsic motivation* is creativity's fourth component. As psychologist Teresa Amabile points out, "People will be most creative when they feel motivated primarily by the interest, enjoyment, satisfaction, and challenge of the work itself—rather than by external pressures" (Amabile & Hennessey, 1992). Creative people focus not so much on extrinsic motivators—meeting deadlines, impressing people, or making money—as on the intrinsic pleasure and challenge of their work.

■ creativity the ability to produce novel and valuable ideas.

After picking up a Nobel prize in Stockholm, physicist Richard Feynman stopped in Queens, New York, to look at his high school record. "My grades were not as good as I remembered," he reported, "and my IQ was [a good, though unexceptional] 124" (Faber, 1987).

Imaginative thinking
Cartoonists often display creativity as they see things in new ways or make unusual connections.

Everyone held up their crackers as David threw the cheese log into the ceiling fan.

FURIOUS GEORGE

■ **emotional intelligence** the ability to perceive, understand, and manage emotions.

■ **Wechsler Adult Intelligence Scale (WAIS)** the WAIS is the most widely used intelligence test; contains verbal and performance (nonverbal) subtests.

"You're wise, but you lack tree smarts."

"I worry about [intelligence] definitions that collapse assessments of our cognitive powers with statements about the kind of human beings we favor."

Howard Gardner, "*Rethinking the Concept of Intelligence***," 2000**

Athleticism, like intelligence, is many things
Some football and basketball coaches have encouraged players to develop their finesse by taking dance classes.

■ A *creative environment* sparks, supports, and refines creative ideas. After studying the careers of 2026 prominent scientists and inventors, Dean Keith Simonton (1992) noted that the most eminent among them were in fact not lone geniuses. Rather they were mentored, challenged, and supported by their relationships with colleagues. Such people often have the emotional intelligence needed to network effectively with peers.

Emotional Intelligence

PREVIEW QUESTION 4 Is our ability to manage our own emotions and to empathize with others a form of intelligence?

Also distinct from academic intelligence is what Nancy Cantor and John Kihlstrom (1987) first called *social intelligence*—the know-how involved in comprehending social situations and managing oneself successfully. A critical part of social intelligence is what Peter Salovey and John Mayer (1990; Mayer & Salovey, 1993, 1995, 1997) call **emotional intelligence**—the ability to perceive, understand, and manage emotions. Emotionally intelligent people are especially self-aware. They manage their emotions without being hijacked by overwhelming depression, anxiety, or anger. They can delay gratification in pursuit of long-range rewards, rather than being overtaken by immediate impulses. Their empathy enables them to read others' emotions. They handle others' emotions skillfully, knowing what to say to a grieving friend, how to encourage colleagues, and how to manage conflicts well. Simply said, they are emotionally smart, and thus they often succeed in careers, marriages, and parenting where other academically smarter (but emotionally less intelligent) people fail.

Given the significance of practical, creative, and emotional intelligence, researchers are now wondering: Can we assess these alternative intelligences? Can we teach practical and emotional intelligence to schoolchildren? Can we stimulate their creative problem-solving abilities and their abilities to read and manage emotions (Goleman, 1995; Mayer & others, 2000a,b)? Such questions define a new frontier in the study of intelligence.

Other scholars, however—including even multiple intelligence man Howard Gardner (1999)—think that concepts such as *emotional intelligence* and *moral intelligence* stretch *intelligence* too far. It is wise to stretch the concept to include not only our processing of words, numbers, and logic, but also space, music, and information about ourselves and others, says Gardner. But let us also, he says, respect emotional sensitivity, creativity, motivation, and morality as important but different. Stretch a word to mean everything we prize and it will lose its meaning.

In defense of academic smarts—the *g* factor—researchers point to studies in which traditional intelligence scores *do* to some extent predict both occupational status and job performance (Brody, 1997; Schmidt & Hunter, 1998). For example, intelligence matters most in mentally demanding jobs. Meteorology more than meter reading requires intelligence to excel. However, once admitted to a vocation, those who become highly successful have other traits as well—they are conscientious, well-connected, and doggedly energetic. Thus, high intelligence does more to get you into a profession (via the schools and training programs that take you there) than it does to make you successful, once there.

So it seems that the academic aptitude tapped by intelligence tests is indeed important. Yet our competence in everyday living requires much that traditional intelligence tests do not measure. We might, then, liken mental abilities to physical abilities. Athleticism is not one thing but many. The ability to run fast is distinct from the eye-hand coordination required to throw a ball on target. A champion weightlifter rarely has the potential to be a skilled ice skater. Yet there remains some tendency for good things to come packaged together—for running speed and throwing accuracy to correlate, thanks to general athletic ability. Similarly, intelligence involves several distinct abilities, which cluster together in the same individual often enough to define a small general intelligence factor.

Assessing Intelligence

PREVIEW QUESTION 5 What do intelligence tests measure, and by what criteria can we judge these tests?

How do we assess intelligence? Movie hero Forrest Gump's answer, "Stupid is as stupid does," catches the spirit of psychology's simplest answer: Intelligent is as intelligent does on an intelligence test. In other words, intelligence is whatever intelligence tests measure. So, what are these tests, and what makes a test credible?

Today's most widely used intelligence test, the **Wechsler Adult Intelligence Scale (WAIS),** was created by psychologist David Wechsler, who, as a 6-year-old Romanian, was among the Eastern European immigrants of the early 1900s who were mistakenly classified as feeble-minded because they did not know their new culture. Wechsler later developed a similar test for school-age children, called the *Wechsler Intelligence Scale for Children (WISC),* and still later a test for preschool children. The WAIS consists of 11 subtests, as illustrated in **FIGURE 22.2**. It yields not only an overall intelligence score, as does the Stanford-Binet, but also separate "verbal" and "performance" (nonverbal) scores. Striking differences between the two scores alert the examiner to possible learning problems. For example, a verbal score much lower than the same person's performance score might indicate a reading or language disability. The tests also provide clues to cognitive strengths that a teacher or an employer might build upon.

Matching patterns
Block design puzzles test the ability to analyze patterns. Wechsler's individually administered intelligence test comes in forms suited for adults (WAIS) and children (WISC).

FIGURE 22.2
Sample items from the Wechsler Adult Intelligence Scale (WAIS) subtests
(From Thorndike & Hagen, 1977.)

VERBAL

General Information
What day of the year is Independence Day?

Similarities
In what way are *wool* and *cotton* alike?

Arithmetic Reasoning
If eggs cost 60 cents a dozen, what does 1 egg cost?

Vocabulary
Tell me the meaning of corrupt.

Comprehension
Why do people buy fire insurance?

Digit Span
Listen carefully, and when I am through, say the numbers right after me.

7   3   4   1   8   6

Now I am going to say some more numbers, but I want you to say them backward.

3   8   4   1   6

PERFORMANCE

Picture Completion
I am going to show you a picture with an important part missing. Tell me what is missing.

'85

SUN	MON	TUE	WED	THU	FRI	SAT
1	2	3	4	5	6	7
8	9	10	11	12	13	14
15	16	17	18	19	20	21
22	23	24	25	26	27	28
29	30					

Picture Arrangement
The pictures below tell a story. Put them in the right order to tell the story.

Block Design
Using the four blocks, make one just like this.

Object Assembly
If these pieces are put together correctly, they will make something. Go ahead and put them together as quickly as you can.

Digit-Symbol Substitution

Code

△	○	⬭	×	8
1	2	3	4	5

Test

△	8	×	○	△	⬭	8	×	△	8

CLOSE-UP:

EXTREMES OF INTELLIGENCE

One way to glimpse the validity and significance of any test is to compare people who score at the two extremes of the normal curve. The two groups should differ noticeably, and they do.

In one famous project begun in 1921, Lewis Terman studied more than 1500 California schoolchildren with IQ scores over 135. Contrary to the popular notion that intellectually gifted children are frequently maladjusted because they are "in a different world" from their nongifted peers, Terman's high-scoring children were healthy, well adjusted, and unusually successful academically. When restudied over the next seven decades, most had attained high levels of education (Holahan & Sears, 1995). The group included many doctors, lawyers, professors, scientists, and writers. Johns Hopkins University studies have similarly tracked mathematically precocious youngsters into early scientific achievement (Lubinski & Benbow, 2000; Stanley, 1997). These whiz kids remind one of Jean Piaget, who by age 7 was devoting his free time to studying birds, fossils, and machines; who by 15 began publishing scientific articles on mollusks; and who later went on to become the twentieth century's most

A gifted child At age 10, Lenny Ng became the youngest child to score a perfect 800 on the SAT math test. At age 16, his math project won a $20,000 scholarship in the 1993 Westinghouse Science Talent Search. At age 20, he was a second-year graduate student in mathematics at MIT, after graduating with highest honors from Harvard and winning a national math competition. Contrary to the notion that such precocious children suffer socially, high-aptitude children are typically well adjusted.

famous developmental psychologist (Hunt, 1993).

At another extreme are those whose intelligence test scores fall below 70. To be labeled as having **mental retardation,** a child must have both a low test score *and* difficulty adapting to the normal demands of independent living. Only about 1 percent of the population meets both criteria, with males outnumbering females by 50 percent (American

Psychiatric Association, 1994). As Table 22.1 indicates, most individuals with mental retardation can, with support, live in mainstream society.

Mental retardation sometimes has a known physical cause. One such case is **Down syndrome,** a disorder of varying severity caused by an extra chromosome in the person's genetic makeup.

During the last two centuries, the pendulum of opinion about how best to care for people with mental retardation has made a complete swing. Until the mid-nineteenth century, they were cared for at home. Many of those with the most severe disabilities died, but people with milder forms of retardation often found a place in a farm-based society. Then, residential schools for slow learners were established. By the twentieth century, many of these institutions had become warehouses, providing residents no privacy, little attention, and no hope. Parents often were told to separate themselves permanently from their impaired child before they became attached.

In the last half of the twentieth century, the pendulum swung back to normalization—encouraging people to live in their own communities as normally as their functioning permits. Children with mild retardation are educated in less restrictive environments, and many are integrated, or *mainstreamed,* into regular classrooms. Most grow up with their own families, then move into a protected living arrangement, such as a group home. The hope, and often the reality, is a happier and more dignified life.

- **mental retardation** a condition of limited mental ability, indicated by an intelligence score below 70 and difficulty in adapting to the demands of life; varies from mild to profound.

- **Down syndrome** a condition of retardation and associated physical disorders caused by an extra chromosome in one's genetic makeup.

TABLE 22.1

DEGREES OF MENTAL RETARDATION

Level	Typical Intelligence Scores	Percentage of Persons With Retardation	Adaptation to Demands of Life
Mild	50–70	85%	May learn academic skills up to sixth-grade level. Adults may, with assistance, achieve self-supporting social and vocational skills.
Moderate	35–49	10%	May progress to second-grade level academically. Adults may contribute to their own support by laboring in sheltered workshops.
Severe	20–34	3–4%	May learn to talk and to perform simple work tasks under close supervision but are generally unable to profit from vocational training.
Profound	Below 20	1–2%	Require constant aid and supervision.

Source: Reprinted with permission from the *Diagnostic and Statistical Manual of Mental Disorders,* Fourth Edition. Copyright 1994 American Psychiatric Association.

Principles of Test Construction

To be widely accepted, psychological tests—whether tests of **aptitude** (the capacity to learn) or **achievement** (what has already been learned)—must meet three criteria: They must be *standardized, reliable,* and *valid.* The Stanford-Binet and Wechsler tests meet these requirements.

Standardization

The number of questions you answered correctly on an intelligence test would tell us almost nothing. To evaluate your performance, we need a basis for comparing it with others' performance. To enable meaningful comparisons, test-makers first give the test to a representative sample of people. When others take the test following the same procedures, their scores can be compared with the standards defined by the sample. This process of defining meaningful scores relative to a pretested group is called **standardization.**

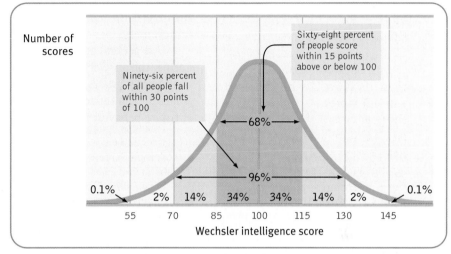

Recall that Terman and his colleagues recognized that items developed for Parisians did not provide a satisfactory standard for evaluating Americans. So they revised the test and standardized the new version by testing 2300 native-born, white Americans of differing socioeconomic levels. Ironically, they used this standard to evaluate nonwhite American and immigrant groups (Van Leeuwen, 1982).

Standardized test results typically form a *normal distribution,* a bell-shaped pattern of scores that forms the **normal curve** (**FIGURE 22.3**). No matter what we measure—people's heights, weights, or mental aptitudes—scores often form a roughly symmetrical, bell-shaped distribution clustered around the average. On an intelligence test, we call this average score 100. As we move out from the average (toward either extreme) we find fewer and fewer people. Within each age group, the Stanford-Binet and the Wechsler tests assign any person a score according to how much that person's performance deviates above or below the average. As Figure 22.3 shows, a performance higher than all but 2 percent of all scores earns an intelligence score of 130. A raw score that is comparably *below* 98 percent of all the scores earns an intelligence score of 70.

Reliability

Comparing your test scores to those of the standardizing group still won't tell us much about you unless the test has **reliability.** A good test must yield dependably consistent scores. To check a test's reliability, researchers retest people using either the same test or another form of it. If the two scores generally agree, or *correlate,* the test is reliable. As an alternative, the researcher may split a test in half and see whether scores derived from odd and even questions agree.

The higher the correlation between the *test-retest* or the *split-half* scores, the higher the test's reliability. The tests we have considered so far—the Stanford-Binet, the WAIS, and the WISC—all have reliabilities of about +0.9, which is very high. When retested, people's scores generally match their first score closely.

Validity

High reliability does not ensure a test's **validity**—the extent to which the test actually measures what it is supposed to measure or predicts what it is supposed to predict. If you use an inaccurate tape measure to measure people's heights, your height report would have high reliability (consistency) but low validity. How, then, is a test's validity determined? It is enough for some tests that they have **content validity,** meaning

FIGURE 22.3

The normal curve

Scores on aptitude tests tend to form a normal, or bell-shaped, curve. For example, the Wechsler scale calls the average score 100.

- **aptitude tests** tests designed to predict a person's future performance. Aptitude is the capacity to learn.

- **achievement tests** tests designed to assess what a person has learned.

- **standardization** defining meaningful scores by comparison with the performance of a pretested "standardization group."

- **normal curve** the symmetrical bell-shaped curve that describes the distribution of many physical and psychological attributes. Most scores fall near the average, and fewer and fewer scores lie near the extremes.

- **reliability** the extent to which a test yields consistent results, as assessed by the consistency of scores on two halves of the test, on alternative forms of the test, or on retesting.

- **validity** the extent to which a test measures or predicts what it is supposed to. (See also *content validity* and *predictive validity.*)

- **content validity** the extent to which a test samples the behavior that is of interest (such as a driving test that samples driving tasks).

■ **criterion** the behavior (such as college grades) that a test (such as the SAT) is designed to predict; thus, the measure used in defining whether the test has predictive validity.

■ **predictive validity** the success with which a test predicts the behavior it is designed to predict; it is assessed by computing the correlation between test scores and the criterion behavior. Also called *criterion-related validity*.

the test taps the pertinent behavior. The road test for a driver's license has content validity because it samples the tasks a driver routinely faces. Course exams have content validity if they assess one's mastery of a representative sample of course material.

Other tests are evaluated in terms of how well they agree with some **criterion,** an independent measure of what the test aims to assess. For some tests, the criterion is future performance. For example, aptitude tests must have **predictive validity** (also called *criterion-related validity*), which means they predict future achievement.

Are general aptitude tests as predictive as they are reliable? As critics are fond of noting, the answer is plainly no. The predictive power of aptitude tests is fairly strong in the early grades, but later it weakens. A better predictor of future grades is past grades, which reflect both aptitude and motivation. More generally, the best predictor of future behavior is a large sample of past behavior of the same sort.

rehearse it!

1. Intelligence quotient, or IQ, was originally defined as the ratio of mental age to chronological age multiplied by 100. By this definition, a 6-year-old child with a measured mental age of 6 would have an IQ of 100. Likewise, a 6-year-old with a measured mental age of 9 would have an IQ of
   a. 67.   c. 86.
   b. 133.   d. 150.

2. Savant syndrome is retardation combined with incredible ability in one specific area. The existence of savant syndrome seems to support
   a. Sternberg's distinction among three aspects of intelligence.
   b. Spearman's notion of general intelligence, or *g* factor.
   c. Gardner's theory of multiple intelligences.
   d. Binet's conception of mental age.

3. Intelligence tests predict school grades reasonably well but are less successful at predicting achievement in other areas. Robert Sternberg has therefore identified three aspects of intelligence, which are

   a. spatial, academic, and artistic intelligence.
   b. musical, athletic, and academic intelligence.
   c. academic, practical, and creative intelligence.
   d. emotional, practical, and spatial intelligence.

4. Creativity is the ability to produce novel and valuable ideas. Which of the following is not a characteristic of a creative person?
   a. Expertise
   b. Extrinsic motivation
   c. A venturesome personality
   d. Imaginative thinking skills

5. Emotionally intelligent people are characterized by
   a. the tendency to seek immediate gratification.
   b. the ability to understand their own emotions but not those of others.
   c. high practical intelligence.
   d. self-awareness.

6. The Wechsler Adult Intelligence Scale (WAIS) yields an overall intelligence score as well as

   separate verbal and performance (nonverbal) scores. The WAIS is best able to tell us
   a. what part of an individual's intelligence is determined by genetic inheritance.
   b. whether the test-taker will succeed in a job.
   c. how the test-taker compares with other adults in vocabulary and arithmetic reasoning.
   d. whether the test-taker has specific skills for music and the performing arts.

7. The Stanford-Binet, the Wechsler Adult Intelligence Scale, and the Wechsler Intelligence Scale for Children are known to have very high reliability (about +0.9). This means that
   a. a pretest has been given to a representative sample.
   b. the test yields consistent results (for example, on retesting).
   c. the test measures what it is supposed to measure.
   d. the results of the test will be distributed on a bell-shaped curve.

Genetic and Environmental Influences on Intelligence

PREVIEW QUESTION 6 Is intellect influenced more by heredity or by environment?

Intelligence seems to run in families. But why? Are our intellectual abilities mostly inherited? Or primarily molded by our environment?

Few issues arouse such passion or have such serious political implications. Consider: If we mainly inherit our differing mental abilities, and if success reflects those abilities, then people's socioeconomic standing will correspond to their inborn differences. This could lead to those on top believing their intellectual birthright justifies their social positions.

If, on the other hand, mental abilities are primarily nurtured by the environments that raise and inform us, then children from disadvantaged environments can expect to lead disadvantaged lives. In this case, people's standing will result from their unequal opportunities, a situation often regarded as basically unjust. For now, as best we can, let us set aside such political implications and examine the evidence.

Genetic Influences

Do people who share the same genes also share comparable mental abilities? As you can see from **FIGURE 22.4**, which summarizes many studies, the answer is clearly yes. In support of the genetic contribution to intelligence, researchers cite four sets of findings:

- The intelligence test scores of 163 identical twins reared apart are virtually as similar as those of the same person taking the same test twice (Lykken, 1999). So similar are their scores that twin researcher Thomas Bouchard (1996) estimates that "about 70 percent" of intelligence score variation "can be attributed to genetic variation." Other researchers have offered estimates nearer 50 percent (Devlin & others, 1997; Plomin, 1999).
- Even identical twins whose parents do not dress or treat them identically are virtual carbon copies of each other in intelligence test scores (Loehlin & Nichols, 1976). Fraternal twins, who share only half their genes, are much less similar in their scores.
- Among the many genes that combine to influence intelligence, one, located on chromosome 6, has recently been identified. In two studies, the gene was carried by about one-third of children with very high intelligence scores but by only one-sixth of those with average scores (Chorney & others, 1998).
- By inserting an extra gene into fertilized mouse eggs, researchers have produced smarter mice—mice that excel at learning and remembering the location of a hidden underwater platform or recognizing cues that signal impending shock (Tsien, 2000). The gene engineers a neural receptor involved in memory.

"I am, somehow, less interested in the weight and convolutions of Einstein's brain than in the near certainty that people of equal talent have lived and died in cotton fields and sweatshops."

Stephen Jay Gould, *The Panda's Thumb*, 1980

"There are more studies addressing the genetics of g than any other human characteristic."

Robert Plomin (1999)

FIGURE 22.4

Intelligence: Nature and nurture
The most genetically similar people have the most similar intelligence scores. Remember: 1.0 indicates a perfect correlation; zero indicates no correlation at all. (Data from McGue & others, 1993.)

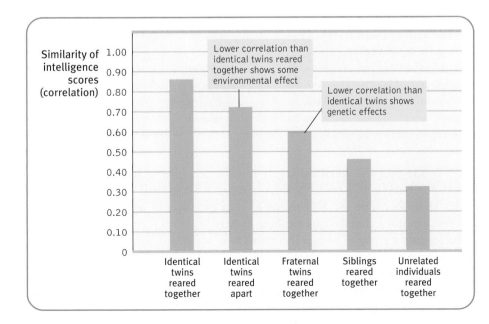

Smart mouse, smart scientist
Working with Ya-Ping Tang and others, Princeton University biologist Joe Z. Tsien genetically engineered a strain of smart mice. Such work may shed new light on the biology of human intelligence.

But there is also some evidence pointing to an effect of environment. Fraternal twins, who are genetically no more alike than any other siblings, but who are treated more alike because they are the same age, tend to score more alike than other siblings.

Seeking to disentangle genes and environment, researchers have also asked whether adopted children and their siblings, thanks to their shared environment, share similar aptitudes. During childhood, the intelligence test scores of adoptive siblings correlate modestly. Researchers have also compared the intelligence test scores of adopted children with those of their biological parents, the people from whom they received their genes, and with those of their adoptive parents, the providers of their home environment. Over time, adopted children accumulate experience in their differing adoptive families. So would you expect the family environment effect to grow with age and the genetic legacy effect to shrink?

If, like many people, you would, behavior geneticists have a surprise for you. With age, mental similarities between adopted children and their adoptive families disappear as the effect of common rearing wanes; by adulthood, the correlation is roughly zero (McGue & others, 1993). Such findings contradict the widely held belief that, as we accumulate life experience, the environmental influence on traits such as intelligence increases. In fact, the *opposite* seems true: With age, genetic influences become more apparent (Bouchard, 1995, 1996a). Adopted children's intelligence scores become more like those of their biological parents, and identical twins' similarities continue or increase into their eighties (McClearn & others, 1997; Plomin & others, 1997; see **FIGURE 22.5**).

FIGURE 22.5

Whom do adopted children resemble?

As the years went by in their adoptive families, Colorado Adoption Project children's verbal ability scores became modestly more like their *biological* parents' scores. (Adapted from Plomin & DeFries, 1998.)

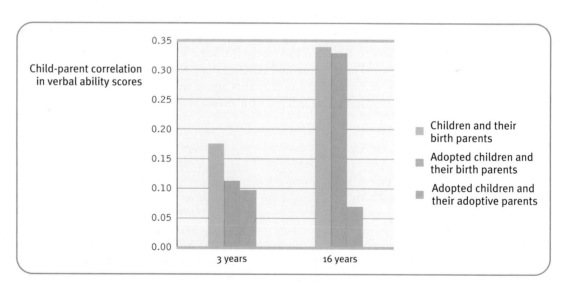

■ **heritability** the proportion of variation among individuals that we can attribute to genes. The heritability of a trait may vary, depending on the range of populations and environments studied.

To say that the **heritability** of intelligence—the variation in intelligence test scores attributable to genetic factors—is roughly 50 percent does *not* mean that your genes are responsible for 50 percent of your intelligence and your environment for the rest. It means that we can attribute to heredity 50 percent *of the variation in intelligence within a group of people*. This point is so often misunderstood that I repeat: We can never say what percentage of an *individual's* intelligence is inherited. Heritability refers instead to the extent to which *differences among people* are attributable to genes. Heritability *never* pertains to an individual, only to why people differ.

Even this conclusion must be qualified, because heritability can vary from study to study. For example, environmental differences are more predictive of intelligence scores among children of less-educated parents—among whom family environments may vary widely (Rowe & others, 1999). The effects of heredity would be very clear if we were to follow a proposal Mark Twain once made—that we should raise boys in barrels to age 12, feeding them through a hole. Given the boys' equal environments, differences in their individual intelligence test scores at age 12 could be explained only by their heredity. Thus, heritability for their differences would be nearly 100 percent. But if we raise people with similar heredities in drastically different environments (barrels versus advantaged homes), heritability—differences due to genes—will be low.

Remember, too, that genes and environment interact. For example, students with a natural aptitude for mathematics are more likely to select math courses in high school and later to score well on math aptitude tests—thanks *both* to their natural math aptitude *and* to their math experience. Our genes shape the experiences that shape us.

"I told my parents that if grades were so important they should have paid for a smarter egg donor."

Environmental Influences

We have seen that our genes make a difference. Even if we were all raised in the same intellectually stimulating environment, we still would not have the same aptitudes. But we have also seen that heredity doesn't tell the whole story. Within the limits dictated by our genes, our life experiences do matter. Human environments are rarely as impoverished as the dark and barren cages inhabited by deprived rats that develop thinner-than-normal brain cortexes (Rosenzweig, 1984). Yet severe life experiences do leave marks on us. Biology and experience intertwine (**FIGURE 22.6**).

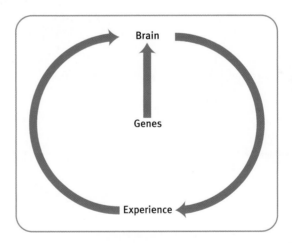

FIGURE 22.6
Nature and nurture
The plastic brain is shaped by genes and experience, working together.

Early Intervention Effects

Psychologist J. McVicker Hunt (1982) both observed the dramatic effects of early experiences and demonstrated the impact of early intervention effects in a destitute Iranian orphanage in Tehran. The typical child Hunt observed there could not sit up unassisted at age 2 or walk at age 4. The little care the infants received was not in response to their crying, cooing, or other behaviors. The children were therefore not developing any sense of personal control over their environment. As a result, they were becoming passive "glum lumps." Extreme deprivation was bludgeoning native intelligence.

Aware of the benefits of responsive caregiving, Hunt began a program of "tutored human enrichment." For instance, he trained caregivers to play vocal games with the infants. They first imitated the babies' babbling. Then they led the babies in vocal follow-the-leader by shifting from one familiar sound to another. Then they began to teach sounds from the Persian language.

The results were dramatic. All 11 infants who received these language-fostering experiences could name more than 50 objects and body parts by 22 months. So charming had the infants become that most were adopted—an unprecedented success for the orphanage.

Hunt's findings testify to the importance of environment. There is no doubt that severe disadvantage takes a toll on children (Ramey & Ramey, 1992). And when the infant malnutrition associated with severe poverty is relieved with nutritional supplements, poverty's effect on physical and cognitive development lessens (Brown & Pollitt, 1996).

Do such findings indicate a way to "give your child a superior intellect"? Some popular books claim that with intensive preschool training such is possible, but most experts are doubtful (Bruer, 1999). Although malnutrition, sensory deprivation, and social isolation can retard normal brain development, the difference between normal and "enriched" environments matters less. There is no environmental recipe for superbabies, beyond normal exposure to sights, sounds, and speech. Sandra Scarr's (1984) verdict still is widely shared: "Parents who are very concerned about providing special educational lessons for their babies are wasting their time."

Hunt would probably agree with Scarr that extra instruction has little effect on the intellectual development of children from stimulating environments. But he was optimistic when it came to children from disadvantaged environments. Indeed, his 1961 book, *Intelligence and Experience,* helped launch Project Head Start in 1965.

> "There is a large body of evidence indicating that there is little if anything to be gained by exposing middle-class children to early education."
>
> **Developmental psychologist Edward F. Zigler (1987)**

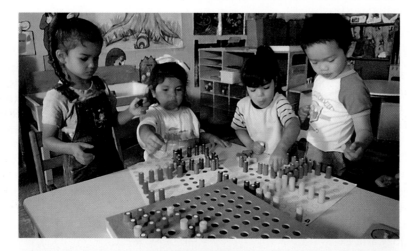

Head Start, a $4 billion U.S. government–funded preschool program, serves some 800,000 children, most of whom come from families below the poverty level (Ripple & others, 1999). It aims to enhance children's chances for success in school and beyond by boosting their cognitive and social skills.

Does it succeed? Researchers study Head Start and other preschool programs by comparing children who do experience the program with their counterparts who don't. Research findings indicate that high-quality programs for disadvantaged children produce at least short-term cognitive gains, even on intelligence tests (Haskins, 1989). Quality programs also increase school readiness, decreasing the likelihood of a child's repeating a grade or being placed in special education. Although the aptitude benefits dissipate over time (reminding us that life experience *after* Head Start matters, too), psychologist

Getting a head start
To increase readiness for schoolwork and expand children's notions of where school might lead them, Project Head Start offers educational activities. Here children in a classroom learn about colors and those on a field trip learn what fire fighters do.

Edward Zigler, the program's first director, believes there are long-term benefits (Zigler & Muenchow, 1992). High-quality preschool programs improve emotional intelligence—creating better attitudes toward learning and reducing school dropouts and criminality.

One intensive intervention program provided year-round quality day care for the children of poor and uneducated North Carolina families from infancy to age 5. Craig Ramey and Sharon Ramey (1998) report that at age 15, the intervention group maintained an intelligence test score advantage of five points over their peers in a control group, were still performing better on math and reading achievement tests, and were less likely to have repeated a school grade.

Schooling Effects

Schooling itself is an intervention that pays dividends reflected in intelligence scores. Stephen Ceci and Wendy Williams (1997) have amassed evidence that schooling and intelligence contribute to each other (and that both enhance later income). High intelligence is conducive to prolonged schooling. But it is also true that intelligence scores tend to rise during the school year and drop over the summer months. They decline when students' schooling is discontinued. Completing high school elevates intelligence scores over those obtained by comparable children who leave school early. And consider this: Children whose birthdays just make the cutoff point for school entrance temporarily have higher intelligence scores than those born just slightly later, who are a year behind them in school (**FIGURE 22.7**).

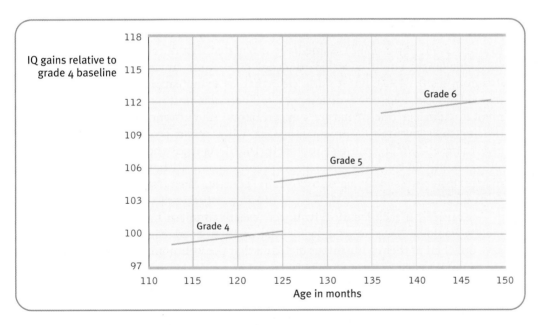

FIGURE 22.7

The schooling effect

On a test of nonverbal intelligence administered by Sorel Cahan and Nora Cohen of Hebrew University, older children within a grade tend to score slightly higher than their younger classmates. The large gap between the end of one line and the beginning of the next reflects the extra year of schooling among children who are virtually the same age.
(From Neisser, 1997.)

Group Differences in Intelligence Test Scores

PREVIEW QUESTION 7 How, and why, do ethnic and gender groups differ in aptitude test performance?

If there were no group differences in aptitude scores, psychologists could politely debate hereditary and environmental influences in their ivory towers. But there are group differences. What are they? And what shall we make of them?

Ethnic Similarities and Differences

Fueling this discussion are two disturbing but agreed-upon facts:

- Racial groups differ in their average scores on intelligence tests.
- High-scoring people (and groups) are more likely to attain high levels of education and income.

A statement by 52 intelligence researchers explains: "The bell curve for Whites is centered roughly around IQ 100; the bell curve for American Blacks roughly around 85; and those for different subgroups of Hispanics roughly midway between those for Whites and Blacks" (Avery & others, 1994). Comparable results come from other academic aptitude tests. In recent years, the Black-White difference has diminished somewhat, and among children has dropped to 10 points in some recent studies (Neisser & others, 1996). Yet the test score gap persists.

There are differences among other groups as well. European New Zealanders outscore native Maori New Zealanders. Israeli Jews outscore Israeli Arabs. Most Japanese outscore the stigmatized Japanese minority, the Burakumin. And those who can hear outscore those born deaf (Braden, 1994; Steele, 1990; Zeidner, 1990).

Everyone further agrees that such *group* differences provide little basis for judging individuals. Women outlive men by six years, but knowing someone's sex doesn't tell us with any precision how long that person will live. Even Charles Murray and Richard Herrnstein (1994), whose writings have drawn attention to Black-White differences, reminded us that "millions of Blacks have higher IQs than the average White."

If heredity contributes to individual differences in intelligence, does it also contribute to group differences? Some psychologists believe it does (Herrnstein & Murray, 1994; Rowe, 1997). Some have speculated that different climates and survival challenges could have led to racial differences in aptitudes (Lynn, 1991; Rushton, 1990, 1995). But it's also clear that, as in our earlier barrel-versus-home-reared boys example, group differences in a heritable trait may be entirely environmental. Consider one of nature's experiments: Allow some children to grow up hearing their culture's dominant language, while others, born deaf, do not. Then give them an intelligence test rooted in that language, and (no surprise) those with expertise in the test's language will score highest. Although individual performance differences may be substantially genetic, the group difference is not (**FIGURE 22.8**).

Consider: If each identical twin were exactly as tall as his or her co-twin, heritability would be 100 percent. Imagine that we then separated some young twins and gave only half of them a nutritious diet, and that the well-nourished twins all grew to

FIGURE 22.8

Group differences and environmental impact

Even if the variation among members within a group reflects genetic differences, the average difference between groups may be wholly due to the environment. Imagine that seeds from the same mixture are sown in poor and fertile soil. Although height differences within each pot will be genetic, the height difference between the two groups will be environmental. (From Lewontin, 1976.)

Variation within group

Variation within group

Seeds

Poor soil

Fertile soil

Difference between groups

be exactly 3 inches taller than their counterparts—an environmental effect comparable to that actually observed in both Britain and America, where adolescents are several inches taller than their counterparts were half a century ago (Angoff, 1987; Lynn, 1987). What would the heritability of height be now for our well-nourished twins? Still 100 percent, because the variation in height within the group would remain entirely predictable from the heights of their malnourished identical siblings. So even perfect heritability within groups would not eliminate the possibility of a strong environmental impact on the group differences.

So, is there evidence that the racial gap may be similarly environmental? Consider these findings:

- Genetics research reveals that under the skin, the races are remarkably alike (Cavalli-Sforza & others, 1994; Lewontin, 1982). Individual differences within a race are much greater than differences between races. The average genetic difference between two Icelandic villagers or between two Kenyans greatly exceeds the group difference between Icelanders and Kenyans. Moreover, looks can deceive. Europeans and Africans are genetically closer than are Africans and Aboriginal Australians.

- Asian students outperform North American students on math achievement and aptitude tests. But this difference appears to be a recent phenomenon and may reflect conscientiousness rather than competence. Asian students also attend school 30 percent more days per year and spend much more time in and out of school studying math (Geary & others, 1996; Larson & Verma, 1999; Stevenson, 1992).

- The intelligence test performance of today's better-fed and better-educated population exceeds that of the 1930s population by the same margin that the intelligence test score of the average White today exceeds that of the average Black. No one attributes the generational group difference to genetics.

- White and black infants have scored equally well on an infant intelligence measure (preference for looking at novel stimuli—a predictor of future intelligence scores; Fagan, 1992).

- In different eras, different ethnic groups have experienced golden ages—periods of remarkable achievement. Twenty-five hundred years ago it was the Greeks and the Egyptians, then the Romans; in the eighth and ninth centuries, genius seemed to reside in the Arab world; 500 years ago it was the Aztec Indians and the peoples of northern Europe. Today, people marvel at Asians' technological genius. Cultures rise and fall over centuries; genes do not. That fact makes it difficult to attribute a natural superiority to any race.

Since 1850, the average Dutch man has grown from 5 feet 4 inches to today's 5 feet 10 inches (Bogin, 1997).

In prosperous country X everyone eats all they want. In country Y the rich are well fed, but the semistarved poor are often thin. In which country will the heritability of body weight be the greatest? (See page 346.)

The culture of scholarship
The children of Indochinese refugee families studied by Nathan Caplan, Marcella Choy, and James Whitmore (1992) typically excel in school. On weekday nights after dinner, the family clears the table and begins homework. Family cooperation is valued, and older siblings help younger ones.

"Do not obtain your slaves from Britain, because they are so stupid and so utterly incapable of being taught."

Cicero, 106–43 B.C.

Gender Similarities and Differences

In science, as in everyday life, differences, not similarities, excite interest. Compared with the anatomical and physiological similarities between men and women, our sex differences are relatively minor. Yet it is the differences we find exciting.

Similarly, in the psychological domain, gender similarities vastly outnumber gender differences, but the differences often capture our attention. To some, it is news that there is no gender gap in overall intelligence scores. But most people find differences more newsworthy.

- Girls are better spellers: At the end of high school, only 30 percent of males spell better than the average female (Lubinski & Benbow, 1992).
- Girls are more verbally fluent and more sensitive to touch, taste, and odor (Halpern, 1997).
- Boys outnumber girls at the low extremes and therefore in special education classes (Kleinfeld, 1998).
- Boys tend to talk later and to stutter more often. In remedial reading classes, boys outnumber girls three to one (Finucci & Childs, 1981).
- In high school, underachieving boys outnumber girls by two to one (McCall & others, 1992).

Despite the gender equivalence in intelligence test scores, males are more likely than females to overestimate their own test scores. Both males and females tend to rate their fathers' scores higher than their mothers', and their sons' scores higher than their daughters' (Furnham & Gasson, 1998; Furnham & Rawles, 1995).

World Math Olympics Champs
After outscoring 350,000 of their U.S. peers, these boys all had perfect scores in competition with math whizzes from 68 other countries.

In the first 56 years of the Putnam Mathematical Competition—the Olympics of college math—all of the nearly 300 awardees were men (Arenson, 1997). In 1997, a woman broke the male grip by joining 5 men in the winner's circle.

Math and Spatial Aptitudes

In math grades, the average girl typically equals or surpasses the average boy (ETS, 1992; Kimball, 1989). And on math tests given to more than 3 million representatively sampled people in 100 independent studies, males and females obtained nearly identical average scores (Hyde & others, 1990). But again—despite greater diversity within the genders than between them—group differences make the news. Although females have an edge in math computation, males in 20 of 21 countries scored higher in math problem solving (Bronner, 1998; Hedges & Nowell, 1995). For example, male high school seniors average 45 points higher on the 200- to 800-point Scholastic Assessment Test (SAT) math test (literally meaning that they average 4 more correct answers on the 60-question test). Because U.S. National Merit Scholarships are based on SAT scores, only about 35 percent of these awards have gone to girls (despite their generally higher grades).

The score differences are sharpest at the extremes. Among precocious 12-year-olds scoring extremely high on SAT math, boys have outnumbered girls 13 to 1 (Lubinski & Benbow, 1992). In other Western countries, virtually all math prodigies participating in the International Mathematics Olympiad have been males. Female math prodigies have, however, reached the top levels in non-Western countries such as China (Halpern, 1991). The average male edge seems most reliable in tests like the one shown in **FIGURE 22.9**, which involve speedily rotating three-dimensional objects in one's mind (Collins & Kimura, 1997; Masters & Sanders, 1993; Voyer & others, 1995). Such spatial ability helps when fitting suitcases into a car trunk, playing chess, or doing certain types of geometry problems.

Working from an evolutionary perspective, David Geary (1995, 1996) and Irwin Silverman and his colleagues (1992, 1998) speculate that skills in navigating within three-dimensional space also helped our ancestral fathers in tracking their prey and making their way home. In contrast, the survival of our ancestral mothers was enhanced by keen memory for the location of edible plants—a legacy that lives today in women's superior memory for objects and their location.

In studies of more than 100,000 American adolescents, girls also modestly surpassed boys in memory for picture associations (Hedges & Nowell, 1995). And

Which two circles contain a configuration of blocks identical to the one in the circle at the left?

Standard

Responses

FIGURE 22.9

The mental rotation test

This is a test of spatial abilities. Which two responses show a different view of the standard? (From Vandenberg & Kuse, 1978.) (See page 347 for answers.)

among nearly 200,000 students taking Germany's Test for Medical Studies, young women year after year have surpassed men in remembering facts from short medical cases (Stumpf & Jackson, 1994). (My wife, who remembers many of my experiences for me, tells me that if she died I'd be a man without a past.)

Do natural sex differences therefore explain why most mathematicians and more than 9 in 10 rated chess players and American architects, engineers, and mapmakers are men? Or why the world chess body has therefore found it necessary to hold separate competitions for men and women? Exposure to high levels of male sex hormones during the prenatal period does enhance spatial abilities (Berenbaum & others, 1995). But social expectations also shape boys' and girls' interests and abilities (Crawford & others, 1995; Eccles & others, 1990). Traditionally, math and science have been considered masculine subjects. For example, many parents send their sons to computer camps and give their daughters more encouragement in English. Thus, the male edge in math problem solving grows with age, becoming detectable only after elementary school.

Emotion-Detecting Ability

Recall that part of emotional intelligence is empathic accuracy in reading others' emotions. Some of us are more sensitive to emotional cues. Robert Rosenthal, Judith Hall, and their colleagues (1979; McClure, 2000) demonstrated this by showing hundreds of people brief film clips of portions of a person's emotionally expressive face or body, sometimes with a garbled voice added. For example, after a two-second scene revealing only the face of an upset woman, the researchers asked whether the woman was criticizing someone

Who wants to be a millionaire?

In the first half year of this once popular quiz show, only 1 in 10 American contestants who made it to the hot seat were women. The qualifying questions—requiring a competitive, speed-based, sequential ordering of information—seemed to favor men. A different format, such as challenging contestants to detect facial emotions, might have favored women.

for being late or was talking about her divorce. Rosenthal and Hall reported that some people are much better emotion detectors than others are, and that women are better at it than men.

Some psychologists speculate that women's ability to detect emotions helped our ancestral mothers read emotions in their infants and would-be lovers, which may in turn have fueled cultural tendencies to encourage women's empathic skills. Such skills may explain women's somewhat greater responsiveness in both positive and negative emotional situations.

Answer to question on page 343:
Heritability—differences due to genes—
will be greater in country X, where
environmental differences in nutrition are
minimal.

The Question of Bias

PREVIEW QUESTION 8 Are intelligence tests biased and discriminatory?

Knowing there are group differences in intelligence test scores leads us to wonder whether intelligence tests are biased. The answer depends on two very different definitions of *bias*. One meaning is that the tests detect not only innate differences in intelligence but also differences caused by cultural experiences. In this sense, everyone agrees that intelligence tests are biased. No one claims that heritability is 100 percent responsible for any test score. An intelligence test measures a person's developed abilities at a particular time. These abilities necessarily reflect that person's experiences *and* environment.

Another meaning of *bias* hinges on whether a test is less valid for some groups than for others. If the SAT accurately predicts the college achievement of one race but not that of another, then the test would be biased. The near-consensus among psychologists, as summarized by the National Research Council's Committee on Ability Testing and the American Psychological Association's Task Force on Intelligence, is that the major aptitude tests are *not* biased in this statistical meaning of the term (Neisser & others, 1998; Wigdor & Garner, 1982). The predictive validity of the SAT or of a standard intelligence test is roughly the same for Blacks and Whites and for rich and poor. If an intelligence test score of 95 predicts C grades, the rough prediction usually applies equally to all ethnic and economic groups. If anything, the SAT overpredicts the college achievements of non-Asian minority students (Steele, 1997).

To predict school performance accurately, an aptitude test must mirror any gender or racial bias in school teaching and testing. Among students given a difficult math test by Steven Spencer and his colleagues (1997), men outperformed equally capable women—except when the women had been led to expect that women usually do as well as men on the test. Otherwise, the women apparently felt apprehensive and despairing, affecting their performance. Claude Steele and Joshua Aronson (1996) observed the same self-fulfilling effect of negative beliefs. They found black students' verbal aptitude scores were lower when they took tests under conditions designed to make black students feel threatened. Women students, too, perform worse on math problems when tested with men rather than with two women (Inzlicht & Ben-Zeev, 2000). Steele (1995, 1997) concluded that if you tell students they probably won't succeed (as remedial "minority support" programs often do), this stereotype will eventually erode their performance both on aptitude tests and in school. Over time, such students may "disidentify" with school achievement. They may detach their self-esteem from academics and look for self-esteem elsewhere—which would explain why they tend to underachieve relative to their abilities. (Indeed, as African-American boys progress from eighth to twelfth grade, the disconnect between their grades and their self-esteem becomes pronounced [Osborne, 1997].) Minority students in university programs that instead challenge them to believe in their potential produce markedly higher grades and have lower dropout rates.

"Math class is tough!"

**"Teen talk" talking Barbie doll (introduced
February 1992, recalled October 1992)**

Untested compassion
Intelligence test scores are only one part of the picture of a whole person. They don't measure the abilities, talent, and commitment of, for example, people who devote their lives to helping others.

What then can we realistically conclude about aptitude tests and bias? The tests do seem biased in one sense—sensitivity to performance differences caused by cultural experience. But they are not biased in another—statistical prediction for different groups.

Does this mean the tests are discriminatory? Again, the answer can be yes or no. In one sense, yes, their purpose is to discriminate—to distinguish among individuals. In another sense, their purpose is to reduce discrimination by reducing reliance on subjective criteria for school and job placement—criteria such as whom you know, what you look like, or how much the interviewer happens to like "your kind of person." Many pioneers of mental testing saw themselves as social progressives who were sometimes uncovering abilities—diamonds in the rough—when few expected to find them. (The educational system is very good at finding those who score in the top 1 or 2 percent on intelligence-related tests and then offering a first-class education that may lead to a first-class job.) Banning aptitude tests would lead those who decide on admissions and jobs to rely more on other considerations, such as their personal opinions. Civil service tests, for example, were devised to discriminate more fairly and objectively, by reducing the political, racial, and ethnic discrimination that preceded their use.

"Almost all the joyful things of life are outside the measure of IQ tests."

Madeleine L'Engle, *A Circle of Quiet*, **1972**

Perhaps, then, our aim should be threefold. First, we should realize the benefits that Alfred Binet foresaw for intelligence tests—to enable schools to recognize who might best benefit from early intervention. At the same time, we must remain alert to Binet's fear that test scores may be misinterpreted as literal measures of a person's worth and fixed potential. And finally, we must remember that *intelligence test scores reflect only one aspect of personal competence*. Our practical and emotional intelligence matter, too, as do other forms of talent and character. The competence that intelligence tests sample is important but far from all-inclusive. The spatial ability of the carpenter differs from the logical ability of the computer programmer, which differs from the verbal ability of the poet. Differences are not deficits. Because there are many ways of being successful, our personal and cultural differences—regardless of their origins—are variations on the human theme of adaptability.

Answers to the mental rotation test on page 345: the first and fourth alternatives.

rehearse it!

8. A current view is that between 50 and 60 percent of intelligence score variation among individuals can be attributed to heredity. The strongest support for the influence of heredity on intelligence is the finding that
   a. identical twins, but not other siblings, have nearly identical IQ scores.
   b. the correlation between IQ scores of fraternal twins is higher than that for other siblings.
   c. unrelated people living in the same environment tend not to have similar IQ scores.
   d. the IQ scores of adopted children do not closely correlate with those of their biological or adoptive parents.

9. The heritability of a trait may vary, depending on the range of populations and environments studied. To say that the heritability of intelligence is 60 percent means that 60 percent of
   a. an individual's intelligence is due to genetic factors.
   b. the similarities among groups of people are attributable to genes.
   c. the variation in intelligence within a group of people is attributable to genetic factors.
   d. intelligence is due to the mother's genes and the rest is due to the father's genes.

10. Within the limits set by heredity, experiences help shape intelligence. The experience that has the clearest, most profound effect on intellectual development is
    a. being enrolled in a Head Start program.
    b. growing up in an economically disadvantaged home or neighborhood.
    c. being raised in a very neglectful home or institution.
    d. being exposed to very stimulating toys and lessons in infancy.

Intelligence

1. When and why were intelligence tests created?

Intelligence can be defined as the mental abilities needed to select, adapt to, and shape environments. In the early 1900s, French
psychologist Alfred Binet and his colleague Théodore Simon developed questions in an attempt to measure mental age and thus to
help predict children's future progress in the Paris school system.
Lewis Terman of Stanford University adapted Binet's test and offered his Stanford-Binet test as a way to direct people toward occupations for which they were deemed well suited. William Stern
derived the intelligence quotient (IQ) to define performance on
Terman's test.

2. Is intelligence a single general ability or several distinct abilities?

Psychologists agree that people have specific abilities, such as
verbal and mathematical aptitudes. However, they debate whether
a general intelligence (*g*) factor runs through all these specific
abilities. Factor analysis and studies of special conditions, such as
the savant syndrome, have identified clusters of mental aptitudes.
Howard Gardner has identified multiple intelligences, and Robert
Sternberg specifies three components of intelligence: academic,
practical, and creative.

3. What is creativity, and what fosters this ability?

Intelligence correlates weakly with creativity. Creative people generally have a reasonable level of intelligence, but also a developed
expertise, imaginative thinking skills, a venturesome personality,
intrinsic motivation, and a supportive environment.

4. Is our ability to manage our own emotions and to em-pathize with others a form of intelligence?

Psychologists have recently described emotional intelligence as
the ability to describe, understand, and control emotions. Emotionally intelligent people are especially self-aware, and their empathy enables them to read others' emotions.

5. What do intelligence tests measure, and by what criteria can we judge these tests?

The most widely used intelligence test is the Wechsler Adult Intelligence Scale (WAIS). All good tests—whether aptitude tests (designed to predict ability to learn a particular skill) or achievement
tests (designed to assess current competence)—must be *standardized,* so that any person's performance can be meaningfully
compared with others'. They must also be *reliable,* so they yield
dependably consistent scores. And they must be *valid,* so they
measure what they are supposed to measure *(content validity)* or
predict, on the basis of a specified *criterion,* what they are supposed to predict *(predictive validity)*. Test scores usually fall into a
bell-shaped distribution, the normal curve. The average score is
assigned an arbitrary number (such as 100 on an intelligence test).
Aptitude tests are highly reliable, but their validity is more modest
(as judged by their predictions of academic success).

At the extremes of the bell curve are the gifted and those with
mental retardation. One cause of mental retardation is Down syndrome.

6. Is intellect influenced more by heredity or by environment?

Studies of twins, family members, and adopted children point to a
significant hereditary contribution to intelligence scores. Heritability, differences attributable to genes, increases as environmental
differences decrease. These studies, plus others that compare
children reared in extremely impoverished or in enriched environments or in different cultures, indicate that life experiences also
significantly influence intelligence test performance.

7. How, and why, do ethnic and gender groups differ in apti-tude test performance?

Like individuals, groups vary in intelligence test scores. Hereditary
variation *within* a group need not signify a hereditary explanation
of *between*-group differences. In the case of the racial gaps in test
scores, the evidence suggests that environmental differences are
largely, perhaps entirely, responsible. Girls have tended to score
higher on spelling tests, boys on math aptitude tests (though not
in math grades). Although some psychologists believe that a gender difference in spatial ability explains the gender gap in math
performance, the difference is shrinking as more girls develop
their math ability.

8. Are intelligence tests biased and discriminatory?

If by *biased* one means sensitive to differences caused by cultural
experience, then aptitude tests are necessarily biased. But if one
means what psychologists commonly mean—that a test predicts
less validly for one group than for another—then the current tests
considered in this module seem not to be biased. Indeed, tests
are designed specifically to avoid more subjective forms of discrimination.

TERMS AND CONCEPTS TO REMEMBER

intelligence, p. 327
mental age, p. 327
Stanford-Binet, p. 328
intelligence quotient (IQ), p. 328
factor analysis, p. 329
general intelligence (*g*), p. 329

savant syndrome, p. 329
creativity, p. 331
emotional intelligence, p. 332
Wechsler Adult Intelligence Scale
  (WAIS), p. 333
mental retardation, p. 334

Down syndrome, p. 334
aptitude test, p. 335
achievement test, p. 335
standardization, p. 335
normal curve, p. 335
reliability, p. 335

validity, p. 335
content validity, p. 335
criterion, p. 336
predictive validity, p. 336
heritability, p. 338

REHEARSE IT ANSWER KEY

1. a   2. c   3. c   4. b   5. d   6. c   7. b   8. a   9. c   10. c

Motivation

"What's my motivation?" the actor asks the director. In our everyday conversation, the question "What motivated you to do that?" is a way of asking "What *caused* your behavior? *Why* did you act that way?" To psychologists, a *motivation* is a need or desire that serves to *energize* behavior and to *direct* it toward a goal. Like intelligence, motivation is a hypothetical concept. We infer motivation from behaviors we observe. Consider motivation in these situations:

- David Mandel (1983), a former Nazi concentration camp inmate, recalled how a starving "father and son would fight over a piece of bread. Like dogs." One father, whose 20-year-old son stole his bread from under his pillow while he slept, went into a deep depression, asking over and over again how his son could do such a thing. The next day the father died. "Hunger does something to you that's hard to describe," Mandel explained. "I can't believe it myself today, so how can I expect anyone else to understand it?"

- In the Old Testament's *Song of Solomon* love poems, a man and a woman express their intense sexual passion for one another. "I am sick with love," she declares. "O that his left hand were under my head, and that his right hand embraced me!" He, in turn, pronounces her "delectable." "You are stately as a palm tree, and your breasts are like its clusters. I say I will climb the palm tree and lay hold of its branches."

- In Texas, a school truant officer discovers Alfredo Gonzales, age 14, picking fruit and sends him off to the first day of school in his life. Although placed at the lowest skill level and paddled for asking questions in Spanish—he knows no English—Alfredo decides "I could do better." Today he is a highly educated college administrator who works to motivate youth to wake up, as he did, to "their own potential and to gain a desire to achieve it."

In Modules 23 through 25, we explore motivation by focusing on these three motives—hunger, sex, and achievement. Although other identifiable motives exist (including thirst and curiosity), a close look at these three reveals the interplay between nature (the physiological "push") and nurture (the cognitive and cultural "pulls"). Module 23 begins with a look at how psychologists have approached the study of motivation.

23 Introduction to Motivation: Hunger

"What do you think . . . should we get started on that motivation research or not?"

Motivational Concepts

To psychologists, a **motivation** is a need or desire that serves to *energize* behavior and to *direct* it toward a goal. Three perspectives have been influential: instinct theory (now replaced by an evolutionary perspective), drive-reduction theory (emphasizing the interaction between inner pushes and external pulls), and arousal theory (emphasizing the urge for an optimum level of stimulation).

Instincts and Evolutionary Psychology

PREVIEW QUESTION 1 What is the underlying assumption shared by instinct theory and evolutionary psychology?

Early in the twentieth century, as the influence of Charles Darwin's evolutionary theory grew, it became fashionable to classify all sorts of behaviors as instincts. If people criticized themselves, it was because of their "self-abasement instinct." If they boasted, it reflected their "self-assertion instinct." After scanning 500 books, one sociologist compiled a list of 5759 supposed human instincts! Before long, this fad for naming instincts collapsed under its own weight. Rather than *explaining* human behaviors, the early instinct theorists were simply *naming* them. It was like "explaining" a bright child's low grades by labeling the child an "underachiever." To name a behavior is *not* to explain it.

To qualify as an **instinct,** a complex behavior must have a fixed pattern throughout a species and be unlearned (Tinbergen, 1951). Such behaviors are common in other species (imprinting in birds, for example, or the return of salmon to their birthplace). Human behavior, too, exhibits certain innate tendencies, including simple fixed patterns such as an infant's rooting and sucking. Most psychologists, though, view human behavior as directed by physiological needs *and* psychological wants.

Same motive, different wiring
The more complex the nervous system, the more adaptable the organism. Both the weaverbird and the woman satisfy their need for shelter in ways that reflect their inherited capacities. The woman's behavior is flexible; she can learn whatever skills she needs to build a house. The bird's behavior pattern is fixed; it can build only this kind of nest.

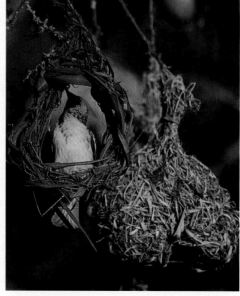

Although instinct theory failed to explain human motives, the underlying assumption that genes predispose species-typical behavior remains as strong as ever. Evolutionary psychology is now in its heyday, and psychologists working from this perspective search for explanations of some human behaviors in the genetic blueprint shared by our species. They are interested, for example, in how evolution might influence our phobias, our helping behaviors, and our romantic attractions.

Drives and Incentives

PREVIEW QUESTION 2 How does drive-reduction theory help us understand the forces that energize and direct some of our behavior?

When the original instinct theory of motivation collapsed, it was replaced by **drive-reduction theory**—the idea that a physiological need creates an aroused state that *drives* the organism to reduce the need by, say, eating or drinking. With few exceptions, when a physiological need increases, so does a psychological drive—an aroused, motivated state.

The physiological aim of drive reduction is **homeostasis**—the maintenance of a steady internal state. An example of homeostasis (literally "staying the same") is the body's temperature-regulation system, which works like a thermostat. Both systems operate through feedback loops: Sensors feed room temperature to a control device. If room temperature cools, the control device switches on the furnace. Likewise, if our body temperature cools, blood vessels constrict to conserve warmth, and we feel driven to put on more clothes or seek a warmer environment. Similarly, if the water level in our cells drops, sensors detect our need for water and we feel thirsty (**FIGURE 23.1**).

FIGURE 23.1
Drive theory

> ■ **motivation** a need or desire that energizes and directs behavior.
>
> ■ **instinct** a complex behavior that is rigidly patterned throughout a species and is unlearned.
>
> ■ **drive-reduction theory** the idea that a physiological need creates an aroused tension state (a drive) that motivates an organism to satisfy the need.
>
> ■ **homeostasis** a tendency to maintain a balanced or constant internal state; the regulation of any aspect of body chemistry, such as blood glucose, around a particular level.
>
> ■ **incentive** a positive or negative environmental stimulus that motivates behavior.

Not only are we *pushed* by our "need" to reduce drives, we also are *pulled* by **incentives**—positive or negative stimuli that lure or repel us. This is one way our individual learning histories influence our motives. Depending on our learning, the aroma of fresh roasted peanuts (or toasted ants), the sight of someone we find attractive, and the threat of disapproval can all motivate our behavior. Our internal needs energize and direct our behavior, but these external incentives do as well. The lure of money may energize us quite apart from any need-based drive.

When there is both a need and an incentive, we feel strongly driven. The food-deprived person who smells baking bread feels a strong hunger drive. In the presence of that drive, the baking bread becomes a compelling incentive. For each motive, we can therefore ask, "How is it pushed by our inborn physiological needs and pulled by incentives in the environment?"

Optimum Arousal

PREVIEW QUESTION 3 What types of motivated behavior does arousal theory attempt to explain?

We are much more than homeostatic systems, however. Our biological rhythms cycle through times of arousal. Also, far from reducing a physiological need or minimizing tension, some motivated behaviors *increase* arousal. Well-fed animals

■ **hierarchy of needs** Maslow's pyramid of human needs, beginning at the base with physiological needs that must first be satisfied before higher-level safety needs and then psychological needs become active.

will leave their shelter to explore, seemingly in the absence of any need-based drive. From taking such risks, animals may, however, gain information and resources (Renner, 1992).

Curiosity drives monkeys to monkey around trying to figure out how to unlock a latch that opens nothing or how to open a window that allows them to see outside their room (Butler, 1954). It drives the 9-month-old infant who investigates every accessible corner of the house. It drives the scientists whose work this text discusses. And it drives the explorers and adventurers. Asked why he wanted to climb Mount Everest, George Mallory answered, "Because it is there." Those who, like Mallory, enjoy high arousal are most likely to enjoy intense music, novel foods, and risky behaviors (Zuckerman, 1979).

Driven by curiosity
Baby monkeys and small people are fascinated by things they've never handled before. Their drive to explore the relatively unfamiliar is one of several motives that do not fill any immediate physiological need.

In experiments on sensory restriction, volunteers have spent hour after hour isolated in a monotonous chamber. Their experience—though peaceful and quiet—sensitized them to any available stimulation. Despite having all our biological needs satisfied, we feel driven to experience stimulation. Without it, we feel bored and look for a way to increase arousal to some optimum level. However, with too much stimulation comes stress, and we then look for a way to decrease arousal.

A Hierarchy of Motives

PREVIEW QUESTION 4 What is the basic idea behind Maslow's hierarchy of needs?

Some needs take priority over others. At this moment, with your needs for air and water satisfied, other motives—such as your desire to achieve—energize and direct your behavior. Let your need for water go unsatisfied and your thirst will preoccupy you. But if you were deprived of air, your thirst would disappear.

"Nobody wants to kiss when they are hungry."

Dorothea Dix, 1801–1887

Abraham Maslow (1970) described these priorities as a **hierarchy of needs** (**FIGURE 23.2**). At its base are our physiological needs, such as those for food and water. Only if these needs are met are we prompted to meet our need for safety, and then to meet the uniquely human needs to give and receive love and to enjoy self-esteem. Beyond this, said Maslow (1971), lies the highest of human needs: to actualize one's full potential.

Maslow's hierarchy is somewhat arbitrary. Moreover, the order of such needs is not universally fixed. People have starved themselves to make a political statement. Nevertheless, the simple idea that some motives are more compelling than others

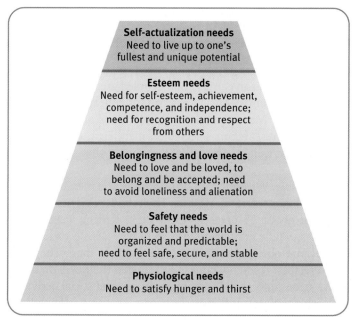

Self-actualization needs
Need to live up to one's fullest and unique potential

Esteem needs
Need for self-esteem, achievement, competence, and independence; need for recognition and respect from others

Belongingness and love needs
Need to love and be loved, to belong and be accepted; need to avoid loneliness and alienation

Safety needs
Need to feel that the world is organized and predictable; need to feel safe, secure, and stable

Physiological needs
Need to satisfy hunger and thirst

FIGURE 23.2
Maslow's hierarchy of needs
Once our lower-level needs are met, we are prompted to satisfy our higher-level needs. (From Maslow, 1970.)

does provide a framework for thinking about motivation. And surveys of life satisfaction in 39 nations have confirmed what Maslow would have predicted: Financial satisfaction is more strongly predictive of subjective well-being in poorer nations, whereas home-life satisfaction matters more in wealthy nations and self-esteem in individualist nations (Oishi & others, 1999). Where there is little money, money—which buys shelter and food—matters.

rehearse it!

1. Although instinct theory fails to explain most human behavior, the existence of simple fixed patterns such as an infant's rooting and sucking suggests some innate tendencies in humans. Indeed, the underlying assumption of instinct theory—that _____ —is as strong as ever.
   a. physiological needs arouse psychological states
   b. genes predispose species-typical behavior
   c. physiological needs increase arousal
   d. external needs energize and direct behavior

2. Drive reduction motivates many behaviors necessary for survival. A need, or deprivation (for example, a lack of water), leads to an aroused state or drive; this in turn motivates the organism to act to reduce this drive (drink a glass of water) and restore internal

stability. Drive reduction also motivates behaviors such as
   a. eating and breathing.
   b. satisfaction of curiosity.
   c. nest building and other instincts.
   d. pursuit of stimulation.

3. The aim of drive reduction is internal stability. For example, if we are too hot, we perspire; if we are dehydrated, we feel thirsty—and drink. The maintenance of a balanced internal state is called
   a. instinct.
   b. sensory restriction.
   c. a hierarchy of needs.
   d. homeostasis.

4. Behavior is also influenced by incentives in the environment. For example, a pile of leaves in the driveway may motivate you to get out the rake; your neighbor's disapproval may motivate you to turn down your radio. To explain the effects of external incentives, we must refer to

   a. biological needs.
   b. instinct.
   c. individual learning histories.
   d. homeostasis.

5. Motivated behaviors satisfy a variety of needs. Experiments on sensory restriction indicate that one such need can be to
   a. reduce physiological needs.
   b. search out respect from others.
   c. increase arousal.
   d. ensure stability.

6. According to Abraham Maslow, we are not prompted to satisfy psychological needs, such as the need to be accepted or loved, until we have satisfied more basic needs. The most basic needs are physiological needs, including the need for food, water, and oxygen; just above these are
   a. safety needs.
   b. self-esteem needs.
   c. belongingness needs.
   d. psychological needs.

■ **glucose** the form of sugar that circulates in the blood and provides the major source of energy for body tissues. When its level is low, we feel hunger.

The Physiology of Hunger

PREVIEW QUESTION 5 What physiological factors cause us to feel hungry?

A vivid demonstration of the supremacy of physiological needs came about following reports of starvation in World War II prison camps and occupied areas. To learn more about the results of semistarvation, scientist Ancel Keys and his colleagues (1950) solicited volunteers for an experiment. More than 100 conscientious objectors to the war volunteered and from them the researchers selected 36 men. First, they fed them just enough to maintain their initial weight. Then, for six months, they cut this food level in half.

The effects soon became visible. Without thinking about it, the men began conserving energy; they appeared listless and apathetic. Their body weights dropped rapidly, eventually stabilizing at about 25 percent below their starting weights. But the psychological effects were especially dramatic. Consistent with Maslow's idea of a needs hierarchy, the men became obsessed with food. They talked food. They daydreamed food. They collected recipes, read cookbooks, and feasted their eyes on delectable forbidden foods. At the same time, they lost interest in sex and social activities. They became preoccupied with their unfulfilled basic needs. As one participant reported, "If we see a show, the most interesting part of it is contained in scenes where people are eating. I couldn't laugh at the funniest picture in the world, and love scenes are completely dull."

Keys' semistarved subjects felt their hunger in response to a homeostatic system designed to maintain normal body weight and an adequate nutrient supply. But what precisely triggers hunger? Is it the pangs of an empty stomach? That is how it feels. And so it seemed after A. L. Washburn, working with Walter Cannon (Cannon & Washburn, 1912), intentionally swallowed a balloon. When inflated in his stomach, the balloon transmitted his stomach contractions to a recording device (**FIGURE 23.3**). While his stomach was being monitored, Washburn pressed a key each time he felt hungry. The discovery: Washburn was indeed having stomach contractions whenever he felt hungry. Some diet aids reduce this feeling of an empty stomach by filling the stomach with indigestible fibers that swell as they absorb water.

Alas, there is more to hunger than the pangs of an empty stomach. Researchers discovered this a quarter-century later when they removed some rats' stomachs and attached their esophagi to their small intestines (Tsang, 1938). Without stomach pangs, did hunger persist? Did the rats continue to eat regularly? Indeed they did. Hunger persists similarly in humans whose ulcerated or cancerous stomachs have been removed. In fact, one can feel hungry even on a full stomach. Animals that fill their stomachs by eating low-calorie food will eat more than animals that consume a less filling, high-calorie diet (McHugh & Moran, 1978). If the pangs of an empty stomach are not the only source of our hunger, what else matters?

"The full person does not understand the needs of the hungry."

Irish proverb

Subject swallows balloon, which measures stomach contractions.

Subject presses key each time he feels hungry.

Stomach contractions

Hunger pangs

0 1 2 3 4 5 6 7 8 9 10
Time in minutes

FIGURE 23.3
Monitoring stomach contractions
Using this procedure, Washburn showed that stomach contractions (transmitted by the stomach balloon) accompany our feelings of hunger (indicated by a key press). (From Cannon, 1929.)

Body Chemistry

Changes in body chemistry also affect hunger. People and other animals automatically regulate their caloric intake to prevent energy deficits and maintain a stable body weight. This suggests that the body is somehow, somewhere, keeping tabs on its available resources. One such resource is the blood sugar **glucose.** Increases in the hormone insulin diminish blood glucose, partly by converting it to stored fat. The body is normally adept at maintaining blood glucose levels. But if the blood glucose level drops, hunger increases. As we will soon see, however, insulin and glucose are not the only hunger-regulating chemicals.

The Brain

Low blood glucose triggers hunger. But you do not consciously feel this change in your blood chemistry. Rather, the brain automatically monitors information on your body's internal state. Signals from the stomach, the intestines, and the liver (indicating whether glucose is being deposited or withdrawn) all signal the brain to motivate eating or not. But where in the brain are these messages integrated? During the 1940s and 1950s, researchers located hunger controls within the hypothalamus, a small but complex neural traffic intersection buried deep in the brain (**FIGURE 23.4**).

Actually, there are two distinct hypothalamic centers that help control eating. Experiments during the 1960s suggested that activity along the sides of the hypothalamus, known as the *lateral hypothalamus,* brings on hunger. When electrically stimulated there, a well-fed animal would begin to eat; when the area was destroyed, even a starving animal had no interest in food. When a rat is deprived of food and its blood sugar levels wane, the lateral hypothalamus churns out a hunger-triggering hormone, orexin. When given orexin, rats become ravenously hungry (Sakurai & others, 1998).

Activity in the lower mid-hypothalamus, the *ventromedial hypothalamus,* depresses hunger. Stimulate this area and an animal will stop eating; destroy it and the animal's stomach and intestines will

FIGURE 23.4
The hypothalamus
The hypothalamus (colored red) performs various body maintenance functions, including control of hunger. Blood vessels supply the hypothalamus, enabling it to respond to our current blood chemistry as well as to incoming neural information about the body's state.

Evidence for the brain's control of eating
A lesion near the ventromedial (middle) area of the hypothalamus caused this rat's weight to triple.

■ **set point** the point at which an individual's "weight thermostat" is supposedly set. When the body falls below this weight, an increase in hunger and a lowered metabolic rate may act to restore the lost weight.

■ **basal metabolic rate** the body's resting rate of energy expenditure.

process food more rapidly, causing it to eat more often and to become extremely fat (Duggan & Booth, 1986; Hoebel & Teitelbaum, 1966). This discovery explained why some patients with tumors near the base of the brain (in what we now realize is the hypothalamus) eat excessively and become very overweight (Miller, 1995).

How do these complementary areas of the hypothalamus work? One theory is that they influence how much glucose is converted to fat and how much is left available to fuel immediate activity (and minimize hunger). After ventromedial lesions, rats produce more fat and use less fat for energy, rather like a miser who runs every bit of extra money to the bank and resists taking any out (Pinel, 1993). Recent experiments also suggest that a distributed brain system monitors the body's state and reports to the hypothalamus, which processes the information and sends it along to the frontal lobes, which decide behavior (Winn, 1995).

An older theory is that manipulating the lateral and ventromedial hypothalamus alters the body's "weight thermostat," which predisposes us to keep our body at a particular weight level, called its **set point** (Keesey & Corbett, 1983). When semistarved rats fall below their normal weight, biological pressures act to restore the lost weight: Hunger increases and energy expenditure decreases. If body weight rises—as happens when rats are force-fed—hunger decreases and energy expenditure increases. This stable weight toward which semistarved and overstuffed rats return is their set point. In rats and in humans, heredity influences body type and set point.

Human bodies also regulate weight much as rats' bodies do—through the control of food intake and energy output. Despite day-to-day variations in your eating, your body regulates your weight much better than you could through conscious efforts to control food intake precisely. If your body weight rises above its set point, you will tend to feel less hungry; if your weight drops below, you will tend to eat more. Consider that over the next 40 years you will eat about 20 tons of food. If during those years you increase your daily intake by just .01 ounce more than required for your energy needs, you will gain 24 pounds (Martin & others, 1991). With astonishing precision, your body will automatically balance your energy intake and expenditure.

To maintain its set-point weight, your body adjusts not only food intake and energy output but also its **basal metabolic rate**—its rate of energy expenditure in maintaining basic body functions when the body is at rest. By the end of their 24 weeks of semistarvation, the subjects in the World War II experiment had stabilized at three-quarters of their normal weight—while eating half of what they previously did. The stabilization resulted from reduced energy expenditure, achieved partly by physical lethargy and partly by a 29 percent drop in their basal metabolic rate. In a reverse experiment—in which volunteers were overfed 1000 calories a day for eight weeks—those who gained the least weight tended to spend the caloric energy by fidgeting more (Levine & others, 1999).

Some researchers, however, doubt that the body has a precise set point that drives hunger. They believe that slow, sustained changes in body weight can, for example, alter one's set point. Given unlimited access to tasty foods, people and other animals tend to overeat and gain weight. This casts doubt on the idea that our bodies have a preset tendency to maintain optimum weight (Assanand & others, 1998). Hunger is determined by many factors, including learned incentives.

The Psychology of Hunger

PREVIEW QUESTION 6 What psychological influences affect our eating behavior and our feelings of hunger?

Our eagerness to eat is indeed pushed by our physiological state—our body chemistry and hypothalamic activity. Yet there is more to hunger than meets the stomach. This was strikingly apparent when Paul Rozin and his trickster colleagues (1998) tested two patients with amnesia who had no memory for events occurring more than a minute ago. If, 20 minutes after eating a normal lunch, the patients were offered another, both readily consumed it . . . and usually a third meal offered 20 minutes after the second was finished. This suggests that part of knowing when to eat is our memory of our last meal. As time accumulates since we last ate, we anticipate eating again and start feeling hungry.

External Incentives and Hunger

Like the dogs in Ivan Pavlov's experiments, people learn to salivate in anticipation of appealing foods. As the hours pile up since last eating, food becomes a strong incentive. Anticipating pleasure from eating, we eat. Some people are especially responsive to appealing foods, and tend to gain the most weight, when food is abundant.

Consider the 9- to 15-year-old girls studied by Judith Rodin and Joyce Slochower (1976) at an eight-week summer camp. During the first week of camp, some could not resist munching readily visible M&M's, even after a full meal. These girls were typical of a category the researchers called *externals*—people whose eating is triggered more by the presence of food than by internal factors. In the seven weeks that followed, the "external" girls gained the most weight.

In a delicious demonstration of how internal and external factors interact, Rodin (1984) invited other research subjects to her laboratory for lunch. They had gone 18 hours without food. While blood samples were being taken, a large, juicy steak was wheeled in, crackling as it finished grilling. As the hungry subjects sat watching, hearing, and smelling the soon-to-be-eaten steak, Rodin monitored their rising blood insulin levels and their accompanying feelings of hunger. When stimulated by the sight, sound, and aroma of the steak, "externals" had the greatest insulin increase and accompanying hunger response. This illustrates how certain individuals' psychological experience of an external incentive (the steak) can affect their internal physiological state.

Taste Preference: Biology or Culture?

Psychologists have studied how we eat and how our eating is influenced by hunger and taste. As our hunger diminishes, our eating behavior changes. Eliot Stellar (1985) discovered this after outfitting people with a special dental retainer engineered to record each chew and swallow. The device answers questions about our eating that you may never have thought to ask. During a meal of sandwich snacks, how often does the average person swallow? Every 14 seconds. How many chews per swallow? On average, 19. How fast do people chew? Some 1.8 chews per second. As the meal progresses and both hunger and food tastiness decrease, people chew more. Ironically, the better a food tastes, the *less* time we leave it in our mouth.

Body chemistry and environmental factors together influence not only when we feel hunger, but what we feel hungry for—our taste preference. When feeling tense or depressed, do you crave sweet or starchy carbohydrate-laden foods? Carbohydrates help boost levels of the neurotransmitter serotonin, which has calming effects.

Our preferences for sweet and salty tastes are genetic and universal. Other taste preferences are conditioned, as when people given highly salted foods develop a liking for excess salt (Beauchamp, 1987) or when people develop an aversion to a food eaten before becoming violently ill. (The frequency of children's illnesses provides many chances for them to learn food aversions.)

Culture affects taste, too. Bedouins enjoy eating the eye of a camel, which most North Americans would find repulsive. Similarly, most North Americans and Europeans shun dog, rat, and horse meat, all of which are prized elsewhere, but welcome beef, which Hindus would not think of eating. Such preferences vary with exposure (Pliner & Pelchat, 1991; Rozin, 1976). We humans have a natural dislike of many things that are unfamiliar, including novel foods (especially novel animal-based

PEANUTS

An acquired taste

For Alaskan Eskimos, but not for most other North Americans, whale blubber is a tasty treat. People everywhere learn to enjoy the fatty, bitter, or irritating foods that are prescribed by their culture.

CLOSE-UP:

EATING DISORDERS

Psychological influences on eating behavior are strikingly evident in those for whom normal homeostatic pressures are overwhelmed by a motive for abnormal thinness. Consider two eating disorder cases.

Mary is a 5 foot, 3 inch 15-year-old who, having reached 100 pounds, decided she needed to lose weight to enhance her attractiveness. After gradually reducing her food intake to a few vegetables a day and then adding a vigorous exercise program, she now weighs a mere 80 pounds. Yet she still feels "fat" and plans to continue dieting. Mary has been having difficulty sleeping, has at times been depressed, and no longer has regular menstrual periods. She is socially inactive, but she is very successful academically. Mary does not regard herself as ill or needing treatment.

Alice is a 5 foot, 9 inch 17-year-old who weighs 160 pounds and says she has always been a little chubby. For the last five years, she has often eaten in binges, followed by vomiting. She will eat a quart of ice cream or an entire pie and then, to control her weight, make herself vomit in secret. Alice wants to date, but she doesn't, partly because she is so self-conscious about her looks. She has at times taken diet pills to try to lose weight.

Mary is diagnosed as having **anorexia nervosa**—a disorder in which a person becomes significantly underweight (typically, 15 percent or more) yet feels fat and is obsessed with losing weight. Even when ema-

"Gee, I had no idea you were married to a supermodel."

ciated, the person continues to limit food intake. The disorder usually develops in adolescence, 9 times out of 10 in females.

Alice's condition is more common. **Bulimia nervosa** is a disorder marked by repeated episodes of overeating followed by compensatory vomiting, laxative use, fasting, or excessive exercise. Bulimia patients eat the way some alcoholics drink—in spurts, sometimes under the influence of friends who are bingeing (Crandall, 1988). Most binge-purge eaters are women in their late teens or early twenties. Like those with anorexia, they are preoccupied with food (craving sweet and high-fat foods), are fearful of becoming overweight, and are depressed or anxious (Hinz & Williamson, 1987). Their depression and shame are felt most keenly during and following binges. About half of those with anorexia also

display the binge-purge-depression symptoms of bulimia. But unlike anorexia, bulimia is marked by weight fluctuations within or above normal ranges, making the condition easy to hide.

Researchers report that the families of bulimia patients have a higher-than-usual incidence of alcoholism, obesity, and depression. In contrast, anorexia patients often come from families that are competitive, high-achieving, and protective (Pate & others, 1992; Yates, 1989, 1990). They set high standards, fret about falling short of expectations, and are intensely concerned with how others perceive them (Heatherton & Baumeister, 1991; Striegel-Moore & others, 1993). Eating disorders do *not*, however, provide (as some have speculated) a telltale sign of childhood sexual abuse (Kinzl & others, 1994; Pope & others, 1992, 1994; Rorty & others, 1994).

Genetics, too, may influence susceptibility to eating disorders. If twins

"Diana remained throughout a very insecure person at heart, almost child-like in her desire to do good for others, so she could release herself from deep feelings of unworthiness, of which her eating disorders were merely a symptom."

Charles, Ninth Earl of Spencer, eulogizing his sister Princess Diana, 1997

rather than vegetarian foods). This "neophobia" surely was adaptive for our ancestors, protecting them from potentially toxic substances. In experiments, people have tried novel fruit drinks or ethnic foods. With repeated exposure, their appreciation for the new taste typically increases; moreover, exposure to one set of novel foods increases our willingness to try another (Pliner, 1982; Pliner & others, 1993).

Part of the cultural pressure is surely transmitted by the view of women exemplified in fashion magazines, advertisements, and even in some toys. What do you suppose happens when young women repeatedly encounter magazine images of fashion models, who tend to be unnaturally thin (Tovee & others, 1997)? Eric Stice and are identical rather than fraternal, the chances of the other twin's sharing the disorder are much greater (Fichter & Noegel, 1990). People with eating disorders may also have abnormal supplies of certain neurotransmitters that put them at risk for anxiety or depression (Fava & others, 1989).

There is, however, a cultural explanation for the fact that anorexia and bulimia occur mostly in women

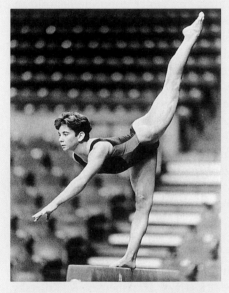

Dying to be thin Champion U.S. gymnast Christy Henrich, shown here at the 1989 World Games, was plagued by anorexia and bulimia. She was at times training nine hours a day and eating one apple. "My life is a horrifying nightmare. It feels like there's a beast inside of me," she exclaimed before dying in 1994, a 60-pound tragedy who barely dented her hospital mattress (Deardorff, 1994).

and mostly in weight-conscious cultures. Mothers of girls with eating disorders are themselves often focused on their own weight and on their daughters' weight and appearance (Pike & Rodin, 1991). Anorexia nervosa always begins as a weight-loss diet, and the self-induced vomiting of bulimia nearly always begins after a dieter has broken diet restrictions and gorged. Facing a diet, the person's body seems to revolt and overcomes the dieter's willpower by demanding food to restore lost fat. Those whose natural weight is well above their thin-ideal weight are especially vulnerable (Seligman, 1994).

Ideals of beauty have varied over the centuries, but women in every era have struggled to make their bodies conform to the particular ideal of their day. The sickness of today's eating disorders lies not just within the victims but also within our weight-obsessed culture—a culture that says, in countless ways, "Fat is bad," that motivates millions of women to be "always dieting," and that encourages eating binges by pressuring women to live in a constant state of semistarvation. "You can't be too rich or too thin," declared the Duchess of Windsor. Eating disorder specialists disagree. As obesity researchers Susan Wooley and Orland Wooley (1983) noted, "An increasingly stringent cultural standard of thinness for women has been ac-

companied by a steadily increasing incidence of serious eating disorders in women."

A recent analysis of 222 studies of 141,000 people over 50 years revealed "dramatic increases in the numbers of women . . . who have poor body image" (Feingold & Mazzella, 1998). In one 1993 national survey, nearly one-half of U.S. women reported feeling negative about their appearance and preoccupied with being or becoming overweight (Cash & Henry, 1995). Those vulnerable to eating disorders are those with greater body dissatisfaction (Cash & Deagle, 1997). In one lighthearted experiment, a research team led by Barbara Fredrickson (1998) had University of Michigan men and women put on a sweater or a swim suit and complete a math test while alone in a changing room. For the women but not the men, wearing the swimsuit triggered self-consciousness and shame that disrupted their math performance.

■ **anorexia nervosa** an eating disorder in which a normal-weight person (usually an adolescent female) diets and becomes significantly (15 percent or more) underweight, yet, still feeling fat, continues to starve.

■ **bulimia nervosa** an eating disorder characterized by episodes of overeating, usually of highly caloric foods, followed by vomiting, laxative use, fasting, or excessive exercise.

Heather Shaw (1994) and Heidi Posavac and colleagues (1998) report that women tend to feel more ashamed, depressed, and dissatisfied with their own bodies—the very attitudes that predispose eating disorders. Further evidence of the effect of cultural pressure on ideal body image came in 1995, when satellites began beaming television signals to a remote region of Fiji in the South Pacific. Within three years, the percentage of teen girls who induced vomiting to control their weight had quintupled. Those who watched TV three or more nights a week were 50 percent more likely to describe themselves as "too big or fat" and 30 percent more likely to be dieting, which was uncommon before 1995 (Goode, 1999). But even ultra-thin actresses and

"Why do women have such low self-esteem? There are many complex psychological and societal reasons, by which I mean Barbie."

Dave Barry, 1999

models do not define the impossible standard of the Barbie fashion doll. Adjusted to a height of 5 feet 7 inches, her 32-16-29 figure (in centimeters, 82 bust, 41 waist, and 73 hips) defines a body shape approximated by fewer than 1 in 100,000 women (Norton & others, 1996).

Obesity and Weight Control

PREVIEW QUESTION 7 What factors predispose some people to become and remain obese?

People wonder: Why do some people gain weight while others eat the same amount and seldom add a pound? And why do so few overweight people win the battle of the bulge? What hope is there for the one American in three who is, according to the National Center for Health Statistics, overweight?

First, the good news about fat. It is an ideal form of stored energy that provides the body with a high-caloric fuel reserve to carry it through periods when food is scarce—a common occurrence in the feast-or-famine existence of our prehistoric ancestors. Eating three or more meals every day is actually a relatively recent phenomenon and a luxury hundreds of millions of people still do not enjoy. In circumstances of alternating feast and famine, overeating and storing the excess as fat is adaptive; it prepares the body to withstand famine. Think of that spare tire around the middle as an energy storehouse—biology's counterpart to a hiker's waist-borne snack pack. This may explain why in most developing societies today, as in Europe in earlier centuries—in fact, wherever people face famine—obesity is a sign of affluence and social status (Furnham & Baguma, 1994).

Cultures without a thin-ideal for women are also cultures without eating disorders. For example, Ghanians idealize a larger body size than do Americans—and experience fewer eating disorders (Cogan & others, 1996). The same is true of African-American women compared with European-American women (Parker & others, 1995).

The bad news is that in those parts of the world where food and sweets are now abundantly available, the adaptive tendency to store fat has become maladaptive. Being slightly overweight poses no health risks (Ernsberger & Koletsky, 1999; Miller, 1999). Fitness matters more than being a little overweight. But the National Institutes of Health report that significant obesity increases the risk of diabetes, high blood pressure and heart disease, gallstones, arthritis, sleep disorders, and certain types of cancer. This is more true for apple-shaped people who carry their weight in pot bellies than for pear-shaped people with ample hips and thighs (Greenwood, 1989).

Not surprisingly, then, a massive recent study—following more than 1 million Americans over 14 years—revealed that being significantly overweight can cut life short (Calle & others, 1999). This was especially true for white men: White men with the highest body mass index (BMI) were 2

Rubens' The Garden of Love
In other times and places, fatter bodies have been idealized.

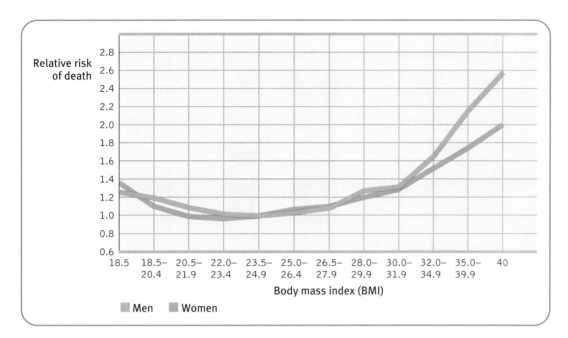

FIGURE 23.5
Obesity and mortality
Relative risk of death among
healthy nonsmokers rises with
extremely high or low body mass
index. (Data from 14-year study of
1.05 million Americans; Calle &
others, 1999.)

to 6 times more likely to have died than were those with a BMI of 24. The heaviest
white women were twice as likely to have died as those with a BMI of 23, while the
heaviest black men and women had lower relative risks of death (1.4 and 1.2) than
their counterparts who were not significantly overweight. For all men and women,
being moderately over or under normal weight was less of a risk factor (**FIGURE 23.5**).

Obesity is not just a threat to physical health. Being perceived as obese can affect
both how you are treated and how you feel about yourself. People often stereotype anyone who is obese as slow, lazy, and sloppy (Crandall, 1994, 1995; Ryckman & others,
1989). Widen people's images on a video monitor (making them look fatter) and they
suddenly seem less sincere, less friendly, meaner, and more obnoxious (Gardner &
Tockerman, 1994). Curiously, black women are less denigrating of large black women
than white women are of large white women (Hebl & Heatherton, 1998).

Obese people—sometimes victims of ridicule and job discrimination—know the
stereotype. In studies of patients who were especially unhappy with their weight—
those who had lost an average of 100 pounds after short-cutting digestion with in-
testinal bypass surgery—4 in 5 said their children had asked them not to attend school
functions. Nine in 10 said they would rather have a leg amputated than be obese again
(Rand & Macgregor, 1990, 1991). As the parents of Samuel Graham—5 feet, 4 inches
and weighing 174 pounds—can testify, overweight children suffer, too. No longer able
to bear classmates' taunts about his weight, Samuel, age 12, hanged himself (Cogan &
Ernsberger, 1999).

The social effects of obesity were clear in a study that followed 370 obese 16- to
24-year-old women (Gortmaker & others, 1993). When restudied seven years later,
two-thirds of the women were still obese. They also were less likely to be married, and
they were making less money than a comparison group of some 5000 other women.
Even after correcting for aptitude test scores, race, and parental income, the obese
women's incomes were $7000 a year below average.

In one clever experiment, Regina Pingitore and her colleagues (1994) videotaped mock job interviews in which professional actors appeared as either normal-
weight or overweight applicants. In one condition, they wore makeup and prostheses
that made them look 30 pounds heavier. When appearing overweight, the same person, using the same lines, intonation, and gestures, was rated as less worthy of hiring.

Government guidelines encourage a body
mass index (BMI) under 25.

$$BMI = \frac{\text{weight in kg (pounds} \times 0.45)}{\text{squared height in meters (inches divided by 39.4)}}$$

The World Health Organization and many
countries define obesity as a BMI of
30 or more.

FIGURE 23.6

Gender and weight discrimination

When women applicants were made to look overweight, university students were less willing to think they would hire them. Among men applicants, weight mattered less. (Data from Pingitore & others, 1994.)

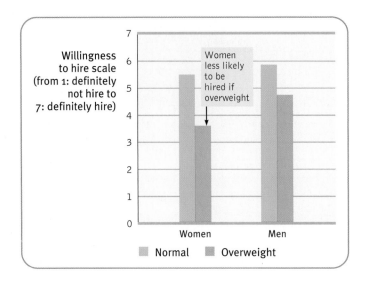

The weight bias was especially strong against women applicants (**FIGURE 23.6**). Other studies reveal that weight discrimination is greater than race and gender discrimination, and that it occurs at every stage of the employment cycle—hiring, placement, promotion, compensation, discipline, and discharge (Roehling, 2000).

The Physiology of Obesity

Research on the physiology of obesity challenges the popular stereotype of severely overweight people being weak-willed gluttons or self-indulgent overeaters with a personality problem. First, consider the arithmetic of weight gain: People get fat by consuming more calories than they expend. The energy equivalent of a pound of fat is 3500 calories; therefore, dieters have been told they will lose a pound for every 3500-calorie reduction in their diet. Surprise: This conclusion is false. Why? The answer lies in the physiology of fat.

Fat Cells

The immediate determinants of body fat are the size and number of fat cells. A typical adult has about 30 billion of these miniature fuel tanks, half of which lie near the skin's surface. A fat cell can vary from relatively empty, like a deflated balloon, to overly full. In an obese person, fat cells may swell to two or three times their normal size and then divide. Once the number of fat cells increases—due to genetic predisposition, early childhood eating patterns, or adult overeating—it never decreases. Fat cells may shrink on a diet, but they never disappear (Sjöstrum, 1980).

This unyielding nature of our fat cells is but one way, once we become fat, our bodies maintain fat. Another way is that fat tissue has a low metabolic (energy expenditure) rate. Compared with other tissue, fat takes less food energy to maintain. Thus, once we become fat, we require less food to maintain our weight than we did to attain it.

Set Points and Metabolism

There is another reason why most obese people find it so difficult to lose weight permanently. Their bodies' "weight thermostats" are set to maintain body weight within a higher-than-average range. When their weight drops below the set-point range, their hunger increases and metabolism decreases.

As many a dieter can testify, the drop in resting metabolic rate can be particularly frustrating. After the rapid weight losses that occur during the initial three weeks or so of a rigorous diet, any further weight loss comes slowly. In a classic experiment (Bray, 1969), obese patients whose daily food intake was reduced from 3500 to 450 calories lost only 6 percent of their weight—partly because their metabolic rates dropped about 15 percent (**FIGURE 23.7**). Thus, the body adapts to starvation by burning off fewer calories, and to extra calories by burning off more. That is why reducing your food intake by 3500 calories may not reduce your weight by 1 pound. And that is why when a diet ends and the body is still conserving energy, amounts of food that worked to maintain weight before the diet may now increase it.

FIGURE 23.7

The effects of a severe diet on obese patients' body weight and metabolism
After seven days on a 3500-calorie diet, six obese patients were given only 450 calories a day for the next 24 days. Body weight declined only 6 percent and then leveled off, because metabolism dropped about 15 percent. (From Bray, 1969.)

Individual differences in resting metabolism explain why—contrary to the stereotype of the overweight glutton—it is possible for two people of the same height, age, and activity level to maintain the same weight, even if one of them eats much more than the other does. Or why it is possible for a person to eat less than another similarly active person, yet weigh more. This appears true despite findings that people—obese people, especially—tend to overestimate their physical activity and underestimate their caloric intake (Brownell & Wadden, 1992; Lichtman & others, 1992).

The Genetic Factor

Studies of adoptees and twins reveal a genetic influence on body weight. Consider:

- Despite shared family meals, the body weights of adoptive siblings are uncorrelated with one another and with those of their adoptive parents. Rather, people's weights resemble those of their biological parents (Grilo & Pogue-Geile, 1991).
- Identical twins have closely similar weights, even when reared apart (Plomin & others, 1997; Stunkard & others, 1990). Across studies, their weight correlates 0.74. The much lower 0.32 correlation among fraternal twins suggests that genes explain two-thirds of our varying BMI (Maes & others, 1997). Being overweight is therefore not simply a matter of scarfing too many hot fudge sundaes. And losing weight is not merely a matter of mind over platter.

The genetic influence is surely complex, with some genes influencing when our intestines signal "full," others dictating how efficiently we burn calories or convert extra calories to fat, or how much we fidget. But recent experiments do reveal one genetic mechanism for weight control. As a normal mouse's fat cells become bloated, its genes produce leptin, a protein that is monitored by the brain.

The lean look
Contemporary clothing ads and films present an ideal of thinness that most women cannot attain. The message is so pervasive in Western cultures that even those who have what others might consider a flawless appearance are often worried about their bodily "imperfections."

Fat-signaling hormone
The obese mouse at left has a defective gene for producing the fat-signaling hormone, leptin. When the genetically similar mouse at right was treated with leptin, it shed 40 percent of its body weight.

When researchers injected obese mice with daily doses of leptin, the mice then ate less, became more active, and lost weight. So, might injections of leptin similarly serve as virtual fat for humans, fooling the brain into making a fat body trimmer? Or, as newer research suggests, are the leptin receptors of obese humans insensitive to leptin (Considine & others, 1996)? If so, might a slightly different drug be designed that activates insensitive leptin receptors? Or might we look forward to a drug that blocks hypothalamic receptors that activate eating (Gerald & others, 1996)? Given the huge potential market for such drugs, the race to define them is on.

Genes aren't the whole story behind obesity, however. Genes cannot explain why obesity is six times more common among lower-class than among upper-class women, more common among Americans than among Europeans, and more common among Americans today than in 1900. Exercise and diet—Big Gulps, Double Whoppers, and Frosted Flakes—can. Compared with their counterparts in the early 1900s, people are eating a higher-fat, higher-sugar diet, expending fewer calories, and suffering more diabetes at younger ages (Thompson, 1998).

Across the developed world, the increase in population pudginess has accelerated. In Britain, the average woman's dress size has increased from size 12 in 1951 to size 16 today (Merriman, 1999). And so it goes, pretty much everywhere this book is being read. As recently as 1960, 43 percent of Americans were classified as overweight, with a BMI of 25 or over; today 55 percent are, and nearly twice as many—23 percent—are obese, at a BMI of 30 or more (Flegal & others, 1998; NIH, 1998). Australia, too, classifies 55 percent of its population as overweight (Australian Bureau of Statistics, 1999). In Canada, the proportion of people classified as overweight has increased by 60 percent since 1985 (Statistics Canada, 1999). Public seating is now expanding to accommodate this population growth. As the century turned, airlines and theaters were offering wider seats for today's wider bodies. The Washington State Ferries abandoned its 50-year-old standard of 18 inches per person. "Eighteen-inch butts are a thing of the past," explained a spokesperson (Shepherd, 1999).

In Britain, as elsewhere, not all pounds are sterling
We humans were not designed for a world filled with energy-saving cars and tools, and high-calorie foods. In hunting-and-gathering societies, obesity is almost unknown (Brown, 1993).

Note how these findings reinforce a familiar lesson: There can be high levels of heritability (genetic influence on individual differences) without heredity explaining group differences. Genes mostly determine why one person today is heavier than another. Environment mostly determines why people are heavier today than 50 years ago.

Ironically, the expanding waistlines of the American population coincide with an increasing idealization of the thin-and-fit look. Consider:

- Most models and actresses have hardly more than half the 22 to 26 percent body fat of an average woman (Brownell, 1991). When young women look at magazine pictures of ultra-thin models, they report an increase in their feelings of shame, guilt, and body dissatisfaction (Stice & Shaw, 1994).

- In 1950, department-store mannequins looked nearly like real women. Since then, they have lost about 3 inches around their hips, which now average only 31 inches—quite unlike today's average young adult woman's 37 inches. In fact, women with as little body fat as these mannequins likely would not menstruate (University of California, 1993).

- While the average North American woman weighs more than her counterpart of 40 years ago and obesity rates are increasing, today's average Miss America contestant weighs about 15 pounds less (**FIGURE 23.8**).

FIGURE 23.8
The thinning of Miss America
(Rubinstein & others, 2000).

Trend in Body Mass Index (BMI) of Miss America Pageant Winners, 1922 to 1999

Rosemary La Planche
1941

Elizabeth Ward
1982

Losing Weight

Perhaps you shake your head in sympathy with obese people: "Slim chance they (or we) have of becoming and staying thin. If they lose weight on a diet, their metabolism slows and their hungry fat cells cry out, 'Feed me!'" Indeed, the condition of an obese person's body reduced to average weight is much like that of a semi-starved body. Held under normal set point, each body "thinks" it is starving. Having lost weight, formerly obese people look normal, but their fat cells may be abnormally small, their metabolism slowed, and their minds obsessed with food.

All this explains why most people who succeed on a weight-loss program eventually gain nearly all of the weight back (Garner & Wooley, 1991; Wing & Jeffery, 1979). One study followed 207 obese patients who had lost large amounts of weight during a 2-month hospital fast (Johnson & Drenick, 1977). Within 3 years, half had gained back all the weight they had lost, and virtually all were again obese within 9 years. Programs that modify one's life-style and ongoing eating behavior have better carryover to postdiet weight management. Yet the participants in these programs,

"After years of research, after tens of millions of dieters, after tens of billions of dollars, no one has found a diet that keeps the weight off in any but a small fraction of dieters."

Martin E. P. Seligman, *What You Can Change and What You Can't*, 1994

FIGURE 23.9

Weight-loss programs and weight change

Behavior management weight-loss programs promote weight loss, but most lost weight is regained. (From Brownell & Jeffery, 1987.)

BOTTOM LINERS

"It works as well as most other diet plans.... I've lost over $200 in less than three weeks."

too, typically regain much of their lost weight (**FIGURE 23.9**). When cultural ideals of slimness collide with hunger, hunger usually wins. Commercial weight-loss programs can justifiably proclaim that they help people lose weight, *temporarily.* For most people, however, the only long-term result is a thinner wallet: Americans spend $30 billion a year trying to lose weight (Gura, 1997). In 1999, 52 percent of Americans—up from 31 percent in 1951—said they would like to lose weight (Gallup, 1999).

And yet, the battle of the bulge rages on, and it is most intense among people with two X chromosomes. In one survey of 108,000 adults, 29 percent of men and 44 percent of women were actively trying to lose weight (Serdula & others, 1999). Asked if they would rather "be five years younger or weigh 15 pounds less," 29 percent of men and 48 percent of women said they would prefer losing the weight (*Responsive Community,* 1996). The gender difference for teenagers is even larger: 15 percent of boys and 44 percent of girls report trying to lose weight (Centers for Disease Control, 1991).

Although preserving weight loss is a constant challenge, Stanley Schachter (1982) was less pessimistic than most obesity researchers about the likelihood of doing it successfully. While he recognized the overwhelming rate of failure among those in structured weight-loss programs, he also noted that these are a special group of people, probably people who have been unable to help themselves. Moreover, the failure rates recorded for these programs are based on single attempts at weight loss. Perhaps when people try repeatedly to lose weight, more of them do eventually succeed. When Schachter interviewed a haphazard sample of people, he found that one-fourth had at one time been significantly overweight and had tried to slim down. Of these, 6 out of 10 had *succeeded:* They weighed at least 10 percent less than their maximum prediet weight (an average loss of 35 pounds) and were no longer obese. A 1993 survey of 90,000 *Consumer Reports* readers found 25 percent of dieters claiming an enduring weight loss. Aided by media publicity, the National Weight Control Registry has identified 2500 Americans who have maintained a weight loss for at least one year and are being studied over time (Fritsch, 1999; McGuire & others, 1999).

There is another option for overweight people, and one chosen by 13 percent of the people Schachter interviewed—simply to accept one's weight. We all do well to note that researchers have *not* identified guilt, hostility, oral fixation, or any similar personality maladjustment as causes of obesity. Nor is obesity simply a matter of a

CLOSE-UP:

HELPFUL HINTS FOR LOSING WEIGHT

With fat cells, set points, metabolism, and genetic factors all tirelessly conspiring to make losing weight a big problem, what advice can psychology offer if you wish to shed any excess pounds?

Minimize exposure to tempting food cues

Keep tempting foods out of the house or out of sight. Stay out of the sweets and chips shops. Go to the supermarket only on a full stomach.

Take steps to boost your metabolism

Inactive people are often overweight (**FIGURE 23.10**). One of the few predictors of successful long-term weight loss is exercise both during and after changing your eating patterns (Foreyt & others, 1996; McGuire & others, 1999; Wadden & others, 1998). Exercise, such as brisk walking, running, and swimming, not only empties fat cells, builds muscle, and makes you feel better, it also temporarily speeds up metabolism and can help lower your set point (Bennett, 1995; Kolata, 1987; Thompson & others, 1982). Even brief bouts of exercise—four 10-minute walks a day—provide benefits (Jakicic & others, 1999). Lack of exercise helps explain why so few succeed in losing weight permanently. In a Centers for Disease Control study of 107,000 adults, only one in five of those trying to lose weight were following the government recommendation to both count calories and exercise 150 minutes weekly (Serdula & others, 1999).

Be realistic and moderate

Being moderately heavy is less risky than being extremely thin (Ernsberger & Koletsky, 1999). Permanent weight loss is not easy. Take it gradually. "A reasonable *time line* for a 10 percent reduction in body weight is six months," advises the National Institutes of Health (1998).

FIGURE 23.10

Couch potatoes beware: a correlational study of TV watching and obesity

In a 1980s study of 6671 young people 12 to 17 years old, and in a 1990s follow-up study of 4063 children, ages 8 to 16, obesity was more common among those who watched the most television (Ander-

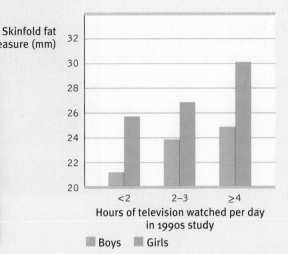

Skinfold fat measure (mm)

Hours of television watched per day in 1990s study
■ Boys ■ Girls

sen & others, 1998; Dietz & Gortmaker, 1985). As life-styles have become more sedentary and TV watching has increased, so has the percentage of overweight people in Britain, North America, and elsewhere (Vines, 1995). When California children were placed in a TV-reduction educational program, they watched less—and lost weight (Robinson, 1999).

Modify both your metabolic rate and your hunger by changing the food you eat

Findings suggest that complex carbohydrates (pasta, grains, potatoes) increase metabolism and are less readily converted to body fat than are the same calories eaten as fats (Rodin, 1979, 1985). Complex carbohydrates and fructose (the sugar in fruits) stimulate less of the hunger-producing insulin jump than does refined sugar (sucrose).

Don't starve all day and eat one big meal at night

This eating pattern, common among overweight people, slows metabolism.

Beware of the binge

Among people who consciously restrain their eating, drinking alcohol or feeling anxious or depressed can unleash the urge to eat (Herman & Polivy, 1980). Once the diet is bro-

ken, the person often thinks "what the heck" and then binges (Polivy & Herman, 1985, 1987). A lapse need not become a full collapse: Remember, most people occasionally lapse. Remind yourself that you've succeeded before, and continue with your plan.

Set realistic goals

Targeting an ambitiously low weight usually dooms a person to eventual defeat. Setting a realistic objective—such as walking several times a week—can promote effort and persistence.

Begin only if you are prepared to exercise and restrict your eating permanently

For most people, permanent weight loss requires making a career of staying thin—a lifelong change in eating habits combined with gradually increased exercise.

An unusual success story

Tammy and Jeffrey Munson—two volunteers in the National Weight Control Registry—shown before and after she lost 147 pounds and he lost 100 pounds.

"Fat! So?"

Popular T-shirt at the 1999 convention of the National Association to Advance Fat Acceptance

lack of willpower. If dieters are more likely to binge when under stress or after breaking their diets, this may be largely a consequence of their constant dieting. Indeed, the relentless pursuit of thinness puts people at risk not only for binge eating and food obsession, but also for taxing weight fluctuations, malnutrition, smoking, depression, and harmful side effects of weight-loss drugs (Cogan & Ernsberger, 1999).

"Fat is not a four-letter word," proclaims the National Association to Advance Fat Acceptance, so "a waist is a terrible thing to mind." Such statements discount the health risks linked with significant obesity, but they do convey a valid point: It is surely better to accept oneself as a bit chubby than to diet and binge and feel continually out of control and guilty. Fans loved Oprah Winfrey before she lost 67 pounds. They loved her after she put them back on. They loved her when she shed them again. And they will love her still, chubby or not.

rehearse it!

7. The hypothalamus, a structure deep within the brain, controls feelings of hunger and fullness, in part by evaluating changes in blood chemistry. Hunger occurs in response to high blood insulin and
   a. high blood glucose.
   b. low blood glucose.
   c. decreased energy expenditure.
   d. stimulation of any part of the hypothalamus.

8. One theory maintains that our bodies tend to stay at a particular weight level, or set point. Changes in the basal metabolic rate help keep us at this weight. For example, when our weight falls below the set point, we feel hungrier (and eat more) and lethargic (and reduce our energy expenditure). The operation of this "weight thermostat" is an example of
   a. homeostasis.
   b. an eating disorder.

   c. individual learning.
   d. binge-purge episodes.

9. Some of our responses to food and eating are learned; others are genetic and universal. Which of the following is a genetically disposed response to food?
   a. An aversion to eating cats and dogs
   b. An interest in novel foods
   c. A preference for sweet and salty foods
   d. An aversion to carbohydrates

10. Both anorexia nervosa and bulimia nervosa are eating disorders characterized by a preoccupation with food and body weight. Which of the following is true regarding bulimia nervosa?
   a. People with bulimia continue to want to lose weight even when they are underweight.
   b. Bulimia is marked by weight fluctuations within or above normal ranges.

   c. Bulimia patients often come from middle-class families that are competitive, high-achieving, and protective.
   d. If one twin is diagnosed with bulimia, the chances of the other twin's sharing the disorder are greater if they are fraternal rather than identical twins.

11. Obese people find it very difficult to lose weight permanently. This is due to several factors, including the fact that
   a. with dieting, fat cells shrink and then disappear.
   b. the set point of obese people is lower than average.
   c. with dieting, basal metabolic rate increases.
   d. there is a genetic influence on body weight.

Introduction to Motivation: Hunger

1. What is the underlying assumption shared by instinct theory and evolutionary psychology?

Under Darwin's influence, early theorists viewed behavior as controlled by biological forces, such as instincts. But when it became clear that people were naming, not explaining, various behaviors by calling them instincts, this idea fell into disfavor. The underlying idea—that genes predispose species-typical behavior—is, however, still influential in evolutionary psychology.

2. How does drive-reduction theory help us understand the forces that energize and direct some of our behavior?

Most physiological needs create aroused psychological states that drive us to reduce or satisfy those needs. The aim of *drive reduction* is internal stability, or homeostasis. Thus, drive reduction motivates survival behaviors such as eating and drinking.

3. What types of motivated behavior does arousal theory attempt to explain?

Rather than reducing a physiological need or tension state, some motivated behaviors increase arousal. Curiosity-driven behaviors, for example, suggest that too little as well as too much stimulation can motivate people to seek an optimum level of arousal. Not only are we pushed by our internal drives, we are pulled by external incentives. Our individual learning histories also help explain which external incentives, such as certain foods or erotic images, will arouse our desires.

4. What is the basic idea behind Maslow's hierarchy of needs?

Maslow's hierarchy of needs expresses the idea that, until satisfied, some motives are more compelling (that is, more basic) than others. At the base of his hierarchy are physiological needs and at the top are self-actualization needs.

5. What physiological factors cause us to feel hungry?

Hunger's inner push primarily originates not from the stomach's contractions but from variations in body chemistry. For example, we are likely to feel hungry when our blood glucose levels are low. This information is monitored by the hypothalamus, which regulates the body's weight as it influences our feelings of hunger and fullness. To maintain weight at its set point, the body also adjusts its basal metabolic rate of energy expenditure.

6. What psychological influences affect our eating behavior and our feelings of hunger?

Especially in "external" people, the sight and smell of food can trigger hunger and eating, partly by stimulating a rise in insulin level. Our preferences for certain tastes are partly genetic and universal, but also partly learned in a cultural context. The effect of psychological factors on eating behavior is most obvious in people (usually young women) with anorexia nervosa and bulimia nervosa.

7. What factors predispose some people to become and remain obese?

Fat is a concentrated fuel reserve stored in fat cells. Under genetic influence, the number and size of these cells determine one's body fat. Obese people find it difficult to lose weight permanently because the number of fat cells is not reduced by a diet, because fat cells require less energy expenditure than muscle cells to maintain themselves, and because the overall metabolic rate decreases when body weight drops below its set point. Those who nevertheless wish to diet should minimize exposure to food cues, boost energy expenditure through exercise, and make a lifelong change in eating patterns.

TERMS AND CONCEPTS TO REMEMBER

motivation, p. 352	homeostasis, p. 353	glucose, p. 357	anorexia nervosa, p. 360
instinct, p. 352	incentive, p. 353	set point, p. 358	bulimia nervosa, p. 360
drive-reduction theory, p. 353	hierarchy of needs, p. 354	basal metabolic rate, p. 358	

REHEARSE IT ANSWER KEY

1. b	3. d	5. c	7. b	9. c	11. d
2. a	4. c	6. a	8. a	10. b	

24 Sexual Motivation

Sex is part of life. Had this not been so for all your ancestors, you would not be reading this book. Sexual motivation is nature's clever way of making people procreate, thus enabling our species' survival. When two people feel attracted, they hardly stop to think of themselves as guided by their genes. As the pleasure we take in eating is nature's inventive method of getting our body nourishment, so the pleasure of sex is our genes' way of preserving and spreading themselves.

Describing Sexual Behavior

PREVIEW QUESTION 1 What behavior patterns must a theory of sexual motivation explain?

Before looking at what energizes and directs sexual arousal, let's consider the behavior patterns that a theory of sexual motivation must explain.

Unable to answer his students' questions about people's sexual practices, Indiana University biologist Alfred Kinsey and his colleagues (1948, 1953) set out to find some answers. Kinsey's confidential interviews with 18,000 people—85 percent conducted by himself or his associate Wardell Pomeroy—asked more than 350 rapid-fire questions. Social scientists were quick to point out what Kinsey readily acknowledged—that his nonrandom sample contained an overrepresentation of well-educated white urbanites.

Because we do not know whether Kinsey's sample accurately represented the nation's sexual practices in the 1940s, let alone those of today, his precise findings can be misleading. Moreover, Kinsey and Pomeroy's questioning encouraged (some say, demanded) admission of sexual activity. They never asked subjects *whether* they had engaged in a particular activity; they asked them *when* they had first engaged in it (thus making it easier for people to divulge their behavior). Pomeroy (1972, pp. 113, 124, 127) reported that he and Kinsey "went on the broad assumption that everybody had done everything." If Kinsey or Pomeroy doubted a subject's denial, they might respond, "Yes, I know you have never done that, but how old were you the *first* time you did it?" or even "Look, I don't give a damn what you've done, but if you don't tell

"I love the idea of there being two sexes, don't you?"

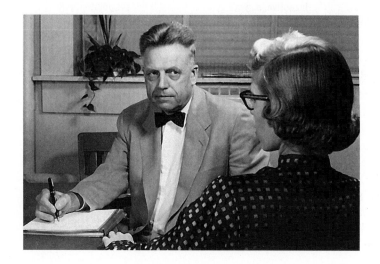

Alfred Kinsey

The controversial biologist, shown here conducting one of his interviews, did not begin with sexually explicit questions. Rather, he first helped people feel at ease by asking nonthreatening questions about family background, health, and education.

me the straight of it, it's better that we stop this history right here. Now, how old were you the first time this or that happened?" Even his motives are suspect. Kinsey, his biographers report, was driven by a desire to overthrow the "Victorian repression" of his father's strict Methodist morality and to justify his own sexual compulsions (Ericksen, 1998; Jones, 1997a,b).

By today's standards of random sampling and nonleading questioning, Kinsey's tactics, and thus his results, are suspect. Yet his surveys were less misleading than some of the haphazard sexual surveys reported more recently in the popular press. Some of these popular "sex reports" have relied on a biased sample of people (such as subscribers to selected magazines) and have received replies from only 3 percent of this nonrandom sample—good reason to doubt the generality of their findings.

The Physiology of Sex

Like hunger, sexual arousal depends on the interplay of internal and external stimuli. To understand sexual motivation, we must consider both.

The Sexual Response Cycle

PREVIEW QUESTION 2 What are the stages of the human sexual response cycle?

The headlines created by Kinsey's 1940s surveys reappeared after some 1960s studies in which scientists recorded the physiological responses of volunteers who masturbated or had intercourse. With the help of 382 female and 312 male volunteers—an atypical sample, consisting only of people able and willing to display arousal and orgasm while being observed in a laboratory—gynecologist-obstetrician William Masters and his collaborator Virginia Johnson (1966) monitored or filmed more than 10,000 sexual "cycles."

Their description of the **sexual response cycle** identified four stages, similar in men and women. During the initial *excitement phase,* the genital areas become engorged with blood, causing the man's penis to become partially erect and the woman's clitoris to swell and the inner lips covering her vagina to open up. Her vagina also expands and secretes lubricant, and her breasts and nipples may enlarge.

In the *plateau phase,* excitement peaks as breathing, pulse, and blood pressure rates continue to increase. The penis becomes fully engorged and some fluid—frequently containing enough live sperm to enable conception—may appear at the tip of the penis. Vaginal secretion continues to increase, the clitoris retracts, and orgasm feels imminent.

Masters and Johnson observed muscle contractions all over the body during *orgasm;* these were accompanied by further increases in breathing, pulse, and blood pressure rates. A woman's arousal and orgasm facilitate conception by helping propel semen from the penis, positioning the uterus to receive sperm, and drawing the sperm farther inward. A woman's orgasm therefore not only reinforces intercourse, which is essential to natural reproduction, it also increases retention of deposited sperm (Furlow & Thornhill, 1996). In the excitement of the moment, men and women are hardly aware of all this but are more aware of their rhythmic genital contractions that create a pleasurable feeling of sexual release. The feeling apparently is much the same for both sexes. In one study, a panel of experts could not reliably distinguish between descriptions of orgasm written by men and those written by women (Vance & Wagner, 1976).

After orgasm, the body gradually returns to its unaroused state as the engorged genital blood vessels release their accumulated blood—relatively quickly if orgasm has occurred, relatively slowly otherwise. (It's like the nasal tickle that goes away rapidly if you have sneezed, slowly otherwise.) During this *resolution phase,* the male enters a

A nonsmoking 50-year-old male has about a 1 in a million chance of a heart attack during any hour. This increases to merely 2 in a million during the hour following sex (with no increase for those who exercise regularly). Compared with risks associated with heavy exertion or anger, this risk seems not worth losing sleep (or sex) over (Muller & others, 1996).

■ **sexual response cycle** the four stages of sexual responding described by Masters and Johnson—excitement, plateau, orgasm, and resolution.

■ **refractory period** a resting period after orgasm, during which a man cannot achieve another orgasm.

■ **estrogen** a sex hormone, secreted in greater amounts by females than by males. In nonhuman female mammals, estrogen levels peak during ovulation, promoting sexual receptivity.

■ **testosterone** the most important of the male sex hormones. Both males and females have it, but the additional testosterone in males stimulates the growth of the male sex organs in the fetus and the development of the male sex characteristics during puberty.

refractory period, lasting from a few minutes to a day or more, during which he is incapable of another orgasm. The female's refractory period is not very long, which may make it possible for her to have another orgasm if restimulated during or soon after resolution.

Hormones and Sexual Behavior

PREVIEW QUESTION 3 What role do hormones play in human sexuality?

Sex hormones have two effects: They direct the development of male and female sex characteristics, and (especially in nonhuman animals) they activate sexual behavior. In most mammals, nature neatly synchronizes sex with fertility. The female becomes sexually receptive ("in heat") when production of the female hormone **estrogen** peaks at ovulation. (In experiments, researchers stimulate receptivity by injecting female animals with estrogen.) Male hormone levels are more constant, and researchers cannot so easily manipulate the sexual behavior of male animals by hormone treatments (Feder, 1984). Nevertheless, castrated male rats—having lost their testes, which manufacture the male sex hormone **testosterone**—gradually lose much of their interest in receptive females. They gradually regain it if injected with testosterone.

Hormones do not, however, so neatly control human sexual behavior. At ovulation, women's sexual desire is only slightly higher than at other times (Harvey, 1987; Meuwissen & Over, 1992). Women's sexuality also differs from that of other mammalian females in being more responsive to testosterone level than to estrogen level (Andersen & Cyranowski, 1995; Reichman, 1998). If a woman's testosterone level is low, her sexual interest may wane, but it can be restored by a testosterone replacement drug.

In men, normal fluctuations in testosterone levels, from man to man and hour to hour, have little effect on sex drive (Byrne, 1982). Indeed, fluctuations in male hormones are partly a response to sexual stimulation. When James Dabbs and his colleagues (1987) had male collegians converse separately with a male and with a female student, the men's testosterone levels rose with the social arousal, but especially after talking with the female. Sexual arousal can be a cause as well as a consequence of increased testosterone levels.

Although normal short-term hormonal changes have little effect on men's and women's desire, large hormone shifts over the life span have a greater effect. A person's interest in dating and sexual stimulation usually increases with the pubertal surge in sex hormones. If the hormonal surge is precluded—as happened during the 1600s and 1700s with prepubertal boys who were castrated to preserve their soprano voices for Italian opera—the normal development of sex characteristics and sexual desire does not occur (Peschel & Peschel, 1987). Among adult men who suffer castration, sex drive typically falls along with declining testosterone levels (Hucker & Bain, 1990). Likewise, male sex offenders lose much of their sexual urge when voluntarily taking Depo-Provera, a drug that reduces testosterone level to that of a prepubertal boy (Money & others, 1983). In later life, as sex hormone levels decline, the frequency of sexual fantasies and intercourse declines as well (Leitenberg & Henning, 1995).

Hormones influence sexual arousal via the brain's hypothalamus, which both monitors variations in blood hormone levels and activates the appropriate neural circuits. In rats, destroying a key area of the hypothalamus may extinguish sexual activity; stimulating this area, either electrically or by directly inserting minute quantities of hormones, may activate sexual behavior.

To summarize: We might compare human sex hormones, especially testosterone, to the fuel in a car. Without fuel, a car will not run. But if the fuel level is minimally adequate, adding more fuel to the gas tank won't change how the car runs.

The analogy is imperfect, because the interaction between hormones and sexual motivation is two-way. However, the analogy correctly suggests that biology is a necessary but not sufficient explanation of human sexual behavior. The hormonal fuel is essential, but so are the psychological stimuli that turn on the engine, keep it running, and shift it into high gear.

The Psychology of Sex

PREVIEW QUESTION 4 How do internal and external stimuli contribute to sexual arousal?

Hunger and sex are different sorts of motives. Hunger responds to a *need*. If we do not eat, we die. Sex is not in this sense a need. If we do not have sex, we may feel like dying, but we do not. Nevertheless, there are similarities between hunger and sexual motivation. Both depend on internal physiological factors. And both are influenced by external stimuli.

"Fill'er up with testosterone."

External Stimuli

Many studies confirm that men become aroused when they see, hear, or read erotic material. Surprising to many (because sexually explicit materials are sold mostly to men) is that most women—at least the less-inhibited women who volunteer to participate in such studies—report nearly as much arousal to the same stimuli (Stockton & Murnen, 1992).

In one such study, psychologist Julia Heiman (1975) had sexually experienced university volunteers attach instruments that detected arousal (changes in penis circumference or in vaginal color). The students then listened to one of four tapes: a sexually explicit erotic tape, a romantic tape (of a couple expressing love without physical contact), a combined erotic-romantic tape, or a neutral control tape. Which do you suppose the men were most aroused by? And the women? Both found the tape of explicit sex most arousing, especially when a woman initiated the sex and the depiction centered on her responses. In other studies both sexes have shown arousal to sexual stimuli, though men's arousal has tended to exceed women's somewhat (Murnen & Stockton, 1997).

People may find such arousal either pleasing or disturbing. (Those who find it disturbing often limit their exposure to such materials, just as those wishing to control hunger limit their exposure to tempting cues.) With repeated exposure, the emotional response to any erotic stimulus often "habituates" (lessens). During the 1920s, when Western women's hemlines first reached the knee, an exposed leg was a mildly erotic stimulus, as were modest (by today's standards) two-piece swim suits and movie scenes of a mere kiss.

Can sexually explicit material have adverse effects? Research indicates that it can. Depictions of women being sexually coerced—and enjoying it—tend to increase the viewers' acceptance of the false idea that women enjoy rape and tend to increase male viewers' willingness to hurt women (Malamuth & Check, 1981; Zillmann, 1989). Images of sexually attractive women and men may also lead people to devalue their own partners and relationships. After male collegians watch TV or magazine depictions of sexually attractive women, they often find an average woman, or their own girlfriends or wives, less attractive (Kenrick & Gutierres, 1980; Kenrick & others, 1989; Weaver & others, 1984). Viewing X-rated sex films similarly tends to diminish people's satisfaction with their own sexual partners (Zillmann, 1989). Erotica may create expectations that few men and women can hope to live up to.

"Ours is a society which stimulates interest in sex by constant titillation. . . . Cinema, television, and all the formidable array of our marketing technology project our very effective forms of titillation and our prejudices about man as a sexy animal into every corner of every hovel in the world."

Germaine Greer, 1984

Imagined Stimuli

Sexual motivation arises from the interplay of our physiology and our environment. But the stimuli inside our heads—our imaginations—also influence sexual arousal and desire (**FIGURE 24.1**). The brain, it has been said, is our most significant sex organ. People who, because of a spinal cord injury, have no genital sensation, can still feel sexual desire (Willmuth, 1987). Consider, too, the erotic potential of dreams. Sleep researchers have discovered that genital arousal accompanies all types of dreams, even though most dreams have no sexual content. But in nearly all men and some 40 percent of women (Wells, 1986), dreams sometimes do contain sexual imagery that leads to orgasm. In men, these nocturnal emissions ("wet dreams") are more likely when orgasm has not occurred recently.

FIGURE 24.1

Forces affecting sexual motivation

Physiology, imagination, and the environment all affect sexual motivation.

Wide-awake people become sexually aroused not only by memories of prior sexual activities but also by fantasies. Fantasies need not correspond to actual behavior. In one survey of masturbation-related fantasies (Hunt, 1974), 19 percent of women and 10 percent of men reported imagining being taken by someone overwhelmed with desire for them. Fantasy is not reality, however. To paraphrase Susan Brownmiller (1975), for women there's a big difference between fantasizing that Leonardo DiCaprio just won't take no for an answer and having a hostile stranger actually force himself on you.

About 95 percent of both men and women say they have had sexual fantasies. But men (whether gay or straight) fantasize about sex more often, more physically, and less romantically—and prefer less personal and faster-paced sex content in books and videos (Leitenberg & Henning, 1995). Fantasizing about sex does *not* indicate a sexual problem or dissatisfaction. (If anything, sexually active people have more sexual fantasies.)

"There is no difference between being raped and being run over by a truck except that afterward men ask if you enjoyed it."

Marge Piercy, "Rape Poem," 1976

Adolescent Sexuality

PREVIEW QUESTION 5 What factors influence teenagers' sexual attitudes and behaviors?

Adolescents' physical maturation fosters a sexual dimension to their emerging identity. Yet sexual expression also varies dramatically with time and culture.

Culture

We humans are one species, driven by similar motives that enhance our survival and spread our genes. Yet our attitudes toward behaviors such as premarital sex and nonmarital childbearing vary widely across the planet. These cultural differences in sexual attitudes are manifest in sexual behavior. In the United States, about half of ninth- to twelfth-graders report having had sexual intercourse, as do 42 percent of Canadian 16-year-olds (Boroditsky & others, 1995; Smith, 1998). Teen intercourse rates are higher in Western Europe but much lower in Arab and Asian countries and among

CLOSE-UP:

SEXUAL DISORDERS AND THERAPY

Masters and Johnson sought not only to describe the human sexual response cycle but also to understand and treat the inability to complete it. **Sexual disorders** are problems that consistently impair sexual functioning. Some involve sexual motivation, especially lack of sexual energy and arousability. In a national survey of 18- to 59-year-old Americans, 3 in 10 men reported *premature ejaculation* (before they or their partners wish) and 1 in 10 acknowledged *impotence* (the inability to have or maintain an erection) (Laumann & others, 1999). Among women respondents, 3 in 10 reported low sexual desire and 1 in 4 acknowledged *orgasmic disorder* (infrequently or never experiencing orgasm).

What causes such problems? The idea that personality disorders are to blame has been largely discounted. Men who experience premature ejaculation are similar, even in their sexual arousal patterns, to men who do not; they simply ejaculate at lower levels of arousal—something that often occurs with young men who have had long periods of sexual abstinence (Grenier & Byers, 1995; Spiess & others, 1984).

When Barbara Andersen (1983) reviewed research on the diagnosis and treatment of orgasmic disorder in women, she, too, could find no associated personality traits. Furthermore, she reported that treating orgasmic disorder through traditional psychotherapy (as though it were a disorder of personality) has been unsuccessful. She did, however, report a nearly 100 percent success rate with a behavioral treatment that trains women to enjoy their bodies and to give themselves orgasms, with a vibrator if necessary. Women who undergo such training are then sometimes able to generalize their new sexual responsiveness to interactions with their mates (Rosen & Leiblum, 1995; Wakefield, 1987). Some success has also been reported in training men to control their premature ejaculations by repeatedly stimulating the penis and then stopping stimulation (or even firmly squeezing the head of the penis) when the urge to ejaculate arises. Alternatively, men can reduce their excitability by simply having more orgasms (LoPicolo & Stock, 1986).

■ **sexual disorder** a problem that consistently impairs sexual arousal or functioning.

North Americans of Asian descent (McLaughlin & others, 1997). In one survey, only 2.5 percent of 4688 unmarried Chinese students entering Hong Kong's six universities reported having had sexual intercourse (Meston & others, 1996). The variations in sexual standards from country to country help to explain the cultural differences in rates of nonmarital childbearing (**FIGURE 24.2**).

Sexual attitudes and behaviors also vary with time within the same culture. Among American women born before 1900, a mere 3 percent had experienced premarital sex by age 18; among today's 18-year-old women, slightly more than half have done so (Smith, 1998). (Seventy-two percent of 12- to 17-year-old girls who have had sex say they regret it [Reuters, 2000].) This increase in sexual activity has led to an increase in the adolescent pregnancy rate. The often impoverished futures of teen mothers and of children in father-absent homes have in turn prompted new research on teen sexuality and adolescents' use of contraceptives.

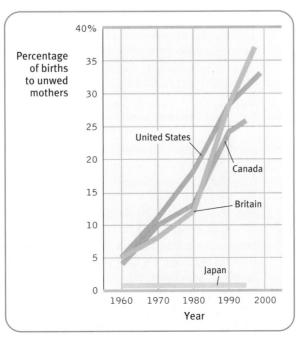

FIGURE 24.2

Births to unwed parents

Since 1960, the percentage of babies born to unmarried Canadian, British, and American women—one-third of whom were teens—has more than quintupled. This increase stems from two trends: a decreasing birthrate among married women and a doubling of the birthrate among unmarried women. (Data from National Center for Health Statistics; Bureau of the Census [1998], Table 1347; and British Annual Abstract of Statistics, 1999.)

Short of abstinence, contraceptives are the surest strategy for preventing pregnancy. Yet only one-third of sexually active male teens used condoms consistently (Sonenstein, 1992). Why? Among the contributing factors are these:

1. ***Ignorance*** In eight surveys, fewer than half the adolescents could correctly identify the safe and risky times of the menstrual cycle (Morrison, 1985). Half of sexually active Canadian teen girls have mistaken ideas about which birth control methods will protect them from pregnancy and sexually transmitted diseases (Immen, 1995). Thus, most unwed teens report surprise at finding themselves pregnant (Brooks-Gunn & Furstenberg, 1989).

2. ***Guilt related to sexual activity*** Although sexual inhibitions reduce sexual activity, they also result in lack of planned birth control for those who do engage in sex (Gerrard & Luus, 1995). Not wanting to appear deliberately sexual or promiscuous, teens may hesitate to carry and produce a condom. When, as sometimes happens, passion overwhelms intentions, the result may be conception.

3. ***Minimal communication about birth control*** Many teenagers are uncomfortable discussing contraception with their parents, partners, and peers (Kotva & Schneider, 1990; Milan & Kilmann, 1987). Teens who talk freely with friends or parents and are in an exclusive relationship with a partner with whom they communicate openly are more likely to use contraceptives.

4. ***Alcohol use*** Sexually active teens are typically alcohol-using teens (National Research Council, 1987). By depressing the brain centers that control judgment, inhibition, and self-awareness, alcohol tends to break down normal restraints, a phenomenon well known to sexually coercive males.

5. ***Mass media norms of unprotected promiscuity*** The Planned Parenthood Federation (1986) has complained that television and movies help define sexual norms, which today are "Go for it *now*." An average hour of prime-time television on the three major U.S. networks contains approximately 15 sexual acts, words, and innuendos. Nearly all of these instances involve unmarried partners, and few communicate any concern for birth control or sexually transmitted disease (Sapolsky & Tabarlet, 1991). Planned Parenthood contends that repeated portrayals of unsafe sex, without consequence, amount to a campaign of sex disinformation.

Unprotected sex has led not only to an increase in teen pregnancies but also to increased rates of sexually transmitted disease (STD). More than 60 percent of new infections occur in persons under 25. Teenage girls, because of their less mature biological development and lower levels of protective antibodies, seem especially vulnerable to STD and associated risks of becoming infertile and developing certain cancers (Guttmacher, 1994; Morell, 1995). One response to these facts of life has been a shift to include teen abstinence within comprehensive sex education.

To comprehend the mathematics of sexually transmitted disease, imagine an island on which all people were virgins until they first began having sex a year ago. Pat has sex with 9 people, each of whom over the same time period has sex with 9 other people, who in turn have sex with 9 others. How many "phantom" sex partners (past partners of partners) will Pat have? Ohio State researchers Laura Brannon and Timothy

> "Will your child learn to multiply before she learns to subtract?"
>
> Anti–teen-pregnancy poster, Children's Defense Fund

> "All of us who make motion pictures are teachers, teachers with very loud voices."
>
> Film producer George Lucas, Academy Award ceremonies, 1992

FEIFFER

Brock (1994) report that the actual number—511—is more than five times what the average student guess is.

Given these odds, the rapid spread of STDs is not surprising. Although condoms sometimes fail, they reduce tenfold the risk of contracting HIV (human immuno-deficiency virus—the virus that causes AIDS) from an infected partner (Pinkerton & Abramson, 1997). With certain other skin-to-skin STDs—notably the human papilloma virus, which is responsible for most genital cancers—condoms are virtually useless (Medical Institute, 1994).

Throughout history, the pendulum of sexual values has swung—from the European eroticism of the early 1800s to the conservative Victorian era of the late 1800s, from the libertine flapper era of the 1920s to the family values period of the 1950s. With new voices decrying family disintegration and calling for a balance between sexual expression and restraint, the pendulum may have begun a new swing toward commitment in the twenty-first century. In West Germany, the percentage of teens who link sex with committed love is up significantly since 1970 (Schmidt & others, 1994). And would you agree or disagree that "if two people like each other, it's all right for them to have sex even if they've known each other for a very short time"? The percentage of first-year American college and university students who agree dropped from 52 percent in 1987 to 41 percent in 1999 (Sax & others, 1999).

Sexual Orientation

PREVIEW QUESTION 6 What does current research tell us about why some people are attracted to members of their own sex and others are attracted to members of the other sex?

To motivate is to energize and direct behavior. So far, we have considered the energizing of sexual motivation but not its direction. We express the direction of our sexual interest in our **sexual orientation**—our enduring sexual attraction toward members of a particular sex. Cultures vary in their attitudes toward homosexuality. As far as we know, all cultures in all times have been predominantly heterosexual (Bullough, 1990). Whether a culture condemns or accepts homosexuality, heterosexuality prevails and homosexuality survives.

Gay men and lesbians often recall childhood play preferences like those of the other sex (Bailey & Zucker, 1995). But most homosexual people report not becoming aware of same-sex attraction until during or shortly after puberty, and not thinking of themselves as gay or lesbian until around age 20 (Garnets & Kimmel, 1990).

How many people are exclusively homosexual? Until recently, the popular press assumed a homosexuality rate of 10 percent. But in both Europe and the United States, more than a dozen national surveys in the early 1990s explored sexual orientation, using methods that protected the respondent's anonymity. Their results agree in suggesting that a more accurate figure is about 3 or 4 percent of men and 1 or 2 percent of women (Laumann & others, 1994; National Center for Health Statistics, 1991; Smith, 1998). Fewer than 1 percent of the respondents' reported being actively bisexual, but a larger number of adults reported having had an isolated homosexual experience. And most people said they had had an occasional homosexual fantasy.

Health experts find it helpful to know sexual statistics, but numbers do not decide issues of human rights. Similarly, it's helpful in manufacturing school desks to know that about 10 percent of people are left-handed. But whether left-handers are 3 percent or 10 percent of the population doesn't answer the moral question of whether lefties should enjoy equal rights.

What does it feel like to be homosexual in a heterosexual culture? If you are heterosexual, one way to understand is to imagine how you would feel if you were ostracized or fired for openly admitting or displaying your feelings toward someone of

■ **sexual orientation** an enduring sexual attraction toward members of either one's own sex (homosexual orientation) or the other sex (heterosexual orientation).

"It has been maintained for years that we each use only about 10 percent of our brain capacity; that the condom failure rate is 10 percent; and until just last year, that 10 percent of Americans are homosexual. Such statistics are partly artifacts, I suspect, of our decimal system; in a base 12 system, we'd no doubt show a similar affinity for statistics that were multiples of 8.333 percent."

John Allen Paulos, "Counting on Dyscalculia," 1993

the other sex; if you overheard people making crude jokes about heterosexual people; if most movies, TV shows, and advertisements portrayed (or implied) homosexuality; and if your family members were pleading with you to change your heterosexual lifestyle and to enter into a homosexual marriage.

Facing such reactions, homosexual people often struggle with their sexual orientation. They may at first try to ignore or deny their desires, hoping they will go away. But they don't. Then they may try to change, through psychotherapy, willpower, or prayer. But the feelings typically persist, as do those of heterosexual people—who are similarly incapable of becoming homosexual (Haldeman, 1994). Eventually, homosexuals may accept their orientation—by electing celibacy (as do some heterosexuals); by engaging in promiscuous sex (a choice more commonly made by men than by women); by attempting suicide (which homosexual people are at increased risk for); or by entering into a committed, long-term love relationship (a choice more often made by women than by men) (Peplau, 1982; Remafedi, 1999; Weinberg & Williams, 1974).

Most psychologists today view sexual orientation as neither willfully chosen nor willfully changed. Sexual orientation in some ways is like handedness: Most people are one way, some (mostly men) the other. A very few are truly ambidextrous. Regardless, the way one is endures. Nor is sexual orientation linked with psychological disorder or sexual crime. "Child molester" is not a sexual orientation. Some child molesters are homosexual, but most are heterosexual males (Gonsiorek, 1982). Partly for these reasons, the American Psychiatric Association in 1973 dropped homosexuality from its list of "mental illnesses."

Understanding Sexual Orientation

If our sexual orientation is indeed something we do not choose and seemingly cannot change, then where do these preferences come from? How do we move toward either a heterosexual or a homosexual orientation? See if you can anticipate the consensus that has emerged from hundreds of research studies by responding yes or no to the following questions:

1. Is homosexuality linked with problems in a child's relationships with parents, such as with a domineering mother and an ineffectual father, or a possessive mother and a hostile father?
2. Does homosexuality involve a fear or hatred of people of the other gender, leading individuals to direct their sexual desires toward members of their own sex?
3. Is sexual orientation linked with levels of sex hormones currently in the blood?
4. As children, were many homosexuals molested, seduced, or otherwise sexually victimized by an adult homosexual?

Contrary to widely held ideas about homosexuality, the answer to all these questions is no (Storms, 1983). Consider the findings of lengthy Kinsey Institute interviews with nearly 1000 homosexuals and 500 heterosexuals (Bell & others, 1981; Hammersmith, 1982). The investigators assessed nearly every imaginable psychological cause of homosexuality—parental relationships, childhood sexual experiences, peer relationships, dating experiences. Their findings: Homosexuals were no more likely than heterosexuals to have been smothered by maternal love, neglected by their father, or sexually abused. And consider this: If "distant fathers" were more likely to produce homosexual sons, then shouldn't boys growing up in father-absent homes more often be gay? (They are not.) And shouldn't the rising number of such homes have led to a noticeable increase in the gay population? (It has not.)

More recent studies have also found that sons of homosexual men were *not* more likely to become gay if they lived with their gay dad, and that 9 in 10 children of lesbian mothers developed into heterosexuals (Bailey & others, 1995; Golombok &

Personal values affect sexual orientation less than they affect other forms of sexual behavior. Compared with people who rarely attend church, for example, those who attend regularly are one-third as likely to have cohabited before marriage, and they report having had many fewer sex partners. But (if male) they are just as likely to be homosexual (Smith, 1998).

Note that the scientific question is not "What causes homosexuality?" (or "What causes heterosexuality?") but "What causes differing sexual orientation?" In pursuit of answers, psychological science compares the backgrounds and physiology of people whose sexual orientations differ.

Tasker, 1996). If even being reared by a homosexual parent has no marked influence on sexual orientation, then having a gay or lesbian teacher or bus driver also seems unlikely to have an appreciable influence.

Homosexual people do, however, appear more often in certain populations:

- In America's dozen largest cities, the percentage of men identifying themselves as gay jumps to 9 percent, compared with only 1 percent in rural areas (Binson & others, 1995; Laumann & others, 1994).
- One study (Ludwig, 1995) of the biographies of 1004 eminent people found homosexual and bisexual people overrepresented (11 percent of the sample), especially among poets (24 percent), fiction writers (21 percent), and artists and musicians (15 percent).
- Men who have older brothers are somewhat more likely to be gay, reports Ray Blanchard (1997). Assuming the odds of homosexuality are roughly 3 percent among first sons, they rise to 4 percent among second sons and 5 percent for third sons. The reason for this curious phenomenon is unclear, though Blanchard suspects a maternal immune response that becomes stronger after each pregnancy with a male fetus.

Erick has two moms
Maria Christina Vlassidis (left) and Marie Tatro (center), who are lesbians, tell playmates of their son Erick, 8, that they are both his moms. Both women attend school conferences and support other aspects of his life. Studies suggest that being reared by lesbian or gay parents does not appreciably affect a child's sexual orientation.

So, what then does determine sexual orientation? One theory proposes that people develop same-sex erotic attachments if segregated by gender at the time their sex drive matures (Storms, 1981). But even in a tribal culture in which homosexual behavior is expected of all boys before marriage, heterosexuality prevails (Money, 1987). (As this illustrates, homosexual *behavior* does not always indicate a homosexual *orientation*.) Another theory proposes the opposite: that people develop romantic attachments to those who *differ* from, and thus are more fascinating than, the peers they associated with while growing up (Bell, 1982). The bottom line from a half-century's theory and research: If there are environmental factors that influence sexual orientation, we do not yet know what they are. If someone were to ask me, "What can I do to influence my child's sexual orientation?" my answer would have to be "I haven't a clue."

The Brain and Sexual Orientation

New research indicates that sexual orientation is at least partly physiological. Researcher Simon LeVay (1991) discovered this while studying sections of the hypothalamus taken from deceased heterosexual and homosexual people. As a gay scientist, LeVay wanted to do "something connected with my gay identity." He knew he had to avoid biasing the results, so he did the study "blind," without knowing which donors were gay. For nine months he peered through his microscope at a cell cluster he thought might be important. Then one morning, LeVay sat down and broke the codes. His discovery: The cell cluster was reliably larger in heterosexual men than in women and homosexual men. As the brain difference became apparent, "I was almost in a state of shock. . . . I took a walk by myself on the cliffs over the ocean. I sat for half an hour just thinking what this might mean" (LeVay, 1994).

It should not surprise us that brains differ with sexual orientation. Remember the maxim of this text: Although we find it convenient to talk separately of psychological and biological explanations, *everything psychological is simultaneously biological.* The critical question is, When did the brain difference begin? At conception? In the womb? During childhood or adolescence? Did experience produce the difference? Or did genes or prenatal hormones (or genes via prenatal hormones)?

LeVay does not view this neural center as a sexual orientation center; rather, he sees it as an important part of the neural pathway engaged in sexual behavior. He

"Gay men simply don't have the brain cells to be attracted to women."

Simon LeVay, *The Sexual Brain*, 1993

acknowledges that it's possible that sexual behavior patterns influence the brain's anatomy. In fish, birds, rats, and humans, brain structures vary with experience—including sexual experience, reports Marc Breedlove (1997). But LeVay believes it more likely that brain anatomy influences sexual orientation. Laura Allen and Roger Gorski (1992) offered a similar conclusion after discovering that a section of the fibers connecting the right and left hemispheres is one-third larger in homosexual men than in heterosexual men. "The emerging neuroanatomical picture," notes Brian Gladue (1994), "is that, in some brain areas, homosexual men are more likely to have female-typical neuroanatomy than are heterosexual men."

Genes and Sexual Orientation

The evidence suggests that genetic influence plays a role in sexual orientation (Hershberger, 1997; Whitam & others, 1993). One research team studied the twin brothers of homosexual men. Among their identical twin brothers, 52 percent were homosexual, as were 22 percent of fraternal twin brothers (Bailey & Pillard, 1991, 1995). In a follow-up study of homosexual women, a similar 48 percent of their identical twins were homosexual, as were 16 percent of their fraternal twins (Bailey & others, 1993). With half the identical twin pairs differing, we know that genes are not the whole story. Moreover, new studies using a diverse sample of Australian twins found somewhat lower rates of sexual similarity—although, again, identical twins were more likely than fraternal twins to share homosexual feelings (Bailey & others, 1997, 2000). This is the sort of pattern we expect to see when genes are having an *influence*. Moreover, with a single transplanted gene, scientists can now cause male fruit flies to display homosexual behavior (Zhang & Odenwald, 1995).

Prenatal Hormones and Sexual Orientation

The elevated rate of homosexual orientation even in fraternal twins might also result from their sharing the same prenatal environment. In animals and some exceptional human cases, sexual orientation has been altered by abnormal prenatal hormone conditions. German researcher Gunter Dorner (1976, 1988) pioneered this research by manipulating a fetal rat's exposure to male hormones, thereby "inverting" its sexual behavior. Female sheep will likewise show homosexual behavior if their pregnant mothers are injected with testosterone during a critical gestation period (Money, 1987).

With humans, a critical period for the brain's neural-hormonal control system may exist between the middle of the second and fifth months after conception (Ellis & Ames, 1987; Gladue, 1990; Meyer-Bahlburg, 1995). Exposure to the hormone levels typically experienced by female fetuses during this time appears to predispose the person (whether female or male) to be attracted to males in later life. Some tests reveal that homosexual men have spatial abilities like those typical of heterosexual women—a pattern consistent with the hypothesis that homosexuals were exposed to atypical prenatal hormones (Gladue, 1994; McCormick & Witelson, 1991; Sanders & Wright, 1997).

Curiously, gay men also have fingerprint patterns rather like those of heterosexual women. Most people have more fingerprint ridges on their right hand than on their left. Jeff Hall and Doreen Kimura (1994) observed that this difference is less true of females and gay males than of heterosexual males—a difference these researchers believe is due to prenatal hormones.

Lesbians may likewise have more male-typical anatomy. For example, the cochlea and hearing system of lesbians develop in a way that is "intermediate to those of heterosexual females and heterosexual males" (McFadden & Pasanen, 1998, 1999).

Because the physiological evidence is preliminary and controversial, some scientists remain skeptical. Rather than specifying sexual orientation, perhaps biological factors predispose a temperament that influences sexuality "in the context of individual learning and experience" (Byne & Parsons, 1993). Perhaps, theorizes Daryl Bem

> "Studies indicate that male homosexuality is more likely to be transmitted from the mother's side of the family."
>
> Robert Plomin, John DeFries, Gerald McClearn, and Michael Rutter, *Behavioral Genetics*, 1997

Lesbians are also nearly twice as likely as heterosexual women to be left-handed (Lalumiére & others, 2000).

(1996, 2000), genes code for prenatal hormones and brain anatomy, which predispose *temperaments* that lead children to prefer gender-typical or gender-atypical activities and friends. These preferences may later lead children to feel attracted to whichever sex feels different from their own. The dissimilar-seeming sex (whether or not it conforms to one's own anatomy) becomes associated with anxiety and other forms of arousal, which eventually gets transformed into romantic arousal. The exotic becomes erotic.

Regardless of the process, the consistency of the genetic, prenatal, and brain findings has swung the pendulum toward a physiological explanation. Nature more than nurture, most psychiatrists now believe, predisposes sexual orientation (Vreeland & others, 1995). If biological influences prove critical, such would explain why sexual orientation is so difficult to change.

Still, some people wonder: Should the cause of sexual orientation matter? Perhaps it shouldn't, but people's assumptions matter. Those who believe, as do most homosexual people, that sexual orientation is a biological given—disposed identity, not a choice—express more accepting attitudes toward homosexual persons (Allen & others, 1996; Furnham & Taylor, 1990; Whitley, 1990). In American surveys, agreement that homosexuality is "something a person is born with" rose from 13 to 31 percent between 1977 and 1998 (Newport, 1998). Over roughly the same period, support for equal job rights for gays and lesbians increased from 59 to 80 percent (Moore, 1993). And agreement "that homosexuality should be an acceptable alternative life-style" increased between 1982 and 1996 from 34 to 44 percent (Gallup, 1996; see also **FIGURE 24.3**). Acceptance is most common among women and those with a gay or lesbian friend or relative (Herek & Capitanio, 1996; Kite & Whitley, 1996).

To gay and lesbian activists, the new biological research is a double-edged sword (Diamond, 1993). If sexual orientation, like skin color and sex, is genetically influenced, that offers a further rationale for civil rights protection. Moreover, it may alleviate parents' concerns about their children having gay teachers and role models. It does, however, raise the haunting possibility that genetic markers of sexual orientation could someday be identified through fetal testing, and the fetus be aborted simply for being pre-homosexual.

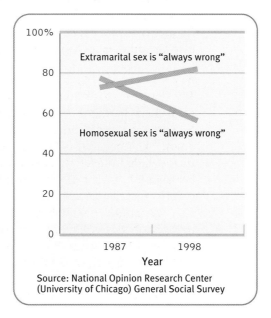

FIGURE 24.3
Changing attitudes
National Opinion Research Center surveys indicate that attitudes remain conservative regarding extramarital sex but are becoming more tolerant of homosexual sex in at least some circumstances.

Sex and Human Values

PREVIEW QUESTION 7 What roles do personal values play in sex research and sex education?

Recognizing that values are both personal and cultural, most sex researchers and educators strive to keep their writings on sexuality value-free.

But can the study of sexual behavior and what motivates it ever be free of values? Those who think not say that the very words we use to describe behavior often reflect our personal values. When sex researchers label sexually restrained individuals as "erotophobic" and as having "high sex guilt," they express their own values. Whether we label sexual acts we do not practice as "perversions," "deviations," or part of an "alternative sexual life-style" depends on our attitudes toward the behaviors. Labels describe, but they also evaluate.

CLOSE-UP:

THE NEED TO BELONG

We are what Aristotle called "the social animal." We have a need to affiliate with others, even to become strongly attached to certain others in enduring, close relationships. Human beings, contended the personality theorist Alfred Adler, have an "urge to community" (Ferguson, 1989). Roy Baumeister and Mark Leary (1995) have assembled evidence for this deep *need to belong*.

Aiding survival

Social bonds boosted our ancestors' survival rate. By keeping children close to their caregivers, attachments served as a powerful survival impulse. As adults, those who formed attachments were more likely to come together to reproduce and to stay together to nurture their offspring to maturity.

Cooperation in groups also enhanced survival. In solo combat, our ancestors were not the toughest predators. But as hunters they learned that six hands were better than two. Those who foraged in groups also gained protection from predators and enemies. If those who felt a need to belong were also those who survived and reproduced most successfully, their genes would in time predominate. The inevitable result: an innately social crea-

ture. People in every society on Earth belong to groups and tend to prefer and favor "us" over "them."

Wanting to belong

The need to belong colors our thoughts and emotions. We spend a great deal of time thinking about our actual and hoped-for relationships. When relationships form, we often feel joy. Falling in mutual love, people have been known to feel their cheeks ache from their irrepressible grins. Asked, "What is necessary for your happiness?" or "What is it that makes your life meaningful?" most people mention—before anything else—close, satisfying relationships with family, friends, or romantic partners (Berscheid, 1985). Happiness hits close to home.

Acting to increase social acceptance

When we feel included, accepted, and loved by those important to us, our self-esteem rides high. Indeed, say Mark Leary and his colleagues (1998), our self-esteem is a gauge of how valued and accepted we feel. Much of our social behavior therefore aims to increase our belonging—our social acceptance and inclusion. To avoid rejection, we generally conform to group standards and seek to make favorable impressions. To win friendship and esteem, we monitor our behavior, hoping to create the right impressions. Seeking love and belonging, we spend billions on clothes, cosmetics, and diet and fitness aids—all motivated by our quest for acceptance.

The need to belong
For most adults, the sharing of love in a sexual relationship fulfills not only a biological motive, but a social need for intimacy.

When education about sex is separated from the context of human values, some students may get the idea that sexual intercourse is simply a recreational activity. Diana Baumrind (1982), a University of California child-rearing expert, has observed that adolescents interpret sex education that pretends to be "value-free" as meaning that adults are neutral about adolescent sexual activity. Such an implication is unfortunate, she added, because "promiscuous recreational sex poses certain psychological, social, health, and moral problems that must be faced realistically."

Other researchers have found that teenagers who have had formal sex education are no more likely to engage in premarital sex than those who have not (Furstenberg & others, 1985; Zelnik & Kim, 1982). Moreover, we enrich our lives by knowing ourselves, by realizing that others share our feelings, by understanding what is likely

Like sexual motivation, which feeds both love and exploitation, the need to belong feeds both deep attachments and menacing threats. Out of our need to define a "we" come loving families, faithful friendships, and team spirit, but also teen gangs, ethnic rivalries, and fanatic nationalism.

Maintaining relationships

For most of us, familiarity breeds liking, not contempt. We resist breaking social bonds. Thrown together at school, at summer camp, on a vacation cruise, people resist the group's dissolution. Hoping to maintain our relationships, we promise to call, to write, to come back for reunions. Parting, we feel distress. The dark side of this is that attachments can keep people in abusive relationships; the fear of being alone may seem worse than the pain of emotional or physical abuse. The fear has some basis in reality. Children who move through a series of foster homes, with repeated disruption of budding attachments, may come to have difficulty forming deep attachments.

When something threatens or dissolves our social ties, negative emotions overwhelm us. For chil-

dren, even a brief time-out in isolation can be an effective punishment. For adults as well as children, social ostracism can be even more painful. To be shunned—given the cold shoulder or the silent treatment, with others' eyes avoiding yours—is to have one's need to belong threatened, observe Kipling Williams and Lisa Zadro (2001). People often respond to social ostracism with depressed moods, initial efforts to restore their acceptance, and then withdrawal. "It's the meanest thing you can do to someone, especially if you know they can't fight back. I never should have been born," said Lea, a lifelong victim of the silent treatment by her mother and grandmother. "I came home every night and cried. I lost 25 pounds, had no self-esteem and felt that I wasn't worthy," reported Richard, after two years of silent treatment by his employer.

Exile, imprisonment, and solitary confinement are progressively more severe forms of punishment. The bereaved often feel life is empty, pointless. Children reared in institutions without a sense of belonging to anyone, or locked away at home under extreme neglect, become pathetic creatures—withdrawn, fright-

ened, speechless. Adults denied acceptance and inclusion may feel depressed. Anxiety, jealousy, loneliness, and guilt all involve threatened disruptions of our need to belong. Even when bad relationships break, people suffer. In one 16-nation survey, separated and divorced people were only half as likely as married people to say they were "very happy" (Inglehart, 1990). After such separations, feelings of loneliness and anger—and sometimes even a strange desire to be near the former partner—are commonplace.

Fortifying health

Do you have close friends—people with whom you freely disclose your ups and downs? People who feel supported by close relationships live with better health and at lower risk for psychological disorder and premature death than do those who lack social support. Married people, for example, are less at risk for depression, suicide, and early death than are unattached people. All this evidence affirms Baumeister and Leary's (1995) contention that "human beings are fundamentally and pervasively motivated by a need to belong."

to please or displease our loved one. Witness the crumbling of falsehoods about homosexuality. Witness the growing realization that certain sexually explicit material can lead people to devalue and hurt others.

Perhaps we can agree that the knowledge provided by sex research is preferable to ignorance and yet also agree that researchers' values should be stated openly, enabling us to debate them and to reflect on our own values. We should remember that scientific research on sexual motivation does not aim to define the personal meaning of sex in our own lives. You could know every available fact about sex—that the initial spasms of male and female orgasm come at 0.8-second intervals, that the female nipples expand 10 millimeters at the peak of sexual arousal, that systolic blood pressure rises some 60 points and the respiration rate to 40 breaths per minute—but fail to understand the human significance of sexual intimacy (see Close-Up box).

"The relationship between women and men should be characterized not by patronizing behavior or exploitation, but by love, partnership, and trustworthiness. . . . Sexuality should express and reinforce a loving relationship lived by equal partners."

Towards a Global Ethic, 1993 **Parliament of the World's Religions**

Surely one significance of sexual intimacy is its expression of our profoundly social nature. Sex is a socially significant act. Men and women can achieve orgasm alone, yet most people find greater satisfaction while embracing their loved one. There is a yearning for closeness in sexual motivation. Sex at its human best is life-uniting and love-renewing, so helps satisfy our need to belong.

rehearse it!

1. In the 1940s, Alfred Kinsey and his colleagues used questionnaires to investigate human sexual behavior. Their results have been criticized because
   a. their sample was not large enough.
   b. their sample was not representative of the population as a whole.
   c. they asked leading questions.
   d. both b. and c. are true.

2. In describing the sexual response cycle, Masters and Johnson noted that
   a. a plateau phase followed orgasm.
   b. men experience a refractory period during which they could not experience orgasm.
   c. the feeling that accompanies orgasm is stronger in men than in women.
   d. testosterone is released in the female as well as in the male.

3. Daily and monthly fluctuations in hormone levels do not greatly affect sexual desire in humans. Over the life span, however, hormonal changes have significant effects. A striking effect of hormonal changes on human sexual behavior is the
   a. arousing influence of erotic materials.
   b. sharp rise in sexual interest at puberty.
   c. increase in women's sexual desire at the time of ovulation.
   d. increase in testosterone levels in castrated males.

4. Sexual behavior is motivated by internal biological factors, by external stimuli, and by imagined stimuli. An example of an external stimulus that might influence sexual behavior is
   a. blood level of testosterone.
   b. the onset of puberty.
   c. a sexually explicit film.
   d. an erotic fantasy or dream.

5. Aside from abstinence, contraception is the surest way of preventing pregnancy. More than half of all sexually active teens, however, either do not use contraceptives or do not use them regularly. Factors contributing to the epidemic of teen pregnancies include ignorance about reproduction and contraception, guilt about sexual behavior, mass media norms of promiscuity, insufficient communication about contraception, and
   a. the "just say no" attitude.
   b. the unavailability of abortion.
   c. the decreased rates of sexually transmitted diseases.
   d. alcohol use.

6. Sexual orientation refers to our enduring sexual attraction to members of a particular gender. Current research suggests several possible contributors to sexual orientation. Which of the following is *not* one of those contributors?
   a. Certain cell clusters in the hypothalamus
   b. Gender segregation during the time the sex drive matures
   c. A section of fibers connecting the right and left hemispheres of the brain
   d. Exposure to hormone levels typically experienced by female fetuses

REVIEWING

Sexual Motivation

1. What behavior patterns must a theory of sexual motivation explain?

A theory of sexual motivation should attempt to explain the broad range of sexual behaviors that vary across time and place. Kinsey's early data-collection efforts, although criticized for their methodology, were an attempt to survey these behaviors.

2. What are the stages of the human sexual response cycle?

Biologically, the human sexual response cycle normally follows a pattern of excitement, plateau, orgasm, and resolution. During the resolution phase, males enter a refractory period during which another orgasm is not possible.

3. What role do hormones play in human sexuality?

Sex hormones such as estrogen and testosterone help our bodies develop and function as either male or female. In many nonhuman animals, hormones also help to stimulate sexual activity, but in humans, they influence sexual behavior more loosely, especially once minimally sufficient hormone levels are present.

4. How do internal and external stimuli contribute to sexual arousal?

External stimuli can trigger sexual arousal in both men and women. Sexually explicit materials may also lead people to perceive their partners as comparatively less appealing and to devalue their relationships. In combination with the internal hormonal push and the external pull of sexual stimuli, imagined stimuli (fantasies) help trigger sexual arousal. Some sexual disorders respond well to behavioral treatment, which assumes that people can learn to modify their sexual responses.

5. What factors influence teenagers' sexual attitudes and behaviors?

Adolescents' physical maturation fosters a sexual dimension to their emerging identity. But culture is a big influence, too, as is apparent from varying rates of teen intercourse and pregnancy. Epidemic rates of sexually transmitted diseases have triggered new research and educational programs pertinent to adolescent sexuality.

6. What does current research tell us about why some people are attracted to members of their own sex and others are attracted to members of the other sex?

One's heterosexual or homosexual orientation seems neither willfully chosen nor able to be willfully changed. Evidence discounts certain environmental explanations of sexual orientation. Preliminary new evidence links sexual orientation with genetic influences, prenatal hormones, and the size of certain brain structures.

7. What roles do personal values play in sex research and sex education?

Sex research and education are not value-free. Sex-related values should therefore be discussed openly, recognizing the social significance of sexual expression.

TERMS AND CONCEPTS TO REMEMBER

sexual response cycle, p. 373
refractory period, p. 374

estrogen, p. 374
testosterone, p. 374

sexual disorder, p. 377

sexual orientation, p. 379

REHEARSE IT ANSWER KEY

1. d   2. b   3. b   4. c   5. d   6. b

25 Achievement Motivation

What is your greatest achievement to date? What is your greatest future ambition—to attain fame? Fortune? Creative accomplishment? Security? Love? Power? Wisdom? Spiritual wholeness?

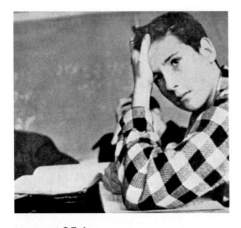

FIGURE 25.1

What is this boy daydreaming about? By analyzing responses to ambiguous photos like this, motivation researchers have sought clues to people's level of achievement motivation.

The biological perspective on motivation—the idea that physiological needs drive us to satisfy those needs—only partially explains what energizes and directs our behavior. Hunger and sex have both social and physiological components. Moreover, there are motives that, unlike hunger and sex, do not appear to satisfy any physical need. Billionaire entrepreneurs may be motivated to make ever more money, celebrities to become even more famous, dictators to achieve more power, daredevils to seek greater thrills. When fed, such motives, like our need to belong, seem not to diminish. The more we achieve, the more we may need to achieve.

Identifying Achievement Motivation

PREVIEW QUESTION 1 What characteristics are shared by people with a high need to achieve?

Think of someone you know who strives to succeed by excelling at any task where evaluation is possible. Now think of someone who is less driven. Psychologist Henry Murray (1938) defined the first person's high need for achievement, or **achievement motivation,** as a desire for significant accomplishment, for mastering skills or ideas, for control, and for rapidly attaining a high standard.

To study this motive, we first need a way to measure it. Studies on semistarved volunteers show that if driven by hunger we begin to fantasize about food. Our sexual orientation is similarly reflected in our prevalent sexual fantasies. If socially isolated, we think about those we love. Do these examples suggest a way to assess a person's need to achieve?

Murray and investigators David McClelland and John Atkinson presumed that people's fantasies would reflect their concern for achievement. So they asked research participants to invent stories about ambiguous pictures. If a person who was shown the daydreaming boy in **FIGURE 25.1** said the boy was preoccupied with pursuit of a goal, that he imagined himself performing a heroic act, or that he was feeling pride about some success, the researchers scored the response as indicating achievement concerns. If people's stories consistently included such themes, McClelland and Atkinson regarded them as having a high need for achievement.

Would you expect people whose stories express high achievement to prefer tasks that are easy, moderately challenging, or very difficult? People whose stories suggest low achievement motivation tend to choose either very easy or very difficult tasks, where failure is either unlikely or not embarrassing (Geen, 1984). Those whose stories express high achievement motivation tend to prefer moderately difficult tasks, where success is attainable yet attributable to their skill and effort. In a ring-toss game they often stand at an intermediate distance from the stake, enabling some successes while providing a suitable challenge. When things get difficult, people with a strong need to achieve do persist more (Cooper, 1983). By contrast, high school underachievers persist less in completing college degrees, holding on to jobs, and maintaining their marriages (McCall, 1994).

As you might expect from their persistence and eagerness for realistic challenges, people with high achievement motivation do achieve more. One study followed the lives of 1528 California children whose intelligence test scores were in the top 1 percent. Forty years later, when researchers compared those who were most and least successful professionally, they found a motivational difference. Those most successful were more ambitious, energetic, and persistent. As children, they had more active hobbies. As adults, they participated in more groups and favored participating in sports over being a spectator (Goleman, 1980).

Another study of outstanding scholars, athletes, and artists found that all were highly motivated and self-disciplined, willing to dedicate hours every day to the pursuit of their goals (Bloom, 1985). These superstar achievers were distinguished not so much by their extraordinary natural talent as by their extraordinary daily discipline. When their preparation met an opportunity, the result was success.

By their early twenties, top violinists have accumulated some 10,000 lifetime practice hours—double the practice time of other violin students aiming to be teachers (Ericsson & others, 1993). From his studies, Herbert Simon (1998), a psychologist who won the Nobel Prize for economics, estimates that world-class experts in a field typically have invested "at least 10 years of hard work—say, 40 hours a week for 50 weeks a year." Great achievement, it seems, mixes a teaspoon of inspiration with a gallon of perspiration.

Analyses of the life histories of great scientists, philosophers, political leaders, writers, and musicians confirm the importance of disciplined motivation. Great achievers, consumed by a passion to perfect their gift, are often continuously productive from an early age, notes Dean Keith Simonton (1994). So much so that a small proportion of contributors to any field produce most of its achievements. And we are not looking merely at intelligence. Intelligence is distributed like a *bell-shaped curve*—most scores fall near the average, with fewer and fewer scores lying near the extreme high or low ends of the scale. Achievements do not follow the same pattern—and that tells us that achievement involves much more than raw ability.

Sources of Achievement Motivation

PREVIEW QUESTION 2 Why are some of us driven to excel but others are not?

Why, despite having similar potentials, does one person become more motivated to achieve than another? Highly motivated children (and those least likely to drop out of school) often have parents and teachers who encourage their independence from an early age and praise and reward them for their successes (Teevan & McGhee, 1972; Vallerand & others, 1997). Such parents encourage their children to dress and feed themselves and to do well in school. When their children achieve, they express delight.

Theorists speculate that the high achievement motivation displayed by such children has *emotional* roots. They learn to associate achievement with positive emotions. There may also be *cognitive* roots, as children learn to attribute their achievements to their own competence and effort, raising their expectations (Dweck & Elliott, 1983). Experiments show that even children who are bribed into an activity such as writing will sustain their interest if led to attribute their involvement internally: "You look like the kind of [girl/boy] who understands how important it is to write correctly, and who really wants to be good at it" (Cialdini & others, 1998).

Intrinsic Motivation and Achievement

PREVIEW QUESTION 3 What is intrinsic motivation, and how can it be nurtured?

In the classroom, at work, and on the athletic field, two types of achievement motivation operate. **Intrinsic motivation** is the desire to perform a behavior for its own sake and to be effective. Intrinsically motivated people approach work or play seeking

■ **achievement motivation** a desire for significant accomplishment: for mastery of things, people, or ideas; for attaining a high standard.

■ **intrinsic motivation** a desire to perform a behavior for its own sake and to be effective.

"The more I practice the luckier I get."

Gary Player, golf professional

"They can because they think they can."

Virgil, *Aeneid*, 19 B.C.

The image of achievement
What motivates a person to study to the level of a Ph.D., learn five languages, and become a leading expert in international issues—as did Madeleine Albright, before becoming the U.S. representative to the United Nations and then the U.S. secretary of state?

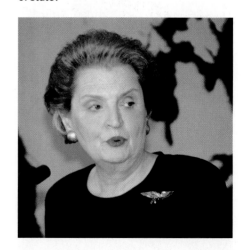

■ **extrinsic motivation** a desire to perform a behavior due to promised rewards or threats of punishment.

■ **industrial/organizational psychology** a subfield of psychology that studies and advises on workplace behavior. Industrial/organizational (I/O) psychologists help organizations select and train employees, boost morale and productivity, and design products and assess responses to them.

enjoyment, interest, self-expression, or challenge. **Extrinsic motivation** is seeking external rewards and avoiding punishments.

To sense the difference between extrinsic and intrinsic motivation, you might reflect on your own current experience. Are you feeling pressured to get this reading finished before a deadline? Worried about your course grade? Eager for rewards that depend on your doing well? If yes, then you are extrinsically motivated (as, to some extent, almost all students are). Are you also finding the course material interesting? Does learning it lead you to feel more competent? If there were no grade at stake, might you be curious enough to want to learn the material for its own sake? If yes, intrinsic motivation also fuels your efforts.

In sports, as in other activities, excessive external pressures and incentives can undermine our intrinsic enjoyment. When researcher Dean Ryan (1980) studied university football players, he found that those on athletic scholarships (who were, in a sense, playing for pay) enjoyed playing less than did the nonscholarship players. Had pay and pressure turned play into labor? Perhaps. But rewards can increase intrinsic motivation if their effect is to inform the players of their athletic competence (as with a "most improved player" award).

So, should coaches emphasize extrinsic pressures, rewards, and competition? Studies by motivation researchers Edward Deci and Richard Ryan indicate that it also depends on the goal (1985, 1992). For some, as for legendary football coach Vince Lombardi, "Winning isn't everything; it's the only thing." If so, it may pay to control the players with pressures and rewards for winning. But what if the goal is—as it should be for most programs of physical education, fitness, and amateur sports—the promotion of an enduring interest and participation in physical activity? In that case, as Deci and Ryan observed, "External pressures, competitive emphasis, and evaluative feedback are in contradiction to this goal." If children's soccer coaches want the kids to continue playing in the future, they should focus not on winning but on the joy of playing one's best.

Researchers in the psychology of religion have also explored intrinsic versus extrinsic motivation (Bergin, 1991; Gorsuch, 1988). Some religiously active people score high on tests of *extrinsic* religious motivation, by reporting their religion is a means to other ends. (They might agree, for example, that "a primary reason for my interest in religion is that my church is a congenial social activity.") Others score high on *intrinsic* religious motivation, by reporting their religion is an end in itself. ("My religious beliefs are what really lie behind my whole approach to life.") Compared with the extrinsically religious, intrinsically religious people tend to score lower on tests of prejudice and anxiety. They also tend to live with a greater sense of control over their lives and a clearer sense of purpose (Wulff, 1991).

Tiger Woods

"I remember a daily ritual that we had: I would call Pop at work to ask if I could practice with him. He would always pause a second or two, keeping me in suspense, but he'd always say yes. . . . In his own way, he was teaching me initiative. You see, he never pushed me to play" (quoted in *USA Weekend*, 1997).

Motivating People

PREVIEW QUESTION 4 How can effective leaders motivate others to seek higher levels of achievement?

This question is one of many that interest researchers in **industrial/organizational psychology,** which includes studies of how managers might best

■ promote teamwork and group achievement.
■ match people with jobs, by identifying motivated, well-suited personnel.
■ make jobs suit people, by creating work environments that boost morale and output.
■ evaluate performance and create incentives for excellence.

What every leader wants to know is "How can I manage in ways that enhance people's motivation, productivity, satisfaction?" (Satisfied workers aren't always more productive, but they are less likely to be absent or to quit.) Effective leaders cultivate intrinsic motivation, attend to people's motives, set goals, and choose an appropriate leadership style.

Cultivate Intrinsic Motivation

Given that intrinsic motivation stimulates achievement, especially in situations where people work independently (as students, teachers, executives, artists, and scientists often do), how can we encourage it? Here, from hundreds of studies, are the consistent answers: First, provide tasks that challenge and trigger curiosity (Malone & Lepper, 1986). Second, avoid snuffing out people's sense of self-determination with an overuse of controlling extrinsic rewards (Ryan & Deci, 2000).

Note that we can use extrinsic rewards in two ways: to *control* ("If you clean up your room, you can have some ice cream") or to *inform* someone of successes ("That was outstanding—congratulations!"). Attempts to *control* people's behaviors through rewards and surveillance may be successful as long as these controls are present. But, if taken away, people's interest in the activity often drops. Teachers who try hardest to boost their students' achievement on competency tests tend to be most controlling, thus ironically undermining their students' intrinsic interest. On the other hand, rewards that *inform* people that their efforts are paying off can boost their feelings of competence and intrinsic motivation (**FIGURE 25.2**).

There is an important practical principle here. Because the use of rewards to control undermines intrinsic motivation, parents, teachers, and managers should take care not to be overcontrolling. It is important to expect, support, challenge, and inform, but if you want to encourage internally motivated, self-directed achievements, do not overly control.

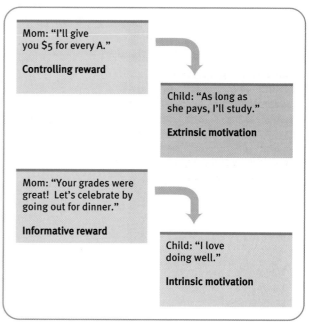

FIGURE 25.2
Rewards
The type of reward affects motivation.

Attend to People's Motives

Effective managerial styles vary with the people managed. To motivate people, Martin Maehr and Larry Braskamp (1986; Braskamp, 1987) advised managers to assess their people's motives and then adjust their managerial style accordingly. Challenge employees who value *accomplishment* to try new things and to strive for excellence. Give those who value *recognition* the attention they desire. Place those who value *affiliation* in a unit that has a family feeling and shares decision making. Motivate those who value *power* with competition and opportunities for triumphant success. Different strokes for different folks, but for each a way to motivate.

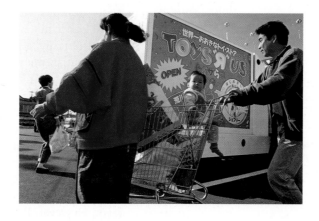

Toys "R" everywhere
Hiring Japanese top executives who know their own culture and listening to what they have to say has enabled Toys "R" Us and some other Western firms to succeed in Japanese markets.

Set Specific, Challenging Goals

In study after study, specific, challenging goals have motivated higher achievement, especially when combined with progress reports (Locke & Latham, 1990; Mento & others, 1987; Tubbs, 1986). Clear objectives, such as those you might set in planning your course work, serve to direct attention, promote effort, and stimulate creative strategies. When people find a goal reasonable, their reaching it or not affects their self-evaluation (White & others, 1995). So, to motivate high productivity, effective leaders work with people to define explicit goals and elicit commitments, and they provide feedback on progress.

"I knew exactly where I wanted to go and I focused on getting there. . . . Whether it's golf, basketball, business, family life, or even baseball, I set goals—realistic goals—and I focus on them." Michael Jordan, *I Can't Accept Not Trying*, 1994

■ **task leadership** goal-oriented leadership that sets standards, organizes work, and focuses attention on goals.

■ **social leadership** group-oriented leadership that builds teamwork, mediates conflict, and offers support.

"Good leaders don't ask more than their constituents can give, but they often ask—and get—more than their constituents intended to give or thought it was possible to give."

John W. Gardner, *Excellence,* **1984**

Choose an Appropriate Leadership Style

Whether a directive or a democratic leadership style works best depends on the situation and the leader. The best leadership style for leading a discussion is not the best style for leading troops on a charge (Fiedler, 1981). Moreover, different leaders are suited to different styles. Some excel at **task leadership**—setting standards, organizing work, and focusing attention on goals. Being goal-oriented, task leaders are good at keeping a group centered on its mission. Typically, they have a directive style, which can work well if the leader is bright enough to give good orders (Fiedler, 1987).

Other managers excel at **social leadership**—mediating conflicts and building the sort of team spirit that leads to high performance (Evans & Dion, 1991). Social leaders often have a democratic style: They delegate authority and welcome the participation of team members. Many experiments show that social leadership is good for morale. Subordinates usually feel more satisfied and motivated when they can participate in decision making (Burger, 1987; Spector, 1986).

John Williams and Deborah Best (1990, p. 15) have suggested an imaginary scenario in which we hear about two people: One is "adventurous, autocratic, coarse, dominant, forceful, independent, and strong." The other is "affectionate, dependent, dreamy, emotional, submissive, and weak." Did you picture the first person as a woman and the second as a man? If so, you are likely nearly alone. The world around, people perceive the first set of traits as more descriptive of men, the second set more of women. As leaders, men indeed tend to be directive, even autocratic, and women tend to be more democratic (Eagly & Johnson, 1990). When people interact, men are more likely to utter opinions, women to express support (Aries, 1987; Wood, 1987). In everyday behavior, men are more likely than women to act the ways powerful people do—to talk assertively, to interrupt, to initiate touching, to smile less, to stare (J. Hall, 1987; Major & others, 1990). Thus, despite great variations within each gender, women do more often excel at social leadership, men at task leadership (Eagly & Karau, 1991).

Ironically, a major influence on the "Japanese-style participative management" that has grown increasingly popular in North America was MIT social psychologist Kurt Lewin. In laboratory and factory experiments, Lewin and his students demonstrated the effects of worker participation on productivity. Shortly before World War II, Lewin visited Japan and explained his findings to industrial and academic leaders (Nisbett & Ross, 1991).

Because effective leadership styles vary with the situation and the person, the once-popular "great person" theory of leadership—that all great leaders share certain traits—fell out of favor. However, Peter Smith and Monir Tayeb (1989) have compiled data from studies in India, Taiwan, and Iran indicating that effective managers—whether in coal mines, banks, or government offices—often exhibit a high degree of *both* task and social leadership. As achievement-minded people, effective managers certainly care about how well work is done, yet at the same time they are sensitive to their subordinates' needs.

Effective leaders of laboratory groups, work teams, and large corporations also tend to exude a self-confident "charisma" (House & Singh, 1987; Shamir & others, 1993). Their charisma is a mix of a *vision* of some goal, an ability to *communicate* it clearly and simply, and enough optimism and faith in their group to *inspire* others to follow. Leadership of this kind motivates others to identify with and commit themselves to the group's mission.

Identifiable physiological mechanisms drive some motives, such as hunger (though external incentives and learned tastes matter, too). Other motives, such as achievement, are more obviously driven by psychological factors, such as an intrinsic quest for mastery and the external rewards of recognition. What unifies all motives is their common effect: the energizing and directing of behavior.

rehearse it!

1. Achievement motivation is defined as a desire for significant accomplishment, for mastering skills or ideas, for control, and for rapidly attaining a high standard. Given a choice of tasks, high achievers would select one that is
   a. very difficult, so they have an excuse for failure.
   b. very easy, so that they can avoid failure.
   c. moderately challenging, so that their success will be attributed to their skill and effort.
   d. extremely difficult, so that when they do complete the task, they can feel superior to others performing the same task.

2. Psychologists know that achievements are not distributed in a bell curve, as intelligence scores are. Achievement therefore must be more than just raw ability. Studies of highly motivated children have found that
   a. their parents tend to encourage their independence and praise and reward their successes.
   b. their teachers and caregivers use primarily extrinsic rewards.
   c. these children are aggressive, antisocial, and self-absorbed.
   d. these children are distinguished by extraordinary natural talent.

3. Psychologists identify two types of achievement motivation: extrinsic and intrinsic. Intrinsic motivation is a desire to perform a behavior because it is enjoyable and leads to feelings of mastery. For a violinist, an example of an intrinsic motive is the desire to
   a. earn enough to maintain an extravagant life-style.
   b. be promoted to concertmaster.
   c. perfect a difficult piece of music.
   d. obtain a positive grade or evaluation.

4. Task leadership is goal-oriented, while social leadership is group-oriented. Research indicates that effective managers exhibit
   a. only task leadership.
   b. only social leadership.
   c. task leadership for building teams and social leadership for setting standards.
   d. both task and social leadership, depending on the situation and the person.

REVIEWING

Achievement Motivation

1. What characteristics are shared by people with a high need to achieve?

Some human behaviors are energized and directed without satisfying any apparent biological need. Achieving personal goals, for example, may be motivated by a person's social needs for competence and independence. People with a high need to achieve tend to prefer moderately challenging tasks and tend to persist in accomplishing them.

2. Why are some of us driven to excel but others are not?

To understand why people with similar abilities often differ widely in their achievements, psychologists have studied highly motivated children. Many achievement-motivated children have parents and teachers who encourage and affirm independent achievement rather than overly controlling them with external rewards and threats.

3. What is intrinsic motivation, and how can it be nurtured?

Intrinsic motivation is the desire to be effective and to perform a behavior for its own sake. Rewards that boost people's sense of competence or inform them of improvement may increase intrinsic motivation. Rewards used to control behavior (extrinsic motivation) do not.

4. How can effective leaders motivate others to seek higher levels of achievement?

Industrial/organizational psychologists explore how best to create a motivated, productive, and satisfied work force. Rewards may increase intrinsic motivation if used not to control people but to boost their sense of competence or to inform them of improvement. Effective managers adjust their managerial style in response to workers' motives; set specific, challenging goals; and combine goal-oriented task leadership with group-oriented social leadership, according to the needs of the situation.

TERMS AND CONCEPTS TO REMEMBER

achievement motivation, p. 388
intrinsic motivation, p. 389

extrinsic motivation, p. 390
industrial/organizational
  psychology, p. 390

task leadership, p. 392

social leadership, p. 392

REHEARSE IT ANSWER KEY

1. c   2. a   3. c   4. d

Emotions, Stress, and Health

No one needs to tell you that feelings add color to your life, or that in times of stress they can disrupt your life or save it. Of all the species, we seem the most emotional (Hebb, 1980). More often than any other creature, we express fear, anger, sadness, joy, and love.

Fictional characters help us imagine life without emotion. Data, the human-appearing android in *Star Trek: The Next Generation,* embodied cool, rational, emotionless intelligence. Data's brilliance and cool logic gave him superhuman analytical intelligence. And yet he realized something was missing. He tried to write poetry, but without the passions of the heart it fell flat. Data's intellectual curiosity led him to wonder about fear, anger, and joy. But try as he might, he could not create such feelings. Data was all cognition, no emotion.

Back in the real world, consider the case of Elliot. Elliot has normal intelligence and memory. But since removal of a brain tumor he has lived without emotion. "I never saw a tinge of emotion in my many hours of conversation with him," reported neuroscientist Antonio Damasio (1994, p. 45), "no sadness, no impatience, no frustration." Shown disturbing pictures of injured people, destroyed communities, and natural disasters, Elliot shows—and realizes he feels—no emotion. He knows but he cannot feel. And lacking emotional signals, his social intelligence plummeted. He lost his job. He went bankrupt. His marriage collapsed. He remarried and divorced again. And he is now dependent on custodial care from a sibling and a disability check.

What do we know about emotions? How do our emotional responses affect our well-being? The research findings on the three components of emotion—the physiological response to stimuli, the expressive behaviors, and the conscious experience of the emotion—are the topics of Modules 26 and 27. Then in Modules 28 and 29 we consider what stress is, how it affects our health, and what we can do to cope with life's stresses and promote good health.

26 Theories and Physiology of Emotion

Not only emotion, but most psychological phenomena (vision, sleep, memory, sex, and so forth) can be approached these three ways—physiologically, behaviorally, and cognitively.

■ **emotion** a response of the whole organism, involving (1) physiological arousal, (2) expressive behaviors, and (3) conscious experience.

■ **James-Lange theory** the theory that our experience of emotion is our awareness of our physiological responses to emotion-arousing stimuli.

■ **Cannon-Bard theory** the theory that an emotion-arousing stimulus simultaneously triggers (1) physiological responses and (2) the subjective experience of emotion.

PREVIEW QUESTION 1 What are the components of an emotion?

Where do emotions come from? What are they made of? Imagine that, while walking home along a deserted street late at night, you hear the rumble of an engine and think someone in a car is stalking you. Emotions are your body's adaptive response. They focus your attention and prepare you for action. Your heart begins to race, you quicken your pace, you wonder about the driver's intent, and you feel scared. As this illustrates, **emotions** are a mix of (1) physiological activation (heart pounding), (2) expressive behaviors (quickened pace), and (3) conscious experience (interpreting the person's intent and feeling fearful). The puzzle is how these three pieces fit together: Did you first notice your heart racing and your faster step, and then feel afraid? Or did your sense of fear come first, stirring your heart and legs to respond?

Theories of Emotion

The James-Lange and Cannon-Bard Theories

PREVIEW QUESTION 2 Does physiological arousal precede or follow an emotional experience? (Does your heart pound because you are afraid, or are you afraid because you feel your heart pounding?)

Common sense tells most of us that we cry because we are sad, lash out because we are angry, tremble because we are afraid. First comes conscious awareness, then the physiological trimmings. But to pioneering psychologist William James this commonsense view of emotion was 180 degrees out of line. According to James, "We feel sorry because we cry, angry because we strike, afraid because we tremble" (1890, p. 1066). After you evade an oncoming car in your lane, you may notice your racing heart and *then* feel shaken with fright. Your feeling of fear follows your body's response. James' idea, which was also proposed by Danish physiologist Carl Lange, is called the **James-Lange theory.**

The James-Lange theory struck U.S. physiologist Walter Cannon (1871–1943) as implausible. Cannon thought the body's responses were not distinct enough to evoke the different emotions. Does a racing heart signal fear, anger, or love? Also, changes in heart rate, perspiration, and body temperature seemed too slow to trigger sudden emotion. Cannon, and later another physiologist, Philip Bard, concluded that physiological arousal and our emotional experience occur simultaneously: The emotion-triggering stimulus is routed simultaneously to the brain's cortex, causing the subjective awareness of emotion, and to the sympathetic nervous system, causing the body's arousal. Thus, this **Cannon-Bard theory** implies that your heart begins pounding as you experience fear; one does not cause the other (**FIGURE 26.1**).

As long as the evidence suggested that our physiological reactions to different emotions were much the same, the James-Lange assumption that we experience our emotions through differing body states seemed improbable. But then new evidence showed subtle physiological distinctions among the emotions, and the James-Lange theory again became plausible. James struggled with his own feelings of depression and grief, and in doing so he came to believe that we can control emotions by going

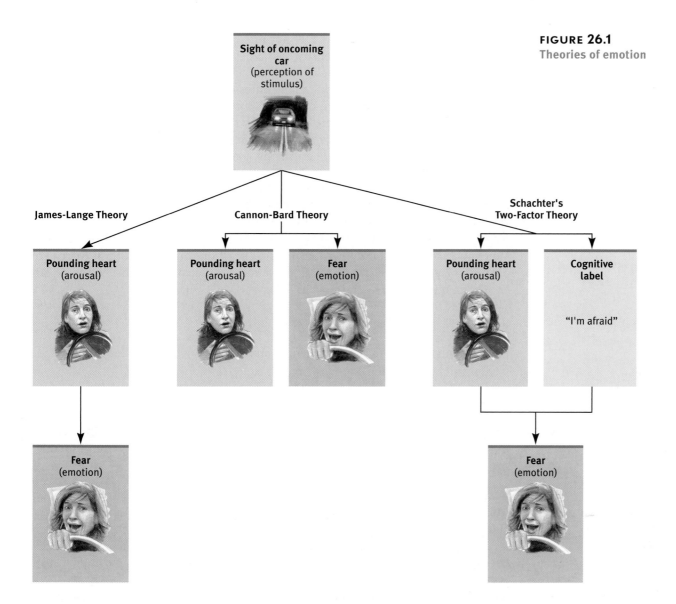

FIGURE 26.1
Theories of emotion

"through the outward motions" of whatever emotion we want to experience. "To feel cheerful," he advised, "sit up cheerfully, look around cheerfully, and act as if cheerfulness were already there." The last few decades' findings concerning emotional effects of facial expressions, as we will see, are precisely what James might have predicted.

Let's check your understanding of the James-Lange and Cannon-Bard theories. Imagine that your brain could not sense your heart pounding or your stomach churning. According to each theory, how would this affect your experienced emotions?

Cannon and Bard would have expected you to experience emotions normally, because they believed emotions occur separately from (though simultaneously with) the body's arousal. James and Lange would have expected greatly diminished emotions because they believed that to experience emotion you must first perceive your body's arousal.

The condition you imagined actually exists in people with severed spinal cords. Psychologist George Hohmann (1966) interviewed 25 soldiers who suffered such injuries in World War II. He asked them to recall emotion-arousing incidents that occurred before and after their spinal injuries. Those with injuries in the lower part of the spine, who had lost sensation only in their legs, reported little change in

"Whenever I feel afraid
I hold my head erect
And whistle a happy tune."

Richard Rodgers and Oscar Hammerstein,
The King and I, 1958

■ **two-factor theory** Schachter's theory that to experience emotion one must (1) be physically aroused and (2) cognitively label the arousal.

"Every moment is more intense."

Paralyzed actor Christopher Reeve (1995)

their emotions. Those who could feel nothing below the neck reported a considerable decrease in emotional intensity (as James and Lange would have expected). These soldiers said that although they might act much the same as before in emotional situations, the anger, as one man confessed, "just doesn't have the heat to it that it used to. It's a mental kind of anger." But emotions expressed mostly in body areas above the neck are felt more intensely by those with spinal cord injury. Virtually all the men Hohmann interviewed reported increases in weeping, lumps in the throat, and getting choked up when saying good-bye, worshipping, or watching a touching movie.

Although such evidence breathed new life into the James-Lange theory, most researchers agree with Cannon and Bard that our experienced emotions also involve cognition (Averill, 1993). Whether we fear the man behind us on the dark street depends entirely on whether we interpret his actions as threatening or friendly. With James and Lange we can say that our physical reactions are an important ingredient of emotion. And with Cannon and Bard we can say that there is more to the experience of emotion than reading our physiology.

Cognition and Emotion

PREVIEW QUESTION 3 To experience emotions, must we consciously interpret and label them?

Now, a second and more recent controversy: Put simply, what is the connection between what we *think* and how we *feel*? Which is the chicken and which the egg? Do our emotions always grow from our thoughts? Are our feelings always subject to our mind's appraisal of a situation? Or can we experience emotion apart from thinking? The issue has practical implications for self-improvement.

Schachter's Two-Factor Theory of Emotion

Most psychologists today believe that our cognitions—our perceptions, memories, and interpretations—are an essential ingredient of emotion. One such theorist, Stanley Schachter, proposed a **two-factor theory,** in which emotions have two ingredients: physical arousal and a cognitive label (Figure 26.1). Like James and Lange, Schachter presumed that our experience of emotion grows from our awareness of our body's arousal. Yet like Cannon and Bard, Schachter also believed that emotions are physiologically similar. Thus, in his view, an emotional experience requires a conscious interpretation of the arousal.

The spillover effect
Arousal from a soccer match can fuel disorder, as happened in Hillsborough, England, in 1989. Too many people were trying to squeeze into too small an area, and in the charged atmosphere of the game, many people were hurt and crushed to death.

Sometimes our arousal response to one event spills over into our response to the next event. Imagine that after an invigorating run you arrive home to find a message that you got a longed-for job. With arousal lingering from the run, would you feel more elated than if you had received this news after awakening from a nap?

To find out whether this spillover effect exists, Schachter and Jerome Singer (1962) aroused college men with injections of the hormone epinephrine. Picture yourself as one of these students: After receiving the injection, you go to a waiting room, where you find yourself with another person (actually an accomplice of the experimenters) who is acting either euphoric or irritated. As you observe this person, you begin to feel your heart race, your body flush, and your breathing become more rapid. If told to expect these effects from the injection, what would you feel? The students in Schachter and Singer's study felt little emotion—because they attributed their arousal to the drug. But if told the injection would produce no effects, what would you feel? Perhaps you would react, as another group of participants did, by "catching" the apparent emotion of the person you are with—becoming happy if the accomplice is acting euphoric, and testy if the accomplice is acting irritated.

This discovery—that a stirred-up state can be experienced as one emotion or another very different one, depending on how we interpret and label it—has been replicated in dozens of experiments. Although emotional arousal is not as undifferentiated as Schachter believed, arousal can intensify just about any emotion (Reisenzein, 1983; Sinclair & others, 1994). Insult people who have just been aroused by pedaling an exercise bike or watching rock videos and they will find it easy to misattribute their arousal to the provocation. Their feelings of anger will be greater than those of people who were similarly provoked but were not previously aroused. Arousal from emotions as diverse as anger, fear, and sexual excitement can spill from one emotion to another (Zillmann, 1986). In anger-provoking situations, sexually aroused people react with more hostility; and the arousal that lingers after an intense argument or a frightening experience may intensify sexual passion (Palace, 1995). Arousal fuels emotion; cognition channels it.

Must Cognition Precede Emotion?

So, to experience an emotion, must we first label our arousal? If Robert Zajonc (pronounced ZI-yence; 1980, 1984a) is right, the answer is no. He argues that our emotional reactions can be quicker than our interpretations of a situation; we therefore feel some emotions *before* we think. When people repeatedly view stimuli flashed too briefly for them to perceive and recall, they nevertheless come to prefer these stimuli. Without being consciously aware of having seen the stimuli, they rather like them. A subliminally flashed smiling or angry face can also prime us to feel better or worse about a follow-up stimulus (Murphy & others, 1995).

Research on neurological processes shows how we can experience emotion before cognition. Some neural pathways involved in emotion bypass the cortical areas involved in thinking. One such pathway runs from the eye or ear via the thalamus to the amygdala, an emotional control center. This shortcut enables a quick, precognitive emotional response before the intellect intervenes. Indeed, the amygdala sends more neural projections up to the cortex than it receives back; this makes it easier for our feelings to hijack our thinking than for our thinking to rule our feelings, note Joseph LeDoux and Jorge Armony (1999). After the cortex has further interpreted a threat, the thinking brain can take over (**FIGURE 26.2** on page 400). In the forest, we jump at the sound of rustling leaves nearby, leaving the cortex to decide later whether the sound was made by a predator or just the wind. Such an experience supports Zajonc's belief that *some* of our emotional reactions involve no deliberate thinking and that cognition is not always necessary for emotion. The heart is not always subject to the mind.

FIGURE 26.2

The brain's shortcut for emotions
Sensory input may be routed through the thalamus both to the cortex and directly to the amygdala for a more instant emotional reaction.

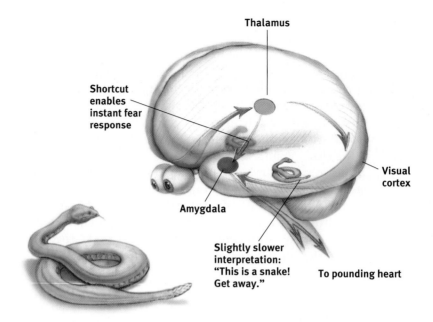

Thalamus

Shortcut enables instant fear response

Visual cortex

Amygdala

Slightly slower interpretation: "This is a snake! Get away."

To pounding heart

Can you recall disliking something or someone immediately, without knowing why?

Emotion researcher Richard Lazarus (1991, 1998) disagrees. He does concede that our brains process and react to vast amounts of information without our conscious awareness, and he willingly grants that some emotional responses do not require *conscious* thinking. Nevertheless, he points out, even instantaneously felt emotions require some sort of cognitive appraisal of the situation; otherwise, how do we *know* what we are reacting to? The appraisal may be effortless and we may not be conscious of it, but it is still a mental function (**FIGURE 26.3**). Emotions arise when we *appraise* an event as beneficial or harmful to our well-being, whether we truly know it is or not. We appraise the sound of the rustling leaves as the presence of a predator. We learn after the appraisal that it was "just the wind."

For us, the important conclusion concerns what Lazarus and Zajonc agree on: Some emotional responses—especially simple likes, dislikes, and fears—involve no conscious thinking. We may fear the spider, even if we "know" it is harmless. Such responses are difficult to alter by changing our thinking.

Other emotions—including moods such as depression and complex feelings such as hatred and love—are greatly affected by our interpretations, memories, and expectations. For these emotions, learning to *think* more positively about ourselves and the world around us helps us *feel* better. This seemingly simple idea has been an important part of therapy for some psychological disorders.

FIGURE 26.3

Two routes to emotion
As Zajonc emphasizes, some emotional responses are immediate, before any conscious appraisal. As Lazarus and Schachter emphasize, our appraisal and labeling of events also determine our emotional responses.

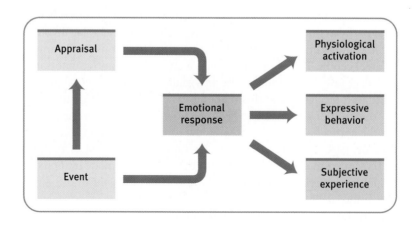

Appraisal

Physiological activation

Emotional response

Expressive behavior

Event

Subjective experience

1. Two important theories of emotion are the James-Lange theory and the Cannon-Bard theory. The James-Lange theory states that our experience of an emotion is a consequence of our physiological response to a stimulus; we are afraid because our heart pounds. The Cannon-Bard theory proposes that the physiological response (like heart pounding) and the subjective experience of, say, anger
   a. are unrelated.
   b. occur simultaneously.
   c. occur in the opposite order (with feelings of fear first).
   d. are regulated by the thalamus.

2. Assume that after spending an hour on a treadmill, you receive a letter saying that your scholarship to college has been approved. The two-factor theory of emotion would predict that your physical arousal will
   a. weaken your happiness.
   b. intensify your happiness.
   c. transform your happiness into relief.
   d. have no particular effect on your happiness.

3. Research suggests that we can experience an aroused state as one of several different emotions, depending on how we interpret and label the arousal. If physically aroused by swimming, then heckled by an onlooker, we may interpret our arousal as anger and
   a. become less physically aroused.
   b. feel angrier than usual.
   c. feel less angry than usual.
   d. feel sexually aroused.

4. Robert Zajonc maintains that some of our emotional reactions occur before we have had the chance to label or interpret them. Richard Lazarus disagrees. The two psychologists differ about whether emotional responses occur in the absence of
   a. physical arousal.
   b. the hormone epinephrine.
   c. cognitive processing.
   d. learning.

THE PHYSIOLOGY OF EMOTION

Arousal

PREVIEW QUESTION 4 What physiological changes accompany emotional arousal?

Emotion physically arouses you. Some physical responses you easily notice. As you hear a motorcycle rumbling up alongside you on a dark street, your muscles tense, your stomach develops butterflies, your mouth becomes dry.

Your body also mobilizes for action in less noticeable ways. To provide energy, your liver pours extra sugar into your bloodstream. To help burn the sugar, your respiration increases to supply needed oxygen. Your digestion slows, diverting blood from your internal organs to your muscles. With blood sugar driven into the large muscles, running becomes easier. Your pupils dilate, letting in more light. To cool your stirred-up body, you perspire. If you were wounded, your blood would clot more quickly. After your next crisis, think of this: Without any conscious effort, your body's response to danger was wonderfully coordinated and adaptive—preparing you to fight or flee.

Your *autonomic nervous system* controls all these aspects of arousal (**FIGURE 26.4**). Its sympathetic division activates arousal by directing the adrenal glands atop the kidneys to release the stress hormones epinephrine (adrenaline) and norepinephrine (noradrenaline). The surge in epinephrine and norepinephrine increases heart rate, blood pressure, and blood sugar levels. When the crisis passes, the parasympathetic neural centers become active, calming the body. Even after the parasympathetic division inhibits further release of stress hormones, those already in the bloodstream linger awhile, so arousal diminishes gradually.

Prolonged arousal, produced by sustained stress, taxes the body. Yet in many situations arousal is adaptive. Too little arousal (say, sleepiness) can be as disruptive as extremely high levels of arousal. When you're taking an exam, it pays to be moderately aroused—alert, but not trembling with nervousness.

"Fear lends wings to his feet."

Virgil, *Aeneid*, 19 B.C.

One explanation of sudden death caused by a voodoo "curse" is that the terrified person's parasympathetic nervous system, which calms the body, overreacts to the extreme arousal by slowing the heart to a stop (Seligman, 1974).

FIGURE 26.4

Emotional arousal

Emotional arousal involves autonomic nervous system activation.

Autonomic nervous system controls physiological arousal

Sympathetic division (arousing)		Parasympathetic division (calming)
Pupils dilate	EYES	Pupils contract
Decreases	SALIVATION	Increases
Perspires	SKIN	Dries
Increases	RESPIRATION	Decreases
Accelerates	HEART	Slows
Inhibits	DIGESTION	Activates
Secrete stress hormones	ADRENAL GLANDS	Decrease secretion of stress hormones

FIGURE 26.5

Arousal and performance

Performance peaks at lower levels of arousal for difficult tasks, and at higher levels for easy or well-learned tasks.

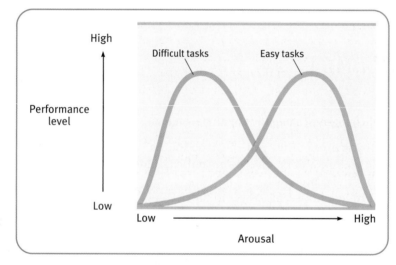

Although we usually perform best when our arousal is moderate, the level of arousal for optimal performance varies for different tasks. With easy or well-learned tasks, peak performance comes with relatively high arousal, which enhances the dominant, usually correct, response. With more difficult or unrehearsed tasks, the optimal arousal is somewhat lower (**FIGURE 26.5**). Runners, who are performing a well-learned task, usually achieve their peak performances when highly aroused by competition. Basketball players shooting free throws—a less automatic skill—may not perform quite as well if a packed fieldhouse makes them hyperaroused (Sokoll & Mynatt, 1984). Likewise, students who feel great anxiety during exams perform more poorly than those equally able but more confident. Teaching anxious students how to relax before an exam often enables them to perform better (Hembree, 1988).

Physiological States Accompanying Specific Emotions

PREVIEW QUESTION 5 Do different emotions activate different physiological responses?

Imagine conducting an experiment exploring physiological signs of arousal. In each of four rooms, you have someone watching a movie: In the first, the person is viewing a horror show; in the second, a film sure to provoke anger; in the third, a sexually arousing film; in the fourth, an utterly boring movie. From the control center you monitor each person's physiological responses, examining their perspiration, breathing, and heart rates. Do you think you could tell who was frightened? Who was angry? Who was sexually aroused? Who was bored?

With training, you could probably pick out the bored viewer. But discerning physiological differences among fear, anger, and sexual arousal, with their similar symptoms of arousal, is much more difficult (Cacioppo & others, 1997; Zillmann, 1986).

Fear, anger, and sexual arousal certainly *feel* different (and, as we shall see, cognitively *are* different). If you are terrified, you may feel a clutching, sinking sensation in your chest and a knot in your stomach. If angry, you may feel "hot under the collar" and will likely experience a pressing inner tension. If sexually stimulated, you will experience a genital response. Yet despite similar arousal, frightened and angry people also *look* different—"paralyzed with fear" and "ready to explode." Knowing this, is it possible to pinpoint some distinct physiological indicators of each emotion?

The finger temperatures and hormone secretions that accompany fear and rage sometimes differ (Ax, 1953; Levenson, 1992). The arousal that accompanies negative fear and positive excitement may lead to similar increases in heart rate but different versions of muscle tension, recorded above the eyes in a subtle frown or below them in a smile (Witvliet & Vrana, 1995). Different emotions also arise through different brain circuits (Kalin, 1993; Panksepp, 1982). Stimulate one area of a cat's limbic system (the brain structures associated with emotions) and it will pull back in terror at the sight of a mouse. Stimulate another limbic area and the cat will look enraged—pupils dilated, fur and tail erect, claws out, hissing furiously.

As people experience negative emotions such as disgust, their right hemisphere becomes more electrically active. One man, having lost part of his right frontal lobe in brain surgery, became, his not-unhappy wife reported, less irritable and more affectionate (Goleman, 1995). The left hemisphere activates when processing positive emotions (Davidson, 1999). For some infants and adults, the left frontal lobe shows more activity than the right. These individuals are typically more cheerful and less

> "No one ever told me that grief felt so much like fear. I am not afraid, but the sensation is like being afraid. The same fluttering in the stomach, the same restlessness, the yawning. I keep on swallowing."
>
> C. S. Lewis, *A Grief Observed*, 1961

In 1966, a young man named Charles Whitman killed his wife and mother and then climbed to the top of a tower at the University of Texas and shot 38 people. An autopsy later revealed a tumor in his limbic system.

Emotional arousal
Elated excitement and panicky fear involve similar physiological arousal. That allows us to flip rapidly between the two emotions.

LIE DETECTION

Given the physical indicators of emotion, might we, like Pinocchio, give some telltale sign whenever we lie? The *lie detector,* or **polygraph,** was once used mainly in law enforcement and national security work. But by the mid-1980s, 2 million Americans annually were reportedly being tested, usually by corporations trying to screen applicants for honesty or to uncover employee theft (Holden, 1986a).

Just what does a polygraph do? First of all, it does not literally detect lies. Rather, it measures several of the arousal responses that accompany emotion, such as changes in breathing, blood pressure, and perspiration. While you try to relax, the examiner measures your physiological responses as you answer questions. Some of these, called *control questions,* are designed to make anyone a little nervous. If asked, "In the last 20 years, have you ever taken something that didn't belong to you?" many peo-

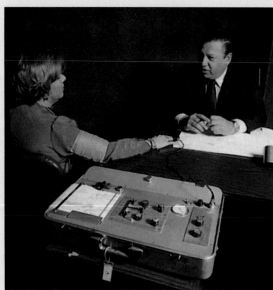

Who's lying? Can polygraph tests like this identify liars, or are its promoters putting something over on a gullible public? To learn more about this disputed issue, read on.

ple will tell a white lie and say no, causing arousal that the polygraph would detect. If your physiological reactions to the critical questions ("Did you ever steal anything from your previous employer?") are weaker than to the control ques-

tions, the examiner infers you are telling the truth. The assumption is that only a thief becomes agitated when denying a theft.

But there are two problems with this approach. First, our physiological arousal is much the same from one emotion to another. The polygraph cannot distinguish among anxiety, irritation, and guilt—they all appear as arousal. Second, an innocent person might also respond with heightened tension to the accusations implied by the critical questions. Many rape victims, for example, "fail" lie detector tests when reacting emotionally while telling the truth about their assailant (Lykken, 1992).

Thus, these tests err about one-third of the time. The "lie detector" could more accurately be called a fear detector. The test more often labels the innocent guilty—when the relevant question upsets the honest person—than the guilty innocent (**FIGURE 26.6**).

readily threatened or depressed than those with more active right frontal lobes. The left frontal lobe's rich supply of dopamine receptors may help explain why a peppy left hemisphere correlates with a perky disposition.

So, although emotions as varied as fear and anger involve a similar general autonomic arousal (thanks to the sympathetic nervous system), there are real, if subtle, physiological differences that help explain why we experience them so differently. Moreover, the physical accompaniments of emotion appear innate and universal—the same in a village on Sumatra as in one in North America (Levenson & others, 1991).

FIGURE 26.6

How often do lie detectors lie?

Benjamin Kleinmuntz and Julian Szucko (1984) had polygraph experts study the polygraph data of 50 theft suspects who later confessed to being guilty and 50 suspects whose innocence was later established by someone's confession. Had the polygraph experts been the judges, more than one-third of the innocent would have been declared guilty, and almost one-fourth of the guilty would have been declared innocent.

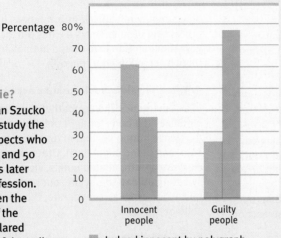

Percentage

Innocent people | Guilty people

■ Judged innocent by polygraph
■ Judged guilty by polygraph

Because the polygraph cannot discriminate the arousal of guilty lying from fearful honesty, "tens of thousands of polygraph screening exams administered by the CIA, the FBI, and the National Security Agency have yet to uncover a single spy," noted Robert Park (1999). Meanwhile Aldrich Ames, who enjoyed an unexplained lavish lifestyle while a Russian spy within the CIA, went undetected. Ames "took scores of polygraph tests and passed them all," notes Park. "Nobody thought to investigate the source of his sudden wealth—after all, he was passing the lie detector tests." The truth is, lie detectors can lie.

The fear-detection ability of the polygraph has not gone unnoticed. Although polygraphs are too error-prone for use in testing applicants and employees, police sometimes use them to induce confessions from criminals—by scaring them into thinking that any lies will be transparent. Even so, more than 9 in 10 psychophysiologists and research psychologists agreed in a recent survey that savvy criminals and spies could beat the test by augmenting their arousal to control questions, such as biting their tongue (Iacono & Lykken, 1997). A more effective approach uses the *guilty knowledge test,* which assesses a suspect's physiological responses to the details of a crime known only to the police and the guilty person. If a camera and money had been stolen, the polygraph examiner could notice whether the suspect reacts strongly to the specific brand name of the camera and the dollar amounts. Presumably, only one guilty of the crime would have such responses. Given enough such specific probes, an innocent person would seldom be wrongly accused.

■ **polygraph** a machine, commonly used in attempts to detect lies, that measures several of the physiological responses accompanying emotion (such as perspiration, heart rate, blood pressure, and breathing changes).

---

rehearse it!

5. Emotions such as fear and anger involve a general autonomic arousal that is orchestrated by the sympathetic nervous system. In many situations, arousal is adaptive. For example, with a challenging task, such as taking an exam, performance is likely to be best when arousal is

   a. very high.
   b. moderate.
   c. low.
   d. diminishing.

6. Although feelings of fear and anger involve a similar general autonomic arousal, they involve different brain areas. For example, stimulate one area of a cat's _____ and the cat draws back in terror; stimulate another area and the cat hisses with rage.

   a. cortex
   b. thalamus
   c. frontal lobes
   d. limbic system

REVIEWING

Theories and Physiology of Emotion

1. What are the components of an emotion?

Emotions are psychological responses of the whole organism that involve an interplay among (1) physiological arousal, (2) expressive behaviors, and (3) conscious experience.

2. Does physiological arousal precede or follow an emotional experience? (Does your heart pound because you are afraid, or are you afraid because you feel your heart pounding?)

This is one of the oldest theoretical controversies regarding emotion. William James and Carl Lange proposed that we feel emotion after we notice our body responses. Walter Cannon and Philip Bard believed that we feel emotion *at the same time* that our bodies respond. Most researchers today agree with Cannon and Bard but also note that, as James and Lange pointed out, physical reactions are an important ingredient of emotion.

3. To experience emotions, must we consciously interpret and label them?

Can we experience human emotions apart from cognition? Can we feel before we think? Stanley Schachter's two-factor theory of emotion contends that the cognitive labels we put on our states of arousal are an essential ingredient of emotion. Richard Lazarus agrees that cognition is essential: Many important emotions arise from our interpretations or inferences. Robert Zajonc, however, believes that some simple emotional responses occur instantly, not

only outside our conscious awareness but before any cognitive processing occurs. The issue has practical implications: To the degree that emotions are rooted in thinking, we can hope to change them by changing our thinking.

4. What physiological changes accompany emotional arousal?

In an emergency, the sympathetic nervous system automatically mobilizes the body for fight or flight, directing the adrenal glands to release hormones that in turn increase heart rate, blood pressure, and blood sugar level. Other changes include tensed muscles, dry mouth, dilated pupils, slowed digestion, and increased sweating. In day-to-day life, our performance on a task is usually best when arousal is moderate, though this varies with the difficulty of the task.

5. Do different emotions activate different physiological responses?

The physical arousal that occurs with one emotion is in most ways indistinguishable from that which occurs with another. However, scientists have discovered subtle differences in the brain pathways and hormones associated with different emotions.

Polygraphs measure several physiological indicators of emotion. They detect lies at a rate better than chance but not nearly well enough to justify their use in business and government. They are more likely to label the innocent guilty than the reverse.

TERMS AND CONCEPTS TO REMEMBER

emotion, p. 396
James-Lange theory, p. 396

Cannon-Bard theory, p. 396

two-factor theory, p. 398

polygraph, p. 404

REHEARSE IT ANSWER KEY

1. b   2. b   3. b   4. c   5. b   6. d

Expressing and Experiencing Emotion

Expressing Emotion

We express our emotions in many subtle and not-so-subtle visible ways. And we interpret these outward expressions in other people to decipher their emotions: We read their bodies, listen to their tone of voice, and study their faces.

Nonverbal Communication

PREVIEW QUESTION 1 How do we communicate nonverbally?

All of us communicate nonverbally as well as verbally. If irritated, we may tense our bodies, press our lips together, and turn away. With a gaze, an averted glance, or a stare we can communicate intimacy, submission, or dominance (Kleinke, 1986). Among those passionately in love, gazing into one another's eyes is typically prolonged and mutual (Rubin, 1970). Joan Kellerman, James Lewis, and James Laird (1989) wondered if such intimate gazes would stir such feelings between strangers. To find out, they asked unacquainted male-female pairs to gaze intently for two minutes either at one another's hands or into one another's eyes. After separating, the couples reported feeling a greater tingle of attraction and affection.

Most of us are good enough at reading nonverbal cues to decipher the emotions in an old silent film. We are especially good at detecting nonverbal threats. In a crowd of faces, a single angry face will "pop out" faster than a single happy one (Hansen & Hansen, 1988). By exposing different parts of emotion-laden faces, Robert Kestenbaum (1992) discovered that we read fear and anger mostly from the eyes, happiness from the mouth.

Some of us are more sensitive than others to these cues. Robert Rosenthal, Judith Hall, and their colleagues (1979) discovered this by showing hundreds of people brief film clips of portions of a person's emotionally expressive face or body, sometimes adding a garbled voice. For example, after a 2-second scene revealing only the face of an upset woman, the researchers would ask whether the woman was criticizing someone for being late or was talking about her divorce. Rosenthal and Hall reported that some people are much better than others at detecting emotion. Introverts tend to do better at reading others' emotions, although extraverts are themselves easier to read (Ambady & others, 1995).

Gender and Nonverbal Behavior

Studies also consistently find females better at reading people's emotional cues (Hall, 1987). Women's nonverbal sensitivity, perhaps a by-product of traditional gender roles, may help explain their greater emotional responsiveness in positive and negative situations (Grossman & Wood, 1993; Sprecher & Sedikides, 1993; Stoppard & Gruchy, 1993).

When surveyed, women are far more likely than men to describe themselves as empathic. If you have empathy, you identify with others, rejoicing with those who rejoice and weeping with those who weep. Physiological measures of empathy, such as one's heart rate while seeing another's distress, reveal a much smaller gender gap than reported in surveys (Eisenberg & Lennon, 1983). Nevertheless, females are more likely to *express* empathy—to cry and to report distress when observing someone in distress. Ann Kring and Albert Gordon (1998) observed this gender difference from videotapes of men and women students as they watched film clips that were sad

"Your face, my thane, is a book where men may read strange matters."

Lady Macbeth to her husband, in William Shakespeare's *Macbeth*.

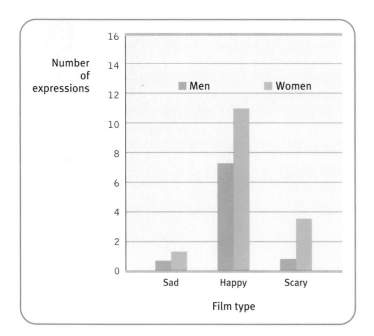

FIGURE 27.1

Gender and expressiveness

Although male and female students did not differ dramatically in self-reported emotions or physiological responses while viewing emotional films, the women's faces *showed* much more emotion. (From Kring & Gordon, 1998.)

(children with a dying parent), happy (slapstick comedy), or frightening (a man nearly falling off the ledge of a tall building). As **FIGURE 27.1** shows, the women reacted more visibly to each of the films.

Detecting Emotion

Working with high-tech equipment, psychologists are now linking various emotions with specific facial muscles (**FIGURE 27.2**). Hard-to-control facial muscles reveal signs of emotions you may be trying to conceal. Lifting just the inner part of your eyebrows, which few people do consciously, reveals distress or worry. Eyebrows raised and pulled together signal fear. Activated muscles under the eyes and raised cheeks suggest a natural smile. A feigned smile, such as one we make for a photographer, often continues for more than four or five seconds. Most authentic expressions have faded by that time. Feigned smiles also get switched on and off more abruptly than a genuine smile (Bugental, 1986).

Our brains are rather amazing emotion detectors. Elisha Babad, Frank Bernieri, and Robert Rosenthal (1991) discovered just *how* amazing after videotaping teachers talking to unseen schoolchildren. A mere 10-second clip of either the teacher's voice or face provided enough clues for both young and old viewers to determine whether the teacher liked and admired the child he or she was addressing. Teachers may think they can conceal their feelings and stay objective, but their students can sense what their expressions and gestures reveal.

The growing awareness that we communicate through the body's silent language has led to studies of how job applicants and interviewers communicate (or miscommunicate) nonverbally. Popular guidebooks and articles offer advice on how to interpret nonverbal signals when negotiating a business deal, selling a product, or flirting. It pays to be able to read feelings that leak through via subtle facial expres-

FIGURE 27.2

Smiles as indicators of emotions

Paul Ekman's system for classifying a particular smile consists of a specific code for each facial muscle used to create it. Notice how different these smiles are. (a) A smile that masks anger (the woman has just been told she is being dismissed). (b) An overly polite smile (the man is telling a patient to enjoy her hospital stay). (c) A smile softening verbal criticism ("I'd appreciate it if you wouldn't come to rehearsal drunk"). And (d) a reluctant, compliant smile ("I guess I don't have any choice, so OK").

(a) (b)

(c) (d)

sions, body movements, and postures. Fidgeting, for example, may reveal anxiety or boredom. It's important to remember that more specific interpretations of postures and gestures are risky because different expressions may convey the same emotion: Either a cold stare or the avoidance of eye contact may signify hostility. And a single gesture can convey very different emotions: Folded arms, for example, can signify either irritation or relaxation.

Such gestures, facial expressions, and tones of voice are all absent in computer-based communication. E-mail communications sometimes include sideways "emoticons," such as ;-) for a knowing wink and :-(for a frown. But e-mail letters and Internet discussions otherwise lack nonverbal cues to status, personality, and age. Nobody knows what you look or sound like, or anything about your background—you are judged solely on your words. It's no wonder then that when first meeting an e-mail pen pal face to face, people are often surprised at the person they encounter.

A silent language of emotion
The art of nonverbal communication reached a pinnacle early in the twentieth century as silent films became widely available. For a nickel, rapt audiences could watch performers mime a wide range of unmistakable emotions. Here Chester Conklin woos a woman on horseback while Louise Fazenda fumes.

Culture and Emotional Expression

PREVIEW QUESTION 2 Are nonverbal expressions of emotion universally understood?

The meaning of gestures varies with the culture. Some years ago, psychologist Otto Klineberg (1938) observed that in Chinese literature people clapped their hands to express worry or disappointment, laughed a great "Ho-Ho" to express anger, and stuck out their tongues to show surprise. Similarly, the North American "thumbs up" and "A-OK" signs would be insults in certain other cultures. (When former U.S. President Nixon made the latter sign in Brazil, he didn't realize he was saying "Let's have sex.") Just how important cultural definitions of gestures can be was demonstrated in 1968, when North Korea photographed supposedly happy officers from a captured U.S. Navy spy ship. In the photo, three of the men raised their middle-fingers; they had told captors it was a "Hawaiian good luck sign" (Fleming & Scott, 1991).

Do facial expressions also have different meanings in different cultures? To find out, two investigative teams—one led by Paul Ekman and Wallace Friesen (1975, 1987, 1994), the other by Carroll Izard (1977, 1994)—showed photographs of different facial expressions to people in different parts of the world and asked them to

Open palm *Greece:* an insult dating to ancient times; *West Africa:* You have five fathers, an insult akin to calling someone a bastard

Thumbs-up *Australia:* up yours; *Germany:* the number one; *Japan:* the number five; *Saudi Arabia:* I'm winning; *Ghana:* an insult; *Malaysia:* the thumb is used to point rather than the finger

Thumb and forefinger *Most countries:* money; *France:* something is perfect; *Mediterranean:* a vulgar gesture

OK sign *France:* you're a zero; *Japan:* please give me coins; *Brazil:* an obscene gesture; *Mediterranean countries:* an obscene gesture

Understanding gestures
Volunteers working with international visitors during the 1996 Olympics were briefed on the cultural meanings of gestures.

FIGURE 27.3

Culture-specific or culturally universal expressions?

As people of differing cultures and races, do our faces speak differing languages? Which face expresses disgust? Anger? Fear? Happiness? Sadness? Surprise? The answers are on page 412. (From Matsumoto and Ekman, 1989.)

"For news of the heart, ask the face."

Guinean proverb

While weightless, astronauts' fluids move toward their upper body and their faces become puffy. This makes nonverbal communication more difficult, increasing the risks of misunderstanding, especially among multinational crews (Gelman, 1989).

guess the emotion. You can try this yourself. Match the six emotions with the six faces of **FIGURE 27.3**.

You probably did pretty well regardless of your cultural background. A smile's a smile the world around. Ditto for anger, and to a lesser extent the other basic expressions (Elfenbein & Ambady, 1999). (There is no culture where people frown when they are happy.) Despite some differences, cultures and languages share many similarities in the ways they categorize emotions—as anger, fear, and so on. The physiological indicators of emotion also cross cultural boundaries (Levenson & others, 1992; Mesquita & Frijda, 1992). Thus, Americans, Jordanians, and Indians are similarly adept at detecting videotaped lying, whether the lie is told by someone from their own country or one of the other two (Bond & Atoum, 2000).

Do people from different cultures make and interpret facial expressions similarly because they experience similar influences, such as American movies, the BBC, and CNN? Apparently not. Ekman and his team asked isolated people in New Guinea to display various emotions in response to such statements as, "Pretend your child has died." When the researchers showed videotapes of the New Guineans' facial reactions to North American collegians, the students read them easily. Children's facial expressions—even those of blind children who have never seen a face—are also universal (Eibl-Eibesfeldt, 1971). People blind from birth spontaneously exhibit the common facial expressions associated with such emotions as joy, sadness, fear, and anger (Galati & others, 1997). The world over, children cry when distressed, shake their heads when defiant, and smile when they are happy.

The discovery that the facial muscles speak a fairly universal language would have come as no surprise to pioneering emotion researcher Charles Darwin (1809–1882). He speculated that in prehistoric times, before our ancestors communicated in words, their ability to convey threats, greetings, and submission with facial expressions helped them survive. That shared heritage, he believed, is why all humans express the basic emotions with similar facial expressions. A sneer, for example, retains elements of an animal's baring its teeth in a snarl.

Smiles, too, are social phenomena as well as emotional reflexes. Bowlers don't smile when they score a strike—they smile when they turn to face their companions (Jones & others, 1991; Kraut & Johnston, 1979). Even euphoric winners of Olympic gold medals typically don't smile when they are awaiting their ceremony but do when interacting with officials and facing the crowd and cameras (Fernández-Dols & Ruiz-Belda, 1995).

It has also been adaptive for us to *interpret* faces in particular contexts. People judge an angry face set in a frightening situation as afraid. They judge a fearful face set in a painful situation as pained (Carroll & Russell, 1996). Movie directors harness this phenomenon by creating contexts and soundtracks that amplify our perceptions of particular emotions.

Emotional expressions may enhance our survival in other ways, too. Surprise raises the eyebrows and widens the eyes, enabling us to take in more information. Disgust wrinkles the nose, closing it from foul odors.

Although cultures share a universal facial language for basic emotions, they do differ in how much emotion they express. In cultures that encourage individuality, as in Western Europe, Australia, New Zealand, and North America, emotional displays often are intense and prolonged. People focus on their own goals and attitudes and express themselves accordingly. Watching a film of someone's hand being cut, Americans grimace (whether alone or with other viewers). In contrast, Japanese viewers hide their emotions when in the presence of others (Triandis, 1994). Asians rarely and briefly display negative or self-aggrandizing emotions that might disrupt communal feeling within close-knit groups (Markus & Kitayama, 1991; Matsumoto & others, 1988). Moreover, in Asian and other cultures that emphasize social connections and interdependence, displays of emotions such as sympathy, respect, and shame are more common than in the West.

The Effects of Facial Expressions

PREVIEW QUESTION 3 Do our facial expressions influence our feelings?

Expressions not only communicate emotion, they also amplify and regulate it. In his 1872 book, *The Expression of the Emotions in Man and Animals,* Darwin contended that "the free expression by outward signs of an emotion intensifies it. . . . He who gives way to violent gestures will increase his rage" (p. 365).

Was Darwin right? I was driving in my car one day when the song "Put On a Happy Face" came on the radio. How phony, I thought. But I tested Darwin's hypothesis anyway, as you can, too. Fake a big grin. Now scowl. Can you feel the "smile therapy" difference?

The subjects in dozens of experiments have felt a difference. For example, James Laird and his colleagues (1974, 1984, 1989) subtly induced students to make a frowning expression by asking them to "contract these muscles" and "pull your brows together" (supposedly to help the researchers attach facial electrodes). The results? The students reported feeling a little angry. Students similarly induced to smile felt happier, found cartoons more humorous, and recalled happier memories than did the frowners. People instructed to mold their faces in ways that mimicked expressions of other basic emotions also experienced those emotions. For example, they reported feeling more fear than anger, disgust, or sadness when made to construct an expression of fear: "Raise your eyebrows. And open your eyes wide. Move your whole head back, so that your chin is tucked in a little bit, and let your mouth relax and hang open a little" (Duclos & others, 1989). Going through the motions awakens the emotions.

In the absence of competing emotions, this "facial feedback" effect is subtle, yet detectable. Consider these findings:

- If subtly manipulated into furrowing their brows (**FIGURE 27.4**), people feel sadder while looking at sad photos.
- Saying the speech sounds *e* and *ah,* which activate smiling muscles, puts people—believe it or not—in a better mood than saying the German *ü* (rather like saying the English *e* and *u* together), which activates muscles associated with negative emotions (Zajonc & others, 1989).
- Just activating one of the smiling muscles by holding a pen in the teeth (rather than with the lips, which activates a frowning muscle) is enough to make cartoons seem more amusing (Strack & others, 1988). A heartier smile, made not

FIGURE 27.4

How to make people frown without telling them to frown Randy Larsen, Margaret Kasimatis, and Kurt Frey's (1992) solution: Attach two golf tees above the eyebrows and ask the subjects to make the tee tips touch. Subjects felt sad while viewing scenes of war, sickness, and starvation, and even sadder with their "sad face" muscles activated.

just with the mouth but with raised cheeks as well, works even better (Ekman & others, 1990). Looking at oneself in a mirror further amplifies the effect (Kleinke & others, 1998). Smile warmly on the outside and you feel better on the inside. Scowl and the whole world seems to scowl back.

Which smile makes Paul Ekman feel happy?
The smile on the right, which engages the face muscles of a natural smile.

Sara Snodgrass and her associates (1986) observed the behavior feedback phenomenon with walking. You can duplicate her subjects' experience: Walk for a few minutes while taking short, shuffling steps, keeping your eyes downcast. Now walk around taking long strides, with your arms swinging and your eyes looking straight ahead. Can you feel your mood shift?

If assuming an emotional expression triggers a feeling, then would imitating others' expressions help us feel what they are feeling? Again, the laboratory evidence is supportive. Kathleen Burns Vaughn and John Lanzetta (1981) asked some students but not others to make a pained expression whenever an electric shock was apparently delivered to someone they were watching. With each apparent shock, the grimacing observers perspired more and had a faster heart rate than the other observers. So one small way to become more empathic—to feel what others feel—is to let your own face mimic the other person's expression. Acting as another acts helps us feel what another feels. Indeed, natural mimicry of others' emotions helps explain why emotions are contagious (Dimberg & others, 2000; Neumann & Strack, 2000).

> "Refuse to express a passion and it dies. . . . If we wish to conquer undesirable emotional tendencies in ourselves, we must . . . go through the outward movements of those contrary dispositions which we prefer to cultivate."
>
> **William James,** *Principles of Psychology,* 1890

rehearse it!

1. We can successfully interpret nonverbal threats and certain other silent messages regardless of the national origin of the sender. However, some nonverbal behaviors are *not* universal. People in different cultures are most likely to differ in their interpretations of

   a. adults' facial expressions.
   b. children's facial expressions.
   c. smiles.
   d. postures and gestures.

2. When people are induced to assume fearful expressions, they will feel their heart rates increase. This suggests

that the autonomic nervous system responds to
   a. signals from the facial muscles.
   b. conscious feelings of emotion.
   c. physiological responses involved in deception.
   d. electrical stimulation.

Experiencing Emotion

The ingredients of emotion include not only physiology and expressive behavior but also our conscious experience. How many distinct emotions are there? Carroll Izard (1977) isolated 10 such basic emotions (joy, interest-excitement, surprise, sadness, anger, disgust, contempt, fear, shame, and guilt), most of which are present in infancy (**FIGURE 27.5**). Izard reported that other emotions are combinations of these 10. Although Phillip Shaver and his colleagues (1996) believe that love, too, may be a basic emotion, Izard viewed it as a mixture of joy and interest-excitement.

Here we will focus on two important emotions: anger and happiness. What functions do they serve? What influences our experience of them?

Anger

PREVIEW QUESTION 4 What are the causes and consequences of anger?

Answers to the questions in Figure 27.3 (page 410): From left to right, top to bottom: happiness, surprise, fear, sadness, anger, disgust.

Anger, the sages have said, is "a short madness" (Horace, 65–8 B.C.) that "carries the mind away" (Virgil, 70–19 B.C.) and that can be "many times more hurtful than the injury that caused it" (Thomas Fuller, 1654–1734). But they have also said, "noble anger"

(a) Joy (mouth forming smile, cheeks lifted, twinkle in eye)

(b) Anger (brows drawn together and downward, eyes fixed, mouth squarish)

(c) Interest (brows raised or knitted, mouth softly rounded, lips may be pursed)

FIGURE 27.5
Infants' naturally occurring emotions
To identify the emotions present from birth, Carroll Izard analyzed the facial expressions of very young infants.

(d) Disgust (nose wrinkled, upper lip raised, tongue pushed outward)

(e) Surprise (brows raised, eyes widened, mouth rounded in oval shape)

(f) Sadness (brow's inner corners raised, mouth corners drawn down)

(g) Fear (brows level, drawn in and up, eyelids lifted, mouth corners retracted)

(William Shakespeare, 1564–1616) "makes any coward brave" (Cato, 234–149 B.C.) and "brings back . . . strength" (Virgil).

What makes us angry? To find out, James Averill (1983) asked people to recall or keep careful records of their experiences with anger. Most reported becoming at least mildly angry several times a week, some several times a day. The anger was often a response to friends' or loved ones' perceived misdeeds and was especially common when another person's act seemed willful, unjustified, and avoidable. But blameless annoyances—foul odors, high temperatures, a traffic jam, aches and pains—also have the power to make us angry (Berkowitz, 1990).

What do we do with our anger? And what *should* we do with it? When anger fuels physically or verbally aggressive acts we later regret, it becomes maladaptive. And it can harm us—chronic hostility is linked to heart disease. But controlled expressions of anger are more adaptive than either hostile outbursts or pent-up angry feelings. Averill's subjects recalled that when they were angry they often reacted assertively rather than hurtfully. Their anger frequently led them to talk things over with the offender, thereby lessening the aggravation.

Popular books and articles on aggression at times advise that even releasing angry feelings as hostile outbursts can be better than internalizing them. When irritated, should we go ahead and curse, tell a person off, or retaliate? Are "recovery movement" leaders right in encouraging us to rage at our dead parents, imaginatively curse the boss, or confront our childhood abuser?

Such encouragement to vent our rage is typical in individualized cultures, but it would seldom be heard in cultures where people's identity is centered more on the group. People who keenly sense their *inter*dependence see anger as a threat to group harmony (Markus & Kitayama, 1991). In Tahiti, for instance, people learn to be considerate and gentle. From infancy on in Japan, expressions of anger are less common than in Western cultures.

But even in Western cultures "vent your anger" advice presumes that emotional expression provides emotional release, or **catharsis.** The catharsis hypothesis maintains that we reduce anger by releasing it through aggressive action or fantasy. Experi-

"I thought it would be nice if we had a forum where we could get together and have screaming tantrums."

■ **catharsis** emotional release. In psychology, the catharsis hypothesis maintains that "releasing" aggressive energy (through action or fantasy) relieves aggressive urges.

menters report that this sometimes occurs. When people retaliate against someone who has provoked them, they may indeed calm down—*if* their counterattack is directed against the provoker, *if* their retaliation seems justifiable, and *if* their target is not intimidating (Geen & Quanty, 1977; Hokanson & Edelman, 1966). In short, expressing anger can be *temporarily* calming *if* it does not leave us feeling guilty or anxious.

However, despite the afterglow—people sometimes feel better afterward—catharsis usually fails to cleanse one's rage. More often, expressing anger breeds more anger. For one thing, it may provoke retaliation, thus escalating a minor conflict into a major confrontation. For another, expressing anger can magnify anger. (Recall Darwin's suggestion that violent gestures increase anger.) Ebbe Ebbesen and his colleagues (1975) saw this when they interviewed 100 frustrated engineers and technicians just laid off by an aerospace company. They asked some of the workers questions that released hostility, questions such as, "What instances can you think of where the company has not been fair with you?" When these people later filled out a questionnaire that assessed their attitudes toward the company, did this opportunity to "drain off" their hostility reduce it? Quite the contrary. Compared with those who had not vented their anger, those who had let it all out exhibited *more* hostility. Even when provoked people hit a punching bag *believing* it will be cathartic the effect is the opposite—leading them to exhibit *more* cruelty (Bushman & others, 1999).

Thus, although "blowing off steam" may temporarily calm us, it may also amplify the underlying hostility. And—ironically—when angry outbursts actually do calm us, they may actually be reinforcing and therefore habit forming. If stressed managers find they can drain off some of their tension by berating their employees, then the next time they feel irritated and tense they may be more likely to explode again. Think about it: The next time you are angry you are likely to do whatever has relieved your anger in the past.

> "Anger will never disappear so long as thoughts of resentment are cherished in the mind."
>
> **The Buddha, 500 B.C.**

A cool culture

Caregivers who turn abusive against other family members are rare in Micronesia. This photo of community life on Pulap Island suggests one possible reason: Family life takes place in the open in the South Pacific. Relatives and neighbors who witness angry outbursts can step in before the emotion escalates into child, spouse, or elder abuse.

What then is the best way to handle our anger? Experts offer two suggestions. First, wait. You can bring down the level of physiological arousal of anger by waiting. "It is true of the body as of arrows," noted Carol Tavris (1982), "what goes up must come down. Any emotional arousal will simmer down if you just wait long enough." Second, deal with anger in a way that involves neither being chronically angry over every little annoyance nor passively sulking, merely rehearsing your reasons for your anger. Ruminating inwardly about the causes of your anger serves only to increase it (Rusting & Nolen-Hoeksema, 1998). Don't join those who stifle their feelings over a series of provocations, and then suddenly overreact to a single incident (Baumeister & others, 1990). Calm yourself in other ways, such as by exercising, playing an instrument, or confiding your feelings to a friend.

Anger can actually benefit a relationship when it expresses a grievance in ways that promote reconciliation rather than retaliation. Civility means not only keeping silent about trivial irritations but also communicating important ones clearly and assertively. A nonaccusing statement of feeling—perhaps letting one's housemate know that "I get irritated when you leave your dirty dishes for me to clean up"—can help resolve the conflicts that cause anger.

Happiness

PREVIEW QUESTION 5 What are the causes and consequences of happiness?

"How to gain, how to keep, how to recover happiness is in fact for most men at all times the secret motive for all they do," observed William James (1902, p. 76). Understandably so, for one's state of happiness or unhappiness colors everything. People who are happy perceive the world as safer, make decisions more easily, rate job applicants more favorably, are more cooperative, and report greater satisfaction with their whole lives (Myers, 1993). When your mood is gloomy and your thinking preoccupied, life as a whole seems depressing. Let your mood brighten and your thinking broadens and becomes more playful and creative (Fredrickson, 1998, 2000). Your relationships, your self-image, and your hopes for the future also seem more promising.

Moreover—and this is one of psychology's most consistent findings—when we feel happy we are more willing to help others. In study after study, a mood-boosting experience (finding money, succeeding on a challenging task, recalling a happy event) made people more likely to give money, pick up someone's dropped papers, volunteer time, and so forth. Psychologists call it the **feel-good, do-good phenomenon** (Salovey, 1990).

Despite the significance of happiness, psychology throughout its history has more often focused on negative emotions. Since 1887, *Psychological Abstracts* (a guide to psychology's literature) has included 8072 articles mentioning anger, 57,800 mentioning anxiety, and 70,856 mentioning depression. For every 14 articles on these topics, only one dealt with the positive emotions of joy (851), life satisfaction (5701), or happiness (2958). There is, of course, good reason to focus on negative emotions; they can make our lives miserable and drive us to seek help. But researchers are becoming increasingly interested in **subjective well-being,** assessed either as feelings of happiness (sometimes defined as a high ratio of positive to negative feelings) or as a sense of satisfaction with life. "Positive psychology" is on the rise.

On this subject, as on so many others, whatever psychological research reveals will have been anticipated by someone. We have inherited any number of contradictory maxims concerning happiness: that it comes from knowing the truth, or from preserving illusions; from living for the present, or from living for the future; from being with others, or from living in peaceful solitude (Tatarkiewicz, 1976). The list goes on, and the scientific task is clear: to ask which of these competing ideas fit reality. Sifting the actual predictors of happiness from the plausible hunches requires research.

In their research on happiness, psychologists have studied influences on both our temporary moods and our long-term life satisfaction. Studying people's reports of daily moods confirms that stressful events—an argument, a sick child, a car problem—trigger bad moods. No surprise there. But by the next day, the gloom nearly always lifts (Affleck & others, 1994; Bolger & others, 1989; Stone & Neale, 1984). If anything, people tend to rebound from bad days to a *better*-than-usual good mood the following day. When in a bad mood, can you usually depend on rebounding within a day or two? Are your times of elation similarly hard to sustain? Over the long ride, our emotional ups and downs tend to balance.

Apart from prolonged grief over the loss of a loved one or lingering anxiety after a trauma (such as child abuse, rape, or the terrors of war), even tragedy is not permanently depressing. The finding is surprising but reliable. Those who become blind or paralyzed usually recover near-normal levels of day-to-day happiness. Consider these findings:

- Able-bodied University of Illinois students described themselves as happy 50 percent of the time, unhappy 22 percent of the time, and neutral 29 percent of the

---

- **feel-good, do-good phenomenon** people's tendency to be helpful when already in a good mood.
- **subjective well-being** self-perceived happiness or satisfaction with life. Used along with measures of objective well-being (for example, physical and economic indicators) to evaluate people's quality of life.

"Everything important has been said before."

Philosopher Alfred North Whitehead (1861–1947)

"Weeping may tarry for the night, but joy comes with the morning."

Psalms 30:5

"If I couldn't know the joy of dancing, I could know the ecstasy of creating."

Christy Brown, *My Left Foot*, 1954

time. To within 1 percentage point, students with disabilities rated their emotions identically (Chwalisz & others, 1988).

- Students perceive their friends with disabilities as just as happy as their other friends (Allman, 1989).

- In one survey of 128 people with all four limbs paralyzed, most acknowledged having considered suicide after their injury. However, more than a year later, only 10 percent rated their quality of life as poor; most described it as good or excellent (Whiteneck & others, 1985). When 233 emergency room caregivers imagined how they would feel about themselves years after such an injury, only 39 percent guessed they would feel "satisfied with myself, on the whole." But that is exactly how 95 percent of the actual patients felt (Gerhart & others, 1994). And 98 percent of them agreed that "I feel I am a person of worth."

In less time than most people suppose, the emotional impact of significant events dissipates. Learning that one is HIV-positive is devastating. Yet after five weeks of adapting to the grim news, those who tested positive felt less emotionally distraught than they had expected (Sieff & others, 1999). Likewise, faculty members up for tenure expect their lives would be deflated by a negative decision. Actually, 5 to 10 years later, those denied are not noticeably unhappier than those who were awarded tenure, report Daniel Gilbert and colleagues (1998). The same is true of romantic breakups, which at the time may seem to have ruined one's life. The surprising reality: We overestimate the long-term emotional impact of very bad news and underestimate our capacity to adapt.

It may come as a disappointment, but the effect of dramatically positive events is similarly temporary. Once their rush of euphoria wears off, state lottery winners typically find their overall happiness unchanged (Brickman & others, 1978). Other research confirms that there is much more to well-being than being well-off. Many people (including most new collegians, as **FIGURE 27.6** suggests) believe they would be happier if they had more money. They probably would be—temporarily. But in the long run, increased affluence hardly affects happiness. Within most affluent countries, people with lots of money are not much happier than those with just enough to afford life's necessities. Wealth is like health: Its utter absence breeds misery, yet having it is no guarantee of happiness.

During the last four decades, the average U.S. citizen's buying power doubled. The 1957 per-person after-tax income, inflated to 1995 dollars, was $8500; by 1998,

Faced with adversity

In 1995, an accident transformed *Superman* actor Christopher Reeve into an immobile person needing others to feed, dress, and care for him. "Maybe I should just check out," he told his wife, Dana, shortly after the accident. But within four months he reported in a Barbara Walters interview "genuine joy in being alive."

FIGURE 27.6

The changing materialism of entering college students

From 1970 through most of the 1980s, annual surveys of more than 200,000 entering U.S. college students revealed an increasing desire for wealth. (From *The American Freshman* surveys, UCLA, 1966 to 2000.)

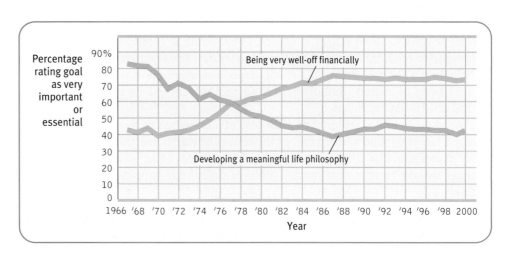

thanks partly to the rich getting richer and to women's increasing employment, it was $20,000. Did this doubled wealth—enabling twice as many cars per capita, and color TVs, VCRs, personal computers, air conditioning, and answering machines galore—also buy more happiness? As **FIGURE 27.7** shows, the average American is now

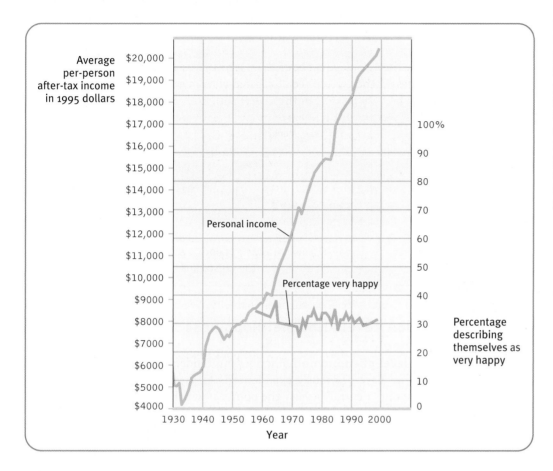

FIGURE 27.7

Does money buy happiness?
It surely helps us to avoid certain types of pain. Yet, though buying power has doubled since the 1950s, the average American's reported happiness has remained almost unchanged. (Happiness data from Niemi & others, 1989, and T. Smith, personal correspondence; income data from *Historical Statistics of the United States* and *Economic Indicators*.)

twice as rich but not a bit happier. In 1957, some 35 percent said they were "very happy," as did slightly fewer—32 percent—in 1998.

Indeed, if we can judge from statistics—a doubled divorce rate, tripled teen suicide and teen violent crime rates, and mushrooming depression—contemporary Americans seem to be more often miserable. The same is true of the European countries and of Japan: In these countries, people enjoy better nutrition, health care, education, and science, and are somewhat happier than those in very poor countries, and yet the increasing real incomes have *not* produced increasing happiness. The findings lob a bombshell at modern materialism: *Economic growth in affluent countries has provided no apparent boost to psychological morale or social bonds.*

A further bombshell comes from studies showing that individuals who strive most for wealth tend to live with lower well-being, a finding that "comes through very strongly in every culture I've looked at," reports Richard Ryan (1999). His collaborator, Tim Kasser (2000), concludes from their studies that those who instead strive for "intimacy, personal growth, and contribution to the community" experience a higher quality of life. Ryan and Kasser's research echoes an earlier finding by H. W. Perkins (1991): Among 800 college alumni surveyed, those with "Yuppie values"—preferring a high income and occupational success and prestige to having very close friends and a close marriage—were twice as likely as their former classmates to describe themselves as "fairly" or "very" *un*happy. A similar correlation appears

"This lovely car has not brought us happiness. You agree, Morris? That is why I am now thinking in terms of having the entire house recarpeted."

among 7167 college students surveyed in 41 countries. Those who value love more than money report much higher satisfaction with life than do their money-hungry peers (**FIGURE 27.8**).

Two psychological principles explain why, for all but the very poor, more money buys no more than a temporary surge of happiness and why our emotions seem attached to elastic bands that pull us back from highs or lows. In its own way, each principle suggests that happiness is relative.

FIGURE 27.8

Values and life satisfaction
Among college and university students worldwide, those who report high life satisfaction give priority to love over money. (From Diener & Oishi, 2000.)

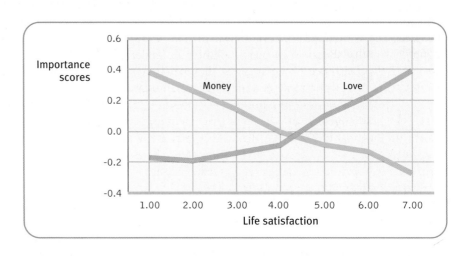

> "No happiness lasts for long."
>
> Seneca, *Agamemnon*, A.D. 60

> "Continued pleasures wear off. . . . Pleasure is always contingent upon change and disappears with continuous satisfaction."
>
> Dutch psychologist Nico Frijda (1988)

> "I have also learned why people work so hard to succeed: It is because they envy the things their neighbors have. But it is useless. It is like chasing the wind. . . . It is better to have only a little, with peace of mind, than be busy all the time with both hands, trying to catch the wind."
>
> Ecclesiastes 4:4

The Adaptation-Level Principle: Happiness Is Relative to Our Prior Experience

The **adaptation-level phenomenon** describes our tendency to judge various stimuli relative to those we have previously experienced. As psychologist Harry Helson explained, we adjust our "neutral" levels—the points at which sounds seem neither loud nor soft, temperatures neither hot nor cold, events neither pleasant nor unpleasant—based on our experience. We then notice and react to variations up or down from these levels. Adaptation researcher Allen Parducci (1995) recalls a striking example: "On the Micronesian island of Ponope, which is almost on the equator, I was told of a bitter night back in 1915 when the temperature dropped to a record-breaking 69 degrees [Fahrenheit; 21 degrees Celsius]!"

So, could we ever create a permanent social paradise? Donald Campbell (1975) answered no: If you woke up tomorrow to your utopia—perhaps a world with no bills, no ills, all A's, someone who loves you unreservedly—you would feel euphoric, for a time. But before long, you would soon recalibrate your adaptation level. Before long you would again sometimes feel gratified (when achievements surpass expectations), sometimes feel deprived (when they fall below), and sometimes feel neutral. That helps explain why, despite the realities of triumph and tragedy, million-dollar lottery winners and people who are paralyzed report roughly similar levels of happiness. *The point to remember:* Satisfaction and dissatisfaction, success and failure—all are relative to our recent experience. Satisfaction, as Richard Ryan (1999) says, "has a short half-life."

The Relative Deprivation Principle: Happiness Is Relative to Others' Attainments

Happiness is relative not only to our past experience but also to our comparisons with others. We are always comparing ourselves with others. And whether we feel good or bad depends on who those others are. We are slow-witted or clumsy only when others are smart or agile.

An example: To explain the frustration expressed by U.S. Air Corps soldiers during World War II, researchers formulated the concept of **relative deprivation**—the sense

that we are worse off than others with whom we compare ourselves. Despite a relatively rapid promotion rate for the group, many soldiers were frustrated about their own promotion rates (Merton & Kitt, 1950). Apparently, seeing so many others being promoted inflated the soldiers' expectations. And when expectations soar above attainments, the result is disappointment. News of Alex Rodriguez's $250 million 10-year baseball contract surely diminished other players' satisfaction with their multimillion-dollar contracts.

Such comparisons help us understand why the middle- and upper-income people in a given country, who can compare themselves with the relatively poor, tend to be slightly more satisfied with life than their less fortunate compatriots. Nevertheless, once people reach a moderate income level, further increases do little to increase their happiness. Why? Because as people climb the ladder of success they mostly compare themselves with peers who are at or above their current level (Gruder, 1977; Suls & Tesch, 1978). For one athlete, another is the standard of comparison. For average people, athletes' salaries are emotionally irrelevant. "Beggars do not envy millionaires, though of course they will envy other beggars who are more successful," noted Bertrand Russell (1930, p. 90). Thus, "Napoleon envied Caesar, Caesar envied Alexander, and Alexander, I daresay, envied Hercules, who never existed. You cannot, therefore, get away from envy by means of success alone, for there will always be in history or legend some person even more successful than you are" (pp. 68–69).

By "counting our blessings" when we compare ourselves with those less fortunate, we can, however, increase our satisfaction. Just as comparing ourselves with those who are better off creates envy, so comparing ourselves with those less well off boosts our contentment. Marshall Dermer and his colleagues (1979) demonstrated this by asking University of Wisconsin-Milwaukee women to study others' deprivation and suffering. After viewing vivid depictions of how grim life was in Milwaukee in 1900, or after imagining and then writing about various personal tragedies, such as being burned and disfigured, the women expressed greater satisfaction with their own lives. Similarly, when mildly depressed people read about someone who is even more depressed, they feel somewhat better (Gibbons, 1986). "I cried because I had no shoes," states a Persian saying, "until I met a man who had no feet."

Predictors of Happiness

If, as the adaptation-level phenomenon implies, our emotions tend to balance around normal, why do some people seem so filled with joy and others so gloomy day after day? What makes one person normally happy and another less so? Research reveals several predictors of happiness (Table 27.1). Again, keep in mind that knowing that two variables correlate does not tell us whether one causes the other. For exam-

"Shortly after I realized I had plenty, I realized there was plenty more."

"Our poverty became a reality. Not because of our having less, but by our neighbors having more."

Will Campbell, *Brother to a Dragonfly*, 1977

The effect of comparison with others helps explain why students of a given level of academic ability tend to have a higher academic self-concept if they attend a school where most other students are not exceptionally able (Marsh & Parker, 1984). If you were near the top of your class in high school, you might feel inferior upon entering a college where everyone was near the top of their class.

"The optimist is as often wrong as the pessimist, but far happier."

Anonymous

TABLE **27.1**
HAPPINESS IS . . .

Researchers Have Found That Happy People Tend to
Have high self-esteem (in individualistic countries)
Be optimistic, outgoing, and agreeable
Have close friendships and a satisfying marriage
Have work and leisure that engage their skills
Have a meaningful religious faith
Sleep well and exercise

Source: Summarized from DeNeve and Cooper (1998), Myers (1993, 2000), and Myers and Diener, (1995, 1996).

■ **adaptation-level phenomenon** our tendency to form judgments (of sounds, of lights, of income) relative to a "neutral" level defined by our prior experience.

■ **relative deprivation** the perception that one is worse off relative to those with whom one compares oneself.

ple, many studies indicate that religiously active people tend to report greater happiness and life satisfaction. Is happiness then conducive to faith? Or does faith enhance happiness?

Whether at work or leisure, most of us derive our greatest enjoyment from engaging, challenging activities. Mihaly Csikszentmihalyi (1990) and his colleagues discovered this after giving research volunteers a pager. When beeped, the people would note what they were doing and how they were feeling. Usually, they felt happier if mentally engaged by work or active leisure than if passively vegetating. Ironically, the less expensive a leisure activity is, the more absorbed and happy people often are while doing it. People are happier gardening than sitting on a power boat. They're happier when talking to friends than when watching TV. Happy, says Csikszentmihalyi, are those whose work and leisure absorb them, enabling them to "flow" unself-consciously in focused activity.

Satisfying tasks and relationships affect our happiness, but always within the limits imposed by our genetic leash. From their study of 254 identical and fraternal twins, David Lykken and Auke Tellegen (1996) estimated that 50 percent of the difference among people's happiness ratings is heritable. Even identical twins raised apart are often similarly happy. Depending on our outlooks and recent experiences, our happiness fluctuates around our "happiness set point," which disposes some people to be ever upbeat, and others down. Our happiness, it seems, is like our cholesterol level—genetically influenced yet also influenced by factors under our control.

"I could cry when I think of the years I wasted accumulating money, only to learn that my cheerful disposition is genetic."

A recent study of 137 chimpanzees in zoos revealed that happiness in chimps, as in humans, is genetically influenced (Weiss & others, 1999).

rehearse it!

3. In some situations, venting anger— "blowing up"—seems to calm a person temporarily. In other cases, acting angry increases hostility. Experts suggest that to bring down anger, a good first step is to
   a. retaliate verbally or physically.
   b. wait or "simmer down."
   c. express anger in action or fantasy.
   d. review the grievance silently.

4. After graduating from college, you get a job and move into a large metropolitan city. At first, you find the street noise irritatingly loud, but after a while, it no longer bothers you, thus illustrating the
   a. relative deprivation principle.
   b. adaptation-level principle.

   c. feel-good, do-good phenomenon.
   d. catharsis principle.

5. A philosopher notes that one cannot escape envy by means of success alone: There will always be someone more successful, more accomplished, or richer with whom to compare oneself. In psychology this observation is embodied in the
   a. relative deprivation principle.
   b. adaptation-level principle.
   c. list of predictors of happiness.
   d. feel-good, do-good phenomenon.

6. When happy and unhappy people are compared, researchers find that happy people are optimistic, outgoing, and likely to have satisfying close relation-

ships. One of the most consistent findings of psychological research is that happy people are also
   a. more likely to express anger.
   b. generally luckier than others.
   c. concentrated in the wealthier nations.
   d. more likely to help others.

7. Age, race, and gender seem not to be predictably related to subjective feelings of happiness or well-being. However, researchers have found that happy people tend to
   a. have children.
   b. score high on intelligence tests.
   c. have a meaningful religious faith.
   d. complete high school and some college education.

Expressing and Experiencing Emotion

1. How do we communicate nonverbally?

Much of our communication is through the silent language of the body. Even very thin (seconds-long) videotaped slices of behavior can reveal feelings. Women tend to be better at reading people's emotional cues.

2. Are nonverbal expressions of emotion universally understood?

Gestures appear to be culturally determined, but facial expressions, such as those of happiness and fear, are common the world over. In communal cultures that value interdependence, intense displays of potentially disruptive emotions are infrequent.

3. Do our facial expressions influence our feelings?

Expressions do more than communicate emotion to others. They also amplify our own feelings of emotion and signal our bodies to respond accordingly.

4. What are the causes and consequences of anger?

Anger is most often aroused by events that not only are frustrating or insulting but also are interpreted as willful, unjustified, and avoidable. Blowing off steam (catharsis) may be temporarily calming, but in the long run, it does not reduce anger. Expressing anger can actually arouse more anger.

5. What are the causes and consequences of happiness?

A good mood boosts people's perceptions of the world and their willingness to help others (the *feel-good, do-good phenomenon*). A person's self-perceived happiness or satisfaction with life is his or her subjective well-being. The moods triggered by the day's good or bad events seldom last beyond that day. Even significant good events, such as a substantial rise in income, seldom increase happiness for long. We can explain the relativity of happiness with the adaptation-level phenomenon and the relative deprivation principle. Nevertheless, some people are usually happier than others, and researchers have identified factors that predict such happiness.

TERMS AND CONCEPTS TO REMEMBER

catharsis, p. 413
feel-good, do-good phenomenon, p. 415

subjective well-being, p. 415

adaptation-level phenomenon, p. 418

relative deprivation, p. 418

REHEARSE IT ANSWER KEY

1. d   2. a   3. b   4. b   5. a   6. d   7. c

28 Stress and Illness

- Stress and Stressors
- Stress and Heart Disease
- Stress and Susceptibility to Disease

Worldwide, reports the World Health Organization, nearly a quarter of health care contacts are prompted by psychological problems (Sartorius, 1994).

Walking along the path toward his Rocky Mountain campsite, Karl hears a rustle at his feet. As he glimpses a rattlesnake, his body mobilizes for fight or flight: His muscles tense, his adrenaline flows, his heart pounds, and he flees, racing to the security of camp. Once there, Karl's muscles gradually relax and his heart rate and breathing ease.

Karen leaves her suburban apartment one morning and, delayed by road construction, arrives at the parking lot of the commuter train station just in time to see the 8:05 pull away. Catching the next train, she arrives in the city late and elbows her way through crowds of rush-hour pedestrians. Once at her bank office, she apologizes to her first client, who wonders where Karen has been and why his quarterly investment report is not ready. Karen does her best to mollify the client. Afterward, she notices her tense muscles, clenched teeth, and churning stomach.

Karl's response to stress saved his life; Karen's, if chronic, could increase her risk of heart disease, high blood pressure, and other stress-linked health problems. Moreover, feeling under pressure, she might sleep and exercise less and smoke and drink more, further endangering her long-term health.

Stress and Stressors

PREVIEW QUESTION 1 What is stress?

Stress is a slippery concept. It is sometimes used to describe threats or challenges ("Karen was under a lot of stress"), other times to describe our responses ("When Karl saw the rattler, he experienced acute stress"). Most psychologists would define Karen's missed train as a "stressor," Karl's physical and emotional responses as a "stress reaction," and the process by which Karen and Karl related to their environments as stress.

Thus, **stress** is not just a stimulus or a response. It is the process by which we appraise and cope with environmental threats and challenges (**FIGURE 28.1**). The events of our lives flow through a psychological filter. Stress arises less from events themselves than from how we appraise them (Lazarus, 1998). One person, alone in a house, dismisses its creaking sounds and experiences no stress; someone else suspects an intruder and becomes alarmed. One person regards a new job as a welcome challenge; someone else appraises it as risking failure.

FIGURE 28.1

Stress appraisal

How we appraise an event influences how much stress we experience and how effectively we respond.

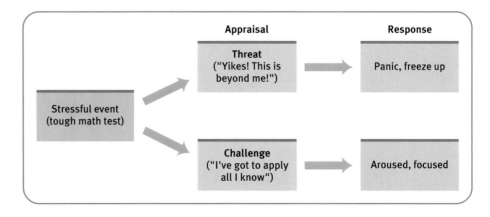

When perceived as challenges, stressors can have positive effects, arousing and motivating us to conquer problems. Championship athletes, successful entertainers, and great teachers and leaders all thrive and excel when aroused by a challenge. Having conquered cancer or rebounded from a lost job, some people emerge with stronger self-esteem and a deepened spirituality and sense of purpose. Indeed, among humans and other animals, some stress and physical stimulation early in life is conducive to later emotional resilience and physical growth (Landauer & Whiting, 1979). As many of us have experienced, bad things sometimes work for good. Adversity sometimes begets growth.

But stressors can also threaten our resources—our status and security on the job, our deeply held beliefs, our self-image (Hobfoll, 1989). And experiencing severe or prolonged stress may harm us. Those who had post-traumatic stress reactions to heavy combat in the Vietnam War went on to suffer greatly elevated rates of circulatory, digestive, respiratory, and infectious diseases (Boscarino, 1997).

The Stress Response System

Although medical interest in stress dates back to Hippocrates (460–377 B.C.), it was not until the 1920s that Walter Cannon (1929) confirmed that the stress response is part of a unified mind-body system. He observed that extreme cold, lack of oxygen, and emotion-arousing incidents all trigger an outpouring of epinephrine (adrenaline) and norepinephrine (noradrenaline). These stress hormones enter the bloodstream from sympathetic nerve endings in the inner part of the adrenal glands. This is but one part of the sympathetic nervous system's response. When alerted by any of a number of brain pathways, the sympathetic nervous system increases heart rate and respiration, diverts blood from digestion to the skeletal muscles, dulls pain, and releases sugar and fat from the body's stores—all to prepare the body for what Cannon called *fight or flight*. All in all, this stress response struck Cannon as wonderfully adaptive.

Canadian scientist Hans Selye's (1936, 1976) 40 years of research on stress extended Cannon's findings and helped make stress a major concept in both psychology and medicine. Selye studied animals' reactions to various other stressors, such as electric shock, surgical trauma, and immobilizing restraint. He discovered that the body's adaptive response to stress was so general—like a single burglar alarm that sounds, no matter what intrudes—that he called it the **general adaptation syndrome (GAS).**

Selye saw the GAS as having three phases (**FIGURE 28.2**). Let's say you suffer a physical or emotional trauma. In Phase 1, you experience an *alarm reaction* due to the sudden activation of your sympathetic nervous system. Your heart rate zooms. Blood is diverted to your skeletal muscles. You feel the faintness of shock. With your resources mobilized, you are now ready to fight the challenge during Phase 2, *resistance.* Your temperature, blood pressure, and respiration remain high, and there is a sudden outpouring of hormones. If persistent, the stress may eventually deplete your body's reserves during Phase 3, *exhaustion.* With exhaustion, you are more vulnerable to illness or even, in extreme cases, collapse and death.

■ **stress** the process by which we perceive and respond to certain events, called stressors, that we appraise as threatening or challenging.

■ **general adaptation syndrome (GAS)** Selye's concept of the body's adaptive response to stress in three stages— alarm, resistance, exhaustion.

FIGURE 28.2
Selye's general adaptation syndrome
After a trauma, the body enters an alarm phase of temporary shock. From this it rebounds, as stress resistance rises. If the stress is prolonged, wear and tear may lead to exhaustion.

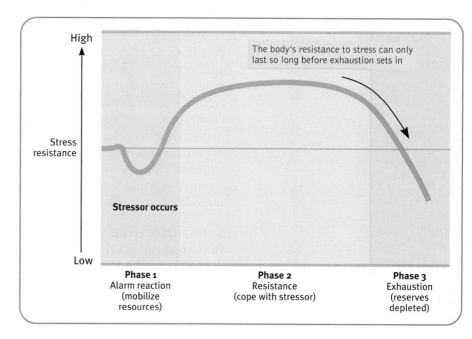

■ **health psychology** a subfield of psychology that provides psychology's contribution to behavioral medicine.

Newer research reveals subtle differences in the body's reactions to different stressors. Nevertheless, few medical experts today quarrel with Selye's basic point: Although the human body comes designed to cope with temporary stress, prolonged stress can produce physical deterioration. Several recent studies have taken MRI (magnetic resonance imaging) brain scans of people who have experienced a prolonged flood of stress hormones, due to sustained child abuse, combat, or an endocrine disease (Sapolsky, 1999). Most have a shrunken hippocampus, the inner brain structure vital to laying down explicit (declarative) memories. In animals, too, various stresses—being subordinate in a group, being physically restrained, being isolated—can cause hippocampal tissue to shrink (McEwen, 1998). Such findings serve as further incentives to today's **health psychologists,** who have joined with physicians to create the interdisciplinary field of *behavioral medicine*. Health psychologists are actively exploring such questions as, What causes stress? What are the effects of stress? And how can we alleviate those effects?

Stressful Life Events

PREVIEW QUESTION 2 What events provoke stress responses?

Research has focused on our responses to three types of stressors: catastrophes, significant life changes, and daily hassles.

Catastrophes

Catastrophes are unpredictable, large-scale events such as war and natural disasters that nearly everyone appraises as threatening. Although people often provide one another with aid as well as comfort after such events, the health consequences can be significant. Two examples:

Toxic stress
Researchers have found that catastrophes such as flooding increase rates of psychological disorders.

- On the day of its 1994 earthquake, Los Angeles experienced a fivefold increase in sudden-death heart attacks—especially in the first two hours after the quake and near its epicenter. Physical exertion (running, lifting debris) was a factor in only 13 percent of the deaths, leaving stress as the likely trigger for the others (Muller & Verrier, 1996).
- In the year following the crash of a 747 jumbo jet at Lockerbie, Scotland, police officers—after being pressed into recovering human remains and patrolling the disaster zone—suffered a 38 percent increase in short-term illnesses (Paton, 1992).

Do other community disasters usually produce effects this great? After digesting data from 52 studies of catastrophic floods, hurricanes, and fires, Anthony Rubonis and Leonard Bickman (1991) found the typical effect more modest but nonetheless genuine. In disaster's wake, rates of psychological disorders such as depression and anxiety rose an average 17 percent. The nuclear accident at Three Mile Island produced similar stress symptoms in area residents (Baum & Fleming, 1993). Refugees fleeing their homeland also suffer increased rates of psychological disorder. Their stress stems from the trauma of uprooting and family separation, and from the challenges of adjusting to a foreign culture's new language, ethnicity, climate, and social norms (Williams & Berry, 1991). In all these cases, the health consequences often come only after prolonged stress.

Significant Life Changes

The second type of life event stressor is a significant personal life change—leaving home, the death of a loved one, the loss of a job, a marriage or divorce. Life transitions and insecurities are often keenly felt during young adulthood. That helps explain why, when 15,000 Canadian adults were asked whether "You are trying to take on too many things at once," responses indicated highest stress levels among the youngest adults.

Some psychologists study the health effects of life changes by following people over time to see if such events precede illnesses. Others compare the life changes recalled by those who have or have not suffered a specific health problem, such as a heart attack. A review of these studies commissioned by the U.S. National Academy of Sciences revealed that people recently widowed, fired, or divorced are more vulnerable to disease (Dohrenwend & others, 1982). A Finnish study of 96,000 widowed people confirmed the phenomenon: Their risk of death doubled in the week following their partner's death (Kaprio & others, 1987). Experiencing a cluster of crises puts one even more at risk.

Daily Hassles

Our happiness tends to stem less from enduring good fortune than from our response to daily events—an A on an exam, a gratifying letter, your team's winning the big game. This principle works for negative events, too. Everyday annoyances may be the most significant sources of stress (Kohn & Macdonald, 1992; Lazarus, 1990; Ruffin, 1993). These daily hassles include rush-hour traffic, aggravating housemates, long lines at the bank or store, too many things to do, and misplacing things. Although some people can simply shrug them off, others are "driven up the wall" by such inconveniences. In fact, 6 in 10 people say they feel "great stress" at least once a week (Harris, 1987).

No end in sight

"It's not the large things that send a man to the madhouse . . . no, it's the continuing series of small tragedies . . . not the death of his love but the shoelace that snaps with no time left" (Charles Bukowski, cited by Lazarus in Wallis, 1983).

Over time, these little stressors can add up and take a toll on our health and well-being. Hypertension (high blood pressure) rates are high among residents of urban ghettos, where the stresses that accompany poverty, unemployment, solo parenting, and overcrowding are part of daily life for some people. And these daily pressures may be compounded by racism, which—like other stressors—can have both psychological and physical consequences. Imagine thinking that some people distrust you, do not like you, or doubt your abilities. Might you not find daily life stressful? Might such stress eventually take a toll on your health, perhaps driving up your blood pressure? Well, that describes the experiences of many African-Americans as they perceive racism in their daily lives, note Rodney Clark and his colleagues (1999).

The dramatic effects of high levels of stress became apparent in Russia from 1990 to 1993, following the collapse of socialism in the former Soviet Union. During that period, Russia experienced mushrooming divorce, murder, suicide, and stress-related disease rates. Life expectancy for Russian men also plummeted by nearly 5 years, to 58.9 years (Holden, 1996).

Perceived Control

Catastrophes, important life changes, and daily hassles and conflicts are especially stressful when we appraise them as both negative *and* uncontrolled. If two rats receive simultaneous shocks, but one can turn a wheel to stop the shocks, the helpless rat becomes more susceptible to ulcers and lowered immunity to disease (Laudenslager & Reite, 1984). In humans, a bacterial infection often combines with uncontrollable stress to produce the most severe ulcers (Overmier & Murison, 1997). The cure is twofold: Kill the bug with antibiotics, but control the acid secretions with reduced stress.

Perceiving a loss of control, we become vulnerable to ill health. Judith Rodin (1986), for example, has shown that elderly nursing home patients who have little perceived control over their activities tend to decline faster and die sooner than do those given more control over their activities. And workers given control over their work environments—by being able to adjust office furnishings and control interruptions and distractions—experience less stress (O'Neill, 1993). This may help explain why British civil service workers at the executive grades outlive those at clerical or laboring grades. The more control workers have, the longer they live (Bosma & others, 1997, 1998; Marmot & others, 1997).

Poverty and Inequality

Control may also help explain a well-established link between economic status and longevity. In one study of 843 grave markers in an old graveyard in Glasgow, Scotland, those with the costliest, highest pillars (indicating the most affluence) tended to live the longest (Carroll & others, 1994). Likewise, Scottish regions with the least overcrowding and unemployment have the greatest longevity. In the United States and Canada, too, poorer people are more at risk for premature death. Even among primates, those at the bottom of the social pecking order are more likely than their higher-status companions to become sick when exposed to a coldlike virus (Cohen & others, 1997).

People also tend to die younger in areas where there is greater income *inequality* (Kawachi & others, 1999; Lynch & others, 1998; Marmot & Wilkinson, 1999). Among developed countries, Britain and the United States, which have large income disparities between rich and poor, have life expectancies two to four years lower than those in Japan and Sweden, where the differences in income are less extreme. And as income inequality has grown over the last decade in Eastern Europe and Russia, life expectancy has decreased. The effect is not confined to nations. Cities and U.S. states with relatively disparate incomes also tend to have lower life expectancy than those where incomes are more equal.

Does the inequality–mortality correlation occur merely because extreme differences in income are flags of substantial poverty? No, the correlation remains after adjusting for average income and for the proportion of the population with low incomes. In fact, report John Lynch and his colleagues (1998, 2000), people at every income level are at greater risk of death if they live in a community with great income inequality.

But *why* does inequality predict mortality? Is it because the risk of violent death is greater? Because receiving relatively low income evokes feelings of frustration and

Equal incomes lead to longer lives
In Kerala state, India, incomes are low, yet life expectancy is greater than in other Indian states. "Indeed," report John Lynch and his co-researchers (2000), thanks to relative equality and to "investment in human resources, . . . [life expectancy approximates] levels seen in rich industrialized countries."

worthlessness? Because investment in public health, education, and housing is lower in such regions? Researchers are now pondering all these questions.

Optimism-Pessimism

One control-related factor that does influence our vulnerability to stress is optimism. Psychologists Michael Scheier and Charles Carver (1992) report that optimists—people who agree with statements such as, "In uncertain times, I usually expect the best"—not only perceive more control, they cope better with stressful events and enjoy better health. During the last month of a semester, students previously identified as optimistic report less fatigue and fewer coughs, aches, and pains. During the stressful first few weeks of law school, those who are optimistic ("It's unlikely that I will fail") enjoy better moods and stronger infection-thwarting immune systems (Segerstrom & others, 1998). Optimists also respond to stress with smaller increases in blood pressure, and they recover more quickly from heart bypass surgery. One study that followed 2428 middle-aged Finnish men for up to 10 years discovered that the number of deaths among men with a bleak, hopeless outlook was more than double that found among their optimistic counterparts (**FIGURE 28.3**).

Why do perceived loss of control and pessimism predict health problems? Animal studies show—and human studies confirm—that losing control provokes an outpouring of stress hormones. When rats cannot control shock or when humans feel unable to control their environment, stress hormone levels rise and immune responses drop (Rodin, 1986). Captive animals therefore experience more stress and are more vulnerable to disease than are wild animals (Roberts, 1988). The crowding that occurs in high-density neighborhoods, prisons, and college dorms is another source of diminished feelings of control—and of elevated levels of stress hormones and blood pressure (Fleming & others, 1987; Ostfeld & others 1987).

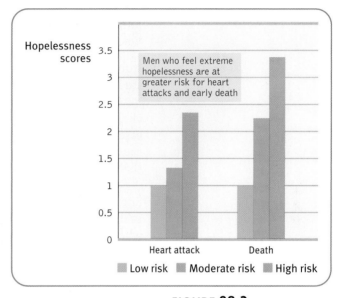

FIGURE 28.3

Toxic hopelessness

Compared with Finnish middle-aged men scoring low in hopelessness, those scoring high were two to four times more vulnerable to a heart attack over the ensuing six years and three to four times more likely to die. (Data from Everson & others, 1996.)

rehearse it!

1. The physiologist Walter Cannon described the role of the sympathetic nervous system in preparing the body for fight or flight. Hans Selye extended Cannon's findings by describing the body's adaptive response to stress in general. Selye's general adaptation syndrome (GAS) consists of an alarm reaction followed by
   a. fight or flight.
   b. resistance and exhaustion.
   c. challenge and recovery.
   d. stressful life events.

2. In the months following a catastrophe, such as an earthquake or a nuclear accident, there is a higher than usual number of short-term illnesses and stress-related psychological disorders. Following widowhood, there is an increased risk of illness and death. These findings suggest that
   a. daily hassles have adverse health consequences.
   b. experiencing a very stressful event increases one's vulnerability to illness and death.
   c. the amount of stress felt is directly related to the number of stressors involved.
   d. having a negative outlook has an adverse effect on recovery from illness.

3. Stressors are events that we appraise as threatening or challenging. Research suggests that the most significant sources of stress are
   a. catastrophes.
   b. traumatic events, such as the loss of a loved one.
   c. daily hassles.
   d. threatening events that we witness.

4. The stress we experience depends on how we perceive the events of our lives. A person (or animal) is most likely to find an event stressful and to suffer reduced immunity and other adverse health effects if the event seems
   a. painful or harmful.
   b. predictable and negative.
   c. uncontrollable and negative.
   d. both repellent and attractive.

coronary heart disease the clogging of the vessels that nourish the heart muscle; the leading cause of death in the United States.

Type A Friedman and Rosenman's term for competitive, hard-driving, impatient, verbally aggressive, and anger-prone people.

Type B Friedman and Rosenman's term for easygoing, relaxed people.

Stress and Heart Disease

PREVIEW QUESTION 3 Why are some of us more prone than others to coronary heart disease?

Although infrequent before 1900, **coronary heart disease**—the closing of the vessels that nourish the heart muscle—became by the 1950s North America's leading cause of death and remains so today. In addition to family history of the disease, many behavioral and physiological factors increase the risk of heart disease—smoking, obesity, a high-fat diet, physical inactivity, elevated blood pressure, and an elevated cholesterol level. The psychological factors of stress and personality also play a big role.

In 1956, cardiologists Meyer Friedman, Ray Rosenman, and their colleagues stumbled upon an indication of how big that role is (Friedman & Ulmer, 1984). While studying the eating behavior of San Francisco Junior League white women and their husbands, Friedman and Rosenman discovered that the women consumed as much cholesterol and fat as their husbands did, yet they were far less susceptible to heart disease. Was it because of their female sex hormones? No, the researchers surmised, because African-American women with the same sex hormones but facing more stress than the Junior Leaguers are as prone to heart disease as their husbands are.

The Junior League president thought she knew the answer. "If you really want to know what is going to give our husbands heart attacks, I'll tell you. It's stress," she said sadly, "the stress they have to face in their businesses, day in, day out. Why, when my husband comes home at night, it takes at least one martini just to unclench his jaws."

To test the idea that stress increases vulnerability to heart disease, Friedman and Rosenman measured the blood cholesterol level and clotting speed of 40 tax accountants. From January through March, both of these coronary warning indicators were completely normal. Then, as the accountants began scrambling to finish their clients' tax returns before the April 15 filing deadline, their cholesterol and clotting measures rose to dangerous levels. In May and June, with the deadline past, the measures returned to normal. The researchers' hunch had paid off: Stress predicted heart attack risk.

The stage was set for Friedman and Rosenman's classic nine-year study of more than 3000 healthy men aged 35 to 59. At the start of the study, they interviewed each man for 15 minutes about his work and eating habits. During the interview, they noted the man's manner of talking and other behavioral patterns. Those who seemed the most reactive, competitive, hard-driving, impatient, time-conscious, supermotivated, verbally aggressive, and easily angered they called **Type A.** A roughly equal number who were more easygoing they called **Type B.** Which group do you suppose turned out to be the most coronary-prone?

By the time the study was complete, 257 of the men had suffered heart attacks; 69 percent were Type A. Moreover, not one of the "pure" Type Bs—the most mellow and laid-back of their group—had suffered a heart attack.

As happens often in science, this exciting discovery provoked enormous public interest. But after the honeymoon period, in which the finding seemed definitive and revolutionary, other researchers began asking, Is the finding reliable? If so, what is the toxic component of the Type A profile: Time-consciousness? Competitiveness? Anger?

Why may Type A people be prone to heart disease? Further research found that reactive Type A individuals are more often "combat ready." When harassed or challenged, their active sympathetic nervous system redistributes bloodflow to the muscles and away from internal organs such as the liver, which removes cholesterol and

TYPE A PERSONALITY

Because it's there!

TYPE B PERSONALITY

Because it's there!

Bannerman © 7/94

In both India and America, Type A bus drivers are literally hard-driving: They brake, pass, and honk their horns more often than their more easygoing Type B colleagues (Evans & others, 1987).

fat from the blood. Thus, their blood may contain excess cholesterol and fat that later get deposited around the heart. Further stress—sometimes conflicts brought on by their own abrasiveness—may trigger the altered heart rhythms that, in those with weakened hearts, can cause sudden death (Kamarck & Jennings, 1991). In such ways, the hearts and minds of people interact.

More recent research has revealed that rather than a fast-paced life-style, Type A's toxic core is negative emotions—especially the anger associated with an aggressively reactive temperament (Miller & others, 1996; Williams, 1993). The effect of an anger-prone personality appears most noticeably in studies in which interviewers assess verbal assertiveness and emotional intensity. (If you pause in the middle of a sentence, an intense, anger-prone person may jump in and finish it for you.) Among young and middle-aged adults, those who react with anger over little things are the most coronary-prone. One study followed Duke University law students over 25 years. Those inclined to be hostile and cynical were five times more likely than their gentler, trusting classmates to die by middle age (Williams, 1989). As Charles Spielberger and Perry London (1982) put it, rage "seems to lash back and strike us in the heart muscle."

> "The fire you kindle for your enemy often burns you more than him."
>
> **Chinese proverb**

Anger is not the only toxic emotion. Depression, too, can be lethal. Centers for Disease Control researchers studied adults who were feeling a sense of hopelessness or at least mild depression. Compared with those without such feelings, these downhearted people were more vulnerable to heart disease in the ensuing 12 years. This was true even after controlling for differences in age, sex, smoking, and other factors linked to heart ailments (Anda & others, 1993). Another study (Whooley & Browner, 1998), of 7406 women age 67 or older with varying levels of depression, found significant differences in mortality, due partly to increased heart disease. Of those with no depressive symptoms, 7 percent died within six years, as did 17 percent of those with three to five depressive symptoms and 24 percent of those with six or more depressive symptoms. In the years following a heart attack, depressed people have a quadrupled risk of further heart problems (Frasure-Smith & others, 1995, 1999; Pratt & others, 1996). The depression that follows a spouse's death similarly increases one's risk of having a heart attack or stroke (National Academy of Sciences, 1984). All in all, the evidence from 57 studies suggests that "depression substantially increases the risk of death, especially death by unnatural causes and cardiovascular disease" (Wulsin & others, 1999).

The toxic effects of negative emotions help explain why about a quarter of medical inpatients suffer a mood or anxiety disorder, and why 4 in 10 chronically ill patients suffer or have suffered a psychiatric disorder (Cohen & Rodriguez, 1995; Katon & Sullivan, 1990). Negative emotions have physical consequences. The fats released during stress linger in the bloodstream and help form the plaque that clogs arteries. While making blood available to the extremities, stress also constricts blood vessels in the heart, decreasing blood flow to parts of the heart. Negative emotions may also contribute to poor health practices and health-related decisions.

> "When the heart is at ease, the body is healthy."
>
> **Chinese proverb**

Stress and Susceptibility to Disease

PREVIEW QUESTION 4 How does stress make us more vulnerable to disease?

Not so long ago, the term *psychosomatic* described psychologically caused physical symptoms. To laypeople, the term implied that the symptoms were unreal—they were "merely" psychosomatic. To avoid such connotations and to describe better the genuine physiological effects of psychological states, most experts today refer instead to **psychophysiological illnesses.** These illnesses, such as hypertension and some headaches, are stress-related. A person under stress may retain excess sodium and fluids, which, together with constriction of the arteries' muscle walls, contribute to increased blood pressure (Light & others, 1983).

■ **psychophysiological illness** literally, "mind-body" illness; any stress-related physical illness, such as hypertension and some headaches.

Stress and the Immune System

Evidence for the reality of psychophysiological ailments comes from hundreds of new experiments that reveal the nervous and endocrine systems' influence on the immune system. Your immune system is a complex surveillance system that defends your body by isolating and destroying bacteria, viruses, and other foreign substances. This system includes two types of white blood cells, called **lymphocytes.** *B lymphocytes* form in the *bone* marrow and release antibodies that fight bacterial infections. *T lymphocytes* form in the *thymus* and other lymphatic tissue and attack cancer cells, viruses, and foreign substances—even "good" ones, such as transplanted organs. Another agent of the immune system is the *macrophage* ("big eater"), which identifies, pursues, and ingests harmful invaders. Age, nutrition, genetics, body temperature, and stress all influence the immune system's activity.

Your immune system can err in two directions. Responding too strongly, it may attack the body's own tissues, causing arthritis or an allergic reaction. Or it may underreact, allowing, say, a dormant herpes virus to erupt or cancer cells to multiply. Women are immunologically stronger than men (Morell, 1995), making them less susceptible to infections. But this very strength also makes them more susceptible to self-attacking diseases, such as lupus and multiple sclerosis.

Your immune system is not a headless horseman. Rather, it exchanges information with your brain and your hormone-secreting endocrine system. The brain regulates the secretion of stress hormones, which in turn suppress the disease-fighting lymphocytes. Thus, when animals are physically restrained, given unavoidable electric shocks, or subjected to noise, crowding, cold water, social defeat, or maternal separation, their immune systems become less active (Maier & others, 1994). One study monitored immune responses in 43 monkeys over six months (Cohen & others, 1992). Twenty-one were stressed by being housed with new roommates—three or four new monkeys—each month. (To empathize with the monkeys, recall the stress of leaving home to attend school or summer camp, and imagine having to repeat this experience monthly.) Compared with monkeys left in stable groups, the socially disrupted monkeys experienced weakened immune systems.

Does stress similarly depress the immune system of humans? Consider:

- In three separate *Skylab* missions, the immune systems of the astronauts showed reduced effectiveness immediately after the stress of reentry and splashdown (Kimzey, 1975; Kimzey & others, 1976).
- Surgical wounds heal more slowly in stressed animals and humans. In one experiment, dental students received "punch wounds" (punching a precise small hole in the skin). Compared with wounds placed during summer vacation, those placed three days before a major exam healed 40 percent more slowly. In fact, report Janice Kiecolt-Glaser and her co-researchers (1998), "no student healed as rapidly during this stressful period as during vacation."
- Students' disease-fighting mechanisms are weaker during high-stress times, such as exam weeks, and on days when they are upset (Jemmott & Magloire, 1988; Stone & others, 1987). In one experiment, 47 percent of subjects living stress-filled lives developed colds after a virus was dropped in their noses, but only 27 percent of those living relatively free of stress caught colds (Cohen & others, 1991).
- Managing stress may be life-sustaining. The one personality trait shared by 169 centenarians (people over 100) was their ability to manage stress well (Silver & Perls, 1999).

The stress effect on immunity makes physiological sense (Maier & others, 1994). As we have seen, stress involves an aroused, fight-or-flight response. Stress diverts energy to the muscles and brain, mobilizing the body for action. The immune

"In the eyes of God or biology or what have you, it is just very important to have women."

Immunologist Normal Talal (1996)

The immune system in action
A large macrophage (at top) is about to trap and ingest a tiny bacterium (lower right). Macrophages constantly patrol our bodies in search of invaders—such as this Escherichia coli bacterium—and debris, such as worn-out red blood cells.

response to disease is a competing energy system. It takes energy to fight infections, produce inflammations, and maintain fevers. Thus, when diseased, our bodies reduce muscular energy output by inactivity and increased sleep. Stress diverts energy from the disease-fighting system, rendering us more vulnerable to illness. The bottom line: Stress does not make us sick, but it does restrain our immune functioning, making us more vulnerable to foreign invaders.

Stress and AIDS

AIDS has become the world's fourth leading cause of death and the number one killer in Africa, where in 1998 it took 1.83 million lives (Balter, 1999). AIDS, as its name tells us, is an immune disorder—an *acquired immune deficiency syndrome* caused by the human immunodeficiency virus (HIV), which is spread by the exchange of bodily fluids, primarily semen and blood. If a disease that is spread by human contact kills very quickly, it likely will not kill many. If, as with HIV, it kills slowly, it ironically can be lethal to more people: Those who carry the disease have time to spread it, often without realizing they are infected. When the HIV infection becomes manifest as AIDS, some years after the initial infection, the person has difficulty fighting off other diseases, such as pneumonia. Worldwide, reports the United Nations, 22 million people had died of AIDS and 36 million people were infected with HIV in 2000 (UNAIDS, 2000).

So if chronic stress serves to suppress immune functioning, could it also exacerbate the course of AIDS? Researchers have found that stress and negative emotions do correlate with a progression from HIV infection to AIDS and with the speed of decline in those infected (Bower & others, 1998; Kiecolt-Glaser & Glaser, 1995; Leserman & others, 1999). HIV-infected men faced with stressful life circumstances, such as the loss of a partner, exhibit somewhat greater immune suppression and a faster disease progression.

Would efforts to reduce stress help control the disease? Although the benefits are small compared with available drug treatments, the answer appears again to be yes. Educational initiatives, bereavement support groups, cognitive therapy, and exercise programs that reduce distress have all had positive consequences for HIV-positive individuals (Baum & Posluszny, 1999; Schneiderman, 1999).

Stress and Cancer

Stress and negative emotions such as anger and depression have also been linked to cancer's rate of progression. To explore a possible connection between stress and cancer, experimenters have implanted tumor cells into rodents or given them cancer-producing substances. Those rodents also exposed to uncontrollable stress, such as inescapable shocks, were more prone to cancer (Sklar & Anisman, 1981). With their immune systems weakened by stress, their tumors developed sooner and grew larger.

In people, some researchers have found no link between stress and cancer (Edelman & Kidman, 1997; Fox, 1998; Petticrew & others, 1999). Concentration camp and prisoner of war survivors, for example, have not exhibited elevated cancer rates. However, other investigators report that people are at increased risk for cancer within a year after experiencing depression, helplessness, or bereavement. For example, cancer occurs slightly more often than usual among those widowed, divorced, or separated. A study of the husbands of women with terminal breast

lymphocytes the two types of white blood cells that are part of the body's immune system: B lymphocytes form in the bone marrow and release antibodies that fight bacterial infections; T lymphocytes form in the thymus and, among other duties, attack cancer cells, viruses, and foreign substances.

Supporting survival
Can support groups delay the course of cancer? One experiment has suggested that they can. Other research, currently under way, will reveal whether this finding is replicable.

cancer pinpointed a possible reason: During the first two months after their wives' deaths, the bereaved men's lymphocyte responses dropped (Schleifer & others, 1979).

Another study gave a personality test to 2018 middle-aged men employed by the Western Electric Company in 1958. During the next 20 years, 7 percent of those with no symptoms of depression died of cancer, as did 12 percent of those who were somewhat depressed (Persky & others, 1987). A large Swedish study revealed that people with a history of workplace stress had 5.5 times greater risk of colon cancer than those who reported no such problems (Courtney & others, 1993). In both studies, the cancer difference was not attributable to differences in age, smoking, drinking, or physical characteristics.

In the first weeks after receiving their diagnosis, cancer patients understandably feel anxious and depressed (Andersen, 1989). Might promoting their fighting spirit aid their survival? Can hope boost the body by alleviating negative emotions that suppress the cancer-fighting immune system?

Although the jury is still out, some studies suggest that mastectomy patients who display a determination to conquer their breast cancer survive longer than do those who are stoic or feel hopeless (Hall & Goldstein, 1986; Pettingale & others, 1985). What is more, in some studies, cancer patients who bottle up their negative emotions have had a somewhat lower chance of survival than those who verbalized their feelings (McKenna & others, 1999; O'Leary, 1990; Temoshok, 1992).

One danger in publicizing reports on attitudes and cancer is that they may lead some patients to blame themselves for their illness—"If only I had been more expressive, relaxed, and hopeful." A corollary danger is a "wellness macho" among the healthy, who credit their health to their healthy character and lay a guilt trip on the ill: "She has cancer? That's what you get for holding your feelings in and being so nice." Dying thus becomes the ultimate failure.

In noting the modest link between emotions and cancer prognosis, we must remember that stress does not create cancer cells. Rather, it affects their growth by weakening the body's natural defenses against a few proliferating, malignant cells. Although a relaxed, hopeful state may enhance these defenses, we should be aware of the thin line that divides science from wishful thinking. The physiological processes at work in advanced cancer or AIDS are not likely to be derailed by avoiding stress or by a relaxed but determined spirit (Kessler & others, 1991).

Conditioning the Immune System

A hay fever sufferer sees the flower on the restaurant table and, not realizing it is plastic, begins to sneeze. Such experiences hint that stress is not the only psychological influence on the body's ailments. Simple classical conditioning may be an added influence. This raises an intriguing question: If conditioning affects the body's overt physiological responses, might it affect the immune system as well?

Psychologist Robert Ader and immunologist Nicholas Cohen (1985) discovered that the answer is yes. Ader came upon this discovery while researching taste aversion in rats. He paired the rats' drinking of saccharin-sweetened water with injections of a drug that happened to suppress immune functioning. After repeated pairings, sweetened water alone triggered immune suppression, as if the drug had been given **FIGURE 28.4**). Such conditioned immune suppression can triple an animal's likelihood of growing a tumor when fed a carcinogen (Blom & others, 1995).

Many questions about the role of the immune system and ways to harness its healing potential remain unanswered. If it is possible to condition the immune system's suppression, should it not also be possible to condition its enhancement? Might this be one way in which placebos—treatments that have no biochemical effect—promote healing? Can a placebo sometimes elicit the same healthful state produced by an actual drug? Research now under way is hoping to answer such questions.

"A cheerful heart is a good medicine, but a downcast spirit dries up the bones."

Proverbs 17:22

"I didn't give myself cancer."

Mayor Barbara Boggs Sigmund, 1939–1990, Princeton, New Jersey

When organic causes of illness are unknown, it is tempting to invent psychological explanations. Before the germ that causes tuberculosis was discovered, personality explanations of TB were popular (Sontag, 1978).

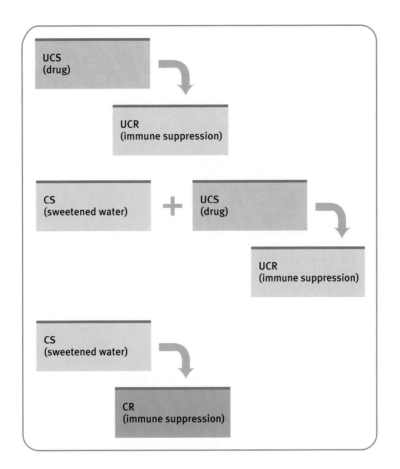

FIGURE 28.4

The conditioning of immune suppression

After Ader and Cohen (1985) associated sweetened water (the conditioned stimulus) with a drug (the unconditioned stimulus) that causes immune suppression in rats (the unconditioned response), the inert substance alone triggered the conditioned immune response.

For now, we can view the toll that stress sometimes takes on our resistance to disease (**FIGURE 28.5**) as a price we pay for the adaptive benefits of stress. Stress invigorates our lives by arousing and motivating us. An unstressed life would hardly be challenging or productive. Moreover, spending our resources in fighting or fleeing an external threat aids our immediate survival. But it does so at the cost of diminished resources for fighting internal threats to our body's health. When the stress is momentary, the cost is negligible. When uncontrollable aggravations persist, however, the cost may become considerable.

This new behavioral medicine research provides yet another reminder of one of contemporary psychology's overriding themes. *Mind and body continuously interact—everything psychological is simultaneously physiological.* Psychological states are physiological events that can influence other parts of our physiological system. Just pausing to *think* about biting into an orange section—the sweet, tangy juice from the pulpy fruit flooding across your tongue—can trigger salivation. As the Indian sage Santi Parva recognized more than 4000 years ago, "Mental disorders arise from physical causes, and likewise physical disorders arise from mental causes." There is interplay between our heads and our health.

FIGURE 28.5

Negative emotions can have a variety of health-related consequences

This is especially so when experienced by "disease-prone" angry, depressed, or anxious persons.

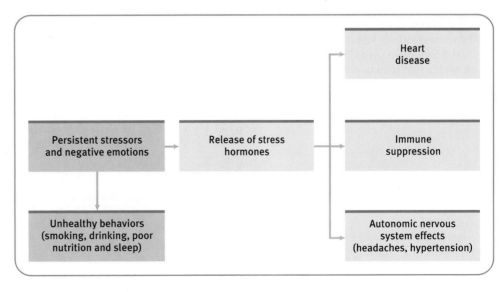

rehearse it!

5. Cardiologists Meyer Friedman, Ray Rosenman, and their colleagues observed that heart attacks were more frequent in Type A men—in those who appeared to be hard-driving, verbally aggressive, and anger-prone. The component of Type A behavior linked most closely to coronary heart disease is
   a. living a fast-paced life-style.
   b. working in a competitive area.
   c. meeting deadlines and challenges.
   d. feeling angry and negative much of the time.

6. Evidence suggests that disease-fighting mechanisms are weakened during times of high stress—for example, following the death of a loved one. Stress hormones suppress the lymphocytes, which ordinarily attack bacteria, viruses, cancer cells, and other foreign substances. The stress

   hormones are released mainly in response to a signal from the
   a. lymphocytes and macrophages.
   b. brain.
   c. upper respiratory tract.
   d. adrenal glands.

7. Research has shown people are at increased risk for cancer a year or so after experiencing depression, helplessness, or bereavement. In describing this link between emotions and cancer, researchers are quick to point out that
   a. accumulated stress that is not relieved by positive emotions poses the greatest threat to people who are genetically vulnerable to cancer.
   b. anger is the negative emotion most closely linked to cancer.
   c. stress does not create cancer cells, but it weakens the body's natural defenses against them.

   d. feeling optimistic about chances of survival ensures that a cancer patient will get well.

8. In testing taste aversion in rats, researchers paired the rats' drinking of saccharin-sweetened water with injections of a drug that suppressed immune functioning. After repeated pairings, sweetened water *alone* triggered immune suppression. These results suggest that
   a. the immune system is under the direct control of the hypothalamus.
   b. classical conditioning may influence the body's ailments.
   c. placebos are as effective as actual drugs in treating the body's ailments.
   d. external threats diminish our body's ability to fight internal threats.

REVIEWING

Stress and Illness

1. What is stress?

Walter Cannon viewed stress, the process by which we appraise and respond to events that challenge or threaten us, as a fight-or-flight system. Hans Selye saw it as a three-stage (alarm-resistance-exhaustion) general adaptation syndrome (GAS).

2. What events provoke stress responses?

Modern research on stress assesses the health consequences of catastrophic events, significant life changes, and daily hassles. The events that tend to provoke stress responses are those that we perceive as both negative and uncontrollable. Optimists seem to cope more successfully with stress and enjoy better health.

3. Why are some of us more prone than others to coronary heart disease?

Coronary heart disease, North America's number one cause of death, has been linked with the competitive, hard-driving, impatient, and (especially) anger-prone Type A personality. Under stress, the body of a reactive, hostile person secretes more of the hormones that accelerate the buildup of plaque on the heart's artery walls. Type B personalities are more relaxed and easygoing.

4. How does stress make us more vulnerable to disease?

Stress diverts energy from the immune system, inhibiting the activities of its B and T lymphocytes and macrophages. Although stress does not cause diseases such as cancer, it may influence the disease's progression. Research indicates that conditioning also influences the immune system's responses.

TERMS AND CONCEPTS TO REMEMBER

stress, p. 422
general adaptation syndrome (GAS), p. 423

health psychology, p. 424
coronary heart disease, p. 428
Type A, p. 428

Type B, p. 428
psychophysiological illness, p. 429

lymphocytes, p. 430

REHEARSE IT ANSWER KEY

1. b   2. b   3. c   4. c   5. d   6. b   7. c   8. b

Promoting Health

PREVIEW QUESTION 1 What tactics can we use to manage stress and reduce stress-related ailments?

Traditionally, people have sought out physicians for the diagnosis and treatment of disease. That, say health psychologists, is like ignoring a car's maintenance and going to a mechanic only when the car breaks down. Now that we realize that our attitudes and behaviors affect our health, attention is turning to health maintenance—on ways of coping with stress, preventing illness, and promoting well-being.

Stressors are unavoidable. This fact, coupled with the growing awareness that recurring stress correlates with heart disease, lowered immunity, and other bodily ailments, gives us a clear message. If we cannot eliminate stress by changing or ignoring a situation, we had best learn to manage it—by confronting or escaping the problem and taking steps to prevent its recurrence. Stress management may include aerobic exercise, biofeedback, relaxation, and social support.

Aerobic Exercise

Aerobic exercise is sustained exercise that increases heart and lung fitness. Clearly, such exercise strengthens the body. Does it also boost the spirit?

Exercise and Mood

Many studies suggest that aerobic exercise can reduce stress, depression, and anxiety. One in 3 Americans and about 4 in 10 Canadians exercise regularly, and studies indicate that they also cope better with stressful events, exhibit more self-confidence, feel more vigor, and feel depressed and fatigued less often than those who exercise less (Brown, 1991; *Prevention,* 1995; *Statistics Canada,* 1999). But if we state this observation the other way around—that stressed and depressed people exercise less—cause and effect become unclear.

Experiments have resolved this ambiguity by randomly assigning stressed, depressed, or anxious people either to aerobic exercise or to other treatments. In one such experiment, Lisa McCann and David Holmes (1984) assigned one-third of a group of mildly depressed female college students to a program of aerobic exercise and another third to a treatment of relaxation exercises; the remaining third, a control group, received no treatment. As **FIGURE 29.1** on page 436 shows, 10 weeks later the women in the aerobic exercise program reported the greatest decrease in depression. Many of them had, quite literally, run away from their troubles.

More than 100 other studies confirm that exercise reduces depression and anxiety (Berger & Motl, 2000; Craft & Landers, 1998). Repeated surveys, some by government health agencies, reveal that Canadians and Americans are more self-confident, self-disciplined, and psychologically resilient if physically fit (Stephens, 1988). Just a 10-minute walk stimulates two hours of increased well-being by raising energy levels and lowering tension (Thayer, 1987, 1993).

Researchers are now wondering *why* aerobic exercise alleviates the effects of stress and negative emotions. They know that exercise

- strengthens the heart, increases blood flow, and lowers both blood pressure and the blood pressure reaction to stress (Perkins & others, 1986; Roviario & others, 1984).

"Is there anyone here who specializes in stress management?"

■ **aerobic exercise** sustained exercise that increases heart and lung fitness; may also alleviate depression and anxiety.

FIGURE 29.1

Aerobic exercise and depression

Mildly depressed college women who participated in an aerobic exercise program showed markedly reduced depression, compared with those who did relaxation exercises or received no treatment. (From McCann & Holmes, 1984.)

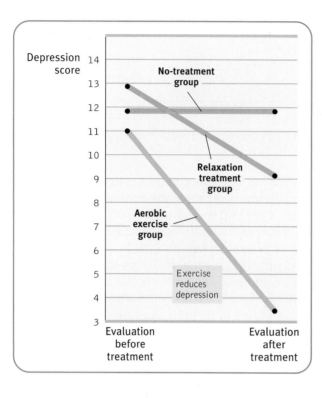

Depression score

- No-treatment group
- Relaxation treatment group
- Aerobic exercise group

Exercise reduces depression

Evaluation before treatment   Evaluation after treatment

- orders up chemicals from our body's internal pharmacy by increasing production of mood-boosting neurotransmitters such as norepinephrine, serotonin, and the endorphins (Jacobs, 1994).
- modestly enhances cognitive abilities, such as memory (Etnier & others, 1997).
- promotes the growth of new brain cells in mice exercising daily on a running wheel regimen (Kempermann & Gage, 1999).

Perhaps the emotional benefits of exercise are also a side effect of increased body arousal and warmth or of the muscle relaxation and sounder sleep that occur afterward. Or perhaps a sense of accomplishment and an improved physique enhance one's emotional state.

The mood boost

Aerobic exercise, such as running, appears to counteract depression partly by increasing arousal (replacing depression's low-arousal state) and by doing naturally what Prozac does—increasing the brain's serotonin activity.

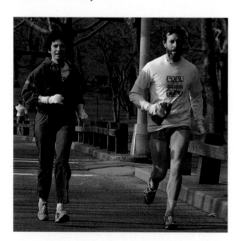

Exercise and Health

Other research reveals that exercise not only boosts our mood, but also benefits our physical health. A digest of data from 43 studies revealed that, compared with inactive adults, people who exercise suffer half as many heart attacks (Powell & others, 1987). Exercise makes the muscles hungry for the "bad fats" that contribute to clogged arteries (Barinaga, 1997). A study following adult Finnish twins for nearly 20 years revealed that, other things being equal, occasional exercise reduced the risk of death by 29 percent, compared with no exercise. Daily conditioning exercise reduced death risk by 43 percent (Kujala & others, 1998).

By one estimate, moderate exercise adds two years to one's expected life. "Perhaps God does not subtract the time spent exercising from your allotted time on Earth," jests Martin Seligman (1994, p. 193). So, couch potatoes, for both a mood boost and better health, off your duffs!

Biofeedback and Relaxation

Knowing the damaging effects of stress, could we train people to bring their heart rate and blood pressure under conscious control? When a few psychologists started experimenting with this idea, many of their colleagues thought them foolish. After all, these functions are controlled by the autonomic ("involuntary") nervous system. Then, in the late 1960s, experiments by respected psychologists began to make the skeptics wonder. Neal Miller, for one, found that rats could modify their heartbeat if given pleasurable brain stimulation when their heartbeat increased or decreased. Later research revealed that some paralyzed humans could also learn to control their blood pressure (Miller & Brucker, 1979).

Miller was experimenting with **biofeedback,** a system of recording, amplifying, and feeding back information about subtle physiological responses. Biofeedback instruments have been likened to a mirror (Norris, 1986). The instruments no more control one's body than a mirror combs one's hair. Rather, by reflecting the results of a person's own efforts, they allow the person to assess which techniques are most effective in controlling a particular physiological response.

In the example in **FIGURE 29.2**, a sensor records tension in the forehead muscle of a person with chronic headaches. A computer processes this physiological information and instantly feeds it back to the person in some easily understood signal. As the person relaxes the forehead muscle, the pointer on the display screen (or a tone) may go lower. The patient's task is to learn to control the pointer or tone and thereby learn to control the tension in the forehead muscle and the accompanying headaches.

System receives signal • Amplifies signal • Processes signal • Feedback • Displays signal • Patient observes signal

FIGURE 29.2
Self-monitoring
Biofeedback systems—such as this one, which records tension in the forehead muscle of a headache sufferer—allow people to monitor their subtle physiological responses.

■ **biofeedback** a system for electronically recording, amplifying, and feeding back information regarding a subtle physiological state, such as blood pressure or muscle tension.

The initial excitement over potential uses for biofeedback triggered some 4000 follow-up studies, including more than 400 in Russia (Sokhadze & Shtark, 1991). But after a decade of study, researchers decided that biofeedback had been oversold (Miller, 1985). The system does enable some people to influence their finger temperature and forehead-muscle tension, and it can help somewhat in reducing the intensity of migraine headaches and chronic pain (King & Montgomery, 1980; Qualls & Sheehan, 1981; Turk & others, 1979). A 1995 National Institutes of Health panel declared that biofeedback works best on tension headaches. But other, simpler methods of relaxation, which require no expensive equipment, produce many of the same benefits.

If relaxation is an important part of biofeedback, then wouldn't relaxation exercises alone be a natural antidote for stress? Cardiologist Herbert Benson (1996) became intrigued with this possibility when he found that experienced meditators could decrease their blood pressure, heart rate, and oxygen consumption and raise their fingertip temperature. You can experience the essence of this *relaxation response,* as Benson calls it, right now: Assume a comfortable position, breathe deeply, and relax your muscles from foot to face. Now, concentrate on a single word or a phrase. (About 80 percent of Benson's patients choose to focus on a favorite prayer.) Close your eyes and let other thoughts drift away when they intrude as you repeat your phrase continually for 10 to 20 minutes.

Many of those who simply set aside a quiet time or two each day report enjoying the tranquility. Stress worsens pain, infertility, and insomnia, and it suppresses the immune system. Meditative relaxation counteracts all these effects, Benson reports. One astonishing study assigned 73 residents of homes for the elderly either to daily meditation or to none. After three years, one-fourth of the nonmeditators had died, while all the meditators were still alive (Alexander & others, 1989).

Meditation is a modern phenomenon with a long history: "Sit down alone and in silence. Lower your head, shut your eyes, breathe out gently, and imagine yourself looking into your own heart. . . . As you breathe out, say 'Lord Jesus Christ, have mercy on me.' . . . Try to put all other thoughts aside. Be calm, be patient and repeat the process very frequently" (Gregory of Sinai, died 1346).

Learning the "relaxation response"
Relaxation training is a component of many stress-reduction programs. At Boston's Deaconess Hospital, hypertension patients learn meditation techniques that counteract stress.

Another relaxation study focused on Type A heart attack victims. If these competitive, hard-driving, impatient, and (especially) anger-prone people could be taught to relax, might their risk of another attack be reduced? To find out, Meyer Friedman and his colleagues randomly assigned hundreds of middle-aged heart attack survivors in San Francisco to one of two groups. The first group received standard advice from cardiologists concerning medications, diet, and exercise habits. The second group received similar advice plus continuing counseling on modifying their life-styles—how to slow down and relax by walking, talking, and eating more slowly; by smiling at others and laughing at themselves; by admitting mistakes; by taking time to enjoy life; and by renewing their religious faith. As **FIGURE 29.3** indicates, during the ensuing three years, the second group experienced half as many repeat heart attacks as the first group. This, wrote the exuberant Friedman, is an unprecedented, spectacular reduction in heart attack recurrence. A smaller-scale British study similarly divided heart-attack–prone people into control and life-style modification groups (Eysenck &

FIGURE 29.3

Recurrent heart attacks and life-style modification

The San Francisco Recurrent Coronary Prevention Project offered survivors of heart attacks counseling from a cardiologist. Those who were also guided in modifying their Type A life-style suffered fewer repeat heart attacks. (From Friedman & Ulmer, 1984.)

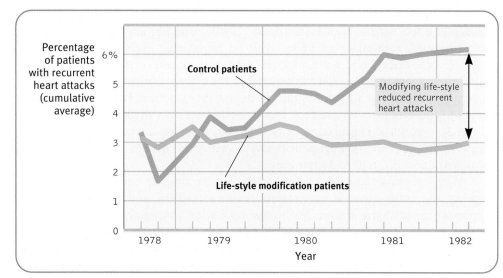

Grossarth-Maticek, 1991). During the next 13 years, it also found a 50 percent reduction in death rate among those trained to alter their thinking and life-style.

Social Support

Linda and Emily had much in common. When interviewed for a study conducted by UCLA social psychologist Shelley Taylor (1989), both Los Angeles women had married, raised three children, suffered comparable breast tumors, and recovered from surgery and six months of chemotherapy. But there was a difference. Linda, a widow in her early fifties, was living alone, her children scattered in Atlanta, Boston, and Europe. "She had become odd in ways that people sometimes do when they are isolated," reported Taylor. "Having no one with whom to share her thoughts on a daily basis, she unloaded them somewhat inappropriately with strangers, including our interviewer."

Interviewing Emily was difficult in a different way. Phone calls interrupted. Her children, all living nearby, were in and out of the house, dropping things off with a quick kiss. Her husband called from his office for a brief chat. Two dogs roamed the house, greeting visitors enthusiastically. All in all, Emily "seemed a serene and contented person, basking in the warmth of her family."

Three years later, the researchers tried to reinterview the women. Linda, they learned, had died two years before. Emily was still lovingly supported by her family and friends and was as happy and healthy as ever.

Because no two cancers are identical, we can't be certain that different social situations led to Linda's and Emily's fates. But they do illustrate a conclusion drawn from several large studies: Social support—feeling liked, affirmed, and encouraged by intimate friends and family—promotes not only happiness but also health.

However, relationships can sometimes be stressful, especially in living conditions that are crowded and lack privacy (Evans & others, 1989). "Hell is others," wrote Jean-Paul Sartre. Peter Warr and Roy Payne (1982) at the University of Sheffield asked a representative sample of British adults what, if anything, had emotionally strained them the day before. Their most frequent answer? "Family." Even when well-meaning, family intrusions can be stressful. And stress, as we have seen, contributes to heart disease, hypertension, and a suppressed immune system.

On balance, however, close relationships more often contribute to health and happiness. Asked what prompted yesterday's times of pleasure, the same British sample, by an even larger margin, again answered, "Family." For most of us, family relationships provide not only our greatest heartaches but also our greatest comfort and joy. Moreover, seven massive investigations, each following thousands of people for several years, revealed that close relationships affect health. Compared with those having few social ties, people are less likely to die prematurely if supported by close relationships with friends, family, fellow workers, religious group members, or other support groups (Cohen, 1988; House & others, 1988; Nelson, 1988).

There are several possible reasons for the link between social support and health (Helgeson & others, 1998). One study following 50,000 young adults through time found, for example, that unhealthy behaviors such as smoking and not exercising drop precipitously after marriage (Marano, 1998). But environments that support our need to belong can also foster stronger immune functioning. Given ample social support, spouses of cancer patients exhibit stronger immune functioning (Baron & others, 1990). Social ties even confer resistance to cold viruses. Sheldon Cohen and his colleagues (1997) demonstrated this after putting 276 healthy volunteers in quarantine for five days after administering

Humans aren't the only source of stress-buffering comfort. After stressful events, Medicare patients who have a dog or other companionable pet are less likely to visit their doctor (Siegel, 1990).

"Woe to one who is alone and falls and does not have another to help."

Ecclesiastes 4:10

"I get by with a little help from my friends."

John Lennon and Paul McCartney, *Sgt. Pepper's Lonely Hearts Club Band*, 1967

nasal drops laden with a cold virus. (The volunteers were paid $800 each to endure this experience.) The cold fact is that the effect of social ties is nothing to sneeze at. Age, race, sex, smoking, and other health habits being equal, those with the most social ties were least likely to catch a cold and they produced less mucus. More than 50 studies further reveal that social support calms the cardiovascular system, lowering blood pressure and stress hormones (Uchino & others, 1996, 1999).

Close relationships also provide the opportunity to *confide* painful feelings, a social support component that has now been extensively studied. In one study, health psychologists James Pennebaker and Robin O'Heeron (1984) contacted the surviving spouses of people who had committed suicide or died in car accidents. Those who bore their grief alone had more health problems than those who could express it openly. Talking about our troubles can be "open heart therapy." Older people, many of whom have lost a spouse and close friends, are somewhat less likely to enjoy such confiding (**FIGURE 29.4**).

FIGURE 29.4

Social support across the life span

Do you have someone you can confide in? Someone to count on in a crisis? Someone to count on for advice? Someone who makes you feel loved and cared for? In a national health survey, 9 in 10 young adult Canadians, but only 7 in 10 over the age of 75, indicated high social support by answering yes to all four questions. (Data from *Statistics Canada*, 1999, page 133.)

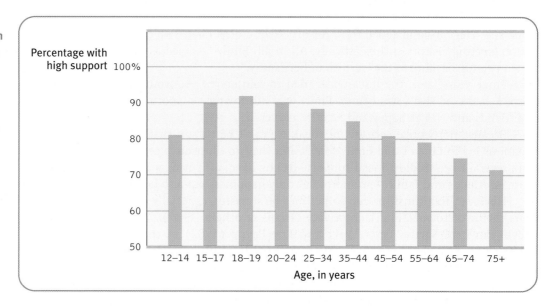

Actively suppressing thoughts can cause them to bubble up intrusively, preoccupying the person (Wegner, 1990). (In the next five seconds, please *don't* picture a white bear.) Disclosing suppressed thoughts may stop their intrusion. In a simulated confessional, Pennebaker asked volunteers to share with a hidden experimenter some upsetting events that had been preying on their minds. He asked some of the volunteers to describe a trivial event before they divulged the troubling one. Physiological measures revealed that their bodies remained tense the whole time they talked about the trivial event; they relaxed only when they later confided the cause of their turmoil. Even writing about personal traumas in a diary can help. When volunteers in other experiments did this,

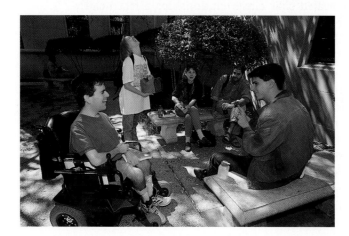

Friendships are good medicine

Several long-term studies of thousands of people have found that individuals with close supportive relationships are less likely than socially isolated people to die prematurely.

they had fewer health problems during the ensuing four to six months (Pennebaker, 1990). As one subject explained, "Although I have not talked with anyone about what I wrote, I was finally able to deal with it, work through the pain instead of trying to block it out. Now it doesn't hurt to think about it."

Suppressed traumas sometimes eat away at us and affect our physical health. When Pennebaker surveyed more than 700 undergraduate women, he found that about 1 in 12 reported a traumatic sexual experience in childhood. Compared with women who had experienced nonsexual traumas, such as parental death or divorce, the sexually abused women—especially those who had kept their secret to themselves—reported more headaches and stomach ailments.

Pennebaker and his colleagues (1989) also invited 33 Holocaust survivors to spend two hours recalling their experiences. Many did so in intimate detail never before disclosed. Most watched and showed family and friends a videotape of their recollections in the weeks following. Again, those who were most self-disclosing had the most improved health 14 months later. Talking about a stressful event can temporarily arouse people, but in the long run it calms them (Mendolia & Kleck, 1993). Confiding is good for the soul.

Let's summarize: Sustained emotional reactions to stressful events can be debilitating. However, the stress experienced depends on the person and the environment. Nothing is stressful until we appraise it as such. When stressful things happen, our personalities and interpretations influence how we react emotionally. Moreover, the toxic impact of stressful events can be buffered by a relaxed, healthy life-style and by the comfort and aid provided by supportive friends and family (**FIGURE 29.5**).

FIGURE 29.5
Coping with stress
Life events can be debilitating or not. It all depends on how we appraise them and whether the stresses are buffered by a stress-resistant disposition, healthy habits, and enduring social support.

Spirituality and Faith Communities

Throughout history, humans have suffered ills and sought healing. In response, the two healing traditions—religion and medicine—historically have joined hands in care of the sick. Religious and healing efforts were often conducted by the same person; the priest was also the healer. Maimonides was a twelfth-century rabbi and a renowned physician. Hospitals were first established in monasteries, then spread by missionaries.

As medical science matured, however, healing and religion diverged. Rather than simply asking God to spare their children from smallpox, people began vaccinating them. Rather than seeking a spiritual healer when burning with bacterial fever, they turned to antibiotics.

This wall between religion and medicine is now breaking down again. "Spirituality" has made a comeback. Pollster George Gallup (1994) detected "the search for spiritual moorings" as a "dominant trend" in the mid-1990s. Since 1995, Harvard Medical School has annually attracted nearly 2000 health professionals from across North America to its Spirituality and Healing in Medicine conferences. Duke University has established a Center for the Study of Religion/Spirituality and Health. And 61 of America's 126 medical schools were offering spirituality and health courses in 1999, up from 3 in 1994 (Levin & others, 1997; McVeigh, 1999). A Yankelovich survey found 94 percent of HMO professionals and 99 percent of family physicians agreeing that "personal prayer, meditation, or other spiritual and religious practices" can enhance medical treatment. This renewed convergence of religion and medicine was also evident in such books as *The Faith Factor* (Viking, 1998), *The Healing Power of Faith* (Simon & Schuster, 1999), and *Religion and Health* (Oxford University Press, 2000). *Time* magazine, not to be left out, devoted a 1996 cover story to "Faith and Healing."

Is there fire underneath all this smoke? Do religion and spirituality actually relate to health, as polls show 4 in 5 Americans believe (Matthews, 1997)? More than a thousand studies have sought to correlate "the faith factor" with health and healing. Consider two:

- Jeremy Kark and his colleagues (1996) compared the death rates for 3900 Israelis either in one of 11 religiously orthodox or in one of 11 matched, nonreligious collective settlements (kibbutz communities). The researchers reported that over a 16-year period, "belonging to a religious collective was associated with a strong protective effect" not explained by age or economic differences. In every age group, those belonging to the religious communities were about half as likely as their nonreligious counterparts to have died. This is roughly comparable to the gender difference in mortality. (In every age group, 64 British and 60 American women die for every 100 men [*Chance News*, 1997].)

- An earlier study of 91,909 persons in one Maryland county found that those who attended religious services weekly were less likely to die during the study period than were those who did not—53 percent less from coronary disease, 53 percent less due to suicide, and 74 percent less from cirrhosis of the liver (Comstock & Partridge, 1972).

In response to such findings, Richard Sloan and his skeptical colleagues (1999) remind us that mere correlations can leave many factors uncontrolled. Consider one obvious possibility: Women are more religiously active than men, and women outlive men. So perhaps religious involvement is merely an expression of the gender effect on longevity.

However, several new studies find the religiosity-longevity correlation among men alone, and even more strongly among women (McCullough & others, 2000). One study that followed 5286 Californians over 28 years found that, after controlling for age, gender, ethnicity, and education, frequent religious attendees were 36 percent less likely to have died in any year (**FIGURE 29.6**). Another followed 3968 elderly North Carolinians for 6 years. It found that 23 percent of those attending religious services at least weekly had died, as had 37 percent of infrequent attendees (Koenig & others, 1999). A National Health Interview Survey (Hummer & others, 1999) followed 21,204 people over 8 years. After controlling for age, sex,

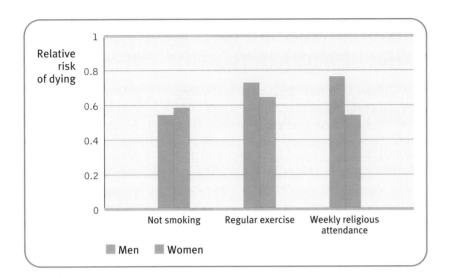

FIGURE 29.6

Not smoking, frequent exercise, and regular religious attendance as predictors of mortality

Epidemiologist William Strawbridge and his co-workers (1997, 1999) followed 5286 Alameda, California, adults over 28 years. After adjusting for age, ethnicity, and education, the researchers found that not smoking, regular exercise, and religious attendance all predicted a lowered risk of death in any given year. "The relative risk of dying" indicates how often nonsmokers, exercisers, and religious attenders died compared to smokers, nonexercisers, and nonattenders. Women attending weekly religious services, for example, were only 54 percent as likely to die in a typical study year as were nonattenders.

race, and region, researchers found that nonattenders were 1.87 times more likely to have died than were those attending more than weekly. This translated into a life expectancy at age 20 of 83 years for frequent attenders and 75 years for infrequent attenders (**FIGURE 29.7**).

These correlational findings do not indicate that if nonattenders start attending, and change nothing else, they will live 8 years longer. But they do indicate that as a *predictor* of health and longevity, religious involvement rivals nonsmoking and exercise effects. Such findings demand explanation. Can you imagine what "intervening variables" might account for the correlation?

First, in all the available studies, the beliefs of religiously active people motivate healthier life-styles; for example, they smoke and drink less. Health-oriented, vegetarian Seventh Day Adventists have a longer-than-usual life expectancy (Berkel & de Waard, 1983). Religiously orthodox Israelis eat less fat than do their nonreligious compatriots. But such differences are not great enough to explain the dramatically reduced mortality in the religious kibbutzim, argued the Israeli researchers. In the recent American studies, too, about a 75 percent longevity difference remains after controlling for unhealthy behaviors such as inactivity and smoking (Musick & others, 1999).

Social support is another variable that helps explain the "faith factor." For Judaism, Christianity, and Islam, faith is not solo spirituality but a communal experi-

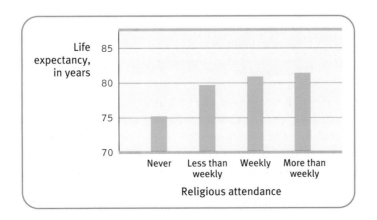

FIGURE 29.7

Religious attendance and life expectancy

In a national health survey financed by the Centers for Disease Control and Prevention, religiously active people had longer life expectancies. (Data from Hummer & others, 1999.)

ALTERNATIVE MEDICINE: NEW WAYS TO HEALTH OR OLD SNAKE OIL?

One health care growth market is **complementary and alternative medicine,** which encompasses acupuncture, massage therapy, homeopathy, spiritual healing, herbal remedies, chiropractic, aromatherapy, and the like. In Germany, herbal remedies and homeopathy are enormously popular. In China, herbal therapies have long flourished, as have acupuncture and acupressure therapies that claim to correct "imbalances of energy flow" (called *Qi* or *Chi*) at identifiable points close to the skin. In the United Kingdom, sales of alternative medical remedies were predicted to double in the five years surrounding 2000 (Ernst, 1998). In the United States, Andrew Weil's eight books on alternative medicine have sold millions of copies, putting him on the cover of *Time* magazine and gaining his Web site a reported 2.5 million monthly hits (Relman, 1998). Facing political pressure to explore such things, the National Institutes of Health established the National Center for Complementary and Alternative Medicine, which the center defines as health care treatments not taught widely in medical schools, not used in hospitals, and not usually reimbursed by insurance companies (Table 29.1). Furthering the alternative medicine boom, Congress increased the center's funding from $20 million in 1998 to $50 million in 1999.

So what shall we make of alternative medicine? Some aspects, such as life-style and stress management, have acknowledged validity. Do the other aspects offer, as some believe, a new medical paradigm for a new millennium? Or do they represent, as others maintain, "voodoo medicine"—a retreat from rationality and science?

Supporters of alternative medicine offer inspirational cases, such as these from Andrew Weil's books (Relman, 1998):

- A young woman diagnosed with bone cancer starts a vigorous exercise program (biking 500 miles and running 60 miles weekly), becomes vegetarian (consuming fresh fruit, juices, and whole grains), and shucks the alleged cancer.
- A woman uses "respiratory biofeedback" to end her Parkinson's-induced seizures.
- A man with scleroderma, a progressive and fatal disease of the skin and internal organs, cures himself with vinegar, lemons, aloe vera juice, and vitamin E.

But critics point out that people consult physicians for diagnosable,

> "Sickness is the manifestation of evil in the body."
>
> **Andrew Weil, *Health and Healing*, 1998**

TABLE 29.1

SUBFIELDS OF ALTERNATIVE MEDICINE

Alternative systems of medical practice	Health care ranging from self-care according to folk principles, to care rendered in an organized health care system based on alternative traditions or practices
Bioelectromagnetic applications	The study of how living organisms interact with electromagnetic (EM) fields
Diet, nutrition, life-style changes	The knowledge of how to prevent illness, maintain health, and reverse the effects of chronic disease through dietary or nutritional intervention
Herbal medicine	Employing plant and plant products from folk medicine traditions for pharmacological use
Manual healing	Using touch and manipulation with the hands as a diagnostic and therapeutic tool
Mind-body control	Exploring the mind's capacity to affect the body, based on traditional medical systems that make use of the interconnectedness of mind and body
Pharmacological and biological treatments	Drugs and vaccines not yet accepted by mainstream medicine

Source: Offered without endorsement by the National Center for Complementary and Alternative Medicine (nccam.nih.gov)

ence that helps satisfy the need to belong. The more than 350,000 faith communities in North America and the millions more elsewhere provide support networks for their active participants—people who are there for one another when stress strikes. Moreover, religion encourages another predictor of health and longevity—marriage. In the religious kibbutzim, for example, divorce is almost nonexistent.

curable diseases and employ alternative medicine when they either are incurably ill or are basically well but feeling subpar. So an otherwise healthy person with a cold, for example, may try an herbal remedy and then credit the subsequent return to good health to alternative medicine, rather than to the body's natural return to its normal state. Alternative medicine will seem especially effective with cyclical diseases, such as arthritis and allergies, as people seek therapy during the downturn and presume its effectiveness during the ensuing upturn. Add to this the healing power of belief—the placebo effect—plus the natural disappearance ("spontaneous remission") of many diseases, and voila: Alternative medicine practices are bound to seem effective, whether they are or not. In the 1700s, even bloodletting *seemed* effective. Sometimes people improved despite the treatment; when they did not, the practitioner inferred the disease was too far advanced to be reversed.

The National Council Against Health Fraud and the editors of leading medical journals and of the *Scientific Review of Alternative Medicine* doubt the efficacy of alternative medicine therapies. They note that for most alternative medicine claims the scientific jury is not out; it hasn't yet convened. Although the U.S. government's National Center for Complementary and Alternative Medicine is funding research, the 30 research grants it awarded in 1993 had, al-most six years later, produced only four studies found among the 3500 medical journals—and none of these controlled for placebo effects (Angell & Kassirer, 1998).

In November 1998, the *Journal of the American Medical Association* published seven new research studies. Three showed alternative medicine treatments to be useless (chiropractic manipulation for tension headaches, a popular herb for weight loss, and acupuncture to control nerve pain caused by HIV). Four other treatments—an herb mixture for inflammatory bowel syndrome, an herbal remedy for bladder problems, yoga for carpal tunnel syndrome pain, and a Chinese method for inducing fetuses in the breech position to turn—showed some benefits. Each now awaits replication, with new controls. As always, the way to discern what works and what does not is to experiment: Randomly assign patients to receive the therapy or a placebo control. Then ask the critical question: When neither the therapist nor the patient knows who is getting the real therapy, is the real therapy effective?

Much of today's mainstream medicine began as yesterday's alternative medicine, not all of which, like bloodletting, was refuted by controlled experiments. Natural botani-

> "In God we trust. All others must have data."
>
> **George Lundberg, Editor, *Journal of the American Medical Association*, 1998**

■ **complementary and alternative medicine** unproven health care treatments not taught widely in medical schools, not used in hospitals, and not usually reimbursed by insurance companies.

cal life has given us digitalis (from purple foxglove), morphine (from the opium poppy), and penicillin (from penicillium mold). In each case, the active ingredient was isolated, synthesized, and carefully verified in controlled trials. We have medical science, not alternative medicine, to thank for the antibiotics, vaccines, surgical procedures, and emergency medicine that helped lengthen our life expectancy by three decades during the last century. If you have acute chest pain, find a lump in your chest, cough up blood, or develop a high fever, you would do well to seek out someone trained in medical science—someone undergirded by research on what treatments really work best for what ailments at what doses for what lengths of time.

Indeed, said *New England Journal of Medicine* editors Marcia Angell and Jerome Kassirer (1998), "There cannot be two kinds of medicine—conventional and alternative. There is only medicine that has been adequately tested and medicine that has not, medicine that works and medicine that may or may not work. Once a treatment has been tested rigorously, it no longer matters whether it was considered alternative at the outset."

But even after controlling for gender, unhealthy behaviors, social ties, and preexisting health problems, the mortality studies find much of the mortality reduction remaining. Researchers therefore speculate that a third set of intervening variables is the stress protection and enhanced well-being associated with a coherent worldview, a sense of hope for the long-term future, feelings of ultimate acceptance, and the relaxed meditation of prayer or Sabbath observance (**FIGURE 29.8**). These variables might also help to explain other recent findings, such as healthier immune functioning and fewer hospital admissions among religiously active people (Koenig & Larson, 1998; Koenig & others, 1997).

FIGURE 29.8
Possible explanations for the correlation between religious involvement and health/longevity
The religion factor is multidimensional.

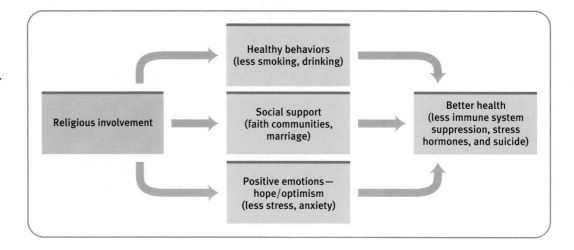

Although the religion-health correlation is yet to be fully explained, Harold Pincus (1997), deputy medical director of the American Psychiatric Association, believes these findings "have made clear that anyone involved in providing health care services . . . cannot ignore . . . the important connections between spirituality, religion, and health."

rehearse it!

1. A number of studies reveal that aerobic exercise raises energy levels and helps alleviate depression and anxiety. The reasons for these emotional effects of exercise are unclear. One explanation is that exercise triggers the release of mood-boosting neurotransmitters such as norepinephrine, serotonin, and
   a. the placebos.
   b. the endorphins.
   c. epinephrine.
   d. acetylcholine.

2. Neal Miller found that rats could learn to control their heartbeat when they were rewarded with pleasurable brain stimulation for doing so. Later research showed that some paralyzed humans could also learn to control blood pressure through biofeedback. Biofeedback was thought to help people exercise control over functions that are usually controlled by
   a. the autonomic nervous system.
   b. conscious thought.
   c. the immune system.
   d. external stimuli.

3. Long-term studies of thousands of people have shown that people who have close relationships—a strong social support system—are less likely to die prematurely than those who do not. These studies provide evidence that
   a. social ties can be a source of stress.
   b. people who lose a close relationship are at risk for illness.
   c. Type A behavior is responsible for many premature deaths.
   d. social support has a beneficial effect on health.

Promoting Health

1. What tactics can we use to manage stress and reduce stress-related ailments?

Among the components of stress management programs are aerobic exercise, biofeedback, and relaxation. Although the degree of mind control over the body that can be gained through biofeedback has fallen short of early expectations, biofeedback sometimes helps control tension headaches and high blood pressure.

Simple relaxation exercises offer some of the same benefits. Counseling Type A heart attack survivors to slow down and relax has helped them lower their rate of recurring attacks. Social support also helps people cope, partly by buffering the impact of stress. Researchers are now trying to understand the active components of the religion-health correlation.

TERMS AND CONCEPTS TO REMEMBER

aerobic exercise, p. 435

biofeedback, p. 436

complementary and alternative medicine, p. 444

REHEARSE IT ANSWER KEY

1. b   2. a   3. d

Personality

Novelist William Faulkner was a master at creating characters with vivid personalities.[1] One of his creations, Ike McCaslin, who appears at various ages in more than a dozen novels and short stories, is highly principled, and consistently so. At age 10 he feels a deep reverence for the wilderness and its creatures. At 21 he forfeits a "tainted" inheritance. In his late seventies he counsels his nephew to use his land responsibly. Ike the adult is clearly an extension of Ike the child.

Another Faulkner character, Jason Compson, is a selfish, whining 4-year-old at the beginning of *The Sound and the Fury,* and a selfish, screaming 34-year-old as the novel closes. As head of the Compson household, he verbally abuses family members and household servants. Lying, threatening, conniving, he was a self-centered child who became a self-centered adult.

Faulkner's characters, as they appear and reappear throughout his fiction, exhibit the distinctiveness and consistency that define personality. Psychology often emphasizes our similarity—how we all develop, perceive, learn, remember, think, and feel. To study personality is to study our individuality. Your individual *personality* is your characteristic pattern of thinking, feeling, and acting. If your behavior pattern is strikingly distinctive and consistent—if you are always outgoing, whether at a party or in a classroom—people are likely to say that you have a "strong" personality.

> "There is no man who is not, at each moment, what he has been and what he will be."
>
> Oscar Wilde, 1854–1900

Much of psychology is concerned with personality: biological influences on personality; personality development across the life span; personality-related aspects of learning, motivation, and emotion; disorders of personality; and social influences on personality.

Modules 30 through 33 explore and evaluate four major perspectives on personality:

- Sigmund Freud's *psychoanalytic* theory proposes that childhood sexuality and unconscious motivations influence personality (Module 30).
- The *trait* perspective identifies personality dimensions that account for our consistent behavior patterns (Module 31).
- The *humanistic* approach focuses on our inner capacities for growth and self-fulfillment (Module 32).
- The *social-cognitive* approach emphasizes how we shape and are shaped by our environment (Module 33).

Module 33 also includes some final reflections on these four perspectives.

---

[1]Faulkner scholar Nancy Nicodemus assisted with these examples.

30 The Psychoanalytic Perspective

- ■ **Exploring the Unconscious**

- ■ **Assessing the Unconscious**

- ■ **Evaluating the Psychoanalytic Perspective**

Ask 100 people on the street to name a notable deceased psychologist, suggests Keith Stanovich (1996, p. 1), and "Sigmund Freud would be the winner hands down." Freud's current influence in psychological science has diminished (Robins & others, 1999). But his influence lingers in literary and film interpretation, psychiatry, pop psychology . . . and Woody Allen movies. So, who was Freud, and what did he teach?

Well before entering the University of Vienna in 1873, a youthful Sigmund Freud showed signs of independence and brilliance. He had a prodigious memory and so loved reading plays, poetry, and philosophy that he once ran up a bookstore debt beyond his means. As a teen he often took his evening meal in his tiny bedroom in order to lose no time from his studies.

Freud went to medical school and after graduation set up a private practice, specializing in neurology. Before long, however, he faced patients whose disorders made no neurological sense. For example, a patient might have lost all feeling in a hand—yet there is no sensory nerve that, if damaged, would numb the entire hand and nothing else. Freud's search for the cause of such disorders set his mind running in a direction destined to change human self-understanding. He laid out the first comprehensive theory of **personality**—individuals' characteristic patterns of thinking, feeling, and acting.

Exploring the Unconscious

PREVIEW QUESTION 1 What was Freud's view of human personality, and what role do unconscious dynamics play in his theory of personality?

While experimenting with hypnosis, Freud "discovered" the unconscious. He decided that the loss of feeling in one's hand might be caused by a fear of touching one's genitals; that blindness or deafness might be caused by not wanting to see or hear something that aroused intense anxiety. He then turned to **free association**—in which he merely told the patient to relax and say whatever came to mind, no matter how embarrassing or trivial. Freud seemed to assume that a line of mental dominoes had fallen from his patients' distant past to their troubled present. Free association, he believed, allowed him to trace that line back, producing a chain of thought leading into the patient's unconscious, thereby retrieving and releasing painful unconscious memories, often from childhood. Freud called his theory and associated techniques **psychoanalysis.**

Sigmund Freud, 1856–1939
"I was the only worker in a new field."

Freud's consulting room
Freud's office was rich with antiquities from around the world, including art work related to his ideas about unconscious motives. His famous couch, piled high with pillows, placed patients in a comfortable reclining position facing away from him to help them focus inward.

Underlying Freud's psychoanalytic conception of personality was his belief that the mind is like an iceberg—mostly hidden. Our conscious awareness is the part of the iceberg that floats above the surface. Below the surface is the much larger, **unconscious** region containing thoughts, wishes, feelings, and memories, of which we are largely unaware. Some of these thoughts we store temporarily in a **preconscious** area, from which we can retrieve them into conscious awareness. Of greater interest to Freud was the mass of unacceptable passions and thoughts that he believed we *repress,* or forcibly block from our consciousness because they would be too unsettling to acknowledge. Freud believed that, although we are not consciously aware of them, these troublesome feelings and ideas powerfully influence us. In his view, our unacknowledged impulses express themselves in disguised forms—the work we choose, the beliefs we hold, our daily habits, our troubling symptoms. In such ways, the unconscious seeps into our thoughts and actions.

For Freud the determinist, nothing was ever accidental. He believed he could glimpse the unconscious seeping through, not only in people's free associations, beliefs, habits, and symptoms, but also in their dreams and slips of the tongue and pen. He illustrated with a financially stressed patient who, not wanting any large pills, said, "Please do not give me any bills, because I cannot swallow them." Similarly, Freud viewed jokes as expressions of repressed sexual and aggressive tendencies, and dreams as the "royal road to the unconscious." The remembered content of dreams (their *manifest content*) he believed to be a censored expression of the dream's unconscious meaning (the dream's *latent content*). By analyzing people's dreams, Freud believed, he could reveal the nature of their inner conflicts and release their inner tensions.

"Good morning, beheaded—uh, I mean beloved."

Personality Structure

PREVIEW QUESTION 2 How did Freud view personality structure and development, and how did he think people defended themselves against anxiety?

In Freud's view, human personality—including its emotions and strivings—arises from a conflict between our aggressive, pleasure-seeking biological impulses and the internalized social restraints against them. Personality is the result of our efforts to resolve this basic conflict—to express these impulses in ways that bring satisfaction without also bringing guilt or punishment.

Freud theorized that the conflict centers on three interacting systems: id, ego, and superego (**FIGURE 30.1**). These abstract psychological concepts are, said Freud, "useful aids to understanding" the mind's dynamics.

FIGURE 30.1

Freud's idea of the mind's structure Consciousness is like an iceberg's visible tip. Note that the id is totally unconscious, but ego and superego operate both consciously and unconsciously. (Adapted from Freud, 1933, page 111.)

- **personality** an individual's characteristic pattern of thinking, feeling, and acting.

- **free association** in psychoanalysis, a method of exploring the unconscious in which the person relaxes and says whatever comes to mind, no matter how trivial or embarrassing.

- **psychoanalysis** Freud's theory of personality that attributes our thoughts and actions to unconscious motives and conflicts; the techniques used in treating psychological disorders by seeking to expose and interpret unconscious tensions.

- **unconscious** according to Freud, a reservoir of mostly unacceptable thoughts, wishes, feelings, and memories. According to contemporary psychologists, information processing of which we are unaware.

- **preconscious** information that is not conscious but is retrievable into conscious awareness.

"I remember your name perfectly but I just can't think of your face."

Oxford professor W. A. Spooner, 1844–1930, famous for his linguistic flip-flops ("spoonerisms"). Spooner rebuked one student for "fighting a liar in the quadrangle" and another who "hissed my mystery lecture," adding "You have tasted two worms."

■ **id** contains a reservoir of unconscious psychic energy that, according to Freud, strives to satisfy basic sexual and aggressive drives. The id operates on the pleasure principle, demanding immediate gratification.

■ **ego** the largely conscious, "executive" part of personality that, according to Freud, mediates among the demands of the id, superego, and reality. The ego operates on the reality principle, satisfying the id's desires in ways that will realistically bring pleasure rather than pain.

■ **superego** the part of personality that, according to Freud, represents internalized ideals and provides standards for judgment (the conscience) and for future aspirations.

■ **psychosexual stages** the childhood stages of development (oral, anal, phallic, latency, genital) during which, according to Freud, the id's pleasure-seeking energies focus on distinct erogenous zones.

■ **Oedipus** [ED-uh-puss] **complex** according to Freud, a boy's sexual desires toward his mother and feelings of jealousy and hatred for the rival father.

The **id** has a reservoir of unconscious psychic energy constantly striving to satisfy basic drives to survive, reproduce, and aggress. The id operates on the *pleasure principle:* If not constrained by reality, it seeks immediate gratification. Think of newborn infants. Governed by the id, they cry out for satisfaction the moment they feel a need, caring nothing for the outside world's conditions and demands.

As the **ego** develops, the young child learns to cope with the real world. The ego, operating on the *reality principle,* seeks to gratify the id's impulses in realistic ways that will bring long-term pleasure rather than pain or destruction. (Imagine what would happen if, lacking an ego, we expressed our unrestrained sexual or aggressive impulses whenever we felt them.) The ego contains our partly conscious perceptions, thoughts, judgments, and memories, making it the personality "executive," mediating the impulsive demands of the id, the restraining demands of the superego, and the real-life demands of the external world.

Beginning around age 4 or 5, Freud theorized, a child's ego recognizes the demands of the newly emerging **superego,** the voice of conscience that forces the ego to consider not only the real but the ideal, and that focuses solely on how one *ought* to behave. The superego strives for perfection, judging actions and producing positive feelings of pride or negative feelings of guilt. Someone with an exceptionally strong superego may be virtuous yet, ironically, guilt-ridden; another with a weak superego may be wantonly self-indulgent and remorseless. Because the superego's demands often oppose the id's, the ego struggles to reconcile the two. The chaste student who is sexually attracted to someone may satisfy both id and superego by joining a volunteer organization to which the desired person belongs.

Personality Development

Analysis of his patients' histories convinced Freud that personality forms during life's first few years. Again and again his patients' symptoms seemed rooted in unresolved conflicts from early childhood. He concluded that children pass through a series of **psychosexual stages** during which the id's pleasure-seeking energies focus on distinct pleasure-sensitive areas of the body called *erogenous zones.*

During the *oral stage,* which lasts throughout the first 18 months, the infant's sensual pleasures focus on sucking, biting, and chewing.

During the *anal stage,* from about 18 months to 3 years, the sphincter muscles become sensitive and controllable, and bowel and bladder retention and elimination become a source of gratification.

During the *phallic stage,* from roughly 3 to 6 years, the pleasure zone shifts to the genitals. Freud believed that during this stage boys seek genital stimulation and develop both unconscious sexual desires for their mother and jealousy and hatred for their father, whom they consider a rival. Given these feelings, boys would also feel guilt and a lurking fear of punishment, perhaps by castration, from their father. Freud called this collection of feelings the **Oedipus complex** after the Greek legend of Oedipus, who unknowingly killed his father and married his mother. Although some psychoanalysts believed that girls

The ego struggles to reconcile the demands of superego and id, said Freud.

"Fifty is plenty."
"Hundred and fifty."

experience a parallel *Electra complex,* Freud (1931, p. 229) said no: "It is only in the male child that we find the fateful combination of love for the one parent and simultaneous hatred for the other as a rival."

Children eventually cope with threatening feelings, said Freud, by repressing them and by identifying with (trying to become like) the rival parent. It's as though something inside the child decides, "If you can't beat 'em (the parent of the same sex), join 'em." Through this **identification** process, children's superegos gain strength as they incorporate many of their parents' values. Freud believed that identification with the same-sex parent provides what we now call our *gender identity*—our sense of being male or female.

Identification

Freud believed that children cope with threatening feelings of competition with their same-sex parent by identifying with that parent.

With their sexual feelings repressed and redirected, children enter a *latency stage.* Freud maintained that during latency, extending from around age 6 to puberty, sexuality is dormant and children play mostly with peers of the same sex.

At puberty, latency gives way to the final stage, the *genital stage,* as the person begins to experience sexual feelings toward others.

In Freud's view, maladaptive behavior in the adult results from conflicts unresolved during earlier psychosexual stages. At any point in the oral, anal, or phallic stage, strong conflict can lock, or **fixate,** the person's pleasure-seeking energies in that stage. For example, people who were either orally overindulged or deprived (perhaps by abrupt, early weaning) might fixate at the oral stage. Orally fixated adults are said to exhibit either passive dependence (like that of a nursing infant) or an exaggerated denial of this dependence—perhaps by acting tough and uttering biting sarcasm. Or they might continue to seek oral gratification by excessively smoking and eating. Similarly, those who never quite resolve the anal conflict between the desire to eliminate at will and the demands of toilet training may be messy and disorganized *(anal expulsive)* or highly controlled and compulsively neat *(anal retentive).* In such ways, believed Freud, the twig of personality is bent at an early age.

"Oh, for goodness' sake! Smoke!"

Defense Mechanisms

To live in social groups, we cannot spontaneously act out our sexual and aggressive impulses willy-nilly. We must control them. When the ego fears losing control of the inner war between the demands of the id and the superego, the result is a dark cloud of unfocused anxiety. Anxiety, said Freud, is the price we pay for civilization. Anxiety is hard to cope with, as when we feel unsettled but are unsure why. Freud proposed that the ego protects itself against anxiety with **defense mechanisms.** These reduce or redirect anxiety in various ways, all of them distorting reality. Some examples:

Repression banishes anxiety-arousing thoughts and feelings from consciousness. According to Freud, *repression underlies all the other defense mechanisms,* each of which disguises threatening impulses and keeps them from reaching consciousness. Freud believed that repression explains why we do not remember our childhood lust for our parent of the other sex. However, he also believed that repression is often incomplete, that repressed urges seep out in dream symbols and slips of the tongue.

- **identification** the process by which, according to Freud, children incorporate their parents' values into their developing superegos.

- **fixation** according to Freud, a lingering focus of pleasure-seeking energies at an earlier psychosexual stage, where conflicts were unresolved.

- **defense mechanisms** in psychoanalytic theory, the ego's protective methods of reducing anxiety by unconsciously distorting reality.

- **repression** in psychoanalytic theory, the basic defense mechanism that banishes anxiety-arousing thoughts, feelings, and memories from consciousness.

Regression
Faced with a mild stressor, children, young monkeys, and others will regress, retreating to the comfort of earlier behaviors.

"The lady doth protest too much, methinks."

William Shakespeare, *Hamlet*, 1600

■ **regression** defense mechanism in which an individual faced with anxiety retreats to a more infantile psychosexual stage, where some psychic energy remains fixated.

■ **reaction formation** defense mechanism by which the ego unconsciously switches unacceptable impulses into their opposites. Thus, people may express feelings that are the opposite of their anxiety-arousing unconscious feelings.

■ **projection** defense mechanism by which people disguise their own threatening impulses by attributing them to others.

■ **rationalization** defense mechanism that offers self-justifying explanations in place of the real, more threatening, unconscious reasons for one's actions.

■ **displacement** defense mechanism that shifts sexual or aggressive impulses toward a more acceptable or less threatening object or person, as when redirecting anger toward a safer outlet.

We also cope with anxiety through **regression**—retreating to an earlier, more infantile stage of development. Like juvenile monkeys that retreat to infantile clinging to their mothers or to one another when anxious (Suomi, 1987), human children facing the anxious first days of school may regress to the oral comfort of thumb-sucking. Even homesick new college students may long for the security and comfort of home.

In **reaction formation**, the ego unconsciously makes unacceptable impulses look like their opposites. En route to consciousness, the unacceptable proposition "I hate him" becomes "I love him." Timidity becomes daring. Feelings of inadequacy become bravado.

Projection disguises threatening impulses by attributing them to others. Thus, "He doesn't trust me" may be a projection of the actual feeling "I don't trust him" or "I don't trust myself." An El Salvadoran saying captures the idea: "The thief thinks everyone else is a thief."

The familiar mechanism of **rationalization** occurs when we unconsciously generate self-justifying explanations in order to hide from ourselves the real reasons for our actions. Habitual drinkers may say they drink with their friends "just to be sociable." Students who fail to study may rationalize, "All work and no play makes Jack [or Jill] a dull person."

Displacement diverts one's sexual or aggressive impulses toward an object or person that is psychologically more acceptable than the one that aroused the feelings. Children who fear expressing anger against their parents may displace it by kicking the family pet. Students upset over an exam may snap at a roommate.

Sublimation is the transformation of unacceptable impulses into socially valued motivations. Freud suggested that Leonardo da Vinci's paintings of Madonnas were a sublimation of his longing for intimacy with his mother, who was separated from him at an early age. In such ways, civilization benefits from sublimation, Freud believed.

Note that all these defense mechanisms function indirectly and unconsciously, reducing anxiety by disguising our threatening impulses. We would never say, "I'm feeling anxious; I'd better project my sexual or hostile feelings onto someone else." Defense mechanisms would not work if we recognized them. Just as the body unconsciously defends itself against disease, so also, believed Freud, does the ego unconsciously defend itself against anxiety.

Assessing the Unconscious

Preview Question 3 What are projective tests, and what do clinicians in the Freudian tradition hope to learn from them?

Those who study personality or provide therapy need ways to evaluate the personality characteristics they consider important. As a result, different personality theorists have developed their own preferred methods of assessment.

Freud's theory maintains that the significant influences on our personalities arise from the unconscious, which contains residues from early childhood experiences. The interpretation of dreams, he said, provides the road into the unconscious mind. Psychoanalysts therefore dismiss objective assessment tools, such as agree-disagree or true-false questionnaires, as merely tapping the conscious surface. Their tool of choice would be a sort of psychological x-ray—a test that sees through our surface pretensions and reveals our hidden conflicts and impulses.

Projective tests aim to provide such a view by presenting an ambiguous stimulus and then asking test-takers to describe it or tell a story about it. The stimulus has no inherent significance, so any meaning people read into it presumably is a projection of their interests and conflicts. Henry Murray (1933) demonstrated a possible basis for such a test at a party hosted by his 11-year-old daughter. Murray engaged the children in a frightening game called "Murder." When shown some photographs after the game, the children perceived the photos as more malicious than they had before the game. These children, it seemed to Murray, had *projected* their inner feelings into the pictures.

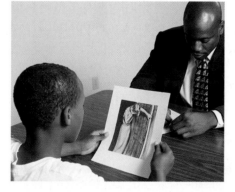

A few years later, Murray introduced the **Thematic Apperception Test (TAT)**—a test in which people view ambiguous pictures and then make up stories about them. One use of storytelling has been to assess achievement motivation. Shown a daydreaming boy, those who imagine he is fantasizing about an achievement are presumed to be projecting their own goals. "As a rule," said Murray, "the subject leaves the test happily unaware that he has presented the psychologist with what amounts to an x-ray of his inner self" (quoted by Talbot, 1999).

Various projective tests ask test-takers to draw a person, to complete sentences ("My mother. . . ."), or to provide the first word that comes to mind after the examiner says a test word. Most widely used is the famous **Rorschach inkblot test,**

The TAT

This psychologist presumes that the hopes, fears, and interests expressed in this boy's descriptions of a series of ambiguous pictures in the Thematic Apperception Test (TAT) are projections of his inner feelings.

The Rorschach test

In this projective test, people tell what they see in a series of symmetrical inkblots. Some who use this test are confident that the interpretation of ambiguous stimuli will reveal unconscious aspects of the test-taker's personality. Others use it as an icebreaker or to supplement other information.

■ **sublimation** in psychoanalytic theory, the defense mechanism by which people rechannel their unacceptable impulses into socially approved activities.

■ **projective test** a personality test, such as the Rorschach or TAT, that provides ambiguous stimuli designed to trigger projection of one's inner dynamics.

■ **Thematic Apperception Test (TAT)** a projective test in which people express their inner feelings and interests through the stories they make up about ambiguous scenes.

■ **Rorschach inkblot test** the most widely used projective test, a set of 10 inkblots, designed by Hermann Rorschach; seeks to identify people's inner feelings by analyzing their interpretations of the blots.

"If a professional psychologist is 'evaluating' you in a situation in which you are at risk and asks you for responses to ink blots . . . walk out of that psychologist's office."

Robyn Dawes, *House of Cards: Psychology and Psychotherapy Based on Myth*, 1994

© 1983 by Sidney Harris; American Scientist Magazine.

"The forward thrust of the antlers shows a determined personality, yet the small sun indicates a lack of self-confidence. . . ."

introduced in 1921 by Swiss psychiatrist Hermann Rorschach [ROAR-shock]. The test assumes that what we see in its 10 inkblots reflects our inner feelings and conflicts. If we see predatory animals or weapons, the examiner may infer we have aggressive tendencies.

Is this reasonable? If so, can a psychologist use the Rorschach to understand one's personality and diagnose an emotional disorder? The two primary criteria of a good test are *reliability* (consistency of results) and *validity* (predicting what it's supposed to). On those criteria, how good is the Rorschach?

The "almost universal agreement among the scientific community" is that it is not very good (Sechrest & others, 1998). No one accepted system for scoring and interpreting the test has been developed. If two raters were not trained in the same scoring system, their agreement on the results of any given test would be minimal. Nor has the test been very successful at predicting behavior or at discriminating between groups (for example, identifying who is suicidal and who is not). The Rorschach is not an emotional x-ray.

With all the criticisms, the Rorschach remains "simultaneously, the most cherished and the most reviled of all psychological assessment tools" (Hunsley & Bailey, 1999). Some clinicians remain confident of the test's validity—not as a device that by itself can provide a diagnosis, but as a source of suggestive leads that supplement other information. Other clinicians use the test as an icebreaker and a revealing interview technique. There is even a research-based, computer-aided scoring and interpretation tool that aims to improve agreement among raters and enhance the test's validity (Erdberg, 1990; Exner, 1993). But the evidence is insufficient to satisfy critics, who still find "no scientific basis for justifying the use of Rorschach scales in psychological assessments" (Hunsley & Bailey, 1999). Freud himself probably would have been uncomfortable with trying to assign each patient a test score and more interested in the therapist–patient interactions that take place during the test.

rehearse it!

1. According to Freud, we block from consciousness the thoughts, wishes, feelings, and memories that are unacceptable or unbearably painful. The blocked material surfaces in disguised forms, for example, in physical symptoms, dreams, or slips of the tongue. This unconscious blocking of unacceptable thoughts is
   a. free association.
   b. repression.
   c. anxiety.
   d. reaction formation.

2. According to Freud's view of personality structure, the "executive" system, the _____, seeks to gratify the impulses of the _____ in more realistic ways.
   a. id; ego
   b. ego; superego
   c. ego; id
   d. id; superego

3. Freud proposed an Oedipus complex, which is resolved through a process called *identification*, during which the child incorporates parental values. This process is closely associated with the development of the "voice of conscience," the part of the personality that internalizes ideals and that Freud called the
   a. ego.
   b. superego.
   c. reality principle.
   d. sublimation.

4. According to the psychoanalytic view of development, the oral, anal, and phallic stages are followed by a latency stage, during which sexuality is largely dormant or submerged. The latency stage extends roughly through
   a. the preschool years.
   b. the early school years.
   c. adolescence.
   d. infancy.

5. Defense mechanisms identified by Freud include regression (in which a person copes with anxiety by retreating to an earlier stage of development) and projection (in which a person disguises threatening impulses by attributing them to others). There are many other defense mechanisms. All of them have in common some distortion or disguising of reality, and all of them are
   a. conscious.
   b. unconscious.
   c. preconscious.
   d. rationalizations.

6. Projective tests are personality tests that present test-takers with an ambiguous stimulus and ask them to respond to it, for example, by describing it or telling a story about it. One well-known projective test, which uses inkblots as stimuli, was created by
   a. the neo-Freudians.
   b. Henry Murray.
   c. Carl Jung.
   d. Hermann Rorschach.

Evaluating the Psychoanalytic Perspective

Knowing what you do about Freud's ideas, listen now to his critics.

Freud's Early Descendants and Dissenters

PREVIEW QUESTION 4 Which of Freud's ideas did his followers accept? Which did they reject?

Freud's writings were controversial, but they soon attracted followers, mostly young, ambitious physicians who formed an inner circle around their strong-minded leader. These pioneering psychoanalysts and others, whom we now call *neo-Freudians,* accepted Freud's basic ideas: the personality structures of id, ego, and superego; the importance of the unconscious; the shaping of personality in childhood; and the dynamics of anxiety and the defense mechanisms. But many veered away from Freud in two important ways: They placed more emphasis on the conscious mind's role in interpreting experience and in coping with the environment. And they doubted that sex and aggression were all-consuming motivations. Instead, they tended to emphasize loftier motives and social interaction. The following examples illustrate.

Alfred Adler and Karen Horney [HORN-eye] agreed with Freud that childhood is important. But they believed that childhood *social,* not sexual, tensions are crucial for personality formation. Adler, who himself struggled to overcome childhood illnesses and accidents, said that much of our behavior is driven by efforts to conquer childhood feelings of inferiority, feelings that trigger our strivings for superiority and power. (Adler proposed the still-popular idea of the "inferiority complex.") Horney said childhood anxiety, caused by the dependent child's sense of helplessness, triggers our desire for love and security. Horney countered Freud's assumptions that women have weak superegos and suffer "penis envy," and she attempted to balance the bias she detected in this masculine view of psychology.

Unlike other neo-Freudians, Carl Jung—Freud's disciple-turned-dissenter—placed less emphasis on social factors and agreed with Freud that the unconscious exerts a powerful influence. But to Jung (pronounced Yoong), the unconscious contains more

> "The female . . . acknowledges the fact of her castration, and with it, too, the superiority of the male and her own inferiority; but she rebels against this unwelcome state of affairs."
>
> Sigmund Freud, *Female Sexuality*, 1931

Alfred Adler
"The individual feels at home in life and feels his existence to be worthwhile just so far as he is useful to others and is overcoming feelings of inferiority" (*Problems of Neurosis*, 1964).

Karen Horney
"The view that women are infantile and emotional creatures, and as such, incapable of responsibility and independence is the work of the masculine tendency to lower women's self-respect" (*Feminine Psychology*, 1932).

Carl Jung
"We can keep from a child all knowledge of earlier myths, but we cannot take from him the need for mythology" (*Symbols of Transformation*, 1912).

■ **collective unconscious** Carl Jung's concept of a shared, inherited reservoir of memory traces from our species' history.

than our repressed thoughts and feelings. He believed we also have a **collective unconscious,** a common reservoir of images derived from our species' universal experiences. Jung said that the collective unconscious explains why, for many people, spiritual concerns are deeply rooted and why people in different cultures share certain myths and images, such as mother as a symbol of nurturance. (Today's psychologists discount the idea of inherited experiences. But many do believe that our shared evolutionary history shaped some universal dispositions.)

Freud died in 1939. Since then some of his ideas have been incorporated into *psychodynamic theory.* "Most contemporary psychodynamic theorists and therapists are not wedded to the idea that sex is the basis of personality," notes Drew Westen (1996). They "do not talk about ids and egos, and do not go around classifying their patients as oral, anal, or phallic characters." What they do assume, with Freud, is that much of our mental life is unconscious, that childhood shapes our personalities and ways of becoming attached to others, and that we often struggle with inner conflicts among our wishes, fears, and values.

Freud's Ideas in the Light of Modern Research

PREVIEW QUESTION 5 How do Freud's ideas hold up today?

We can also critique Freud from the perspective of the beginning of the twenty-first century, a perspective that is itself subject to revision. Freud did not have access to all that we have since learned about human development, thinking, and emotion. Thus, say Freud's admirers, to criticize his theories by comparing them with current concepts is like comparing Henry Ford's Model T with today's Taurus. To Freud's critics, however, his ideas are psychology's historical equivalent of astronomy's flat-earth theory.

Both admirers and critics could agree that recent research contradicts many of Freud's specific ideas. Today's developmental psychologists see our development as lifelong, not fixed in childhood. They doubt that infants' neural networks are mature enough to sustain as much emotional trauma as Freud assumed. Some think Freud overestimated parental influence and underestimated peer influence (and abuse). They also question Freud's idea that conscience and gender identity form as the child resolves the Oedipus complex at age 5 or 6. We gain our gender identity earlier and become strongly masculine or feminine even without a same-sex parent present (Frieze & others, 1978). Freud's ideas about childhood sexuality arose from his rejection of stories of childhood sexual abuse told by his female patients—stories that some scholars believe he suggested or coerced and then attributed to their own childhood sexual wishes and conflicts (Powell & Boer, 1994). Today, we understand how Freud's questioning might have created false memories, and we also know that childhood sexual abuse does happen. Freud's ideas about the natural superiority of men have been thoroughly discounted.

New ideas about why we dream—to consolidate memories, or to make sense of random neural activity, for example—dispute Freud's belief that dreams disguise and fulfill wishes. And slips of the tongue can be explained as competition between similar verbal choices in our memory network. Someone who says "I don't want to do that—it's a lot of brothel" may simply be blending *bother* and *trouble* (Foss & Hakes, 1978). Researchers find little support for Freud's idea that defense mechanisms disguise sexual and aggressive impulses (though our cognitive gymnastics do work to protect our self-esteem). History also has failed to support another of Freud's ideas—that sexual repression causes psychological disorder. From Freud's time to ours, sexual repression has diminished; psychological disorders have not.

"Many aspects of Freudian theory are indeed out of date, and they should be: Freud died in 1939, and he has been slow to undertake further revisions."

Psychologist Drew Westen (1998)

"Studies have begun to converge toward a verdict . . . : there is literally nothing to be said [for] the entire Freudian system."

Frederick Crews (1996)

Is Repression a Myth?

Sigmund Freud's entire psychoanalytic theory rests on his assumption that the human mind often *represses* painful experiences, banishing them into the unconscious. Freud and his followers thought if we could somehow uncover our past experiences, we would find them intact, like long-lost books in a dusty attic. Recover and resolve the painful repressed memories of our childhood and emotional healing would follow. Under Freud's influence, repression has been used to explain hypnotic phenomena, psychological disorders, and apparent lost and recovered memories of childhood traumas (Cheit, 1998). It became one of popular psychology's most widely accepted concepts. In one survey, 88 percent of university students believed that painful experiences commonly get pushed out of awareness and into the unconscious (Garry & others, 1994).

Actually, contend many of today's researchers, repression, if it ever occurs, is a rare mental response to terrible trauma. "Repression folklore is . . . partly refuted, partly untested, and partly untestable," says Elizabeth Loftus (1995). Consider: If the human mind indeed commonly banishes painful experiences, how do we explain these odd findings?

- Shouldn't we expect children who have witnessed a parent's murder to repress the experience? A study of sixteen 5- to 10-year-old children who had this horrific experience found that not one repressed the memory (Malmquist, 1986).

- Shouldn't survivors of Nazi death camps have banished the atrocities from consciousness? With rare exceptions they remember all too well—although many do benefit from disclosing and talking through their experiences (Helmreich, 1992, 1994; Pennebaker, 1990).

- Shouldn't we expect children who have been terrorized while their school bus was hijacked or pinned down by sniper fire to repress the experience? In separate incidents every child remembered it (Pope & Hudson, 1995).

- Shouldn't battle-scarred veterans suffer amnesia for their worst experiences? In one neurological unit in a British hospital, 35 percent of military patients arrived with amnesia after severe combat during World War II (Arrigo & Pezdek, 1997; Karon & Widener, 1997, 1998). But such cases often appear to be either concussion-related or a "false amnesia" tactic for escaping intolerable situations (Holmes, 1990, 1994). Folklore regarding recovered battlefield memories is either unconfirmed or related to therapists' use of suggestive techniques.

- Shouldn't people who have kept a diary of everyday life events later recall negative events significantly less well than positive events? "The memory for the two types of events [is] almost the same," report Charles Thompson and his colleagues (1996).

There are exceptions—one death camp survivor reportedly forgot for over 30 years the snatching and shooting of her infant son (Kraft, 1996). Some researchers believe that extreme, prolonged stress, such as the stress some severely abused children experience, might disrupt memory by damaging the hippocampus, the brain structure that processes memories (Schacter, 1996). But the far more common reality? High stress enhances memory, and negative emotional events are therefore remembered well (Christianson, 1992; Shobe & Kihlstrom, 1997). In fact, too well: Traumatic events, such as rape and torture, haunt survivors, who experience unwanted flashbacks. They are seared onto the soul.

After studying 400 hours of recollections by 120 witnesses to the Holocaust, psychologist Robert Kraft (1996) reported that "the nearly universal response is persistent, intrusive, extended, vivid memory for personally-experienced events." "You see the babies," said survivor Sally H. (1979). "You see the screaming mothers. You see hanging people. You sit and you see that face there. It's something you don't forget."

"Warning. Despite seventy years of research, there is no objective evidence to support the concept of repression."

Psychologist David S. Holmes (1994)

"During the Holocaust, many children . . . were forced to endure the unendurable. For those who continue to suffer [the] pain is still present, many years later, as real as it was on the day it occurred."

Eric Zillmer, Molly Harrower, Barry Ritzler, and Robert Archer, *The Quest for the Nazi Personality*, 1995

The Unconscious Mind

History has been kinder to Freud's "iceberg" view of the mind, at least in part. We now know that we indeed have limited access to all that goes on in our minds (Bargh & Chartrand, 1999; Erdelyi, 1985, 1988). As Freud supposed, mental processes can operate in parallel and sometimes opposing ways. Our thoughts and emotions are sometimes out of sync.

However, the "iceberg" notion held by today's research psychologists differs from Freud's—so much so, argues Anthony Greenwald (1992), that it is time to abandon Freud's view of the unconscious. Many researchers think of the unconscious not as seething passions and repressive censoring but as cooler information processing that occurs without our awareness. To them, the unconscious involves

- the schemas that automatically control our perceptions and interpretations.
- the right hemisphere activity that enables the split-brain patient's left hand to carry out an instruction the patient cannot verbalize.
- the parallel processing of different aspects of vision and thinking.
- the implicit memories that operate without conscious recall, even among those with amnesia.
- the emotions that activate instantly, before conscious analysis.
- the self-concept and stereotypes that automatically and unconsciously influence how we process information about ourselves and others (Bargh, 1997).

More than we realize, we fly on autopilot. This understanding of unconscious information processing is more like the pre-Freudian view of an underground stream of thought from which spontaneous creative ideas surface.

Recent research has, however, provided some support for Freud's idea of defense mechanisms (even if they don't work exactly as Freud supposed). Roy Baumeister and his colleagues (1998) illustrate:

- If confronted with their sexism, racism, or incompetence, people often react with views and actions that seek to prove the opposite. For example, white research participants previously accused of racism give more money to a black panhandler than do their nonaccused counterparts. This curious generosity is akin to Freud's *reaction formation,* which states that we sometimes behave in ways opposite to our true feelings.
- People tend to see their foibles and attitudes in others, a phenomenon called the *false consensus effect.* People who cheat on their taxes or break speed limits tend to think many others do likewise. The evidence has not, however, confirmed Freud's idea that this *projection* has a defensive purpose—to conceal our own bad traits (Holmes, 1978, 1981).

Supportive evidence is meager for defenses (such as displacement and sublimation) that are tied to instinctual energy. More evidence exists for defenses (such as reaction formation) that support self-esteem. Defense mechanisms, Baumeister concludes, are motivated less by the seething impulses that Freud presumed than by our need to protect our self-image.

Freud's Ideas as Scientific Theory

Psychologists also criticize Freud's theory for its scientific shortcomings, noting that good scientific theories explain observations and offer testable hypotheses. Freud's theory rests on few objective observations and offers few hypotheses to verify or reject. (For Freud, his own recollections and interpretations of patients' free associations, dreams, and slips were evidence enough.)

What is the most serious problem with Freud's theory? It offers after-the-fact explanations of any characteristic (of one person's smoking, another's fear of

"Two passengers leaned against the ship's rail and stared at the sea. 'There sure is a lot of water in the ocean,' said one. 'Yes,' answered his friend, 'we've only seen the top of it.'"

Psychologist George A. Miller (1962)

"Sigmund Freud is an empirical void."

Anonymous

horses, another's sexual orientation) yet fails to *predict* such behavior and traits. If you feel angry at your mother's death, you illustrate his theory because "your unresolved childhood dependency needs are threatened." If you do not feel angry, you again illustrate his theory because "you are repressing your anger." That, said Calvin Hall and Gardner Lindzey (1978, p. 68), "is like betting on a horse after the race has been run."

For such reasons, some of Freud's critics offer harsh words. They see a decaying Freudian edifice built on the swamplands of childhood sexuality, repression, dream analysis, and after-the-fact speculation. "When we stand on [Freud's] shoulders, we only discover that we're looking further in the wrong direction," says John Kihlstrom (1997). Freud's most searing critic, Frederick Crews (1998), likens Freud to Peter Sellers' bumbling Inspector Clouseau, albeit with a unique talent for bamboozling an entire century. What is original about Freud's ideas is not supported, and what is supported is not original (the unconscious mind is an idea that dates back to Plato).

Freud's supporters object. "To reject psychodynamic thinking because Freud's instinct theory or his view of women is dated," says Drew Westen (1998), "is like rejecting modern physics because Newton did not understand relativity." Moreover, to criticize Freudian theory for not making testable predictions is like criticizing baseball for not being an aerobic exercise. Is it fair to fault something for not being what it was never intended to be? Unlike many later psychoanalysts, Freud never claimed that psychoanalysis was predictive science. He merely claimed that, looking back, psychoanalysts could find meaning in our state of mind (Rieff, 1979).

Freud's supporters also note that some of his ideas *are* enduring. It was Freud who drew our attention to the unconscious and the irrational, to our defenses against anxiety, to the importance of human sexuality, and to the tension between our biological impulses and our social well-being. It was Freud who challenged our self-righteousness, punctured our pretensions, and reminded us of our potential for evil.

Freud's legacy lives on. Some ideas that many people assume to be true—that childhood experiences mold personality, that many behaviors have disguised motives—are part of that legacy. His early-twentieth-century concepts penetrate our twenty-first-century language. Without realizing their source, we may speak of *ego, repression, projection, sublimation, complex* (as in "inferiority complex"), *sibling rivalry, Freudian slips,* and *fixation.* "Freud's premises may have undergone a steady decline in currency within academia for many years," notes Martin Seligman (1994), "but Hollywood, the talk shows, many therapists, and the general public still love them."

> "We are arguing like a man who should say, 'If there were an invisible cat in that chair, the chair would look empty; but the chair does look empty; therefore there is an invisible cat in it.'"
>
> C. S. Lewis, *Four Loves*, 1958

PEANUTS reprinted by permission of UFS, Inc.

rehearse it!

7. In general, neo-Freudians such as Adler and Horney accepted many of Freud's views but placed more emphasis on
   a. development throughout the life span.
   b. the collective unconscious.
   c. the role of the id.
   d. social interactions.

8. Many of Freud's specific ideas—for example, his ideas on the formation of gender identity and the function of dreams—have been modified by the neo-Freudians or challenged by recent research. However, psychodynamic psychologists would agree with Freud about
   a. the existence of unconscious mental processes.
   b. the Oedipus and Electra complexes.
   c. the predictive value of Freudian theory.
   d. adult psychological problems being the result of inadequate psychosexual development.

The Psychoanalytic Perspective

1. What was Freud's view of human personality, and what role do unconscious dynamics play in his theory of personality?

Sigmund Freud believed that the mind was like an iceberg, with the unconscious region below the surface and the preconscious close enough to the surface for its contents to be retrievable. Freud's treatment of emotional disorders led him to believe that they spring from unconscious dynamics, which he sought to analyze through the techniques of free association and dream analysis. He referred to his theory and techniques as *psychoanalysis.*

2. How did Freud view personality structure and development, and how did he think people defended themselves against anxiety?

Freud saw personality as composed of pleasure-seeking psychic impulses (the id), a reality-oriented executive (the ego), and an internalized set of ideals (the superego). He believed that children develop through psychosexual stages—the oral, anal, phallic, latency, and genital stages. During the phallic stages, boys may experience an Oedipus complex. To cope with threatening feelings about their parents, boys and girls identify with the same-sex parent, which provides their gender identity. Freud suggested that our personalities are influenced by how we have resolved conflicts associated with these stages and whether we have remained fixated at any stage.

Tensions between the demands of id and superego produce anxiety. The ego copes by using protective, reality-distorting defense mechanisms: repression, regression, reaction formation, projection, rationalization, displacement, and sublimation. Of these, Freud believed, repression is the most basic.

3. What are projective tests, and what do clinicians in the Freudian tradition hope to learn from them?

Projective tests attempt to assess personality by presenting ambiguous stimuli that are designed to reveal the unconscious aspects of personality. Although some critics question the reliability and validity of projective tests, such as the Rorschach inkblots, many clinicians continue to use them.

4. Which of Freud's ideas did his followers accept? Which did they reject?

Neo-Freudians, among them Alfred Adler and Karen Horney, accepted many of Freud's ideas but placed more emphasis on conscious experience and on social motivations other than sex and aggression, such as feelings of inferiority and anxiety. Carl Jung expanded Freud's concept of the unconscious to include a collective unconscious that he believed all humans inherit.

5. How do Freud's ideas hold up today?

Critics say many of Freud's specific ideas are implausible, unvalidated, or contradicted by new research, and that his theory offers only after-the-fact explanations. Nevertheless, Freud drew psychology's attention to the unconscious, to the struggle to cope with anxiety and sexuality, and to the conflict between biological impulses and social restraints. His cultural impact has been enormous.

TERMS AND CONCEPTS TO REMEMBER

personality, p. 450
free association, p. 450
psychoanalysis, p. 450
unconscious, p. 451
preconscious, p. 451
id, p. 452
ego, p. 452

superego, p. 452
psychosexual stages, p. 452
Oedipus [ED-uh-puss] complex,
   p. 452
identification, p. 453
fixation, p. 453
defense mechanisms, p. 453

repression, p. 453
regression, p. 454
reaction formation, p. 454
projection, p. 454
rationalization, p. 454
displacement, p. 454

sublimation, p. 454
projective test, p. 455
Thematic Apperception Test (TAT),
   p. 455
Rorschach inkblot test, p. 455
collective unconscious, p. 458

REHEARSE IT ANSWER KEY

1. b   2. c   3. b   4. b   5. b   6. d   7. d   8. a

The Trait Perspective

31

PREVIEW QUESTION 1 How do psychologists use traits to describe personality, and which aspects of traits seem to provide the most useful information about human variation?

Sigmund Freud's *psychoanalytic theory* attempts to explain personality in terms of the dynamics that underlie behavior. It peers beneath the surface searching for hidden motives. In 1919, Gordon Allport, a curious 22-year-old psychology student, interviewed Freud in Vienna and discovered just how preoccupied the founder of psychoanalysis was with finding hidden motives.

> Soon after I had entered the famous red burlap room with pictures of dreams on the wall, he summoned me to his inner office. He did not speak to me but sat in expectant silence, for me to state my mission. I was not prepared for silence and had to think fast to find a suitable conversational gambit. I told him of an episode on the tram car on my way to his office. A small boy about 4 years of age had displayed a conspicuous dirt phobia. He kept saying to his mother, "I don't want to sit there . . . don't let that dirty man sit beside me." To him everything was *schmutzig* (filthy). His mother was a well-starched *Hausfrau,* so dominant and purposive looking that I thought the cause and effect apparent.
>
> When I finished my story Freud fixed his kindly therapeutic eyes upon me and said, "And was that little boy you?" Flabbergasted and feeling a bit guilty, I contrived to change the subject. While Freud's misunderstanding of my motivation was amusing, it also started a deep train of thought (1967, pp. 7–8).

That train of thought ultimately led Allport to do what Freud did not do—to describe personality in terms of fundamental **traits**—people's characteristic behaviors and conscious motives. Meeting Freud, said Allport, "taught me that [psychoanalysis], for all its merits, may plunge too deep, and that psychologists would do well to give full recognition to manifest motives before probing the unconscious." Allport came to define personality in terms of identifiable behavior patterns. He was concerned less with *explaining* individual traits than with *describing* them.

How then do trait theorists describe and classify personalities? An analogy may help. Imagine that you want to describe and classify apples. Someone might correctly say that every apple is unique. Still, you might find it useful to begin by classifying apples as distinct *types*—Granny Smith, McIntosh, Red or Golden Delicious, and so forth. Based on children's physiological and psychological reactivity, Jerome Kagan (1989b) has classified children's temperaments as either shy-inhibited or fearless-uninhibited types. Some health psychologists classify people as intense, *Type A,* or as laid-back, *Type B,* personalities.

More popular today, especially in business and career counseling, is an effort to classify people according to Carl Jung's personality types, based on their responses to 126 questions written by Isabel Briggs Myers (1987) and her mother, Kathleen Briggs. The *Myers-Briggs Type Indicator* is quite simple. It offers choices, such as "Do you usually value sentiment more than logic, or value logic more than sentiment?" Then it counts the test-taker's preferences, labels them as indicating, say, a "feeling" or "thinking" type, and feeds them back to the person in complimentary terms. Feeling types, for example, are told they are sensitive to values and "sympathetic, appreciative, and tactful"; thinking types are told they "prefer an objective standard of truth" and are "good at analyzing."

Whoopi the extravert
Whoopi Goldberg seems as outgoing as her stage name implies. Trait labels such as *extraversion* can describe our temperaments and typical behaviors.

■ **trait** a characteristic pattern of behavior or a disposition to feel and act, as assessed by self-report inventories and peer reports.

Most people agree with their announced type profile. It, after all, mirrors their declared preferences. They may also accept their label as a basis for being matched with work partners and tasks that supposedly suit their temperaments (although critics wonder if labeling people creates self-fulfilling prophecies). A National Research Council report, however, noted that the test's initial use outran research on its value as a predictor of job performance and that "the popularity of this instrument in the absence of proven scientific worth is troublesome" (Druckman & Bjork, 1991, p. 101; see also Pittenger, 1993). With more than 300 articles on the Myers-Briggs now published in the *Journal of Psychological Type* (Carskadon & McCarley, 1997), advocates hope that verdict may change.

Exploring Traits

Classifying people as one or another distinct personality type fails to capture their full individuality. So how else could we describe their personalities? To return to our apple analogy, we might describe an apple along several trait dimensions—relatively large or small, red or yellow, sweet or sour. We know that variations on just three color dimensions—hue, saturation, and brightness—create many thousands of colors. Similarly, by placing people on several trait dimensions simultaneously, psychologists can describe countless individual personality variations.

What trait dimensions describe personality? Allport and his associate H. S. Odbert (1936) literally counted all the words in an unabridged dictionary with which one could describe people. How many were there? Almost 18,000! How, then, could psychologists condense the list to a manageable number of basic traits?

Factor Analysis

One way has been to propose traits, such as anxiety, that some theory regards as basic. A newer technique is *factor analysis,* a statistical procedure that has been used to identify clusters of test items that tap basic components of intelligence (such as spatial ability, reasoning ability, or verbal skill). Imagine that people who describe themselves as outgoing also tend to say that they like excitement and practical jokes and dislike quiet reading. Such a statistically correlated cluster of behaviors reflects a basic trait, or factor—in this case, a trait called *extraversion.*

British psychologists Hans Eysenck and Sybil Eysenck [EYE-zink] believed that we can reduce many of our normal individual variations to two or three genetically influenced dimensions, including *extraversion–introversion* and *emotional stability–instability* (**FIGURE 31.1**). Their *Eysenck Personality Questionnaire* has been given to people in 35 countries around the world, from China to Uganda to Russia. When people's answers are analyzed, the extraversion and emotionality factors inevitably emerge as basic personality dimensions (Eysenck, 1990, 1992).

The Big Five

Most researchers believe that while the Eysencks' dimensions are important, they do not tell the whole story. A slightly expanded set of factors—dubbed the *Big Five*—does a better job (Goldberg, 1993; John, 1990; Wiggins, 1996). If a test specifies where you are on the five dimensions of Table 31.1, it has said much of what there is to say about your personality. Around the world, people describe others in terms roughly consistent with the Big Five—how agreeable they are, how extraverted they are, and so forth. The Big Five is not the last word, but for now the winning number in the personality lottery is five. The Big Five was the most active personality research topic during the 1990s and is currently our best approximation of the basic trait dimensions

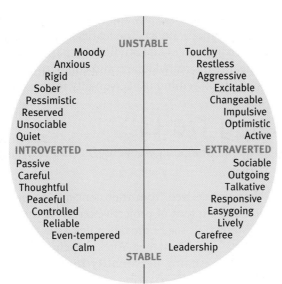

UNSTABLE

INTROVERTED	EXTRAVERTED
Moody	Touchy
Anxious	Restless
Rigid	Aggressive
Sober	Excitable
Pessimistic	Changeable
Reserved	Impulsive
Unsociable	Optimistic
Quiet	Active
Passive	Sociable
Careful	Outgoing
Thoughtful	Talkative
Peaceful	Responsive
Controlled	Easygoing
Reliable	Lively
Even-tempered	Carefree
Calm	Leadership

STABLE

FIGURE 31.1

Two personality factors
Mapmakers can tell us a lot by using two axes (north-south and east-west). Hans Eysenck and Sybil Eysenck use two primary personality factors—extraversion-introversion and stability-instability—as axes for describing personality variation. Varying combinations define other, more specific traits. (From Eysenck & Eysenck, 1963.)

(Endler & Speer, 1998). If you could ask five questions about the personality of a stranger—say, a blind date you were soon to meet—querying where the person is on these five dimensions would be most revealing.

The recent wave of Big Five research explores various questions:

- **How stable are these traits?** In adulthood, the Big Five traits are quite stable, with some tendencies (instability, extraversion, and openness) waning a bit in the decades after college, and others (agreeableness and conscientiousness) rising (McCrae & others, 1999).

- **How heritable are they?** Heritability of individual differences varies with the diversity of people studied, but it generally runs 50 percent or a tad more for each dimension (Loehlin & others, 1998).

- **How well do they apply to other cultures?** The Big Five dimensions describe personality in various cultures reasonably well (McCrae & others, 1998).

- **Do the Big Five traits predict other personal attributes?** Yes again. An example: Highly conscientious people are more likely to be morning types; evening types are marginally more ex-traverted (Jackson & Gerard, 1996). Another example: When one's partner scores lower on agreeableness, stability, and openness, marital and sexual satisfaction may suffer (Botwin & others, 1997).

By exploring such questions, Big Five research has rejuvenated trait psychology and renewed appreciation for the importance of personality.

TABLE 31.1

THE "BIG FIVE" PERSONALITY FACTORS

Trait Dimension	Endpoints of the Dimension
Emotional stability	Calm ——— Anxious Secure ——— Insecure Self-satisfied ——— Self-pitying
Extraversion	Sociable ——— Retiring Fun-loving ——— Sober Affectionate ——— Reserved
Openness	Imaginative ——— Practical Preference for variety ——— Preference for routine Independent ———Conforming
Agreeableness	Soft-hearted ——— Ruthless Trusting ——— Suspicious Helpful ——— Uncooperative
Conscientiousness	Organized ——— Disorganized Careful ——— Careless Disciplined ——— Impulsive

Source: Adapted from McCrae & Costa (1986, p. 1002).

Biology and Personality

Genetic predispositions influence most personality traits. Jerome Kagan, for example, attributes differences in children's shyness and inhibition to their autonomic nervous system reactivity. Our genes have much to say about the temperament and the behavioral style that help define our personality—more, it seems, than the way our parents handled us (although parents are very important for other internal realities such as beliefs and values). New molecular genetic studies are beginning to isolate genes that predispose babies to welcome novelty and to grow into adults who seek sensation and take risks (Ebstein & others, 1998). The fearless, curious child may become the rock-climbing or fast-driving adult. And studies comparing identical and fraternal twins, comparing identical twins reared apart, and comparing adoptees with their adoptive and biological parents all remind us: Personality forms under the influence of genes.

Assessing Traits

PREVIEW QUESTION 2 What are personality inventories, and how do trait theorists use them?

Assessment techniques derived from trait concepts do not reveal hidden personality dynamics (which is the intent of projective tests). Rather, they profile a person's behavior patterns. Many trait scales provide quick assessments of a single trait, such as extraversion, anxiety, or self-esteem. Alternatively, psychologists can assess several traits at once by administering **personality inventories**—longer questionnaires on which people respond to items covering a wide range of feelings and behaviors.

The most extensively researched and widely used personality inventory is the **Minnesota Multiphasic Personality Inventory (MMPI).** Although it assesses "abnormal" personality tendencies rather than normal personality traits, the MMPI illustrates a good way of developing a personality inventory. One of its creators, Starke Hathaway (1960), compared his effort to that of Alfred Binet. Binet developed the first intelligence test by selecting items that discriminated children who would have trouble progressing normally in French schools. The MMPI items, too, were **empirically derived.** That is, from a large pool of items Hathaway and his colleagues selected those that discriminated particular diagnostic groups. They then grouped the questions into 10 clinical scales.

They initially gave hundreds of true-false statements ("No one seems to understand me"; "I get all the sympathy I should"; "I like poetry") to groups of psychologically disordered patients and to "normal" people. They retained any statement—no matter how silly it sounded—on which the patient group's answer differed from that of the normal group. "Nothing in the newspaper interests me except the comics" may seem senseless, but it just so happened that depressed people were more likely to answer "true." (Nevertheless, people have had fun spoofing the MMPI with their own mock items, such as: "Weeping brings tears to my eyes," "Frantic screams make me nervous," and "I stay in the bathtub until I look like a raisin" [Frankel & others, 1983].)

Today's new MMPI-2, renormed on a full cross-section of Americans and containing revised items, still contains 10 clinical scales (**FIGURE 31.2**). Like its predecessor, it has several validity scales, including the so-called lie scale that assesses the extent to which a person is faking in order to make a good impression (by responding "false" to statements such as "I get angry sometimes"). And it has 15 content scales assessing, for instance, work attitudes, family problems, and anger.

In contrast to the subjectivity of projective tests, personality inventories are scored objectively—so objectively and automatically that a computer can administer and score them. (The computer can also provide descriptions of people who previously responded similarly.) Objectivity does not, however, guarantee validity. For example, sophisticated test-takers taking the MMPI for employment purposes can give fake answers to create a good impression. (They consistently answer in socially desirable ways, except on those items like "I get angry sometimes," for which nearly any honest person would say yes.) Moreover, the ease of computerized testing tempts untrained administrators—including many personnel officers, educational admissions officers, and physicians—to use the test in ways for which it has not been validated (Matarazzo, 1983). Nevertheless, for better or worse, the objectivity of the MMPI contributes to its popularity and to its translation into more than 100 languages.

■ **personality inventory** a questionnaire (often with true-false or agree-disagree items) on which people respond to items designed to gauge a wide range of feelings and behaviors; used to assess selected personality traits.

■ **Minnesota Multiphasic Personality Inventory (MMPI)** the most widely researched and clinically used of all personality tests. Originally developed to identify emotional disorders (still considered its most appropriate use), this test is now used for many other screening purposes.

■ **empirically derived test** a test (such as the MMPI) developed by testing a pool of items and then selecting those that discriminate between groups.

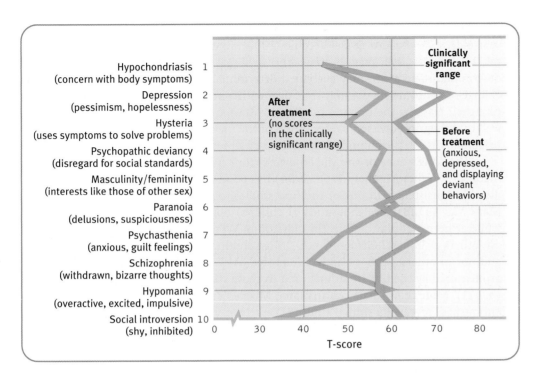

FIGURE 31.2
Minnesota Multiphasic Personality Inventory (MMPI) test profile
High T-scores suggest a psychological disorder; an average score is 50. This graph plots the scores of Ed, a depressed and anxious young man, before and after psychotherapy. (Scores are converted to a "T-scale," such that an average score is called 50 and about two-thirds of people fall between 40 and 60.) (Adapted from Butcher, 1990.)

Evaluating the Trait Perspective

PREVIEW QUESTION 3 Does research support the consistency of personality traits over time and across situations?

Are our personality traits stable and enduring? Or does our behavior depend on where we are and whom we are with? William Faulkner created characters, like the self-centered Jason Compson in *The Sound and the Fury*, whose personality traits were consistent across various times and places. The Italian playwright Luigi Pirandello had a different view. For him, personality was ever-changing, tailored to the particular role or situation. In Pirandello's play *It Is So!* (*If You Think So*), Lamberto Laudisi describes himself: "I am really what you take me to be; though, my dear madam, that does not prevent me from also being really what your husband, my sister, my niece, and Signora Cini take me to be—because they also are absolutely right!" To which Signora Sirelli responds, "In other words you are a different person for each of us."

The Person-Situation Controversy

Who, then, typifies human personality, Faulkner's consistent Jason Compson or Pirandello's inconsistent Laudisi? Both. Our behavior is influenced by the interaction of our inner disposition with our environment. Still, the question lingers: Which is *more* important? Are we *more* as Faulkner or as Pirandello imagined us to be? Forced to choose, most people would probably side with Faulkner. Until the late 1960s, most psychologists would have, too. Isn't it obvious that some people are dependably conscientious and others unreliable, some cheerful and others dour, some outgoing and others shy?

When we explore this *person-situation controversy,* we look for genuine personality traits that persist over time *and* across situations. If we are to consider friendliness a trait, friendly people must act friendly at different times and places. Do they? Faulkner would not have been surprised: Data from 152 long-term studies reveal that personality trait scores correlate with scores obtained seven years later. The results

"There is as much difference between us and ourselves, as between us and others."

Michel de Montaigne, *Essays,* 1588

were as follows: children, +.31; collegians, +.54; 30-year-olds, +.54; and 50- to 70-year-olds, +.74 (Roberts & Del Vecchio, 2000). Interests may change—the avid collector of tropical fish may become the avid gardener. Careers may change—the determined salesperson may become a determined social worker. Relationships may change—the hostile spouse may start over with a new partner. But most people recognize their traits as their own, note Robert McCrae and Paul Costa (1994), "and it is well that they do. A person's recognition of the inevitability of his or her one and only personality is . . . the culminating wisdom of a lifetime."

The consistency of specific *behaviors* from one situation to the next is another matter. As Walter Mischel (1968, 1984) has pointed out, people do not act with predictable consistency. In one of the first studies to reveal this, Hugh Hartshorne and Mark May (1928) gave thousands of children opportunities to lie, cheat, and steal while at home, at play, and in the classroom. Were some children consistently honest, others dishonest? Generally not. "Most children will deceive in certain situations and not in others," the researchers reported. A child's "lying, cheating, and stealing as measured by the test situations used in these studies are only very loosely related" (p. 411). More than a half-century later, Mischel's studies of college students' conscientiousness revealed a similar finding. There was virtually no relation between a student's being conscientious on one occasion (say, showing up for class on time) and being similarly conscientious on another occasion (say, turning in assignments on time). Pirandello would not have been surprised.

Mischel has also pointed out that people's scores on personality tests only mildly predict their behaviors. For example, people's scores on an extraversion test do not neatly predict how sociable they actually will be on any given occasion. If we remember such results, says Mischel, we will be more cautious about labeling and pigeonholing individuals. We will be more restrained when asked to predict whether someone is likely to violate parole, commit suicide, or be an effective employee. Years in advance, science can tell us the phase of the moon for any given date. A day in advance, meteorologists can often predict the weather. But despite the best efforts of those who would foresee your future, we are much further from being able to predict how *you* will feel and act tomorrow.

"Mr. Coughlin over there was the founder of one of the first motorcycle gangs."

In the margin:
Roughly speaking, the temporary, external influences on behavior are the focus of social psychology, and the enduring, inner influences are the focus of personality psychology. In actuality, behavior always depends on the interaction of persons with situations.

In defense of traits, Seymour Epstein (1983a,b) maintained that trying to predict a specific act on the basis of a personality test result is like trying to predict your answer to a specific aptitude question on the basis of an intelligence test result. Your answer to any given question is unpredictable because it depends on so many variables (your reading of the question, your understanding of the topic, your concentration level at the moment, luck). Your *average* accuracy over many questions on several tests is more predictable. Similarly, people's *average* outgoingness, happiness, or carelessness over *many* situations is predictable, Epstein observed. When rating someone's shyness or agreeableness, this consistency enables people who know someone well to agree (Kenrick & Funder, 1988). As our best friends can verify, we *do* have personality traits—genetically influenced traits, we now know. Moreover, our traits are socially significant. They influence our health, our thinking, and our job performance (Deary & Matthews, 1993; Hogan, 1998).

Consistency of Expressive Style

In unfamiliar, formal situations—perhaps when a guest in the home of a person from another culture—our traits may remain hidden as we attend carefully to social cues. In familiar, informal situations—just hanging out with friends—we feel less constrained, allowing our traits to emerge (Buss, 1989). In such situations, our expressive styles are impressively consistent. Thus, we often form lasting impressions within a few moments of meeting someone and noting the person's animation, manner of speaking, and gestures. Nalini Ambady and Robert Rosenthal (1992, 1993) video-taped 13 Harvard University graduate students teaching undergraduate courses. Observers then viewed three thin slices of each teacher's behavior—mere 10-second clips from the beginning, middle, and end of a class—and rated each teacher's level of confidence, activeness, warmth, and so forth. These behavior ratings, based on 30 *seconds* of teaching from an entire semester, predicted amazingly well the teacher's average student ratings at the semester's end. Observing even thinner slices—three 2-second clips—yielded ratings that still correlated as high as +.72 with the student evaluations. Some people's first impressions, derived from expressive behavior, predicted other people's lasting impressions!

To sum up, we can say that at any moment the immediate situation powerfully influences a person's behavior, especially when the situation makes clear demands. We can better predict drivers' behavior at traffic lights from knowing the color of the lights than from knowing the drivers' personalities. Averaging our behavior across many occasions does, however, reveal distinct personality traits. Moreover, we can in a flash perceive individual differences in some traits, such as expressiveness.

rehearse it!

1. Trait theory describes personality in terms of characteristic behaviors, or traits, such as agreeableness or extraversion. A pioneering trait theorist was
   a. Sigmund Freud.
   b. Walter Mischel.
   c. Gordon Allport.
   d. Carl Jung.

2. Hans Eysenck and Sybil Eysenck defined personality in terms of two primary factors—extraversion-introversion and stability-instability. Most researchers today believe that the Eysenck dimensions are too limiting and prefer the so-called Big Five personality factors. Which of the following is *not* one of the Big Five?
   a. Conscientiousness
   b. Anxiety
   c. Extraversion
   d. Agreeableness

3. Trait theorists assess personality by developing a profile of a person's traits. For example, they administer personality inventories, long questionnaires that ask people to report their characteristic feelings and behaviors. The most widely used of all personality inventories is the
   a. extraversion-introversion scale.
   b. Myers-Briggs.
   c. MMPI.
   d. Rorschach.

4. The MMPI's items were empirically derived. This means, for example, that the designers of the test figured out which responses indicated schizophrenia by

   a. taking case histories before and after the test.
   b. analyzing the content of the items in the light of their understanding of the disorder.
   c. comparing the responses of people known to have schizophrenia with the responses of "normal" people.
   d. assessing the degree of deception, using validity scales.

5. People's scores on personality tests are only mildly predictive of their behavior. Such tests best predict
   a. a person's behavior on a specific occasion.
   b. a person's average behavior across many situations.
   c. behavior involving a single trait, such as conscientiousness.
   d. behavior that depends on situation or context.

HOW TO BE A "SUCCESSFUL" ASTROLOGER OR PALM READER

How should we evaluate alternative ways of assessing traits? Does the alignment of the stars and planets at the time of one's birth affect who we are? Is one's handwriting revealing? Do our palms expose deep secrets?

While astronomers scoff at the naiveté of astrology—the constellations have shifted in the millennia since astrologers formulated their predictions (Kelly, 1997, 1998)—psychologists ask questions. Does it work? Are birth dates correlated with character traits? Given someone's birth date, can astrologers surpass chance when asked to identify the person from a short lineup of different personality descriptions? Can people pick out their own horoscopes from a lineup of horoscopes? The consistent answers have been: no, no, no, and no (British Psychological Society, 1993; Carlson, 1985; Kelly, 1997). Graphologists, who make predictions from handwriting samples, have similarly been found to do no better than chance when trying to discern people's occupations from examining several pages of their handwriting (Beyerstein & Beyerstein, 1992; Dean & others, 1992).

How, then, do astrologers and the like persuade thousands of newspapers and millions of people worldwide to buy their advice? Ray Hyman (1981), palm reader turned research psychologist, has revealed the suckering methods of astrologers, palm readers, and crystal-ball gazers.

Their first technique, the "stock spiel," builds on the observation that each of us is in some ways like no one else and in other ways just like everyone. That some things are true

of us all enables the "seer" to offer statements that seem impressively accurate: "I sense that you're nursing a grudge against someone; you really ought to let that go." "You worry about things more than you let on, even to your best friends." "You are adaptable to social situations and your interests are wide-ranging."

Such generally true statements can be combined into a personality description. Imagine that you take a

I SEE BY YOUR HANDWRITING YOU LIKE BANANAS.

© 2000 by Rob Pudim / Skeptical Inquirer

personality test and then receive the following character sketch:

You have a strong need for other people to like and to admire you. You have a tendency to be critical of yourself. . . . You pride yourself on being an independent thinker and do not accept other opinions without satisfactory proof. You have

found it unwise to be too frank in revealing yourself to others. At times you are extraverted, affable, sociable; at other times you are introverted, wary, and reserved. Some of your aspirations tend to be pretty unrealistic (Davies, 1997; Forer, 1949).

In experiments, college students have received stock assessments like this one, drawn from statements in a newsstand astrology book. When they think the bogus feedback was

prepared just for them and when it is favorable and pretty general, they nearly always rate the description as either "good" or "excellent" (Davies, 1997). Peter Glick and his co-workers (1989) found that even skeptics of astrology, when given a flattering description attributed to an astrologer, begin to think that "maybe there's something to this astrology stuff after all."

French psychologist Michael Gauguelin placed an ad in a Paris newspaper offering a free personal horoscope. Ninety-four percent of those receiving the horoscope praised the description as accurate. Whose horoscope had they all actually received? That of France's Dr. Petiot, a notorious mass murderer (Kurtz, 1983).

This acceptance is called *the Barnum effect,* named in honor of master showman P. T. Barnum's dictum, "There's a sucker born every minute." So powerful is the Barnum effect that, given a choice between this stock spiel and an individualized personality description actually based on a real test, most people choose the phony description as being more accurate.

Even some popular psychological labels are made plausible by Barnum statements. Mary Beth Logue and her colleagues (1992) report that adult children of alcoholics also rate descriptions of their supposed traits ("You are sensitive to the difficulties of others" or "You sometimes project a front, hiding your true feelings") as accurate. But people who are *not* children of alcoholics also rate the same statements as self-descriptive.

A second technique used by seers is to "read" our clothing, physical features, nonverbal gestures, and reactions to what they are saying. Imagine yourself as the character reader who was visited by a young woman in her late twenties or early thirties. Hyman described the woman as "wearing expensive jewelry, a wedding band, and a black

dress of cheap material. The observant reader noted that she was wearing shoes which were advertised for people with foot trouble." Do these clues suggest anything?

Drawing on these observations, the character reader proceeded to amaze his client with his insights. He assumed that the woman had come to see him, as did most of his female customers, because of a love or financial problem. The black dress and the wedding band led him to reason that her husband had died recently. The expensive jewelry suggested that she had been financially comfortable during the marriage, but the cheap dress suggested that

"Madame Zelinski can provide an even more accurate reading with your date of birth and social security number."

her husband's death had left her impoverished. The therapeutic shoes signified that she was now on her feet more than she had been used to, implying that she had been working to support herself since her husband's death.

If you are not as shrewd as this character reader (who correctly guessed that the woman was won-

dering if she should remarry in hope of ending her economic hardship), Hyman says it hardly matters. If people seek you out for a reading, start with some safe sympathy: "I sense you're having some problems lately. You seem unsure what to do. I get the feeling another person is involved." Then tell them what they want to hear. Memorize some Barnum statements from astrology and fortune-telling manuals and use them liberally. Tell people it is their responsibility to cooperate by relating your message to their specific experiences. Later they will recall that you predicted the specifics. Phrase statements as questions, and

when you detect a positive response assert the statement strongly. Be a good listener, and later, in different words, reveal to people what they earlier revealed to you. If you dupe them, they will come.

Better yet, beware of those who, by exploiting people with these techniques, are fortune takers rather than fortune tellers.

REVIEWING

The Trait Perspective

1. How do psychologists use traits to describe personality, and which aspects of traits seem to provide the most useful information about human variation?

Rather than explain the hidden aspects of personality, trait theorists describe the predispositions that underlie our actions. For example, through factor analysis, researchers have isolated five important dimensions of personality: emotional stability, extraversion, openness, agreeableness, and conscientiousness. Genetic predispositions influence most such traits.

2. What are personality inventories, and how do trait theorists use them?

To assess traits, psychologists have devised self-report personality inventories (like the MMPI)—questionnaires on which people respond to items designed to gauge a wide range of feelings and behaviors. Items on the test are empirically derived, and the tests are objectively scored. But people can fake their answers to create a good impression, and the ease of computerized testing may lead to misuse of these tests.

3. Does research support the consistency of personality traits over time and across situations?

Critics of trait theory question the consistency with which traits are expressed. Although people's traits persist through time, human behavior varies widely from situation to situation. Nevertheless, people's *average* behavior across different situations tends to be fairly consistent.

TERMS AND CONCEPTS TO REMEMBER

trait, p. 463
personality inventory, p. 466

Minnesota Multiphasic Personality
Inventory (MMPI), p. 466

empirically derived test, p. 466

REHEARSE IT ANSWER KEY

1. c   2. b   3. c   4. c   5. b

The Humanistic Perspective

By 1960, some personality psychologists had become discontented both with the negativity of Sigmund Freud's psychoanalytic approach to personality and with the objectivity of trait psychology. In contrast to Freud's study of the base motives of "sick" people, these *humanistic psychologists* focused on the ways "healthy" people strive for self-determination and self-realization.

Exploring the Self

PREVIEW QUESTION 1 What do humanistic psychologists view as the central feature of personality, and what is their goal in studying personality?

Two pioneering theorists—Abraham Maslow (1908–1970) and Carl Rogers (1902–1987)—illustrate the humanistic approach, with its emphasis on human potential and seeing the world through the person's (not the researcher's) eyes.

Abraham Maslow's Self-Actualizing Person

Maslow proposed that we are motivated by a hierarchy of needs, with physiological needs at the base. If our physiological needs are met, we become concerned with personal safety; if we achieve a sense of security, we then seek to love, to be loved, and to love ourselves; with our love needs satisfied, we seek self-esteem. Having achieved self-esteem, we ultimately seek **self-actualization,** the process of fulfilling our potential.

Abraham Maslow

"Any theory of motivation that is worthy of attention must deal with the highest capacities of the healthy and strong person as well as with the defensive maneuvers of crippled spirits" (*Motivation and Personality*, 1970).

Maslow (1970) developed his ideas by studying healthy, creative people rather than troubled clinical cases. He based his description of self-actualization on a study of those who seemed notable for their rich and productive lives—among them, Abraham Lincoln, Thomas Jefferson, and Eleanor Roosevelt. Maslow reported that these people shared certain characteristics: They were self-aware and self-accepting, open and spontaneous, loving and caring, and not paralyzed by others' opinions. Secure in their sense of who they were, their interests were problem-centered rather than self-centered. They focused their energies on a particular task, one they often regarded as their mission in life. Most enjoyed a few deep relationships rather than many superficial ones. Many had been moved by spiritual or personal *peak experiences* that surpassed ordinary consciousness.

These, said Maslow, are mature adult qualities, ones found in those who have learned enough about life to be compassionate, to have outgrown their mixed feelings toward their parents, to have found their calling, to have "acquired enough courage to be unpopular, to be unashamed about being openly virtuous, etc." Maslow's work with college students led him to speculate that those likely to become self-actualizing adults were likable, caring, "privately affectionate to those of their elders who deserve it," and "secretly uneasy about the cruelty, meanness, and mob spirit so often found in young people."

■ **self-actualization** according to Maslow, the ultimate psychological need that arises after basic physical and psychological needs are met and self-esteem is achieved; the motivation to fulfill one's potential.

■ **unconditional positive regard** according to Rogers, an attitude of total acceptance toward another person.

■ **self-concept** all our thoughts and feelings about ourselves, in answer to the question, "Who am I?"

Carl Rogers' Person-Centered Perspective

Fellow humanistic psychologist Carl Rogers agreed with much of Maslow's thinking. Rogers believed that people are basically good and are endowed with self-actualizing tendencies. Unless thwarted by an environment that inhibits growth, each of us is like an acorn, primed for growth and fulfillment. Rogers (1980) believed that a growth-promoting climate required three conditions—genuineness, acceptance, and empathy.

According to Rogers, people nurture our growth by being *genuine*—by being open with their own feelings, dropping their facades, and being transparent and self-disclosing.

People also nurture growth by being *accepting*—by offering us what Rogers called **unconditional positive regard.** This is an attitude of grace, an attitude that values us even knowing our failings. It is a profound relief to drop our pretenses, confess our worst feelings, and discover that we are still accepted. We hope to enjoy this gratifying experience in a good marriage, a close family, or an intimate friendship in which we no longer feel a need to explain ourselves. In the best of relationships, we are free to be spontaneous without fearing the loss of others' esteem.

Finally, people nurture growth by being *empathic*—by sharing and mirroring our feelings and reflecting our meanings. "Rarely do we listen with real understanding, true empathy," said Rogers. "Yet listening, of this very special kind, is one of the most potent forces for change that I know."

The picture of empathy
Being open and sharing confidences is easier when the listener shows real understanding. Within such relationships people can relax and fully express their true selves.

Genuineness, acceptance, and empathy are the water, sun, and nutrients that enable people to grow like vigorous oak trees, according to Rogers. For "as persons are accepted and prized, they tend to develop a more caring attitude toward themselves" (Rogers 1980, p. 116). As persons are empathically heard, "it becomes possible for them to listen more accurately to the flow of inner experiencings."

Rogers believed that genuineness, acceptance, and empathy nurture growth not only in the relationship between therapist and client but also between parent and child, leader and group, teacher and student, administrator and staff member—in fact, between any two human beings. He would have been pleased by a finding published shortly after his death: Preschool children whose parents exhibit such attitudes usually become creative adolescents (Harrington & others, 1987).

For Maslow, and even more for Rogers, a central feature of personality is one's **self-concept**—all the thoughts and feelings we have in response to the question, "Who am I?" If our self-concept is positive, we tend to act and perceive the world positively. If it is negative—if in our own eyes we fall far short of our "ideal self"—said Rogers, we feel dissatisfied and unhappy. A worthwhile goal for therapists, parents, teachers, and friends is therefore, he said, to help others know, accept, and be true to themselves.

College of Positive Self-Image 7. University of Low Self-Esteem o.

Assessing the Self

PREVIEW QUESTION 2 How do humanistic psychologists attempt to assess the self? What have we learned from research on the self?

If a humanistic psychologist were to assess your personality, you might be asked to fill out a questionnaire that would evaluate your self-concept. One questionnaire, inspired by Carl Rogers, asks people to describe themselves both as they would ideally like to be and as they actually are. When the ideal and the actual self are nearly alike, said Rogers, the self-concept is positive. When assessing his clients' personal growth during therapy, he looked for successively closer ratings of actual and ideal self.

Some humanistic psychologists believe that any standardized assessment of personality is depersonalizing, that even a questionnaire detaches the psychologist from the living human. Rather than forcing the person to respond to narrow categories, these humanistic psychologists believe that interviews and intimate conversation enable a better understanding of each person's unique experiences.

Research on the Self

Psychology's concern with people's sense of self dates back at least to William James, who, in his 1890 *Principles of Psychology,* devoted more than 100 pages to the topic. By 1943, Gordon Allport lamented that the self had become "lost to view." Even humanistic psychology's emphasis on the self did not instigate much scientific research, but it did help renew the concept of self and keep it alive. Now, more than a century after James and outside humanistic psychology, the self is one of Western psychology's most vigorously researched topics. Every year, new studies galore appear on self-esteem, self-disclosure, self-awareness, self-schemas, self-monitoring, and so forth—more than 110,000 articles in all since 1967.

An example of thinking about self is the concept of *possible selves* put forth by Hazel Markus and her colleagues (Inglehart & others, 1989; Markus & Nurius, 1986). Your possible selves include your visions of the self you dream of becoming— the rich self, the successful self, the loved and admired self. They also include the self you fear becoming—the unemployed self, the lonely self, the academically failed self. Such possible selves motivate us by laying out specific goals and calling forth the energy to work toward them. University of Michigan students in a combined undergraduate/medical school program earn higher grades if they undergo the program with a clear vision of themselves as successful doctors. Dreams do often give birth to achievements.

Underlying this research is an assumption (shared by humanistic psychologists) that the self, as organizer of our thoughts, feelings, and actions, is a pivotal center of personality. From our self-focused perspective we too readily presume that others are noticing and evaluating us. Thomas Gilovich (1996) demonstrated this "spotlight effect" by having individual Cornell University students don Barry Manilow T-shirts before entering a room with other students. Feeling self-conscious, the T-shirt wearers guessed that nearly half of their peers would take note of the shirt as they walked in. In reality, only 23 percent did. This absence of attention applies not only to our dorky clothes and bad hair but also to our nervousness, irritation, or attraction—fewer people notice than we presume (Gilovich & Savitsky, 1999).

How we *feel* about ourselves is also important. Research studies confirm the benefits of positive self-esteem and also hint at the hazards of pride.

The Benefits of Self-Esteem

High **self-esteem**—a feeling of self-worth—pays dividends. People who feel good about themselves (who strongly agree with self-affirming questionnaire statements) have fewer sleepless nights, succumb less easily to pressures to conform, are less likely to use drugs, are more persistent at difficult tasks, are less shy and lonely, and are just plain happier (Crocker & Wolfe, 1999; Leary, 1999; Tafarodi & Vu, 1997).

Psychotherapy researcher Hans Strupp (1982) noted that "As soon as one listens to a patient's story, one encounters unhappiness, frustration, and despair. . . . Basic to all these difficulties are impairments in self-acceptance and self-esteem." Those whose self-esteem is low do not necessarily see themselves as worthless or wicked, but they seldom say good things about themselves. Such low self-esteem exacts costs. Unhappiness and despair often coexist with low self-esteem.

"The first step to better times is to imagine them."

Chinese fortune cookie

Possible selves
By giving them a chance to try out many possible selves, pretend games offer children important opportunities to grow emotionally, socially, and cognitively. Although this young boy may not grow up to be a physician, playing adult roles will certainly bear fruit in terms of an expanded vision of what he might become.

■ **self-esteem** one's feelings of high or low self-worth.

LOW SELF-ESTEEM

Dear diary, Sorry to bother you again.

"There's a lot of talk about self-esteem these days. It seems pretty basic to me. If you want to feel proud of yourself, you've got to do things you can be proud of."

Oseola McCarty, Mississippi washerwoman, after donating $150,000 to the University of Southern Mississippi

Low self-esteem comes in different forms. Those vulnerable to depression often feel they are falling short of their *hopes*. Those vulnerable to anxiety often feel they are falling short of what they *ought* to be (Higgins, 1987). For such people, the pain of anticipated social rejection, experienced as low self-esteem, is sometimes adaptive. As with other forms of pain, it may aid survival by motivating them to behave in ways that sustain their inclusion within a supportive group (Leary & others, 1995).

The correlational links between low self-esteem and personal problems have other possible interpretations. Psychologists William Damon (1995), Robyn Dawes (1994), Mark Leary (1999), and Martin Seligman (1994) doubt that self-esteem is really "the armor that protects kids" from life's problems. Could it not be the other way around? Couldn't problems and failures cause low self-esteem? Maybe self-esteem simply reflects reality. Maybe feeling good *follows* doing well. Maybe it's a side effect of meeting challenges and surmounting difficulties. Maybe self-esteem is a gauge that reads out the state of our relationships with others. If so, isn't pushing the gauge artificially higher akin to forcing a car's low fuel gauge to display "full"? And will the best boost to self-esteem therefore come not so much from our repeatedly telling children how wonderful they are as from their own effective coping and hard-won achievements?

However, an *effect* of low self-esteem does appear in experiments. Temporarily deflate people's self-image (say, by telling them they did poorly on an aptitude test or by disparaging their personality) and they will be more likely to disparage others or to express heightened racial prejudice (Ybarra, 1999). Those who are negative about themselves also tend to be thin-skinned and judgmental (Baumeister, 1993; Baumgardner & others, 1989; Pelham, 1993). Some "love their neighbors as themselves"; others loathe their neighbors as themselves. In experiments, those made to feel insecure often become excessively critical, as if to impress others with their own brilliance (Amabile, 1983). Such findings are consistent with Maslow's and Rogers' presumptions that a healthy self-image can pay dividends. Accept yourself and you'll find it easier to accept others.

Culture and Self-Esteem

Is it true, as so many assume, that ethnic minorities, people with disabilities, and women live lives handicapped by impoverished self-esteem? The accumulated evidence says no. For example, 261 comparisons of more than half a million people have revealed slightly *higher* self-esteem scores for black than for white children, adolescents, and young adults (Gray-Little & Hafdahl, 2000). The National Institute of Mental Health's 1980s study *Psychiatric Disorders in America* similarly reveals that the rates of depression and alcoholism among African- and Hispanic-Americans are roughly comparable to those among other Americans (if anything, America's ethnic minorities suffer slightly less depression [Robins & Regier, 1991]).

Some people wonder: How can this be? Some members of "stigmatized" groups (people of color, those with disabilities, women) have faced discrimination and lower status, yet maintain their self-esteem in three ways, according to Jennifer Crocker and Brenda Major (1989):

- They value the things at which they excel.
- They attribute problems to prejudice.
- They do as everyone does—they compare themselves to those in their own group.

These findings help us understand why, despite the realities of prejudice, such groups report roughly comparable levels of happiness.

The Pervasiveness of Self-Serving Bias

Carl Rogers (1958) once objected to the religious doctrine that humanity's problems arise from excessive self-love, or pride. He noted that most people he had known "despise themselves, regard themselves as worthless and unlovable." Mark Twain had the idea: "No man, deep down in the privacy of his heart, has any considerable respect for himself."

Actually, most of us have a good reputation with ourselves. In studies of self-esteem, even those who score low respond in the midrange of possible scores. (A "low" self-esteem person responds to statements such as "I have good ideas" with qualifying adjectives such as *somewhat* or *sometimes*.) Moreover, one of psychology's most provocative and firmly established recent conclusions concerns our potent **self-serving bias**—our readiness to perceive ourselves favorably. Consider these findings (Brown, 1991; Myers, 1999):

People accept more responsibility for good deeds than for bad, and for successes than for failures. Athletes often privately credit their victories to their own prowess and their losses to bad breaks, lousy officiating, or the other team's exceptional performance. After receiving poor grades on an exam, most students in a half-dozen studies criticized the exam, not themselves. On insurance forms, drivers have explained accidents in such words as: "An invisible car came out of nowhere, struck my car, and vanished." "As I reached an intersection, a hedge sprang up, obscuring my vision, and I did not see the other car." "A pedestrian hit me and went under my car." The question "What have I done to deserve this?" is one we usually ask of our troubles, not our successes—those, we assume we deserve.

Most people see themselves as better than average. This is true for nearly any subjective and socially desirable dimension. In national surveys, most business executives say they are more ethical than their average counterpart. In several studies, 90 percent of business managers and more than 90 percent of college professors rated their performance as superior to that of their average peer. In Australia, 86 percent of people rate their job performance as above average, and only 1 percent as below average. Although the phenomenon is notably less striking in Asia, where people value modesty, self-serving biases have been observed worldwide: among

PEANUTS

Dutch, Australian, and Chinese students; Japanese drivers; Indian Hindus; and French people of most walks of life. The world, it seems, is Garrison Keillor's Lake Wobegon writ large—a place where "all the women are strong, all the men are good-looking, and all the children are above average."

And who is at least "somewhat likely" to go to heaven? Of Americans surveyed by *U.S. News & World Report* (1997), 19 percent thought O. J. Simpson would make it. They were more optimistic about Bill Clinton (52 percent), Princess Diana (60 percent), and Michael Jordan (65 percent). The public figure closest to a perceived heavenly shoo-in was Mother Teresa (79 percent). But she was topped by the survey's respondents, 87 percent of whom believed they themselves were destined for eternal bliss.

Self-serving bias flies in the face of today's pop psychology. "All of us have inferiority complexes," wrote John Powell (1989, p. 15). "Those who seem not to have such a complex are only pretending." But additional findings remove any doubts (Myers, 2002):

■ We remember and justify our past actions in self-enhancing ways.
■ We exhibit an inflated confidence in the accuracy of our beliefs and judgments.
■ We overestimate how desirably *we* would act in situations where most people behave less than admirably.

> "To love oneself is the beginning of a life-long romance."
>
> **Oscar Wilde, *An Ideal Husband*, 1895**

> "The [self-]portraits that we actually believe, when we are given freedom to voice them, are dramatically more positive than reality can sustain."
>
> **Shelley Taylor, *Positive Illusions*, 1989**

■ **self-serving bias** a readiness to perceive oneself favorably.

■ **individualism** giving priority to one's own goals over group goals, and defining one's identity in terms of personal attributes rather than group identifications.

■ **collectivism** giving priority to the goals of one's group (often one's extended family or work group) and defining one's identity accordingly.

"The enthusiastic claims of the self-esteem movement mostly range from fantasy to hogwash. The effects of self-esteem are small, limited, and not all good."

Roy Baumeister (1996)

"If you compare yourself with others, you may become vain and bitter; for always there will be greater and lesser persons than yourself."

Max Ehrmann, "Desiderata," 1927

■ We often seek out favorable, self-enhancing information.
■ We are quicker to believe flattering descriptions of ourselves than unflattering ones, and we are impressed with psychological tests that make us look good.
■ We exhibit group pride—a tendency to see our group (our school, our country, our race) as superior.

Moreover, pride does often go before a fall. Self-serving perceptions underlie conflicts ranging from blaming one's spouse for marital discord to arrogantly promoting one's own ethnic superiority. It was national self-righteousness that led both the Americans and Soviets during the arms race to say, "Your weapons threaten us, ours are for our defense." No wonder religion and literature so often warn against the perils of excessive pride.

Finding their self-esteem threatened, people with large egos may do more than put others down; they may react violently. Someone with a swelled head that gets deflated by insult or rejection is potentially dangerous. Brad Bushman and Roy Baumeister (1998) experimented with this dark side of high self-esteem. They had 540 undergraduate volunteers write a paragraph, in response to which another supposed student gave them either praise ("Great essay!") or stinging criticism ("One of the worst essays I have read!"). Then the essay writers played a reaction-time game against the other student. After wins, they could assault their opponent with noise of any intensity for any duration.

Can you anticipate the result? After criticism, those with unrealistically high self-esteem were "exceptionally aggressive." They delivered three times the auditory torture of those with normal self-esteem. It is "threatened egotism," not low self-esteem, that predisposes aggression, the researchers concluded. Moreover, people with excessive self-regard are prone to excessive risks (Baumeister & others, 1993). Would you rather ride with people who overestimate or underestimate their ability to maintain control while driving fast?

Despite the demonstrated perils of pride, many people reject the idea of self-serving bias, insisting it overlooks those who feel worthless and unlovable and seem to despise themselves. If self-serving bias prevails, why do so many people disparage themselves? For at least two reasons. Sometimes self-directed put-downs are subtly strategic: They elicit reassuring strokes. Saying "No one likes me" may at least elicit "But not everyone has met you!" At other times, such as before a game or an exam, self-disparaging comments prepare us for possible failure. The coach who extols the superior strength of the upcoming opponent makes a loss understandable, a victory noteworthy.

Even so, it's true: All of us some of the time, and some of us much of the time, *do* feel inferior—especially when we compare ourselves with those who are a step or two higher on the ladder of status, looks, income, or ability. The deeper and more frequently we have such feelings, the more unhappy, even depressed, we are. But for most people—the 98 percent who at any time are *not* suffering depression—thinking has a naturally positive bias.

We can therefore affirm what humanistic psychologists rightly emphasize: For the individual, self-affirming thinking is generally adaptive. To a point, our positive illusions are beneficial. They maintain our self-confidence, protect against anxiety and depression, and sustain our sense of well-being. "Life is the art of being well-deceived," observed the English essayist William Hazlitt.

Recognizing both the perils of self-righteousness and the dividends of positive self-esteem, psychologists Roy Baumeister (1989), Jonathan Brown (1991), and Shelley Taylor (1989) have all suggested that humans function best with modest self-enhancing illusions. Like the Japanese and European magnetic levitation trains, Brown noted, we function optimally when riding just off the rails—not so high that we gyrate and crash, yet not so in touch that we grind to a halt.

Culture and the Individual Self

PREVIEW QUESTION 3 What distinguishes individualist and collectivist views of self?

If someone were to rip away your social connections, making you a solitary refugee in a foreign land, how much of your identity would remain intact? The answer might depend in large part on whether your culture gives greater priority to the independent self that marks **individualism** or the interdependent self that marks **collectivism.**

If our solitary traveler were an individualist, a great deal of the person's identity would remain intact—the very core of his or her being, the sense of "me," the awareness of his or her personal convictions and values. Individualists give relatively greater priority to personal goals and define their identity mostly in terms of personal attributes. They strive for personal control and individual achievement. Although individualism varies from person to person within any culture, cross-cultural psychologists have mostly studied how it varies across cultures, ranging from the extreme individualism of the United States outside the Deep South to the extreme collectivism of rural Asia (Hofstede, 1980; Triandis, 1994; Vandello & Cohen, 1999).

A collectivist, if set adrift in a foreign land, might experience a much greater loss of identity. Cut off from family, groups, and loyal friends, the person would lose connections that have defined who he or she is. In a collectivist culture, a social network provides one's bearings. What is most important is not "me" but "we." Collectivists give priority to the goals of their groups—often their family, clan, or company—and define their identity accordingly. By their group identifications, collectivists gain a sense of belonging, a set of values, a network of caring individuals, an assurance of security.

The individual identity that is usually primary for Westerners gives way to a collective identity that is more often primary for Asians. Compared with American students, for example, students in Japan, China, and India are much less likely to complete the sentence "I am . . ." with personal traits ("I am sincere," "I am confident") and are much more likely to declare their social identities ("I am a Keio University student," "I am the third son in my family") (Cousins, 1989; Dhawan & others, 1995; Triandis, 1989a,b). And the individualized latté—"decaf, single shot, skinny, extra hot"—that feels so good to a North American in an espresso shop might sound more like a selfish demand in Seoul, note Heejung Kim and Hazel Markus (1999). In Korea, their studies confirm, people place less value on uniqueness and more on tradition and shared practices.

Being self-contained, individualists more easily move in and out of social groups. They feel relatively free to switch churches, leave one job for another, or even to leave their extended families and migrate to a new place. Marriage is often for as long as they both shall love. In contrast, collectivists may act shy in new groups and are more easily embarrassed (Singelis & others, 1995, 1999). They have deeper, more stable attachments to their familiar groups and friends. Relationships are long-term. Loyalties run strong between employer and employees.

Valuing communal solidarity, people in collectivist cultures place a premium on maintaining harmony and making sure others never lose face. Direct confrontation and blunt honesty are rare, as are expressions of personal egotism. What people say reflects not only what they feel (their inner attitudes) but also what they presume others feel (Kashima & others, 1992). Elders and superiors are given respect. To pre-

Collectivism

By identifying with family and other groups, these yak herders in northern India gain a sense of "we," a set of values, a network of care. Like athletes who take more pleasure in their team's victory than in their own performance, collectivists find satisfaction in advancing their groups' interests, even at the expense of personal needs.

No wonder, says Harry Triandis (1989b), that modern world colonization was led not by Asians, who were reluctant to cut social and family ties, but by the more individualist Europeans. And no wonder that countries colonized by Europeans willing to leave friends and family are today highly individualistic.

"One needs to cultivate the spirits of sacrificing the *little me* to achieve the benefits of the *big me*."

Chinese saying

serve group spirit, people avoid uncomfortable topics, defer to others' wishes, and display a polite, self-effacing humility (Markus & Kitayama, 1991). People remember those who have done them favors, and reciprocation becomes a social art. The collectivist self is not independent but *inter*dependent (Table 32.1). Among collectivists—especially those influenced by the Confucian idea of self as embedded in "a web of interrelatedness"—no one is an island (Kim & Lee, 1994). Happiness is being attuned to others (Kitayama & Markus, 2000).

TABLE 32.1

VALUE CONTRASTS BETWEEN INDIVIDUALISM AND COLLECTIVISM

Concept	Individualism	Collectivism
Self	Independent (identity from individual traits)	Interdependent (identity from belonging)
Life task	Discover and express one's uniqueness	Maintain connections, fit in
What matters	Me—personal achievement and fulfillment; rights and liberties; self-esteem	Us—group goals and solidarity; social responsibilities and relationships
Coping method	Change reality	Accommodate to reality
Morality	Defined by individuals (self-based)	Defined by social networks (duty-based)
Relationships	Many, often temporary or casual; confrontation acceptable	Few, close and enduring; harmony valued
Attributing behavior	Behavior reflects one's personality and attitudes	Behavior reflects social norms and roles

Sources: Adapted from Thomas Schoeneman (1994) and Harry Triandis (1994).

Both individualism and collectivism offer benefits that come at a cost. People in competitive, individualistic cultures have more personal freedom, take more pride in personal achievements, are less geographically bound to their families, and enjoy more privacy. Their less-unified cultures offer a smorgasbord of life-styles and invite individuals to construct their own identities. These cultures also celebrate innovation and creativity, and they tend to respect individual human rights. Such may help explain Ed Diener, Marissa Diener, and Carol Diener's (1995) finding that people in individualistic cultures report experiencing greater happiness than do those in collectivist cultures. When individualists pursue their own ends and all goes well, life can seem rewarding.

Curiously, though, within individualist cultures, people with the strongest social ties express greatest satisfaction with their lives (Bettencourt & Door, 1997). Moreover, the seeming benefits of individualism can come at the cost of more loneliness, more divorce, more homicide, and more stress-related disease (Popenoe, 1993; Triandis & others, 1988). Individualists demand more romance and personal fulfillment in marriage, which subjects the marriage relationship to more pressure (Dion & Dion, 1993). In one survey, "keeping romance alive" was rated as important to a good marriage by 78 percent of American women but only 29 percent of Japanese women (*American Enterprise*, 1992). In China, love songs often express enduring commitment and friendship (Rothbaum & Tsang, 1998). As one song put it, "we will be together from now on . . . I will never change from now to forever."

In recent decades, Western individualism has increased, while the priority placed on social obligations and family ties has decreased (Yankelovich, 1993). Martin Seligman (1988) has argued that "rampant individualism carries with it two seeds of its own destruction. First, a society that exalts the individual to the extent ours now does will be ridden with depression. . . . Second, and perhaps most important, is meaninglessness [which occurs when there is no] attachment to something larger than you are."

Evaluating the Humanistic Perspective

PREVIEW QUESTION 4 How has the humanistic perspective on personality influenced psychology? What criticisms have been leveled against this perspective?

One thing said of Freud can also be said of the humanistic psychologists: Their impact, though waning, has been pervasive. Their ideas have influenced counseling, education, child-rearing, and management. They have also influenced—sometimes in ways they did not intend—much of today's popular psychology.

Through popular psychology many people have absorbed some of what Maslow and Rogers taught—that a positive self-concept is the key to happiness and success, that acceptance and empathy help nurture positive feelings about oneself, and that people are basically good and capable of self-improvement. One study found that, by a four-to-one margin, Americans believe "human nature is basically good" rather than "fundamentally perverse and corrupt" (NORC, 1985). Humanistic psychologists can also take satisfaction in the changed response to one of the items on the Minnesota Multiphasic Personality Inventory (MMPI): Among those in the 1930s normal baseline sample, only 9 percent agreed that "I am an important person"; in the mid-1980s, more than half agreed (Holden, 1986b). Responding to a 1989 Gallup poll, 85 percent of Americans rated "having a good self-image or self-respect" as *very* important; 0 percent rated it unimportant. And 89 percent of people responding to a 1992 *Newsweek* Gallup poll rated self-esteem as very important for "motivating a person to work hard and succeed." Humanistic psychology's message has been heard.

Perhaps one reason that message has been so well received is that its emphasis on the individual self reflects and reinforces Western cultural values. As self-reliant individualism has grown, with increased priority given to personal identity and aspirations, the popular media have celebrated the rugged individual. Movie plots feature heroes who, true to themselves, buck social convention or take the law into their own hands. Popular songs proclaim "I Did It My Way" and remind us that to love yourself is "The Greatest Love of All" (Schoeneman, 1994).

But the prominence of the humanistic perspective also set off a backlash of criticism. First, said the critics, its concepts are vague and subjective. Consider the description of self-actualizing people as open, spontaneous, loving, self-accepting, and productive. Is this a scientific description? Isn't it merely a description of Maslow's personal values and ideals? Maslow, noted M. Brewster Smith (1978), offered impressions of his own personal heroes. Imagine another theorist who began with a different set of heroes—perhaps Napoleon, Alexander the Great, and John D. Rockefeller, Sr. This theorist would likely describe self-actualizing people as "undeterred by the needs of others," "motivated to achieve," and "obsessed with power."

Critics raised a second objection to the idea that, as Carl Rogers put it, "The only question which matters is, 'Am I living in a way which is deeply satisfying to me, and which truly expresses me?'" (quoted by Wallach & Wallach, 1985). The individualism encouraged by humanistic psychology—trusting and acting on one's feelings, being true to oneself, fulfilling oneself—can lead to self-indulgence, selfishness, and

"We do pretty well when you stop to think that people are basically good."

an erosion of moral restraints (Campbell & Specht, 1985; Wallach & Wallach, 1983). Indeed it is those who focus beyond themselves who are most likely to experience social support, to enjoy life, and to cope effectively with stress (Crandall, 1984).

Humanistic psychologists counter that belligerence, hostility, and insensitivity are often traceable to a poor self-concept. Moreover, they argue, a secure, nondefensive self-acceptance is actually the first step toward loving others.

A final accusation leveled against humanistic psychology is that it fails to appreciate the reality of our human capacity for evil. Faced with assaults on the environment, overpopulation, and the spread of nuclear weapons, we may become apathetic from either of two rationalizations. One is a naive optimism that denies the threat ("People are basically good; everything will work out"). The other is a dark despair ("It's hopeless; why try?"). Action requires enough realism to fuel concern and enough optimism to provide hope. Humanistic psychology, say the critics, encourages the needed hope but not the equally necessary realism about evil.

rehearse it!

1. Abraham Maslow theorized that human beings are motivated by a hierarchy of needs. When basic physiological and psychological needs are satisfied, he wrote, people become motivated to fulfill their potential through self-actualization. Maslow based his ideas on
   a. Freudian theory.
   b. his experiences with patients.
   c. a series of laboratory experiments.
   d. his study of healthy, creative people.

2. According to Carl Rogers, a growth-promoting environment is one that offers genuineness, acceptance, and empathy. The total acceptance Rogers advocated is called
   a. self-concept.
   b. unconditional positive regard.
   c. self-actualization.
   d. the "ideal self."

3. Researchers have found that high self-esteem is beneficial, noting that people who feel good about themselves have

fewer sleepless nights, are less likely to use drugs, and are happier, for example. On the other hand, low self-esteem is linked with life problems. How should this link between low self-esteem and life problems be interpreted?
   a. Life problems cause low self-esteem.
   b. The answer isn't clear because the link is correlational and does not indicate cause and effect.
   c. Low self-esteem leads to life problems.
   d. Because of the self-serving bias, we must assume that external factors cause low self-esteem.

4. Researchers have found that people tend to accept responsibility for their successes or good qualities and blame circumstances or luck for their failures. This is an example of
   a. low self-esteem.
   b. self-actualization.
   c. self-serving bias.
   d. empathy.

5. Individualists and collectivists have differing identities. Compared with collectivists, individualists more often define themselves in terms of their
   a. family connections.
   b. nationality.
   c. social roles.
   d. personal achievements.

6. The humanistic perspective is most concerned with the potential for human growth and self-fulfillment; ideas of the humanistic psychologists have found their way into counseling, education, child-rearing, and popular psychology. The humanistic perspective has been so well received because
   a. its emphasis on the individual fits well with the erosion of moral restraints in modern society.
   b. it feeds people's optimism about the good in human nature.
   c. it negates the idea that humans have a basic capacity for evil.
   d. its emphasis on the individual self reflects and reinforces Western cultural values.

REVIEWING

The Humanistic Perspective

1. What do humanistic psychologists view as the central feature of personality, and what is their goal in studying personality?

Humanistic psychologists have sought to turn psychology's attention away from basic motives and environmental conditioning and toward the growth potential of healthy people, as seen through the individual's own experiences and self-concept. Abraham Maslow believed that if basic human needs are fulfilled, people will strive to actualize their highest potential. To describe self-actualization, he studied some exemplary personalities and summarized his impressions of their qualities. To nurture growth in others, Carl Rogers advised unconditional positive regard by being genuine, accepting, and empathic. In such a climate, people can develop a deeper self-awareness and a more realistic and positive self-concept.

2. How do humanistic psychologists attempt to assess the self? What have we learned from research on the self?

Humanistic psychologists assess personality through questionnaires that rate self-concept and in therapy by seeking to understand others' subjective personal experiences. Research on the self documents the importance of high self-esteem and the po-tency of the self-serving bias. We know that self-esteem is an adaptive quality and that most people do perceive and explain themselves favorably.

3. What distinguishes individualist and collectivist views of self?

Individuals and cultures vary in giving priority to "me" or "us"—to personal control and individual achievement or to social connections and solidarity. Self-reliant *individualism* defines identity in terms of personal goals and attributes; socially connected *collectivism* gives priority to group goals and to one's social identity and commitments.

4. How has the humanistic perspective on personality influenced psychology? What criticisms have been leveled against this perspective?

Humanistic psychology helped to renew psychology's interest in the concept of self. Nevertheless, humanistic psychology's critics complain that its concepts are vague and subjective, its values individualistic and self-centered, and its assumptions naively optimistic.

TERMS AND CONCEPTS TO REMEMBER

self-actualization, p. 473
unconditional positive regard,
 p. 474

self-concept, p. 474
self-esteem, p. 475

self-serving bias, p. 477
individualism, p. 479

collectivism, p. 479

REHEARSE IT ANSWER KEY

1. d   2. b   3. b   4. c   5. d   6. d

The Social-Cognitive Perspective and Reflections on the Four Key Perspectives

PREVIEW QUESTION 1 In the view of social-cognitive psychologists, what three influences shape an individual's personality?

One major perspective on personality derives from psychological principles of learning, cognition, and social behavior. Called the *social-cognitive perspective* by psychologist Albert Bandura (1986), and the *cognitive social learning perspective* by others, its proponents emphasize the importance of external events and how we interpret them.

Exploring Behavior in Situations

Like learning theorists, social-cognitive theorists believe that we learn many of our behaviors either through conditioning or by observing others and modeling our behavior after theirs. They also emphasize the importance of mental processes: What we think about our situations affects our behavior. Instead of focusing solely on how our environment controls us (behaviorism), social-cognitive theorists focus on how we and our environment interact: How do we interpret and respond to external events? How do our schemas, our memories, and our expectations influence our behavior patterns?

Reciprocal Influences

Bandura (1986) called the process of interacting with our environment **reciprocal determinism.** "Behavior, internal personal factors, and environmental influences," he said, "all operate as interlocking determinants of each other" (**FIGURE 33.1**). For example, children's TV-viewing habits (past behavior) influence their viewing preferences (personal factor), which influence how television (environmental factor) affects their current behavior. The influences are mutual.

FIGURE 33.1

Reciprocal determinism

The social-cognitive perspective proposes that our personalities are shaped by the interaction of personal/cognitive factors (our thoughts and feelings), our environment, and our behaviors.

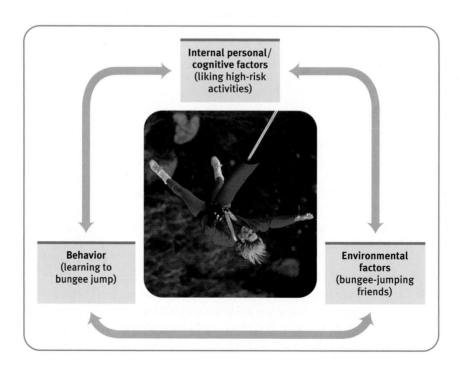

Internal personal/cognitive factors (liking high-risk activities)

Behavior (learning to bungee jump)

Environmental factors (bungee-jumping friends)

Consider three specific ways in which individuals and environments interact:

1. *Different people choose different environments.* The school you attend, the reading you do, the television programs you watch, the music you listen to, the friends you associate with—all are part of an environment you have chosen, based partly on your dispositions (Ickes & others, 1997). *You choose your environment and it then shapes you.*

2. *Our personalities shape how we interpret and react to events.* Anxious people, for example, are more likely to be attuned to potentially threatening events than are nonanxious people (Eysenck & others, 1987). Thus, anxious people perceive the world as more threatening than do those who are nonanxious, and they react accordingly.

3. *Our personalities help create situations to which we react.* Many experiments reveal that how we view and treat people influences how they in turn treat us. If we expect someone to be angry with us, we may give the person a cold shoulder, touching off the very behavior we expect. If we have an easygoing temperament we will likely enjoy close, supportive friendships (Kendler, 1997).

Personality is seen in individual differences, as it shapes how people interpret and react to events.

In such ways, we are both the products and the architects of our environments.

If all this has a familiar ring, it may be because it parallels and reinforces a pervasive theme in psychology: *Behavior emerges from the interplay of external and internal influences.* Boiling water turns an egg hard and a potato soft. A threatening environment turns one person into a hero, another into a scoundrel. *At every moment,* our behavior is influenced by our genes, our experiences, and our personalities.

Personal Control

PREVIEW QUESTION 2 What are the causes and consequences of personal control?

In studying how we interact with our environment, social-cognitive psychologists emphasize our sense of **personal control**—whether we learn to see ourselves as controlling, or as controlled by, our environment. Psychologists have two basic ways to study the effect of personal control (or any personality factor). One: *Correlate* people's feelings of control with their behaviors and achievements. Two: *Experiment,* by raising or lowering people's sense of control and noting the effects. Let's take these one at a time.

Locus of Control

Consider your own feelings of control. Do you believe that your life is beyond your control? That the world is run by a few powerful people? That getting a good job depends mainly on being in the right place at the right time? Or do you more strongly believe that what happens to you is your own doing? That the average person can influence government decisions? That being a success is a matter of hard work, not luck?

Hundreds of studies have compared people who differ in their perceptions of control. On the one side are those who have what psychologist Julian Rotter called an **external locus of control**—the perception that chance or outside forces determine their fate. On the other are those who perceive an **internal locus of control** and believe that to a great extent they control their own destiny. In study after study, "internals" achieve more in school, act more independently, enjoy better health, and feel less depressed than do "externals" (Lachman & Weaver, 1998; Lefcourt, 1982; Presson & Benassi, 1996). Moreover, they are better able to delay gratification and cope with various stresses, including marital problems (Miller & others, 1986).

- **reciprocal determinism** the interacting influences between personality and environmental factors.

- **personal control** our sense of controlling our environment rather than feeling helpless.

- **external locus of control** the perception that chance or outside forces beyond one's personal control determine one's fate.

- **internal locus of control** the perception that one controls one's own fate.

■ **learned helplessness** the hopelessness and passive resignation an animal or human learns when unable to avoid repeated aversive events.

Learned Helplessness Versus Personal Control

People who feel helpless and oppressed often perceive control as external. This perception may then deepen their feelings of resignation. In fact, this is precisely what researcher Martin Seligman (1975, 1991) and others found in experiments with both animals and people. Dogs strapped in a harness and given repeated shocks, with no opportunity to avoid them, learned a sense of helplessness. Later placed in another situation where they *could* escape the punishment by simply leaping a hurdle, the dogs cowered without hope. Repeatedly faced with traumatic events over which they have no control, people, too, come to feel helpless, hopeless, and depressed. Psychologists call this passive resignation **learned helplessness** (**FIGURE 33.2**). In contrast, animals able to escape the shocks in the first situation learned personal control and easily escaped the shocks in the new situation.

FIGURE 33.2

Learned helplessness

When animals and people experience no control over repeated bad events, they often learn helplessness.

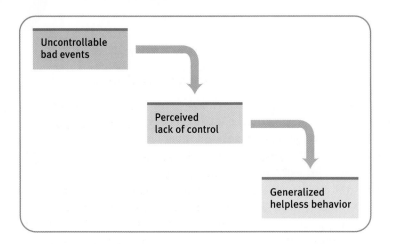

In prisons, factories, colleges, and nursing homes, people given little control experience a similar lowering of their morale and an increase in stress. Part of the shock we feel in an unfamiliar culture comes from a diminished sense of control when unsure how people in the new environment will respond (Triandis, 1994). Measures that increase control—allowing prisoners to move chairs and control room lights and the TV, having workers participate in decision making, offering nursing home patients choices about their environment—noticeably improve health and morale (Miller & Monge, 1986; Ruback & others, 1986; Wener & others, 1987). In one famous study of nursing home patients, 93 percent of those encouraged to exert more control became more alert, active, and happy (Rodin, 1986). As researcher Ellen Langer (1983, p. 291) concluded, "Perceived control is basic to human functioning." She recommended that "for the young and old alike," it is important that we create environments that enhance our sense of control and personal efficacy.

The verdict of these studies is reassuring: Under conditions of democracy, personal freedom, and empowerment, people thrive. Small wonder that the citizens of stable democracies report higher levels of happiness than people elsewhere (Inglehart, 1990). Shortly before the democratic revolution in the former East Germany, psychologists Gabriele Oettingen and Martin Seligman (1990) compared the telltale body language of working-class men in East and West Berlin bars. Compared with their counterparts on the other side of the Wall, the empowered West Berliners much

RUBES® **BY LEIGH RUBIN**

Control affects well-being

Nursing home residents who can arrange their own possessions, control other aspects of their daily lives, and pursue their own interests are more vigorous and happy than those who do not have these opportunities.

more often laughed, sat upright rather than slumped, and had upward- rather than downward-turned mouths. To paraphrase the Roman philosopher Seneca, happy are those who choose their own path.

Optimism

One measure of how helpless or effective you feel is where you stand on the trait dimension of optimism-pessimism. How do you characteristically explain negative and positive events? Perhaps you have known students whose *attributional* style is negative—who attribute poor performance to their lack of ability ("I can't do this") or to situations beyond their control ("bad" teachers, textbooks, or exam questions). Such students are more likely to persist in getting low grades than are students who adopt the more hopeful attitude that effort, good study habits, and self-discipline can make a difference (Noel & others, 1987; Peterson & Barrett, 1987).

CLOSE-UP:

TOWARD A MORE POSITIVE PSYCHOLOGY

During its first century, psychology understandably focused much of its attention on understanding and alleviating negative states. We have studied abuse and anxiety, depression and disease, prejudice and poverty, and since 1887, articles on selected negative emotions have outnumbered those on positive emotions by 14 to 1. Similarly, the 14,964 articles on "crime" dwarfed the 1155 articles on "virtue." "Anger" (8166 articles) outstripped "forgiveness" (416). And "fear" (18,602 articles) triumphed over "courage" (671).

In ages past, notes 1998 American Psychological Association president Martin Seligman (1998a,b), times of relative peace and prosperity have enabled cultures to turn their attention from repairing weakness and damage to promoting "the highest qualities of life." Prosperous fifth-century B.C. Athens nurtured philosophy and democracy. Flourishing fifteenth-century Florence nurtured great art. Victorian England, flush with the bounty of the British empire, nurtured honor, discipline, and duty. As we enter the new millennium, Seligman believes that thriving Western cultures have a parallel opportunity to create, as a "humane, scientific monument," a more **positive psychology**—a psy-

chology concerned not only with weakness and damage but also with strength and virtue.

Positive psychology shares with humanistic psychology an interest in advancing human fulfillment, but its origins and methodology are scientific. From these roots have grown not only the new studies of happiness and health, but also the shift in emphasis from learned helplessness and depression to optimism and thriving. Taken together, satisfaction with the past, happiness with the present, and optimism about the future define the movement's first pillar: *positive subjective well-being.*

The second pillar, *positive character,* focuses on exploring and enhanc-

Martin E. P. Seligman
"The main purpose of a positive psychology is to measure, understand and then build the human strengths and the civic virtues."

ing virtues such as creativity, courage, compassion, integrity, self-control, leadership, wisdom, and spirituality. Current research examines the roots and fruits of such virtues, sometimes by studying individuals who exemplify them in extraordinary ways.

The third pillar, *positive groups, communities, and cultures,* seeks to foster a positive social ecology, including healthy families, communal neighborhoods, effective schools, socially responsible media, and civil dialogue.

Will psychology have a more positive mission in this new century? Without slighting the need to repair damage and cure disease, the supporters of positive psychology hope so. With *American Psychologist* millennial issues (January 2000, and January 2001) devoted to this topic, and with a forthcoming *Handbook of Positive Psychology* (Snyder & Lopez, 2002), an upcoming book series, and new prizes for outstanding positive psychology scholarship, these psychologists have reason to be positive.

■ **positive psychology** the scientific study of optimal human functioning; aims to discover and promote conditions that enable individuals and communities to thrive.

"We just haven't been flapping them hard enough."

"O God, give us grace to accept with serenity the things that cannot be changed, courage to change the things which should be changed, and the wisdom to distinguish the one from the other."

Reinhold Niebuhr, *"The Serenity Prayer,"* 1943

In their study of professional achievement, Seligman and Peter Schulman (1986) compared sales made by new life insurance representatives who were more or less optimistic in their outlooks. Those who put an optimistic spin on their setbacks—seeing them as flukes or as a means to learning a new approach, rather than viewing them as signs of incompetence—sold more policies during their first year and were half as likely to quit. Seligman's finding came to life for him when Bob Dell, one of the optimistic recruits who began selling for Metropolitan Life after taking Seligman's optimism test, later dialed him up and sold him a policy.

Health, too, benefits from a basic optimism. A depressed hopelessness dampens the body's disease-fighting immune system. In repeated studies, optimists have been found to outlive pessimists or to live with fewer illnesses.

If positive thinking in the face of adversity pays dividends, so, too, can a dash of realism. Anxiety over possible failure can actually fuel energetic efforts to avoid the dreaded fate (Goodhart, 1986; Norem, 2000; Showers, 1992). Overconfident students often perform less well than their equally able peers who, concerned about bombing the upcoming exam, study thoroughly and get a top grade. Edward Chang (2000) reports that, compared with European-American students, Asian-American students express somewhat greater pessimism—which he suspects helps explain their more impressive academic achievements. Success requires enough optimism to provide hope and enough pessimism to prevent complacency.

Excessive optimism can also blind us to real risks. Neil Weinstein (1980, 1982, 1996) has shown how our natural positive-thinking bias can promote "an unrealistic optimism about future life events." Most college students perceive themselves as less likely than their average classmate to develop drinking problems, drop out of school, or have a heart attack by age 40. Most late adolescents see themselves as much less vulnerable than their peers to the AIDS virus (Abrams, 1991).

Given illusory optimism, documented in some 200 research reports, people may fail to take sensible precautions. Most young Americans know that half of U.S. marriages end in divorce, but they are confident that *theirs* will not (Lehman & Nisbett, 1985). Most cigarette smokers smoke high-tar brands, but only 17 percent believe their brand has a more hazardous tar level than most others (Segerstrom & others, 1993). Compared with other women at their university, sexually active undergraduate women—especially those who do *not* consistently use effective contraception—perceive themselves as *less* vulnerable to unwanted pregnancy (Burger & Burns, 1988). Individuals who optimistically venture into ill-

DOONESBURY   **BY GARRY TRUDEAU**

fated relationships, deny the effects of smoking, or engage in unprotected sex remind us that, like pride, blind optimism may go before a fall.

Ironically, people often are most overconfident when most incompetent. That's because it often takes competence to recognize competence, note Justin Kruger and David Dunning (1999). They found that most students scoring at the low end of tests of grammar and logic believed they had scored in the top half. If you do not know what good grammar is, you may be unaware that your grammar is poor. The difficulty in recognizing one's own incompetence helps explain why so many low-scoring students are dumbfounded after doing badly on an exam.

Assessing Behavior in Situations

PREVIEW QUESTION 3 How do social-cognitive researchers evaluate personality?

Social-cognitive researchers explore the effect of differing situations on people's behavior patterns and attitudes. They study, for example, how viewing aggressive or nonaggressive models affects behavior. They assess the impact of dehumanizing situations on people's attitudes. And they examine the consistency of people's personalities in varying circumstances.

An ambitious example of such research, and one that predates social-cognitive theory, is the U.S. Army's World War II strategy for assessing candidates for spy missions. Rather than using paper-and-pencil tests, army psychologists subjected the candidates to simulated undercover conditions. They tested their ability to handle stress, solve problems, maintain leadership, and withstand intense interrogation without blowing their covers. Although it was time-consuming and expensive, this assessment of behavior in a realistic situation helped predict later success on actual spy missions (OSS Assessment Staff, 1948).

Military and educational organizations and 4 in 5 Fortune 500 companies are continuing this strategy in their evaluations of hundreds of thousands of people each year in assessment centers (Bray & others, 1991, 1997). AT&T has observed prospective managers doing simulated managerial work. Many colleges assess potential faculty members' teaching abilities by observing them teach. Armies assess their soldiers by observing them during military exercises. Most American cities with populations of 50,000 or more use assessment centers in evaluating police and fire officers (Lowry, 1997).

These procedures exploit the principle that the best means of predicting future behavior is neither a personality test nor an interviewer's intuition. Rather, it is the person's past behavior patterns in similar situations (Mischel, 1981; Ouellette & Wood, 1998; Schmidt & Hunter, 1998). As long as the situation and the person remain much the same, the best predictor of future job performance is past job performance; the best predictor of future grades is past grades; the best predictor of future aggressiveness is past aggressiveness; the best predictor of drug use in young adulthood is drug use in high school. If you can't check the person's past behavior, the next-best thing is to create an assessment situation that simulates the demands of the task so you can see how the person handles them.

Evaluating the Social-Cognitive Perspective

PREVIEW QUESTION 4 What has the social-cognitive perspective contributed to the study of personality, and what criticisms have been leveled against it?

The social-cognitive perspective on personality sensitizes researchers to how situations affect, and are affected by, individuals. More than do the other perspectives, it builds from psychological research on learning and cognition.

"I didn't think it could happen to me."

Earvin "Magic" Johnson, *My Life*, 1993 (after contracting the HIV virus)

"Ignorance more freely begets confidence than does knowledge."

Charles Darwin, *The Descent of Man*, 1871

One criticism is that the theory focuses so much on the situation that it fails to appreciate the person's inner traits. Where is the person in this view of personality, ask the dissenters (Carlson, 1984), and where are human emotions? True, the situation does guide our behavior. But, say the critics, in many instances our unconscious motives, our emotions, and our pervasive traits shine through. Consider Percy Ray Pridgen and Charles Gill. They each faced the same situation: They jointly won a $90 million lottery jackpot (Harriston, 1993). When he learned of the winning numbers, Pridgen began trembling uncontrollably, huddled with a friend behind a bathroom door while confirming the win, then sobbed. Gill told his wife and then went to sleep.

Reflections on the Personality Perspectives

Each of the four major perspectives on personality (summarized in Table 33.1) can teach us something. The psychoanalytic perspective draws our attention to the unconscious and irrational aspects of human existence. The trait perspective systematically describes and classifies important components of personality. The humanistic perspective reminds us of the importance of our sense of self and of our potential for self-actualization. The social-cognitive perspective teaches us that we always act in the context of situations that we help to create.

Seldom in life does a single perspective on any issue give us a complete picture of another human being. Human personality reveals its different aspects when we view it from different perspectives, and each perspective can enlarge our vision of the whole person.

> "Nature is always more subtle, more intricate, more elegant than what we are able to imagine."
>
> Carl Sagan, "Science—Who Cares?" 1991

TABLE 33.1

THE FOUR PERSPECTIVES ON PERSONALITY

Perspective	Explanation of Behavior	Assessment Techniques	Evaluation
Psychoanalytic	Unconscious conflicts between pleasure-seeking impulses and social restraints	Projective tests aimed at revealing unconscious motivations	A speculative, hard-to-test theory with enormous cultural impact
Trait	Expressing biologically influenced dispositions, such as extraversion or introversion	Personality inventories that assess the strengths of different traits	A descriptive approach criticized as sometimes underestimating the variability of behavior from situation to situation
Humanistic	Processing conscious feelings about oneself in the light of one's experiences and needs	Questionnaire assessments of self-concept	A theory that reinvigorated contemporary interest in the self; criticized as subjective and sometimes naively self-centered and optimistic
Social-cognitive	Reciprocal influences between people and their situations, colored by perceptions of control	Correlational and experimental studies of people's feelings of control	An interactive theory that integrates research on learning, cognition, and social behavior; criticized as underestimating the importance of emotions and enduring traits

rehearse it!

1. Albert Bandura, a social-cognitive theorist, believes that interacting with our environment involves reciprocal determinism, or mutual influences among personal factors, environmental factors, and behavior. An example of an environmental factor is
   a. the presence of books in a home.
   b. a preference for outdoor play.
   c. the ability to read at a fourth-grade level.
   d. the fear of violent action on television.

2. Researchers have found that when elderly patients are given an active part in the management of their care and surroundings, their morale and health tend to improve. The assumption is that the patients do better when they perceive
   a. learned helplessness.
   b. an external locus of control.

   c. an internal locus of control.
   d. reciprocal determinism.

3. Martin Seligman described an attitude of passive resignation, which he called *learned helplessness*. Working with animals and people, Seligman identified the circumstances under which learned helplessness develops. For example, a dog will respond with learned helplessness if it has received repeated shocks and has had
   a. the opportunity to escape.
   b. no control over the shocks.
   c. pain or discomfort.
   d. no food or water prior to the shocks.

4. A goal of many personality theories is to be able to predict a person's behavior in a particular situation. A theory that is very sensitive to the way people affect, and are affected by, particular situations, but that says little

   about enduring traits, is the
   _____ theory.
   a. psychoanalytic
   b. trait
   c. humanistic
   d. social-cognitive

5. What conclusion can we draw regarding the four perspectives on personality: the psychoanalytic, trait, humanistic, and social-cognitive perspectives?
   a. The usefulness of each depends on the behavior being studied.
   b. Together, they provide a complete picture of the whole person.
   c. The trait and social-cognitive perspectives are currently the most useful for understanding personality.
   d. They need to be supplemented by a biological perspective on personality.

REVIEWING

The Social-Cognitive Perspective and Reflections on the Four Key Perspectives

1. In the view of social-cognitive psychologists, what three influences shape an individual's personality?

The social-cognitive perspective applies principles of learning, cognition, and social behavior to personality, with particular emphasis on the ways in which our personality influences and is influenced by our interaction with the environment. It assumes reciprocal determinism—that personal-cognitive factors interact with the environment to influence people's behavior.

2. What are the causes and consequences of personal control?

By studying variations among people in their perceived personal control and in their experiences of learned helplessness or mastery and competence, researchers have found that people with an internal locus of control are better able to cope with life than are those with an external locus of control.

3. How do social-cognitive researchers evaluate personality?

Social-cognitive researchers study how people's behaviors and beliefs both affect and are affected by their situations. They have found that the best way to predict someone's behavior in a given situation is to observe that person's behavior in similar situations.

4. What has the social-cognitive perspective contributed to the study of personality, and what criticisms have been leveled against it?

Though faulted for underemphasizing the importance of unconscious dynamics and inner traits, the social-cognitive perspective builds on psychology's well-established concepts of learning and cognition and reminds us of the power of social situations.

TERMS AND CONCEPTS TO REMEMBER

reciprocal determinism, p. 484
personal control, p. 485

external locus of control, p. 485
internal locus of control, p. 485

learned helplessness, p. 486

positive psychology, p. 487

REHEARSE IT ANSWER KEY

1. a   2. c   3. b   4. d   5. b

Psychological Disorders and Their Treatment

I felt the need to clean my room at home in Indianapolis every Sunday and would spend four to five hours at it. I would take every book out of the bookcase, dust and put it back. At the time I loved doing it. Then I didn't want to do it anymore, but I couldn't stop. The clothes in my closet hung exactly two fingers apart. . . . I made a ritual of touching the wall in my bedroom before I went out because something bad would happen if I didn't do it the right way. I had a constant anxiety about it as a kid, and it made me think for the first time that I might be nuts.

Marc, diagnosed with obsessive-compulsive disorder (from Summers, 1996)

Whenever I get depressed it's because I've lost a sense of self. I can't find reasons to like myself. I think I'm ugly. I think no one likes me. . . . I become grumpy and short-tempered. Nobody wants to be around me. I'm left alone. Being alone confirms that I am ugly and not worth being with. I think I'm responsible for everything that goes wrong.

Greta, diagnosed with depression (from Thorne, 1993, p. 21)

Voices, like the roar of a crowd came. I felt like Jesus; I was being crucified. It was dark. I just continued to huddle under the blanket, feeling weak, laid bare and defenseless in a cruel world I could no longer understand.

Stuart, diagnosed with schizophrenia (from Emmons & others, 1997)

W̲e are fascinated by the exceptional, the unusual, and the abnormal, especially in people. But why such fascination with disturbed people? Do we see in them something of ourselves? At various moments, all of us feel, think, or act the way disturbed people do much of the time. We, too, get anxious, depressed, withdrawn, suspicious, deluded, or antisocial, just less intensely and more briefly. It's no wonder then that studying psychological disorders may at times evoke an eerie self-recognition, one that illuminates the dynamics of our own personality. "To study the abnormal is the best way of understanding the normal," proposed William James (1842–1910).

Another reason for our curiosity is that so many of us have felt, either personally or through friends or family members, the bewilderment and pain of a psychological disorder—unexplained physical symptoms, irrational fears, or the feeling that life is not worth living.

Module 34 provides a general introduction to psychological disorders and describes those that are classified as *anxiety disorders*. Module 35 focuses on *mood disorders* and *personality disorders*, with a brief essay on *dissociative disorders*. Module 36 focuses on *schizophrenia*. Module 37 addresses the ways in which people with psychological disorders are treated through various types of psychotherapies and biomedical therapies.

"We are all mad at some time or another."

Battista Mantuanus, *Eclogues*, 1500

"The sun shines and warms and lights us and we have no curiosity to know why this is so, but we ask the reason of all evil, of pain, and hunger, and [unusual] people."

Ralph Waldo Emerson, 1803–1882

34 Introduction to Psychological Disorders: Anxiety Disorders

"Who in the rainbow can draw the line where the violet tint ends and the orange tint begins? Distinctly we see the difference of the colors, but where exactly does the one first blendingly enter into the other? So with sanity and insanity?"

Herman Melville, *Billy Budd, Sailor*, 1924

Some 400 million people worldwide suffer psychological disorders, reports the World Health Organization's mental health director (Sartorius, 1994). The WHO also reports that, worldwide, mental disorders account for 15.4 percent of the years of life lost due to death or disability—scoring slightly below cardiovascular conditions and slightly above cancer (Murray & Lopez, 1996). And no known culture is free of the two terrible psychological maladies—depression and schizophrenia (Castillo, 1997; Draguns, 1990a,b, 1997). As members of the human family, few of us go through life unacquainted with the reality of psychological disturbance.

Perspectives on Psychological Disorders

PREVIEW QUESTION 1 Where should we draw the line between normality and disorder?

Most people would agree that someone who is too depressed to get out of bed for weeks at a time has a psychological disorder. But what about those who, having experienced a loss, are unable to resume their usual social activities? Where should we draw the line between sadness and depression? Between zany creativity and bizarre irrationality? Between normality and abnormality? How should we *define* psychological disorders? Equally important, how should we *understand* disorders—as sicknesses that need to be diagnosed and cured, or as natural responses to a troubling environment? Finally, how should we *classify* psychological disorders? Can we do so in a way that allows us to help disturbed people without stigmatizing them with labels?

Defining Psychological Disorders

Many mental health workers view **psychological disorders** as *harmful dysfunctions* (Spitzer, 1997; Wakefield, 1997). *Dysfunction* refers to not functioning as natural selection predisposes our species to behave, and *harmful* is a judgment of undesirability. Thus, they label behavior as disordered when they judge it to be *atypical, disturbing, maladaptive,* and *unjustifiable.*

Being different from most other people in one's culture is *part* of what it takes to define a psychological disorder. But there is more to a disorder than being atypical. Olympic gold medalists are abnormal in their physical abilities, and they are heroes. To be considered disordered, an atypical behavior must also be one that other people find *disturbing.*

Standards of acceptability for behaviors vary. In some cultures, people routinely behave in ways (such as going about naked) that in other cultures would be grounds for arrest.

A benign obsession
British street cleaner Snowy Farr's eccentric behavior may indeed be atypical, but clinicians would not label it disordered because it is neither particularly disturbing nor maladaptive.

In at least one cultural context—wartime—even mass killing may be viewed as heroic. One person's homicidal "terrorist" is another person's "freedom fighter."

Standards of acceptability also vary over time. On December 9, 1973, homosexuality was an illness. By day's end on December 10 it was not. The American Psychiatric Association had dropped homosexuality as a disorder (because it no longer equated being gay with having psychological problems). Later it *added* nicotine dependence (because it deemed smoking both addictive and self-destructive).

Atypical and disturbing behaviors are more likely to be considered disordered when judged harmful. Indeed, many clinicians define disorders as behaviors that are *maladaptive*—as when a smoker's nicotine dependence causes physical damage. By this yardstick, even typical behaviors, such as the occasional despondency that many college students feel, may signal a psychological disorder—if they become disabling.

Finally, abnormal behavior is most likely to be considered disordered when others find it rationally *unjustifiable*. Those who claim to hear voices have usually been presumed to be deranged. But actress Shirley MacLaine could wear a crystal on her neck and say, "See the outer bubble of white light watching you. It is part of you," and not be seen as disordered because enough people found her rational (Friedrich, 1987).

> "If a man is in a minority of one, we lock him up."
>
> Oliver Wendell Holmes, 1841–1935

Understanding Psychological Disorders

PREVIEW QUESTION 2 What theoretical models or perspectives can help us understand psychological disorders?

To explain puzzling behavior, people in earlier times often presumed that strange forces—the movements of the stars, godlike powers, or evil spirits—were at work. "The devil made him do it," you might have said if you had lived during the Middle Ages. The cure might have been to get rid of the evil force—by placating the great powers or exorcising the demon. Until the last two centuries, "mad" people were sometimes caged in zoolike conditions or given "therapies" appropriate to a demon: They were sometimes beaten, burned, or castrated. In other times, the therapy included pulling teeth, removing lengths of intestines, and cauterizing the clitoris. Some people considered "mad" even had their own blood removed and replaced with transfusions of animal blood (Farina, 1982). These views have given way to two other interpretations: the medical perspective and the bio-psycho-social perspective.

The Medical Perspective

In opposition to the brutal treatment of the Middle Ages, reformers such as Philippe Pinel (1745–1826) in France insisted madness was not demon possession but a sickness caused by severe stresses and inhumane conditions. For Pinel and other reformers, treatment included boosting patients' morale by unchaining them, talking with them, and replacing brutality with gentleness, isolation with activity, and filth with clean air and sun.

When physicians later discovered that syphilis infects the brain and distorts the mind, health reformers and medical workers began to focus on physical causes for disorders and treatments that would cure them. Today, the medical perspective is familiar and recognizable to us in the terminology of the mental *health* movement: A mental *illness* (also called a psycho*pathology*) needs to be *diagnosed* on the basis of its *symptoms* and *cured* through *therapy*, which may include *treatment* in a psychiatric hospital. In the 1800s, the assumption of this **medical model**—that psychological disorders are sicknesses—provided the impetus for much-needed reform. Comfort replaced chains, therapy replaced torture, and hospitals replaced asylums.

The medical perspective has gained credibility from recent discoveries. Genetically influenced abnormalities in brain structure and biochemistry contribute to a

■ **psychological disorder** a "harmful dysfunction" in which behavior is judged to be atypical, disturbing, maladaptive, and unjustifiable.

■ **medical model** the concept that diseases have physical causes that can be diagnosed, treated, and, in most cases, cured. When applied to psychological disorders, the medical model assumes that these "mental" illnesses can be diagnosed on the basis of their symptoms and cured through therapy, which may include treatment in a psychiatric hospital.

■ **bio-psycho-social perspective** a contemporary perspective which assumes that biological, psychological, and sociocultural factors combine and interact to produce psychological disorders.

■ **DSM-IV** the American Psychiatric Association's *Diagnostic and Statistical Manual of Mental Disorders* (Fourth Edition), a widely used system for classifying psychological disorders.

number of disorders. "Mental illnesses are diagnosable disorders of the brain," declares a White House fact sheet on mental illness (1999). Two of the most troubling, depression and schizophrenia, are often treated medically. But psychological factors, such as traumatic stress, also play an important role.

The Bio-Psycho-Social Perspective

Today's psychologists contend that *all* behavior, whether called normal or disordered, arises from the interaction of nature (genetic and physiological factors) and nurture (past and present experiences). To presume that a person is "mentally ill" attributes the condition solely to an internal problem—to a "sickness" that must be found and cured. Maybe there *is* no deep, internal problem. Maybe instead there is a growth-blocking difficulty in the person's environment, in the person's current interpretations of events, or in the person's bad habits and poor social skills.

Evidence of environmental effects comes from links between disorder and culture. Some major disorders such as depression and schizophrenia occur worldwide. From Asia to Africa and across the Americas, the core symptoms of schizophrenia include irrationality and incoherent speech (Brislin, 1993; Draguns, 1990b). Other disorders are culture-bound (Beardsley, 1994; Castillo, 1997). Different cultures have different sources of stress and produce different ways of coping. The eating disorders anorexia nervosa and bulimia, for example, occur mostly in Western cultures. *Susto,* marked by severe anxiety, restlessness, and a fear of black magic, is found in Latin America. *Taijin-kyofusho,* which combines social anxiety about one's appearance with a readiness to blush and a fear of eye contact, appears in Japan. Such disorders may share an underlying dynamic (such as anxiety) while differing in the symptoms (an eating problem or a type of fear) manifested in a particular culture.

Today, most mental health workers assume that disorders are influenced by genetic predispositions and physiological states. And by inner psychological dynamics. And by social and cultural circumstances. To get the whole picture, we need an interdisciplinary **bio-psycho-social perspective** (**FIGURE 34.1**).

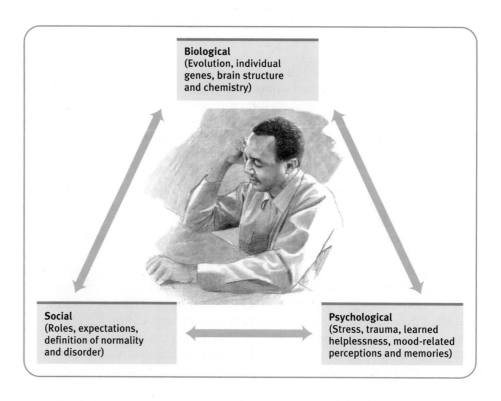

FIGURE 34.1

The bio-psycho-social perspective

Today's psychology studies how biological, psychological, and social factors interact to produce specific psychological disorders.

Biological
(Evolution, individual genes, brain structure and chemistry)

Social
(Roles, expectations, definition of normality and disorder)

Psychological
(Stress, trauma, learned helplessness, mood-related perceptions and memories)

Classifying Psychological Disorders

PREVIEW QUESTION 3 How and why do clinicians classify psychological disorders?

In biology and the other sciences, classification creates order. To classify an animal as a mammal says a great deal—that it is warm-blooded, has hair or fur, and nourishes its young with milk. In psychiatry and psychology, too, classification both orders and describes clusters of symptoms. To classify a person's disorder as "schizophrenia" suggests that the person talks incoherently, hallucinates or has delusions (bizarre beliefs), shows either little emotion or inappropriate emotion, or is socially withdrawn. Thus, the diagnostic term simply provides a handy shorthand for describing a complex disorder.

In psychiatry and psychology, diagnostic classification ideally aims to describe a disorder, predict its future course, imply appropriate treatment, and stimulate research into its causes. Indeed, to study a disorder we must first name and describe it. The current authoritative scheme for classifying psychological disorders is the American Psychiatric Association's *Diagnostic and Statistical Manual of Mental Disorders* (Fourth Edition), nicknamed **DSM-IV.** This 1994 volume and an accompanying book of case illustrations provide the basis for much of the material in this chapter. DSM-IV was developed in coordination with the tenth edition of the World Health Organization's *International Classification of Diseases* (ICD-10).

The very idea of "diagnosing" people's problems in terms of their "symptoms" presumes a mental "illness." As a result, some practitioners are not enthralled with this medical terminology, but most find DSM-IV a helpful and practical tool. It is also financially necessary: Most North American health insurance companies require a DSM-IV diagnosis.

For a DSM-IV category to be valid, it must first be reliable. If one psychiatrist or psychologist diagnoses someone as having, say, "catatonic schizophrenia," what are the chances that another mental health worker will independently give the same diagnosis? With the DSM-IV's diagnostic guidelines, the chances are good. The guidelines work by asking clinicians a series of objective questions about observable behaviors, such as, "Is the person afraid to leave home?" In one study, 16 psychologists used this structured-interview procedure to diagnose 75 psychiatric patients as suffering from (1) depression, (2) generalized anxiety, or (3) some other disorder (Riskind & others, 1987). Without knowing the first psychologist's diagnosis, another psychologist viewed a videotape of each interview and offered a second opinion. For 83 percent of the patients, the two opinions agreed.

Some critics fault the manual for casting too wide a net and bringing "almost any kind of behavior within the compass of psychiatry" (Eysenck & others, 1983). These critics point to behaviors ranging from irrational fear of humiliation and embarrassment (social phobia) to persistently breaking rules at home or school (conduct disorder). As the number of disorder categories has swelled, from 60 in the 1950s' DSM to 400 in today's, so has the number of adults who meet the criteria for at least one psychiatric ailment—nearly 30 percent in one recent year according to one national survey (Regier & others, 1998).

"I'm always like this, and my family was wondering if you could prescribe a mild depressant."

Labeling Psychological Disorders

PREVIEW QUESTION 4 Why do some psychologists criticize the use of diagnostic labels?

The DSM has other critics who register a more fundamental complaint—that these labels are at best arbitrary and at worst value judgments masquerading as science. Once we label a person, we view that person differently (Farina, 1982). Labels create preconceptions that can bias our perceptions and our interpretations. It is better,

"One of the unpardonable sins, in the eyes of most people, is for a man to go about unlabelled. The world regards such a person as the police do an unmuzzled dog, not under proper control."

T. H. Huxley, *Evolution and Ethics*, 1893

some clinicians say, to study the roots of specific symptoms, such as delusions or hallucinations, than to study catchall categories, such as schizophrenia (Persons, 1986).

In the most controversial demonstration of the biasing power of diagnostic labels, David Rosenhan (1973) and seven of his friends and Stanford University colleagues went to mental hospital admissions offices, complaining of "hearing voices" that were saying "empty," "hollow," and "thud." Apart from this complaint and giving false names and occupations, they answered all the questions truthfully. All eight were diagnosed as mentally ill.

That these normal people were misdiagnosed is unsurprising. As one psychiatrist noted, if someone swallowed blood, went to an emergency room, and spat it up, would we fault the doctor for diagnosing a bleeding ulcer? What followed the diagnosis *was* startling. Until being released (an average of 19 days later), the "patients" exhibited no further symptoms. Yet the clinicians were able to "discover" the causes of their disorders after analyzing their (quite normal) life histories. They said one person was reacting to mixed emotions about his parents. Even the normal behaviors of the "patients," such as taking notes, were often misinterpreted as symptoms.

Other studies also confirm that labels affect how we perceive people. Ellen Langer and her colleagues (1974, 1980) had people rate an interviewee they thought was either normal (a job applicant) or out of the ordinary (a psychiatric or cancer patient). All the raters saw the identical videotape. Those who watched unlabeled interviewees perceived them as normal; those who watched supposed patients perceived them as "different from most people." Therapists (who thought they were evaluating a psychiatric patient) perceived the interviewee as "frightened of his own aggressive impulses," a "passive, dependent type," and so forth. A label can serve a useful purpose. But as Rosenhan discovered, it can also have "a life and an influence of its own."

The stigmatizing power of labels was illustrated when a female associate of psychologist Stewart Page (1977) called 180 people in Toronto who were advertising furnished rooms for rent. When she merely asked if the room was still available, the answer was nearly always yes. When she said she was about to be released from a mental hospital, the answer three times out of four was no (as it was when she said she was calling for her brother who was about to be released from jail). Some who answered no were later called by a second person who simply asked if the room was still available. Nearly always it was. Surveys in Western Europe have uncovered similar attitudes toward those labeled mentally ill. But as we have come to understand psychological disorders as diseases of the brain, not failures of character, the stigma seems to be lifting (Solomon, 1996). More and more public figures are feeling free to "come out" and speak with candor about their struggles with disorders such as depression. And the more often people have contact with mental health patients, the more accepting their attitudes are (Kolodziej & Johnson, 1996).

Given the images of psychological disorder in the popular media, it is hardly surprising that stereotypes linger. Television researcher George Gerbner (1985) reported that 1 in 5 prime-time and daytime programs depicted a psychologically disordered person, and 7 in 10 of such programs portrayed this character as violent or criminal. Movies, too, stereotype mental health patients, sometimes as homicidal (Anthony Hopkins' role in *Silence of the Lambs*) or as freaks (Woody Allen as *Zelig*) (Hyler & others, 1991; Wahl, 1992). People with schizophrenia are indeed more likely than others to commit violent crime, especially if they also abuse alcohol (Citrome & Volavka, 1999; Tiihonen & others, 1997). However, at least 9 in 10 people with disorders are *not* dangerous; instead, they are anxious, depressed, or withdrawn. And *if* they steer clear of alcohol and drugs, those released from mental hospitals are no more prone to violence than are their neighbors (Steadman & others, 1998). Indeed, reports the U.S. Surgeon General's Office (1999, p. 7), "There is very little risk of violence or harm to a stranger from casual contact with an individual who has a mental disorder."

Tipper Gore

"I had clinical depression, recognized it, and went to a social worker. I got diagnosed and then successfully treated. I hope that will encourage people to seek treatment if they think they are suffering from depression."

ferent to planes not in their immediate neighborhood (Mineka & Zinbarg, 1996). Evolution has not prepared us to learn to fear bombs dropping from the sky.

Just as our phobias focus on dangers faced by our ancestors, our compulsive acts typically exaggerate behaviors that contributed to our species' survival. Grooming gone wild becomes hair pulling. Washing up becomes ritual hand washing. Checking territorial boundaries becomes checking and rechecking an already locked door (Rapoport, 1989).

Genes

Some people more than others seem genetically predisposed to particular fears and high anxiety. Identical twins often develop similar phobias, in some cases even when raised separately (Carey, 1990; Eckert & others, 1981). One pair of 35-year-old identical female twins independently developed claustrophobia. They also became so afraid of water that each would gingerly wade backward into the ocean, and then only up to the knees. Among monkeys, fearfulness runs in families. Individual monkeys react more strongly to stress if their close biological relatives are anxiously reactive (Suomi, 1986). Among humans, vulnerability to anxiety disorder rises when the afflicted relative is an identical twin (Barlow, 1988; Kendler & others, 1992, 1999; Roy & others, 1995).

Physiology

General anxiety, panic attacks, and even obsessions and compulsions are biologically measurable as an overarousal of brain areas involved in impulse control and habitual behaviors. PET scans of persons with obsessive-compulsive disorder reveal unusually high activity in an area of the frontal lobes just above the eyes (**FIGURE 34.3**) (Rauch & Jenike, 1993; Resnick, 1992). Fear-learning experiences also serve to create fear circuits within the amygdala, deep in the brain (Armony & others, 1998). Some antidepressant drugs dampen this fear-circuit activity, and the associated obsessive-compulsive behavior.

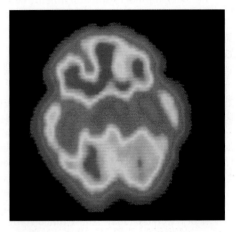

FIGURE 34.3

A PET scan of the brain of a person with obsessive-compulsive disorder
The scan reveals an abnormally high metabolic activity (red areas) in the frontal lobes, seen at the top of the photo. This is visible in a region of the left hemisphere's frontal lobe involved in directing attention.

rehearse it!

8. When anxiety is so distressing, uncontrollable, or persistent that it results in maladaptive behavior, the person is said to have an anxiety disorder. If a person's anxiety takes the form of an irrational fear of a specific object or situation—for example, an irrational fear of thunderstorms or closed spaces—the disorder is called
   a. a phobia.
   b. a panic attack.
   c. generalized anxiety.
   d. an obsessive-compulsive disorder.

9. The experience of anxiety often involves physical symptoms, such as trembling, dizziness, chest pains, or choking sensations. An episode of intense dread, which is typically accompanied by such symptoms and by feelings of terror, is called

   a. generalized or chronic anxiety.
   b. a social phobia.
   c. a panic attack.
   d. an obsessive fear.

10. Marina has always been concerned with cleanliness and neatness. Her mother never had to remind her to clean her room. When Marina became consumed with the need to clean the entire house and refused to participate in any other activities, her family consulted a therapist, who diagnosed her as having
    a. obsessive-compulsive disorder.
    b. generalized anxiety disorder.
    c. a phobia.
    d. learned helplessness.

11. Rats subjected to unpredictable shocks in the laboratory become chronically anxious. To the learning researcher this suggests that anxiety is a response to

    a. a phobia.
    b. biological factors.
    c. the pressures of the superego.
    d. helplessness.

12. Psychologists have different ideas about the causes of phobias. For example, some psychologists stress the importance of biological predispositions, noting that we seem predisposed to fear certain stimuli. Psychologists of the learning perspective, on the other hand, maintain that phobias are
    a. the result of individual genetic makeup.
    b. a way of repressing unacceptable impulses.
    c. conditioned fears.
    d. a symptom of having been abused as a child.

Introduction to Psychological Disorders: Anxiety Disorders

1. Where should we draw the line between normality and disorder?

Between normality and abnormality lies not a gulf but a fine and somewhat arbitrary line. Where we draw that line depends on how atypical, disturbing, maladaptive, and unjustifiable a person's behavior is.

2. What theoretical models or perspectives can help us understand psychological disorders?

The medical model's assumption that psychological disorders are mental "illnesses" has displaced earlier views that demons and evil spirits were to blame. Recent interest in the link between disorders and genetically influenced abnormalities in brain structure and biochemistry has renewed interest in the medical model. However, critics question the medical model's labeling of psychological disorders as sicknesses. They argue that the disorders are socially defined and that some disorders are found only in certain cultures. Most mental health workers today believe that disorders are influenced by genetic predisposition, physiological states, psychological dynamics, and social circumstances (the bio-psycho-social perspective).

3. How and why do clinicians classify psychological disorders?

Many psychiatrists and psychologists believe that a system for naming and describing psychological disorders facilitates treatment and research. The current edition of the *Diagnostic and Statistical Manual of Mental Disorders* (DSM-IV) provides an authoritative classification scheme. Diagnostic labels facilitate mental health professionals' communications and research, and most health insurance policies in North America require DSM-IV diagnoses before they will pay for therapy.

4. Why do some psychologists criticize the use of diagnostic labels?

Critics point out the price we pay for the benefits of classifying disorders: Labels can create preconceptions that unfairly stigmatize people and bias our perceptions of their past and present behavior.

5. How many people suffer, or have suffered, from a psychological disorder? Does the risk vary with ethnicity or gender?

A 1980s National Institute of Mental Health survey of nearly 20,000 institutionalized and community residents revealed that 1 in 3 American adults has at some time experienced a psychological disorder, and that 1 in 5 does so currently. Risk does vary with ethnicity and gender, and the incidence of serious disorders is doubly high below the poverty line. The three most common disorders are phobias and mood disorder (with women outnumbering men 2 to 1) and alcohol abuse or dependence (with men outnumbering women 5 to 1).

6. What are anxiety disorders, and how do they differ from the ordinary worries and fears we all experience?

For most of us, worries and anxiety are not intensely distressing, persistent, and maladaptive—the hallmarks of anxiety disorders. Those who suffer a *generalized anxiety disorder* may for no clear reason feel persistently and uncontrollably tense and uneasy. Anxiety escalates into periodic episodes of intense dread for those suffering *panic disorder*. Those with a *phobic disorder* may be irrationally afraid of a specific object or situation. Persistent and repetitive thoughts and actions characterize *obsessive-compulsive disorder*.

7. What are the sources of the anxious feelings and thoughts that characterize anxiety disorders?

Freud's psychoanalytic perspective views anxiety disorders as the discharging of repressed impulses. The learning perspective sees them as a product of fear conditioning and observational learning. The biological perspective considers possible evolutionary, genetic, and physiological influences.

TERMS AND CONCEPTS TO REMEMBER

psychological disorder, p. 494
medical model, p. 495
bio-psycho-social perspective,
  p. 496

DSM-IV, p. 497
anxiety disorders, p. 502
generalized anxiety disorder,
  p. 502

panic disorder, p. 502
phobia, p. 502

obsessive-compulsive disorder,
  p. 502

REHEARSE IT ANSWER KEY

1. c	3. c	5. c	7. c	9. c	11. d
2. a	4. c	6. d	8. a	10. a	12. c

Mood Disorders and Personality Disorders

PREVIEW QUESTION 1 What are mood disorders, and what forms do they take?

The emotional extremes of **mood disorders** come in two principal forms: (1) *major depressive disorder,* in which the person experiences prolonged hopelessness and lethargy until usually rebounding to normality; and (2) *bipolar disorder* (formerly called *manic depressive disorder*), in which the person alternates between depression and *mania,* an overexcited, hyperactive state.

Major Depressive Disorder

Perhaps you know what depression feels like. If you are like most college students, at some time during this year—more likely the dark months of winter than the bright days of summer—you will probably experience a few of the symptoms of depression (Beck & Young, 1978). You may feel deeply discouraged about the future, dissatisfied with your life, or isolated from others. You may lack the energy to get things done or even to force yourself out of bed; be unable to concentrate, eat, or sleep normally; or even wonder if you would be better off dead. Perhaps academic success came easily to you in high school, and now you find that disappointing grades jeopardize your goals. You may feel lonely and isolated as a "nontraditional" student—returning after attending to other work or family commitments. Maybe social stresses, such as feeling you don't belong or the breakup of a romance, have plunged you into despair. And maybe brooding has at times only worsened your self-torment.

You are not alone. Depression is the "common cold" of psychological disorders—an expression that effectively describes its pervasiveness but certainly not its seriousness. Although phobias—the persistent, irrational fears occurring in some anxiety disorders—are more common, depression is the number one reason people seek mental health services.

As anxiety is a response to threat of future loss, depression is often a response to past and current loss. To feel bad in reaction to profoundly sad events (such as a significant loss) is to be in touch with reality. In such times, depression is like a car's low-oil-pressure light—a signal that warns us to stop and take protective measures. Recall that, biologically speaking, life's purpose is not happiness but survival and reproduction. To this end, coughing, vomiting, and various forms of pain protect the body from dangerous toxins. Similarly, depression is a sort of psychic hibernation: It slows us down, helps us avoid attracting predators, and evokes support. To grind temporarily to a halt and ruminate, as depressed people do, is to reassess one's life when feeling threatened. From this perspective, there is sense to suffering. Withdrawal may be strategic.

But when does this response become seriously maladaptive? The line separating life's normal "downs" from major depression is difficult to draw. Joy, contentment, sadness, and despair are different points on a continuum, points at which any of us may be found at any given moment.

Major depressive disorder occurs when signs of depression (including lethargy, feelings of worthlessness, or loss of interest in family, friends, and activities) last two weeks or more without any notable cause. The difference between a blue mood after bad news and a mood disorder is like the difference between gasping for breath after a hard run and being chronically short of breath. To sense what depression feels like, suggest some clinicians, imagine combining the anguish of grief with the sluggishness of jet lag.

- **mood disorders** psychological disorders characterized by emotional extremes. See *major depressive disorder, manic episode,* and *bipolar disorder.*
- **major depressive disorder** a mood disorder in which a person, for no apparent reason, experiences two or more weeks of depressed moods, feelings of worthlessness, and diminished interest or pleasure in most activities.

For some people, recurring depression during winter's dark months constitutes a seasonal affective disorder. For others, winter darkness means more blue moods. When asked "Have you cried today?" Americans answered yes more often in the winter:

	Men (answered yes)	Women (answered yes)
August	4%	7%
December	8%	21%

Source: Time/CNN survey, 1994

"My life had come to a sudden stop. I was able to breathe, to eat, to drink, to sleep. I could not, indeed, help doing so; but there was no real life in me."

Leo Tolstoy, *My Confession*, 1887

Bipolar Disorder

With or without therapy, episodes of major depression usually end, and people temporarily or permanently return to their previous behavior patterns. However, some people rebound to or from the opposite emotional extreme—a euphoric, hyperactive, wildly optimistic **manic episode.** If depression is living in slow motion, mania is fast forward. Alternation between depression and mania signals **bipolar disorder.** During the manic phase of bipolar disorder, the person is typically overtalkative, overactive, elated (though easily irritated if crossed); has little need for sleep; and shows fewer sexual inhibitions. Speech is loud, flighty, and hard to interrupt.

One of mania's maladaptive symptoms is grandiose optimism and self-esteem, which may lead to reckless investments and spending sprees. Although people in a manic state find advice irritating, they need protection from their own poor judgment. In milder forms, however, the energy and free-flowing thinking of mania can fuel creativity. History offers many examples of creative bipolar people, from Walt Whitman and Ernest Hemingway to actress Margot Kidder. Bipolar disorder is especially common among creative artists (Jamison, 1993, 1995). George Frideric Handel (1685–1759), who many believe suffered a mild form of bipolar disorder, composed his nearly four-hour-long *Messiah* during three weeks of intense, creative energy (Keynes, 1980). Creative professionals who rely on precision and logic (architects, designers, journalists) are less vulnerable to bipolar disorder than are those who rely on emotional expression and vivid imagery (poets, novelists, entertainers), reports Arnold Ludwig (1995).

Creativity and bipolar disorders
History has given us many creative artists, composers, and writers with bipolar disorder, including Walt Whitman, Virginia Woolf, Edgar Allan Poe, Samuel Clemens (Mark Twain), Ernest Hemingway, and Margot Kidder.

It is as true of emotions as of everything else: What goes up comes down. Before long, the elated mood either returns to normal or plunges into a depression. Though as maladaptive as major depression, bipolar disorder is much less common, occurring in about 1 percent of the population. Unlike major depression, it afflicts as many men as women.

Explaining Mood Disorders

PREVIEW QUESTION 2 What causes mood disorders, and what might explain the Western world's rising incidence of depression among youth and young adults?

Because depression profoundly affects so many people, it understandably has been the subject of thousands of studies. Psychologists are working to develop a theory of mood disorders that will suggest ways to treat and prevent them. Researcher Peter Lewinsohn and his colleagues (1985, 1998) summarized the facts that any theory of depression must explain. Among them are the following:

- **Many behavioral and cognitive changes accompany depression.** Depressed people are inactive and feel unmotivated. They are sensitive to negative happen-

■ **manic episode** a mood disorder marked by a hyperactive, wildly optimistic state.

■ **bipolar disorder** a mood disorder in which the person alternates between the hopelessness and lethargy of depression and the overexcited state of mania.

ings, expect negative outcomes, and more often recall negative information. When the depression lifts, these behavioral and cognitive accompaniments disappear. Nearly half the time they exhibit symptoms of another disorder, such as anxiety or drug or alcohol abuse.

- **Depression is widespread.** Its commonality suggests that its causes, too, must be common.

- **Compared with men, women are twice as vulnerable to major depression** (**FIGURE 35.1**). In general, women are most vulnerable to passive disorders—internalized states, such as depression, anxiety, and inhibited sexual desire. Men's disorders are more active—alcohol abuse, antisocial conduct, lack of impulse control. When women get sad, they often get sadder than men do. When men get mad, they often get madder than women do. Curiously, the gender difference in depression is quite small among college students (Regeth & Lewis, 1995).

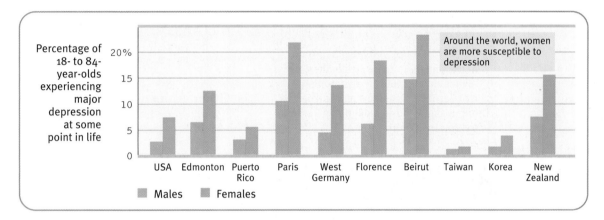

Percentage of 18- to 84-year-olds experiencing major depression at some point in life

Around the world, women are more susceptible to depression

USA Edmonton Puerto Rico Paris West Germany Florence Beirut Taiwan Korea New Zealand

■ Males ■ Females

FIGURE 35.1

Gender and depression
Interviews with 38,000 adults in 10 countries confirm what many smaller studies have found: Women's risk of major depression is double that of men's. Note, too, that lifetime risk of depression varies by culture—from 1.5 percent in Taiwan to 19 percent in Beirut. (Data from Weissman & others, 1996.)

- **Most major depressive episodes last less than six months.** Therapy can speed recovery, yet most people suffering major depression return to normal without professional help. The plague of depression comes and, a few weeks or months later, it usually goes.

- **Stressful events related to work, marriage, and close relationships often precede depression.** A family member's death, a job loss, a marital crisis, or a physical assault increase one's risk of depression. One study followed 2000 people over time. It found that the risk of the onset of depression in the ensuing month ranged from less than 1 percent among those who had experienced no stressful life event to 24 percent among those with three such stresses (Kendler & others, 1998). The early loss of a parent due to death or separation also increases later vulnerability to depression (Agid & others, 1999).

About 50 percent of those who recover from depression will suffer another episode within two years. Recovery is more likely to be enduring the longer patients stay well, the fewer their previous episodes, the less stress they experience, and the more social support they have (Belsher & Costello, 1988).

To these facts we can add one more: *With each new generation, the rate of depression is increasing and the disorder is striking earlier* (now often in the late teens). This is true not only in Canada and the United States but also in Germany, Italy, France, Lebanon, New Zealand, Taiwan, and Puerto Rico (Cross-National Collaborative Group, 1992). In North America, today's young adults are three times as likely as their grandparents to report recently—or ever—suffering depression (despite the grandparents' having had many more years at risk). In one National Institute of Mental Health study of 18,244 Americans, only 1 percent of those born before 1905 had suffered major depression by age 75. Of those born since 1955, 6 percent had experienced depression by age 25. The increase appears authentic, *not* simply the result of younger adults being more willing to disclose depression. Young adult Canadians are similarly most vulnerable to depression (*Statistics Canada*, 1999).

CLOSE-UP:

SUICIDE

"But life, being weary of these worldly bars, Never lacks power to dismiss itself."

William Shakespeare, *Julius Caesar*, 1599

Each year some three-quarters of a million despairing people worldwide will say no to life by electing a permanent solution to what may be a temporary problem (Retterstøl, 1993).

To find out who commits suicide, researchers have compared the suicide rates of different groups.

- **National differences** The suicide rates of England, Italy, and Spain are little more than half those of Canada, Australia, and the United States; Austrian, Danish, and Finnish suicide rates are about double (U.S. Bureau of the Census, 1998). Within Europe, the most suicide-prone people (Hungarians) are 20 times more likely to kill themselves than the least (Albanians) (Schmidtke, 1997).
- **Racial differences** White Americans are nearly twice as likely as black Americans to kill themselves (U.S. Bureau of the Census, 1998).
- **Gender differences** Women are much more likely than men to attempt suicide. But men are two to four times more likely (depending on the country) to succeed (**FIGURE 35.2**). (There is one exception—China—whose 500 daily female suicides account for at least half the world total [Rosenthal, 1999].) Men are more likely to use lethal methods, such as firing a bullet into the head, the method of choice in 6 of 10 U.S. suicides. (A study of 238,000 California hand gun purchasers found them 57 times more likely than other Californians to kill themselves in the week following their purchase [Wintemute & others, 1999].)
- **Age differences** Due partly to improved reporting (Gist & Welch, 1989), the known suicide rate among 15- to 19-year-olds has more than doubled in the United States since 1950. It now nearly equals the traditionally higher suicide rate among adults (**FIGURE 35.3**). In Canada, the suicide rate among 15- to 18-year-olds has increased sixfold since 1955 (NFFRE, 1996).
- **Other group differences** Suicide rates are much higher among

FIGURE 35.2

Suicide rates by gender and age

In the United States, suicide rates are higher among males than among females. The highest rates of all are found among older men. (From Centers for Disease Control, 1999.)

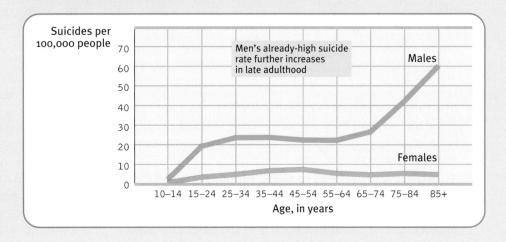

As you might expect, researchers understand and interpret these facts in ways that reflect their different perspectives. Psychoanalytic theory applies Freud's ideas about the importance of early childhood experiences and unconscious impulses. It suggests that depression occurs when significant losses evoke feelings associated with losses experienced in childhood. Loss of a romantic relationship or a job might evoke feelings associated with the loss of the intimate relationship with one's mother. Alternatively, unresolved anger toward one's parents might be turned inward against the self. Today's bio-psycho-social perspective is replacing these Freudian explanations with biological and cognitive explanations of depression.

The Biological Perspective

Most recent mental health research dollars have funded explorations of biological influences on mood disorders. Depression is a whole-body disorder. It involves genetic predispositions, biochemical imbalances, melancholy mood, and negative thoughts.

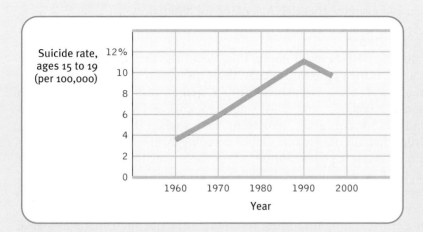

FIGURE 35.3

Increasing rates of teen suicide

Teen suicide soared from 1960 to 1990, and then tapered off. (From National Center for Health Statistics.)

the rich, the nonreligious, and those who are single, widowed, or divorced (Hoyer & Lund, 1993; Stack, 1992; Stengel, 1981). In both the United States and Australia, the teen suicide surge was almost entirely among males (Hassan & Carr, 1989).

People seldom commit suicide while in the depths of depression, when energy and initiative are lacking. It is when they begin to rebound and become capable of following through that the risk increases. Teenage sui-

cides may follow a traumatic event, such as a romantic breakup or a guilt-provoking antisocial act; they are often linked with drug and alcohol abuse (Fowler & others, 1986; Kolata, 1986). Compared with people who suffer no disorder, those addicted to alcohol are roughly 100 times more likely to commit suicide; some 3 percent of them do (Murphy & Wetzel, 1990). Even among those who have attempted suicide, those who abuse alcohol are five times more likely than others to kill themselves eventually (Beck & Steer, 1989).

Social suggestion may trigger the final act. Following highly publicized suicides and TV programs featuring suicide, known suicides increase. So

do fatal auto "accidents" and private airplane crashes.

Among the elderly, suicide is sometimes chosen as an alternative to current or future suffering. In people of all ages, suicide is not necessarily an act of hostility or revenge, but may instead be a way of switching off unendurable pain (Shneidman, 1987).

In retrospect, families and friends may recall signs that they believe should have forewarned them—verbal hints, giving possessions away, or withdrawal and preoccupation with death. Most people who commit suicide have been depressed. One-third have tried before to kill themselves.

Few who talk of suicide or think suicidal thoughts (a number that includes one-third of all adolescents and college students) actually attempt suicide, and few of those who attempt it complete the act (Yip, 1998). The United States, for example, records about 30,000 suicides annually and half a million emergency room visits for attempted suicide (Surgeon General, 1999). Still, most who do commit suicide had talked of it. And anyone who does threaten suicide is at least sending a signal of being desperate or feeling despondent. So, if a friend talks suicide, it's important to listen and to direct the friend to professional help.

Genetic Influences

We have long known that mood disorders run in families. The risk of major depression and bipolar disorder increases if you have a parent or sibling who became depressed before age 30 (Pauls & others, 1992; Weissman & others, 1986). If one identical twin is diagnosed as suffering major depressive disorder, the chances are about 1 in 2 that at some time the other twin will be, too. If one identical twin has bipolar disorder, the chances are 7 in 10 that the other twin will at some point be diagnosed similarly. Among fraternal twins, the corresponding odds are just under 1 in 5 (Tsuang & Faraone, 1990). The greater similarity of identical twins' depressive tendencies even occurs among twins reared apart (DiLalla & others, 1996). Moreover, adopted people who suffer a mood disorder often have close biological relatives who suffer mood disorders, become dependent on alcohol, or commit suicide (Wender & others, 1986).

A search for the genes that put people at risk for depression is now under way. At least 15 groups worldwide are sleuthing the genes that make one vulnerable to

Gene-hunters' pursuit of bipolar–DNA links
Linkage studies seek to identify aberrant genes in family members suffering the disorder. These Pennsylvania Amish family members—an isolated population sharing a common life-style and some vulnerability to the disorder—have been among the volunteer subjects.

bipolar disorder (Veggeberg, 1996). To tease out which genes are implicated, researchers use *linkage analysis*. First, they find families that have had the disorder across several generations. Then they draw blood from both affected and unaffected family members and examine their DNA, looking for differences.

The Depressed Brain

Genes act by directing biochemical events that, down the line, influence behavior. The biochemical key is the neurotransmitters, those messenger molecules that shuttle signals between nerve cells. Norepinephrine, a neurotransmitter that increases arousal and boosts mood, is overabundant during mania and scarce during depression. A second neurotransmitter, serotonin, also appears to be scarce during depression. Drugs that alleviate mania reduce norepinephrine; drugs that relieve depression tend to increase norepinephrine or serotonin supplies by blocking either their reuptake (as Prozac, Zoloft, and Paxil do with serotonin) or their chemical breakdown. Repetitive physical exercise, such as jogging, also increases serotonin and helps reduce depression (Jacobs, 1994).

Using modern scanning machines, researchers are also spotting neurological signs of depression. Many recent studies have found the brains of depressed people to be less active, indicating a slowed-down state (**FIGURE 35.4**). The left frontal lobe, which is active during positive emotions, is likely to be inactive in depressed states (Davidson, 1999). MRI scans have even shown the frontal lobes to be 7 percent smaller in severely depressed patients (Coffey & others, 1993).

FIGURE 35.4

The ups and downs of bipolar disorder
PET (position emission tomography) scans show that brain energy consumption rises and falls with the patient's emotional switches. Red areas are where the brain rapidly consumes glucose. (Courtesy of Lewis Baxter and Michael E. Phelps, UCLA School of Medicine.)

Depressed state   Manic state   Depressed state

The Social-Cognitive Perspective

Some people slide into depression for no obvious reason, even when life has been going well. Often, however, biological factors accompany psychological reactions to experience (**FIGURE 35.5**). The mind's negative thoughts somehow influence biochemical events that in a vicious cycle amplify depressing thoughts.

Recent research reveals how *self-defeating beliefs* feed the vicious cycle. Depressed people view life through dark glasses. Their intensely negative assumptions about themselves, their situations, and their futures lead them to magnify bad experiences and minimize good ones. Listen to Norman, a Canadian college professor, recalling his depression:

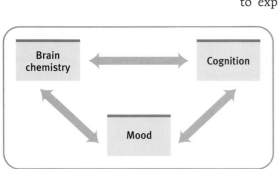

FIGURE 35.5

Depression—an ailing mind in an ailing body
Altering any one component of the chemistry-cognition-mood circuit can alter the others.

> I [despaired] of ever being human again. I honestly felt subhuman, lower than the lowest vermin. Furthermore, I was self-deprecatory and could not understand why anyone would want to associate with me, let alone love me. . . . I was positive that I was a fraud and a phony and that I didn't deserve my Ph.D. I didn't deserve to have tenure; I didn't deserve to be a Full Professor. . . . I didn't deserve the research grants I had been awarded; I couldn't understand how I had written books and journal articles . . . I must have conned a lot of people. (Endler, 1982, pp. 45–49)

Self-defeating beliefs may arise from *learned helplessness.* Studies show that both dogs and humans act depressed, passive, and withdrawn after experiencing uncontrollable painful events. Gender differences in uncontrollable stress help explain why women have been twice as vulnerable to depression. Women more often than men have been abused or made to feel helpless (Hamida & others, 1998; Nolen-Hoeksema, 1990). Thirty-nine percent of women and 20 percent of men entering American colleges feel "frequently overwhelmed by all I have to do" (Sax & others, 1999). (Men report spending more of their time in "light anxiety" activities such as sports, TV watching, and partying, possibly avoiding activities that might make them feel overwhelmed.)

Negative Thoughts Feed Negative Moods

Why do life's unavoidable failures lead some people, but not others, to become depressed? The difference lies partly with people's *attributions* of blame. We have some choice of whom or what to blame for our failures. If you fail a test and blame yourself, you may feel stupid and depressed. If you externalize the blame—perhaps attributing your failure to an unfair test—you are more likely to feel angry.

Depressed people tend to explain bad events in terms that are *stable* ("It's going to last forever"), *global* ("It's going to affect everything I do"), and *internal* ("It's all my fault"). Lyn Abramson, Gerald Metalsky, and Lauren Alloy (1989) theorize that the result of these pessimistic, overgeneralized, self-blaming attributions is a depressing sense of hopelessness. If you tend to see bad grades, social rejection, and work problems as inevitable and your own fault, and if you ruminate about such things, then when bad things happen you will probably experience the blues.

Martin Seligman (1991, 1995) argues that depression is common among young Westerners because of epidemic hopelessness stemming from the rise of individualism and the decline of commitment to religion and family. When facing failure or rejection, contends Seligman, the self-focused individual takes on personal responsibility for problems and has nothing to fall back on for hope. In non-Western cultures, where close-knit relationships and cooperation are the norm, major depression is less common and less tied to self-blame over personal failure. In Japan, for example, depressed people instead tend to report feeling shame over letting others down (Draguns, 1990a).

Negative Moods Feed Negative Thoughts

There is, however, a chicken-and-egg problem with the social-cognitive explanation of depression. Self-defeating beliefs, self-blame, and negative attributions surely do support depression. But do they *cause* depression, any more than a speedometer's reading 70 mph causes a car's speed? Peter Barnett and Ian Gotlib (1988) note that such cognitions are *indicators* of depression. Depressing thoughts *coincide* with a depressed mood. But before or after being depressed, people's thoughts are less negative. Perhaps this is because a depressed mood triggers negative thoughts. If you temporarily put people in a bad or sad mood, their memories, judgments, and expectations suddenly become more pessimistic.

Depression's Vicious Cycle

"A recipe for severe depression is preexisting pessimism encountering failure," noted Martin Seligman (1991, p. 78). Depression, as we have seen, is often brought on by stressful experiences—losing a job, getting divorced or rejected, suffering physical trauma—anything that disrupts your sense of who you are and why you are a worthy human being. Such brooding after failure can be adaptive; one may gain insights during times of depressed inactivity that can later lead to more effective strategies for interacting with the world. But depression-prone people respond to bad events in an especially self-focused, self-blaming way (Pyszczynski &

"I have learned to accept my mistakes by referring them to a personal history which was not of my making."

B. F. Skinner (1983)

"Man never reasons so much and becomes so introspective as when he suffers, since he is anxious to get at the cause of his sufferings."

Luigi Pirandello, *Six Characters in Search of an Author,* **1922**

Surviving depression

CBS correspondent Mike Wallace became debilitated by severe depression during a tough libel trial. "Depression is palpable," he says. "You begin to feel like a fake and a fraud. You second-guess everything about everything."

others, 1991; Wood & others, 1990a,b). Their self-esteem fluctuates up more rapidly with boosts and down with threats (Butler & others, 1994). When down, their brooding amplifies their negative feelings, which in turn trigger depression's other cognitive and behavioral symptoms.

This phenomenon also helps explain women's doubled risk of depression. When trouble strikes, women tend to think, men tend to act. Women often have vivid recall for both wonderful and horrid experiences; men more vaguely recall such experiences (Seidlitz & Diener, 1998). This gender difference in emotional recall may feed women's greater rumination over negative events. A woman may fret and act anxious or depressed, while a man may distract himself by drinking, acting out, delving into work, or watching sports (Nolen-Hoeksema, 2000; Seligman, 1994).

When bad events happen, those who ruminate and catastrophize with pessimistic, self-blaming thoughts are more at risk for depression. In research demonstrating this effect, Susan Nolen-Hoeksema and Jannay Morrow (1991) happened to assess Stanford University students' moods and ruminations 2 weeks before the 1989 earthquake devastated much of their area. Those identified as prone to brood over negative events showed more symptoms of depression both 10 days and 7 weeks after the earthquake. If you have an optimistic way of interpreting events, a failure or stress is unlikely to provoke depression (Seligman, 1991). And even if you do fall prey to depression, you are more likely to recover quickly (Metalsky & others, 1993; Needles & Abramson, 1990).

And what might you expect of new college students who are not depressed but do exhibit a pessimistic cognitive style (some of whom are about to satisfy Seligman's depression recipe: pessimism encountering failure)? Lauren Alloy and her collaborators (1999) monitored Temple University and University of Wisconsin students every 6 weeks for 2.5 years. Among those identified as having optimistic thinking styles only 1 percent had a first episode of major depression, as did 17 percent of those who began college with pessimistic thinking styles. Their simple conclusion: Negative thinkers are vulnerable to depression.

So there is two-way traffic between depressed mood and negative thinking. Depression causes self-focused negative thinking. And a self-focused, self-blaming style of explaining events puts one at risk for depression when bad events strike.

Knowing this, might we train depression-prone people to think more positively? That is one aim of cognitive therapy. It's also the aim of the Penn Optimism Program for 9- to 13-year-old children targeted as at risk for depression. The program puts children through 12 small-group sessions, each lasting two hours, in which they learn to tune into their thoughts when facing tough situations and to imagine alternatives to negative thoughts. The leader might, for example, present a cartoon depicting a child being called a name and invite the children to brainstorm positive ways to cope. In early experiments, the training has halved the proportion of children suffering depression for up to two ensuing years (Gillham & Reivich, 1999).

When successful, such therapy helps disrupt depression's vicious cycle. Being withdrawn, self-focused, and complaining elicits rejection (Furr & Funder, 1998; Gotlib & Hammen, 1992). In one study, researchers Stephen Strack and James Coyne (1983) noted that "depressed persons induced hostility, depression, and anxiety in others and got rejected. Their guesses that they were not accepted were not a matter of cognitive distortion." Weary of the person's fatigue, hopeless attitude, and lethargy, a spouse may threaten to leave or a boss may begin to question the person's

CLOSE-UP:

LONELINESS

Loneliness—the painful awareness that one's social relationships are deficient—is both a contributor to depression and its own problem. The deficiency stems from a mismatch between one's actual and desired social contacts. One person may feel lonely when isolated, another when in a crowd.

Aloneness often breeds loneliness. People who are alone—unmarried, unattached, and often young—are more likely to feel lonely. Dutch psychologist Jenny de Jong-Gierveld (1987) has speculated that the emphasis on individual fulfillment and the downgrading of stable relationships and commitment to others are "loneliness-provoking factors." Work-related moves also make for fewer long-term family and social ties and increased loneliness (Dill & Anderson, 1999).

People commonly experience one or more of four types of loneliness (Beck & Young, 1978). To be lonely is to feel *excluded* from a group you would like to belong to; to feel *unloved* and uncared about by those around you; to feel *constricted* and unable to share your private concerns with anyone; or to feel *alienated,* or different, from those in your community.

Like people suffering from depression, lonely people tend to blame themselves, attributing their deficient social relationships to their own inadequacies (Snodgrass, 1987). There may be a basis for this self-blame:

Chronically lonely people tend to be shy, self-conscious, and lacking in self-esteem, and to be perceived as less socially competent and attractive (Cheek & Melchior, 1990; Lau & Gruen, 1992; Vaux, 1988). They often find it hard to introduce themselves, make phone calls, and participate in groups (Rook, 1984; Spitzberg & Hurt, 1987). In addition, believing in their own social unworthiness restricts them from noticing and remembering positive feedback and from taking steps that would reduce their loneliness (Frankel & Prentice-Dunn, 1990). Thus, the very factors that work to create and maintain the cycle of depression can also produce a cycle of loneliness.

competence. Indeed, people in the throes of depression are at high risk for divorce, job loss, and other stressful life events. Misery may love another's company, but company does not love another's misery.

We can now assemble the pieces of the depression puzzle (**FIGURE 35.6**): (1) Negative, stressful events interpreted through (2) a ruminating, pessimistic explanatory style create (3) a hopeless, depressed state that (4) hampers the way the person thinks and acts. This, in turn, fuels (1) negative experiences such as rejection.

It's a cycle we can all recognize. Bad moods feed on themselves: When we *feel* down, we *think* negatively and remember bad experiences. On the brighter side, we can break the cycle of depression at any of these points—by moving to a different environment, by reversing our self-blame and negative attributions, by turning our attention outward, or by engaging in more pleasant activities and more competent behavior.

Winston Churchill called depression a "black dog" that periodically hounded him. Poet Emily Dickinson was so afraid of bursting into tears in public that she spent much of her adult life in seclusion (Patterson, 1951). Abraham Lincoln was so withdrawn and brooding as a young man that his friends feared he might take his own life (Kline, 1974). As each of these lives reminds us, people can and do struggle through depression. Most regain their capacity to love, to work, and even to succeed at the highest levels.

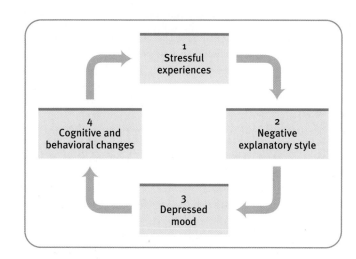

FIGURE 35.6

The vicious cycle of depression

This cycle can be broken at any point. A variety of therapeutic techniques attempt to intervene at one or more of the four points in the cycle. (Adapted from Lewinsohn & others, 1985.)

■ **personality disorders** psychological disorders characterized by inflexible and enduring behavior patterns that impair social functioning.

■ **antisocial personality disorder** a personality disorder in which the person (usually a man) exhibits a lack of conscience for wrongdoing, even toward friends and family members. May be aggressive and ruthless or a clever con artist.

Types of Personality Disorders

PREVIEW QUESTION 3 What characteristics are typical of personality disorders?

Personality disorders are inflexible and enduring patterns of behavior that impair one's social functioning. One cluster of disorders expresses anxiety, such as a fearful sensitivity to rejection that predisposes the withdrawn *avoidant personality disorder.* A second cluster expresses eccentric behaviors, such as the social disengagement of the *schizoid personality disorder.*

A third cluster exhibits dramatic or impulsive behaviors. A person with a *histrionic personality disorder* displays shallow, attention-getting emotions and goes to great lengths to gain others' praise and reassurance. Those with *narcissistic personality disorder* exaggerate their own importance, aided by success fantasies. They find criticism hard to accept, often reacting with rage or shame. Those with *borderline personality disorder* have an unstable identity, unstable relationships, and unstable emotions. If personality is one's enduring pattern of thinking, feeling, and acting, then a markedly unstable sense of self defines a "borderline personality."

The most troubling of these impulsive personality disorders is the **antisocial personality disorder.** The person (formerly called a *sociopath* or a *psychopath*) is typically a male whose lack of conscience becomes plain before age 15, as he begins to lie, steal, fight, or display unrestrained sexual behavior. About half of such children become antisocial adults—unable to keep a job, irresponsible as a spouse and parent, and assaultive or otherwise criminal (Farrington, 1991). When the antisocial personality combines a keen intelligence with amorality, the result may be a charming and clever con artist—or worse.

Despite their antisocial behavior, most criminals do not fit the description of antisocial personality disorder. Why? Because most criminals actually show responsible concern for their friends and family members. Antisocial personalities feel little and fear little, and in extreme cases, the results can be horrifyingly tragic. Henry Lee Lucas reported that at age 13 he strangled a woman who refused to have sex with him. He at one time confessed to having bludgeoned, suffocated, stabbed, shot, or mutilated some 360 women, men, and children during his 32 years of crime. During the last 6 years of his reign of terror, Lucas teamed with Elwood Toole, who reportedly slaughtered about 50 people whom he "didn't think was worth living anyhow." It ended when Lucas confessed to stabbing and dismembering his 15-year-old common-law wife, who was Toole's niece.

The antisocial personality expresses little regret over violating others' rights. "Once I've done a crime, I just forget it," said Lucas. Toole was equally matter-of-fact: "I think of killing like smoking a cigarette, like another habit" (Darrach & Norris, 1984).

Understanding Personality Disorders

As with mood disorders and schizophrenia, the antisocial personality disorder is woven of both biological and psychological strands. No single gene codes for a complex behavior such as crime, but twin and adoption studies reveal that biological relatives of certain individuals are at increased risk for criminality (Brennan & Mednick, 1993; DiLalla & Gottesman, 1991; Lyons & others, 1995). Their genetic vulnerability appears as a fearless approach to life. When they await aversive events, such as electric shocks or loud noises, they show little autonomic nervous system arousal (Hare, 1975). Even as youngsters, before committing any crime, they react with lower levels of stress hormones than do others their age (**FIGURE 35.7**).

FIGURE 35.7

Cold-blooded arousability and risk of crime
Levels of the stress hormone adrenaline were measured in two groups of 13-year-old Swedish boys. In both stressful and nonstressful situations, those who were later convicted of a crime (as 18- to 26-year-olds) showed relatively low arousal. (From Magnusson, 1990.)

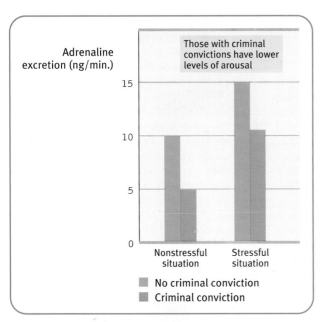

Adrenaline excretion (ng/min.)

Those with criminal convictions have lower levels of arousal

■ No criminal conviction
■ Criminal conviction

Some studies have detected the early signs of antisocial behavior in children as young as ages 3 to 6 (Caspi & others, 1996; Tremblay & others, 1994). Boys who later became aggressive or antisocial as adolescents tended, as young children, to have been impulsive, uninhibited, unconcerned with social rewards, and low in anxiety. If channeled in more productive directions, such fearlessness may lead to courageous heroism or adventurism. Lacking a sense of social responsibility, the same disposition produces a cool con artist or killer (Lykken, 1995).

Genetic influences help wire the brain. Adrian Raine (1999) compared PET scans of 41 murderers' brains with those from people of similar age and sex. Raine found reduced activity in the murderers' frontal lobe, which helps control impulses (**FIGURE 35.8**). This was especially true for those who murdered impulsively. In a follow-up study, Raine and his colleagues (2000) found that violent, antisocial people had less gray matter in their frontal lobes.

Genetics alone is hardly the whole story of antisocial crime, however. Relative to 1960, the average American in 1995 (before the late 1990s crime decline) was twice as likely to be murdered, four times as likely to report being raped, four times as likely to report being robbed, and five times as likely to report being assaulted (FBI, *Uniform Crime Reports*). Violent crime was also surging in other Western nations. Yet the human gene pool had hardly changed. Or consider the British social experiment begun in 1787, exiling 160,000 criminals to Australia. The descendants of these exiles, carrying their ancestors' supposed "criminal genes," have helped create a civilized democracy whose crime rate is similar to Britain's. Genetic predispositions do put some individuals more at risk for antisocial conduct than others; biological as well as environmental influences explain why 5 to 6 percent of offenders commit 50 to 60 percent of crimes (Lyman, 1996). But we must look to sociocultural factors to explain the modern epidemic of violence.

FIGURE 35.8

Murderous minds

PET scans illustrate reduced activation in a murderer's frontal cortex—a brain area that helps brake impulsive, aggressive behavior. (From Raine, 1999.)

Non-murderer's brain

Murderer's brain

rehearse it!

1. An example of a disorder that is so common it has been called the "common cold" of psychological disorders is
   a. amnesia.
   b. depression.
   c. bipolar disorder.
   d. schizophrenia.

2. With bipolar disorder, the person alternates between the lethargy of depression and the overexcited state of mania. Although bipolar disorder is as maladaptive as depression, it is much less common and it affects
   a. all ethnic groups equally.
   b. primarily scientists and doctors.
   c. as many men as women.
   d. younger people more than older people.

3. Depression affects many people, often following a stressful event, such as divorce or job change. In a depressive episode, a person tends to be inactive and unmotivated and overly sensitive to negative happenings. In most cases the depressive episode lasts
   a. three months.
   b. less than six months.
   c. six months to one year.
   d. two years.

4. Depression tends to run in families. It can often be alleviated by drugs that block the reuptake of the neurotransmitters norepinephrine and serotonin. These findings suggest that an explanation for depression may well be found in
   a. psychoanalytic theory.
   b. learned helplessness.
   c. stressful events.
   d. biological factors.

5. Depressed people are more likely than others to blame themselves, rather than external factors, for their failures. Such self-defeating beliefs often arise from feelings of helplessness or futility. Psychologists who emphasize the importance of negative perceptions, beliefs, and thoughts in depression are working within the _____ perspective.
   a. psychoanalytic
   b. biological
   c. behavioral
   d. social-cognitive

6. Unlike other psychological disorders, personality disorders need not involve any apparent anxiety, depression, or loss of contact with reality. A personality disorder, such as antisocial personality, is characterized by
   a. the presence of multiple personalities.
   b. disorganized thinking.
   c. enduring and maladaptive personality traits.
   d. mood disturbances.

DISSOCIATION AND MULTIPLE PERSONALITIES

"Multiple personalities" is not a form of personality disorder, but rather one of the rare **dissociative disorders,** in which a person appears to experience a sudden loss of memory or change in identity. When a situation becomes overwhelmingly stressful, people are said to dissociate themselves from it. Their conscious awareness becomes separated from painful memories, thoughts, and feelings. (Note that this explanation presumes the existence of repressed memories, which have recently been questioned.)

Certain symptoms of dissociation are not so rare. Now and then, many people may have a sense of being unreal, of being separated from their body, of watching themselves as if in a movie. Perhaps you can recall getting in your car and driving to some unintended location while your mind was preoccupied elsewhere. Facing trauma, such detachment may actually protect a person from being overwhelmed by emotion. Only when such experiences are severe and prolonged do they suggest a dissociative disorder.

The king of dissociative disorders is the massive dissociation of self from ordinary consciousness in those with **dissociative identity disorder.** These people are said to have two or more distinct identities that alternately control the person's behavior. The person with this disorder may be prim and proper one moment and loud and flirtatious the next. Each personality has its own voice and mannerisms, and the original one typically denies any awareness of the other(s).

Although people diagnosed as having multiple personalities are usually not violent, there have been cases in which the person reportedly became dissociated into a

The "Hillside Strangler" Kenneth Bianchi is shown here at his trial.

"good" and a "bad" or aggressive personality—a modest version of the Dr. Jekyll/Mr. Hyde split immortalized in Robert Louis Stevenson's story. Freud would have said that, rid of the original "good" personality's awareness, the wanton second personality is free to discharge forbidden impulses. One unusual case that for a time seemed to support this interpretation involved Kenneth Bianchi, who was on trial for the "Hillside Strangler" rapes and murders of 10 California women. During a hypnosis session with Bianchi, psychologist John Watkins (1984) "called forth" a hidden personality: "I've talked a bit to Ken, but I think that perhaps there might be another part of Ken that I haven't talked to, another part that maybe feels somewhat differently from the part that I've talked to. . . . Would you talk with me, Part, by saying, 'I'm here'?" Bianchi answered "Yes" and then claimed to be "Steve."

When speaking as Steve, Bianchi stated that he hated Ken because Ken was nice and that he (Steve), aided by a cousin, had murdered women. He also claimed that Ken knew nothing about his existence and that Ken was innocent of the murders. Was Bianchi's second personality a ruse, simply a way of disavowing responsibility for his actions? Yes. Bianchi— a practiced liar who had read about multiple personalities in psychology books—was later convicted.

Exploring our capacity for personality shifts, Nicholas Spanos (1986, 1994, 1996) asked college students to pretend they were accused murderers being examined by a psychiatrist. When given the same hypnotic treatment Bianchi received, most spontaneously expressed a second personality. This discovery made Spanos wonder: Are dissociative identities simply a more extreme version of our normal human capacity to vary the "selves" we present—as when we might display a goofy, loud self while hanging out with friends, and a subdued, respectful self around grandparents? Are clinicians who discover multiple personalities merely triggering fantasy-prone people's enactment of a role? If so, can such people then convince themselves of the authenticity of their own role enactments? Are they like actors, who commonly report "losing themselves" in their roles?

Spanos also raised these questions about the hypnotic state. Given that most multiple personalities patients are highly hypnotizable, whatever explains one condition—dissociation or role playing—may help explain the other.

Those who accept dissociative identity as a genuine disorder find support in the distinct brain and body states associated with differing personalities (Putnam, 1991). Handedness, too, sometimes switches with personality (Henninger, 1992). Subtle memories of one personality's experience sometimes fail to transfer to another personality (Eich & others, 1997). In one study, ophthalmologists detected shifting visual acuity and eye-muscle balance as patients switched personalities. These changes did not occur among control subjects trying to simulate multiple personalities (Miller & others, 1991).

Skeptics nevertheless find it suspicious that the disorder became so popular in the late 1900s. In North America, the number of diagnoses exploded from only 2 reported cases per decade from 1930 to 1960 to more than 20,000 in the 1980s (McHugh, 1995a). The average number of displayed personalities also mushroomed—from 3 to 12 per patient (Goff & Sims, 1993). How could such a dramatic disorder have gone unnoticed for so long? Isn't the sudden increase just what one would expect after the role of multiple personalities was well publicized in books and films of that time, including *The Three Faces of Eve* and *Sybil*? Many clinicians have never encountered a case of dissociative identity and the disorder is almost nonexistent outside North America, although in other cultures some people are said to be "possessed" by an alien spirit (Aldridge-Morris, 1989; Kluft, 1991). In Britain, the diagnosis—which some consider "a wacky American fad" (Cohen, 1995)—is rare. In India and Japan it is essentially nonexistent.

To skeptics, these findings point to a cultural phenomenon—a disorder created by therapists in a particular social context (Merskey, 1992). Skeptics note how some therapists go fishing for it: "Have you ever felt like another part of you does things you can't control? Does this part of you have a name? Can I talk to the angry part of you?" Once patients permit a therapist to talk, by name, "to the part of you that says those angry things" they have begun acting out the fantasy. Moreover, say skeptics, "It is no coincidence" that multiple personalities studies began among practitioners of hypnosis and that symptoms are most dramatic *after* beginning therapy (Goff, 1993; Piper, 1998).

With the dissociative disorders, as with the anxiety disorders, both psychoanalytic and learning perspectives see the symptoms as ways of dealing with anxiety. Psychoanalysts see them as defenses against the anxiety caused by the eruption of unacceptable impulses. Learning theorists see them as behaviors reinforced by anxiety reduction.

Others view dissociative disorders as what psychiatrist Frank Putnam (1995) calls "post-traumatic disorders"—a natural, protective response to "histories of childhood trauma." Researchers debate whether most dissociative identity disorder patients suffered physical, sexual, or emotional abuse as children (Gleaves, 1996; Lilienfeld & others, 1999). One study of 12 murderers diagnosed with dissociative identity disorder did find that 11 of them had suffered severe, torturous child abuse (Lewis & others, 1997). One was set afire by his parents. Another was used in child pornography and was scarred from being made to sit on a stove burner. Perhaps, then,

multiple personalities are the desperate efforts of the traumatized to flee inward.

But then why, wonder the skeptics, did the children of the Holocaust, after enduring boxcars, concentration camps, and their parents' murders, not develop dissociative identity disorders? Is it because the condition is either contrived by fantasy-prone, emotionally variable people, or constructed out of the therapist-patient interaction? If so, history's verdict will not be sympathetic. "This epidemic will end in the way that the witch craze ended in Salem," predicts psychiatrist Paul McHugh (1995b). "The [multiple personalities phenomenon] will be seen as manufactured, the 're-pressed memory' explanation will be recognized as misguided, and psychiatrists will become immunized against the practices that generated these artifacts."

■ **dissociative disorders** disorders in which conscious awareness becomes separated (dissociated) from previous memories, thoughts, and feelings.

■ **dissociative identity disorder** a rare dissociative disorder in which a person exhibits two or more distinct and alternating personalities. Also called *multiple personality disorder*.

Mood Disorders and Personality Disorders

1. What are mood disorders, and what forms do they take?

Mood disorders are characterized by emotional extremes. The two principal forms are *major depressive disorder* and *bipolar disorder*. In major depressive disorder, the person—without apparent reason—descends for weeks or months into deep unhappiness, lethargy, and feelings of worthlessness before rebounding to normality. In the less common bipolar disorder, the person alternates between the hopelessness and lethargy of depression and the hyperactive, wildly optimistic, impulsive phase of mania.

2. What causes mood disorders, and what might explain the Western world's rising incidence of depression among youth and young adults?

Current research on depression is vigorously exploring two sets of influences. The first focuses on genetic predispositions and neurotransmitter abnormalities. The second views the cycle of depression from a social-cognitive perspective, in the light of a vicious cycle of self-defeating beliefs, learned helplessness, negative attributions, and stressful experiences.

3. What characteristics are typical of personality disorders?

Personality disorders are enduring, maladaptive personality traits. One cluster of these disorders expresses anxiety, another expresses eccentric behaviors, and a third cluster exhibits dramatic or impulsive behaviors. For society, the most troubling personality disorder is the remorseless and fearless antisocial personality.

TERMS AND CONCEPTS TO REMEMBER

mood disorders, p. 509
major depressive disorder, p. 509

manic episode, p. 510
bipolar disorder, p. 510

personality disorders, p. 518
antisocial personality disorder,
   p. 518

dissociative disorders, p. 520
dissociative identity disorder,
   p. 520

REHEARSE IT ANSWER KEY

1. b   2. c   3. b   4. d   5. d   6. c

Schizophrenia

If depression is the common cold of psychological disorders, chronic schizophrenia is the cancer. Nearly 1 in 100 people will develop schizophrenia, joining the millions across the world who have suffered one of humanity's most dreaded disorders. It typically strikes as young people are maturing into adulthood, it knows no national boundaries, and it affects males and females about equally often (though men tend to be struck earlier and more severely).

Symptoms of Schizophrenia

PREVIEW QUESTION 1 What patterns of thinking, perceiving, feeling, and behaving characterize schizophrenia?

Literally translated, **schizophrenia** means "split mind." It refers not to a multiple-personality split but rather to a split from reality that shows itself in disorganized thinking, disturbed perceptions, and inappropriate emotions and actions.

Disorganized Thinking

Imagine trying to communicate with Maxine, a young woman whose thoughts spill out in no logical order. Her biographer, Susan Sheehan (1982, p. 25), observed her saying aloud to no one in particular,

> This morning, when I was at Hillside [Hospital], I was making a movie. I was surrounded by movie stars. The X-ray technician was Peter Lawford. The security guard was Don Knotts. That Indian doctor in Building 40 was Lou Costello. I'm Mary Poppins. Is this room painted blue to get me upset? My grandmother died four weeks after my eighteenth birthday.

As this strange monologue illustrates, the thinking of a person with schizophrenia is fragmented, bizarre, and distorted by false beliefs, called **delusions** ("I'm Mary Poppins"). Jumping from one idea to another may occur even within sentences, creating a sort of "word salad." One young man begged for "a little more allegro in the treatment," and suggested that "liberationary movement with a view to the widening of the horizon" will "ergo extort some wit in lectures." Those with *paranoid* tendencies are particularly prone to delusions of persecution.

Many psychologists believe disorganized thoughts result from a breakdown in selective attention. We normally have a remarkable capacity for selective attention—for, say, giving our undivided attention to one voice at a party while filtering out competing sensory stimuli. Schizophrenia sufferers cannot do this (Gjerde, 1983). They also have difficulty clearing their working memory of distracting information (Schooler & others, 1997). Thus, an irrelevant stimulus or an extraneous part of the preceding thought easily distracts them. Minute stimuli, such as the grooves on a brick or the inflections of a voice, may distract their attention from the whole scene or from the speaker's meaning. As one former patient recalled, "What had happened to me . . . was a breakdown in the filter, and a hodgepodge of unrelated stimuli were distracting me from things which should have had my undivided attention" (MacDonald, 1960, p. 218).

■ **schizophrenia** a group of severe disorders characterized by disorganized and delusional thinking, disturbed perceptions, and inappropriate emotions and actions.

■ **delusions** false beliefs, often of persecution or grandeur, that may accompany psychotic disorders.

Disturbed Perceptions

A person with schizophrenia may perceive things that are not there. Such *hallucinations* (sensory experiences without sensory stimulation) are usually auditory. The person may hear voices that make insulting statements or give orders. The voices may tell the patient that she is bad or that he must burn himself with a cigarette lighter. Less commonly, people see, feel, taste, or smell things that are not there. Such hallucinations have been compared to dreams breaking into waking consciousness. When the unreal seems real, the resulting perceptions are at best bizarre, at worst terrifying.

Inappropriate Emotions and Actions

The emotions of schizophrenia are often utterly inappropriate. Maxine's emotions seemed split off from reality. She laughed after recalling her grandmother's death. On occasion, she became angry for no apparent reason or cried when others laughed. Other victims of schizophrenia sometimes lapse into *flat affect,* a zombielike state of apparent apathy.

Motor behavior may also be inappropriate. The person may perform senseless, compulsive acts, such as continually rocking or rubbing an arm. Those who exhibit *catatonia* may remain motionless for hours on end and then become agitated.

As you can imagine, such disorganized thinking, disturbed perceptions, and inappropriate emotions and actions profoundly disrupt social relationships. During their most severe periods, people with schizophrenia live in a private inner world, preoccupied with illogical ideas and unreal images. Given a supportive environment, some recover to enjoy a normal life or experience bouts of schizophrenia only intermittently. Others remain socially withdrawn and isolated throughout much of their lives. Rarely is schizophrenia a one-time episode that is "cured," never to return.

Art by people diagnosed with schizophrenia
Commenting on the kind of art work shown here, poet and art critic John Ashbery wrote: "The lure of the work is strong, but so is the terror of the unanswerable riddles it proposes."

Types of Schizophrenia

PREVIEW QUESTION 2 What forms does schizophrenia take?

We have thus far described schizophrenia as if it were a single disorder. Actually, it is a cluster of disorders. The subtypes share some common features, but they also have some distinguishing symptoms (Table 36.1). Schizophrenia patients with *positive symptoms* may experience hallucinations, are often disorganized and deluded in their talk, and may exhibit inappropriate laughter, tears, or rage. Those with *negative symp-*

toms have toneless voices, expressionless faces, or mute and rigid bodies. Thus positive symptoms are the *presence* of inappropriate behaviors and negative symptoms are the *absence* of appropriate behaviors. Because schizophrenia is more than one disorder, these varied symptoms could have more than one cause.

Sometimes, as in the case of Maxine, schizophrenia develops gradually, emerging from a long history of social inadequacy (which partially explains why those predisposed to schizophrenia often end up in the lower socioeconomic levels, or even homeless). Other times it appears suddenly, seemingly as a reaction to stress. One rule holds true around the world (World Health Organization, 1979): When the schizophrenia is a slow-developing process (called *chronic,* or *process,* schizophrenia), recovery is doubtful. When, in reaction to particular life stresses, a previously well-adjusted person develops schizophrenia rapidly (*acute,* or *reactive,* schizophrenia), recovery is much more likely. Those with chronic schizophrenia often exhibit the negative symptom of withdrawal. The outlook is better for those exhibiting positive symptoms—they more often have a reactive condition that responds to drug therapy (Fenton & McGlashan, 1991, 1994; Fowles, 1992). (For one person's experiences with positive symptoms, see the Close-Up: Experiencing Schizophrenia.)

TABLE 36.1

SUBTYPES OF SCHIZOPHRENIA

Paranoid:	Preoccupation with delusions or hallucinations
Disorganized:	Disorganized speech or behavior, or flat or inappropriate emotion
Catatonic:	Immobility (or excessive, purposeless movement), extreme negativism, and/or parrotlike repeating of another's speech or movements
Undifferentiated:	Many and varied symptoms
Residual:	Withdrawal, after hallucinations and delusions have disappeared

CLOSE-UP:

EXPERIENCING SCHIZOPHRENIA

These recollections of a schizophrenia patient illustrate some of the thoughts and feelings of those who suffer the positive symptoms of schizophrenia. Note the hallucinations and the delusions of persecution and grandeur.

One night I was invited to listen to a talk by a worker in the foreign service. I was suspicious of him and thought he thought I was a Communist spy. I didn't say anything. I just leaned over and stared at him.

I thought the Government was spying on my room with a telescope in a building across the street. I thought people were loading down my food in the cafeteria with salt. In criminology class I thought the professor and the other students were laughing about me. I thought they were directing the poisoning of my food in the cafeteria. When I went to the cafeteria my hand shook as the waitress poured what I thought was poisonous coffee into my cup. I thought everyone in the cafeteria knew I was going to die. They all thought it was too bad but I was so evil it was necessary.

On a Saturday I drank lemonade to try to neutralize the poison. Then I would take showers to try to sweat the poison out. I was so nervous I could hardly think. I thought I might only have hours left to live. I thought of taking a bus home to my parents. But no, I thought, it was too late for that.

One day when my strange behavior landed me in a jail cell, the walls began to buzz like bees. I felt there were thousands of bees in the walls buzzing. The buzzing went on and on. There was no relief. It was maddening. Finally, I felt my father's hand rest on my head and I felt peace.

When someone asks me to explain schizophrenia I tell them, you know how sometimes in your dreams you are in them yourself and some of them feel like real nightmares? My schizophrenia was like I was walking through a dream. But everything around me was real. At times, today's world seems so boring and I wonder if I would like to step back into the schizophrenic dream, but then I remember all the scary and horrifying experiences. *(Excerpted and paraphrased with permission from Stuart Emmons, Craig Geisler, Kalman J. Kaplan, and Martin Harrow,* Living With Schizophrenia. *Muncie, IN: Taylor & Francis, 1997.)*

Understanding Schizophrenia

PREVIEW QUESTION 3 What causes schizophrenia?

Schizophrenia is not only the most dreaded psychological disorder but also one of the most heavily researched. Most of the new research studies link it with brain abnormalities and genetic predispositions. Schizophrenia is a disease of the brain exhibited in symptoms of the mind.

Brain Abnormalities

The idea that imbalances in brain chemistry might underlie schizophrenia has long intrigued scientists. Strange behaviors, they knew, could have strange chemical causes. The saying "mad as a hatter" refers to the psychological deterioration of British hatmakers whose brains, it was later discovered, were slowly poisoned as they moistened the brims of mercury-laden felt hats with their lips (Smith, 1983). Scientists are clarifying the mechanism by which chemicals such as LSD produce hallucinations, and their discoveries hint that schizophrenia symptoms might have a biochemical key.

Dopamine Overactivity

One such key to schizophrenia involves the neurotransmitter dopamine. When researchers examined patients' brains after death, they found an excess of receptors for dopamine—in fact, a sixfold excess for the so-called D4 dopamine receptor (Seeman & others, 1993; Wong & others, 1986). The researchers speculate that such a high level may intensify brain signals in schizophrenia, creating positive symptoms such as hallucinations and paranoia. As we might therefore expect, drugs that block dopamine receptors often lessen the symptoms; drugs that increase dopamine levels, such as amphetamines and cocaine, sometimes intensify them (Swerdlow & Koob, 1987). Dopamine overactivity may underlie patients' overreacting to irrelevant external and internal stimuli.

Brain Anatomy

Modern brain-scanning techniques reveal that many people with chronic schizophrenia have abnormal brain activity. Some have abnormally low brain activity in the frontal lobes (Pettegrew & others, 1993; Resnick, 1992). One recent study took PET scans of brain activity while people were hallucinating (Silbersweig & others, 1995). When participants heard a voice or saw something, their brains became vigorously active in several core regions, including the thalamus, a structure deep in the brain that filters incoming sensory signals and transmits them to the cortex.

Enlarged, fluid-filled areas and a corresponding shrinkage of cerebral tissue seem characteristic of schizophrenia, especially in men (Cannon & Marco, 1994; Elkis & others, 1995). The greater the shrinkage, often involving the hippocampus and amygdala in the brain's limbic system, the worse the thought disorder tends to be (Nelson & others, 1998; Shenton & others, 1992). The thalamus, too, is smaller than normal, which may explain why people with schizophrenia have difficulty filtering sensory input and focusing attention (Andreasen & others, 1994). The bottom line of various brain studies, reports Nancy Andreasen (1997), is that schizophrenia involves not a single brain abnormality but problems with several brain regions and their interconnections.

Naturally, scientists wonder what causes these brain abnormalities. One possibility is a prenatal problem. Low birth weight and birth complications are known risk factors for schizophrenia (Buka & others, 1999; Zornberg & others, 2000). People conceived during the peak of the Dutch wartime famine also later displayed a doubled rate of schizophrenia (Susser & others, 1996). A midpregnancy viral infection that might impair fetal brain development is another possible culprit (Waddington, 1993).

Can you imagine some ways to test this fetal-virus idea? Scientists exploring this possibility have asked the following questions:

- Are people at increased risk of schizophrenia if, during the middle of their fetal development, their country experienced a flu epidemic?
- Are people born in densely populated areas, where viral diseases spread more readily, at greater risk for schizophrenia?
- Are those born during the winter and spring months—after the fall-winter flu season—also at increased risk?

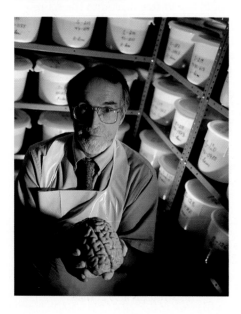

Studying the neurophysiology of schizophrenia

Psychiatrist E. Fuller Torrey is collecting the brains of hundreds of those who died as young adults and suffered disorders such as schizophrenia and bipolar disorder. Torrey is making tissue samples available to researchers worldwide.

- In the Southern Hemisphere, where the seasons are the reverse of the Northern Hemisphere, are the months of above-average schizophrenia births similarly reversed?
- As infectious disease rates have declined, has there been a correlated decline in the later incidence of schizophrenia?

The answer to all these questions is yes, suggesting that prenatal viral infections do play a contributing role (Myers, 2001).

Genetic Factors

Might people also inherit a predisposition to certain brain abnormalities? The evidence strongly suggests that, yes, some do. The nearly 1 in 100 odds of any person's being diagnosed with schizophrenia become 1 in 10 among those who have an afflicted sibling or parent, and close to 1 in 2 among those who have an afflicted identical twin (**FIGURE 36.1**). Although there are barely more than a dozen such known cases, it appears that an identical twin of a person with schizophrenia retains that 1-in-2 chance, whether the twins are reared together or apart (Plomin & others, 1997).

Even with identical twins there may be a prenatal environmental component. About two-thirds of identical twins share the same placenta and blood. (They usually also have opposite handedness to their co-twin.) If one has an identical twin with schizophrenia, the odds are 6 in 10 that the co-twin will be similarly afflicted if they shared a single placenta, but only 1 in 10 if the twins had separate placentas (Davis & others, 1995a,b; Phelps & others, 1997). Twins who share a placenta are more likely to experience the same prenatal viruses. So it's possible that shared germs as well as shared genes produce identical twin similarities.

Adoption studies, however, confirm that the genetic link is real (Gottesman, 1991). Children adopted by someone who develops schizophrenia seldom "catch" the disorder. Rather, adopted children have an elevated risk if a biological parent is diagnosed with schizophrenia.

With the genetic factor established, researchers are now sleuthing specific genes that, in some combination, might predispose schizophrenia-inducing brain abnormalities. So far, the evidence has produced a confusing mix of findings. But several linkage studies have implicated chromosomes 6, 8, and 22 as sites of genes that make some people susceptible (DeLisi, 1999).

The genetic contribution to schizophrenia is beyond question. But the genetic role is not straightforward, as in the inheritance of eye color. After all, about half the twins who share identical genes with a schizophrenia victim do *not* develop the disorder. Thus, behavior geneticists Susan Nicol and Irving Gottesman (1983) concluded that some people "have a genetic predisposition to

Lifetime risk, per 100 people, of developing schizophrenia for relatives of a person with schizophrenia

Schizophrenia risk increases with genetic closeness to relatives with schizophrenia

Relationship to person with schizophrenia

FIGURE 36.1

Risk of developing schizophrenia
The lifetime risks of developing schizophrenia vary with one's genetic relatedness to someone having this disorder. (From family and twin studies conducted between 1920 and 1987 in Europe; Irving Gottesman, 1991.)

Identical twin *with* schizophrenia

Identical twin *without* schizophrenia

Schizophrenia in identical twins
When twins differ, only the one afflicted with schizophrenia typically has enlarged, fluid-filled cranial cavities (Suddath & others, 1990). The difference between the twins implies some nongenetic factor, such as a virus, is also at work.

the disorder but that this predisposition by itself is not sufficient for the development of schizophrenia." Other factors—including prenatal viral infections, nutritional deprivation, and oxygen deprivation at birth—also may be ingredients for the disease.

Our knowledge of the human genome and of genetic influences upon maladies such as schizophrenia and bipolar disorder is exploding. So, can scientists develop genetic tests that reveal who is at risk? If so, will people in the future subject their embryos to genetic testing (and gene repair or abortion if they are at risk for a psychological or physical malady)? Or might they take their egg and sperm to the genetics lab for screening before combining them to produce an embryo? Or will children be tested for genetic risks and given appropriate preventive treatments? Although there is a growing possibility of such a test, the patterns of inheritance seem too complex to expect that a single gene abnormality will prove predictive (Gottesman, 1993). Yet given the explosion in gene and brain research technologies, scientists are optimistic that schizophrenia will soon be better understood.

Psychological Factors

If genetically predisposed physiological abnormalities do not, by themselves, cause schizophrenia, neither do prenatal and psychological factors alone. It remains true, as Nicol and Gottesman (1983) noted nearly two decades ago, that "no environmental causes have been discovered that will invariably, or even with moderate probability, produce schizophrenia in persons who are not related to a schizophrenic." Psychologists long ago ceased blaming cold and capricious "refrigerator mothers."

Nevertheless, if genes predispose some people to *react* to particular experiences by developing schizophrenia, then there must be identifiable triggering experiences. Researchers have asked: Can stress trigger schizophrenia? Can difficulties in family communications be a contributing factor?

The answer to each question is a strong maybe. The psychological triggers of schizophrenia have proved elusive, partly because they may vary with the type of schizophrenia and its speed of onset—whether it is a slow-developing, chronic schizophrenia, or a sudden, acute reaction to stress. True, young people with schizophrenia tend to have unusually disturbed communications with their parents. But is this a cause or a result of their disorder? True, stressful experiences, biochemical abnormalities, and schizophrenia's symptoms often occur together. But as the bio-psycho-social perspective emphasizes, the traffic between brain biochemistry and psychological experiences runs both ways. True, schizophrenic withdrawal often occurs in adolescence or early adulthood, coinciding with the stresses of having to become independent, assert oneself, and achieve social success and intimacy. So, is schizophrenia the maladaptive coping reaction of biologically vulnerable people? For example, abnormalities in the dopamine system and in brain anatomy may render a patient hypersensitive to stress, which worsens symptoms by augmenting dopamine activity (Walker & Diforio, 1997).

The Genain quadruplets
The odds of any four people picked at random all being diagnosed with schizophrenia are 1 in 100 million. But Nora, Iris, Myra, and Hester Genain all have the disease. Two of the sisters have more severe forms of the disorder than the others, suggesting the influence of environmental as well as biological factors.

Most of us can relate more easily to the ups and downs of mood disorders than to the strange thoughts, perceptions, and behaviors of schizophrenia. Sometimes our thoughts do jump around, but we do not talk nonsensically. Occasionally we feel unjustly suspicious of someone, but we do not fear that the world is plotting against us. Often our perceptions err, but rarely do we see or hear things that are not there. We have felt regret after laughing at someone's misfortune, but we rarely giggle in response to bad news. At times we just want to be alone, but we do not live in social isolation. However, millions of people around the world do talk strangely, suffer delusions, hear nonexistent voices, see things that are not there, laugh or cry at inappropriate times, or withdraw into private imaginary worlds. The quest to solve the cruel puzzle of schizophrenia therefore continues.

rehearse it!

1. Schizophrenia patients often show disorganized thinking and disturbed perceptions. They may speak illogically and may hear voices urging self-destruction. Hearing voices in the absence of any auditory stimulation is an example of a(n)
   a. delusion or false belief.
   b. inappropriate emotion.
   c. word salad.
   d. hallucination.

2. Schizophrenia is actually a cluster of disorders characterized by positive or negative symptoms. A person with positive symptoms is most likely to experience
   a. catatonia.   c. withdrawal.
   b. delusions.   d. flat emotion.

3. Stressful events, faulty family communications, and, especially, inherited abnormalities in brain chemistry and structure are all possible factors in the development of schizophrenia. Chances for recovery are best when
   a. onset is sudden, in response to stress.
   b. deterioration occurs gradually, during childhood.
   c. no environmental causes can be identified.
   d. there is a detectable brain abnormality.

REVIEWING

Schizophrenia

1. What patterns of thinking, perceiving, feeling, and behaving characterize schizophrenia?

Schizophrenia typically strikes during late adolescence. It affects men and women about equally, and it seems to occur in all cultures. Schizophrenia shows itself in disorganized thinking (nonsensical talk and delusions, which may stem from a breakdown of selective attention); disturbed perceptions (including hallucinations); and inappropriate emotions and actions. It is rarely a one-time episode.

2. What forms does schizophrenia take?

Schizophrenia is a set of disorders. The subtypes vary in having positive symptoms (the presence of inappropriate behaviors) or negative symptoms (the absence of appropriate behaviors). The subtypes also vary in their cause and onset. The disorders may emerge either gradually from a chronic history of social inadequacy (in which case the outlook is dim) or suddenly in reaction to stress (in which case the prospects for recovery are brighter).

3. What causes schizophrenia?

Researchers have linked certain forms of schizophrenia with brain abnormalities, such as enlarged, fluid-filled cerebral cavities, or increased receptors for the neurotransmitter dopamine, known to be a major player in this disorder. Prenatal viral infections are one possible cause. Twin and adoption studies also point to a genetic predisposition that, in conjunction with environmental factors, may bring about schizophrenia.

TERMS AND CONCEPTS TO REMEMBER

schizophrenia, p. 523   delusions, p. 523

REHEARSE IT ANSWER KEY

1. d   2. b   3. a

Therapy

Dorothea Dix (1802–1887)
"I . . . call your attention to the state of the Insane Persons confined within this Commonwealth, in cages."

- **psychotherapy** an emotionally charged, confiding interaction between a trained therapist and someone who suffers from psychological difficulties.

- **eclectic approach** an approach to psychotherapy that, depending on the client's problems, uses techniques from various forms of therapy.

- **psychoanalysis** Sigmund Freud's therapeutic technique. Freud believed the patient's free associations, resistances, dreams, and transferences—and the therapist's interpretations of them—released previously repressed feelings, allowing the patient to gain self-insight.

We have treated psychological disorders with a bewildering variety of methods, harsh and gentle: by cutting holes in the head and by giving warm baths and massages; by restraining, bleeding, or "beating the devil" out of people; by placing them in sunny, serene environments; by administering drugs and electric shocks; and by talking—talking about childhood experiences, about current feelings, about maladaptive thoughts and behaviors.

The transition from brutal to gentler treatments occurred thanks to the efforts of reformers such as Philippe Pinel in France and Dorothea Dix in the United States, Canada, and Scotland. Both advocated constructing mental hospitals to offer more humane methods of treatment. As we shall see, however, the introduction of therapeutic drugs and community-based treatment programs has largely emptied mental health hospitals since the mid-1950s.

Today's favored treatment depends on the therapist's viewpoint. Those who believe that psychological disorders are learned will tend to favor psychological therapies. Those who view disorders as biologically rooted are likely to advocate medication as well. Those who believe that disorders are responses to social conditions will, in addition, want to reform the "sick" environment. Many therapists seek to integrate insights from each of these views.

We can classify therapies into two main categories: The *psychological therapies* employ structured interactions (usually verbal) between a trained professional and a client with a problem. The *biomedical therapies* act directly on the patient's nervous system.

The Psychological Therapies

Psychological therapy, or **psychotherapy,** is "a planned, emotionally charged, confiding interaction between a trained, socially sanctioned healer and a sufferer" (Frank, 1982). There are 250 or more types of psychotherapy (Parloff, 1987). We will look at only the most influential. Each is built on one or more of psychology's major personality theories: psychoanalytic, humanistic, behavioral, and cognitive.

While each technique is distinctive, there are common threads. Therapists who view disorders as an interplay of bio-psycho-social influences may welcome a combination of treatments. Indeed, half of psychotherapists describe themselves as taking an **eclectic approach,** by using a blend of therapies (Beitman & others, 1989; Castonguay & Goldfried, 1994). Depending on the client and the problem, an eclectic therapist will draw from a variety of techniques. Closely related to eclecticism is *psychotherapy integration.* Rather than picking and choosing methods, integration advocates aim to combine them into a single, coherent system.

Psychoanalysis

PREVIEW QUESTION 1 What are the aims and methods of psychoanalysis and psychodynamic therapy?

Although few of today's therapists practice therapy as Sigmund Freud did, many of his psychoanalytic techniques survive. **Psychoanalysis** is part of our modern vocabulary, and its assumptions influence many other therapies. To understand the Freud-influenced "psychodynamic" therapies, let's first look at classical psychoanalysis as practiced by Freud himself.

The history of treatment
William Hogarth's (1697–1764) engraving
(left) of St. Mary of Bethlehem hospital
(commonly called Bedlam) in London depicts
the treatment of mental disorders in the
eighteenth century. Visitors paid to gawk at
the patients as if they were viewing zoo
animals. The chair on the right was designed
by Benjamin Rush (1746–1813) "for the
benefit of maniacal patients." Rush, a
founder of the movement for more humane
treatment of the mentally ill, believed that
they required restraint to regain their
sensibilities.

Aims

Sigmund Freud believed that the mind was like an iceberg, with the *unconscious* region below the surface and the *preconscious* close enough to the surface for its contents to be retrievable. He saw personality as composed of a reservoir of pleasure-seeking psychic impulses (the *id*), a reality-oriented executive (the *ego*), and an internalized set of ideals (the *superego*). Psychoanalysis assumes that many psychological problems are fueled by childhood's residue of supposedly repressed impulses and conflicts. Psychoanalysts try to bring these repressed feelings into conscious awareness where the patient can deal with them. By gaining insight into the origins of the disorder—by fulfilling the ancient imperative to "know thyself" in a deep way—the patient "works through" the buried feelings. The theory presumes that healthier, less anxious living becomes possible when patients release the energy they had previously devoted to id-ego-superego conflicts.

Methods

Psychoanalysis is historical reconstruction, its goal being to unearth the past in hope of unmasking the present. But how?

Freud came to believe that one path to the past was *free association.* Imagine yourself as a patient using the free association technique. The analyst invites you to relax, perhaps by lying on a couch. He or she will probably sit out of your line of vision, helping you focus attention on your thoughts and feelings. Beginning with a childhood memory, a dream, or a recent experience, you say aloud whatever comes to your mind from moment to moment. It sounds easy, but soon you notice how often you edit your thoughts as you speak, omitting what seems trivial, irrelevant, or shameful. Even in the safe presence of the analyst, you may pause momentarily before uttering an embarrassing thought. You may make a joking remark or change the subject to something less threatening. Sometimes your mind may go blank or you may find yourself unable to remember important details.

Classical psychoanalysis
The placement of the analyst's chair
out of the patient's view is thought
to minimize distraction and make it
easier for the patient—relaxed on a
couch—to verbalize whatever comes
to mind.

■ **resistance** in psychoanalysis, the blocking from consciousness of anxiety-laden material.

■ **interpretation** in psychoanalysis, the analyst's noting supposed dream meanings, resistances, and other significant behaviors in order to promote insight.

■ **transference** in psychoanalysis, the patient's transfer to the analyst of emotions linked with other relationships (such as love or hatred for a parent).

Woody Allen, after awakening from suspended animation in the movie *Sleeper*: **"I haven't seen my analyst in 200 years. He was a strict Freudian. If I'd been going all this time, I'd probably almost be cured by now."**

To the psychoanalyst, these blocks in the flow of your free associations indicate **resistance.** They hint that anxiety lurks and that you are repressing sensitive material. The analyst will want to explore these sensitive areas, first making you aware of your resistances and then interpreting their underlying meaning. The analyst's **interpretations**—suggestions of underlying wishes, feelings, and conflicts—aim to provide you with *insight*. If offered at the right moment, the analyst's interpretation—of, say, your not wanting to talk about your mother—may illuminate what you are avoiding. You may then discover what your resistances mean and how they fit with other pieces of your psychological puzzle.

Freud believed that another clue to repressed impulses is your dreams' *latent content*—their underlying but censored meaning. Thus, after inviting you to report a dream, the analyst may offer a dream analysis, suggesting its meaning.

During many such sessions you will probably disclose to your analyst more of yourself than you have ever revealed to anyone. Because psychoanalytic theory emphasizes the formative power of childhood experiences, much of what you reveal will pertain to your earliest memories. You will also probably find yourself experiencing strong positive or negative feelings for your analyst. Such feelings may express the dependency or mingled love and anger that you earlier experienced toward family members or other important people in your life. When this happens, Freud would say you are actually *transferring* your strongest feelings from those other relationships to the analyst. Analysts and other therapists believe that this **transference** exposes long-repressed feelings, giving you a belated chance to work through them with your analyst's help. But psychoanalysis is not just about excavating your childhood past. By examining your feelings toward the analyst you may also gain insight into your current relationships.

But critics note that much of psychoanalysis is built on the assumption that repressed memories exist, an assumption that is now questioned. This challenge—to an assumption so basic to much of professional and popular psychology—is provoking intense debate. Critics also say psychoanalysts' interpretations are hard to refute. If, in response to the analyst's suggested interpretation, you say, "Yes! I see now," your acceptance confirms the analyst's interpretation. If you emphatically say, "No! That just doesn't ring true," your denial may be taken as more resistance, also confirming the interpretation. Psychoanalysts acknowledge it's hard to prove or disprove their interpretations. But they insist that interpretations often are a great help to patients.

Traditional psychoanalysis takes time, up to several years of several sessions a week, and it is expensive. (Three times a week for just two years at $100 or more per hour comes to $30,000 or more.)

Psychodynamic Therapy

Although there are relatively few traditional psychoanalysts, psychoanalytic assumptions influence many therapists, especially those who make *psychodynamic* assumptions. Psychodynamic therapists try to understand a patient's current symptoms by exploring childhood experiences. They probe for supposed repressed, emotion-laden information, seeking to help the person gain insight into the unconscious roots of problems and work through newly resurrected feelings. Although influenced by Freud's psychoanalysis, these therapists may talk to the patient face to face (rather than out of the line of vision), once a week (rather than several times weekly), and for only a few weeks or months (rather than several years).

No brief excerpt can exemplify psychodynamic therapy's probing of the past, but we can illustrate these therapists' goal of enabling insight via their interpretations. In the following interaction, therapist David Malan responds to all that he has heard from a depressed patient by suggesting insights into her problems. Note how Malan interprets the woman's earlier remarks and suggests that her relationship with him reveals a characteristic pattern of behavior (1978, pp. 133–134).

Malan: I get the feeling that you're the sort of person who needs to keep active. If you don't keep active, then something goes wrong. Is that true?

Patient: Yes.

Malan: I get a second feeling about you and that is that you must, underneath all this, have an awful lot of very strong and upsetting feelings. Somehow they're there but you aren't really quite in touch with them. Isn't this right? I feel you've been like that as long as you can remember.

Patient: For quite a few years, whenever I really sat down and thought about it I got depressed, so I tried not to think about it.

Malan: You see, you've established a pattern, haven't you? You're even like that here with me, because in spite of the fact that you're in some trouble and you feel that the bottom is falling out of your world, the way you're telling me this is just as if there wasn't anything wrong.

Face-to-face therapy
In this type of therapy session the couch has disappeared. But the influence of psychoanalytic theory may not have, especially if the therapist probes for the origin of the patient's symptoms by seeking information from the patient's childhood.

Humanistic Therapies

PREVIEW QUESTION 2 What are the basic themes of humanistic therapy, such as Rogers' client-centered approach?

The humanistic perspective emphasizes people's inherent potential for self-fulfillment. Not surprisingly, then, humanistic therapists aim to boost self-fulfillment by helping people grow in self-awareness and self-acceptance. Unlike psychoanalytic therapists, humanistic therapists tend to focus on

- the *present* and *future* instead of the past. They explore feelings as they occur, rather than achieving insights into the childhood origins of the feelings.
- *conscious* rather than unconscious thoughts.
- taking immediate *responsibility* for one's feelings and actions rather than uncovering hidden determinants.
- promoting *growth* instead of curing illness. Thus, those in therapy are "clients" rather than "patients."

The most widely used humanistic technique is Carl Rogers' (1961, 1980) **client-centered therapy.** A client-centered therapist focuses on the person's conscious self-perceptions rather than on the therapist's own interpretations. The therapist listens, without judging or interpreting, and refrains from directing the client toward certain insights, a strategy labeled *nondirective* therapy.

Believing that most people already possess the resources for growth, Rogers encouraged therapists to exhibit *genuineness, acceptance,* and *empathy.* When therapists drop their facades and genuinely express their true feelings, when they enable their clients to feel unconditionally accepted, and when they empathically sense and reflect their clients' feelings, the clients may increase in self-understanding and self-acceptance. As Rogers (1980, p. 10) explained:

Hearing has consequences. When I truly hear a person and the meanings that are important to him at that moment, hearing not simply his words, but him, and when I let him know that I have heard his own private personal meanings, many things happen. There is first of all a grateful look. He feels released. He wants to tell me more about his world. He surges forth in a new sense of freedom. He becomes more open to the process of change.

I have often noticed that the more deeply I hear the meanings of the person, the more there is that happens. Almost always, when a person realizes he has been deeply heard, his eyes moisten. I think in some real sense he is weeping for joy. It is as though he were saying, "Thank God, somebody heard me. Someone knows what it's like to be me."

■ **client-centered therapy** a humanistic therapy, developed by Carl Rogers, in which the therapist uses techniques such as active listening within a genuine, accepting, empathic environment to facilitate clients' growth. (Also called *person-centered therapy*.)

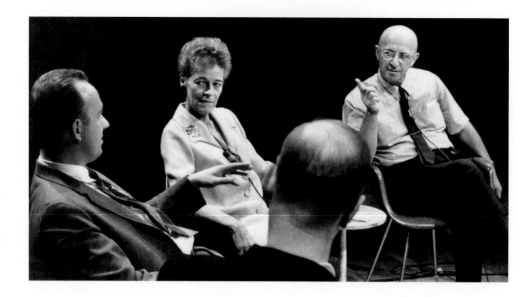

Active listening
Carl Rogers (right), shown here empathizing with a client during a group therapy session.

"We have two ears and one mouth that we may listen the more and talk the less."

Zeno, 335–263 B.C., *Diogenes Laertius*

"Hearing" refers to Rogers' technique of **active listening**—echoing, restating, and seeking clarification of what the person expresses (verbally or nonverbally) and acknowledging the expressed feelings. Active listening is now an accepted part of therapeutic counseling practices in many schools, colleges, and clinics. The counselor listens attentively and interrupts only to restate and confirm the client's feelings, to accept what the client is expressing, or to seek clarification. In counseling a male client, Rogers illustrated active listening:

Client: I just ain't no good to nobody, never was, and never will be.

Rogers: Feeling that now, hm? That you're just no good to yourself, no good to anybody. Never will be any good to anybody. Just that you're completely worthless, huh?—Those really are lousy feelings. Just feel that you're no good at all, hm?

Client: Yeah. (Muttering in low, discouraged voice) That's what this guy I went to town with just the other day told me.

Rogers: This guy that you went to town with really told you that you were no good? Is that what you're saying? Did I get that right?

Client: M-hm.

Rogers: I guess the meaning of that if I get it right is that here's somebody that—meant something to you and what does he think of you? Why, he's told you that he thinks you're no good at all. And that just really knocks the props out from under you. (Client weeps quietly.) It just brings the tears. (Silence of 20 seconds)

Client: (Rather defiantly) I don't care though.

Rogers: You tell yourself you don't care at all, but somehow I guess some part of you cares because some part of you weeps over it.

(Meador & Rogers, 1984, p. 167)

This brief excerpt illustrates how the client-centered counselor seeks to provide a psychological mirror that helps clients see themselves more clearly. But can a therapist be a perfect mirror, without selecting and interpreting what is reflected? Rogers conceded that one cannot be *totally* nondirective. Nevertheless, he believed that the therapist's most important contribution is to accept and understand the client. Given a nonjudgmental, grace-filled environment that provides *unconditional positive regard,* people internalize unconditional positive self-regard; they may accept even their worst traits and feel valued and whole.

If you want to listen more actively in your own relationships, three hints may help (keep in mind that practicing these is not easy):

"You say, 'Off with her head,' but what I'm hearing is, 'I feel neglected.'"

1. *Paraphrase.* Check your understandings by summarizing the speaker's words in your own words.
2. *Invite clarification.* "What might be an example of that?" may encourage the speaker to say more.
3. *Reflect feelings.* "That must be frustrating" might mirror what you're sensing from the speaker's body language and intensity.

rehearse it!

1. All of the psychological therapies involve verbal interactions between a trained professional and a client with a problem. A therapist who encourages clients to relate their dreams and searches for the unconscious roots of their problems is drawing from
   a. psychoanalysis.
   b. humanistic therapies.
   c. person-centered therapy.
   d. nondirective therapy.

2. According to psychoanalytic theory, a patient's emotional relationship with the therapist mirrors other important relationships in the patient's life—for example, an early relationship with a parent. In psychoanalysis, the development of strong feelings for the therapist is an important part of the therapeutic process and is called
   a. transference.
   b. resistance.
   c. interpretation.
   d. empathy.

3. Humanistic therapists focus on present experience—on becoming aware of feelings as they arise and taking responsibility for them. Compared with psychoanalytic therapists, humanistic therapists are more likely to emphasize
   a. hidden or repressed feelings.
   b. childhood experiences.
   c. psychological disorders.
   d. self-fulfillment and growth.

4. Especially important to Carl Rogers' person-centered therapy is the technique of active listening. The therapist who practices active listening
   a. engages in free association.
   b. exposes the patient's resistances.
   c. restates and clarifies the client's statements.
   d. directly challenges the client's self-perceptions.

Behavior Therapies

PREVIEW QUESTION 3 What are the assumptions and techniques of the behavior therapies?

All the therapies we have considered so far assume that, for rational people at least, psychological problems diminish as self-awareness grows. The psychoanalyst expects problems to subside as people gain insight into their unresolved and unconscious tensions. The humanistic therapist expects problems to abate as people "get in touch with their feelings." Behavior therapists, however, do not believe that self-awareness is a magic bullet. They assume that the problem behaviors *are* the problems. You can, for example, become aware of why you are highly anxious during exams and still be anxious. So, instead of trying to alleviate distressing behaviors by resolving a presumed underlying problem, **behavior therapy** applies well-established learning principles to eliminate the unwanted behavior. To treat phobias or sexual disorders, behavior therapists do not delve deep below the surface looking for inner causes. Rather, they try to replace problem thoughts and maladaptive behaviors with constructive ways of thinking and acting.

Classical Conditioning Techniques

One cluster of behavior therapies derives from principles developed in Ivan Pavlov's conditioning experiments in the early twentieth century. As Pavlov and others showed, we learn various behaviors and emotions through classical conditioning. So, are maladaptive symptoms also conditioned responses? If, say, a claustrophobic fear of elevators is a learned response to the stimulus of being in an enclosed space, then might one unlearn the fear by counterconditioning the fear response? **Counterconditioning** pairs the trigger stimulus with a new response that is incompatible with fear. For example, if we repeatedly pair the enclosed space of the elevator with a relaxed response, the fear response may be displaced.

■ **active listening** empathic listening in which the listener echoes, restates, and clarifies. A feature of Rogers' client-centered therapy.

■ **behavior therapy** therapy that applies learning principles to the elimination of unwanted behaviors.

■ **counterconditioning** a behavior therapy procedure that conditions new responses to stimuli that trigger unwanted behaviors; based on classical conditioning. Includes *systematic desensitization* and *aversive conditioning*.

What might a psychoanalyst say about this therapy for bed-wetting? How might a behavior therapist reply?

In classical conditioning terminology, an *unconditioned stimulus* (UCS), such as the smell of food, produces an *unconditioned response* (UCR), such as salivation. During conditioning, the subject learns to associate an originally neutral *conditioned stimulus* (CS), such as the sound of a bell, with the UCS, the smell of food. After conditioning, the bell alone (the CS) can produce salivation—now a *conditioned response* (CR).

THE FAR SIDE

Professor Gallagher and his controversial technique of simultaneously confronting the fear of heights, snakes, and the dark.

■ **systematic desensitization** a type of counterconditioning that associates a pleasant relaxed state with gradually increasing anxiety-triggering stimuli. Commonly used to treat phobias.

Another classical conditioning therapy was developed by learning theorist O. H. Mowrer for chronic bed-wetters. The child sleeps on a liquid-sensitive pad connected to an alarm. Moisture on the pad triggers the alarm, waking the child. With sufficient repetition, this association of urinary relaxation with waking up stops the bed-wetting. In three out of four cases the treatment is effective, and the success provides a boost to the child's self-image (Christophersen & Edwards, 1992; Houts & others, 1994).

Two specific counterconditioning techniques are *systematic desensitization* and *aversive conditioning.*

SYSTEMATIC DESENSITIZATION Picture this scene reported in 1924 by Mary Cover Jones, an associate of the behaviorist John B. Watson: Three-year-old Peter is petrified of rabbits and other furry objects. Jones aims to replace Peter's fear of rabbits with a conditioned response that is incompatible with fear. Her strategy is to associate the fear-evoking rabbit with the pleasurable, relaxed response associated with eating.

As Peter begins his midafternoon snack, Jones introduces a caged rabbit on the other side of the huge room. Peter, eagerly munching away on his crackers and drinking his milk, hardly notices. On succeeding days, she gradually moves the rabbit closer and closer. Within two months, Peter is tolerating the rabbit in his lap, even stroking it while he eats. Moreover, his fear of other furry objects subsides as well, having been "countered," or replaced, by a relaxed state that cannot coexist with fear (Fisher, 1984; Jones, 1924).

Unfortunately for those who might have been helped by her counterconditioning procedures, Jones' story of Peter and the rabbit did not immediately become part of psychology's lore. It was more than 30 years later that psychiatrist Joseph Wolpe (1958; Wolpe & Plaud, 1997) refined Jones' technique into what has become the most widely used method of behavior therapy: **systematic desensitization.** Wolpe assumed, as did Jones, that you cannot simultaneously be anxious and relaxed. Therefore, if you can repeatedly relax when facing anxiety-provoking stimuli, you can gradually eliminate your anxiety. The trick is to proceed gradually.

Let's see how this might work with a common phobia. Imagine yourself afraid of public speaking. A behavior therapist might first ask for your help in constructing a hierarchy of anxiety-triggering speaking situations. Your anxiety hierarchy could range from mildly anxiety-provoking situations, such as speaking up in a small group of friends, to panic-provoking situations, such as having to address a large audience.

Using *progressive relaxation,* the therapist trains you to relax one muscle group after another, until you achieve a drowsy state of complete relaxation and comfort. Then the therapist asks you to imagine, with your eyes closed, a mildly anxiety-arousing situation: You are having coffee with a group of friends and are trying to decide whether to speak up. If imagining the scene causes you to feel any anxiety, you signal your tension by raising your finger, and the therapist instructs you to switch off the mental image and go back to deep relaxation. This imagined scene is repeatedly paired with relaxation until you can feel no trace of anxiety.

The therapist progresses up the client's anxiety hierarchy, using the relaxed state to desensitize the person to each imagined situation. After several therapy sessions, you practice what you had imagined in actual situations, beginning with relatively easy tasks and gradually moving to more anxiety-filled ones. Conquering your anxiety in an actual situation, not just in your imagination, raises your self-confidence (Foa & Kozak, 1986; Williams, 1987). Eventually, you may even become a confident public speaker.

Virtual reality technology can now expose clients to situations more vividly than their own imaginations could. The individual wears a head-mounted display unit that projects a three-dimensional virtual world, immersing its wearer into a lifelike series of scenes. For those unable to vividly imagine the anxiety-arousing situation and too terrified or embarrassed to experience the situation in reality, virtual reality offers an efficient middle ground. Experiments led by several research teams in Atlanta and elsewhere have treated people with fears of flying,

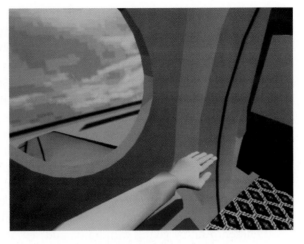

Virtual reality exposure therapy
Within the confines of a room, virtual reality technology exposes patients to vivid simulations of feared stimuli, such as a plane's takeoff.

fears of heights, fears of particular animals, and fears of public speaking (North & others, 1998; Rothbaum & others, 1995, 1997; Vincelli & Molinari, 1998). For example, patients with a fear of flying can experience peering out a virtual window of a simulated plane, feeling vibrations, and hearing the engine roar as the plane taxis down the runway and takes off. In initial experiments, those experiencing this *virtual reality exposure therapy* have experienced greater relief from their fears—in real life—than those in control groups.

Therapists sometimes combine systematic desensitization with other techniques. For clients with phobias, they may have someone model appropriate behavior in a fear-arousing situation. If you were afraid of snakes, you would first observe someone handling a snake. Then you would be coaxed in gradual steps to approach, touch, and handle it yourself (Bandura & others, 1969). By applying this principle of observational learning, therapists have helped people overcome disruptive fears of snakes, spiders, and dogs (**FIGURE 37.1**).

Notice that the systematic desensitization and modeling procedures make no attempt to help you achieve insight into your fear's underlying cause. If you are afraid of heights, the therapist will not spend much time probing when you first experienced

FIGURE 37.1
Systematic desensitization of a phobia
Beverly, who is terribly afraid of spiders, is exposed to stimuli that are progressively more threatening, but she adapts to each one in turn, as shown by her fairly consistent pulse rate. She tolerates first a picture of a spider, then a toy spider, then a dead spider, and finally a live one. (Adapted from Gilling & Brightwell, 1982.)

Pulse rate in beats per minute

Time

■ **aversive conditioning** a type of counterconditioning that associates an unpleasant state (such as nausea) with an unwanted behavior (such as drinking alcohol).

the fear or what may have caused it. Nor do behavior therapists worry (as psychoanalysts might) that eliminating your fear of heights will leave an underlying problem that may now be expressed as, say, a fear of elevators. On the contrary, they find that overcoming maladaptive behaviors helps people feel better about themselves.

AVERSIVE CONDITIONING In systematic desensitization, the therapist helps the client substitute a positive (relaxed) response for a negative (fearful) response to a harmless stimulus. In **aversive conditioning,** the therapist tries to replace a positive response to a harmful stimulus (such as alcohol) with a negative (aversive) response. Thus, aversive conditioning is the reverse of systematic desensitization.

The procedure is simple: It associates unpleasant feelings with the unwanted behavior. To treat nail biting, one can paint the fingernails with a yucky-tasting nail polish (Baskind, 1997). Similarly, by giving child molesters electric shocks as they view photos of nude children, aversion therapists try to eliminate the molesters' sexual response to children. And by giving withdrawn and self-abusing autistic children harmless "aversives," such as a spray of cold water in the face, therapists hope to suppress the child's self-injury while reinforcing more appropriate behavior. Because this therapy involves an unpleasant experience, it is practiced sparingly, with the appropriate consent.

Aversion therapy has also been used to treat alcoholism. The therapist offers the client appealing drinks laced with a drug that produces severe nausea. By linking the drinking of alcohol with violent nausea, the therapist seeks to transform the person's reaction to alcohol from positive to negative (see **FIGURE 37.2**). Arthur Wiens and Carol Menustik (1983) studied 685 alcoholic patients who completed an aversion therapy program at a Portland, Oregon, hospital. One year later, after returning for several booster treatments of alcohol–sickness pairings, 63 percent were still successfully abstaining. But after three years, only 33 percent had remained abstinent.

Does aversive conditioning work? In the short run it may. But, in therapy (as in research experiments), cognition influences conditioning. People know that

FIGURE 37.2

Aversion therapy for alcoholism
After repeatedly imbibing an alcoholic drink (conditioned stimulus) mixed with a drug that produces severe nausea (unconditioned stimulus), some people with a history of alcohol abuse develop at least a temporary conditioned aversion to alcohol.

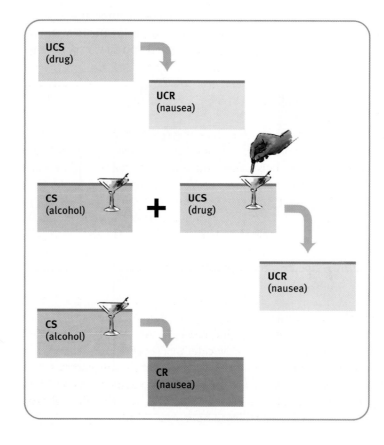

outside the therapist's office they can drink without fear of nausea or engage in sexually deviant behavior without fear of shock. A person's ability to discriminate between the aversive conditioning situation and all other situations can limit the treatment's effectiveness. Thus, it is often used in combination with another treatment.

Operant Conditioning

The work of B. F. Skinner teaches us a basic principle of operant conditioning: Voluntary behaviors are strongly influenced by their consequences. This simple fact enables behavior therapists to reinforce desired behaviors and to withhold reinforcement for, or to punish, undesired behaviors. Using operant conditioning to solve specific behavior problems has raised hopes for some cases thought to be hopeless. Children with mental retardation have been taught to care for themselves. Socially withdrawn children with autism have learned to interact. People with schizophrenia have been helped to behave more rationally in their hospital ward. In such cases, therapists use positive reinforcers to shape behavior by rewarding closer and closer approximations of a desired behavior.

In extreme cases, treatment must be intensive. In one study (Lovaas, 1987), 19 withdrawn, uncommunicative 3-year-olds with autism participated in a 2-year, 40-hour-a-week program in which their parents attempted to shape their behavior. The combination of positively reinforcing desired behaviors and ignoring or punishing aggressive and self-abusive behaviors worked wonders. By first grade, 9 of the 19 children were functioning successfully in school and exhibiting normal intelligence. Only 1 of 40 comparable children who did not undergo this treatment showed similar improvement.

The rewards used to modify behavior vary. For some people, the reinforcing power of attention or praise is sufficient. Others require concrete rewards, such as food. In institutional settings, therapists may create a **token economy.** When patients display appropriate behavior, such as getting out of bed, washing, dressing, eating, talking coherently, cleaning up their rooms, or playing cooperatively, they receive a token or plastic coin as a positive reinforcer. Later, they can exchange their accumulated tokens for various rewards, such as candy, watching television, trips to town, or better living quarters. Token economies have been successfully applied in various settings (homes, classrooms, hospitals, institutions for the delinquent) and among members of various populations (including disturbed children and people with schizophrenia and other mental disabilities).

Critics of such *behavior modification* express two concerns. One concern is practical: What happens when the reinforcers stop, as when the person leaves the institution? Could the person become so dependent on extrinsic rewards that the appropriate behaviors quickly disappear? If so, how can behavior therapists make the appropriate behaviors durable? Proponents of behavior modification respond that they may wean patients from the tokens by shifting them toward rewards, such as social approval, that are more typical of life outside the institution. They may also train patients to behave in ways that are intrinsically rewarding. For example, as a withdrawn person becomes more socially competent, the intrinsic satisfactions of social interaction may help the person maintain the behavior.

The second concern is ethical: Is it right for one human to control another's behavior? Those who set up token economies typically deprive people of something they desire and then decide which behaviors they will reinforce. To critics, the whole behavior modification process has an authoritarian taint. Advocates reply that control already exists; rewards and punishers are already maintaining destructive behavior patterns. So why not reinforce adaptive behavior instead? They argue that being treated with positive rewards is more humane than being institutionalized or punished, and that the right to effective treatment and to an improved life justifies temporary deprivation.

■ **token economy** an operant conditioning procedure that rewards desired behavior. A patient exchanges a token of some sort, earned for exhibiting the desired behavior, for various privileges or treats.

Cognitive Therapies

PREVIEW QUESTION 4 What are the goals and techniques of the cognitive therapies?

We have seen how behavior therapists treat specific fears and problem behaviors. But how do they deal with major depression or general anxiety? One can reinforce healthier behaviors and train people to avoid "high-risk" situations. Still, when anxiety has no focus, developing a hierarchy of anxiety-triggering situations is difficult. The cognitive revolution that has profoundly changed psychology during the last four decades has also influenced how therapists treat these less clearly defined psychological problems (**FIGURE 37.3**).

FIGURE 37.3

The cognitive revolution

Half of all faculty in accredited clinical psychology doctoral programs now align themselves with a cognitive or cognitive-behavior therapy orientation. (Data from Mayne & others, 1994. Note: Some faculty identify with more than one perspective.)

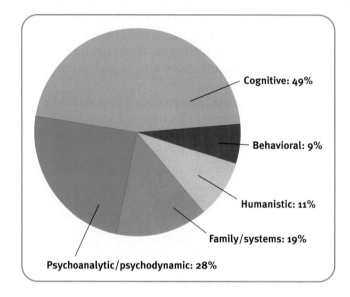

Cognitive: 49%

Behavioral: 9%

Humanistic: 11%

Family/systems: 19%

Psychoanalytic/psychodynamic: 28%

FIGURE 37.4

A cognitive perspective on psychological disorders

The person's emotional reactions are produced not directly by the event but by the person's thoughts in response to the event.

Lost job

Internal beliefs: I'm worthless. It's hopeless.

Depression

Lost job

Internal beliefs: My boss is a jerk. I deserve something better.

No depression

The **cognitive therapies** assume that our thinking colors our feelings (**FIGURE 37.4**), that between the event and our response is the mind. Self-blaming and overgeneralized explanations of bad events are an integral part of the vicious cycle of depression. The person with depression interprets suggestions as criticism, disagreement as dislike, praise as flattery, friendliness as pity. Ruminating on such thoughts sustains the bad mood. (That explains why distracting oneself, perhaps by getting absorbed in a task, can alleviate a bad mood [Erber & Tesser, 1992; Lyubomirsky & Nolen-Hoeksema, 1994].) If depressing thinking patterns are learned, then surely they can be replaced. Cognitive therapists therefore try in various ways to teach people new, more constructive ways of thinking.

Cognitive therapist Aaron Beck was originally trained in Freudian techniques. As Beck analyzed the dreams of patients with depression, he found recurring negative themes of loss, rejection, and abandonment that extended into their waking thoughts. So in his form of cognitive therapy, Beck and his colleagues (1979) seek to reverse clients' catastrophizing beliefs about themselves, their situations, and their futures. They attempt to convince depressed people to take off the dark glasses through which they view life, and their technique is a gentle questioning that aims to help people discover their irrational ities (Beck & others, 1979, pp. 145–146):

Patient: I agree with the descriptions of me but I guess I don't agree that the way I think makes me depressed.

Beck: How do you understand it?

Patient: I get depressed when things go wrong. Like when I fail a test.

Beck: How can failing a test make you depressed?

Patient: Well, if I fail I'll never get into law school.

Beck: So failing the test means a lot to you. But if failing a test could drive people into clinical depression, wouldn't you expect everyone who failed the test to have a depression? . . . Did everyone who failed get depressed enough to require treatment?

Patient: No, but it depends on how important the test was to the person.

Beck: Right, and who decides the importance?

Patient: I do.

Beck: And so, what we have to examine is your way of viewing the test (or the way that you think about the test) and how it affects your chances of getting into law school. Do you agree?

Patient: Right.

Beck: Do you agree that the way you interpret the results of the test will affect you? You might feel depressed, you might have trouble sleeping, not feel like eating, and you might even wonder if you should drop out of the course.

Patient: I have been thinking that I wasn't going to make it. Yes, I agree.

Beck: Now what did failing mean?

Patient: (tearful) That I couldn't get into law school.

Beck: And what does that mean to you?

Patient: That I'm just not smart enough.

Beck: Anything else?

Patient: That I can never be happy.

Beck: And how do these thoughts make you feel?

Patient: Very unhappy.

Beck: So it is the meaning of failing a test that makes you very unhappy. In fact, believing that you can never be happy is a powerful factor in producing unhappiness. So, you get yourself into a trap—by definition, failure to get into law school equals "I can never be happy."

Cognitive therapists often combine the reversal of self-defeating thinking with efforts to modify behavior. This integrated therapy, called **cognitive-behavior therapy,** aims to alter the way people act (behavior therapy) and to alter the way they think (cognitive therapy). It seeks to make people aware of their irrational negative thinking, to replace it with new ways of thinking, *and* to practice the more positive approach in everyday settings.

An example: We often think in words. Therefore, getting people to change what they say to themselves is an effective way to change their thinking. Perhaps you can identify with the anxious students who before an exam make matters worse with self-defeating thoughts: "This exam's probably going to be impossible. All these other students seem so relaxed and confident. I wish I were better prepared. Anyhow, I'm so nervous I'll forget everything." To change such negative patterns, Donald Meichenbaum (1977, 1985) offers *stress inoculation training.* He trains people to restructure their thinking in stressful situations. Sometimes it may be enough simply to say more positive things to oneself: "Relax. The exam may be

■ **cognitive therapy** therapy that teaches people new, more adaptive ways of thinking and acting; based on the assumption that thoughts intervene between events and our emotional reactions.

■ **cognitive-behavior therapy** a popular integrated therapy that combines cognitive therapy (changing self-defeating thinking) with behavior therapy (changing behavior).

"Life does not consist mainly, or even largely, of facts and happenings. It consists mainly of the storm of thoughts that are forever blowing through one's mind."

Mark Twain, 1835–1910

rehearse it!

5. Behavior therapies apply learning principles to the treatment of problems such as sexual disorders, phobias, and alcoholism. In treating people with these problems, the goal of the behavior therapist is to
   a. identify and treat the underlying causes of the problem.
   b. improve learning and insight.
   c. eliminate the unwanted behavior.
   d. improve communication and social sensitivity.

6. Behavior therapists assume that phobias and other maladaptive behaviors are conditioned responses. Behaviorists attempt either to extinguish these responses or to countercondition a client by conditioning a new response to stimuli that trigger maladaptive or unwanted responses. Two countercon-

ditioning techniques are systematic desensitization and
   a. positive reinforcement.
   b. aversive conditioning.
   c. transference.
   d. token economy.

7. The technique of systematic desensitization, developed by Joseph Wolpe, teaches people to relax in the presence of progressively more anxiety-provoking stimuli. Systematic desensitization has been found to be especially effective in the treatment of
   a. phobias.
   b. depression.
   c. alcoholism.
   d. bed-wetting.

8. Some institutions, such as homes for people who are mentally retarded or delinquent, use a token economy to

shape behavior. They hand out tokens, which may later be exchanged for other rewards, to a person who displays a desired behavior or takes a step in the right direction. The token economy is an application of
   a. classical conditioning.
   b. counterconditioning.
   c. cognitive therapy.
   d. operant conditioning.

9. Aaron Beck's form of cognitive therapy teaches people to stop attributing failures to personal inadequacy and success to external circumstances. This form of cognitive therapy has been shown to be especially effective in treating
   a. mental retardation.
   b. phobias.
   c. alcoholism.
   d. depression.

---

hard, but it will be hard for everyone else, too. I studied harder than most people. Besides, I don't need a perfect score to get a good grade."

Evaluating Psychotherapies

Advice columnist Ann Landers frequently advised her troubled letter writers to get professional help. One response urged the writer "not to give up. Hang in there until you find [a psychotherapist] who fills the bill. It's worth the effort." On the same day, she advised a second letter writer, "There are many excellent mental health facilities in your city. I urge you to make an appointment at once" (Farina & Fisher, 1982). Therapy advocate Tipper Gore (1994) would concur: "The data show high levels of success in treating large numbers of people suffering [mental illnesses]." Many share Ann Landers' and Tipper Gore's confidence in psychotherapy's effectiveness. The National Institute of Mental Health estimates that 15 percent of Americans seek help for psychological and addictive disorders each year (**FIGURE 37.5**).

Before 1950, the primary mental health providers were psychiatrists. Since then, demand has outgrown the psychiatric profession, and now most psychotherapy is done by clinical and counseling psychologists; clinical social workers; pastoral, marital, abuse, and school counselors; and psychiatric nurses. Much of it is done through *community mental health* programs, which provide outpatient therapy, crisis phone lines, and halfway houses for those making the transition from hospitalization to independent living. With such an enormous outlay of time, money, effort, and hope, it is important to ask: Is the faith that Ann Landers placed and millions of others worldwide place in these therapists justified? And is the *Wall Street Journal* (1999) therefore wrong to suppose that including psychotherapy in health insurance plans would lead to "endless payments for dubious benefits of apparently marginal problems"?

FIGURE 37.5

Where do people turn for help?
The National Institute of Mental Health reports that 19 million Americans a year seek help for psychological difficulties. About two in five seek out a mental health worker, such as a psychologist or psychiatrist. (Data from Regier & others, 1993.)

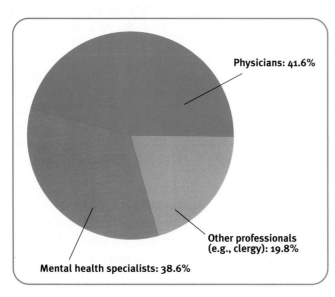

Physicians: 41.6%

Other professionals (e.g., clergy): 19.8%

Mental health specialists: 38.6%

Is Psychotherapy Effective?

PREVIEW QUESTION 5 Does psychotherapy work? Who decides?

These questions, though simply put, are not simply answered. For one thing, measuring therapy's effectiveness is not like taking your body's temperature to see if your fever has gone away. If you and I were to undergo psychotherapy, how would we gauge its effectiveness? By how we feel about our progress? How our therapist feels about it? How our friends and family feel about it? How our behavior has changed? Some other way?

Clients' Perceptions

If clients' testimonials were the only yardstick, we could strongly affirm the effectiveness of psychotherapy. Three out of four clients have reported themselves satisfied, and one in two have said they are "very satisfied" (Lebow, 1982). When 2900 readers of *Consumer Reports* (1995; Kotkin & others, 1996; Seligman, 1995) reported on their experiences with mental health professionals, 89 percent were at least "fairly well satisfied." Among those who recalled feeling *fair* or *very poor* when beginning therapy, 9 in 10 now were feeling *very good, good,* or at least *so-so.* We have their word for it—and who should know better?

THINKING CRITICALLY ABOUT:

"REGRESSING" FROM UNUSUAL TO USUAL

Clients' and therapists' perceptions of therapy's effectiveness are vulnerable to inflation from two phenomena. One is the power of *belief* in a treatment, called the *placebo effect.* An inert placebo is often used as a control treatment in drug experiments. If you *think* a treatment is going to be effective, it just may be (thanks to the healing power of your positive expectation).

The second phenomenon is **regression toward the mean**—the tendency for unusual events (or emotions) to "regress" (return) toward their average state. Thus, extra-

"The real purpose of [the] scientific method is to make sure Nature hasn't misled you into thinking you know something that you actually don't."

Robert Pirsig, *Zen and the Art of Motorcycle Maintenance,* 1974

■ **regression toward the mean** the tendency for extremes of unusual scores to fall back (regress) toward their average.

ordinary happenings (feeling low) tend to be followed by more ordinary ones (a return to our more usual state). Because we returned to that more usual state, anything we tried in the interim may seem to have been effective. Indeed, when things hit bottom, we may try anything, and whatever we try—going to a psychotherapist, starting yoga, doing aerobic exercise—is more likely to be followed by improvement than by further descent.

The point may seem obvious, yet we regularly miss it: We sometimes attribute what may be a normal regression (the expected falling back to normal) to something we have done. Consider:

- Students who score much lower or higher on an exam than they usually do are likely, when retested, to return to their average.
- Unusual ESP subjects who defy chance when first tested nearly always lose their "psychic powers" when retested (a phenomenon parapsychologists have called the "decline effect").

- Scientists who win a Nobel Prize—an extraordinary accomplishment—almost always experience diminished accomplishments thereafter, leading some to believe that winning a Nobel hinders creativity.
- Some people also believe there is a *"Sports Illustrated* jinx"—that athletes whose peak performances get them on the cover of the magazine will then suffer a decline in their performance.

In each case, the effect may be genuine. More likely, however, each represents the natural tendency for behavior to regress from the unusual to the more usual. And this defines a task for therapy effectiveness research: to discern whether improvement following a particular therapy exceeds what we could expect from the placebo and regression effects.

"Once you become sensitized to it, you see regression everywhere."

Psychologist Daniel Kahneman (1985)

We should not dismiss these testimonials lightly. People enter therapy because they are suffering, and most leave feeling better about themselves. But there are several reasons why client testimonials do not persuade psychotherapy's skeptics:

- ■ ***People often enter therapy in crisis.*** When, with the normal ebb and flow of events, the crisis passes, people may attribute their improvement to the therapy. (See Thinking Critically About "Regressing" From Unusual to Usual.)

- ■ ***Clients may need to believe the therapy was worth the effort.*** To admit investing time and money in something ineffective is like admitting to having one's car serviced repeatedly by a mechanic who never fixes it. Self-justification is a powerful human motive.

- ■ ***Clients generally like their therapists and speak kindly of them.*** Even if the clients' problems remain, say the critics, "they work hard to find something positive to say. The therapist had been very understanding, the client had gained a new perspective, he learned to communicate better, his mind was eased, anything at all so as not to have to say treatment was a failure" (Zilbergeld, 1983, p. 117).

Clinicians' Perceptions

If clinicians' perceptions accurately reflected therapeutic effectiveness, we would have even more reason to celebrate. Case studies of successful treatment abound. Furthermore, every therapist treasures compliments from clients as they say good-bye or later express their gratitude. The problem is that clients justify entering psychotherapy by emphasizing their woes, justify leaving therapy by emphasizing their well-being, and stay in touch only if satisfied. Therapists are aware of failures, but they are mostly the failures of *other* therapists—those whose clients, having experienced only temporary relief, are now seeking a new therapist for their recurring problems. Thus, the same person with the same recurring difficulty—the same old weight problem, depression, or marital difficulty—may represent "success" stories in several therapists' files.

Because people enter therapy when they are extremely unhappy, and usually leave when they are less extremely unhappy, most therapists, like most clients, testify to therapy's success—regardless of the treatment. Although "treatments" have varied widely, from chains to counseling, every generation views its own approach as more enlightened.

Outcome Research

How, then, can we objectively measure the effectiveness of psychotherapy? What types of people and problems are best helped, and by what type of psychotherapy? The questions have both academic and personal relevance. If you or someone you care about feels anxious or depressed, or suffers some psychological disorder, it is crucial for you to understand the likelihood of psychotherapy's being of help.

In hopes of better assessing psychotherapy's effectiveness, psychologists have turned to controlled research studies. Similar research in the 1800s transformed medicine from concocted treatments (bleeding, purging, infusions of plant and metal substances) into a science. The transformation occurred when skeptical physicians began to realize that many patients got better on their own, that most of the fashionable treatments were doing no good, and that sorting fact from superstition required following illnesses closely—with and without a particular treatment. Typhoid fever patients, for example, often improved after being bled, convincing most physicians that the treatment worked. Not until a control group was given mere bed rest—and 70 percent were observed to improve after five weeks of fever—did physicians learn, to their shock, that their treatments were, at best, worthless (Thomas, 1992).

In psychology, the opening challenge in what became a spirited debate over such research was issued by British psychologist Hans Eysenck (1952). He summarized studies showing that after undergoing psychotherapy, two-thirds of those suffering nonpsychotic disorders improve markedly. To this day, no one disputes that optimistic estimate.

So why then are we still debating psychotherapy's effectiveness? Because Eysenck also reported similar improvement among *untreated* persons, such as those who were on waiting lists. With or without psychotherapy, he said, roughly two-thirds improved noticeably. Time was a great healer.

The avalanche of criticism prompted by Eysenck's conclusions did reveal shortcomings in his analyses. Also, in 1952 Eysenck could find only 24 studies of psychotherapy outcomes to analyze. Today, there are hundreds. The best of these studies randomly assign people on a waiting list to therapy or to no therapy. Afterward, researchers evaluate.

In the first statistical digest of these studies, Mary Lee Smith and her colleagues (1980) combined the results of 475 investigations. For psychotherapists, the welcome result was that "the evidence overwhelmingly supports the efficacy of psychotherapy" (p. 183). **FIGURE 37.6** depicts their finding—that the average therapy client ends up better off than 80 percent of the untreated individuals on waiting lists. The claim is more modest than it first appears—by definition, about 50 percent of untreated people also are better off than the average untreated person. Nevertheless, Smith and her collaborators exulted that "psychotherapy benefits people of all ages as reliably as schooling educates them, medicine cures them, or business turns a profit" (p. 183).

> "Fortunately, [psycho]analysis is not the only way to resolve inner conflicts. Life itself still remains a very effective therapist."
>
> **Karen Horney, *Our Inner Conflicts*, 1945**

FIGURE 37.6

Treatment versus no treatment
These two normal distribution curves based on data from 475 studies show the improvement of untreated people and psychotherapy clients. The outcome for the average therapy client surpassed that for 80 percent of the untreated people. (Adapted from Smith & others, 1980.)

Newer research summaries confirm that psychotherapy works (Kopta & others, 1999; Shadish & others, 2000). In one ambitious study, the National Institute of Mental Health compared three depression treatments: cognitive therapy, "interpersonal therapy," and a standard drug therapy. Twenty-eight experienced therapists at research sites in Norman, Oklahoma; Washington, DC; and Pittsburgh, Pennsylvania, were trained in one of the three methods and randomly assigned their share of the 239 people with depression who participated. Patients in all three groups improved more than did those in a control group who received merely an inert medication and supportive attention, encouragement, and advice. Among patients who completed a full 16-week treatment program, the depression had lifted for slightly more than half of those in each treatment group—but for only 29 percent of those in the control group (Elkin & others, 1989). This verdict echoes the results of the earlier outcome studies: *Those not undergoing therapy often improve, but those undergoing therapy are more likely to improve.*

Often, however, the improvement was not permanent. Only one in four patients undergoing psychotherapy and one in six undergoing drug therapy both recovered and experienced no relapse within 18 months (Shea & others, 1992). So, extravagant expectations that psychotherapy will transform your life and personality seem unwarranted. Still, Eysenck's pessimism also seems unwarranted. *On average,* psychotherapy is somewhat effective—and is also cost-effective when compared with the greater costs of medical care for psychologically related ailments. When people seek psychological treatment, their search for medical treatment drops—by 16 percent in one digest of 91 studies (Chiles & others, 1999). The annual cost of psychological disorders and substance abuse—including crime, accidents, lost work, and treatment—is staggering. Thus, just as an investment in prenatal and well-baby care *reduces* long-term costs, so will an investment in almost any effective treatment for psychological problems. Anything that boosts employees' psychological well-being will reduce medical costs, improve work efficiency, and diminish absenteeism. Studies by health insurers show that mental health treatment can more than pay for itself with reduced medical costs (American Psychological Association, 1991).

But note that *on average* refers to no one therapy in particular. It is like saying, "Surgery is somewhat effective," or like reassuring lung-cancer patients that "on the average" medical treatment of health problems is effective. What people want to know is not the effectiveness of therapy in general but the effectiveness of particular treatments for their particular problems.

In general, therapy is most effective when the problem is clear-cut (Singer, 1981). Those who experience phobias, who are unassertive, or who are frustrated by sexual performance problems can hope for improvement. Those who have chronic schizophrenia or who wish to change their whole personality are unlikely to benefit from psychotherapy alone (Zilbergeld, 1983). The more specific the problem, the more hope there is.

The Relative Effectiveness of Different Therapies

PREVIEW QUESTION 6 Are some therapies more effective than others?

People considering therapy, and those paying for it, want to know *which* psychotherapy will be most effective for their problem. The statistical summary conducted by Mary Lee Smith and her colleagues (1977, 1980) compared different therapies. What do you suppose it revealed? Despite claims of superiority by advocates of different types of therapy, Smith's comparison of therapies revealed no one type of therapy that was actually superior. (*Consumer Reports* [1995] readers, too, were equally satisfied, no matter what type of therapy they received and whether treated by a psychiatrist, psychologist, or social worker.) Moreover—and more astonishing—the group or individual context of the therapy made no discernible difference, nor did the level of training and experience of the therapist. Now, two decades after Smith's analysis, the evidence still indicates little if any connection between clinicians' experience, training, supervision, and licensing and their clients' outcomes (Bickman, 1999). It seems as though the dodo bird in *Alice in Wonderland* was right: "Everyone has won and all must have prizes."

Some therapies are, however, well suited to particular disorders. For example, behavioral conditioning therapies achieve especially favorable results with specific behavior problems such as phobias, compulsions, or sexual disorders (Bowers & Clum, 1988; Giles, 1983). Just as physicians offer particular treatments for specific medical problems, so psychotherapists are aiming toward particular treatments for specific psychological problems.

"Whatever differences in treatment efficacy exist, they appear to be extremely small, at best."

Bruce Wampold and colleagues (1997)

"Different sores have different salves."

English proverb

Evaluating Alternative Therapies

PREVIEW QUESTION 7 How do alternative therapies stand up to psychology's critical thinking methods?

The tendency of abnormal states of mind to "regress" to normal, combined with the *placebo effect,* creates fertile soil for pseudotherapies. Bolstered by anecdotes, heralded by the media, praised on the Internet, alternative therapies can spread like wildfire. Princess Diana typified the modern fascination with alternative healers by seeking out spiritualists, a hypnotherapist, an "anger-release" therapist, reflexologists, aromatherapists, colonic irrigationists, and a "mind-body" therapist (Smith, 1999).

What can we say of such alternative therapies? Testimonials aside—every therapy, whether effective or not, will *seem* effective to some—what does the evidence say? Which are empirically validated?

About most, there is no evidence, because their proponents and devotees feel no need for controlled research. For them, personal experience is evidence enough. So which therapies do get systematically evaluated? To gauge scientific versus popular interest in various treatments and assessment techniques, clinical researcher Scott Lilienfeld (1998) suggests comparing the number of times each is mentioned in electronic searches of psychology's literature and on the World Wide Web. As Table 37.1 shows, some topics exist mostly in one realm or the other.

TABLE 37.1

COMPARISON OF PSYCHOLOGY CITATIONS AND WEB SITES

Topic	Psychology Journal Citations*	Web Sites**	Ratio
Systematic desensitization	2,224	1,806	1.2 to 1
Cognitive-behavior therapy	6,121	2,974	2 to 1
Interpersonal psychotherapy	4,351	994	4 to 1
Therapeutic touch	249	8,301	1 to 33
St. John's wort (herbal remedy)	57	40,952	1 to 718
Enneagram (personality typing)	16	31,645	1 to 1,998

*Using PsychInfo
**Using AltaVista

Let's evaluate here three alternative therapies: therapeutic touch, eye movement desensitization and reprocessing (EMDR), and light exposure therapy. As we do, remember that sifting sense from nonsense requires the scientific attitude: being skeptical but not cynical, open to surprises but not gullible.

Therapeutic Touch

Among the most popular recent alternative therapies is *therapeutic touch.* Its tens of thousands of practitioners worldwide (many of whom are nurses) move their hands a few inches from a patient's body, purportedly "pushing energy fields into balance." Advocates say these manipulations help heal everything from headaches to burns to cancer (Krieger, 1993). Skeptics say the evidence shows no healing power beyond the placebo effect (Scheiber & Selby, 1997).

To put therapeutic touch to the test, fourth-grader Emily Rosa and her mother, a nurse, schemed a simple experiment (Rosa & others, 1998). Why not test healers' ability to detect the supposed energy field by inviting them to rest their hands, palms up, on a flat surface? (Thanks to a screen, the healers wouldn't see their or Emily's hands.) After

Testing the energy field

Could therapeutic touch practitioners detect a nearby hand? To find out, Emily Rosa tossed a coin and, unobserved by the healer, held a hand over the healer's right or left hand.

the toss of a coin, Emily would hover a hand over one of the practitioner's hands (the experimental hand) to see if the practitioner could detect that this hand rather than the other (the control hand) was receiving the energy field. Shortly before, skeptic James Randi had offered $742,000 to anyone who could detect a human energy field under similar conditions. Only one person agreed to be tested by Randi, and that volunteer had left the experiment in a huff after achieving only chance results in guessing which hand was close to another's.

Apparently less threatened by a 9-year-old girl doing a science fair project, and not fully realizing that this was a serious research project, 21 practitioners agreed to be tested by Emily for 10 trials each. Could they beat chance—50 percent? They could not, averaging but 47 percent correct. A year later when the trials were repeated—this time allowing each practitioner to "feel" Emily's energy field in each hand and then choose which hand Emily would use—the practitioners got 41 percent correct. The results, published in the prestigious *Journal of the American Medical Association*, caused its editor to conclude that the supposed human energy field "does not exist" and that, barring new evidence, patients should "save their money." Perhaps, say critics of this experiment, Emily's hands were held too far from the practitioner's hands. But other research suggests that, when body heat is shielded by a thin sheet of glass, people cannot detect the presence of unseen hands (Long & others, 1999). Thus, the tentative scientific verdict is that therapeutic touch (actually not-touch) does not work, nor is there any credible theory that predicts why it might.

Eye Movement Desensitization and Reprocessing (EMDR)

Walking in a park one day, Francine Shapiro (1989) observed that anxious thoughts vanished as her eyes spontaneously darted about. From this experience she developed a novel anxiety treatment. While patients imagine traumatic scenes, the therapist triggers eye movements by waving a finger in front of their eyes. When Shapiro tried this on 22 people who were haunted by old traumatic memories, all experienced marked reductions in their distress after just one therapeutic session. This extraordinary result triggered an enormous response from mental health professionals, 22,000 of whom have reportedly paid $350 or more to attend Shapiro's training workshops (McNally, 1999; Rosen & Lohr, 1997). Not since the similarly charismatic Franz Anton Mesmer introduced "animal magnetism" (hypnosis) more than two centuries ago (also after feeling inspired by an outdoor experience) has a new therapy attracted so many devotees so quickly.

Does it work? For 84 to 100 percent of single-trauma victims participating in four recent studies, the answer is yes, reports Shapiro (1999). (When EMDR did not fare well in other trials, Shapiro argued that the therapists were not properly trained.) Moreover, the treatment need take no more than three 90-minute sessions. A Society of Clinical Psychology task force on empirically validated treatments acknowledges that the treatment is "probably efficacious" for the treatment of civilian post-traumatic stress disorder (Chambless & others, 1997). Encouraged by their seeming successes, EMDR therapists are now applying the technique to other anxiety disorders, such as panic disorder, and, with Shapiro's (1995) encouragement, to a wide range of complaints including pain, grief, paranoid schizophrenia, rage, and guilt.

EMDR is a therapy that thousands adore, and thousands more dismiss as a sham. Why should rapidly moving one's eyes while recalling traumas be therapeutic, wondered skeptics. Indeed, when they tested the therapy without the eye movements—with finger tapping, for example, or with eyes fixed straight ahead while the therapist's finger wagged—the therapeutic results were the same (Cahill & others, 1999; Lohr & others, 1999). Eye movements, it seems, are not the therapeutic ingredient. What is therapeutic, the skeptics suspect, is the combination of desensitization—repeatedly reliving traumatic memories in a safe and reassuring context—and a robust placebo effect. Had Mesmer's pseudotherapy been compared with no treatment at all, notes Richard McNally (1999), it, too (thanks to the healing power of positive belief), could have been found "probably efficacious."

Light Exposure Therapy

Have you ever found yourself oversleeping, gaining weight, and feeling lethargic during the dark mornings and overcast days of winter? For some people, especially women and those living far from the equator, the wintertime blahs constitute a form of depression known as *seasonal affective disorder,* for which the appropriate acronym is SAD. To counteract these dark spirits, National Institute of Mental Health researchers in the early 1980s had a bright idea: Give SAD people a timed daily dose of intense light. Light exposure can tweak the circadian clock, our regular 24-hour cycle of bodily rhythms. When clinical experience indicated that light exposure could also relieve symptoms associated with wintertime depression, manufacturers produced "light boxes" that can now be rented or purchased from health supply and lighting stores.

Light therapy
To counteract winter depression, some people spend time each morning in front of a box that emits intense light that mimics natural outdoor light.

Is this another placebo effect, attributable to people's expectations? Three new studies shed light on this therapy. In one, Charmane Eastman and her colleagues (1998) exposed some SAD patients to 90 minutes of bright light and others to a sham placebo treatment—a hissing "negative ion generator" about which the staff expressed similar enthusiasm (but which unknown to the patients was not turned on). After four weeks of exposure, 61 percent of those exposed to morning light had greatly improved, as had 50 percent of those exposed to evening light and 32 percent of those exposed to the placebo treatment. Another study, led by Michael Terman (1998), found that 30 minutes of light exposure produced relief for 54 percent of people receiving morning light therapy and 33 percent receiving evening light therapy. The third study, led by Alfred Lewy (1998), replicated the morning light effect and identified a possible biological mechanism. With SAD patients, morning light exposure shifted secretion of the hormone melatonin to an earlier time. The verdict: For many people, morning bright light does indeed dim SAD symptoms.

Commonalities Among Psychotherapies

PREVIEW QUESTION 8 What three elements are shared by all forms of psychotherapy?

Despite their differences, each therapy's effectiveness may derive from certain underlying commonalities. Jerome Frank (1982), Marvin Goldfried (Goldfried & Padawer, 1982), and Hans Strupp (1986) studied the common ingredients of various therapies and suggested that they all offer at least three benefits: hope for demoralized people; a new perspective on oneself and the world; and an empathic, trusting, caring relationship. These "nonspecific" factors aren't all that therapy offers, but they are important (Barker & others, 1988; Jones & others, 1988; Roberts & others, 1993). They are part of what the growing number of self-help and support groups offer their members. And they have been part of what traditional healers offer (Jackson, 1992). Healers—special people to whom others disclose their suffering—have for centuries listened in order to understand and to empathize, reassure, advise, console, interpret, or explain.

Hope for Demoralized People

People who seek therapy typically feel anxious, depressed, devoid of self-esteem, and incapable of turning things around. What any therapy offers is the expectation that, with commitment from the patient, things can and will get better. Apart from the particular therapeutic technique, this belief may itself promote improved morale, new feelings of self-efficacy, and diminished symptoms (Prioleau & others, 1983). This benefit derived from a person's belief in a treatment is, of course,

"I utilize the best from Freud, the best from Jung, and the best from my Uncle Marty, a very smart fellow."

the placebo effect. In psychotherapy experiments, the placebo treatment may be listening to inspirational tapes, attending group discussions, or taking a fake pill.

The finding that improvement is greater for placebo-treated people than for untreated people (although not as great as for those receiving actual psychotherapy) suggests that one reason therapies help is that they offer hope. Said another way, therapy outcomes vary with the client's attitude—the client's motivation, confidence, and commitment. Each therapy, in its individual way, may harness the client's own healing powers. And that, says psychiatrist Jerome Frank, helps us understand why all sorts of treatments—including some folk healing rites known to be powerless apart from the patient's belief—may in their own time and place produce cures.

A New Perspective

Every therapy offers people a plausible explanation of their symptoms and an alternative way of looking at themselves or responding to their worlds. Therapy can offer new experiences as well, ones that help people change their behaviors and their views of themselves. Armed with a believable fresh perspective, they may approach life with a new attitude.

An Empathic, Trusting, Caring Relationship

To say that all therapies are about equally effective is not to say that all *therapists* are equally effective. Regardless of their therapeutic technique, effective therapists are empathic people who seek to understand another's experience; whose care and concern the client feels; and whose respectful listening, reassurance, and advice earn the client's trust and respect. In a National Institute of Mental Health depression-treatment study, the most effective therapists were those who were perceived as most empathic and caring and who established the closest therapeutic bonds with their clients (Blatt & others, 1996). In another study, Marvin Goldfried and his associates (1998) analyzed taped therapy sessions from 36 recognized master therapists. Some were cognitive-behavior therapists, others were psychodynamic-interpersonal therapists. Regardless, the striking finding was how similar the therapists were during the parts of their sessions they considered most significant. At key moments, the empathic therapists of both persuasions would help clients evaluate themselves, link one aspect of their lives with another, and gain insight into their interactions with others. Indeed, some believe that warmth and empathy are hallmarks of healers everywhere, whether psychiatrists, witch doctors, or shamans (Torrey, 1986).

That all therapies offer *hope* through a *fresh perspective* offered by a *caring person* is supported by an analysis of 39 studies. Each study compared treatment offered by professional therapists with treatment offered by laypeople: friendly professors, people who had had a few hours' training in empathic listening skills, and college students supervised by a professional clinician. The result? The "paraprofessionals," as these briefly trained people are called, typically proved as effective as the professionals (Christensen & Jacobson, 1994). Although most of the problems they treated were mild, the trained paraprofessionals were—believe it or not—as effective as professionals even when dealing with more disturbed adults, such as those diagnosed with serious depression.

To recap, people who seek help usually improve. So do many of those who do not undergo psychotherapy, a tribute to our human resourcefulness and to our capacity to care for one another. Nevertheless, though the therapist's orientation and experience appear not to matter much, people who receive some psychotherapy usually improve more than those who do not. Mature, articulate people with specific emotional or behavioral problems often improve the most.

Part of what all therapies offer is hope, a fresh way of looking at life, and an empathic, caring relationship. That may explain why the empathy and friendly

A caring relationship
Effective therapists form a bond of trust with their patients.

"Therapy that reviews childhood endlessly has a century-long history of being ineffective. All therapy that works for depression, anxiety, and sexual problems focuses on exactly what is going wrong now and on how to correct it."

Martin E. P. Seligman, *What You Can Change and What You Can't,* 1994

A CONSUMER'S GUIDE TO PSYCHOTHERAPISTS

When should a person seek the help of a mental health professional? Life for everyone is marked by a mix of serenity and stress, blessing and bereavement, good moods and bad. When troubling thoughts and emotions interfere with your normal living, you might consider talking to a professional. The American Psychological Association offers these common trouble signals:

- Feelings of hopelessness
- Deep and lasting depression
- Self-destructive behavior such as alcohol and drug abuse
- Disruptive fears
- Sudden mood shifts
- Thoughts of suicide
- Compulsive rituals such as hand washing
- Sexual difficulties

If you are looking for a therapist, it may be wise to first have a preliminary consultation with two or three. You can describe your problem and learn each therapist's treatment approach. You can ask questions about the therapist's values, credentials (Table 37.2), and fees. And you can assess your own feelings about each one.

TABLE 37.2

THERAPISTS AND THEIR TRAINING

Type	Description
Clinical psychologists	Most are psychologists with a Ph.D. and expertise in research, assessment, and therapy, supplemented by a supervised internship. About half work in agencies and institutions, half in private practice.
Clinical or psychiatric social workers	A two-year Master of Social Work graduate program plus postgraduate supervision prepares some social workers to offer psychotherapy, mostly to people with everyday personal and family problems. About half have earned the National Association of Social Workers' designation of clinical social worker.
Counselors	Marriage and family counselors specialize in problems arising from family relations. Pastoral counselors provide counseling to countless people. Abuse counselors work with substance abusers and with spouse and child abusers and their victims.
Psychiatrists	Physicians who specialize in the treatment of psychological disorders. Not all psychiatrists have had extensive training in psychotherapy, but as M.D.s they can prescribe medications. Thus, they tend to see those with the most serious problems. Many have a private practice.

counsel of paraprofessionals are often as helpful as professional psychotherapy. And that may also explain why people who feel supported by close relationships—who enjoy the fellowship and friendship of caring people—are less likely to need or seek therapy (Frank, 1982; O'Connor & Brown, 1984).

Culture and Values in Psychotherapy

PREVIEW QUESTION 9 How do differences in culture and values influence the relationship between a therapist and a client?

All therapies offer hope, and nearly all therapists attempt to enhance their clients' sensitivity, openness, personal responsibility, and sense of purpose (Jensen & Bergin, 1988). But on certain matters of moral and cultural diversity, therapists may differ from one another and from their clients (Kelly, 1990). In Canada and the United States, for example, about 1 person in 25 is a self-proclaimed atheist or agnostic, as are (depending on the survey) one-fifth to one-half of psychiatrists and clinical psychologists (Gallup, 1993; Lukoff & others, 1992). In Britain, two-thirds of psychiatrists say they are atheists (Neeleman & Persaud, 1995). That raises an issue: What values prevail in psychotherapy? What values *should* prevail? Should it matter that highly religious people prefer religiously similar therapists (Worthington & others, 1996)?

Albert Ellis, a well-known therapist, and Allen Bergin, co-editor of the *Handbook of Psychotherapy and Behavior Change,* illustrate how sharply values can differ. Ellis (1980) assumes that "no one and nothing is supreme," that "self-gratification" should be encouraged, and that "unequivocal love, commitment, service, and . . . fidelity to any interpersonal commitment, especially marriage, leads to harmful consequences." Bergin (1980) assumes the opposite—that "because God is supreme, humility and the acceptance of divine authority are virtues," that "self-control and committed love and self-sacrifice are to be encouraged," and that "infidelity to any interpersonal commitment, especially marriage, leads to harmful consequences." Bergin and Ellis disagree more radically than most therapists regarding what values are healthiest. In so doing, however, they illustrate what they agree on: that psychotherapists' personal beliefs and values influence their practice. Knowing that clients tend to adopt their therapists' values (Worthington & others, 1996), Bergin and Ellis also agree that therapists should divulge their values more openly.

Value differences also can become significant when a therapist from one culture meets a client from another. In North America, Europe, and Australia, for example, most therapists reflect their culture's individualism (often giving priority to personal desires and identity). Clients who are immigrants from Asian countries, which expect people to be mindful of others' expectations, may therefore have problems with therapies that require them to think only of their own well-being. Such differences help explain the reluctance of some minority populations to use mental health services (Sue, 1990). Recognizing that therapists and clients may differ in values, communication styles, and language, many therapy training programs now provide training in cultural sensitivity and recruit members of underrepresented culture groups.

rehearse it!

10. The question "Is psychotherapy effective?" has been the subject of hundreds of scientific studies and innumerable personal accounts. The most enthusiastic or optimistic view of psychotherapy comes from
    a. outcome research.
    b. psychologist Hans Eysenck.
    c. reports of clinicians and clients.
    d. a government study of treatment for depression.

11. On average, troubled people who undergo therapy are more likely to improve than those who do not, and therapy tends to be most effective when the problem is clearcut and specific. Studies show that _____ therapy is most effective overall.
    a. behavior   c. psychodynamic
    b. humanistic   d. no one type of

12. Psychologists have observed that people's belief that a treatment will help them is often sufficient to cause some improvement. A neutral treatment, such as an inert pill, that results in improved morale and diminished symptoms has produced
    a. a placebo effect.
    b. preventive mental health.
    c. an empathic perspective.
    d. clinical treatment.

13. Those who offer or receive alternative therapies usually feel that testimonials are enough evidence of the success of the therapy. One alternative therapy that has passed the test of critical evaluation is
    a. hypnotherapy.
    b. light exposure therapy.
    c. eye movement desensitization and reprocessing.
    d. therapeutic touch.

The Biomedical Therapies

Psychotherapy is one way to treat psychological disorders. The other is physically changing the brain's functioning—by altering its chemistry with drugs, by overloading its circuits with electroconvulsive shock, or by disconnecting its circuits through psychosurgery. Although psychologists can provide "talking" therapies, only psychiatrists (as medical doctors) offer most biomedical therapies.

Drug Therapies

PREVIEW QUESTION 10 What are the most common forms of drug therapy? What criticisms have been leveled against drug therapies?

By far the most widely used biomedical treatments today are the drug therapies. When introduced in the 1950s, drug therapy greatly reduced the need for psychosurgery or hospitalization. The discoveries in **psychopharmacology** (the study of drug effects on mind and behavior) revolutionized the treatment of people with severe disorders, liberating hundreds of thousands from confinement in mental hospitals. Thanks to drug therapy—and to political and legal efforts to minimize involuntary hospitalization and to return hospitalized people to their communities, aided by community mental health programs—the resident population of state and county mental hospitals in the United States today is but 20 percent of what it was half a century ago (**FIGURE 37.7**).

FIGURE 37.7

The emptying of U.S. mental hospitals

After the widespread introduction of antipsychotic drugs, starting in about 1955, the number of residents in state and county mental hospitals declined sharply. But in the rush to deinstitutionalize the mentally ill, many people who were ill-equipped to care for themselves were left homeless on city streets. (Data from the National Institute of Mental Health and Bureau of the Census, 1999.)

Almost any new treatment, including drug therapy, is greeted by an initial wave of enthusiasm as many people apparently improve. But that enthusiasm often diminishes after researchers subtract the rate of (1) normal recovery among untreated persons and (2) recovery due to the placebo effect, which arises from the positive expectations of patients and mental health workers alike. So, to evaluate the effectiveness of any new drug, researchers use the *double-blind technique.* Half the patients receive the drug, the other half a similar-appearing placebo. Neither the staff nor the patients know who gets which. The good news: In double-blind studies, several types of drugs have proved useful in treating psychological disorders.

Antipsychotic Drugs

The revolution in drug therapy for psychological disorders began with the accidental discovery that certain drugs, used for other medical purposes, calmed psychotic patients. These antipsychotic drugs, such as chlorpromazine (sold as Thorazine), dampen responsiveness to irrelevant stimuli. Thus they provide the most help to schizophrenia patients experiencing what are called positive symptoms, such as auditory hallucinations and paranoia (Lehman & others, 1998; Lenzenweger & others, 1989). Patients exhibiting negative symptoms such as apathy and withdrawal often do not respond well to these antipsychotic drugs. A newer drug, clozapine (marketed as Clozaril), does sometimes enable "awakenings" in such people. It also sometimes helps those who have positive symptoms but have not responded to other drugs. In 1 or 2 percent of cases, clozapine has a toxic effect on white blood cells, necessitating regular blood tests.

■ **psychopharmacology** the study of the effects of drugs on mind and behavior.

Herself renewed
Thanks to clozapine, Daphne Moss went "from hating the sunshine in the morning to loving it." No longer suffering from the paranoid delusion that her parents were witches, Moss began teaching school and living independently.

Researchers are testing possible cousin drugs that would offer the same benefits without the blood problem. For now, clozapine remains the most effective schizophrenia treatment available (Wahlbeck & others, 1999).

The molecules of antipsychotic drugs are similar enough to molecules of the neurotransmitter dopamine to occupy its receptor sites and block its activity (Pickar & others, 1984; Taubes, 1994). (Clozapine also blocks serotonin activity.) This finding—that most antipsychotic drugs block dopamine receptors—reinforces the idea that an overactive dopamine system contributes to schizophrenia.

Antipsychotics such as Thorazine are powerful drugs. They can produce sluggishness, tremors, and twitches similar to those of Parkinson's disease, which is marked by too little dopamine (Kaplan & Saddock, 1989). (Clozapine, thankfully, has few such side effects.) Another complication is that what is an effective dose for some people may be an overdose for others. Asians, for example, seem to require lower doses than do Caucasians (Holden, 1991). Only by carefully monitoring the dosage and its effects can therapist and patient tread the fine line between relieving symptoms and causing extremely unpleasant side effects. But with the appropriate dosage, combined with life-skills programs and family support, hundreds of thousands of people with schizophrenia who had been consigned to the back wards of mental hospitals have returned to work and to near-normal lives.

Antianxiety Drugs

Among the most heavily prescribed and also abused drugs are the antianxiety agents, such as Valium and Librium. Like alcohol, these drugs depress central nervous system activity. Because they reduce tension and anxiety without causing excessive sleepiness, they have been prescribed for even minor emotional stresses. Used in combination with other therapy, an antianxiety drug can help a person learn to cope with frightening situations and fear-triggering stimuli.

The criticism sometimes made of the behavior therapies—that they reduce symptoms without resolving underlying problems—is also made of antianxiety drugs. Unlike the behavior therapies, they may be used as an ongoing treatment. However, routinely "popping a Valium" at the first sign of tension can produce psychological dependence on the drug. (The immediate relief reinforces a person's tendency to take drugs when anxious.) When heavy users stop taking the drug, they may experience both increased anxiety and insomnia, driving them back to the drug for relief.

Antidepressant Drugs

Just as the antianxiety drugs can calm people down from a state of anxiety, the antidepressants sometimes lift people up from a state of depression. Most antidepressants work by increasing the availability of the neurotransmitters norepinephrine or serotonin, which elevate arousal and mood and appear scarce during depression. Consider fluoxetine, which users worldwide know as Prozac. Prozac and other serotonin-enhancing drugs have been prescribed not only to patients with depression but also to those with obsessive-compulsive disorder, two-thirds of whom respond with "partial symptom reduction" (Pigott & Seay, 1997).

Prozac blocks the reabsorption and removal of serotonin from synapses (**FIGURE 37.8**). Prozac, and its cousins Zoloft and Paxil, are therefore called serotonin-reuptake-inhibitor drugs. The 77 million prescriptions written for these drugs in 1998 (at a cost of $5.6 billion) made them the world's most widely prescribed psychiatric drugs (Kaufman, 1999). Other antidepressants work by blocking the reabsorption of both norepinephrine and serotonin or by inhibiting an enzyme that breaks down neurotransmitters such as serotonin. These drugs, though no less effective, have more potential side effects, such as dry mouth, weight gain, or dizzy spells (Anderson, 2000; Mulrow & others, 1999).

"If this doesn't help you don't worry, it's a placebo."

Message is sent across synaptic gap.

- Sending neuron

Vesicles containing neurotransmitters

- Action potential

Synaptic gap

Neurotransmitter molecule

Receptors

Receiving neuron

(a)

Message is received; excess neurotransmitter molecules are reabsorbed by sending neuron.

Reuptake

(b)

Prozac blocks normal reuptake of the neurotransmitter serotonin; excess serotonin in the synapse enhances its mood-lifting effect.

Prozac

Serotonin

(c)

FIGURE 37.8
Biology of antidepressants
Shown here is the action of Prozac, one of the serotonin-reuptake inhibitor drugs.

But be advised: Patients who begin taking antidepressants do not wake up the next day singing "Oh, what a beautiful morning!" Although the influence of antidepressants on neurotransmission does occur within hours, their full psychological effect often requires four weeks, sometimes aided by cognitive therapy to help the patient reverse a now-habitual negative thinking style.

Everyone agrees that people with depression often improve after a month on antidepressants. But after allowing for natural recovery (the regression to normal called "spontaneous recovery") and the placebo effect, how big is the drug effect? Not big, report Irving Kirsch and Guy Sapirstein (1998) from their analysis of 19 double-blind clinical trials: "Inactive placebos produced improvement that was 75 percent of the effect of the active drug." A new study of 7315 participants in 45 government clinical trials confirmed this conclusion: 41 percent of those receiving antidepressants experienced reduced symptoms. But so did 31 percent of those given placebos (Khan & others, 2000). We should also remember that antidepressant drugs are not the only way to give the body a lift. Aerobic exercise, which helps calm people who feel anxious and energize those who feel depressed, does about as much good, and with positive side effects that include increased arousal, increased serotonin levels, and decreased blood pressure.

For those suffering the manic-depressive mood swings of a bipolar disorder, the simple salt **lithium** can be an effective mood stabilizer. Australian physician John Cade discovered this in the 1940s when he administered lithium to a severely manic patient. Although his reason for doing so was misguided—he thought lithium had calmed excitable guinea pigs when actually it had made them sick—Cade found that in less than a week the patient became perfectly well (Snyder, 1986). With continued lithium use, emotional highs and lows typically level. After suffering mood swings for years, about 7 in 10 people with bipolar disorder benefit from a long-term daily dose of this cheap salt (Solomon & others, 1995). Their risk of suicide is but one-sixth that of bipolar patients not taking lithium (Tondo & others, 1997). Although we do not fully understand why, lithium works.

Current drug therapies reduce or increase activity at all the receptors for a given neurotransmitter. This has been likened to watering one's garden by closing and opening floodgates. Drug researchers hope that the next generation of therapeutic drugs will target specific receptors that control specific symptoms, rather like watering individual plants. If so, such drugs may offer greater potency with fewer side effects (Goleman, 1996).

"No twisted thought without a twisted molecule."

Attributed to psychologist Ralph Gerard

"First of all I think you should know that last quarter's sales figures are interfering with my mood-stabilizing drugs."

■ **lithium** a chemical that provides an effective drug therapy for the mood swings of bipolar (manic-depressive) disorders.

Electroconvulsive Therapy

PREVIEW QUESTION 11 What is electroconvulsive therapy? When is it used?

The medical use of electricity is an ancient practice. Physicians treated the Roman Emperor Claudius (10 B.C.–A.D. 54) for headaches by pressing electric eels to his temples.

A more controversial brain manipulation occurs through shock treatment, or **electroconvulsive therapy (ECT).** When ECT was first introduced in 1938, the wide-awake patient was strapped to a table and jolted with roughly 100 volts of electricity to the brain, producing racking convulsions and brief unconsciousness. ECT therefore gained a barbaric image, one that lingers still. Today, however, patients first receive a general anesthetic so they are not conscious, and a muscle relaxant to prevent injury from convulsions. Then a psychiatrist momentarily electrically shocks the unconscious patient's brain. Within 30 minutes the patient awakens and remembers nothing of the treatment or of the hours preceding it.

Psychiatrists usually limit ECT to treatment of severe depression. (It is usually ineffective in treating other psychological disorders.) After three such sessions each week for two to four weeks, 80 percent or more of people receiving ECT improve markedly, showing some memory loss for the treatment period but no discernible brain damage (Bergsholm & others, 1989; Coffey, 1993). "A miracle had happened in two weeks," reported noted research psychologist Norman Endler (1982) after ECT alleviated his deep depression. A 1985 panel of the National Institutes of Health, as well as newer research reviews, confirm that ECT is an effective treatment for severe depression in patients who have not responded to drug therapy (Consensus Conference, 1985; Parker & others, 1992). Thus, reports the American Psychiatric Association (1990), ECT has regained respectability as a "major treatment" for depression (**FIGURE 37.9**).

How does ECT work? After more than 50 years, no one knows for sure (Kapur & Mann, 1993). One recipient likened ECT to smallpox vaccine, which was saving lives before we knew how it worked. Perhaps electrical shock increases the release of norepinephrine, a neurotransmitter that elevates arousal and mood and seems in short supply during depression. Or perhaps the shock-induced seizures cause the brain to react by calming neural centers where overactivity produces depression.

ECT is credited with saving many from suicide and is now administered with briefer pulses that disrupt memory less (Fink, 1998). Yet its Frankensteinlike image continues. No matter how impressive the results, the idea of electrically shocking people into convulsions still strikes many as barbaric, especially given our ignorance about why ECT works. Moreover, ECT-treated patients, like other patients with a history of depression, are vulnerable to relapse. Nevertheless, electroconvulsive therapy is, in the minds of many psychiatrists and patients, a lesser evil than depression's misery, anguish, and risk of suicide.

FIGURE 37.9

Electroconvulsive therapy

Although ECT is controversial, it is the preferred treatment for depression that does not respond to drug therapy.

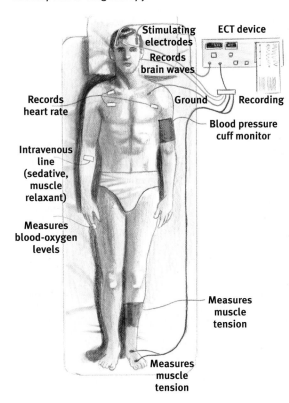

Psychosurgery

PREVIEW QUESTION 12 Under what conditions might psychosurgery be considered for changing behavior or moods?

Because its effects are irreversible, **psychosurgery**—surgery that removes or destroys brain tissue—is the most drastic and the least-used biomedical intervention for changing behavior. In the 1930s, Portuguese physician Egas Moniz developed what became the best-known psychosurgical operation: the **lobotomy.** Moniz found that cutting the nerves connecting the frontal lobes with the emotion-controlling centers of the inner brain calmed uncontrollably emotional and violent patients. After shocking the patient into a coma, a neurosurgeon would hammer an icepicklike instrument through each eye socket into the brain, then wiggle it to sever connections running up to the frontal lobes. The whole procedure was crude but easy and inexpensive, and it took only about 10 minutes. During the 1940s and 1950s, tens of thousands of severely disturbed people were "lobotomized," and Moniz was honored with a Nobel Prize (Valenstein, 1986).

Although the intention was simply to disconnect emotion from thought, the effect was often more drastic: The lobotomy produced a permanently lethargic, immature, impulsive personality. During the 1950s, after some 35,000 people had been lobotomized in the United States alone, calming drugs became available and psychosurgery was largely abandoned. Today, lobotomies are almost never performed, and other psychosurgery is used only in extreme cases. For example, if a patient suffers uncontrollable seizures, surgeons can deactivate the specific nerve clusters that cause or transmit the convulsions. MRI-guided precision surgery is also occasionally done to cut the circuits involved in severe obsessive-compulsive disorder (Sachdev & Sachdev, 1997). Because such beneficial operations are irreversible, however, neurosurgeons perform them only as a last resort.

The effectiveness of the biomedical therapies reminds us of a fundamental lesson: We find it convenient to talk of separate psychological and biological influences, but everything psychological is also biological. Every thought and feeling depends on the functioning brain. Every creative idea, every moment of joy or anger, every period of depression emerges from the electrochemical activity of the living brain. The influence is two-way: When therapy relieves obsessive-compulsive behavior, PET scans reveal a calmer brain (Schwartz & others, 1996).

Preventing Psychological Disorders

PREVIEW QUESTION 13 What is the rationale for preventive mental health programs?

Psychotherapies and biomedical therapies tend to locate the cause of psychological disorders within the person with the disorder. We infer that people who act cruelly must be cruel and that people who act "crazy" must be "sick." We attach labels to such people, thereby distinguishing them from "normal" folks. It follows, then, that we try to treat "abnormal" people by giving them insight into their problems, by changing their thinking, and/or by controlling them with drugs.

There is an alternative viewpoint: We could interpret many psychological disorders as understandable responses to a disturbing and stressful society. According to this view, it is not just the person who needs treatment, but also the person's social context. Better to prevent a problem by reforming a sick situation and by developing people's coping competencies than to wait for a problem to arise and then treat it.

A story about the rescue of a drowning person from a rushing river illustrates this viewpoint: Having successfully administered first aid to the first victim, the rescuer spots another struggling person and pulls her out, too. After a half-dozen repetitions, the rescuer suddenly turns and starts running away while the river sweeps yet another floundering person into view. "Aren't you going to rescue that fellow?" asks a bystander. "Heck no," the rescuer replies. "I'm going upstream to find out what's pushing all these people in."

Preventive mental health is upstream work. It seeks to prevent psychological casualties by identifying and alleviating the conditions that cause them. George Albee (1986) believes there is abundant evidence that poverty, meaningless work, constant criticism, unemployment, racism, and sexism undermine people's sense of competence, personal control, and self-esteem. Such stresses increase their risk of depression, alcoholism, and suicide.

Albee contends that we who care about preventing psychological casualties should therefore support programs that alleviate poverty, discrimination, and other demoralizing situations. We eliminated smallpox not by treating the afflicted but by inoculating the unafflicted. We conquered yellow fever by controlling mosquitos. Prevention of

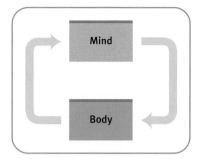

Mind-body interaction
The biomedical therapies assume that mind and body are a unit: Affect one and you will affect the other.

"It's no measure of health to be well adjusted to a profoundly sick society."

Krishnamurti, 1895–1986

"It is better to prevent than to cure."

Peruvian folk wisdom

■ **electroconvulsive therapy (ECT)** a biomedical therapy for severely depressed patients in which a brief electric current is sent through the brain of an anesthetized patient.

■ **psychosurgery** surgery that removes or destroys brain tissue in an effort to change behavior.

■ **lobotomy** a now-rare psychosurgical procedure once used to calm uncontrollably emotional or violent patients. The procedure cut the nerves that connect the frontal lobes to the emotion-controlling centers of the inner brain.

psychological problems means empowering those who have learned an attitude of helplessness, changing environments that breed loneliness, renewing the disintegrating family, and bolstering parents' and teachers' skills at nurturing children's achievements and resulting self-esteem. Indeed, "Everything aimed at improving the human condition, at making life more fulfilling and meaningful, may be considered part of primary prevention of mental or emotional disturbance" (Kessler & Albee, 1975, p. 557).

There is, however, more to the story of psychological disorders than toxic environments and pessimism. Anxiety disorders, major depression, bipolar disorder, and schizophrenia are known biological events. Yet Albee reminds us of one of this book's themes: *A human being is an integrated bio-psycho-social system.* For years we have trusted our bodies to physicians and our minds to psychiatrists and psychologists. That neat separation no longer seems valid. Stress affects body chemistry and health. And chemical imbalances, whatever their cause, can produce schizophrenia and depression. *"Mens sana in corpore sano,"* says an ancient Latin adage: A healthy mind in a healthy body.

"Mental disorders arise from physical ones, and likewise physical disorders arise from mental ones."

The Mahabharata, c. A.D. 200

rehearse it!

14. Antipsychotic drugs are used to calm schizophrenia patients so that they can live outside the hospital. The drugs often bring relief from auditory hallucinations and other troubling symptoms. However, some of them can have unpleasant side effects, most notably
    a. hyperactivity.
    b. convulsions and momentary memory loss.
    c. sluggishness, tremors, and twitches.
    d. paranoia.

15. Valium and Librium, which depress central nervous system activity, are among the most heavily prescribed and abused drugs. These drugs are referred to as _____ drugs.
    a. antipsychotic
    b. antianxiety

    c. antidepressant
    d. antineurotic

16. The antidepressant drugs seem to increase the availability of the neurotransmitters norepinephrine or serotonin, which appear to be scarce during depression. One antidepressant drug that often brings relief to patients suffering the manic-depressive mood swings of a bipolar disorder is
    a. dopamine.
    b. Librium.
    c. lithium.
    d. Valium.

17. Two controversial biomedical therapies are electroconvulsive therapy (shock treatment) and lobotomy (a type of psychosurgery). Lobotomy, once used to treat uncontrollably vio-

lent patients, is no longer an accepted treatment. Electroconvulsive therapy, however, remains in use as a treatment for
    a. depression.
    b. severe depression.
    c. schizophrenia.
    d. anxiety disorders.

18. Being poor or unemployed undermines a person's self-esteem and sense of competence. An approach that seeks to alleviate poverty and other demoralizing situations that put people at high risk for developing psychological disorders is
    a. biomedical therapy.
    b. the humanistic approach.
    c. empathy and active listening.
    d. preventive mental health.

REVIEWING

Therapy

1. What are the aims and methods of psychoanalysis and psychodynamic therapy?

The *psychological therapies*, or *psychotherapies*, treat people with psychological disorders through structured interactions between therapist and client. Therapists influenced by the psychoanalytic perspective try to help people gain insight into the unconscious origins of their disorders and to work through the accompanying feelings. To do so, a therapist may draw on techniques such as free association and dream analysis, and interpret resistances and transference to the therapist of long-repressed feelings. Traditional psychoanalysis, which is no longer practiced widely, is criticized for assuming repression, for after-the-fact interpretations,

and for being time-consuming and costly. The more common psychodynamic therapy is influenced by the psychoanalytic perspective's concern for childhood experiences and defense mechanisms. But it offers a briefer treatment form and often incorporates other techniques into the therapy session.

2. What are the basic themes of humanistic therapy, such as Rogers' client-centered approach?

Unlike psychoanalysts, humanistic therapists focus on clients' current conscious feelings and on their taking responsibility for their own growth. Carl Rogers, in his person-centered therapy, used active listening to express genuineness, acceptance, and empathy.

3. What are the assumptions and techniques of the behavior therapies?

Behavior therapists worry less about promoting self-awareness and more about directly modifying problem behaviors. Thus, they may countercondition behaviors through systematic desensitization or aversive conditioning. Or they may apply operant conditioning principles with behavior modification techniques, such as token economies.

4. What are the goals and techniques of the cognitive therapies?

The cognitive therapies, such as Aaron Beck's cognitive therapy for depression, aim to change self-defeating thinking by training people to look at themselves in new, more positive ways. Cognitive behavior therapy also helps clients to regularly practice new ways of thinking and talking.

5. Does psychotherapy work? Who decides?

Because the positive testimonials of clients and therapists cannot prove that therapy is actually effective, psychologists have conducted hundreds of outcome studies of psychotherapy. These studies indicate that (1) people who remain untreated often improve; (2) those who receive psychotherapy are somewhat more likely to improve, regardless of what kind of therapy they receive and for how long; (3) mature, articulate people with specific behavior problems often receive the greatest benefits from therapy; but (4) placebo treatments or the sympathy and friendly counsel of paraprofessionals also tend to produce more improvement than occurs when people receive no treatment.

6. Are some therapies more effective than others?

Statistical analyses of different types of therapies indicate that no one type of therapy is superior to all others. Some therapies do, however, seem to be well-suited to specific psychological examples, such as behavioral conditioning techniques for treatment of phobias.

7. How do alternative therapies stand up to psychology's critical thinking methods?

Three alternative therapies—therapeutic touch, eye movement desensitization and reprocessing (EMDR), and light exposure therapy—were critically evaluated in this module. No credible evidence supports either therapeutic touch or EMDR, but light exposure therapy does seem to relieve the symptoms of seasonal affective disorder (SAD).

8. What three elements are shared by all forms of psychotherapy?

Despite their differences, all psychotherapies offer three benefits to demoralized people: new hope, a new perspective, and (if the therapist is effective) an empathic, trusting, and caring relationship.

9. How do differences in culture and values influence the relationship between a therapist and a client?

Therapists differ in the values that influence their aims. Before seeking therapy, one might ask about the therapist's treatment approach and values, as well as the person's credentials and fees.

10. What are the most common forms of drug therapy? What criticisms have been leveled against drug therapies?

The most widely used *biomedical therapies*, which treat psychological disorders by altering neural functions, are drug therapies. These include the antipsychotic drugs, used in treating schizophrenia, which block dopamine activity; antianxiety drugs, which depress central nervous system activity; and antidepressant drugs, which increase the availability of serotonin and norepinephrine. Lithium is a mood stabilizer prescribed for those with bipolar disorder. Many drugs are hardly more effective than placebo treatments, and some have serious side effects.

11. What is electroconvulsive therapy? When is it used?

ECT is a biomedical therapy in which a brief electric current is sent through the brain of an anesthetized patient. Although controversial, ECT remains an effective treatment for many people with severe depression who have not responded to drug therapy.

12. Under what conditions might psychosurgery be considered for changing behavior or moods?

Although radical psychosurgical procedures such as lobotomy were once popular, neurosurgeons now rarely perform brain surgery to alleviate specific problems. Even when MRI-guided precision surgery is considered, it is a treatment of last resort because its effects are irreversible.

13. What is the rationale for preventive mental health programs?

Advocates of preventive mental health argue that many psychological disorders could be prevented. Their aim is to change oppressive, esteem-destroying environments into more benevolent, nurturing environments that foster individual growth and self-confidence.

TERMS AND CONCEPTS TO REMEMBER

psychotherapy, p. 530
eclectic approach, p. 530
psychoanalysis, p. 530
resistance, p. 532
interpretation, p. 532
transference, p. 532

client-centered therapy, p. 533
active listening, p. 534
behavior therapy, p. 535
counterconditioning, p. 535
systematic desensitization, p. 536
aversive conditioning, p. 538

token economy, p. 539
cognitive therapy, p. 540
cognitive-behavior therapy, p. 541
regression toward the mean, p. 543
psychopharmacology, p. 553

lithium, p. 555
electroconvulsive therapy (ECT), p. 556
psychosurgery, p. 556
lobotomy, p. 556

REHEARSE IT ANSWER KEY

1. a	3. d	5. c	7. a	9. d	11. d	13. b	15. b	17. b
2. a	4. c	6. b	8. d	10. c	12. a	14. c	16. c	18. d